Training & Development Yearbook 2002

CAROLYN NILSON

PRENTICE HALL

© 2002 by Learning Network Direct, Inc.

All rights reserved. No part of this book may be reproduced in any form or by any means without written permission in writing from the publisher.

Printed in the United States of America

10 9 8 7 6 5 4 3 2 1

ISSN 1049-3875

ISBN 0-13-042133-2

ATTENTION: CORPORATIONS AND SCHOOLS

Prentice Hall books are available at quantity discounts with bulk purchase for educational, business, or sales promotional use. For information, please write to: Prentice Hall Special Sales, 240 Frisch Court, Paramus, New Jersey 07652. Please supply: title of book, ISBN, quantity, how the book will be used, date needed.

PRENTICE HALL
Paramus, NJ 07652

http://www.phdirect.com

What This Book Will Do for You

The *Training & Development Yearbook 2002* is the most comprehensive, varied, wide-ranging, accessible collection of high-interest, high-priority information and verified data of importance to the field. Both the organization of the book and the way in which current ideas and developing trends are presented are carefully designed to start you immediately thinking about meaningful change and point you in the right direction to accomplish it. As you read and become familiar with its contents, you will find that the *Yearbook:*

- Reviews the important professional literature of the field,
- Synthesizes the most recent best practices for you,
- Provides contact information for people you can call on for help,
- Focuses your thinking,
- Spurs you into action,
- Pushes your personal performance, and
- Enables you to help your company succeed in these changing times.

In this *Yearbook,* editor's comments written from the perspective of a seasoned training manager, experienced instructional designer, and consultant quickly focus your thinking and suggest the essential issues you'll need to consider as you read further. Having a highly respected and widely published trainer review the published literature defining the field helps you to sort out your thinking and develop your own up-to-date platform for action. Succinct analysis of the kernel of creativity inherent in an idea, experience, report, or program lets you slash away the superficial and extraneous information that constantly bombards you in books, journals, the media, and online.

Thousands of documents comprise the base of material for this book. The unique concept of a yearbook such as this is that only the best practices and most relevant current thinking and reporting are chosen for this book. Because of this, you can finally throw away those shelves full of old magazines, journals, dog-eared downloads, and newsletters. Your annual record of the training and development field is right here in this one volume, on your desk, always at hand for ready reference. The *Yearbook* contains detailed lists of organizations, conferences, seminars, training centers, publishers, publications, reference books, and Websites providing you with a one-stop directory of names, addresses, Websites, telephone and FAX numbers vital to your work. Our Trainer's Almanac, Section 6, is the most comprehensive and information-rich reference on the market today.

This *Yearbook* is built upon the solid conviction that individuals want to be able to help make their companies successful—to do meaningful work that contributes to overall productivity and performance—and build your own career in the process. The specialized field of training and development has traditionally taken the lead in designing and delivering programs that help people learn better ways to do work, and it will continue to carry the banner for workplace learning. Today, however, things are not as simple as they seemed in the past:

- Fewer people are listed as employees on corporate rosters; outsourcing is common everywhere and training consultants are thriving. Leadership for learning is a major organizational challenge.

- Classroom training is changing: There are not as many people to fill up classrooms, budgets are tighter for out of town training trips, and companies are looking for ways to combine time- and money-saving technology-delivered training with classroom training. "Blended learning" is the choice.

- There are growing relationships between the big picture of social and political changes and the smaller picture of why and how workplace learning must take place. Actions in Washington, in state capitals, and in political and cultural centers around the globe affect how trainers do their jobs. Learning leadership for "Enduring Freedom" presents new challenges.

- Advances in the capabilities of computing and telecommunications, satellite and Internet transmission, combined with decreasing prices of personal computer and peripheral hardware have tended to broaden the resource base and to individualize the accessing and choosing of information which forms the foundation for learning. Trainers are struggling with quality issues in both instructional design and training delivery in the online learning environment.
- Building learning communities, digital and face to face, is training's responsibility.
- Collaborative connections with fellow workers and colleagues on the periphery of a business (such as professors, suppliers, and even competitors) drive individuals to enter into working and learning relationships with even more people. Customer training is becoming more important.
- Intellectual capital and knowledge management present opportunities for training managers.
- Worker stress, the 24/7 work environment, an increasingly litigious society, and gun violence add to the reasons trainers need to help preserve "high touch" in a "high tech" environment.
- Those who design, deliver, support, and manage training are particularly challenged to stay focused on learning in the midst of an advertising, entertainment, and information onslaught.
- Those who evaluate the learning event itself, as well as the results of training, must understand business results and added value in addition to simply determining what has been learned.

The *Training & Development Yearbook 2002* reflects the current continued broadening of the training field and the need for trainers to think more inclusively and strategically as training departments dwindle and stabilize after several recent years of corporate downsizing and the terrorist attacks of 2001. The wider conceptual base of this *Yearbook* can bring you more quickly in touch with the current range of ideas in the field and encourage you to take action with the confidence of being well informed. Among other current trends and developments included in the *Training & Development Yearbook 2002* are:

- Growth opportunities for trainers in times of change—e-learning design, development, and management.
- Boosting individual and organizational performance for stability and growth.
- Assessing learning needs, both for individuals and for the enterprise as a whole.
- Nuances in the experiences with the latest technological directions in training, such as delivering lessons online, instructional Websites, distance learning, virtual universities, and better Learning Management software systems.
- New and better tools for delivering and accessing Web-based and online learning.
- New kinds of blended training delivery sites, including combinations of "high touch" and "high tech."
- Corporate collaborations for increased learning, both within companies and with others outside of companies; digital collaboration and face-to-face collaboration.
- Special training challenges of home-based employees and contingent workers; training 24/7.
- Successful welfare-to-work legislation affecting training program design and workplace learning.
- The push for design quality standards in e-learning; ISD in evolution.
- Training that leverages and maximizes the benefits of global workplace diversity.
- How to build flexibility, better decision making, and creativity into your training programs.
- How leadership is changing; facilitation and community-building.
- Knowledge as strategy; managing, protecting, sharing, and increasing intellectual capital.

What This Book Will Do for You

The trainer's familiar systems development framework that begins with analysis and ends with evaluation is as critical today as it has ever been because it provides a way for you to think about identifying and solving problems within whatever large or small workplace environment you work. As the issues around performance and performance support, productivity, organizational learning, and the enterprise as a whole are debated, it's important for you to take off from a base of experience in systems thinking. And, of course, in all such debate, what you as an individual can bring to technology is the important relationship, not the other way around.

The entries in the *Training & Development Yearbook 2002* are fit within the systems framework beginning with those focused on analysis issues relative to the learner and ending with ideas and experiences in evaluation. Rather than simply choosing "interesting topics" at random, the entries in this *Yearbook* have been cited in relationship to each other and to the broad training and development field through the instructional systems design framework. Around this structure, the opening section on managing training places today's management challenges within the big-picture issues from e-learning development to global interconnectivity. Helping you to recognize and benefit from these system relationships is an important reason why this book was written.

The *Training & Development Yearbook 2002* provides models, case studies, data, insight, applications, and a host of individuals to inspire and encourage the kind of innovative thinking and informed risk-taking that trainers must do in order to continue to improve individual and organizational performance and help your company compete. Entries in this book feature committed employees, leaders, and team members in small companies, entrepreneurial operations, mid- and large-size companies, non-profit and government agencies, consultants, academics, writers, gurus, and just plain folks with good ideas. The scope of *Training & Development Yearbook 2002* is purposely broad, encompassing the strongest influences, most interesting ideas, and best practices in America's training and development scene as the new year 2002 begins. Our *Yearbook* is not affiliated with any organization or other commercial venture. We have been free to choose references from the widest possible field, and include them based only on their merits. We have intentionally searched a range of sources from the general business press representing diverse viewpoints on matters of concern to trainers, and we have purposely included in our literature base the publications of numerous professional associations who have important things to say about training. The breadth of our base of ideas and experience far surpasses any similar publication. Our efforts on your behalf are made with one goal in mind—to provide you with the most complete information about workplace learning in this calendar year.

Think of this book not just as a compendium of information, but in addition and more importantly, as a creative source of new ideas for the year 2002—ideas that drive learning, personal performance, and go right to your company's bottom line.

About the Editor

Carolyn Nilson, Ed.D., is a veteran trainer with a wide experience base in traditional and state-of-the-art training assignments. Among the corporations and agencies she has served as consultant in training design are: American Management Association, AT&T, Chemical Bank, Chevron, Dun & Bradstreet, Martin-Marietta, Nabisco, National Institute of Education, National Occupational Competency Testing Institute, National Westminster Bank, NJ Bell, NJ Department of Education, NJ Department of Labor, US Department of Education, The World Bank, and The MASIE Center.

Dr. Nilson was a Member of the Technical Staff at AT&T Bell Laboratories where she was part of the Standards, Audits, and Inspections Group of the Systems Training Center. In this capacity, she developed, implemented, and promoted quality standards in course design and delivery throughout AT&T; she was the Bell Labs' representative on a corporate instructional design team. At Bell Labs, she received commendations for her work one-to-one mentoring technical professionals for whom English was a second language. She also taught the Bell Labs' train-the-trainer course.

She held the position of Manager of Simulation Training at Combustion Engineering, where she managed the training operation and created high-level computer-based training for an international base of clients in various fields of the chemical process industry. At CE, she was a member of a corporate training design team where her specific contribution was design of a performance support system in learner evaluation using expert system technologies.

Dr. Nilson held the Executive position of Director of Training for a systems consulting firm with a broad-based Fortune 500 clientele in the New York City metropolitan area. In this position, she supervised a staff of training consultants and was responsible for training analysis, design, development, implementation, and evaluation across a range of corporations.

She has been a faculty member for Padgett-Thompson seminars, the Ziff Institute, the Center for the Study of Work Teams, the U.S. Armed Services Training Institute, and USAID's Management Development Initiative in Cairo, Egypt. She is an active member of the American Society for Training and Development (ASTD) where she was part of a grass-roots planning task force in the area of human resources development skills and strategies. She was ASTD's guest host for an online nationwide teleconference on dealing with change. She has been a speaker at national conferences of ASTD, the American Management Association, and at a regional conference of the International Society for Performance and Instruction. She received her doctorate from Rutgers University with a specialty in measurement and evaluation in vocational and technical education.

Her work has been featured in *TRAINING Magazine*, *Training & Development*, *Successful Meetings*, *Entrepreneur*, *HRMagazine*, and *Fortune*. She is the author of numerous training papers, speeches, articles, and manuals; her writings are selling worldwide to a diverse customer base. Four of her books currently appear in amazon.com's "50 Bestselling Training Books." She is a Schwartz Business Books 1995 "Celebrity Author" (Milwaukee, WI), on the 1996 "This Year's Bestsellers" list of the Newbridge Book Clubs (Delran, NJ), has been a talk show guest on "Money Radio" (Pomona, CA), and is featured on AMA's Website *amanet.org*. Her books have been used throughout the country in management seminars of the American Management Association. She has been the editor of Prentice Hall's *Training & Development Yearbook* for seven years. Her books have been chosen by Macmillan's Executive Program Book Club, the Newbridge Book Club, the Training Professionals Book Club, and the *Business Week* Book Club. Among her other books are:

Training & Development Yearbook, Prentice Hall, 1996, 97, 98, 99, 2000, 2001

How To Start A Training Program, ASTD, 1999

The Performance Consulting Toolbook, McGraw-Hill, 1999

How To Manage Training, Amacom, 1998

More Team Games for Trainers, McGraw-Hill, 1997

Games That Drive Change, McGraw-Hill, 1995

Peer Training, Prentice Hall, 1994

Team Games for Trainers, McGraw-Hill, 1993

Training for Non-Trainers, Amacom, 1990; and Spanish edition, 1994

Training Program Workbook and Kit, Prentice Hall, 1989

Acknowledgments

Great appreciation for their ideas and implementation skills goes to the many hundreds of individuals who are mentioned in this 2002 edition of the *Training & Development Yearbook*. These are the persons whose writing, strategizing, planning, problem solving, points of view, and program expertise are featured in this book. Their names and affiliations are listed in the expanded citations on pages where their work is featured, and a big thank you goes out to them for moving the field forward through another year of change and growth. Also, names you will not find elsewhere are Noel Nilson, Bert Holtje, Gene Brissie, Herbert Burtis, John Ferris, and Daniel Patel, the most important men in my daily life, whose kindness, support, steadfastness, forbearance, humor, bread and circuses sustain me on the journey of creating a book, especially this one. To Eric, Jeffrey, Kristen, and Bob, I send hugs and kisses across the miles for your genuine interest in and use of my work, and for your encouragement throughout this project. To Betsey, Sari, Charlotte, Alex, Pearl, Jeanne, Marnie, Carla, Kate, Kim, and Lisa who also love reading and writing, and who share ideas with me, I thank you too for your support and enthusiasm in my sisterhood of learners, communicators, and trainers.

My Postmaster, Howard Wisell, and his assistant Bev Fallon were a critical link in the production process. Ruth Dwyer, librarian, keeps Sandisfield reading. To them also, thank you for caring for and believing in books.

And finally, my team at Prentice Hall in Paramus, New Jersey deserves a standing ovation for seeing this particular production through to completion: Ellen Schneid Coleman, Executive Editor, supported us all to keep going forward; Barry Richardson, Senior Editor extraordinaire, somehow managed content, personalities, and me; Joan Pelleteri guided the paperwork through the editorial process and did a hundred things that only she knows. Judy Weiss-Brown and Kathy Coughlin in the Marketing organization, Sandy Hutchinson, Shira Markoff, and Tony Fischetto in Creative, and Beth Carey in Sales dealt with all the details of matching book to reader. Eve Mossman in Production and Susan Peluso in Book Manufacturing, along with compositor Joe Gorman and his staff did magical feats of scheduling and coordination, and turned another tricky manuscript into a book. Susan Sherman, Manager of Sub-Rights, steered us swiftly and surely through legal waters. An enhanced book, wider and deeper in scope, and in the hands of our readers sooner than ever before is the result of good solid teamwork. We should all be proud of what we've done again this year.

Those outside of the Prentice Hall family who have been especially helpful in the development of this particular book or bringing it to market are:

Daphne Ben Ari, Permissions
Forbes and *Forbes ASAP*
New York, NY

Yvonne Burnside, Permissions Manager
Across the Board
The Conference Board
New York, NY

Karen Caldwell, Editorial Assistant
Society for Human Resource Management
Alexandria, VA

Lori Cefus, Permissions Manager, Research
ASTD Benchmarking Service
Alexandria, VA

Kelly Champion, Permissions
Fortune
New York, NY

Nancy Dann, Permissions Administrator
The Systems Thinker
Pegasus Communications
Waltham, MA

Courtney Diffley, Permissions
SHRM Legal Report
Society for Human Resource Management
Alexandria, VA

Robert C. Dockendorff, Campus Director
New England Technical Institute
New Britain, CT

Jeanne De Ycaza, ESL Instructor
PS 144
Forest Hills, NY

Marnie D'Orazio
Vanguard Group of Investments
Wayne, PA

Christy Eidson, Assistant Editor
Across the Board
The Conference Board
New York, NY

Denise Fenrick, Permissions Assistant
Society for Human Resource Management
Alexandria, VA

Patricia A. Fitzpatrick, Permissions Manager
MIT Sloan Management Review
Cambridge, MA

Katherine M. Franklin
CTB/McGraw Hill
Monterey, CA

Amanda Jennings
Human Synergistics
Plymouth, MI

Deborah Keary, Director
SHRM Information Center
Society for Human Resource Management
Alexandria, VA

Ronda Lathian, Editorial Administrator
Workforce
ACC Communications
Costa Mesa, CA

Susan LeClair, Permissions Editor
U.S. News & World Report
New York, NY

Alex Lumb, Permissions Manager
Harvard Business Review
Boston, MA

Abby Marks-Beale
The Reading Edge
Wallingford, CT

The MASIE Center
Saratoga Springs, NY

Jo Mattern, Permissions
Fortune
New York, NY

Dr. Charlotte McDaniel
Candler School, Emory University
Atlanta, GA

Andrea Medley, Permissions
Fortune
New York, NY

Leigh Montville,
Senior Permissions Coordinator
Conde Nast
New York, NY

Jeffrey Mostade, Director
SENEX Counseling and Training
Fairhill Center
Cleveland, OH

Patrick Murphy,
Senior Permissions Assistant
John Wiley & Sons
New York, NY

Sabrina Paris, Manager
Permissions and Electronic Publishing
AMACOM Books/AMA Publishing
New York, NY

Dr. Daniel Patel
East Mountain Medical Assn.
Great Barrington, MA

Drew Pawling, Permissions
Harvard Management Update
Boston, MA

Robin Reader, Customer Service
Copyright Clearance Center
Danvers, MA

Julie Richards, Permissions Assistant
Forbes and *Forbes ASAP*
New York, NY

Karen Silber, Permissions Editor
The Bureau of National Affairs
Washington, DC

Valerie Small, Periodicals Coordinator
ASTD
American Society for Training & Development
Alexandria, VA

Steven M. Smith, Director of Communications
International Association
of Conference Centers
St. Louis, MO

Acknowledgments

Lyle Steele, Permissions Manager
Business Week
New York, NY

Jeremy Stratton, Permissions Editor
TRAINING Magazine
Bill Communications Inc.
Minneapolis, MN

Matt Tews
Training Supersite
www.trainingsupersite.com

Stacy Van der Wall, Editorial Assistant
Society for Human Resource Management
Alexandria, VA

Becky Wilkinson, Permissions Manager
*Lakewood Report on Technology
for Learning* newsletter
Minneapolis, MN

Mark Worth, Account Representative
Copyright Clearance Center
Danvers, MA

Dr. Harvey Zimbler, Associate Professor
University of Massachusetts Medical School
Pittsfield, MA

Contents

Section 1 Training Management 1

    1. E-Learning Management 5
        Pricing E-Learning 5
        10 Tips for Avoiding Failure in E-Learning 9
        General Electric's Strategic Hunt for "Parallel Paths" 10

    2. Thinking Change 14
        Government Action Regarding New Kinds of Learning 14
        New Ways of Thinking at the Top 16

    3. Digital Structures 22
        Learning Management Systems 22
        What the Best Managers Do to Be Really Supportive 23

    4. Global Connections 25
        Use of E-Learning Around the Globe 25
        Dispersed Teams Need to Get Off on the Right Foot 27
        Training Across Cultures: What to Expect 32

    5. The TRAINING 2001 Industry Report 36

Section 2 Needs of Learners 43

    1. Leadership and Culture 49
        Learning to Learn Dialogue with Warrren Bennis 49
        Ford Defines and Trains Transformational Leaders 55
        Individual Career Development at First USA Bank 62
        CEO in Jeans and T-Shirt? 65
        Generation Y: Self-Confident and Goal-Oriented 66

    2. Race and Gender Plus 67
        Surprises in the Census 67
        Institutional Effects of Immigration 69
        Racism in the Workplace 71
        Training's Important Role in Affirmative Action 75
        Learning from Informal Networks of "Girl Gangs" 76
        How and Why to Be Your Own Mentor 81

    3. Technology and Learning Communities 83
        Dealing with Learner Resistance to Technology-Delivered Training ... 83
        What Napster Did for E-Learning 89
        How To Facilitate Online Communities 92

    4. The New Bottom Line 96
        Faster, Cheaper, Smarter: How Rockwell Collins Reinvented Its Training 96
        Results-Oriented Customer Service Training 98
        Wellness at DaimlerChrysler 103
        On That Fateful Day, Two Airlines Faced Their Darkest Scenario ... 106
        The State of the Union, September 20, 2001 112

Section 3 Training Program Design 117

1. ISD Reborn 121
Instructional Design Strategies and Considerations 121
Begin with Projects 124
Out with the Old: Is It Time to Rethink Instructional Design? 127
Liemandt's Feedback for and from New Hires and Customers 131

2. Big Design Issues in E-Learning 139
A Project Manager's Advice: Plan and Communicate 139
Mission E-Possible: The Cisco E-Learning Story 140
Learners Want More Than Technology 149
E-Learning for Free Agents 152

3. E-Learning Design Nuts and Bolts 154
How Online Course Management Systems Affect the Course 154
Shell's Formula for Blending Training Fuels Optimum Learning at Minimum Cost 157
Knowledge Sharing Using a Knowledge Base 159

4. Lonesome Online 161
Challenge for Designers: The Social Dimensions of Learning 161
Strategies to Prevent Online Attrition 164
Know Stuff Versus Do Stuff 167

Section 4 Training Program Delivery 169

1. Blended Delivery 173
Dot.Coms and Doughnuts 173
Better Training Is Just a Click Away 175
Face-to-Face and Online with Harvard and Stanford 180

2. Advances in E-Learning 181
JIU: The Voice of Experience 181
Success in Surprising Places 182
New Letters: WAP and M-Learning 184
Live E-Learning 185
Help for Instructors 186

3. Today's Trainer as Facilitator of Learning 191
What Is an e-Trainer? 191
Surviving the "Technology Tsunami" 195
Facilitated Mentoring: Rx for Stability and Skills 199
Developing e-Employees Who Value Learning 201

Section 5 Evaluation of Training 203

1. E-Learning Evaluation 207
Quality Standards in E-Business 207
A New Business-Driven Learning Strategy at Rockwell Collins 209
ROI Factors in E-Learning 211
Siemens' Knowledge Management (KM) Metrics 213

	2.	**Evaluation of Learners**..	214
		Performance Assessment: A Multi-Systems Approach	214
		Executive Coaching's Return on Investment	217
		The Evaluator's Role in Improved Performance	218
		Getting 360-Degree Feedback Right..	223
		Quarterly Evaluation for Performance Improvement........................	229
	3.	**Tests, Measures, and Certification**...	230
		The "E-learning Value Proposition"...	230
		ASTD's New Certification	231
		Pre- and Post-Testing Tied to Objectives	232
		Court Rulings Favor Performance Measures	233
		Core Measures of Intellectual Capital	240
		GE's "Four Buckets"	242
		More to E-Learning Measures Than Stock Price	243
Section 6		**The Trainer's Almanac**	**247**
		6.1 Professional Organizations	249
		6.2 Training Conferences	259
		6.3 Worldwide Conference Centers	277
		6.4 Training for Trainers	309
		6.5 Non-Profit Organizations	347
		6.6 Training Research and Reference Sources...............................	355
		6.7 Training Journals, Magazines, and Newsletters	367
		6.8 Training Websites...	381
Section 7		**Index**	**395**

Introduction

OVERVIEW

This is the thirteenth edition of the *Training & Development Yearbook,* the latest in a series of what has become the respected annual review of the field of workplace learning. In a field exploding with new information, practices, and ideas, a tool is needed to organize that information, make it accessible and easy to find, and, most of all, to put it into perspective. This comprehensive volume is that tool. It is the only book of its kind—wide in scope, inclusive of hundreds of organizations, featuring the current experiences and ideas of more than a thousand businesses and individuals, based on primary information sources from 143 different publications and publishers. We show you what's working, who's doing it, and how they're getting results—corporations, colleges, government agencies, online universities, associations, consultants, start-ups.

WHY A YEARBOOK SERIES?

This yearbook series is envisioned as a year-by-year archive of the most important writing on training and development during any twelve-month period. Synthesizing the best ideas and practices of the field in the form of a yearbook provides the reader with an organized and coherent view of the profession at the start of the new year. Since literature on workplace learning and performance is being created continuously and is proliferating around the globe in both quantity and depth, on paper and, electronically, the most meaningful way to organize and archive it is chronologically in the yearbook series. Over time, with a complete collection of yearbooks, we can trace any particular subject or company for a better understanding of the trends that inform the knowledge work of today. The series provides historical perspective of the field; the current volume provides perspective for work in the year ahead.

WHAT'S SPECIAL ABOUT THIS THIRTEENTH EDITION

Research for this *Training & Development Yearbook 2002* involved reading thousands of journal and magazine articles, books, research studies, monographs, directories, newsletters, newspapers, conference proceedings, websites, and government documents. Analysis of these sources has produced a "best practices" compilation of ideas and experiences which define the field for a full twelve-month period and provide a unified foundation of ideas to start the new year.

The training field is in particular flux these days, with fewer staff required to do more work, with strategic business decisions being pushed down lower and lower out of the executive suite, with more outsider involvement in all aspects of training and training management, with old ways of delivering training being questioned, with computer and communications technology being used to support individual and organizational learning, and with global effects on training operations.

This book defines the field of training in the context of societal as well as professional influences—influences on the broader field of training that include competency and career development, infrastructure and design challenges of e-learning, performance improvement, and the development and management of intellectual capital. This book is much more than a reference document: it not only includes the essence of the best practices literature of the field, but it also explains the issues contained in that literature and places the highest level training debate within a framework that trainers can readily understand.

Entries in this year's *Training & Development Yearbook* are presented in a content structure that highlights the most important issues in each of the major training functions: management, needs analysis, instructional design, training delivery, and evaluation. Editor's comments focus each of the 72 major entries. A comprehensive introduction is included for each of the six major sections of the book. The most obvious trends and challenges of the field are given meaning for the trainer in this time of change. The ideas are structured within a systems development framework familiar to most trainers and managers. Each section of content is complete within itself. Each could stand alone as a book within a book. Taken together, these sections provide a powerful platform for developing a vital, relevant, value-adding, successful training program for 2002—a program designed to improve individual and organizational performance.

Several hundred books, authors, articles, databases, publishers, and publications have been cited within the text, illustrating the important dialogue within the field. In addition, 143 primary source publishers and publications are listed alphabetically in the following pages for quick and complete reference. Additional publishers who are primarily seminar or conference providers, as well as professional associations and non-profit agencies who also publish newsletters, journals, or other publications, are listed in Section 6, *The Trainer's Almanac,* providing hundreds more sources of printed information.

The publishing industry's long-held standards of excellence, the practice of peer review, editorial and fair use ethics, the rule of copyright law, standards of style and expression, sales and marketing practices that historically have put the consumer first, all make the information contained in this book an objective, verified and accurate representation of facts and ideas. The World Wide Web as a source of information, in contrast, is still struggling with these fundamental checks and balances. A yearbook and a yearbook series is what no Website can ever expect to be. Our *Trainer's Almanac,* alone, contains around 1000 entries, all of which feature multiple fields of data, compounding the quality of information at your fingertips.

WHO SHOULD READ THIS BOOK?

Training consultants, coordinators, managers, directors, multimedia specialists, coaches, mentors, instructional designers, instructors, performance specialists, knowledge officers, and CEOs: This yearbook is committed to helping trainers with all sorts of titles and job descriptions in companies of all sizes to design and build the knowledge infrastructure of their companies. It is for those learning and performance consultants who advise and listen, coach, negotiate, facilitate, and chart strategic directions. It is for men and women inhabiting the skin of the traditional trainer who are now required to stretch the limits of their organizational creativity, their personal and professional commitment to learning, and their capacity for making learning systems work in the deepening and broadening of a business's knowledge base.

WHAT IS COVERED IN THIS BOOK?

Because this is a yearbook, the content which we've chosen to include represents new ideas, experiences, challenges, and insights apparent in a year's worth of business literature. This literature base includes references from literally hundreds of primary sources. If a subject or company does not seem to be represented in this information base, it is probably because the underlying ideas and practices were not particularly new this year, or not part of the public or professional literature base, or not particularly indicative of a trend anticipated for year 2002. This book concentrates on annual best practices as seen through a thorough, focused, annotated literature review of the immediate past forming a foundation for the immediate future.

The content is organized within a systems framework, recognizing that change and development must occur within a structure that relies especially on analysis of a business's as well as a learner's needs, a process of intentional design, an appropriate delivery method, and the use of evaluation and feedback. Content of this book recognizes that trainers must formulate business goals within a learning and performance context, and must view the development and delivery of training as a means to add value to the company through knowledge. Literature reviewed includes some publications not generally considered as part of the field. This is because we believe that societal trends and political actions have an impact on corporate directions and should be considered as important framers of workplace learning and performance improvement.

Introduction

Specifically, more than 300 topics of unique interest have been categorized into the following major sections:

- Section 1: Training Management
- Section 2: Needs of Learners
- Section 3: Training Program Design
- Section 4: Training Program Delivery
- Section 5: Evaluation of Training

A complete listing of topics is found in the book's Table of Contents, with additional detail in the introductions to each section. A comprehensive master index in the back of this book will direct you to individuals and companies, concepts, and topics elaborated on throughout the book. In all, 72 entries make up Sections 1 through 5.

SPECIAL FEATURES

In a literature review of this size, all content does not fall neatly into "article" form. Therefore, within the first five sections of the book, you'll find the following special features:

- **Abstracts:** An abstract is a brief summary of an information source, often an article from a journal or magazine, newspaper or newsletter. This book contains 13 abstracts.
- **Article Reprints:** Articles have been chosen from a wide variety of relevant publications. This book contains 32 article reprints.
- **Book Reviews:** Among the many fine business books from many publishing houses, 5 were selected from 2001 to review. In some cases, a book chosen for relevance to training and development is also a business best-seller; in other cases, it is not. Their inclusion here means that their authors had something particularly new or developmental to contribute to the field of workplace learning in this twelve-month period. Only the latest publication dates are eligible to be included in *Training & Development Yearbook 2002*. This year's books reviewed here are:

Be Your Own Mentor: Strategies from Top Women on the Secrets of Success by Sheila Wellington and Calalyst (New York: Random House, Inc., 2001), $25.95. Sheila Wellington has been President of Catalyst since 1993. Prior to joining Catalyst, she was the first woman Secretary of Yale University. Catalyst is a non-profit research and advisory organization that works to advance women in business.

e-Volve! Succeeding in the Digital Culture of Tomorrow by Rosabeth Moss Kanter (Boston: Harvard Business School Press, 2001), $27.50. Rosabeth Moss Kanter is the Ernest L. Arbuckle Professsor of Business Administration at Harvard Business School and author of several bestselling books. She has been named one of the "50 Most Powerful Women in the World" by *The Times* of London.

e-Learning: Building Successful Online Learning in Your Organization: Strategies for Delivering Knowledge in the Digital Age by Marc J. Rosenberg (New York: The McGraw-Hill Companies, 2001), $29.95. Marc J. Rosenberg is a principal with DiamondCluster International and a former executive with AT&T. He is also a former President of the International Society for Performance Improvement (ISPI).

Free Agent Nation: How America's New Independent Workers Are Transforming the Way We Live by Daniel H. Pink (New York: Warner Books Inc., 2001), $24.95. Daniel H. Pink is a contributing editor at *Fast Company* magazine. He served as a speechwriter at The White House in the Clinton administration.

Managing Generation Y: Global Citizens Born in the Late Seventites and Early Eighties by Carolyn A. Martin, PhD and Bruce Tulgan (Amherst, MA : HRD Press, 2001) $9.95. Carolyn A. Martin is a Master Trainer for RainmakerThinking, Inc. She is also a former Associate Professor and Dean of Student Services at Georgian Court College. Bruce Tulgan is the founder of RainmakerThinking, Inc., consultant, author, and speaker.

- **Case Studies:** A case study focuses on a specific good idea, program, policy, or strategy practiced this year by a particular organization, individual, or group of companies. In each instance, specific and useful approaches are described and explained. This book contains 16 major case studies. Companies and organizations represented in the case studies and elsewhere in the book are:

General Electric	U.S. Census 2000
Ford Motor Company	Lockheed Martin
First USA Bank	Catalyst
Internal Revenue Service (IRS)	PPL Corporation
Napster	Gulf Breeze Hospital
ASTD	Wild Oats Market
DaimlerChrysler	QUALCOMM
United Airlines	The MASIE Center
American Airlines	Chesterton
Trilogy University	University of Phoenix
Cisco Systems	OutlookSoft
Shell	Sunbridge Healthcare Corp.
ACI	Walden Institute
Harvard University	Manchester Consulting
Massachusetts Institute of Technology (MIT)	Synygy Inc.
Jones International University	Lguide
Rockwell Collins	SkillSoft Corp.
Siemens	Click2Learn
Center for Creative Leadership (CCL)	Stanford University

Plus, at least 100 additional businesses, colleges, and organizations are mentioned throughout the text.

- **Research Summaries:** Many agencies, professional organizations, and companies engage in research projects that reflect the field of workplace learning. Results of such research often point toward new directions in policy and practice. In this book, 6 research studies are summarized; in some cases, sponsors have collaborated in doing studies. Throughout the book, numerous additional research studies have been referenced.

THE TRAINER'S ALMANAC

The Trainer's Almanac is a book within a book, organized as a directory of various sources of particular interest to persons responsible for creating policies and programs that facilitate learning. It contains hundreds of names, addresses and telephone numbers, e-mail and Website addresses—approximately 1000 key citations. All these have been updated since the previous edition of the *Training & Development Yearbook*. The Almanac is your verified, one-stop reference for current listings of the most important information you need to know, presented in directory format.

Sections of the *The Trainer's Almanac* include listings of:

- Professional Organizations
- Training Conferences, including a year 2002 calendar of 74 conferences
- Worldwide Conference Centers
- Training for Trainers
- Nonprofit Organizations
- Training Research and Reference Sources
- Training Journals, Magazines, and Newsletters
- Training Websites

Introduction

HOW TO GET A COPY OF AN ITEM CITED IN THIS YEARBOOK

Three major sources of information are easily accessible for getting reprints of articles and documents referenced in the *Abstracts, Articles, Case Studies,* and *Research Summaries* in this yearbook. These sources are:

- The publication or publisher of the cited item, whose addresses and telephone numbers are listed in the following several pages;

- Websites of publications from which sources are referenced;

- The Information Center of the American Society for Training and Development (ASTD), 1040 King Street, Box 1443, Alexandria, VA 2313, 703/683-8184; ASTD's Website is *www.astd.org*.

- The Information Center of the Society for Human Resource Management (SHRM), 1800 Duke Street, Alexandria, VA 22314; 800/283-SHRM; SHRM's Website is *www.shrm.org*.

Back issues of publications are usually available for a modest fee, and research services such as those provided by ASTD and SHRM charge a reprint fee based on the length of the record and the database from which it comes. Quantity reprints can be had at a discount through reprint offices of the publications from which they originate. Another source of training information, including some sources referenced in this *Training & Development Yearbook* is Lakewood Publication's training Website, *www.trainingsupersite.com*.

ASTD and SHRM maintain staff who can help you seek and find information. These two major online sources for published articles and documents in the broad field of training and development make available topics in areas such as learning organizations, individual learning, performance systems and supports, technologies to enhance learning, and methodologies for assessing needs, designing instruction, delivering training by whatever medium, and evaluating training organizations, systems, programs, courses, materials, and learning events. Customer service personnel, librarians, and technologists on staff can direct you to many kinds of resources and guide you through online searching for information related to what you read here in the pages of this yearbook. Public, college, and university librarians can also direct you to reprint services available locally. Books, of course, are available at libraries, through publishers listed here, at book stores, and online from Barnes andnoble.com, amazon.com and Websites of publishers and megabookstores.

Addresses of Publishers and Publications Used As Sources in *Training & Development Yearbook 2002*

The 143 primary publishing sources listed here are in addition to approximately 50 different secondary sources referenced at the end of many article reprints in sections 1 through 5 of this *Yearbook*. Nearly 1,000 additional listings are included in section 6, "The Trainer's Almanac." This is the most comprehensive publication in the field, representing the ideas, practices, models, personalities, challenges, and opportunities in training and development in its evolution at the beginning of calendar year 2002.

ABC TV News
WABC
7 Lincoln Square
New York, NY 10023
www.abcnews.com
212/456-4811

ACC Communications, Inc.
245 Fischer Avenue B-2
Costa Mesa, CA 92626
714/751-1883

Across the Board
The Conference Board
845 Third Avenue
New York, NY 10022
212/759-0900

Advanstar Communications Inc.
131 W. First St.
Duluth, MN 55802
888/527-7008

AMACOM
P.O. Box 1026
Saranac Lake, NY 12983
518/891-5510

American Management Association International
1601 Broadway
New York, NY 10019
212/586-8100

American Productivity & Quality Center (APQC)
123 North Post Oak Lane
Houston, TX 77024
713/681-3705

American Prospect
5 Broad Street
Boston, MA 02109
617/570-8030

American Society for Training and Development (ASTD)
1640 King St. Box 1443
Alexandria, VA 22313
703/683-8183

Americans with Disabilities Act (ADA)
Public Law 101-336

ASTD 2000 International Comparison Report
1640 King St., Box 1443
Alexandria, VA 22313
703/683-8183

Atlantic Monthly
77 N. Washington Street
Boston, MA 02114
617/854-7700

Bill Communications, Inc.
Human Performance Group
50 South Ninth Street
Minneapolis, MN 55402
612/333-0471

Boston Globe
135 Morrissey Blvd.
P.O. Box 2378
Boston, MA 02107
617/929-7900

brandon-hall.com
390 West Fremont Avenue
Sunnyvale, CA 94087
www.brandon-hall.com
408/736-2335

Broadway Books
A Division of Random House, Inc.
1540 Broadway
New York, NY 10036
www.broadwaybooks.com

Bulletin to Management
Bureau of National Affairs, Inc.
1231 25th St. NW
Washington, DC 20016

Bureau of Labor Statistics
U.S. Department of Labor
200 Constitution Ave. NW
Washington, DC 20210
202/606-7828

Bureau of National Affairs, Inc.
1231 25th St. NW
Washington, DC 20037
800/233-6067

Business 2.0
1 California St.
San Francisco, CA 94111
415/468-4684

Business Week
1221 Avenue of the Americas
New York, NY 10020
800/635-1200

Catalyst
120 Wall Street
New York, NY 10005
212/514-7600

Center for Creative Leadership (CCL)
One Leadership Place
P.O. Box 26300
Greensboro, NC 27438
336/545-2810

Conference Board
845 Third Avenue
New York, NY 10022
212/339-0290

Corporate University Xchange Inc.
381 Park Avenue South Suite 713
New York, NY 10016
212/213-8650

Creative Training Techniques Newsletter
Bill Communications, Inc.
50 South Ninth Street
Minneapolis, MN 55402
612/328-4329

eCompany
Time Inc.
Time & Life Building
Rockefeller Center
New York, NY 10020
www.ecompany.com

Addresses of Publishers and Publications Used As Sources

Economist
111 West 57th St.
New York, NY 10019
212/541-5730

Economist Technology Quarterly
111 West 57th Street
New York, NY 10019
212/541-5730

Educational Technology
720 Palisade Avenue
Englewood Ciffs, NJ 07632
201/871-4008

Educational Technology Publications
700 Palisade Avenue
Englewood Cliffs, NJ 07632
201/871-4007

EDUCAUSE
4772 Walnut St., Ste 206
Boulder, CO 80301
303/449-4430

eePulse
905 W. Eisenhower Circle, Ste. 110
Ann Arbor, MI 48103
www.eepulse.com
734/996-2321

e-learning magazine
201 Sandpointe Ave., Ste 600
Santa Ana, CA 92707
714/513-8400

Executive Excellence newsletter
1366 East 1130 South
Provo, UT 84606

Fast Company
77 North Washington Street
Boston, MA 02114-1927
617/973-0300

Federal Communications Communication (FCC)
445 12th Street SW
Washington, DC 20554
888/225-5322

Forbes
60 Fifth Ave.
New York, NY 10011
800/888-9896

Forbes ASAP
Forbes Building
60 Fifth Avenue
New York, NY 10011
212/620-2421

Fortune
Time & Life Building
Rockefeller Center
New York, NY 10020
800/621-8000

The Gallup Organization
Lincoln, NE 68501
402/489-9000

Generation21 Learning Systems
1536 Cole Blvd., Ste. 250
Golden, CO 80401
888/601-1300

Global Workforce
245 Fischer Ave. B-2
Costa Mesa, CA 92626
714/751-1883

Harvard Business Review
60 Harvard Way
Boston, MA 02163
617/495-6192

Harvard Business School Press
60 Harvard Way
Boston, MA 02163
617/495-6800

Harvard Management Communication Letter
60 Harvard Way
Boston, MA 02163
800/688-6705

Harvard Management Update
60 Harvard Way
Boston, MA 02163
800/668-6705

HRD Press
22 Amherst Road
Amherst, MA 01002
800/822-2801

HRMagazine
606 N. Washington St.
Alexandria, VA 22314
703/548-3440

Human Resource Development Quarterly
Jossey-Bass Publishers
350 Sansome Street
San Francisco, CA 94104
415/433-1767

Human Resource Management
John Wiley & Sons
939 Travis Rd.
Fort Collins, CO 80524
800/225-5945

Human Resources Report
Bureau of National Affairs, Inc.
1231 25th Street, NW
Washington, DC 20037
800/372-1033

HR News
Society for Human Resource Management
606 N. Washington St.
Alexandria, VA 22314
703/548-3440

Industry Report 2000
Lakewood Publications,
TRAINING Magazine
50 South Ninth St.
Minneapolis, MN 55402
612/333-0471

InsideCollaboration
online newsletter
Advanstar Communications
Duluth, MN
888/527-7008
www.collaborateexpos.com

InfoLine: Applying Technology to Learning
ASTD
1640 King Street, Box 1443
Alexandria, VA 22313
703/683-8183

International Association of Conference Centers (IACC)
243 North Lindbergh Blvd., Suite 315
St. Louis, MO 63144
314/993-8575

International Data Corporation (IDC)
Five Speen Street
Framingham, MA 01701
www.idc.com
508/872-8200

International Society for Performance Improvement (ISPI)
1300 L Street, NW, Ste. 1250
Washington, DC 20005
202/408-7969

Issues and Observations
Center for Creative Leadership
One Leadership Place, PO Box 26300
Greensboro, NC 27438
910/288-7210

Jossey-Bass Inc., Publishers
350 Sansome Street
San Francisco, CA 94104
415/433-1740

Jossey-Bass Pfeiffer
350 Sansome Street
San Francisco, CA 94104
415/422-1740

Journal of Instruction Delivery Systems
50 Culpeper St.
Warrenton, VA 22186
540/347-0055

Journal of Interactive Instruction Development
50 Culpeper St.
Warrenton, VA 22186
540/347-0055

Lakewood Report on Technology for Learning Newsletter
Bill Communications
50 South Ninth St.
Minneapolis, MN 55402
800/328-4329

Leadership In Action
Center for Creative Leadership (CCL)
One Leadership Place,
P.O. Box 26300
Greensboro, NC 27438
336/545-2810

Learning Decisions Interactive Newsletter
The MASIE Center
P.O. Box 397
Saratoga Springs, NY 12866
518/587-3522
www.learningdecisions.com

Learning Technology Institute
50 Culpeper Street
Warrenton, VA 20186
540/347-0055

Legal Report
SHRM
1800 Duke Street
Alexandria, VA 22314
703/548-3440

Leverage
Pegasus Communications, Inc.
One Moody St.
Waltham, MA 02453
781/398-9700

Management Review
American Management Assn.
International
Publications Division
Box 319, Trudeau Road
Saranac Lake, NY 12983
800/262-9699

Manchester Consulting
1 East Independent Drive
Jacksonville, FL 32202
904/360-2200

McGraw-Hill Companies
1221 Avenue of the Americas
New York, NY 10020
212/512-6285

MIT Sloan Management Review
Room E60–100
77 Massachusetts Avenue
Cambridge, MA 02139
617/258-7485

MIT Press
Massachusett Institute of Technology
Cambridge, MA 02142
617/253-1000

Mobiltape Co., Inc.
25061 W. Ave. Stanford Ste. 70
Valencia, CA 91355
805/295-0504

MOSAICS
SHRM
1800 Duke St.
Alexandria, VA 22314
703/548-3440

NewsScan Inc.
P.O. Box 200549
Austin, TX 78720
512/335-2286

Newsweek
251 West 57th St.
New York, NY 10019
800/631-1040

New Yorker
20 West 43rd Street
New York, NY 10036
212/286-5400

New York Times
229 West 43rd St.
New York, NY 10036
212/556-1234

New York Times Magazine
229 West 43rd Street
New York, NY 10036
212/556-1234

New York Times on the Web
229 West 43rd Street
New York, NY 10036
212/556-1234
www.nytimes.com

Online Learning magazine
Bill Communications, Inc.
50 South Ninth Street
Minneapolis, MN 55402
612/333-0471

ONLINE LEARNING NEWS
online newsletter
VNU Business Media
50 South Ninth Street
Minneapolis, MN 55402
612/333-0471
www.onlinelearningnews.com

ONLINE LEARNING REVIEWS
online newsletter
VNU Business Media
50 South Ninth Street
Minneapolis, MN 55402
612/333-0471
www.onlinelearningreviews.com

Organizational Dynamics
American Management Assn.
International
1601 Broadway
New York, NY 10019
518/891-5510

PC Magazine
One Park Avenue
New York, NY 10016
212/503-5255

PC World
International Data Group
501 2nd Street #600
San Francisco, CA 94107
415/243-0500

Performance Improvement (P&I)
International Society for Performance Improvement (ISPI)
1300 L Street, NW
Washington, DC 20005
202/408-7969

Performance In Practice
ASTD Newsletter for Forums
1640 King Street Box 1443
Alexandria, VA 22313-2043
703/683-8135

Personnel Decisions International
45 S. 7th Street
Minneapolis, MN 55402
612/339-0927

Perspectives newsletter
Catalyst
120 Wall Street
New York, NY 10005
212/514-7600

Addresses of Publishers and Publications Used As Sources

Pfeiffer & Company
8517 Production Ave.
San Diego, CA 92121
619/578-5900

Prentice Hall Direct
240 Frisch Court
Paramus, NJ 07652
201/909-6418

Publishers Weekly
245 W. 17th St.
New York, NY 10011
212/463-6758

Quality Digest
40 Declaration Drive Suite 100-C
Chico, CA 95973
916/893-4095

Quality Progress
American Society for Quality (ASQ)
P.O. Box 3005
Milwaukee, WI 53201
414/272-8575

Ragan's Strategic Training Report
Lawrence Ragan
Communications Inc.
316 N. Michigan Ave., Ste. 300
Chicago, IL 60601
312/960-4408

Random House, Inc.
1540 Broadway
New York, NY 10036
212/782-9000

Reflections,
The SOL Journal
MIT Press
Five Cambridge Center
Cambridge, MA 02142

Smart Business
50 Beale St. 13th Floor
San Francisco, CA 94105
425/430-1663

Society for Applied Learning Technology (SALT)
50 Culpeper Street
Warrenton, VA 22186
540/347-0075

Society for Human Resource Management (SHRM)
606 North Washington St.
Alexandria, VA 22314
703/548-3440

Soundview Executive Book Summaries
3 Pond Lane
Middlebury VT 05753
802/453-4062

Strategy & Business
Booz-Allen & Hamilton
101 Park Avenue
New York, NY 10178
617/523-7047

Systems Thinker
Pegasus Communications
One Moody Street
Waltham, MA 02453
781/398-9700

T+D
ASTD
1640 King Street Box 1443
Alexandria, VA 22313
703/683-8183

TechLearn TRENDS
Online newsletter
The MASIE Center
www.techlearn.com

TDFeNet online newsletter
Training Directors' Forum
Bill Communications Inc.
50 South Ninth Street
Minneapolis, MN 55402
612/328-4329
www.TDFeNet.com

TIME
Time & Life Building
Rockefeller Center
New York, NY 10020
212/586-1212

Training & Development
American Society for Training
and Development (ASTD)
1640 King St. Box 1443
Alexandria, VA 22313
703/683-8100

TRAINING Magazine
Bill Communications, Inc.
50 South Ninth St.
Minneapolis, MN 55402
612/333-4471

2000 ASTD Trends Report
ASTD
1640 King Street Box 1443
Alexandria, VA 22313
703/683-8183

Union Labor Report
Bureau of National Affairs, Inc.
P.O. Box 40949
Washington, DC 20016
800/372-1033

United States Bureau
of the Census, 2000 U.S. Census
U.S. Department of Commerce
14th Street, between Constitution
and Pennsylvania Aves., NW
Washington, DC 20233
301/457-2794

US Department of Defense
SCORM Standards Project
OASD(PA) PIA
1400 Defense Pentagon, Rm. 3A750
Washington, DC 20301-1400
703/697-5737

US Department of Education
400 Maryland Avenue SW
Washington, DC 20202-5327
800/872-5327

United States Department of Labor
200 Constitution Ave. NW
Washington, DC 20210
202/219-9148

United States Government
Printing Office
Superintendent of Documents
North Capitol and H Streets NW
Washington, DC 20401
202/512-1800

US Department of State
Bureau of Public Affairs, Rm 5827
Washington, DC 20520-6810
202/647-6575

USA Today
99 W. Hawthorne Avenue
Valley Stream, NY 11580
516/568-9191

U.S. News & World Report
2400 N Street NW
Washington, DC 20037
202/955-2000

University of Phoenix Online
3157 East Elwood St.
Phoenix, AZ 85034
888/427-4723
www.uoponline.com

Urban Institute
2100 M Street NW
Washington DC 20037
www.urbaninstitute.org
202/833-7200

VNU Business Media
50 South Ninth Street
Minneapolis, MN 55402
612/333-0471

Wall Street Journal
Dow Jones & Company
200 Liberty St.
New York, NY 10281
800/843-0008

Warner Books, Inc.
1271 Avenue of the Americas
New York, NY 10020
212/522-7200

Washington Post
1150 15th Street, NW
Washington, DC 20071-9200
202/334-6000

Web Based Education Commission
www.webcommission.org

Weekly Standard
News America Publishing Inc.
1211 Avenue of the Americas
New York, NY 10036
800/983-7600

Welfare to Work Partnership
1250 Connecticut Avenue NW
Washington, DC 20036
202/955-3005

The White House
Office of Media Affairs
1600 Pennsylvania Avenue
Washington, DC 20500
202/456-1414

Women In Financial Services Fact Sheet
120 Wall Street, 5th Floor
New York, NY 10005
212/514-7600

Workforce
ACC Communications
245 Fischer Ave., B-2
Costa Mesa, CA 92626
714/751-1883

Working Smarter with PowerPoint newsletter
2055 Army Trail Road, Suite 100
Addison, IL 60101
800/424-8668

Working Woman magazine
Working Mother Media
135 W. 50th Street
New York, NY 10020
877/699-3243

Workplace Visions
SHRM
1800 Duke Street
Alexandria, VA 22314
800/283-7476

Worth
575 Lexington Ave.
New York, NY 10022
212/751-4550

W.W. Norton & Company, Inc.
500 Fifth Avenue
New York, NY 10110
212/354-5500

www.onmagazine.com
Time Life Building
1271 Avenue of the Americas
New York, NY 10011
800/444-3404

Yahoo! News
ZDNet
www.zdnet.com

Ziff Davis Smart Business
50 Beale Street 13th Fl.
San Francisco, CA 94105
www.smartbusinessmag.com
850/682-7624

SECTION 1

Training Management

1. E-Learning Management 5
   Pricing E-Learning 5
   10 Tips for Avoiding Failure in E-Learning 9
   General Electric's Strategic Hunt for "Parallel Paths" 10

2. Thinking Change 14
   Government Action Regarding New Kinds of Learning 14
   New Ways of Thinking at the Top 16

3. Digital Structures 22
   Learning Management Systems 22
   What the Best Managers Do to Be Really Supportive 23

4. Global Connections 25
   Use of E-Learning Around the Globe 25
   Dispersed Teams Need to Get Off on the Right Foot 27
   Training Across Cultures: What to Expect 32

5. The TRAINING 2001 Industry Report 36

INTRODUCTION TO TRAINING MANAGEMENT: SECTION 1

Section 1 of *Training & Development Yearbook 2002* focuses on some of the major concerns of training managers as year 2002 unfolds. E-learning in all of its facets—the technology required to set it up and support it, choosing the kinds of learning that are best learned online, getting buy-in from those you want to buy in, quality issues, and with whom to partner and collaborate to maximize cost and effectiveness. These are all issues we deal with in this book; and in this section, we focus on the management of this function and try to eliminate its wow factor.

We organize this section into five sub-sections. Sub-section 1 is *E-Learning Management* in which we give you guidelines on pricing, tips to avoid failure, and a story about Jack Welch and his late entry into the e-business. Sub-section 2 is *Thinking Change*, in which we've chosen articles that illustrate and explain how new kinds of thinking are in order in a smaller and more complicated world. Sub-section 3 focuses on the *Digital Structures* that are so easy to envision, a bit harder to construct, and often are difficult to make sense of without some more humanistic thinking. Sub-section 4 focuses on *Global Connections* that are so popular and interesting, but fraught with difficulties. We show you how to plan and manage global connections, with a learning focus. Sub-section 5 contains excerpts from *TRAINING Magazine*'s 2001 Industry Report.

E-Learning Management

Many training managers look at e-learning as a project, with project management guidelines. Certainly, at the least, an e-learning initiative will have a planning phase, an implementation phase, and an evaluation phase. The American Productivity & Quality Center (APQC) has an online paper about e-learning as a project and an invitation to readers to join in their project. Information about it can be accessed at *www.apqc.org/proposal/6*, for an overview and project summary, description of project objectives and study team. Roger C. Shank of Cognitive Arts Corporation and Northwestern University is subject matter expert for APQC's implementation of the e-learning project. The "project" orientation is an appealing one for managers, and one way to go about starting an e-learning experience or department. We also urge you to carefully consider our "10 Tips for Avoiding Failure in E-Learning." These tips come from online interactive newsletters from readers who've been there, doing the best they can with e-learning. And finally, we honor America's legendary CEO, Jack Welch in his year of retirement from General Electric with a reprint of his story about his own reluctant entry in to the e-world. We think there are some parallels for training managers in his story.

Fortune magazine, March 19, 2001, ran an article about CEOs in the Bush cabinet, and listed "Eight Rules from Rumsfeld" (p. 146) within the article. There are three of these rules that apply to the training manager in the development of e-learning:

- Beware when any idea is promoted primarily because it is bold, exciting, innovative, and new. There are many ideas that are bold, exciting, innovative, and new, but also foolish.
- Look for what's missing. Many advisors can tell a President how to improve what's proposed or what's gone amiss. Few are able to see what isn't there.
- If you are not criticized, you may not be doing much.

Thinking Change

Rosabeth Moss Kanter in *Harvard Business Review*, January 2001, p. 91, says "For companies not born digital, the fundamental problem is change." *The Economist Technology Quarterly* of March 24, 2001 concludes an article on upgrading the Internet with a hope that the current open architecture of the Internet doesn't get compromised by "short-termism and greed" (p. 36). A *Business Week Special Report, Rethinking the Internet* of March 26, 2001 cautions users that we'll have to get used to tolls, and chastises advertisers for being a bit shallow in their clinging to the banner as the primary means of advertising (p. 117). Government and corporations seek more effective uses of the Internet

Changes in the Workplace

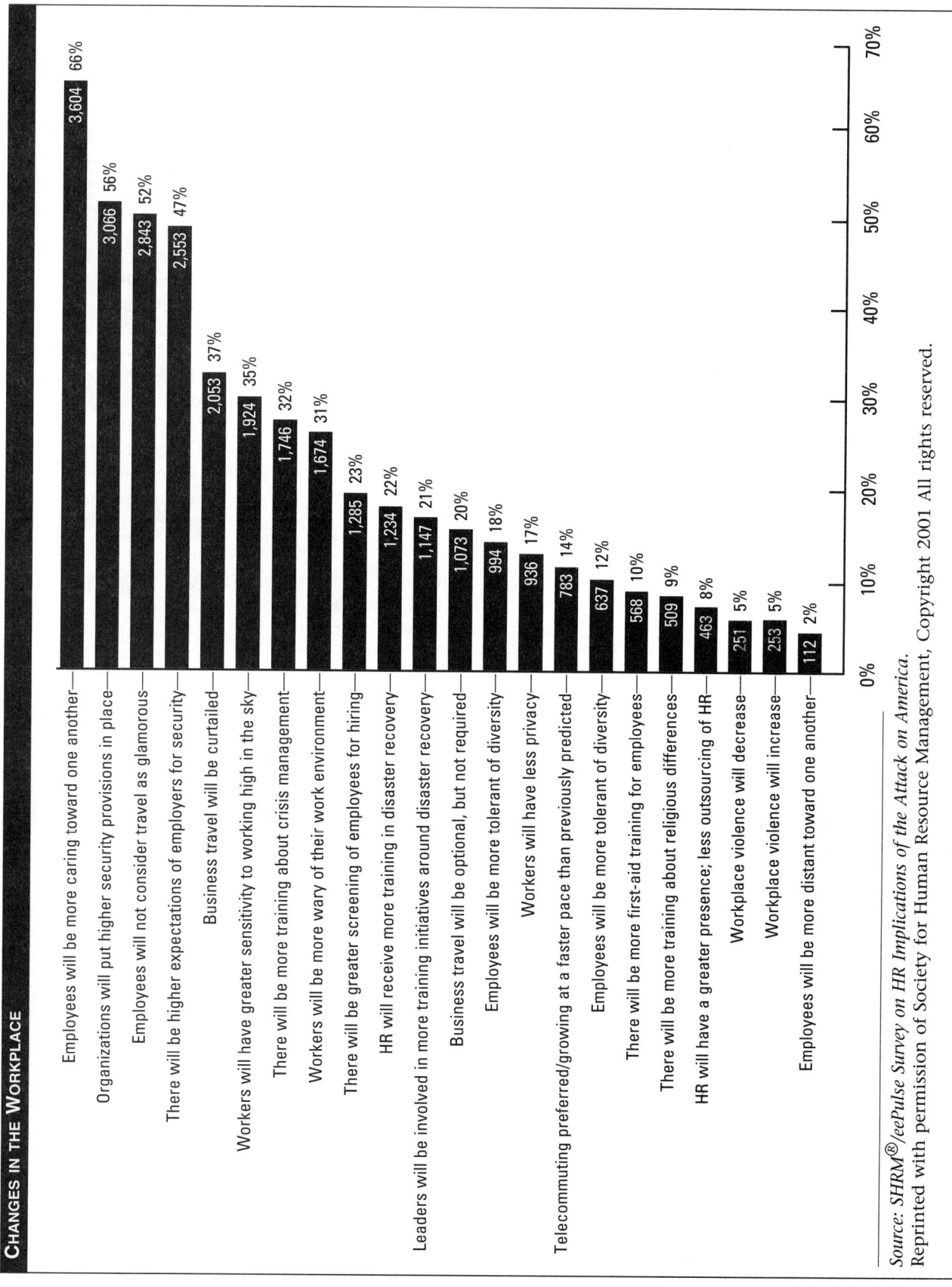

Change	Count	Percent
Employees will be more caring toward one another	3,604	66%
Organizations will put higher security provisions in place	3,066	56%
Employees will not consider travel as glamorous	2,843	52%
There will be higher expectations of employers for security	2,553	47%
Business travel will be curtailed	2,053	37%
Workers will have greater sensitivity to working high in the sky	1,924	35%
There will be more training about crisis management	1,746	32%
Workers will be more wary of their work environment	1,674	31%
There will be greater screening of employees for hiring	1,285	23%
HR will receive more training in disaster recovery	1,234	22%
Leaders will be involved in more training initiatives around disaster recovery	1,147	21%
Business travel will be optional, but not required	1,073	20%
Employees will be more tolerant of diversity	994	18%
Workers will have less privacy	936	17%
Telecommuting preferred/growing at a faster pace than previously predicted	783	14%
Employees will be more tolerant of diversity	637	12%
There will be more first-aid training for employees	568	10%
There will be more training about religious differences	509	9%
HR will have a greater presence; less outsourcing of HR	463	8%
Workplace violence will decrease	251	5%
Workplace violence will increase	253	5%
Employees will be more distant toward one another	112	2%

Source: SHRM®/eePulse Survey on HR Implications of the Attack on America.
Reprinted with permission of Society for Human Resource Management, Copyright 2001 All rights reserved.

and websites, and are collaborating in new ways. We suggest these ways in the articles in this sub-section.

The terrorist attack by three hijacked commercial airliners on September 11, 2001 changed America's innocence forever. The bar chart reprinted here is from *HR News* newsletter of November 2001, published by the Society for Human Resource Management (SHRM), p. 14. The survey was conducted three days after the tragedy and includes the responses of 5,673 human resources professionals. The responses show how this group of people believe that the workplace will change.

In this sub-section we give you a quick look at workplace changes and some of the ways in which new kinds of thinking are helping change to happen.

Digital Structures

ASTD publishes a series of small books known as *InfoLines*. A recent advertisement for *InfoLines* promoted a series known as the *Train the Trainer Series*. The table of contents for Volume 5 of the series is instructional. It's title is "Applying Technology to Learning." It includes:

   Effective Distance Learning
   Learning Technologies
   Intranets
   Needs Assessment for E-Learning
   Evaluating Off-the-Shelf CBT Software
   Implementing WBT
   Training Telecommuters
   EPSS
   Job Oriented Computer Software Training
   Delivering Quick-Response IBT/CBT Training
   Evaluating E-Learning.

These are some of the specifics of the digital environment in which training managers do their jobs these days. In our sub-section 3 we give you an overview of all of these through ideas about Learning Management Systems (LMS) and by the topics in a classic training audit. We suggest that you think creatively about the best ways to support your employees and your learners in this digital environment.

Global Connections

In this sub-section we focus on training's global connections in an increasingly smaller and more complicated world. We particularly include an entry on cultural differences and issues for training managers in developing and implementing overseas projects. We include an ASTD survey of the use of e-learning around the globe and an article on the strengthening of global teams.

TRAINING 2001 Industry Report

We conclude this section with excerpts from *TRAINING Magazine*'s annual survey, the *2001 Industry Report*.

1. E-Learning Management

Pricing E-Learning

Editor's Comment: ASTD's Darin E. Hartley takes the issues head-on here: if it's priced too low, the perceived value will all be low, but if it's priced too high, nobody will take it. He also addresses the issues of comparing apples and oranges, and of applying familiar per-time models to e-learning. Managers need to be thoughtful and careful as you figure out what's best for your training organization.

It's old news that e-learning is sweeping the planet. You can probably count on one hand the number of people who haven't heard of e-learning or aren't at least familiar with the concept of leveraging technology to learn. There are e-learning offerings in nearly every major business or organizational segment, as well as in nearly every learning role.

For instance, e-learning opportunities for people in government organizations cover everything from safety to leadership. There are Web-based courses for credit in institutions of higher learning. There are certification programs for various information technology functions as well as for hardware and software applictions, such as Microsoft Certified Systems Engineer (MCSE).

In a nutshell, as America becomes more technologically savvy and used to self-directed, on-demand learning, there will be more e-learning.

So, with all of the e-learning either already taking place or planned, why is it so darned hard to price this stuff? It's like trying to figure out how much an electron is worth.

❑ Is a four-hour classroom course comparative to a four-hour online learning session?
❑ What models are used to price e-learning?
❑ How do we e-valuate e-learning?
❑ Why is e-learning pricing critical?
❑ What does *price* really mean?

First, let's look at the last question. According to *Webster's Revised Unabridged Dictionary* (1996), price is "the sum or amount of money at which a thing is valued, or the value which a seller sets on his goods in market; that for which something is bought or sold, or offered for sale; equivalent in money or other means of exchange; current value or rate paid or demanded in market or in barter; cost."

One can easily see how pricing works for some items. In almost any grocery store, a dozen jumbo grade A eggs are comparative to a dozen jumbo grade A eggs. You can pick up a dozen eggs at a store in Kansas and a dozen at a store in Florida and pay roughly the same price. Products on the market that have become commodities—such as crude oil, sugar, winter wheat, and pork bellies—are bought and sold on commodities markets. But e-learning offerings are disparate. Can they be made into commodities and as such traded on the open market?

Why is e-learning pricing critical? Part of the success that organizations either experience or don't experience as e-learning proliferates is based on the pricing foundation of e-learning offerings. There's an equitable price that people are willing to pay for any product or service in regard to the definition of price above. Consequently, the way e-learning is priced in organizations is influenced by several factors, including value perception and demand. Let's look at value perception first.

Source: "E-Valuation: Pricing E-Learning/What's This Stuff Supposed to Cost, Anyway?" by Darin E. Hartley in *Training & Development*, April 2001, pp. 25–27. Darin E. Hartley is Developer of New Ventures at ASTD. Reprinted with permission of ASTD, copyright 2001. All rights reserved.

In general, people place more value on things that they pay money for. And, in general, the more money that people pay for something, the more they're likely to value it. Envision someone who has just bought an imported sports car as a special treat for years of hard work. Does this person let his or her new baby that was paid dearly for fall into disrepair and rust? No. The car will get washed regularly and serviced on or ahead of schedule because its value perception is high. Now picture someone with an economy rental car. *Oops!* Spill a little ketchup on the seat? No problem. Just rub it in with a napkin and toss the napkin on the floor. The value perception of a rental car is low.

How does that apply to e-learning pricing? There's a danger of under- or overpricing an e-learning offering above or below its value perception. Cornelia Weggen, an e-learning research analyst with WR Hambrecht + Co, says, "Good-quality e-learning isn't cheap. There's a certain myth out there that e-learning is cheaper, and, in fact, it can reduce costs in many ways. But organizations should expect to pay [a lot] for good e-learning."

Price too low and there's no perceived value in the instruction. That's one reason I worry when I hear e-learning vendors offer courses for 12.5 cents per student. What could that be worth to the student? Have you ever known of a graduate course offered for 12.5 cents? Would anyone even take a course priced at 12.5 cents and not be suspicious of its quality?

But where's the sweet spot for e-learning pricing that's neither too high nor too low? It's critical to try to assess what the market will bear when pricing your e-learning offerings. Now let's look at demand.

Consumption of products is based on laws of supply and demand. That also holds true for e-learning. If quality e-learning is readily available at an equitable price and meets the needs of consumers, the demand should be relatively high. Conversely, if the price is outrageous, the demand will be low or nonexistent.

For instance, a vendor once came to me with a business simulation for a call center. It was computer-based and elegant. After getting interested in the product and toying around with the simulation, I asked my usual closing question: "How much is it?" The vendor gulped visibly and said, "$23 million." The price was beyond anything we could handle, so the demand instantly dropped to zero. So, it's easy to see that e-valuation is critical as you start to implement e-learning in your organization. But how does one e-valuate e-learning?

The Price is Right

Pricing of e-learning happens in a myriad of ways. Here are some of the more common approaches.

Price per seat. This is the most common way to price an e-learning offering. As implied, an organization or individual pays a price per participant. For example, a four-hour e-learning session on coaching might cost out to $89 per participant. Anyone taking the course can have it prepaid by the organization, get his or her cost center charged, or pay by credit card and get reimbursed. The variation is the discount given to organizations that promise a large volume of participants. If many people will use a solution, it's probably worth getting a licensing deal to drive down costs.

One-time flat fee. Sometimes called a subscription model, companies can offer a suite of e-learning courses or an entire set for a one-time flat fee. In such cases, all employees in the company are allowed to take all of the courses as many times as they'd like during the year. Again, a large volume of participants can be a great negotiating point for better pricing.

Pay as you go. With this type of pricing, courses are available and organizations or individuals aren't charged until they take them. In most instances, people are billed at enrollment; in other instances, people are billed after completion. That option, however, lends itself to potential free use of the courseware, simply by not completing it.

This particular approach to e-learning pricing will become more compelling as more companies begin to migrate towards zero-base budgeting.

Per server. Some e-learning providers license their content to servers. A company can pay for the number of servers it uses through additional maintenance and service fees.

Free. What's that you say? Free e-learning? Yes, this is definitely a pricing model that melds nicely with the Internet. You can go to www.google.com, a free search engine, for free

Pros and Cons of Pricing Options

Option	Pros	Cons
Price Per Seat	• High volume can reduce cost per participant.	• Lower volume increases price. • Inaccurate forecasting can skew price per seat high or low.
One-Time Flat Fee (subscription)	• Participants can take multiple courses for one fee; participants with extra initiative can really benefit. • Generally, decreases cost per seat.	• Forecasting should be accurate, or you can pay overage fees. Accurate forecasting is problematic for most organizations. • Generally, much more expensive up front (front-end payment).
Pay as You Go	• Only pay for courses actually taken. • Less expense up front.	• Can be more expensive than paying for courses up front. • Forecasting should be accurate, or you can pay overage fees. Accurate forecasting is problematic for most organizations.
Per Server	• Flat fee per server gives you access to many offerings.	• Sometimes have to buy the entire offering of an e-learning solution provider instead of targeted offering. • Can be easy to forget maintenance fees and requirements.
Free	• It's free! • Can also provide access for participants to related software, books, and other offerings that will enhance learning.	• Can be perceived as too commercial because advertising or product sales are often tied to the learning.
Payment Based on Time	• Pay for use. The cellular phone analogy is familiar to most people.	• Tools and offerings are still being refined to make this a global reality.

Web tools and see how many thousands come up. You'll find free email, free ISPs (Internet service providers), free calendars, free e-greeting cards, free graphics, and free project management systems ad infinitum. So, free e-learning is a natural extension of these Internet times.

A good example of free e-learning is at www.powered.com. Powered Inc., formerly notharvard.com, creates e-learning universities for their clients to help educate their customer bases, improve site stickiness, and sell peripheral products. Some of its clients are Dell Computer and Barnes and Noble.

Payment based on time. Some pricing is based on the time spent in a learning session. A management course might cost $45 per hour; an IT course might cost $125 per hour. I predict that with the advent of robust learning management systems that use standards for data collection, people in the near future will get e-learning bills similar to the cell phone bills they get now:

❑ 12/10 — 12 minutes of a coaching session
❑ 12/11 — 3 minutes downloading a performance management template, 32 minutes streamed video on how to use the performance management template.

Microsoft already offers plug-ins for its streaming-video components to allow chargeback. This model will become more prevalent as classroom time shrinks and people begin getting just the information or tool that they need to do their jobs.

Now that you've seen some of the major pricing models, a logical question is, Which pricing model is the best? That's akin to asking what's the best car on the market. Some people might name an imported sports car; others might say a mini van. Similarly, I can't tell you what the best pricing model is for your organization. You'll need to identify clearly what you're trying to accomplish with your e-learning strategy, business requirements, and operational environment to answer that question. All of the pricing models have strengths and weaknesses. So, you make the decision that will support your goals best.

Here's another question that begs to be asked and answered: Are classroom and e-learning solutions equal? Is a four-hour online session equivalent to a four-hour classroom session? My answer is a resounding no! In a typical four-hour classroom session, participants have to travel (generally speaking) to a campus, classroom, hotel conference room, meeting center, or wherever the training is happening. So, travel expenses are built on. Then, there are the mandatory half-hour introductory sessions, in which the participants and instructor introduce themselves, accompanied by the latest icebreaker. Additionally, there'll be at least two bio-cigarette 10-minute breaks (which will turn out to be 20 minutes each) that chisel away at the actual learning time and time spent debriefing and completing Level 1 evaluations.

In all, the average four-hour classroom session contains about 2.5 hours of viable instruction. Contrast that with a self-paced e-learning session. You know who you are, so there's no need for an icebreaker or introductions. You take shorter breaks because you don't have to wait for the entire herd to return. And most self-paced e-learning lets people pre-assess their knowledge so they can focus on areas needing improvement. In a classroom session, there's only one speed, that of the instructor, which might be too slow or too fast for you.

I don't think we can compare classroom learning with self-paced and other types of e-learning; the dynamics are different. Anyway, classroom instruction is going the way of the dinosaurs. People are going to get the micro sessions they need and go on with the rest of their day, which I think is an important reason for the price-per-time model to develop because it will more closely parallel future learning.

Consider the variety of e-learning pricing models out there, finding the sweet spot for you is crucial. Don't price it so high that there's no demand, and don't price it so low that there's no value perception. Remember: There's no one right model for e-valuating e-learning. You have to pick the model best suited for you and your organization, based on your requirements.

10 Tips for Avoiding Failure in E-Learning

Editor's Comment: E-learning has no doubt encouraged training managers to assess what it is that they want to accomplish with each of their training programs, and has encouraged some reflective and creative thinking also. Many say that e-learning is distinctly different from learning in a classroom, and that training managers need to be sure they understand those differences to avoid the pitfalls of treating both design and delivery systems the same. The key question in any training is how it can narrow the performance gap between the learning moment and a person's job. It's the training manager's job to design the best possible learning situations for individual employees, recognizing the strengths and weaknesses of a variety of choices. The following list of tips for avoiding failure in e-learning are abstracted from the newsletters referenced here.

1. Scalability is a strength of e-learning; be sure you save it for times when you need to get information to large groups of people quickly. (Clark Aldrich, June 12, 2001, pp. 1,2)

2. E-learning typically doesn't work by itself for a host of reasons. It requires "dancing partners"—other instruction, mentoring, coaching, or on-the-job training. Be careful with your assumptions about saving time or money; some kind of blended learning seems to work best. (Mark Van Buren, June 12, 2001, pp. 2,3)

3. Be aware of the need to integrate the learning experiences that you set up when you design a blended learning experience. Fluid content delivery is as important as efficient and effective use of resources. (Mike Cavallo, June 12, 2001, p. 3)

4. Combine the classroom with its social strengths with e-learning's broad reach so that learners can practice what they learned online. (Mike Cavallo, June 12, 2001, p. 3)

5. Design student assessments of online courses so that they can't simply copy the test questions before they are tested. Consider using a randomized assessment of "question pools," available from several vendors. (Greg Ritter, May 24, 2001, p. 7)

6. Don't force employees to make a quick switch from classroom to online. Give them time to gravitate to e-learning. Do an e-mail usage assessment—if employees use e-mail a lot, they're probably ready for online learning (John Coné, June 21, p. 1)

7. Design a distinctive learning screen that's visible across the room, so that passersby will recognize that that person is learning online! Take advantage of the bandwagon effect. (John Coné, June 21, p. 2)

8. Measure the student *drop-in* rate as well as the drop-out rate. Don't be overwhelmed or overimpressed with the drop-out rate. It takes time and experimentation for e-learning to catch on. (John Coné, June 21, p. 2)

9. Be sure you mix people, process, and technology. The most successful projects will have this mix. Involve the IT department, business units, and trainers in the development of e-learning. (Jim Everidge, May 23, 2001, p. 5)

10. When developing an e-learning project, create a "project board" comprised of 3 members—the person who controls the budget, a user representative, and a technical representative. (Hanif Sazen, April 26, 2001, p. 2)

Sources: 4 different issues of the interactive online newsletter, *OLNews* published by VNU Business Media, 50 South Ninth St., Minneapolis, MN 55402. 612/ 333-0471. *OLNews* is weekly and free. To subscribe, go to www.vnulearning.com. These issues are used as sources here: June 21, 2001; June 12, 2001; May 24, 2001; and April 26, 2001. They all feature comments from readers to various questions posed by *OLNews*.

General Electric's Strategic Hunt for "Parallel Paths"

Editor's Comment: We reprint this case study of General Electric's reluctant entry into Internet business—"e-buy, e-make, and e-sell." In Jack Welch's new autobiography, *Jack: Straight from the Gut* (New York: Warner Books, 2001) these are the three essential parts of business that had to make sense for Welch to take them online. Could he "monetize" the operation? was the criterion (pp. 344–349). Although this case study is not about e-learning per se, it gets into the mind of a respected and revered ultimate manager, Jack Welch, in the year of his retirement from GE and has many fundamental ideas that can apply to beginning a strategic e-learning program.

This year has produced a lot of press about the front-end of e-learning management, that is, what steps managers have to take in order for learners to actually sign up for e-learning experiences. Elliott Masie of The MASIE Center, for one, calls this the "Invitation Process" and urges training managers to be much more engaging, innovative, and sophisticated in tweaking the invitation process to suit individual learners (*TechLearn TRENDS*, April 30, 2001, p. 1). Jack Welch had a direct approach that worked for him.

He reports in this book, p. 350, that he borrowed the idea from John Chambers of Cisco Systems. They called this a hunt for the "parallel paths" of behavior and process that stood in the way of people doing business online. For example, all travel was done online; any parallel use of a travel agent was forbidden. Managers were known to have stood at office doors to physically stop the "parallel" processes from happening. Printers were physically removed from offices in order to force people to network their copiers. Reducing the amount of paper flowing around offices in approval processes yielded as much as a 30 percent reduction in overhead costs (p. 351).

The article reprinted here tells a more complete story, one that has strategic parallels for e-learning.

The razzmatazz that once surrounded business-to-business (B2B) e-commerce has vanished, leaving a trail of dead dot-coms. That does not mean an end to the changes that new information and communications technologies are bringing to companies. But from now on, the transformation will occur mainly in established companies, which will continue their quiet search for new electronic ways to carry out familiar tasks.

The coming of the Internet, with its associated technologies, is changing both how companies deal with their suppliers and customers, and how they organise work. Some of these shifts will be profound; others are, for now, mere extensions of the proprietary networks that many big firms were already using. The case studies that we will run over the next few weeks will look at the progress of this revolution in America, Europe, Japan and emerging economies.

One of the companies farthest along the track is General Electric. This old-economy icon now buys and sells more through its private online marketplaces—an estimated $20 billion this year alone—than is traded in all the independent B2B marketplaces together. Management books celebrate the e-business epiphany of its boss, Jack Welch, as proof that even elephants can dance.

Yet, for most of the late 1990s, GE seemed to have blown a spectacular e-business opportunity. When the Internet wave hit, it was one of the world's biggest industrial buyers, with one

---

Source: "E-Strategy brief: GE While Welch Waited" in *The Economist,* May 19, 2001, pp.75–76. Reprinted with permission of *The Economist,* copyright 2001. All rights reserved.

of its biggest electronic buying networks. In 1997 its GE Information Services (GEIS) division was practically the only B2B game in town, albeit based on pre-Internet technologies.

But GEIS faded mysteriously from sight just as such B2B companies as Ariba and Commerce One began to produce fashionable software for electronic commerce. Although GEIS executives knew that they stood on the verge of something big, they were unable to do much about it until it was almost too late.

The reason was a bad case of conglomeritis. GE, the world's largest company, offers vast opportunities to use technology inventively. But its obsession with earnings growth means that it suffers from an inherent conservatism: unprofitable new ventures must win extraordinary executive and board support to go ahead.

In such a culture, it was hard to win support for a new B2B business. Keeping up with the dotcom start-ups would mean spending as profligately as they had, but without the freedom that came, in those golden days, from investors' tolerance of big losses. "We wanted to do some of what Ariba and Commerce One do, but we couldn't do it at the cost of hundreds of millions of dollars of losses," says Harvey Seegers, then GEIS's boss and now in charge of the main part of GE's e-commerce activities. GEIS bosses found it hard to get a green light from headquarters. While they waited, their "first-mover" advantage withered.

The main obstacle was the prospect of cannibalising a profitable proprietary data business: GEIS itself. From the early 1980s until the mid-1990s, e-business referred not to the Internet but to electronic data interchange (EDI), a way of exchanging formatted purchase orders and other documents electronically. EDI transactions tend to be carried over private, secure networks or leased lines, usually run by third-party service providers.

GEIS was the biggest of these. Its data centre in Rockville, Maryland boasted a NASA-like command centre run by former military technicians still sporting crew cuts and smartly addressing supervisors as "sir." It served 100,000 companies that collectively process more than a billion transactions a year.

This offered GE a vision of the future: more and more companies doing business with each other electronically as they automated their internal processes. The natural extension of the "enterprise resource planning" movement led by SAP, a German software company, was connecting one enterprise to another. This laid the groundwork for widespread, automated machine-to-machine transactions between companies.

Enter the Internet

But at the same time the Internet was exploding. GEIS at first saw its potential mostly as a cheap on-ramp to EDI networks for small and medium-sized firms that did not want a full EDI connection. Smaller suppliers often had to be dragged reluctantly on to larger firms' EDI networks: for the minnows, the costs often outweighed the savings. Perhaps the Internet could help there, replacing expensive private networks with cheaper public ones. So GEIS offered a service that would accept EDI forms submitted via a website and transmit them on its own proprietary network to their destination, one of GEIS's larger clients.

But that was as far as it went. For all the Internet's consumer appeal, GEIS reasoned, the business world is far more conservative. For more than two decades, EDI had been the only commonly agreed standard with which to conduct business-to-business transactions. It would not be overturned easily.

Yet EDI has many flaws. In essence it is nothing more than a machine-readable e-mail message with strict rules about what to say. It is not interactive, and it operates, like all e-mail, in an asynchronous fashion, with long delays between call and response.

Thus, Wal-Mart's ordering system might use EDI to send a purchase order to a supplier in the morning; once the supplier accepted the order it might direct its computers to send a confirmation back. Similar formatted messages might travel back and forth as the order is completed, shipped and received. EDI saves companies money, mostly by taking people and errors out of the equation, but it does not fundamentally change the way business is done or who it is done with.

That changed when the Internet came along. B2B exchanges did more than simply take existing relationships and transactions and turn them into digital form: they offered the potential for new relationships and new sorts of transactions, from auctions to direct sales without middlemen and brokers. Between 1995 and 2000, more than 700 such exchanges were founded. Some were independent marketplaces and some were run by big buyers or sellers.

Most of those have since disappeared. Yet B2B continues to grow today, although companies now tend to work with their own suppliers in private marketplaces rather than in independent exchanges. Indeed, many of the virtues of GEIS's model—and especially its focus on improving existing business relationships, rather than reinventing them—are now, ironically, back in vogue.

Fomenting Revolution

A year and a half ago, though, that was not the prevailing wisdom. As B2B dotcom start-ups were going public at multi-billion-dollar valuations, GEIS was starting to have doubts about its continuing focus on traditional EDI. Fears of the Y2K computer bug had distracted it for years, as it spent heavily to avoid trouble. Its customers—mostly larger, established industrial firms—were equally distracted.

Mr Seegers had joined GEIS in 1996. Within the company, a mainframe culture dominated, with an emphasis on white-shirted professionalism and reliability; beyond it, the growth of the Internet was in full spate. Mr Seegers, a former marine, was trained to handle conflict; yet this was a case of two worlds that preferred not to acknowledge each other's existence at all.

GEIS was a small division by GE standards, not even a line item in its annual reports—although its concentration on EDI meant that it certainly satisfied Mr Welch's decree that all divisions must be number one or two in their market. Mr Seegers now began to agitate for a larger role for GEIS. It took Mr Welch's e-business awakening to get it.

That moment has, like most big shifts in GE, taken on an unduly heroic sheen. It was, after all, in early 1999, a time when it was impossible to ignore Internet hype; Mr Welch was hardly a brave pioneer. But it is not easy to turn around the world's biggest firm, even for the most commanding of bosses.

In fact, there had been something of an e-business movement already brewing in GE, from the bottom up and in just a few isolated spots. As early as 1994, GE Plastics, one of the conglomerate's divisions, had a website with some basic information. By 1997, its Polymerland distribution operations had become the first GE unit to allow customers to place online orders. GEIS was also operating a partly web-based service called the Trading Partner Network, which simplified and automated the bid and procurement process for other divisions, led by GE Lighting.

But until 1999, when Mr Welch, after a Christmas watching his family shop online, famously told GE that e-business would be every division's "priority one, two, three and four," progress was slow. Buying from suppliers online was one thing, but selling to customers online risked putting GE's sales force out of business. Big Internet investments risked hurting each division's bottom line, against which bosses are mainly measured. And GEIS, the one division that could have pushed the hardest, was fussing over Y2K.

By the time Y2K had passed, Mr Welch had devised "destroyyourbusiness.com," encouraging each division to reinvent itself before somebody else did. Mr Seegers proposed splitting up GEIS: rather than trying to alter the mainframe culture that ran the EDI networks, he suggested spinning off a more entrepreneurial group to pursue Internet marketplaces. An hour and a half later, Mr Welch said, "Go for it."

So, in March 2000, GEIS became GE Global eXchange Services (GXS), a software and marketplace builder, and GE Systems Services, an EDI network provider. Tellingly, Mr Seegers chose to run GXS, the smaller of the two by assets, but the one with fewer legacy obligations that would hamper innovation.

The Culture Clash

Today, all of GE's big divisions run their own web marketplaces, both for internal and external use. Three initiatives—"e-buy"; "e-sell"; and "e-make"—are digitising the main functions of running the conglomerate, saving money, reaching customers faster and using Internet technology to extend the focus on quality that was the driving-force of Mr Welch's previous passion, six-sigma manufacturing.

The greatest hurdle has been not technology but culture. Sales staff, worried that they might be destroying their jobs, had to be offered bonuses for helping customers to use GE websites to order. Managers had to watch carefully for reprobate employees using "parallel paths" (the telephone, for instance, or a walk to a store) to order supplies, say, or arrange travel. Some offices even closed their mail rooms for all but one day a week (and that only for the incorrigible legal department) to stop employees from using regular post. Others locked their printer rooms except for occasional days when bosses would station themselves at the door and demand from those who came through an explanation for their sad inability to shake old paper habits.

For now, most of this is about cost savings and improved quality. But over time GE hopes its e-business projects will allow it to come up with new products, such as services that turn one-time purchases into recurring revenue streams, and sell to new customers that its existing salesforce cannot reach, such as small businesses. It also hopes to expand its supplier base by letting more firms bid online, through auctions and other marketplaces.

GXS has restored GE's reputation in (depleted) B2B circles. But although the company is now free to invest in its own research and development at a rate closer to that of its independent competitors, it still cannot buy other firms, as they can, with shares. GE may now be flexible about internal e-business spending, but earnings-diluting acquisitions are still hard for it to swallow. This constrains its ability to profit from the industry's consolidation: it must stick mostly to its strategy of organic growth and internal development. GE breaks many moulds, but there are limits to what even the most entrepreneurial arm of a conglomerate can do.

That does not undermine the scale of GXS's achievement; rather, it suggests how hard it is for big companies to keep up with nimble newcomers. Asked if he can think of any other successful high-tech companies that have grown up within a diversified industrial conglomerate, Mr Seegers ponders. "No," he finally concedes with a smile. "We'll be the first."

2. Thinking Change

Government Action Regarding New Kinds of Learning

Editor's Comment: The abstract and synthesis of the articles referenced here profiles a government newly aware that learning challenges are changing and multiplying as the world gets smaller through travel and the Internet. What is particularly interesting about these abstracts is the reaching-out to related agencies in order to solve problems and get things done. This represents a new kind of thinking on the part of agencies formerly entrenched in their own mindsets—a kind of new approach to education and training. These kinds of administrative and representative agencies can be a model for management teams and groups trying to solve similar problems on both local and global scales.

You can find it on the web at *www.webcommission.org*. It is the report of the work of a Congressional panel, the Web Based Education Commission, chaired by Senator Bob Kerrey. The U.S. State Department beginning in April of 2000 became an international voice for educational policy, particularly for "higher or tertiary education, adult education, and training." A coalition of advocates for reform in eldercare in Massachusetts enlarged its focus quickly when it realized that lack of training was a major cause of high turnover in nursing homes. And Elaine Chao, Secretary of the U.S. Department of Labor said at her confirmation that she was concerned about "quality job training," "modernizing the American workforce," and "working with the Department of Education . . . to help workers face the global economy." These statements all reflect a cross-agency or cross-content collaboration that is important for the times in which we live and work. They are a recognition of the importance of global learning and of the particularly strong role government can play in making it happen.

The article referenced in *The New York Times On the Web* considered barriers to "the full educational utility of the Internet" (Jan. 3, 2001, p. 2)—something that training managers need to consider too in the context of their businesses. Other contentious items included the concepts of "can use federal funds" and "must use federal funds" for, in this case, teacher training in the nation's schools. Training managers in corporations, too, have to wrestle with this issue of budgeting, funding, and what's a priority. Protecting online learners, expanding access, ensuring quality of content, working with the Federal Communications Commission

---

Sources: "Will Congressional Web Learning Report Gather Momentum or Only Gather Dust?" by Margaret W. Goldsborough in *The New York Times On the Web*, January 3, 2001, pp. 1, 2; Margaret W. Goldsborough is a freelance writer; "Better-Paid Caregivers, Better Care" by Joan Fitzgerald in *The American Prospect*, May 21, 2001, pp. 30–32; Joan Fitzgerald is Associate Director of the Center for Urban and Regional Policy and an Associate Professor at Northeastern University; "U.S. Government Policy Goes Global—and Takes e-learning With It" by John S. Rudd in *e-learning*, July 2001; John S. Rudd is a freelance writer and consultant; and "Chao Becomes New DOL Secretary" by Karyn-Siobhan Robinson in *HR News*, March 2001, p. 2; Karyn-Siobhan Robinson is a staff writer for *SHRM Online*.

and the Department of Labor's SCORM standards were all concerns raised by the Commission's work. These kinds of issues are also confronting training managers as new ways to learn become part of our workplaces.

The article referenced here in *The American Prospect* is an article about the crisis in American nursing homes in particular and in eldercare in general. It features various state solutions, "piecemeal" at best, to parts of our country's care-giving problem. Of particular interest is a recent nursing home quality initiative in the state of Massachusetts. The legislature there passed a $42 million funding package for direct-care workers including specific items for career-ladder programs, training scholarships, training for people moving off welfare who are employed in nursing homes, and money for post-employment supports also for the welfare to work community (p. 31). The heavy emphasis on training was included as a result of the efforts of the Coalition to Reform Eldercare, a group of labor and advocacy organizations and nursing home operators. *The American Prospect* reports that "the group originally came together to advocate for increased staffing levels, but soon realized the need to address factors causing high turnover first" (p. 31). The case was made that an investment in training this particular workforce was good business sense.

And finally, the article referenced in *e-learning* describes the activity of the Department of State in formulating international educational policy. An April 19, 2000 memo from then President Bill Clinton presented the department with "the twin challenges of preparing our citizens for a global environment while continuing to attract and educate future leaders from around the world." The report of the Educational Study Team included a policy section on boosting the ability of U.S. educators and trainers to supply their services to U.S. and foreign students in other countries on a cross-border basis, through electronic means or through facilities established abroad (p. 22). The report also contained sections on overcoming the barriers to international transmission of learning services, and it encouraged service providers to become involved. The goal of the Study Team is the ambitious one of making the U.S. a leader in international educational policy, as well as a major supplier of worldwide educational products (p. 23).

These reports are examples of government activism in learning, particularly in e-learning. They highlight trends to watch, legislation to support, and ideas to emulate.

New Ways of Thinking at the Top

Editor's Comment: Decision making has long been held to be one of the primary jobs of managers, and from time to time, books and articles examine the process to clarify what it means and how to train for it. This is one such article.

Our workplaces seem to demand both reflection and action. We've seen recent commentaries by professors who disdain experiential workplace research, preferring instead to operate within the confines of academe and academic research standards (Karen Ayas, *Reflections,* spring 2001, p. 65); by consultants who press hard for training managers, especially those responsible for e-learning, to strategically interweave their training plans with those of other departments such as sales, marketing, production, strategic planning, line managers and executives (Fred Poker, *e-learning,* April 2001, p. 126); and of business schools whose MBA enrollments are declining, whose admissions standards are in question, and who often have become irrelevant to business (Jennifer Merritt, *Business Week,* May 7, 2001, pp. 68–69). In many key places and by many key constituencies it seems that decision making is coming under fire. The article reproduced here examines several aspects of decision making and their benefits to managers who understand the differences.

How should decisions be made? Easy, we figured that out long ago. First define the problem, then diagnose its causes, next design possible solutions, and finally decide which is best. And, if course, implement the choice.

But do people always make decisions that way? We propose that this rational, or "thinking first," model of decision making should be supplemented with two very different models—a "seeing first" and a "doing first" model. When practicing managers use all three models, they can improve the quality of their decisions. Healthy organizations, like healthy people, have the capacity for all three.

Consider how a real decision was made, a personal one in this case. It begins with a call from an aunt.

"Hi, kiddo. I want to buy you a housewarming present. What's the color scheme in your new apartment?"

"Color scheme? Betty, you've got to be kidding. I'll have to ask Lisa. Lisa, Betty wants to now the color scheme of the apartment."

> Sometimes decisions defy purely step-by-step logic. To be effective, companies also should embrace intuitive or action-oriented forms of decision making.

"Black," daughter Lisa says.

"Black? Lisa, I've got to live there."

"Black," she repeats.

A few days later, father and daughter find themselves in a furniture store. They try every desk, every chair: Nothing works. Shopper's lethargy sets in. Then Lisa spots a black stool: "Wouldn't that look great against the white counter?" And they're off. Within an hour, they have picked out everything—in black, white and steel gray.

The extraordinary thing about this ordinary story is that our conventional theories of decision making can't explain it. It is not even clear what the final decision was: to buy the stool; to get on with furnishing an apartment; to do

---

Source: "Decision Making: It's Not What You Think" by Henry Mintzberg and Frances Westley in *Sloan Management Review,* Spring 2001, pp. 89–93. Henry Mintzberg and Frances Westley are Professors of Management at McGill University in Montreal, Canada. Reprinted with permission of *Sloan Management Review,* copyright 2001. All rights reserved.

so in black and white; to create a new lifestyle! Decision making can be mysterious.

The Limits of "Thinking First"

Rational decision making has a clearly identified process: define → diagnose → design → decide. However, the rational approach turns out to be uncommon.

Years ago, one of us studied a host of decisions, delineating the steps and then laying them out. A decision process for building a new plant was typical. The process kept cycling back, interrupted by new events, diverted by opportunities and so on, going round and round until finally a solution emerged. The final action was as clear as a wave breaking on the shore, but explaining how it came to be is as hard as tracing the origin of that wave back into the ocean.

Often decisions do not so much emerge as erupt. Here is how Alexander Kotov, the chess master, has described a sudden insight that followed lengthy analysis:

"So, I mustn't move the knight. Try the rook move again. . . . At this point you glance at the clock. 'My goodness! Already 30 minutes gone on thinking about whether to move the rook or the knight. If it goes on like this you'll really be in time trouble.' And then suddenly you are struck by the happy idea—why move rook or knight? What about B-QN1? And without any more ado, without analysis at all, you move the bishop. Just like that."

Perhaps, then, decision making means periods of groping followed by sudden sharp insights that lead to crystallization, as A. Langley and co-authors suggested in a 1995 Organizational Science article.

Or perhaps it is a form of "organized anarchy," as Stanford professor James March and colleagues have written. They characterize decision making as "collections of choices looking for problems, issues and feelings looking for decision situations in which they may be aired, solutions looking for issues to which they might be an answer, and decision makers looking for work."

But is the confusion, as described by those authors, in the process, or is it in the observers? Maybe messy, real-life decision making makes more sense than we think, precisely because so much of it is beyond conscious thought.

"Seeing First"

Insight—"seeing into"—suggests that decisions, or at least actions, may be driven as much by what is seen as by what is thought. As Mozart said, the best part about creating a symphony was being able to "see the whole of it at a single glance in my mind." So, understanding can be visual as well as conceptual.

In W. Koehler's well-known 1920s experiment, an ape struggled to reach a banana placed high in its cage. Then it *saw* the box in the corner—not just noticed it, but realized what could be done with it—and its problem was solved. Likewise after Alexander Fleming really *saw* the mold that had killed the bacteria in some of his research samples (in other words, when he realized how that mold could be used), he and his colleague were able to give us penicillin. The same can be true for strategic vision. Vision requires the courage to see what others do not—and that means having both the confidence and the experience to recognize the sudden insight for what it is.

A theory in Gestalt psychology developed by G. Wallas in the 1920s identifies four steps in creative discovery: preparation → incubation → illumination → verification.

Preparation must come first. As Louis Pasteur put it, "Chance favors only the prepared mind." Deep knowledge, usually developed over years, is followed by incubation, during which the unconscious mind mulls over the issue. Then with luck (as with Archimedes in the bathtub), there is that flash of illumination. That eureka moment often comes after sleep—because in sleep, rational thinking is turned off, and the unconscious has greater freedom. The conscious mind returns later to make the logical argument. But that verification (reasoning it all out in linear order for purposes of elaboration and proof) takes time. There is a story of a mathematician who solved a formula in his sleep. Holding it in his mind's eyes, he was in no rush to write it down. When he did, it took him four months!

Great insights may be rare, but what industry cannot trace its origins to one or more of them? Moreover, little insights occur to all of us all the

Characteristics of the Three Approaches to Making Decisions

"Thinking first" features the qualities of	"Seeing first" features the qualities of	"Doing first" features the qualities of
science	art	craft
planning, programming	visioning, imagining	venture, learning
the verbal	the visual	the visceral
facts	ideas	experiences

time. No one should accept any theory of decision making that ignores insight.

"Doing First"

But what happens when you don't see it and can't think it up? Just do it. That is how pragmatic people function when stymied: They get on with it, believing that if they do "something," the necessary thinking could follow. It's experimentation—trying something so that you can learn.

A theory for "doing first," popularized in academia by organizational-behavior professor Karl Weick, goes like this: enactment → selection → retention.

That means doing various things, finding out which among them works, making sense of that and repeating the successful behaviors while discarding the rest. Successful people know that when they are stuck, they must experiment. Thinking may drive doing, but doing just as surely drives thinking. We don't just think in order to act, we act in order to think.

Show us almost any company that has diversified successfully, and we will show you a company that has learned by doing, one whose diversification strategy emerged through experience. Such a company at the outset may have laid out a tidy strategy on the basis of assessing its weaknesses and strengths (or, if after 1990, its "core competencies"), which it almost certainly got wrong. How can you tell a strength from a weakness when you are entering a new sphere? You have no choice but to try things out. Then you can identify the competencies that are really core. Action is important; if you insist on "thinking first" and, for example, doing formalized strategic planning (which is really part of the same thing), you may in fact discourage learning.

Making Decisions Through Discussion, Collage and Improvisation

Thus the three major approaches to decision making are "thinking first, "seeing first" and "doing first." They correlate with conventional views of science, art and craft. The first is mainly verbal (comprising words in linear order), the second is visual, the third is visceral. Those who favor thinking are people who cherish facts, those who favor seeing cherish ideas and those who favor doing cherish experiences. (See "Characteristics of the Three Approaches to Making Decisions.")

We have for some years conducted workshops on the three approaches with midcareer managers sent by Asian, European and North American companies to our International Masters Program in Practicing Management (www.impm.org). We begin with a general discussion about the relationship between analysis, ideas and action. It soon becomes evident that practicing managers recognize the iterative and connected nature of those elements. We then ask small groups first to discuss an issue for about an hour (one of their own or else what we call a "provocative question." For example: "How do you manage customer service when you never see a customer?" or "How do you organize without structure?"), summarize their conclusions on a flip chart and report back to the full group. Next we give the groups colored paper, pens, scissors and glue. Each small group must create a collage about the issue they discussed in the thinking-first session. At the end of that second workshop, the groups view one another's images and compare "seeing first" with "thinking first"—in terms of both process and results. Finally, each group, with only a few minutes of preparation time permitted, improvises a skit to act out its issue. Again, the groups consider the results.

Reactions to the approaches are revealing. Participants note that in the thinking-first workshop, the initial discussions start off easily enough, no matter what the mix of nationalities or work backgrounds. Participants list comments on flip charts and spontaneously use bulleted items and numbers—with the occasional graph thrown in. Almost no time is spent in discussing *how* to go about analyzing the problem. Groups quickly converge on one of several conventional analytic frameworks: cause and effect, problem and solution, pros and cons, and so on.

Many participants observe that such frameworks, particularly when adopted early, blunt exploration. Quality and depth of analysis may be sacrificed for process efficiency. Thinking-first workshops encourage linear, rational and rather categorical arguments. All too often, the result is a wish list, with disagreements hidden in the different points. In other words, there may be less discipline in thinking first than we believe. Thinking comes too easily to most of us.

But when a group must make a picture, members have to reach consensus. That requires deeper integration of the ideas. "We had to think more to do this," a participant reported. The artistic exercise "really forces you to capture the essence of an issue," another added. People ask more questions in the seeing-first exercise; they become more playful and creative.

"In 'thinking first,' we focused on the problems; in 'seeing first,' we focused on the solutions," one person said. One group believed it had agreement on the issue after the thinking-first workshop. Only when the picture making began did its members realize how superficial that agreement was—more of a compromise. In contrast, when you really do see, as someone said, "The message jumps out at you." But to achieve that, the group members have to find out more about one another's capabilities and collaborate more closely. "I felt it became a group project, not just my project," said a participant who had chosen the topic for his group. The seeing-first exercise also draws out

> In the "seeing first" workshop, midcareer managers find making a picture of problems required deeper integration of ideas.

more emotions; there is more laughter and a higher energy level. This suggests that being able to see a trajectory—having a vision about what you are doing—energizes people and so stimulates action. In comparing the seeing-first exercise with the thinking-first discussion, a participant remarked, "We felt more liberated." The pictures may be more ambiguous than the words, but they are also more involving. A frequent comment: "They invite interpretation."

One particularly interesting observation about the pictures was that "the impression lasts longer." Studies indicate that we remember pictures much longer and more accurately than words. As R. Haber demonstrated in Scientific American in 1970, recall of images, even as many as 10,000 shown at one-second intervals, is nearly 98%—a capability that may be linked to evolution. Humans survived by learning to register danger and safety signals fast. Emotion, memory, recall and stimulation are powerfully bundled in "seeing first." Contrast that with one comment after the thinking-first workshop: "Twenty-four hours later, we won't remember what this meant."

In fact, although many participants have not made a picture since grade school, the art produced in the seeing-first workshops is often remarkable. Creativity flows freely among the managers, suggesting that they could come up with more creative ideas in their home organizations if they more often used symbols beyond words or numbers.

Our multicultural groups may like the art workshop for overcoming language barriers, but groups of managers from the same company, country or language group have responded equally well. One British participant who was working on a joint venture with an American partner found that out. He met with his U.S. counterpart a few days after the workshops. "We talked past each other for two hours," he reported. When he suggested they create a picture of their common concerns, they finally were able to connect.

> ### When Each Decision-Making Approach Works Best
>
> "THINKING FIRST" WORKS BEST WHEN:
> - the issue is clear;
> - the data is reliable;
> - the context is structured;
> - thoughts can be pinned down; and
> - discipline can be applied
>
> as in an established production process.
>
> "SEEING FIRST" WORKS BEST WHEN:
> - many elements have to be combined into creative solutions:
> - commitment to those solutions is key; and
> - communication across boundaries is essential
>
> as in new-product development.
>
> "DOING FIRST" WORKS BEST WHEN:
> - the situation is novel and confusing;
> - complicated specifications would get in the way; and
> - a few simple relationship rules can help people move forward
>
> for example, when companies face a disruptive technology.

The improvisation skits—"doing first"—generate more spontaneity. Participants respond to one another intuitively and viscerally, letting out concerns held back in conversation and even in artwork. For example, turf battles become evident in the way people stand and talk. Humor, power, fear and anger surface. (M. Crossen and M. Sorrenti discuss improvisation at length in a helpful article published in 1997 in Advances in Strategic Management.)

Weick has suggested that a key aspect of effective action in organizations is the ability to remain open to signals from others, even under extreme pressure. He believes that such heedfulness, as he calls it, is a finely honed skill among group improvisers such as jazz musicians. Organizations that recognize opportunities for improvisation—and hone the skills required—increase their capacity for learning. In improvisation, people have to respond with a speed that eliminates many inhibitions. "Having to just act gets rid of the fears," a participant said. Another added, after watching a colleague play the role of a frustrated bank customer, "The output can be scarily real."

Mere words, in contrast, feel more abstract and disconnected—numbers, even more so—just as the aggregations of marketing are more abstract than the experience of selling. The skits bring out what the words and numbers do not say—indeed, what problems they cause. "Not everything is unsayable in words," claimed playwright Eugène Ionesco, "only the living truth." Or as Isadora Duncan, the modern-dance pioneer, insisted, "If I could say it, I wouldn't have to dance it." Thus "doing first" facilitates the dancing that is so lacking in many of today's organizations.

Enough Thinking?

The implications for our large, formalized, thinking-obsessed organizations are clear enough: not to suspend thinking so much as put it in its place, alongside seeing and doing. Isn't it time we got past our obsession with planning and programming, and opened the doors more widely to venturing and visioning? A glance at corporate reports, e-mail and meetings reveals that art is usually something reserved for report covers—or company walls. And when organizations separate the thinking from the doing, with the former coming from the heads of powerful formulators and the latter assigned to the hands of ostensibly docile implementers, those formulators lose the benefits of experimenting—and learning.

Each approach has its own strengths and weaknesses. (See "When Each Decision-Making Approach Works Best.") "Thinking first" works best when the issue is clear, the data reliable and the world structured; when thoughts can be pinned down and discipline applied, as in an established production process. "Seeing first" is necessary when many elements have to be combined into creative solutions and when commitment to those solutions is key, as in much new-product development. The organization has to break away from the conventional, encourage communication across boundaries, bust up cerebral logjams and engage the heart as well as the head. "Doing first" is preferred when the situation is novel and confusing, and things need to be worked out. That is often the case in a new industry—or in an old industry thrown into turmoil by a new technology. Under such circumstances, complicated specifications get in the way, and a few simple relationship rules can help people move forward in a coordinated yet spontaneous manner.

That suggests the advantages of combining all three approaches. In order to learn, a company group might tackle a new issue first by craft, which is tied to doing; then, in order to imagine, by art, which is tied to seeing; finally, in order to program, by science, which is tied to thinking. In ongoing situations, art provides the overview, or vision; science specifies the structure, or plan; and craft produces the action, or energy. In other words, science keeps you straight, art keeps you interested, and craft keeps you going. No organization can do without any one approach. Isn't it time, then, to move beyond our narrow thinking about decision making: to get in *touch*, to *see* another point of view?

3. Digital Structures

Learning Management Systems

Editor's Comment: After the discussions and definitions of intellectual capital and knowledge management of recent years, along comes Learning Management Systems (LMS) as the way to organize, coordinate, and, yes, manage those new, fuzzy relatives of training. The LMS is one of the key digital structures that can be helpful to training managers.

Online interactive newsletters are good sources of what works and what the red flags are as training managers investigate and install Learning Management Systems. The two newsletters referenced here provide some basic information; many other editions of these and other online newsletters contain LMS information.

The vendors multiply and show up in droves at conferences. These two newsletters often report on presentations by conference vendors, especially conferences that the folks at 50 South Ninth Street, Minneapolis, sponsor. Here are some points to consider as you design and implement a Learning Management System:

1. Look at the likely longer term growth expected for your company. Be sure that your LMS is big enough for potential acquisition of employees or functions.

2. Are your employees really ready for the integrating and measuring that typically are key parts of LMS?

3. Will your LMS handle present and future delivery systems—on the job training, mentoring and coaching, classrooms, and e-learning? How about combinations of any or all the above?

4. Is the LMS flexible enough to work with various vendors and contract workers?

5. Do you want to now or later include customers and suppliers in your learning system? Is the LMS able to handle this?

6. Do you need security built into the system to guard against the slippage of proprietary information?

7. A good LMS should have an online browser-based tool for student registration and examining course expectations.

8. A good LMS should have an e-mail feature that notifies all employees about learning events.

9. A good LMS should have management and administration features to allow course set up and documentation.

10. A good LMS should support development efforts with templates for user manuals, with consistent formats for job aids, and with development standards.

11. A good LMS will recognize that the training operation needs to collaborate with other departments and operations within the company and make provision for their input into the system design and management.

12. A good LMS will facilitate learner evaluation in the context of business goals.

Sources: OLReviews online interactive newsletter published by VNU Business Media, June 28, 2001, pp. 3 and 4; and *TDFeNet* online interactive newsletter also published by VNU Business Media June 20, 2001, Minneapolis, MN.

Training Management

What the Best Managers Do to Be Really Supportive

Editor's Comment: The succinct article contributed by an ASTD member to the periodic newsletter, *Performance In Practice*, outlines the content of a Training Audit. It is one way to look at the variety of a training manager's job. It can provide the context for all of the other "softer" sides of the manager's job: listening to employees who need to know how to do something right now; showing them how or finding someone, now, who can show them; deciding when and how to embark on an e-learning adventure; facilitating training courses online or in classrooms when personnel change dramatically or workforces merge; creating communities of learners and of learning. All of these softer sides of training management can be applied to the analytical list in Rita Smith's classic "Training Audit." We urge you to think creatively about the softer side of training management when you read this article; the best managers think and act both ways at once. In this age of pie charts, easy computer graphics, spread sheets, statistical reports, and other digital wizardry that supports things such as training audits, it is more important than ever for those of us who value the development of the *human* resources at work to pay attention continuously to both sides of our jobs as managers.

Is our Training Department as effective and efficient as it can be? Periodically asking this question and actively seeking the answer is the key to a successful training function, whether we are part of an established department, part of a reengineering effort, or brought in to create a new Training Department.

Any high-performing business entity periodically takes a snapshot of its processes, products, and services. Data collected via such an "audit" provides insight into compliance, opportunities for improvement, and a baseline from which to benchmark best practices. As training professionals, we can greatly benefit from periodically conducting a Training Audit. If you have never done one before, ask yourself the following questions:

- What type of information should be collected for the Training Audit?
- How will the audit actually be conducted?
- How should the data be analyzed?
- What type of post-audit reporting is necessary?

Recommended content for the Training Audit includes the following categories (with examples of what each might include in parentheses):

- Training organization (staffing, skills strengths and gaps, organizational structure as it relates to business units supported)
- Governing process (process for making decisions about training investments and priorities, training plan review and approval, process for communicating and monitoring execution of plan)
- Training plan (vision/mission, links to overall business strategy, goals and objectives)
- Training products and services (comprehensive listing)
- Curriculum development (Instructional Systems Design Process, cost models, media selection, development software used, make or buy analysis process)
- Outsourcing/vendor management (sourcing and selecting process, quality management process)

Source: "How Are We Really Doing? The Training Audit" by Rita Smith in *Performance In Practice* newsletter published by ASTD, Summer 2001, pp. 1-2. Rita Smith is Vice President of Training and Development for First Data Merchant Services. Reprinted with permission of ASTD, copyright 2001. All rights reserved.

- Curriculum management (documentation, shelf life, updates and maintenance, disaster recovery process)
- Delivery (hours, number of employees, number of classes per year, cost per employee, type of media used)
- Marketing and communications (brand, marketing plans, methods, media, cost information, communication plans)
- Students (customers, demographics, hardware and software available, numbers served per job family)
- Client relationship management (process for interfacing with business areas to determine training requirements, contact time)
- Training management system (automated system used, student registration process, student records, resource management, customer assistance, technical assistance)
- Measurement and evaluation (quality assurance process, type of evaluation, frequency of evaluations, cost information, improvement processes)

A variety of process options exist for conducting the Training Audit. One option is a workshop format where the training team provides as much data as possible and then gathers whatever information is still missing. Another approach is to assign individual team members a specific data collection category. Of course, enlisting the services of a third party to conduct the audit is yet another option. Whatever option is selected, it is important to acknowledge the concern some team members may have about the concept of an "audit." Open, proactive communication about the audit's intent and processes should allay some concerns.

Analysis can involve assessing current compliance to established practices. It can also include benchmarking against other Training Departments for comparable data. Finally, analysis can include identification of process improvement opportunities. Involving the Training Department's customers in creating process improvement strategies is especially effective for this later analysis.

One product of the Training Audit is a comprehensive report of the findings and recommendations for improvement. Closing the communication loop and sharing these findings with executives and training staff is one of the most important aspects of any Training Audit process.

At the end of the Training Audit process, we are in a much better position to truly answer the question, "How are we really doing?"

4. Global Connections

Use of E-Learning Around the Globe

Editor's Comment: The base of respondents for this large ASTD study is more than 500 organizations from 38 countries. This report presents results from 9 regions:

Asia	China	Latin America
Australia/New Zealand	Europe	the Middle East
Canada	Japan	the United States

The complete report is a 24-page document, available from ASTD, 800/628-2783. We present only the key findings and the narrative on uses of e-learning here.

KEY FINDINGS AND HIGHLIGHTS

Analysis of the responses to the *2000 Measurement Kit*, coupled with comparisons with data from 1997, 1998, and 1999, yielded an interesting mix of similarities and differences as well as trends in training investments and practices across the nine regions. Among the highlights:

- Respondents in Europe reported spending the most ($862) on training per employee, while those in Latin America reported spending the least ($335) on training per employee.

- Training expenditure as a percentage of payroll was the highest in Asian countries (3.8%). Japan reported the lowest percentage of payroll (1.6%) spent on training.

- Respondents in Europe were most likely to outsource training (43.6%), while organizations in the United States were the least likely to do so (18.4%).

- In total training hours per eligible employee, respondents in the Middle East (43.3 hours) and Latin America (38.3 hours) reported the highest number of hours. Japan (25.6 hours) reported the lowest number of hours.

- Training types varied significantly across the regions. For example, training expenditures on customer relations were the lowest in Japan (4.6%) and Australia/New Zealand (5.3%) and highest in Latin America (13%) and the Middle East (9%).

- Quality, competition, and business practice training was relatively high across all regions. Most respondents reported that roughly 11 percent of their resources were invested in this type of training.

- Instructor-led classroom training continued to be the predominant form of training delivery in all regions. However, in every region except China, the United States, and Asia, there was a movement away from instructor-led training and toward

Source: International Comparisons Report 2001 by Michael J. Marquardt, Stephen B. King, and Eustace Koon, published by ASTD, copyright 2001. Page 2, Key Findings and Highlights, and page 11, Use of E-learning. Michael J. Marquardt is Vice President, Research, at ASTD; Stephen B. King is Executive Director, Leadership Management Division, at Management Concepts, Inc.; Eustace Koon is Research Officer, Research, at ASTD. Reprinted with permission of ASTD, copyright 2001. All rights reserved.

other means of delivery, namely learning technologies.
- All regions forecast significant increases in training expenditures, with the highest projections for growth in spending coming from respondents in Japan.

USE OF E-LEARNING

E-learning remains a "hot topic" in the training and development field, as evidenced by professional literature, conference presentations, and Wall Street investments in dot-com companies focused on learning technologies. However, the use of learning technologies showed little change between 1998 and 1999. Moreover, the three-year projections for learning technology this year were more cautious than last year's projections. These findings suggest that most firms around the world continue to believe that learning technologies will play an increasingly important role in the future but have discovered the difficulty in making this a reality.

According to the *Measurement Kit* results, the level of training delivered via learning technologies is on the rise in many regions. The percentage in Australia/New Zealand almost tripled, jumping from 4.2 percent of training delivered via technology in 1998 to 13.3 percent in 1999. The smallest increase was seen in Europe, which reported an increase of only 1.2 percent. The percentage of training delivered via learning technologies ranged from 5 percent in China to 16.2 percent in the Middle East.

Projections on the use of the classroom as a means of training delivery in 2002 were highest in Latin America (73.2%), followed by Japan (70.4%). On the other end of the spectrum, respondents in Australia/New Zealand and Europe estimated 45.0 and 57.5 percent, respectively. The other regions gave figures between 60 and 70 percent.

All regions indicated that more than 12 percent of their training delivery in 2002 would come from innovative learning technologies: Europe (22.9%) and Canada (20.9%) were on the high end, while China and Latin America cited 12.8 and 13.5 percent, respectively. U.S. respondents projected to deliver 18.7 percent of their training via learning technologies in the year 2002.

Dispersed Teams Need to Get Off on the Right Foot

Editor's Comment: Training managers are often called upon to teach team building and to facilitate the on-going work of teams. This article delves deeply into the functioning of geographically dispersed teams, and contains a great deal of lessons from experience in the work of researchers from the Center for Creative Leadership.

The changing global marketplace and technological advancements have led to the creation of teams that are spread across countries and continents. This has occurred so rapidly that organizations' use of geographically dispersed teams has far outstripped knowledge about how such teams operate. In what ways, for instance, do they differ from traditional teams? Now the latest research by CCL sheds light on how members of dispersed teams interact, how to best build and support such teams, and how dispersed teams achieve their goals.

Global markets spread the means of production and the flow of capital as organizations embrace technologies that enable communication and collaboration around the world and across time. Workers find themselves serving on teams with people they have never met and whose native countries they know little about. An increasing number of employees are learning new languages, working extremely odd hours, and relying heavily on colleagues thousands of miles and multiple time zones away. Welcome to the age of the geographically dispersed team (GDT).

As the marketplace undergoes global change and the technological capabilities for communicating across distance and time advance, conventional teams are evolving into GDTs, spread across countries and continents. During this time of change, some management theorists have suggested that the communication and performance challenges posed by dispersed collaboration essentially force the creation of GDTs as entities entirely different from traditional teams. But is that really the case?

The practice of using GDTs has far outpaced the scientific understanding of how they function. Although dispersed collaboration is not exactly new (think of tasks accomplished with the aid of telephones, postal mail, and air travel), recent technological advances and their results—including the public's large-scale adoption of the Internet—have greatly increased the use and proliferation of GDTs among organizations. But there have been few research efforts aimed at better understanding what is needed to build and support GDTs, how GDT members interact, and how GDTs achieve their goals.

What research has been done on GDTs hasn't come up with many conclusive findings. That's not unusual; many organizational trends outpace researchers' ability to construct insightful studies. For its own starting point, the Center for Creative Leadership looked to two fields of research that provide information relevant to GDTs. The first focuses on computer-mediated communication; the second probes the use of group decision support systems.

Source: "Dispersed Teams Need To Get Off on the Right Foot" by Valerie I. Sessa, Michael C. Hansen, Michael E. Kossler, and Sonya Prestridge in *Leadership In Action*, May/June 2001, pp. 14–18. Valerie I. Sessa is a Research Scientist at the Center for Creative Leadership (CCL), Greensboro, NC; Michael C. Hansen works with CCL's geographically dispersed teams research project; Michael K. Kossler is a Senior Program Associate at CCL's Brussels, Belgium, Center; and Sonya Prestridge is a Senior Program Associate at CCL, Greensboro, NC. Reprinted with permission of the Center for Creative Leadership. Copyright 2001. All rights reserved.

Research into computer-mediated communication has frequently compared the communication patterns and effectiveness of groups that collaborate by means of some type of computer system (e-mail or electronic bulletin boards, for example) with those of groups that meet face to face.

Similarly, researchers studying group decision support systems have compared the performances of groups that use computer-based tools for idea generation, evaluation, and decision making against the performances of groups that don't use such tools.

Collectively, findings from these two fields of inquiry suggest that although there are similarities between conventional teams and teams that interact via communication technology, there are also important differences:

- Computer-mediated teams tend to be more task oriented and to have more equal participation among team members than conventional teams.
- Technology may alter social behavior in teams.
- Members of technology-based teams are typically less satisfied with the team experience than are members of conventional teams. However, this doesn't appear to greatly affect the quality of team output.
- Technology-based teams frequently take longer to complete their work than do conventional teams, and they are slower to follow common team-development stages. There is evidence, however, that performance improves for GDTs after they are given time to grow accustomed to their tasks and dispersed situations.

Despite these intriguing findings, laboratory studies haven't sufficiently captured the myriad challenges facing GDTs, including team formation, meeting logistics, and conflict resolution. CCL's research into GDTs bridges the divide between highly controlled laboratory investigations of communication technology's impact and real-life observations of firsthand witnesses about the challenges posed by dispersed teamwork.

CCL began its research with a survey conducted between August 1997 and August 1998 that gathered information from forty-five teams in nineteen organizations. All the teams had members in at least three dispersed locations. Fifteen teams had all their members, including the team leader, based in the United States, and two had all their members, including the team leader, based outside the United States. In twenty-three of the teams the team leader was based in the United States, but some team members were outside the United States. In five of the teams the team leader was based outside the United States, but some team members were based in the United States.

The survey was designed to reveal how organizations form, develop, and maintain GDTs.

Using the core data from the survey, we targeted the second stage of the CCL research along four lines:

- How is being in a GDT similar to or different from being in a traditional, co-located team (that is, a team whose members reside in the same place and work in close physical proximity to one another)? What are the advantages and disadvantages of being in a GDT?
- How do factors such as organizational structure, team design, and individual experience affect a GDT's first team meeting, its team processes, and its performance?
- How does the effectiveness of the first team meeting relate to subsequent team processes, such as ongoing meeting effectiveness, use of technology, team dynamics, and team performance?
- How do team processes relate to team performance?

To help focus our research on group effectiveness within GDTs, we framed our questions using a comprehensive team effectiveness model developed through observation of traditional teams and reviews of the literature on them. In particular we adopted as a guide the Team Effectiveness Leadership Model, which Richard L. Hughes, Robert C. Ginnett, and Gordon J. Curphy published in 1993 (see sidebar).

We placed our four research questions in this framework with the aim of illuminating our understanding of how the first team meeting influences team effectiveness, especially in GDTs. The following overview of our conclu-

Factoring in the Variables

In the framework of the Team Effectiveness Leadership Model, individual, environmental, and team design factors are seen as having an influence on team processes, which are in turn viewed as influencing team results. In the model, these relationships are classified as inputs, process, and outputs.

Inputs. Individual factors connect to what team members bring to the team. These factors include interests and motivations, skills and abilities, values and attitudes, and interpersonal behavior skills. Environmental factors encompass four systems that exist in an organizational structure and that affect an organization's teams: rewards, education, information, and control. Team design factors relate to the team itself—its structure, composition, norms, and authority.

Process. This part of the model includes the amount of effort expended on the task, the knowledge and skills used to accomplish the task, strategies used while working on the task, and the general group dynamics.

Outputs. In defining the results of the team's work, this group of factors comprises three appraisals. First, does the team's output (goods, services, and decisions) meet the quantity, quality, and timeliness standards of the people who use that output? Second, does the group process that occurs while the group is performing its task enhance the ability of the members to work together as a team in the future? And third, does the group experience enhance the personal well-being of the individuals who make up the team?

---

sions will interest all managers and executives who lead, design, sponsor, or otherwise have a stake in the effectiveness and success of GDTs in their organizations.

Team Design Is Key

The importance of team design and structure in the development and work of GDTs emerged as a consistent thread from our data analysis. GDT members saw their team design and structure as both similar to and different from that of co-located teams.

As with traditional teams, good task design—particularly clear and measurable goals—related positively to first-meeting effectiveness, ongoing meeting effectiveness, team dynamics, and team effectiveness. In addition, the team type (a project team or a functional team, for example) had a bearing on similar variables. Project group members reported that they felt more like part of a team after the first meeting than did functional group members. They were less likely than functional team members to spend time on social processes during face-to-face meetings. On the whole, project teams were more effective than functional teams.

GDTs found it particularly difficult to manage projects, schedule meetings, and coordinate work. GDT members reported disadvantages in all these activities. Support from the parent organization, however, partially alleviated these difficulties.

GDT members reported that project management training for the team increased the time they could devote to the task at hand in both face-to-face meetings and electronic meetings. GDTs that received project management training also rated electronic meetings as more effective than did GDTs that did not receive such training.

Team composition, which falls under team design in our model, emerged as another thread from our analysis. GDTs saw their composition as both similar to and different from the composition of traditional teams. That is, members of some teams perceived GDTs and traditional teams as composed of the same types of people in terms of characteristics and competencies. Members of other teams suggested that GDTs are made up of people very different from those on traditional teams. Two main themes stood out:

- GDTs had particular difficulty with cultural differences. Teams whose members represented a large number of nations concentrated more on business issues than on relationships during face-to-face meetings. Members of these teams collaborated less and had fewer strategic conflicts over the ways the team should achieve its goals. (Dealing with strategic conflicts encourages innovation and aids in problem solving, both of which are important to team effectiveness.)

Interestingly, teams that had received training on appreciating cultural differences spent less time on tasks during face-to-face meetings, experienced fewer strategic conflicts, and were less likely to be effective in achieving their goals. These findings contrast with the findings of some other researchers. We hypothesize that the GDTs in our study were struggling with and needed help in developing basic team skills such as project management. Training in cultural differences, although important, is less likely to positively affect performance when GDTs lack basic team skills.

- GDTs had difficulties when team members did not understand why they were selected to the team. When team members lacked this knowledge, they were less focused on the team's task after the first meeting, and during face-to-face meetings they spent more time on relationship building and less time on business issues. Teams with members who didn't know why they were chosen for the team were less likely to be effective.

Growing Pains

Another thread that emerged from our data related to members' perceptions of becoming and working as a team. GDTs were seen as both similar to and different from conventional teams in terms of teamwork. Some GDT members believed that dispersed teams and conventional teams have certain characteristics in common, such as interdependency, cooperation, and collaboration. Other GDT members believed that GDTs and conventional teams do not share these characteristics.

GDT members tended to believe that it was more difficult for them than for members of conventional teams to work as a unit and develop the synergy and cohesiveness needed for effective teamwork. A closely linked finding was communication difficulty—almost 75 percent of the teams indicated that communication within GDTs is generally more difficult, more complex, and more infrequent than communication within conventional teams, in addition to requiring more formal approaches.

> Teams with members who didn't know why they were selected were less likely to be effective.

One strand in this thread was the extent to which GDTs received any type of developmental assistance from their parent organizations. GDTs that received such assistance were more likely than those that did not to conduct electronic meetings and to rate them as being effective. These teams saw themselves as more collaborative. They had more disagreements, which were more likely to be about strategy. They also were less likely to note any impact on their work resulting from team members' being in different time zones.

A second strand in this thread was the importance of GDT's first meetings, specifically the format and effectiveness of these meetings. We used three measures of first-meeting effectiveness: clarity of team goals, the degree to which individuals felt like members of the team, and the degree of commitment individuals felt to the team after the first meeting.

GDT members whose first meetings were face to face were more likely than GDT members whose first meetings occurred electronically to indicate that they never or rarely met electronically as a group and were less likely to discuss business through conference phone calls. These GDT members also indicated that when they did meet electronically they spent a lower percentage of the meeting time on the task at hand. Time zones were less likely to affect GDTs that met electronically the first time.

There was a positive relationship between the effectiveness of the first meeting and the effectiveness of subsequent meetings, whether face to face or electronic. The effectiveness of first meetings also had a positive influence on collaboration in terms of team members relying on one another, but the influence on strategic conflict and overall team effectiveness was mixed.

One important aspect of the first meeting was goal clarity. GDTs whose first meetings produced clear goals were more likely to have strategic conflicts and to be effective. Interestingly, the degree of commitment to the team that individuals felt after an initial meeting had a negative correlation with strategic conflicts and team effectiveness.

> Geographically dispersed teams face myriad challenges, including team formation, meeting logistics, and conflict resolution.

Just Rewards

The importance of rewards emerged as a fourth thread related to the formation of GDTs and to their ongoing work. Both individual and team rewards had a positive effect on team collaboration. GDTs that received individual or team rewards were more likely to make decisions as a team rather than relying on the team leader for decisions. Team members were more likely to get along with each other, to have strategic conflicts, and to discuss conflicts openly, and they were less likely to view time zones as having an impact on the team's work.

A fifth thread was the importance of strategic conflict. The presence of strategic conflict had a positive association with team effectiveness. Effective teams have clear and measurable goals, and we believe that one of the main benefits of a dispersed team is that members naturally bring different perspectives on how to accomplish those goals.

Apples and Oranges?

Several practical implications stem from CCL's study. Most important, individuals in GDTs generally have a strong sense of membership in the team—one of the measures of team effectiveness—and they act accordingly. The differences that team members noted between GDTs and traditional teams—the advantages and disadvantages of each—suggest that the disparities are more a matter of degree than of substance. Consequently, organizations and team leaders can use what they already know about teams—how to design, develop, and manage them for maximum effectiveness—to form, manage, and lead successful GDTs.

Tempering this encouraging news is the fact that in some ways, GDTs struggle even more than traditional teams. Communication is more difficult, for example, as is project management and dealing with cultural differences. Knowing this, organizations should look hard at whether GDTs best fit their needs. If organizations decide that the answer is yes, they should be prepared to supply the resources needed for GDTs to work effectively. These resources include support from the organizational structure and policies, a top-notch technological infrastructure, substantial training and development, and providing the team enough time to complete the task at hand.

One of the most important things that organizations and team leaders can do for GDTs is ensure that they develop clear and measurable goals and objectives as early as possible. CCL's study identified clear and measurable goals as the single most important determinant of GDT dynamics and effectiveness. Developing these goals before or during the first meeting promises the best productivity return for the investment.

Organizations can take other steps to help GDTs produce high-quality results. They should provide teams with user-friendly project management systems and the training to use them. Organizations and team leaders should choose GDT members carefully and make sure that all team members know why they were selected for the team. Because GDTs struggle with challenges such as cultural diversity and the communication problems posed by physical distance, they have a more difficult time developing into and acting as teams than do traditional teams. Organizations and team leaders should provide developmental opportunities to help GDTs meet these challenges. Rewards should be offered to reinforce teamwork. Like the establishment of clear goals, it is best if all these supportive actions are taken as early as possible.

Suggested Reading

Hughes, R. L., Ginnett, R. C., and Curphy, G. J. *Leadership: Enhancing the Lessons of Experience.* Burr Ridge, Ill.: Irwin, 1993.

Kossler, M. E., Hansen, M. C., Sessa, V. I., and Prestridge, S. "A New Kind of Team?" *Leadership in Action*, 2000, *19*(6), 8–12.

Sessa, V. I., Hansen, M. C., Prestridge, S., and Kossler, M. E. *Geographically Dispersed Teams: An Annotated Bibliography.* Greensboro, N.C.: Center for Creative Leadership, 1999.

Training Across Cultures: What to Expect

Editor's Comment: Trainers of all stripes are called on these days to do duty in other countries. The terrorist events of September 11, 2001 and the bioterrorist scares of mid-October brought American citizens together in thinking about what image we portray when we visit or work in other countries. To be sure, persons who make a living in another country must be schooled themselves in the culture of the country where they work, and training materials need to reflect a sensitivity to other beliefs, values, and behaviors in order for that training to be effective.

This article is written as a scenario involving a consultant, trainer, expert, and professor who had a work assignment in another culture. The writer of the article, William A. Weech, suggests four critical dimensions that help explain variation in cultural expectations.

A consultant from California is asked to conduct management training in Guatemala. A Chinese state enterprise hires a trainer from Illinois to conduct a train-the-trainer workshop. A well-known subject matter expert from New York is asked to give a presentation on motivation to a Swedish audience. A Texas oil firm sends a professor to Saudi Arabia to teach a seminar in problem solving.

Even if they are new to the world of training across cultures, each of those people probably recognizes the need to make adjustments for a foreign audience. But how can they know which aspects of their content and training approach should be modified for the places they're going to?

Culture can be defined as the shared values, beliefs, and behaviors that groups pass down from one generation to the next. Our cultures shape our expectations for most interactions, including training events. To maximize training effectiveness in other cultures, trainers need to understand how cultural differences may affect the expectations of their audiences. Though cultures vary in a number of ways, there are four critical dimensions that help explain the variation in cultural expectations.

Egalitarian versus hierarchy (sometimes called *power distance*). Will the audience expect that more attention will be paid to what the class has in common? Or will they expect that more attention will be paid to how participants are different?

Individualism versus collectivism. Will participants expect that individual wants and needs will get priority over group needs, or the opposite?

Achievement versus relationship orientation (sometimes called *cultural masculinity*). Will learners expect that assertiveness, success, and task accomplishment will be valued? Or that compassion, nurturing, and harmonious relationships will be preferred?

Loose versus tight structure (sometimes called *uncertainty avoidance*). Will participants be comfortable agreeing to disagree? Or will they expect to find the one best answer for every problem?

Let's see how each of those dimensions of cultural difference can affect people's expectations for training.

Egalitarian/Hierarchical

Egalitarian cultures minimize inequalities, while hierarchical cultures emphasize the importance of rank and status. Northern European and English-speaking countries are gener-

---

Source: "Training Across Cultures: What To Expect" by William A. Weech in *Training & Development*, January 2001, pp. 62-64. William A. Weech is Associate Director of Executive Programs at the U.S. Department of State's Foreign Service Institute. Reprinted with permission of *Training & Development*, copyright 2001. All rights reserved.

ally egalitarian; Austria, Israel, and Denmark are among the most egalitarian countries in the world. By contrast, Asian, Latin, and Middle Eastern countries are usually more hierarchical.

In egalitarian cultures, participants in training events tend to expect to learn from each other, and they expect dialogue. They typically see their instructors as peers and coaches, and they feel free to speak up in class. In addition, they're generally comfortable with self-directed activities.

In hierarchical cultures, participants expect to learn from the expert, the trainer. They expect more of an instructor-centered design. Learners expect the trainer to provide a clear structure, and they're unlikely to speak up unless called on. Trainees tend to see the instructor as an authority figure who should be respected.

The California consultant conducting management training in Guatemala is going from a relatively egalitarian culture in the United States to a very hierarchical one. What kinds of adjustments should she consider to maximize her effectiveness?

First, the consultant shouldn't hesitate to make her status and expertise known. In a hierarchical culture, participants like to be assured that the trainer really is an expert. The consultant should also make the goals and structure of the workshop clear. Participants from a hierarchical culture aren't likely to be comfortable with emergent designs. If the consultant wants dialogue in the session, she should create a structure for it because it's not likely to happen spontaneously.

When forming small groups, the consultant needs to pay attention to participants' status. Senior-level people are likely to dominate. Last, the consultant should consider whether her materials engender a participative management style that may appear counter-cultural in a hierarchical society.

Once when I was conducting training in a hierarchical country, I noticed that the participants didn't pay attention when I asked small groups to present the results of their group activities. It dawned on me that the participants didn't particularly value the ideas of their peers but only wanted to hear what the expert trainer had to say. To adjust to that difference, I asked each small group to report directly to me. Then I presented a summary of each group's work to the class, to rapt attention.

Compare a John Wayne shoot-'em-up to any Bergman film and you'll see what I mean.

Individualism/Collectivism

Individualist cultures value autonomy and seek self-actualization; collectivist cultures value belonging and seek group harmony. Northern European and English-speaking countries are generally individualist; the United States is the most individualist country in the world. Most Latin, Asian, and African countries are collectivist.

In individualist cultures, people attend training for self-development. They expect to learn the latest ideas concerning the subject matter. They expect to speak up freely in class, and they find intellectual debate stimulating. Individualists are comfortable working alone. When groups are formed in class, they expect that the groupings will be random. By contrast, participants in collectivist cultures are more likely to expect to learn time-tested ways of doing things so that they can earn a certification. They find speaking in front of the class embarrassing, and they're extremely uncomfortable with the open expression of disagreement.

Collectivists prefer to work in groups. When groups are formed, they expect that the groupings will be based on existing associations such as ethnicity, religion, or social class. The Illinois trainer traveling to China is going from an individualist culture in the United States to a collectivist culture in China. What kinds of accommodations are likely to increase his effectiveness? First, the trainer shouldn't expect a great deal of individual initiative or large-group discussion. Instead, he should emphasize small-group activities that minimize the likelihood of conflict or embarrassment. When forming groups, the trainer should be mindful of pre-existing affiliations. As far as the content is concerned, the trainer is likely to find that participants in collectivist cultures want to learn the history and established traditions of the training field before they're exposed to the newest concepts and techniques.

I remember trying to spark class discussions while conducting training in a collectivist culture. I asked, "What do you think is the difference between leadership and management?" No one volunteered a response, and the room filled with awkward silence. Later in the session, as I walked around, several participants slipped me scraps of paper with their written responses. Clearly, they found the question stimulating, but they weren't comfortable expressing their personal opinions in front of the class. I discovered that the session went much better when I assigned such questions to small table groups rather than attempting to stimulate dialogue in the large group. Groups of five or six had lively conversations, and the spokespersons were happy to report the table's consensus to the rest of the class.

Achievement/Relationship

Achievement-oriented cultures value assertiveness, toughness, and winning. Relationship-oriented cultures value compassion and tenderness, and they're sympathetic to failure. North American cultures are usually achievement-oriented; Scandinavian countries are more relationship-oriented. Compare a John Wayne shoot-'em-up to any Bergman film and you'll see what I mean.

In achievement-oriented cultures, learners tend to compete for recognition and expect rewards for performance. People in such cultures go to training hoping to further their careers. If they fail to pass the program, that's usually disturbing to them. In relationship-oriented cultures, learners are likely to avoid competition and expect rewards for being cooperative. People tend to go to training because they find the subject matter interesting. If trainees fail to pass the program, that's disappointing but rarely causes great stress. Interestingly, there's less gender-role differentiation in relationship-oriented cultures.

The New York expert on motivation is going from an achievement-oriented culture to a relationship-oriented culture in Sweden. How should she adjust her training style? First, she should try to be warm and friendly. Although she's an expert, she should downplay her achievements and credentials. To do otherwise would be to appear immodest. Training activities that force learners to compete are likely to make relationship-oriented participants uncomfortable. Activities that require cooperation are usually more popular.

> Our consultant, trainer, expert, and professor each realized that they had to adjust the content and methods of their training to maximize their likelihood of success in foreign cultures.

The expert should also avoid singling out the best learners for praise; that could make everyone uncomfortable. One should always avoid stereotyping on the basis of gender, but it's particularly important in relationship-oriented cultures. As for the content of the presentation, American theories of motivation (such as those of Herzberg and McClelland) tend to stress people's psychological need for achievement, power, and recognition. Discussing motivation in a relationship-oriented culture, the New York expert may want to give equal weight to people's psychological need for affiliation.

Because I work with international groups, I occasionally have trainees whose English is limited. I've noticed that the participants who help strugglers are invariably from relationship-oriented cultures. Relationship-oriented learners typically are concerned that no one gets left behind. By contrast, trainees from achievement-oriented cultures are more likely to pay attention to their most successful classmates. They'll either emulate the valedictorians or compete with them, or both.

Loose/Tight Structures

Loose-structure cultures are tolerant of uncertainty and ambiguity; tight-structure cultures are the opposite. Northern Europe, North America, and much of Africa and Asia have loose-structure cultures. Latin America, the Middle East, and Southern Europe have predominantly tight cultural structures. In cultures with loose structures, there are many ways to solve problems and trainees value innovative answers. Participants tend to be comfortable with broad learning goals and flexible training programs. Intellectual disagreement can be interesting, but it should never be personalized. The instructor should be down-to-earth and approachable.

In tight-structure cultures, trainees expect to learn the single best way to solve a problem, and they value accurate answers. Participants prefer precise learning objectives and a clear program structure. Any intellectual disagreement implies that someone must be wrong, so trainees work hard to achieve consensus. Instructors are expected to be experts who freely use the jargon of their field, even if the participants don't fully understand it.

The Texas professor heading for Saudi Arabia is traveling from a loose-structure culture to a tight-structure culture. He would do well to have complete mastery of his topic and to be not afraid to show it. Participants will expect him to have the correct answers for all of their questions. They'll also expect the class to have a clear structure and for him to teach with conviction and passion. He should avoid any activities that might spark debates, as those will make participants uncomfortable and could even lead to heated arguments. The professor should be well briefed on Saudi culture because conformity to local social norms is particularly important. While reviewing the content of his problem-solving seminar, the professor should remember that participants from tight-structure cultures prefer approaches that lessen uncertainty and ambiguity.

I remember an occasion when I was presenting a technical subject to a multicultural group. I displayed a transparency that outlined a particular process. An Irish participant spoke up and said that his unit followed a procedure that was different from the one I was presenting. After listening to his explanation, I agreed that his approach was as valid as the one that I was teaching. Immediately, I sensed that several participants from the tight-structure cultures were uncomfortable with that exchange. They were uneasy because a participant had openly expressed disagreement with me, the expert on the topic. They were also disappointed in my response, which failed to state which of the two methodologies was the correct one. Like most trainees from tight-structure cultures, they

> Learning another culture gives you another view on the world. Once you have that new perspective, training will never be the same.

expected the instructor to teach them the best way to do their jobs.

Our consultant, trainer, expert, and professor each realized that they had to adjust the content and methods of their training to maximize their likelihood of success in foreign cultures. What should you do when you are invited to train in another country? Learn about the expectations of the intended audience. The best way to ensure that your content and methods are appropriate for local expectations is to have a local partner, preferably a bicultural one. He or she can be a co-trainer who assists you with the design and presentation of the training. Or your partner can be a shadow consultant, reviewing your materials in advance and helping you prepare for the big event.

If it's not possible for you to have a local partner, then you must do your homework before you travel. Get on the phone, get on the Internet, go to the library, tap into your network of colleagues, and learn what you can about your target audience before you head out. Ask about the four cultural dimensions described in this article. The time you spend getting ready helps ensure that you and your audience won't have unmet expectations.

We trainers often say that we learn more from our participants than we teach them. Never is that more true than when we work with groups in other countries. Learning another culture gives you another view on the world. Once you have that new perspective, training will never be the same.

Now that you know what to expect, get ready, pack your bags, and get your passport for training—and learning—across cultures.

5. The TRAINING 2001 Industry Report

Training Industry Report for the Year 2001

Editor's Comment: The "Industry Report" published in *TRAINING Magazine* near the end of each calendar year has come to be known as the most complete snapshot of the training industry in America. The year 2001 report is based on an online survey of randomly selected subscribers to *TRAINING Magazine*. This year's Industry Report covers approximately 35 pages of the magazine; we reprint 4 pages from this Report here plus the "Training Salaries by Region" survey from the November 2001 issue. The full *Industry Report 2000* is available from *TRAINING Magazine* by phoning 800/328-4329.

The population of organizations in this large and comprehensive survey of the field is 166,276 organizations employing 100 or more employees. Only organizations with formal training operations are included. This is about 15,000 more organizations than formed the population for last year's study. To begin the survey, telephone interviews qualified respondents who were then directed to an online questionnaire. This qualification procedure resulted in a remarkable 42.7 percent usable response rate or 1,652 usable responses from a sample pool of 3,873 qualified candidates. Categories in this year's Industry Report include:

- The Money
- The Methods
- The People
- The Delivery
- The Tech Emergence

We also include a map and chart of Training Salaries by Region.

The "2001 Highlights at a Glance" chart indicates some of the trends as the new Millennium takes hold. There's much good news as we enter year 2002. Total dollars budgeted for formal training in the immediate year past is $56.8 billion. This figure does not include training hardware or facilities and overhead, reflecting increasing use of desktop computers, company intranets, and the Internet for training throughout organizations—hardware and facilities that tend to be budgeted in organizations other than training. As in the recent past, managers and professionals get the lion's share of training, and in-house staff share design and delivery with outside trainers and consultants. As in the recent past, the classroom is still a huge favorite for delivery of instructional programs, including information technology (IT) instruction, with a full 77 percent of organizations using classrooms with live instructors. We still have a strong commitment to the preservation of "high touch" in an environment of "high tech" in our workplace learning.

Sources: "Industry Report 2001" in *TRAINING Magazine*, October 2001, pp. 40–75 and November 2001, pp. 60–68. Excerpts are printed with permission from the October 2001 issue and the November 2001 issue of *TRAINING Magazine*. Copyright 2001. Bill Communications, Minneapolis, MN. All rights reserved. Not for resale.

Training Management

2001 Highlights at a Glance

- Total dollars budgeted for formal training this year by U.S. organizations: **$56.8 billion**
- Of that sum, amount that will go to outside providers of training products and services: **$19.3 billion**
- Percentage of companies that employ full-time trainers who draw their salaries from the IT department's budget rather than the training/HR budget: **19%**
- Percentage of companies that anticipated a smaller training budget this year: **15%**

- Percentage of companies that provide weekly customer service skills training: **12%**
- Percentage of companies that do not provide any foreign language training: **62%**
- Percentage of companies that never use computer-based games to train employees: **43%**
- Percentage of companies that often use workbooks or manuals to train employees: **56%**

- Percentage of companies in which the training/HR department controls training purchases: **61%**
- Training dollars spent on nonexempt employees: **$20.4 billion**
- Percentage of training programs delivered via classroom (instructor-led): **77%**
- Percentage of training programs delivered by computer (no instructor): **11%**

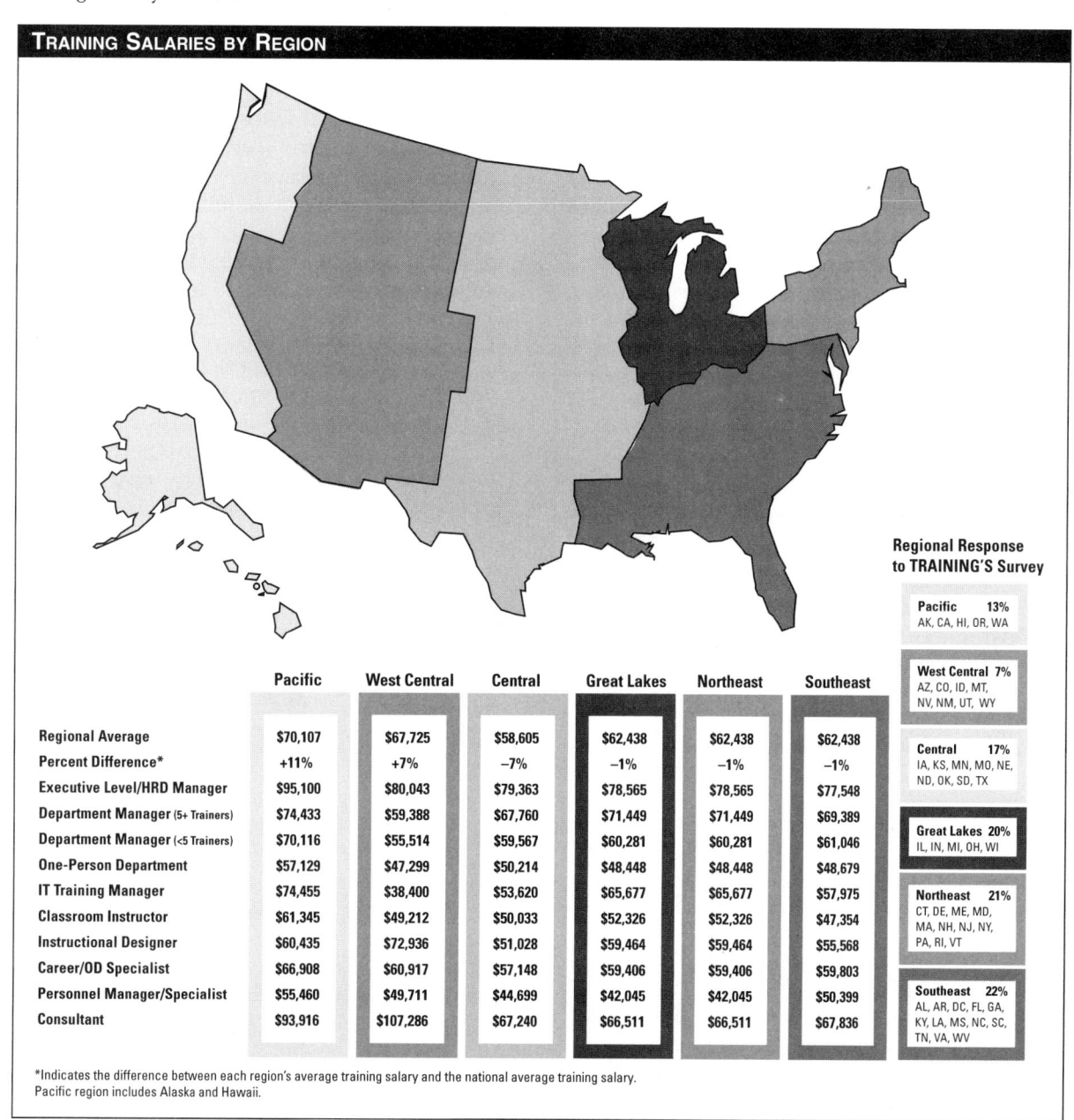

TRAINING SALARIES BY REGION

	Pacific	West Central	Central	Great Lakes	Northeast	Southeast
Regional Average	$70,107	$67,725	$58,605	$62,438	$62,438	$62,438
Percent Difference*	+11%	+7%	–7%	–1%	–1%	–1%
Executive Level/HRD Manager	$95,100	$80,043	$79,363	$78,565	$78,565	$77,548
Department Manager (5+ Trainers)	$74,433	$59,388	$67,760	$71,449	$71,449	$69,389
Department Manager (<5 Trainers)	$70,116	$55,514	$59,567	$60,281	$60,281	$61,046
One-Person Department	$57,129	$47,299	$50,214	$48,448	$48,448	$48,679
IT Training Manager	$74,455	$38,400	$53,620	$65,677	$65,677	$57,975
Classroom Instructor	$61,345	$49,212	$50,033	$52,326	$52,326	$47,354
Instructional Designer	$60,435	$72,936	$51,028	$59,464	$59,464	$55,568
Career/OD Specialist	$66,908	$60,917	$57,148	$59,406	$59,406	$59,803
Personnel Manager/Specialist	$55,460	$49,711	$44,699	$42,045	$42,045	$50,399
Consultant	$93,916	$107,286	$67,240	$66,511	$66,511	$67,836

Regional Response to TRAINING'S Survey

- Pacific **13%** — AK, CA, HI, OR, WA
- West Central **7%** — AZ, CO, ID, MT, NV, NM, UT, WY
- Central **17%** — IA, KS, MN, MO, NE, ND, OK, SD, TX
- Great Lakes **20%** — IL, IN, MI, OH, WI
- Northeast **21%** — CT, DE, ME, MD, MA, NH, NJ, NY, PA, RI, VT
- Southeast **22%** — AL, AR, DC, FL, GA, KY, LA, MS, NC, SC, TN, VA, WV

*Indicates the difference between each region's average training salary and the national average training salary. Pacific region includes Alaska and Hawaii.

The Delivery

Only one delivery method, the instructor-led classroom, increased its share of how training is currently delivered. While traditional classroom-based training accounted for 77 percent of training courses this year, all other categories—instructor-led from a remote location, by computer with no instructor, and other—declined by an average 1.6 percent.

Maintaining the top-choice status for how computer-delivered training is provided is CD-ROM, thanks to its superior ability to handle video, audio and complex graphics. As for online training, like last year, less of it occurs on the Internet than on proprietary, internal networks. Training via those internal networks most commonly is used by companies operating in the business services, finance, banking, real estate and insurance sectors, and is least commonly used in the manufacturing and public administration sectors.

Not surprisingly, computer skills remain the most popular topic to teach via computer-delivered means. And while little variance is shown by organizational size, type of industry plays a much greater role, specifically in the wholesale, distribution and retail trade sector where just 38 percent of computer-delivered courses actually teach computer skills.

Just 23 percent of online training follows the classroom model. That's down 6 percent from last year's survey, in which 29 percent of respondents saw the need for more interactive, computer-based training courses. For companies in the education services and academic institution sectors, however, 43 percent of computer-based training finds the trainee interacting with an instructor or other students.

> How U.S. organizations use classrooms and computers in training.

> Some 82 percent of all training is delivered by live instructors, but in 5 percent of the cases, the instructor is not necessarily in the room with the students. Despite the repeated predictions that online delivery methods will one day take a bite out of the classroom, 77 percent of all training is still conducted in the confines of four walls with an instructor leading the way. Interestingly, training both via computer and instructor-led from a remote location dropped by 2 and 1 percent, respectively. Regarding "other" methods of instruction, respondents mentioned structured, on-the-job training and self-study programs using videos, manuals and workbooks.

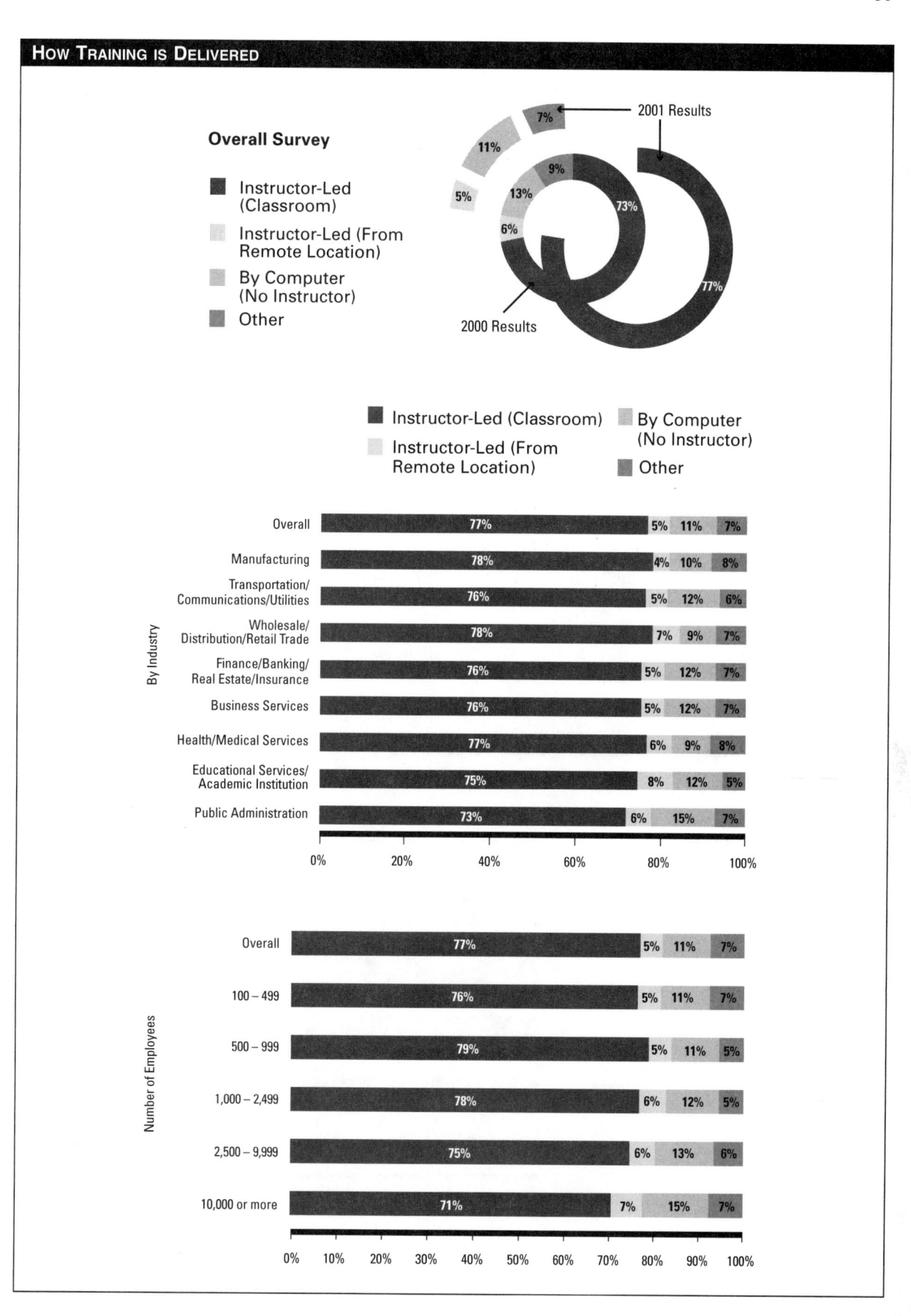

Training Management

How Training is Delivered

Overall Survey

- Instructor-Led (Classroom)
- Instructor-Led (From Remote Location)
- By Computer (No Instructor)
- Other

2001 Results: 73%, 9%, 13%, 7% (with 6% and 11% and 5% segments noted)
2000 Results: 77%

By Industry

Industry	Instructor-Led (Classroom)	Instructor-Led (From Remote Location)	By Computer (No Instructor)	Other
Overall	77%	5%	11%	7%
Manufacturing	78%	4%	10%	8%
Transportation/Communications/Utilities	76%	5%	12%	6%
Wholesale/Distribution/Retail Trade	78%	7%	9%	7%
Finance/Banking/Real Estate/Insurance	76%	5%	12%	7%
Business Services	76%	5%	12%	7%
Health/Medical Services	77%	6%	9%	8%
Educational Services/Academic Institution	75%	8%	12%	5%
Public Administration	73%	6%	15%	7%

Number of Employees

Number of Employees	Instructor-Led (Classroom)	Instructor-Led (From Remote Location)	By Computer (No Instructor)	Other
Overall	77%	5%	11%	7%
100 – 499	76%	5%	11%	7%
500 – 999	79%	5%	11%	5%
1,000 – 2,499	78%	6%	12%	5%
2,500 – 9,999	75%	6%	13%	6%
10,000 or more	71%	7%	15%	7%

How Computer-Delivered Training Breaks Down

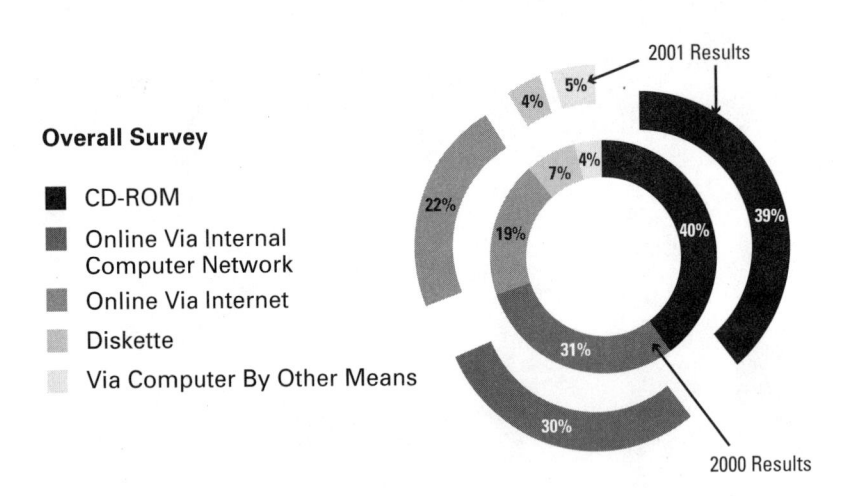

Overall Survey
- CD-ROM
- Online Via Internal Computer Network
- Online Via Internet
- Diskette
- Via Computer By Other Means

2001 Results: 39%, 40%, 31%, 4%, 5%
2000 Results: 39%, 40%, 30%, 19%, 22%, 7%, 4%

CD-ROM once again remains the medium of choice for computer-delivered training thanks to its superior ability to handle video, audio and complex graphics. As for online training, like last year, less of it occurs on the Internet than on proprietary, internal networks—corporate intranets, extranets, local- and wide-area networks (LANs and WANs), etc. Training via those internal networks is most commonly used by companies operating in the business services, finance, banking, real estate and insurance sectors and is least commonly used in the manufacturing and public administration sectors.

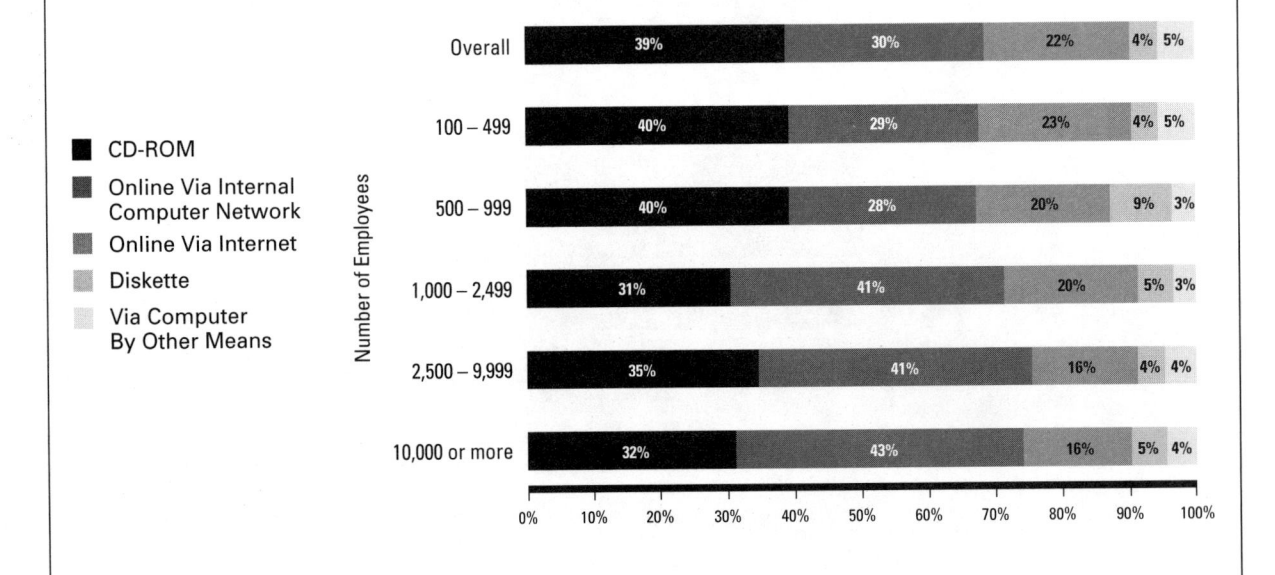

Number of Employees

	CD-ROM	Online Via Internal Computer Network	Online Via Internet	Diskette	Via Computer By Other Means
Overall	39%	30%	22%	4%	5%
100 – 499	40%	29%	23%	4%	5%
500 – 999	40%	28%	20%	9%	3%
1,000 – 2,499	31%	41%	20%	5%	3%
2,500 – 9,999	35%	41%	16%	4%	4%
10,000 or more	32%	43%	16%	5%	4%

Training Management

TRAINING BUDGET BREAKDOWNS 1999-2001

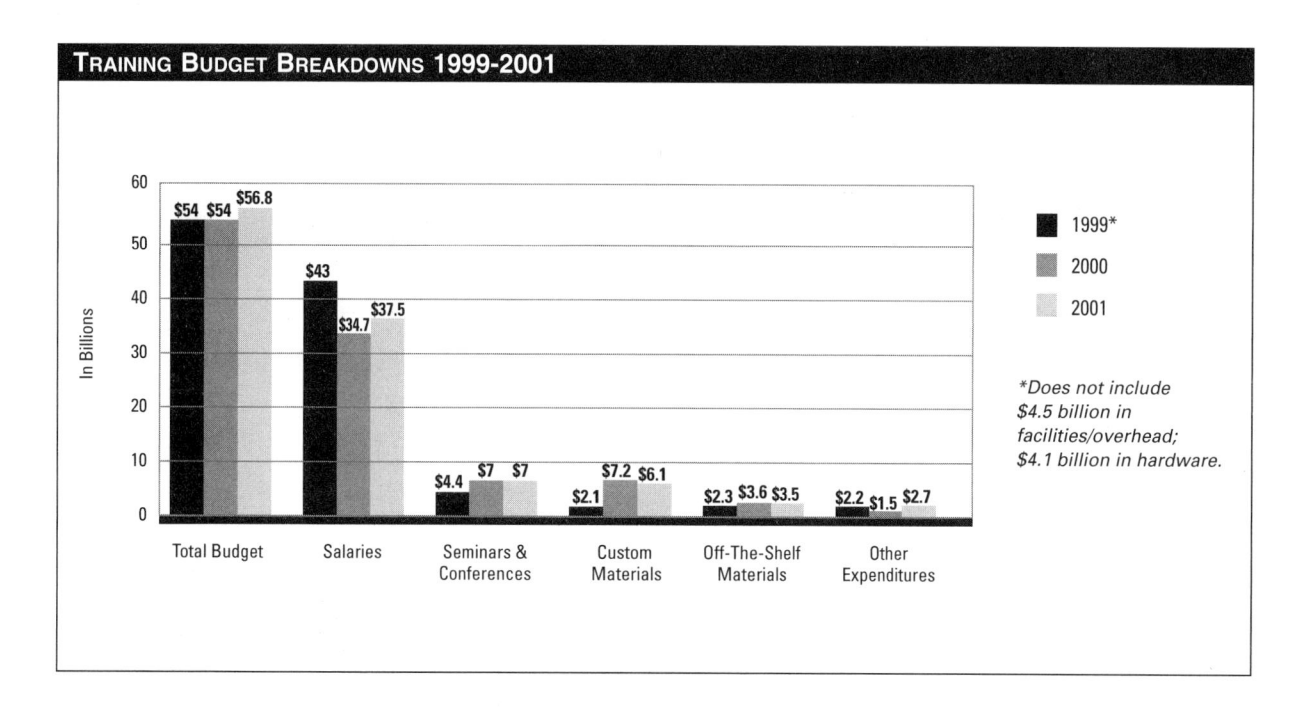

Category	1999*	2000	2001
Total Budget	$54	$54	$56.8
Salaries	$43	$34.7	$37.5
Seminars & Conferences	$4.4	$7	$7
Custom Materials	$2.1	$7.2	$6.1
Off-The-Shelf Materials	$2.3	$3.6	$3.5
Other Expenditures	$2.2	$1.5	$2.7

In Billions

*Does not include $4.5 billion in facilities/overhead; $4.1 billion in hardware.

2001 BUDGET BREAKDOWNS

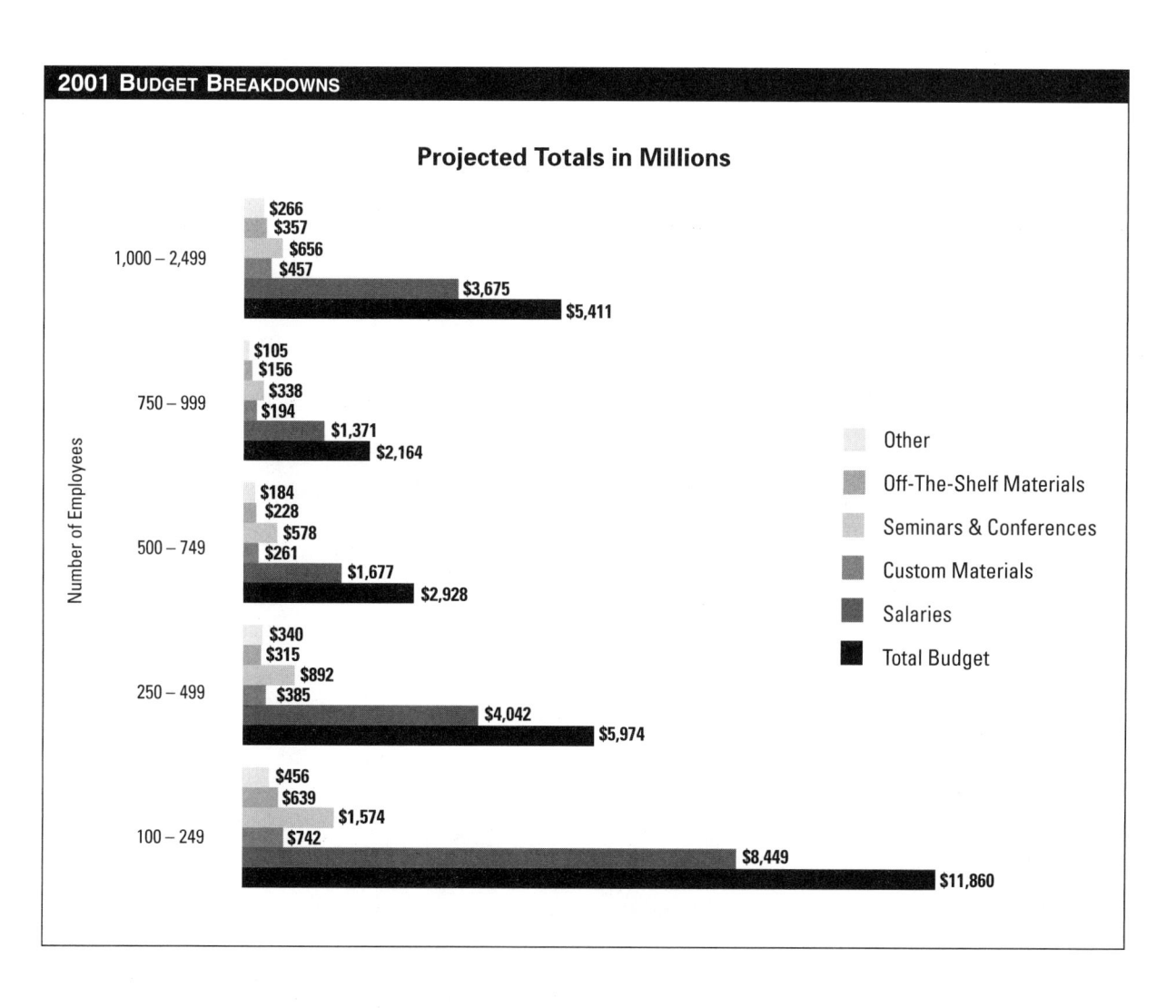

Projected Totals in Millions

Legend (by category): Other, Off-The-Shelf Materials, Seminars & Conferences, Custom Materials, Salaries, Total Budget

Number of Employees: 1,000 – 2,499
- Other: $266
- Off-The-Shelf Materials: $357
- Seminars & Conferences: $656
- Custom Materials: $457
- Salaries: $3,675
- Total Budget: $5,411

Number of Employees: 750 – 999
- Other: $105
- Off-The-Shelf Materials: $156
- Seminars & Conferences: $338
- Custom Materials: $194
- Salaries: $1,371
- Total Budget: $2,164

Number of Employees: 500 – 749
- Other: $184
- Off-The-Shelf Materials: $228
- Seminars & Conferences: $578
- Custom Materials: $261
- Salaries: $1,677
- Total Budget: $2,928

Number of Employees: 250 – 499
- Other: $340
- Off-The-Shelf Materials: $315
- Seminars & Conferences: $892
- Custom Materials: $385
- Salaries: $4,042
- Total Budget: $5,974

Number of Employees: 100 – 249
- Other: $456
- Off-The-Shelf Materials: $639
- Seminars & Conferences: $1,574
- Custom Materials: $742
- Salaries: $8,449
- Total Budget: $11,860

SECTION 2

Needs of Learners

1. **Leadership and Culture** 49
   Learning to Learn Dialogue with Warrren Bennis 49
   Ford Defines and Trains Transformational Leaders 55
   Individual Career Development at First USA Bank 62
   CEO in Jeans and T-Shirt? 65
   Generation Y: Self-Confident and Goal-Oriented 66

2. **Race and Gender Plus** 67
   Surprises in the Census 67
   Institutional Effects of Immigration 69
   Racism in the Workplace 71
   Training's Important Role in Affirmative Action 75
   Learning from Informal Networks of "Girl Gangs" 76
   How and Why to Be Your Own Mentor 81

3. **Technology and Learning Communities** 83
   Dealing with Learner Resistance to Technology-Delivered Training 83
   What Napster Did for E-Learning 89
   How To Facilitate Online Communities 92

4. **The New Bottom Line** 96
   Faster, Cheaper, Smarter: How Rockwell Collins Reinvented Its Training 96
   Results-Oriented Customer Service Training 98
   Wellness at DaimlerChrysler 103
   On That Fateful Day, Two Airlines Faced Their Darkest Scenario 106
   The State of the Union, September 20, 2001 112

INTRODUCTION TO NEEDS OF LEARNERS: SECTION 2

Section 2 of *Training & Development Yearbook 2002* examines four current issues in defining and meeting the needs of workplace learners. There is no question that workplace learning and learners are in transition on several fronts: the obvious one of e-learning and all of the kinds of needs for learning new technology skills as well as learning about the ideas that comprise an e-learning culture—infrastructure, interface, and content. The other obvious new front for learning is that of collaboration and the need to cooperate across business functions often with worldwide partners and with fellow employees sometimes whom you've never met.

The events of September 11, 2001 reinforced America's values of freedom of speech and movement, family and community. A church in Oklahoma planted 5,000 crosses the week after the tragedy to help viewers experience the magnitude of the loss of life; *The New York Times* began a series, "Portraits of Grief," in which they published individual photos, short biographies, and personal tributes to each of the persons lost in the World Trade Center rubble that lasted well into the last quarter of 2001. Airline pilots and friends walked an American flag along the routes of the downed planes, thousands of prayer chains and candlelight vigils were held spontaneously in neighborhoods and in houses of worship across America, thousands of *God Bless America*'s were sung throughout the land including on the steps of the Capitol by our Senators, Congressmen and Congresswomen, and thousands of individuals helped neighbors grieve in thousands of ways for loss of innocence and loss of life. Loss of work, loss of workplaces, and loss of life were mitigated by an enormous outpouring of love, heroism, and generosity.

President George W. Bush's *Remarks* at The National Cathedral three days after the terror strike suggested that "adversity introduces us to ourselves," and that Americans directly after the tragedy "showed a deep commitment to one another, and an abiding love for our country." In the months following those *Remarks*, Americans have been urged to get back to work and to life as usual, the stock market dipped then rallied within a week to pre-9/11 levels, and grounded planes began flying again. In less than a month after the attack, the President announced that a broad-based international coalition of "more than 40 countries in the Middle East, Africa, Europe, and Asia" granted air transit, landing rights, or intelligence help. Europe, NATO, and our Western Hemisphere neighbors joined with us in resolve to fight for freedom (*Presidential Address to the Nation*, The Treaty Room, October 7, 2001).

In spite of October scares of Anthrax poisoning at broadcasting studios, post offices, newspapers, and Congressional offices, Americans did get back to work and faced fears of uncertainty with normalization and resolve to fight for "enduring freedom." The power of technology, communication, and the need for collaboration never seemed greater. These form the foundation of American culture and the framework of learning needs, especially for workers, at the beginning of 2002.

The four sub-sections are: Sub-section 1, *Leadership and Culture*, in which we profile two companies whose workplace learning structure and programs are headed in the right direction, and in which we suggest what to do and what not to do in order for new kinds of learning to occur; Sub-section 2, *Race and Gender Plus*, in which we report on the latest trends in affirmative action and equal opportunity; Sub-section 3, *Technology and Systems*, in which we delve into some of the specific kinds of new needs of learners around technology and systems to maximize learning; and Sub-section 4, *The New Bottom Line*, in which we take a look at the changed workplace and its values after the terror of September 11, 2001.

Leadership and Culture

The cover of the September 2001 issue of *Workforce* magazine, written before the terrorist attacks on America, said in bold red letters on a black background, "HR Takes on Tough Times" with three bullets in white reverse printing: "Hold the Line on Salaries and Benefits/Using Technology to Cut Costs/Training Proves Its Worth." This bold cover reflects the difficult economic times, fueled by the earlier dot.com demise, layoffs in the hundreds of thousands, and stock market roller coaster during the last half of the year. This was before September 11. These *Workforce* cover messages are meant to describe some of the elements of the human resources culture as we approach year's end. Throughout the business press, the cry went out all year for leadership—leaders who could relate to employees and customers in down times, not only to the numbers in the budget or the NASDAQ.

TRAINING Magazine started a somewhat tongue-in-cheek column by Jack Gordon in May of 2000 and continued it throughout the year 2001, called "Portfolio." Gordon and group picked 10 learning-provider stocks, some e-learning companies and some that did not specialize in online learning, and followed their performance. By 4th quarter 2001, the portfolio of learning companies came tumbling down, and the imaginary "Training Mansion" to be purchased with the hoped-for gains was only, for sure, a passing fancy. At one point, Gordon expressed disgust with the whole learning industry, and was ready to give up. Again, from another point of view came the call for a certain kind of leadership that was capable of configuring training and other human resources programs to value and to provide what learners actually need.

Then came September 11 and its aftermath, bringing with it an accelerated sense of a culture of collaboration and community, individual and collective responsibility. Sub-section 1, *Leadership and Culture*, gives you an example of the kinds of thinking in year 2001 around the need for leadership and leadership training to define and solidify a new American workplace culture as year 2002 begins.

Race and Gender Plus

The results of the 2000 U.S. Census were made public during first quarter 2001 by many newspapers and magazines. Numerous agencies and organizations studied the Census results and began building programs and perspectives around specific information that related to them. We call this sub-section *"Race and Gender Plus"* because there are new issues and interpretations raised by Census, particularly in the area of the needs of Hispanic workers. We have also seen a dramatic increase in all kinds of immigrants, about 10 percent more according to the 2000 Census than in the Census ten years ago (*Time for Kids*, March 23, 2001, p. 5). The immigrant population affects trainers at both ends of the skills range—the need for basic skills and work-life programs to maximize and facilitate learning, and the need for more and equitable H-1B visas for immigrant workers to meet the needs for high technology in American companies. The large and diverse Hispanic population and the growing immigrant population present special integration and acculturation challenges as the numbers increase.

The Census also sensitized us to numerous issues in black/white relations and to some newer kinds of inequalities. A major bias suit against Microsoft illustrates this: a class-action suit on behalf of hundreds of current and former black employees was filed in early January 2001 stating unfair performance evaluation processes that often by design skipped managerial levels and were based on subjective measures (*The Wall Street Journal*, January 4, 2001, p. A10). This is a commonly used "360 degree"-type of "flat workplace" evaluation system present and heralded throughout the country in many companies. The commentary in *The Wall Street Journal* is, "Sign of Things to Come?" The $5 billion suit will be watched carefully by many businesses. This is a different kind of legal action from the historical "hostile work environment" based on overt bias and prejudice. While blacks, and women, are making progress in many areas of the workplace, it's the processes that define the workplace culture that seem most difficult to equalize. Trainers will have to become involved in more effective race relations training for whites and blacks in order for things to change.

Affirmative Action will be given a second look in the early days of the new year, as will the Americans with Disabilities Act (ADA). The sensitivities of four distinct age groups currently in the workplace will need to be addressed by workplace learning opportunities. Trainers will become involved in creating programs that meet the needs of the different value systems of veterans, boomers, genXers, and genYs. *TRAINING Magazine* in July 2001 made a very strong point of defining the core values of each of these workplace population cohorts and of challenging trainers to help each group to see what the others value and to find ways to collaborate (p. 46).

Like the black/white statistics that show both positive and negative effects, the statistics for women in the workforce show mixed numbers.

We conclude this sub-section with two entries on women and the challenges to trainers, particularly in meeting the needs of women for management and executive training.

Technology and Learning Communities

In this sub-section, we look at several entries that address the specific problems trainers face in dealing with learners' needs regarding technology and systems, particularly the needs of learners in online learning communities. The training and learning industry is still trying to figure out whether or not learners feel like learners when engaging in e-learning, and if they don't, why not. It's clear from some commercial successes that online communities pay off. For example, in February 2001, eBay had 700,000 new items listed daily. eBay users reported that they'd met good friends on eBay, and that they often traveled together and did other things offline around their common eBay interest (*Fast Company*, May 2001, p. 72). *Fast Company*'s editor, Alan Webber, is quoted in *Reflections* journal as saying his magazine's experiment with "Company of Friends," a web-based community, has not only increased subscription rate to the magazine and brought in more money, but also has caused a potential "fundamental shift in journalism" whereby "The readers are no longer just 'an audience' but co-creators of the product" (winter 2000, p. 81).

Many writers deal with the ideas of both the learning process and the learning content as this year 2002 begins. Experimentation and investigation are proceeding at a rapid pace, and many questions are being asked about the technology and about the kinds of communities of learners that need to be built online.

The New Bottom Line

The terrorist explosions of September 11, 2001 and the bioterrorist attacks of mid-October in media companies, the U.S. Congress, and the U.S. Postal Service caused many Americans to re-think the bottom line. Operation Enduring Freedom was launched around the world against unnamed perpetrators as well as against radicals hiding in Afghanistan. Pollsters, marketers, and psychologists noted that Americans have been good at exporting images of American culture, but that they have often been skewed toward materialistic measures of American success, not the universally acclaimed values of family, community, and charity (*New York Times*, October 14, 2001, p. 14). An image consultant in this same article suggested that corporations should create a new position of "Brand Manager in Charge of America." Other voices urge organizations and businesses to promote America as a country of idealistic and generous people, not one of self-indulgence and imperialism. Business persons began to question just how should the bottom line be defined. Customers received the attention of a whole new spotlight.

Within a month after the attacks on the World Trade Center, New York City had designed a Job Expo and advertised it widely through regional newspapers. One ad in *The New York Times* on October 14, 2001, p. A22, said "thousands of jobs are available" and that representatives from companies in industries would be there including these industries: financial services, food services, technology, retail, healthcare, and security. The Job Expo was held in New York's Madison Square Garden on Wednesday, October 17. *The Wall Street Journal* reported that "hordes of job seekers" showed up, 10,000 persons by some counts, many of whom were willing to take much lower pay than their last job and many of whom were willing to work at any job available. Estimates were that 100,000 jobs were lost in New York as a result of September 11 (*The Wall Street Journal*, October 18, p. B4). *Business Week*'s October 22, 2001 issue contained a special report on the Future of New York, in which writers said, among many other things, that New York contributed $9 billion more to the federal government than it gets back, and that the positive force of "agglomeration" in New York kept people there in a kind of economic and social pull that made the city work. The unasked question was, what will happen to that positive force if the economic infrastructure of the city is gone?

Many of the interactive online newsletters to which I subscribe had reader response items after the events of September 11, 2001 to share ideas about a new awareness throughout American business. Some of the comments were these: "What kind of system interventions can help the First World see that the growing gap (between haves and have nots) will continue to provide fertile soil for violence and terrorist action?"; "The 'Religion of Consumerism' mental model is so deeply in us that it is mostly invisible. It is also so much a part of who we are as a country—our economy depends on it—that it is hard to examine" (*Leverage Points*, published by Pegasus Communications, October 18, 2001, p. 3). The *TechLearn Trends* online newsletter of The MASIE Center, September 26, 2001, p. 1 notified readers of a change in pre-conference workshop offerings to respond to the events of September 11. The TechLearn 2001 Orlando Conference would now include these topics: Learning and Training During Staff Reductions, e-Learning When Investments Are Difficult, Digital Collaboration As an Imperative, and others. The additional workshops addressed the new bottom line characterized by layoffs, a smaller operating and capital budget, less travel, and other reactions to the events of 9/11. The needs of learners for business smarts in this new environment are great, and the good news is that responsible people and organizations are doing what they can to fill those needs.

During the middle weeks of October 2001, Americans along the eastern seaboard were shocked and frightened with anthrax bioterrorism at post offices, including post offices that serve Congress, the White House, and the Supreme Court. Several postal workers and one Congressional staffer died. The workplaces of government workers were closed. Congress itself was closed for business for the first time in its history. The government buildings' mailrooms, tunnels, and ventilation system were searched for anthrax contamination. Reporters reported the news to a worried and newly cautious public. The FBI scrambled to reassess its priorities and hunt down bioterrorists. Our national leaders said publicly that they feared more attacks, yet urged Americans to live our lives normally, although with greater awareness. President Bush in *Newsweek* magazine, October 22, 2001, p. 25 said, "Whoever is behind the anthrax spread may have sophisticated terrorist goals in mind: not just to kill people, but to disrupt the flow of communication that defines our culture." Throughout these difficult months, employees and employers have been reflecting and acting upon new ideas about what really matters. In many cases, the bottom line is forever changed.

We conclude this subsection with the complete text of President George W. Bush's *Address to a Joint Session of Congress and the American People*, on September 20, 2001, in which he describes a new state of the union. This speech is a marker of the current times in which we live and work.

1. Leadership and Culture

Learning to Learn Dialogue with Warren Bennis

Editor's Comment: New tools and new ways of thinking for a world that's gotten bigger—that's what Warren Bennis, leadership guru, said in a roundtable discussion with other leaders sponsored by Linkage, Inc. of Lexington, MA. In times that are increasingly unnerving and unpredictable, leaders are looking for ways of thinking and behaving that legitimize doubt, that allow them to *not* know everything, that encourage them to embrace uncertainty, and that result in their adoption of an overarching learning mindset. Bennis says he'd like to see fewer "great businessmen" on magazine covers and instead see more great teams; and that "a grown-up leader emphasizes teams."

Jason Epstein, distinguished editor and publisher for many years at Random House, wrote a little book called *Book Business*, published by W.W. Norton & Company in mid-2001. Although this is a book about the publishing industry and where books are headed, Epstein has a wonderful Chapter 7, called "Modern Times" in which he comments not only on the challenges writers face in the era of the World Wide Web but also on the nature of human beings who are searching for meaning and who are responsible for its interpretation. Writers, in this regard, are somewhat like leaders—the Bennis-type leaders. Epstein's remarks are also particularly appropriate to the situation leaders face after the terrorism of September 11, 2001. Jason Epstein says (p. 174):

> The critical faculty that selects meaning from chaos is part of our instinctual equipment . . . . Human beings have a genius for finding their way, for creating goods, making orderly markets, distinguishing quality, and assigning value.

Leaders for these kinds of people are what Warren Bennis and this distinguished panel are discussing and defining.

Facilitator: *Warren Bennis, founding chairman of the Leadership Institute of the University of Southern California, Los Angeles.*
Participants: *Candy Albertsson, director of Albertsson Consulting in London; Kevin Cashman, CEO of Minneapolis-based LeaderSource; Paul Hogan, vice chairman and chief risk officer at Fleet Boston Corporation in Boston; David B. Peterson, senior vice president of Personnel Decisions International in Minneapolis; Rich Rosier, vice president of Lexington, Massachusetts-based Linkage Inc., at whose seventh leadership-development conference this roundtable took place; and Alan Stopko, president of Stopko & Associates of Cornelius, North Carolina. Contact the participants at cka@albertsson.demon.co.uk, wbennis@aol.com, kevin@leadersource.com, Paul_F_Hogan@Fleet.com, davidp@pdi-corp.com, rrosier@linkage-inc.com and ASTOP@aol.com.*

Source: "Leading in Unnerving Times" roundtable discussion with Warren Bennis in *MIT Sloan Management Review*, Winter 2001, pp. 97, 98; 101–103. Warren Bennis is founding chairman of the Leadership Institute of the University of Southern California at Los Angeles, and author of many publications on leadership. Reprinted with permission of *MIT Sloan Management Review*, Copyright 2001. All rights reserved.

> Warren Bennis and a panel of experts in leadership development discuss today's "legitimization of doubt," which frees managers to admit they don't know everything and to begin the serious learning that improves competitiveness.

Warren Bennis: I don't recall a time like today. A time when it's clear that we don't have the answers, when younger people may know more than their seniors and the importance of experience is declining, when the foundations of success have morphed from natural resources to human capital, when the economy is changing at warp speed and the life of the proverbial deal-making, world-shaking, tyrannical mogul just doesn't cut it, when employees really are a company's most valuable asset. You can see it all reflected in CEO turnover. Forget that within the last year, the CEOs of Procter & Gamble, Xerox, Kodak and Coke have had to resign. That's small beer when you consider that CEOs appointed after 1985 are three times more likely to be fired than CEOs who were appointed before 1985 and that 34% of Fortune 100 companies have replaced their CEOs since 1995. It has been said of a recently fired CEO, "He didn't get small; the world got bigger."

Most managers find it unnerving to be thrown into situations they can't anticipate. Accustomed to being on top of everything, they are now experiencing doubt. And they should be. As organizational-behavior professor Karl Weick has suggested, our contemporary age should consider the "legitimization of doubt." The really great people know they need new tools and new ways of thinking about leadership. They make it a point of learning how to learn. All of you are leadership educators and have witnessed and participated in the current burst of interest in leadership education. What's your take on it?

Kevin Cashman: We're leaving a period of history and trying to live in it at the same time; people are interested in leadership education because it's necessary for the transition.

David Peterson: But companies are focusing on doing the old leadership programs better; what they need is a new approach.

Paul Hogan: Our businesses are changing in response to competition, the Internet and deregulation. When a management team can't see the problems coming, companies often have to get a team that can. However, the new people may have no experience as managers—hence the interest in leadership education. Also, employees often know more than managers, so managers have to ask for ideas on running the business and then learn how to bring diverse opinions into a cohesive strategy.

Candy Albertsson: The new focus on training and development is a result of the succession vacuum starting to appear at the board level. Boards are looking at succession and saying, "Wait a minute; we don't have anybody. We have to look outside [the organization]." For the cradle-to-grave companies in Europe, that's a shock. The question becomes: What processes will provide a strong pool of candidates for the future? Some European cultures embrace leadership-development processes, but others are 10 years behind—even resistant to 360-degree feedback instruments that assess people's competencies.

David Peterson: Development programs are growing partly because leaders' self-confidence is shaken. Leaders thought they understood how to manage succession development, but how do you motivate a 28-year-old dot-com executive who is worth $14 million? The company has to understand thoroughly what motivates individuals and then make multiple offerings: training, sabbaticals, pets at work, children at work.

Warren Bennis: Have any of you heard clients admit to shakiness?

Alan Stopko: You sense it in companies' planning sessions, when people look for affirmation from outside experts. You also see it in coaching relationships with senior executives.

David Peterson: People are actually asking for coaches now. Leaders don't say they're feeling vulnerable; they say, "I'm the best person to handle this job. I just need help on this one piece."

> Companies that think about how development fits with the strategic agenda recognize that development must start with the CEO and the board.

Thoughts on Leadership from Warren Bennis

- Think "deep generalist," not "specialist."

- Think "applied biology" and "living systems," not "engineering" and "mechanics."

- Encourage others to create meaning for themselves at work.

- Follow organizational-behavior expert Karl Weick's advice and favor compasses over maps.

- Rely as much on the beginner's way of thinking as on experience.

- Question scores, routines and rules, and think "improvisation" and "jamming."

- Vulnerability and the quest to learn are more important than certitude (which is impossible).

- The acronym for today's organizations is no longer COP (control, order, predict). It's more like ACA (align, create, adapt).

- Take a tip from John Keats, and let yourself experience doubt. Writing to his brothers in 1815 about why he so admired Shakespeare, Keats asserted that one of Shakespeare's most important qualities was negative capability—"when man is capable of being in uncertainties, mysteries, doubts, without any irritable reaching after fact and reason."

Warren Bennis: A fascinating change. We are living in developmental times. People are more willing to admit they need to learn some things.

Rich Rosier: There's a media perception that one individual can lead an organization to greatness. So maybe companies think that if they train 20 leaders to be like Cisco's John Chambers, say, they could clinch the future.

Kevin Cashman: Steve Jobs, at Apple, says, "I used to think one great engineer was as valuable as two good engineers. Now I think one great engineer is as good as 50 good engineers." If you work at it, you can replicate one great engineer—or one true leader.

Warren Bennis: Which of you thinks the interest in leadership education comes from people wanting to be John Chambers, GE's Jack Welch or Intel's Andy Grove?

Kevin Cashman: The role models raise the bar. If a company wants 20 great leaders, it will be interested in leadership education.

Warren Bennis: I want to argue against today's emphasis on the great man. (Usually it's a man.) Chambers himself talks about teams, not about great leaders. I don't agree that one great engineer is better than 50 good engineers. We may be placing too much emphasis on the individual—what I call "overpeoplefication." What I would like to see on the covers of business magazines is fewer great men and more teams. A grown-up leader emphasizes teams.

Candy Albertsson: Leadership development is increasingly valued as an attraction-and-retention tool. Prospective employees want to know, Will I strengthen my résumé if I go to this company? It's tough to compete for a new job when one has been at a standstill developmentally.

Warren Bennis: What should a leadership-development expert advise someone who has been successful in the Old Economy and is trying to be a dot-com? Let's say Thomas Stemberg of Staples calls on you. Interesting man, right? A progressive thinker and all that. A Boston firm. Let's say that 10 years ago, you had advised Mr. Stemberg on leadership. What different things would you emphasize today?

Paul Hogan: I'd say, "You don't have time to plan. Try a bunch of things, and see if they work. If they don't, stop doing them. If they do, feed them."

Alan Stopko: I'd say, "If you hire someone to lead, and you believe you have the right person for that job, stay out of the way."

David Peterson: People need learning capabilities. Teaching people how to learn is missing from most leadership-development curricula. How do you learn to cope with ambiguity, for example? You have to get out there and muck

> Maybe the young man Warren described—the big corporation's protégé who went to a dot-com—wasn't asking to develop his capabilities as much as he was asking for more meaning. And for the chance to apply his capabilities to create even more meaning.

around. Figure out what's working. We need to teach people curiosity—how to look at things in a new way. We need to teach them to think clearly, to juggle multiple agendas—to be fast but to leave time for reflection.

Alan Stopko: I'd also emphasize agility of learning—the speed and efficiency of learning something new. Competence, experience and learning agility lead to new expertise.

Candy Albertsson: To be successful in developing new capabilities in an organization, the top people have to look inward first. Do they themselves need new skills? Does their behavior exemplify what they want middle managers to learn? Companies that think about how development fits with the strategic agenda recognize that development must start with the CEO and the board.

Alan Stopko: The issues facing leadership development are best seen in the New Economy. How will the leader of the future motivate the youthful, inexperienced manager who already expects wealth through stock options?

Warren Bennis: Good point. I have a story that illustrates that. A certain famous CEO, now retired, a very good leader, had a protégé with a great future at the corporation. This protégé upped and left for a well-known dot-com. When the CEO asked why, the protégé said, "I want to make more money, and I want to make history." How could the CEO have kept that young man?

Kevin Cashman: He could ask him, "What would you like to do here? What would it take for you to stay?" Then he'd have to decide if it's worth it.

David Peterson: The main question is: How can he make history? Can the company find a way to make that happen?

Paul Hogan: You could ask the guy who's leaving if he'd like to build something new. I think of the way Enron reshaped its playing field.

Warren Bennis: What would the something new be? A company about to commit resources might want to know.

Paul Hogan: I'd say to the person, "You tell us. Create our future. Tell us who you want and what funding you need. We'll build your vision in five years, and you will own everything." You have to inspire people—the way Amazon.com does.

Warren Bennis: I'd probably say, "Before you decide to leave, let's bring a coach in and talk it over."

Candy Albertsson: The best way companies can identify what is required to keep people is to ask them. Today's 30-year-olds may have different ambitions than senior managers had at 30. Once a valued employee's wishes are clear, companies must coach that person regularly. Then if it looks like he or she might leave, the company will be better positioned to take action.

Warren Bennis: So you say, "Here are the things we're going to do to keep you here"?

David Peterson: Well, usually retention plans involve pay and short-term fixes. Long-term fixes require a culture of development.

Warren Bennis: Development for what? When you say "development," what do you really mean?

Candy Albertsson: Making someone capable of meeting the likely challenges.

David Peterson: Providing more career options, so people have more control over their lives.

Paul Hogan: I read about the difficulty of keeping young people in Wall Street funds. At one large firm, a group of young analysts got together and sent a letter to the president with about 30 items they wanted. They got almost everything in about a week. One of the things they wanted was five minutes a week of one-on-one senior-management time. Retention programs suffer when people think, "If somebody senior doesn't have enough interest to talk to me a few minutes a week, then I don't exist as a person."

Kevin Cashman: Maybe the young man Warren described—the big corporation's protégé who went to a dot-com—wasn't asking to develop his capabilities as much as he was asking for more meaning. And for the chance

Needs of Learners

to apply his capabilities to create even more meaning.

Warren Bennis: So we ask the protégé, "What would be most meaningful for you and how can we help you get that?"

Paul Hogan: The problem with most succession planning is that it focuses on the organization's needs without a commensurate investment in what gives meaning to the succession candidate.

Candy Albertsson: People who are wired entrepreneurially are unlikely to remain inside a large organization anyway.

Warren Bennis: According to Dan Tapscott's "Growing Up Digital," someday we'll all be wired entrepreneurially. How does a business operate when everyone is entrepreneurial? Is it possible to develop such people?

David Peterson: Not if companies keep asking, "How do we do training better?" instead of "How do we help people learn better?"

Warren Bennis: Well, David, how *do* you help people learn better?

David Peterson: Self-insight is the first thing people need. Second, motivation. Third, capabilities. Fourth, real-world practice. And fifth, accountability. Most development programs fail to link those pieces.

Warren Bennis: So we make organizations into theaters of inquiry and learning? The idea is good but needs fleshing out. Do any of you really know how you learn? It might be good to organize a conference enlisting the deep thinkers from the learning arena: researchers from linguistics, neurosciences and human development. We haven't listened to them much. Let me ask you: In the last year, what insight did you have that changed the way you looked at things? What were the conditions under which that happened?

David Peterson: People learn in different ways at different times. Let me go back to my model...

Warren Bennis: I don't want your model; that's too abstract. How do you yourself learn?

David Peterson: Well, I *am* going to go back to the model. People are different. For learning to occur, the material has to be relevant.

Warren Bennis: OK. Good. It has to be something that resonates.

> It would be interesting to analyze whether the Jack Welches of the world have been successful at growing leaders because of leadership-development programs like GE's in Crotonville, New York, or because dozens of people inside the organization were inspired to model the behavior of a Welch.

David Peterson: I learn when all five ingredients are present. There is a difference between having the insight and seeing the application, between having the skill and using it. There are 22 functions on my company's new phone system—three of them relevant to me. The training so overwhelmed me I walked out and taught myself how to get voice mail.

Warren Bennis: The need for voice mail was resonant. You were motivated to learn.

Kevin Cashman: That's content learning—learning that impacts a function. There's also transformative learning, which affects every part of your life. It comes from an experience—good or bad—that prevents you from looking at anything the same way afterward.

Paul Hogan: In some environments I have felt everyone would learn better if management just eliminated barriers. Learning occurs when you know you won't get criticized for trying something new. A learning environment is also one where the senior people model the behavior the company says it wants. If the company says it wants a team culture, but the senior people keep operating fiefdoms, that tells young people a lot.

Warren Bennis: How do we embed learning into company culture? Workshops are not enough. We need organizations to become fields of inquiry, where people are continually thinking about learning and helping others learn.

Rich Rosier: It might help to have the CEO walk around and ask people, "What have you learned lately that mattered?"

Warren Bennis: I'm sure that would stump many of them. Personally, I often start learning when I am stumped. I recall lecturing to an M.B.A. class about "meaning" and what is "meaningful," when one of the students asked, "How do you find meaning at work, in life?"

That stumped me. Still does. I told the student I didn't know. When I think about it now, I realize that I could have said, "No one can create meaning for you; you're the only one who can do that." We create our own meaning from our own experiences.

Rich Rosier: The wish to learn is tied to role models. A lot of my leadership capabilities come from people I've worked for. It would be interesting to analyze whether the Jack Welches of the world have been successful at growing leaders because of leadership-development programs like GE's in Crotonville, New York, or because dozens of people inside the organization were inspired to model the behavior of a Welch.

Warren Bennis: Welch does show up at the leadership-development institute every month, but GE's whole system creates opportunities, so it's more than just modeling.

Rich Rosier: Still, how much more learning would happen if instead of talking about leadership qualities in a classroom, you put someone who embodied those characteristics right into the work setting? Suppose you told people, "Here's what this skill looks like. Watch how decisions are made."

Kevin Cashman: Too many senior managers think they don't need to develop. Their behavior communicates negativity about development and blocks creation of a learning organization.

Paul Hogan: We need to redefine some control functions as teaching functions. In a global bank, for example, the risk-management function can control some things but not everything. Employees must learn how to think about risk so they can do the right thing on their own.

Warren Bennis: Let me end with this question: How do you elicit what's relevant to other people when they themselves may not know? Creating that propitious moment for learning is a mystery.

Rich Rosier: A very individual mystery. But we do know that most people want to be successful, so we can tell them exactly what skills are relevant to being successful in the organization. The questions I hear most are: "What does it take to be successful around here?" "Where do I stand?"

Warren Bennis: If you get people to open up with their personal dilemmas, you can spot what would be relevant to them.

Kevin Cashman: It helps to identify the intersection between what the individual cares about and what the organization cares about. At that intersection, the individual finds something relevant to work on, and the organization finds something it can help the individual develop.

Warren Bennis: Very good. It looks like leadership of the future begins with an atmosphere of inquiry and learning. Thank you all. I learned some things.

Ford Motor Company Defines and Trains Transformational Leaders

Editor's Comment: "New Business Leaders" at Ford Motor Company are challenged with the development of "Quantum Ideas"—ideas that stretch an individual's capacity to "think critically, innovate daringly, evaluate choices strategically, and support business objectives wisely." Ford's aim is to create a new leadership mindset that invests in the whole person, capable of contributing at work, at home, and in the community. Ford is taking steps to make a transition from a manufacturing company to a consumer company, and in the process is training its leaders to think differently—the metaphor of changing even its DNA. Ford's program addresses the needs of learners for leadership training in a world that is consumer focused, globally interconnected, and networked electronically and economically. It addresses spiritual and cultural diversity, and focuses on the need for people working together to make sense of their work together.

We live in extraordinary times. Not a day goes by when we don't hear or read about a new discovery, invention, or business initiative that will ultimately affect all of our lives. New media are transforming virtually every aspect of human action. On top of the digital revolution, add new business models, globalization, and new labor market dynamics (such as increased diversity and fresh attitudes about work and one's personal life) and you have a different world than business leaders have ever seen before.

The underlying structure of the global economy is shifting, bringing with it a bewildering array of unprecedented challenges that require a new kind of leadership. Developing the next generation of leaders at a time of momentous change is a monumental task. Yet, those of us in the field of leadership development must continue to ask fundamental questions:

- How can we accelerate the identification of candidates for leadership positions?
- What methods should we use to enable our people to become competitive in the new economy?

> Ford Motor Company created transformational leaders to change itself, and possibly to make a difference in the world.

- How can we challenge our leaders to contribute to the transformation of our company?
- How can we accelerate the preparation of our best leaders for senior executive roles?
- How can we drive our company's vision deep into its culture?
- How can we create a new leadership mindset that invests in the developing leader as a whole person, capable of contributing not only at work, but also at home and in the community?

Ford Motor Company is facing those same questions; senior management has set the direction. In our 2000 Corporate Citizenship Report, chairman William Clay Ford Jr. writes:

"We see no conflict between business goals and social and environmental needs. I believe

---

Source: "Leadership DNA: The Ford Motor Story" by Stewart D. Friedman in *Training & Development*, March 2001, pp. 23–29. Stewart S. Friedman is Director of the Leadership Development Center at Ford Motor Company. Reprinted with permission of ASTD, Copyright 2001. All rights reserved.

the distinction between a good company and a great one is this: A good company delivers excellent products and services; a great one delivers excellent products and services and strives to make the world a better place."

In the same report, our CEO Jacques Nasser observes:

"The transition from a traditional manufacturer to a 21st-century consumer company is critical for our long-term financial success. It requires a new mindset—one focused on connecting not only with our customers, but also with all of our stakeholders to make it work."

THE DNA REVOLUTION

Adopting a consumer mindset as well as one of environmental and social responsibility requires leadership. We need leaders who can make informed business decisions that will make our company better able to meet customer needs and increase shareholder value, as well as honor commitments to the world in which we live. Change like that is easy to talk about but difficult to implement. It will take nothing less than a massive shift in culture to create new leadership DNA. Nothing short of revolution will do.

And that is where our Leadership Development Center enters. Our vision is to be the center for the revolution, developing Ford Motor Company leaders to change the world. Our mission is to accelerate transformation to a consumer- and shareholder-driven business, to accelerate the identification and development of leadership talent, and to drive the company's mission, vision, and values deep into its culture.

How can we do that? We've developed a series of leadership programs centered around these core principles:

- Adopt a transformational mindset.
- Use action learning—learning by doing, leading, and teaching.
- Leverage the power of e-tools.
- Integrate work and life, what I call "total leadership."
- Generate business impact.

Let's examine the first two in depth and the others later on.

Adopt a transformational mindset. The chief way that Ford's Leadership Development Center is fomenting revolution is by creating transformational leaders—men and women who know how to get things done in ways that use the talents of their people for maximum business impact. Our leaders also learn to think "outside of the box" because our programs force them out of their comfort zones in everything from selecting a project to working with new people. Participants return to their positions enthused and ready to look at familiar challenges with fresh eyes and to try new ideas that deliver results.

We nurture the transformational mindset by consistently challenging participants to think of alternative possibilities. That push really begins before participants start the training. The workload of most programs isn't light, and the real work isn't done in the classroom but in the field of real business activity. Participants are expected to do work prior to the classroom phase—mainly, to choose a project and research feasibility. They must devise innovative ways to balance their usual workloads and assume responsibility for meeting program requirements. The challenge is to find ways to eliminate unnecessary tasks and obtain help. Many participants learn to empower their staff and to network with peers to delegate their day-to-day responsibilities. In itself, that is a significant opportunity for leadership lessons.

Transformational leadership at Ford is underscored, as reflected in our expected leadership behaviors, by these values: integrity, flawless execution, and the building of effective relationships with key stakeholders. In other words, while we're asking our people to think and behave differently, we are mindful of our company's culture and respectful of its rich cultural values.

Another aspect of the transformational mindset is the growing need to recognize the triple bottom line of financial success, environmental protection, and social responsibility. Our programs have community service aspects that serve to put our work as a company in the perspective of the larger social context in which we operate, and to which we must contribute. There is a growing realization that a company such as ours (indeed, most companies for that matter) can't continue with traditional business models into the 21st century. We're actively incorporating renewable resource technologies and developing alternatives to the internal combustion engine, for example. Such bold actions require equally bold leaders to implement them. Success in the new century requires the transformational mindset, one found in our new leadership DNA.

Use action learning. All of our programs feature action learning. Participants work individually or in teams with leaders at all levels on projects that challenge them to expand their creative abilities and refine their critical-thinking and execution skills—all in order to drive for improved business results.

Participants receive extensive feedback from multiple sources that enables them to improve and refine their leadership abilities. In addition, alumni of our programs serve as leader-teachers—a practice that helps participants and the instructor grow and develop new capacities for leadership. It's also a critical feature of our strategy to "spread the word."

Action learning creates business impact. The projects participants choose must have a business benefit in terms of customer satisfaction, cost reduction, or enhanced revenue. One of the most notable examples is the QIP—the Quantum Idea Project. It's the key to our New Business Leader program for first-time supervisors of salaried employees. The QIP, intended to drive revolutionary change at Ford, stretches an individual's capacity to think critically, innovate daringly, evaluate choices strategically, and support business objectives wisely. In the process, a manager begins to develop leadership skills that he or she can use every day.

The QIP process is organized according to key milestones, checkoffs, and evaluation processes inherent to a project. Biweekly, participants undergo a cycle of review that occurs in teams with a peer serving as co-strategist or advisor. Review also happens online on password-protected Websites. During these reviews, participants rate their projects as *green* (good to go), *yellow* (not quite sure), or *red* (stuck). Then, they receive feedback and support on how to maintain momentum and progress towards their goals.

Additionally, our programs instill a sense of accountability. Participants are evaluated on the outcome of their projects and how well they performed as leaders. For example, how did they interact with their peers? Did they network successfully? Did they learn new ways of doing things?

Success as a leader depends on more than delivering results; it requires an ability to continually strengthen working alliances and a willingness to test new ideas. The feedback participants receive from multiple sources such as peers, clients, and supervisors adds to their sense of accountability. The feedback also becomes instructive in the development of a person's leadership style and capacity.

FOUR-FIVE PUNCH

At present, the Leadership Development Center at Ford Motor Company offers nine programs—four core and five strategic change initiatives.

The four core programs play a significant role in the identification, selection, and development of Ford's next generation of leaders. For admission, candidates must be rated either as having high potential or recent high performance. The four core programs, targeted for specific leadership levels, are listed in ascending order:

1. *New Business Leader* teaches leadership through the pursuit of innovative ideas designed to transform the business. To date, participants have generated more than 600 QIPs (quantum idea projects), all of which aim for a specific business impact. Participants increase their leadership capacity by building skills in the 12 Ford leadership behaviors as they learn how to take their ideas from conception to implementation.

2. *Leadership for the New Economy* pioneers new ways to work. A primary goal is to enable leaders to deliver strong business results and enrich lives by using new economy tools and by taking what I call a "total leadership" perspective—integrating work, home, community, and self. The lessons emerging from this program are accelerating transformation as participants teach others throughout the company about how they've changed the way work is done.

3. *Experienced Leader Challenge* demonstrates how to deliver improved business results in the form of cost reduction and revenue generation by working in cross-functional teams. Partici-

> Total leadership . . . starts with your life as a whole: your life at work, your life at home, and your life in the community.

pants improve their leadership capacity by working in an environment that develops new business knowledge and that leverages the strengths of broad, cross-functional networks for specific results.

4. *Capstone* prepares people moving into positions of senior leadership. Capstone projects are strategic in nature and are designed to expand leadership capacity to the next level. Corporate officers are sponsors for projects, and senior leaders are involved in teaching, coaching, and evaluating participants.

The Leadership Development Center lends its support through strategic change initiatives, which by nature cut across vertical and horizontal boundaries. At present, there are five change initiative programs underway:

1. *Leadership for Consumer-Driven, Six-Sigma* complements the technical training of Black Belt candidates by teaching the leadership skills required for successful execution of Black Belt projects.

2. *Ford/Supplier BLI* fosters collaborative partnerships with Ford's key suppliers to improve understanding, increase efficiency, and lower costs.

3. *BLI 3 Flawless Execution* builds business leadership competencies in vehicle line, cross-functional teams responsible for designing, engineering, and developing new cars and trucks.

4. *New Leader Impact* rapidly integrates newly hired executives by cultivating networks throughout the company and by reinforcing their role as agents of change.

5. *Global Leadership Forum* brings Ford's top 300 executives together on a quarterly basis to focus on key business initiatives and to strengthen connections among the key players in our company.

THOSE WHO CAN, TEACH

Every program features extensive use of teachers. Graduates of our programs serve as leader-teachers, a practice that helps participants and the instructor grow and develop new capacities for leadership. The concept of leader-teacher isn't unique, but Ford places a high emphasis on teaching. The lesson begins at the top.

More than three years ago, CEO Jacques Nasser inaugurated the Business Leadership Initiative concept with himself as teacher. Now, thousands of managers are teaching other managers about everything from the basics of supervision to the intricacies of Six Sigma. Nowhere is the concept of leader-teacher more prevalent than in the *New Business Leader* program. The active participation of senior leaders in the Quantum Idea Project process is essential. Each QIP must have a senior leader sponsor who serves as a project mentor. The sponsor not only shepherds the project, but he or she also nurtures the leadership capacity of participants.

Another way that leader-teachers contribute is through feedback. Participants in all of our core programs receive extensive feedback from multiple sources to enable them to improve and refine their leadership abilities. The feedback is a two-way street; leader-teachers receive feedback on how they teach. That input is extremely valuable and gives them something to take back to the workplace.

Leader-teachers also create synergy throughout all of the action-learning programs. Graduates become teachers, sponsors, and mentors of participants. That creates cohesion in a spirit of revolutionary change and helps accelerate the transformational process that we're all engaged in.

THE POWER OF E-TOOLS

If we're expecting people to work in the new economy, we need to give them tools to work more effectively. The global 24/7 reality makes working face-to-face often impossible; time zones and distance preclude it. Yet, we need people to work together. Thankfully, technology is making it possible.

The Internet and email are the starting points; virtual collaboration is the next step. For example, in our *Leadership for the New Economy* program, participants work in virtual spaces called "e-rooms" six weeks prior to commencement of the first residential (classroom) session. They also begin working collaboratively in the e-room, using an online tool dedicated to their program sessions and monitored by faculty made up of Ford executives and outside faculty drawn from leading universities and consulting firms. Interestingly, the team set the standard in virtual collaboration as the program was designed and delivered by people who functioned as a virtual team during most of the development.

Taking e-tools to the next step—as a learning exercise as well as a way to have fun—participants took part in an online auction conducted by AutoX-change (later Covisint), bidding on the opportunity to meet individually with outside experts from joint-venture partners and other companies that could offer useful insight and information on specific projects. Not only did the bidding process teach participants lessons about online auctions, but it also enabled them to expand their network of information and resources.

In using e-tools, participants invest time and energy trying out new ways of working that leverage synergies among work, home, and community, thus taking a total leadership approach. That might involve experimenting with telecommuting, flexible schedules, reduced face-time for internal meetings (while making more intelligent use of face-time for customers and other external stakeholders), and other new models for leadership.

To augment our e-leadership mindset, we launched a Website devoted to leadership, with the intention to make it all things to all people at Ford who are interested in leadership. We consider it our virtual community for Ford leadership. Anyone at Ford can visit the site and learn how to gain insight into leadership best practices and get access to leadership materials, including self-nomination forms for admission to our programs. In addition, each program has e-rooms where participants can work independently or cooperatively on their projects.

INTEGRATING WORK AND LIFE

We at Ford are pioneering a new dimension of leadership that seeks to integrate all aspects of a person's life. We call it "total leadership." Total leadership is similar to most leadership approaches in that it aims to achieve superior results. It's different from many prior leadership models because it starts with your life as a whole: your life at work, your life at home, and your life in the community. Total leadership recognizes that the stakeholder expectations in each of those domains can and do affect each other. Therefore, total leadership is about being a leader in all aspects of one's life.

New technologies, specifically the e-tools, permit us to integrate stakeholder domains and even create synergies among them. No longer is business leadership confined to the work domain. Boundaries between diverse domains of life are becoming more permeable and flexible, and leadership now must account for that emerging reality. Leaders will have to leverage resources—financial and human capital, technology, new business models, and so forth—to gain synergies across diverse stakeholder domains: work, home, community, and self.

The total leadership perspective allows for a faster, more agile means to achieve superior business results in the 24/7, global, anytime-anywhere economy. More specifically, because it deemphasizes face-time and focuses on results both within and across domains, the total leadership perspective offers the potential for reduced workload and better results, in all aspects of life.

Business results increase in the short term because of

- increased motivation and commitment
- greater efficiencies in work processes
- reduced cycle times
- lower costs (from less travel, for example)
- enhanced customer focus through explicit emphasis on performance impact across the value chain
- more active engagement by business leaders in home and community life.

With employees having greater control in arranging their life circumstances, long-term business benefits accrue—including greater attraction and retention of top talent in the new labor market, less burnout and stress (potentially related to health-care costs), and decreased downtime from poorly managed connections between work and other aspects of life.

That's the good news, the opportunity. As pioneers facing the frontier of a new economy, the challenge for us is to develop the total leadership capacity necessary to bring the opportunity to reality. It requires understanding more about how to leverage the resources inherent in new-economy tools and models. That means learning how to

- capture synergies across domains of life so that total achievement in life is greater than just the sum of efforts applied at work, at home, in the community, and for one's self
- make more conscious and strategic choices about allocation of time and energy towards valued goals
- rethink the means by which work gets done in ways that force a results-driven focus
- reduce reliance on traditional work methods—face-time and co-location of resources—and use them more wisely
- innovate to better meet performance expectations of key stakeholders at work, at home, in the community, and those you hold for yourself
- aggressively cultivate networks and partnerships that provide the support needed for flexibility and agility in and across domains.

We believe our programs need to continue to develop total leadership capacity further to stay ahead of the curve in the rapidly evolving economic and social environments of business in the 21st century. It isn't a stretch to say that without a total leadership perspective, our company will not be able to compete successfully in the future. Total leadership is essential to Ford's new leadership DNA.

GENERATING BUSINESS IMPACT

All of the programs significantly impact business in two ways: financially and organizationally. Financially, each individual or team project must contribute to customer satisfaction, reduced costs, or increased incremental revenue. And we have some impressive statistics.

Participants in QIP programs have generated more than 600 projects, some with significant business impact such as tire recycling, vehicle customization, and new vehicle servicing models.

A recent *Ford Supplier/Business Leadership Initiative* program identified $300 in cost-reductions per vehicle, which is now in development. Three hundred dollars may not seem like much at first, but when you multiple it by thousands of vehicles, the savings is substantial.

Projects in the *Experienced Leader Challenge* program have identified more than $100 million in cost-savings and another $100 million in incremental revenue. Over the next three to five years, those numbers will likely climb to the billions in savings and earnings.

You can accurately declare that our leadership programs pay for themselves many times over. But that's only part of the story. The second business impact is the effect our programs are having on the organization. We're accelerating the process of creating leaders at every level by having emerging and experienced leaders work individually as well as collaboratively on projects of significant merit. We create synergies further among the programs that, in turn, further facilitate learning and speed the development of leadership capacities.

Bottom line: We are creating transformational leaders, men and women who know how to get things done in ways that use the talents of their people for maximum business impact. For that reason, I believe it's no exaggeration to say that the return on this organizational contribution is exponential. And in the new economy in which we face escalating customer demands, fluid market conditions, and global scale, exponential return is what is required.

Leadership development is an evolutionary process that changes as the needs of an organization change. Core principles, such as action learning or leader-teachers, may remain. But the what, why, and how of a program should change in response to emerging issues. As one who has taught leadership in an academic and now a corporate setting, I suggest these guidelines when creating a leadership development program:

Create a sense of urgency for leadership development. Leadership is not a nice-to-have; it's a must do. Success in the new economy, or any economy, will require men and women to adopt a transformational mindset that enables them to anticipate change, develop strategies to meet new demands, and continue to maximize growth opportunities. In a nutshell, all of that requires leadership.

Our CEO, Jacques Nasser, is brilliant at conveying urgency. Despite years of record earnings, Nasser has been galvanizing Ford to transform itself as quickly as possible in an effort to become a 21st-century company capable of meeting escalating demands and adapting to the rules of the new economy.

Develop a brand for your leadership-development strategy. Every successful consumer product has a readily identifiable brand. Same goes for services. Brand, put simply, is the sum of the attributes, aspirations, and perceptions associated with a product or service. At the heart of successful brands is a sense of trust between the provider and the consumer. That's the kind of trust we're trying to foster with Ford employees whom we encourage to join our programs. Therefore, it makes good sense to develop a strong brand image around the kind of transformational leadership we're trying to create.

Our brand image revolves around creating a new leadership DNA. We even developed a logo (a double helix) and gradually began attributing to it positive characteristics of leadership at Ford. Over time, we believe our brand will become synonymous with the kind of transformational mindset Ford is creating.

Communicate the results of leadership-development activities. Communication is central to leadership, so why would it be any different for a leadership-development program? Tom Grant, program leader for *New Business Leader*, often talks about the time in the not-too-distant future when applicants to the program will exceed its capacity to deliver. Grant is no glutton for excess work, but he understands that when more people want to participate, we'll have achieved a measure of success.

Demand is tied directly to communications, so it's important to use all available means to communicate about your programs: Website, email, video, print materials. Be certain you also communicate your brand in everything you do. Make the logo and its associated images ubiquitous. But a word to the wise: Keep senior leadership in the loop. Invite them to teach, and send them regular updates on what's going on in the programs. Solicit their feedback. Their active support is essential to the long-term health of your programs. Indeed, the Leadership Development Center at Ford isn't an HR initiative; it's owned by senior line management.

Celebrate achievements. Leadership programs should be targeted to achieve business results. When they do, publicize them. Let others in the organization know how the programs are affecting the bottom line. In this way, you can shift the perception of leadership development from a "cost" to a "revenue enhancer." More important, you will demonstrate that leadership development isn't something nice to have but a must-have that not only pays for itself, but also facilitates a mindset and culture that seek to build the business. Frankly, you can't put a price tag on that.

Promote your alumni as leaders of tomorrow. The ultimate measure of any leadership-development program is how well the alumni do. If graduates are moving up in the organization, it's an indication that the lessons of the leadership-development program are effective. As more graduates move up through our organization, the leadership message and example will become part of the culture and transformation process.

A leadership-development program can help its alumni achieve success in the organization in two ways. One, alumni make terrific teachers. Keep bringing them back to your programs. They'll not only help your current participants, but they will also hone their own leadership skills. Two, create an alumni association (similar to what universities do) to help grads of the leadership development programs network with each other and senior leaders.

The success of a program depends on its alumni. The more you can do for them, the better you will do for your leadership development efforts and the organization as a whole.

Make no mistake: The Leadership Development Center is no charm school. It's more like an obstacle course devised by the Marines to bring out the best in Ford's leadership talent by pushing, prodding, and stretching for results.

David Murphy, our vice president of human resources, says, "We aim to be seen by Wall Street as the best-led company in the world, with leaders at all levels, building leadership capacity faster than any other corporation.

"We must become a company where leadership represents intellectual capital at such a level that it will out learn, out compete, and out lead all of the competition to ensure ongoing increases in shareholder value throughout the foreseeable future."

People who graduate from the Leadership Development Center gain improved customer focus, a renewed commitment to business results, and a greater understanding of their role in generating shareholder value. They become transformational leaders—ready, willing, and able to lead Ford Motor Company to meet future challenges. Perhaps the truest measure of our impact will be in the marketplace for talent when Ford is seen as *the* company to go to for the best leadership talent in the business world.

Individual Career Development at First USA Bank

Editor's Comment: Each year, *Workforce* magazine presents "Optimas Awards" to outstanding companies. Ten awards were granted in year 2001, among them the award for "Quality of Life" to First USA Bank of Wilmington, Delaware. Most Quality of Life Programs have focused on issues such as elder-care, child-care on premises, tuition refund for advanced degrees, and community involvement. This program was different; it helped individuals define and pursue their career dreams, and in the process, helped individuals contribute more to their jobs. Company managers said that they wanted "to promote a broader and more pervasive, persistent change in the bank's corporate culture" (p. 55). Through a structured system of career development, individual employees took charge of their own learning, and contributed more to the organization because of it. This article shows why and how First USA Bank developed training for these kinds of learners.

Last year, Jonathan Bender knew he needed a change in his career, but he wasn't sure what to do about it. He worked as a collector for Wilmington, Delaware-based First USA Bank, calling credit card customers who were behind on their payments and helping them reduce their debts. The job was lucrative, since a successful collector can make thousands of dollars in bonuses in addition to his or her salary. But as Bender notes, there's considerable pressure to meet goals, and the pace—collectors must contact at least 16 accounts per hour—can be grueling. "I found myself really starting to get burned out," he says. "I got to the point where I was taking too many breaks, talking to people and complaining, creating for myself the image of someone who didn't really want to work here."

It hadn't always been like that. When Bender had taken the job several years before, he'd seen it as a way to get his foot in the door at First USA. But somewhere along the way he'd gotten off track and lost sight of how to further his ambitions. "This is a huge bank, and I didn't really have a clue as to what else was out there for me to do, what I should learn, who I needed to get to know. I wasn't well organized, and I had trouble focusing on the job and advancing my career at the same time. And I

> The Opportunity Knocks program helps employees zero in on career dreams and achieve them.

couldn't really expect my manager to take a couple of hours and help me figure out what to do with my life."

Fortunately, First USA stepped up and offered Bender and its other employees a way to help themselves. The company's Opportunity Knocks program, now in its third year, is an innovative HR program designed to help employees zero in on their career dreams and achieve them within the organization. What makes the program especially remarkable is the amount of resources the bank has committed to it, and the extent to which it's been integrated into the everyday workplace. First USA not only provides career-development training and follow-up guidance, but it also has outfitted special facilities at its work sites, which it allows employees to use on company time.

The program was born in the summer of 1998, when First USA conducted employee job satisfaction surveys in the wake of a merger. The results were sobering. It found that certain

---

Source: "At First USA Bank, Promotions and Job Satisfaction Are Up" by Patrick J. Kiger in *Workforce*, March 2001, pp. 54–56. Patrick J. Kiger is a freelance writer in Washington, DC. Article reprinted with permission of *Workforce*, Copyright 2001. All rights reserved.

groups were dissatisfied with their jobs, and many seemed pessimistic about their future prospects within the organization. "We already had a sense that career development among our non-exempt employee population was an issue," says Jeff Brown, First USA's assistant vice president for organizational effectiveness. "But the survey really threw it in our faces, and made us realize we had to do something about it."

When First USA's HR team took the grim findings to the organization's site managers, they showed enough wisdom not to dodge the issue or point fingers elsewhere. Instead, management and HR worked together to create an aggressive remedial strategy. That summer, the HR and operations management team plunged into the task of making it happen.

While the team had some specific, measurable short-term goals—improving job satisfaction, reducing attrition, and boosting internal promotions—they also wanted to promote a broader, more pervasive and persistent change in the bank's corporate culture.

"We wanted employees to own their own careers, to take charge of where they were going," Brown says. "We wanted them to choose their path, rather than wait for somebody to choose it for them. But beyond that, we wanted to get away from the idea that the only worthwhile way to grow was to move upward to a higher-ranking job. Promotions are one career path, but they're not the only path. A person can also make lateral moves within an organization, and develop a greater breadth of experience and perspective from working at a different job at the same level. Or a person can follow a path of job enrichment—improving their skills, or maybe reinventing the job itself, to keep it interesting."

At the same time, the team wanted to create an atmosphere in which it was evident that employees' career advancement was not only supported by the bank but also strongly aligned with the organization's own goals. First USA saved time by utilizing the services of Career Systems International, a Scranton, Pennsylvania-based HR consulting firm. CSI provided First USA with CareerPower, a seminar format built around what CSI founder Beverly Kaye calls the "Five Ps."

"The first 'P' is the person—the individual employee." Kaye explains. "The employee needs to understand the sum total of his or her skills, abilities, values, and interests, and to be able to articulate them so that a career fit is possible. The next 'P' is perspective—you need to check out your self-assessment with others, by going back and soliciting feedback, by examining how you interface with your colleagues and your manager and everyone else you deal with. The third 'P' is place. In order to be a good manager of your own career, you have to understand not only your own job and the company you're in, but the whole broader world of work, what's happening in your industry and profession. Part of that is looking for how changes in the workplace and your profession and industry require changes in your skillset and position.

"The fourth 'P' is possibility. You need to get a fix on the different ways you can move within an organization and outside it—the benefits of moving laterally versus moving up, how to accomplish moving vertically if that's what you want to do, how you can enrich yourself. Or, if you decide that leaving is the best option, where you might go. Ideally, you want to have not just one objective, but several possibilities.

"The last 'P' is the plan. If you don't have one, all of those previous ideas aren't worth anything. You need a blueprint for how to develop those new abilities, skills, and competencies that help you move toward your goals."

First USA's team adopted the Five Ps as the core philosophy of its new culture-shift program. To get employees going in the new direction, Brown and his colleagues originally conceived a series of career management skills workshops. But when they reviewed the plan with the bank executives and managers, the latter surprised them by asking for more. "Basically, they told us, 'We're sold on this idea, but if we're going to do this, let's really do it right.' " That feedback helped the team develop a broader vision. "We didn't want to just create another program," Brown explains. "Programs come and go. Instead, we wanted to create a process in which people could take the initiative and develop themselves, after the initial push."

As a result, First USA added two more components to the program, creating Opportunity Knocks. At each of its work sites, the bank set up Career Resource Centers, or CRCs—special rooms equipped with everything from business publications and career-management literature to computers for writing résumés. The CRCs give employees a convenient space where they can sign up to spend a few hours a week—on company time—following up on their career-development plans. In addition, First USA hired employment development advisers, or EDAs, to continue advising and counseling employees after the initial workshops. In keeping with the program's mission of developing First USA's own workforce, the EDAs were 100 percent internal hires, with a variety of backgrounds that included HR, training, and team management.

By the winter of 1998, First USA was ready to roll out pilot programs at two of its work sites. The team marketed the program to employees through "town hall" meetings. They quickly discovered that a hard sell wasn't needed. Employees like Bender were eager for change. Before starting Opportunity Knocks, he'd had a vague ambition to become some sort of manager. The program quickly enabled him to focus on more tangible goals. "One of the first things we did was play a card game," he recalls. "Basically, it showed you things about yourself—are you a people person, or are you more interested in working with computers, or whatever." Further coaching, exercises, and self-examination helped Bender not only to figure out other jobs that he might find satisfying, but also to identify people with whom he had to network.

Ultimately, Opportunity Knocks enabled Bender to move into a different position at the bank. "Now I'm a PFC, a production flow coordinator. I run the dialer system, make sure the computers are running properly, take care of systems issues. It's different and challenging and I like it a lot." Another First USA employee, Christine Lolly-Harvey, says the program helped her realize that she had leadership skills to go with her skill as a collections specialist. She's now breaking in as a team relief manager. "I don't think I'd have thought to make a change on my own," she says.

The Opportunity Knocks program has produced some tangible results, Brown says. Thanks to the preparation and guidance that employees received, internal promotions at First USA increased by more than 50 percent last year. Additionally, when First USA repeated its internal opinion surveys, the bank found that employee satisfaction with career development issues had increased more than 25 percent when compared to 1998 results. The attrition rate among people who participated in the Opportunity Knocks program was about 65 percent lower than that of nonparticipants. This saved First USA $2.2 million in replacement costs.

CEO in Jeans and T-Shirt?

Editor's Comment: This first-person account of being twenty-something and looking for a career presents the reader with a paradox of the dot.com culture: she wears orange snakeskin pants to work but hasn't yet thrown away her closet full of business suits provided by her parents. She illustrates the challenge to those responsible for workplace learning.

She describes what she thought were the essentials of business success: "power suits, pumps, and pearls." What she found when she joined a dot.com were in fact these essentials: "get a tattoo, have something pierced, and get in the groove." She says that she was "groomed for The Old Boys' Club," but now wears orange snakeskin pants to work in a purple office where the CEO wears jeans and a t-shirt.

She says that her dot.comer friends told her that the dot.com workplace values her inexperience as an ability, not a disability; that is, it is evidence of an ability to think freely. Promotions would come every three months if she avoided getting mired in process. She had been taught, however, that inexperience was something that had to be conquered by reason and skill, and that process was something that was good to understand, to learn and to practice. By her education and graduation, she herself feels entitled to be an adult; the dot.com culture wants her to feel entitled to her youth. She wonders where the veterans of the working world were hiding while the dot.comers were feeling their way to success. She wonders how and when she will feel like she's grown up and feel less like a rebel. She wonders if she'll ever wear those power suits; she thinks that maybe growing up might be easier if she did, but her professional world changes too fast to be worried about business suits. She's happy to be a part of the great spirit of American entrepreneurism, but she's not sure she wants to be part of its immaturity.

Source: "These Days, Growing Up Is Hard To Do" My Turn column by Neylan McBaine in *Newsweek*, April 23, 2001, p. 16. Neylan McBaine was educated at Yale University and at a New York City private girls' school; she lives in San Francisco, CA.

Generation Y: Self-Confident and Goal-Oriented

Editor's Comment: These are children of the Baby Boomers, born around 1980, well-educated, optimistic, masters of the Internet and the PC. They are 29 million strong, flooding the workplace with talent, enthusiasm, self-confidence, a global perspective, idealism, technosavvy, and a work ethic that would please their grandparents. At the same time, they are constantly at risk for problems with drugs, sex, and violence: they experienced personal wars just as damaging as Vietnam, Korea, or World War II.

Many articles in business magazines and newspapers have appeared during the past year introducing the cohort of Gen Y and generally describing the young men and women in it in much the same way. This little book by Martin and Tulgan is one of the best and clearest of the commentaries. It is both descriptive and prescriptive, offering insight as well as steps to take to help these new workers to learn and to contribute their best. These are the things managers should *not* do: (pp. 33–45)

1. Be close-minded
2. Delegate ineffectively
3. Lack knowledge and organization skills
4. Have inability to train or to facilitate training
5. Show disrespect for young people
6. Have an intimidating attitude
7. Place an overemphasis on outward appearance.

GenY clearly wants authentic, honest managers who have intact egos. GenYers also want management that is involved as their teachers (pp. 38–39), and they want management to facilitate their continuous learning through mentoring, feedback on their performance, and work that has inherent learning and meaning in it (pp. 54–56).

This is a little book—a paperback, "pocket book" size, of 105 pages. It is easy reading, and made very personal with workplace quotes from numerous 18, 19, 20, and 21 year-olds. After introducing Gen Y workers, the authors explain how not to manage them, and then suggest ways to meet their "14 Expectations." The last 30 pages of the book focus on best practices to meet the 14 expectations, and give the reader an excellent "how to" guide for meeting the needs of this very important worker population.

Source: Managing Generation Y: Global Citizens Born in the Late Seventies and Early Eighties by Carolyn A. Martin, PhD, and Bruce Tulgan. Amherst, Massachusetts: HRD Press, Copyright 2001. *www.hrdpress.com*. 105 pages, $9.95. RainmakerThinking, Inc., New Haven, Connecticut. Carolyn A. Martin is a Master Trainer for RainmakerThinking, Inc. She was formerly Dean of Student Services at Georgian Court College, Lakewood, New Jersey, and a faculty member of the National Seminars Group in Kansas. Bruce Tulgan is the author of numerous HRD Press "Managers' Pocket Guides," and is the founder of RainmakerThinking, Inc.

2. Race and Gender Plus

Surprises in the Census

Editor's Comment: The United States Census is taken every 10 years, as required by *The Constitution* for the express purpose of apportioning seats in Congress fairly according to actual population distribution. For the year 2000 U.S. Census, results were made public during March and April 2001. These results surprised many, and were immediately interpreted for political and private gain in many facets of life having nothing to do with The Constitutional intent of the count. In the following paragraphs, we abstract some of these results from the public information provided by the cited articles here, and suggest how what we know from the 2000 Census might affect workplace learning and learners in year 2002.

Toward a Color-Blind Society: The 2000 Census for the first time offered many racial options—63, in fact, and 2 ethnic possibilities, Hispanic or non-Hispanic, allowing for a total of 126 combinations. Even with all these possibilities, around 10 percent of the population checked "other," in protest at being labeled anything. Mixed and proud of it, was the message. *The Wall Street Journal* editorial suggests that this is a good expression of individuality, that the anthropologists and demographers might not be happy, but that perhaps it might put an end once and for all to Affirmative Action programs that don't work and to government and special interest programs that benefit in an exclusive way from funding to shadowy 'minority' programs rather far removed from *The Constitution*'s simple intent of Congressional apportionment. *The Wall Street Journal*, in a very strong statement, suggests that "the Census has become a primary source of America's regressive identity politics. The irony is that the broader body politic is moving away from rigid racial classifications even as the civic and political leadership digs in its heels, unable to free themselves of the monetary incentives of divisive racial categories." During the next decade until the next U.S. Census, we can expect to see more attempts at blurring racial and ethnic lines and fewer incentives to divisive categorization of individuals and groups. This will change the kinds of diversity programs trainers need to develop and how all workplaces define and implement equal opportunity.

A New, Broad Meaning of 'Hispanic': Census takers and results interpreters were reportedly astonished at the numbers: 35.3 million people in the 2000 Census are Hispanic. One in 8 persons in the United States is counted as Hispanic in year 2000, a 58 percent increase over the last Census in 1990. *U.S. News & World Report* notes that this number is greater than the entire population of Canada (p. 18), and, for the first time in U.S. history, is more

---

Sources: "Sense and the Census" editorial, *The Wall Street Journal*, March 8, 2002; "The Many Faces of America: The surge of Hispanics is changing the way we think of ourselves as a nation" by Michael Barone in *U.S.News & World Report*, March 19, 2001, pp. 18; 20. Michael Barone is a Senior Writer at *U.S. News & World Report*; "Portrait of a Nation: U.S. Now More Diverse, Ethnically and Racially" by Eric Schmitt in *The New York Times*, April 1, 2000, p. 20. Eric Schmitt is a reporter for *The New York Times*; and "Latino Style Is Cool. Oh, All Right: It's Hot" by Ruth La Ferla in *The New York Times*, April 15, 2001, Section 9, pp.1–2. Ruth La Ferla is a writer in the "Sunday Styles" section of *The New York Times*; *Workplace Visions*, the Society for Human Resource Management (SHRM), No. 4, 2001, p. 8.

than the number of persons who consider themselves 'black' on the Census form (p. 20). Hispanics are now the largest minority.

The *U.S. News & World Report* article explains that "Hispanic" is a U.S. government-invented name for persons of Latin American or Spanish descent or Spanish language background. The U.S. Hispanic immigrants come mostly from Mexico and other parts of Latin America, our neighbors in this hemisphere. Over 70 percent are under 40 years of age; workforce participation of Hispanic males is 80 percent, higher than the participation of any other measured group (p. 20). Poverty rates among Hispanics counted in the Census remains high, they have dispersed from the big cities and border towns in the Southwest to suburbs and small towns throughout the country, they have swelled the membership in the Catholic Church, and they have become entrepreneurial in hundreds of ways throughout the land. However, nearly half of adult Hispanics have not graduated from high school, and have children at a rate nearly three times that of non-Hispanic whites (p. 20). Schools, colleges, non-degree certificate programs, ESL tutoring, and workplace basic skills training are all expanding to accommodate the needs of this large and important segment of the workforce.

Diversity among Hispanics is a new phenomenon that public schools, public media, consumer products, politicians running for office, and government programs now need to address. Hispanics are no more homogeneous in their tastes than any other group of people identified in the Census. Mexicans, Cubans, Puerto Ricans, Central Americans, and South Americans simply can't be lumped together for information, advertising, or media campaigns.

Ruth La Ferla's article in *The New York Times* says with enthusiasm, "Wildly heterogeneous, its members come from more than 20 countries and represent a mixture of races, backgrounds, and even religions. What Latinos share. . . is a common language, Spanish, and rapidly expanding cultural clout" (Section 9, p. 1). Trainers, at the very least, need to be aware of Hispanic heterogeneity in workplaces, and work to develop programs of language assistance, work/life programs that address the particular needs of this family-oriented population, and tap into the "cultural clout" for business advantage as businesses grow and change.

Work-Life Balance Issues: The other major surprise in the 2000 Census was the altered state of the American family. For the first time, the majority of women giving birth to their first child are unmarried, and only 1 in 4 households now contains married couples with children. SHRM reports this as a "transformation that affects everything from child-rearing to government policies aimed at families" (p. 8). An examination of laws governing social policies for the workplace can be expected to alter and expand current work-life balance programs in areas such as flextime, working at home, childcare on work premises, workshops on parenting, eldercare services, and specialized services for women with children. Trainers may very well become involved in designing and delivering programs to meet the needs of working families that look entirely different from the families of the previous generation. Trainers may also become involved in helping employees shed their previous assumptions about work and family, before effective work-life balance programs are developed.

Institutional Effects of Immigration

Editor's Comment: The results of the 2000 U.S. Census have heightened our sensitivities about immigration. During March and April 2001, when many magazines, TV programs, and scholarly and professional reports were widely circulated, the issues surrounding immigration were given public airing. The data that emerged from Census reports and interpretations of that data often focused the reader's attention on the institutional effects of our current state of immigration. This abstract from the four sources cited here presents some of these ideas.

Questions of service to more than a 35 percent increase: The 2000 Census showed us that there were in fact 281 million persons, 6 million more than anticipated, who were counted as immigrant—both illegal and legal. And, the immigrant group crosses racial, ethnic, and national origin designations. Already, 20 percent of children in U.S. schools are from immigrant families. Robert J. Samuelson quotes *The Washington Post*, March 27, 2001: "Those who teach, counsel and heal low-income immigrants say they are struggling to help a group that has swelled beyond official estimates." Hospitals, government assistance programs, schools, and entry-level employers have been particularly affected by the large numbers of persons who have come in search of an American dream of self-sufficiency and freedoms of movement, association, speech, worship, and peace of mind. The sheer numbers of the immigrant increase present major challenges to the institutions of American life, including businesses (*Newsweek*, p. 42).

Basic skills challenge: In an effort to find solutions to a shortage of basic reading, writing, and math skills, the U.S. Department of Labor convened the first National Skills Summit in April 2001 to find out, among other things, how businesses across the country were meeting the challenge of finding skilled workers (ASTD, p. 11). The U.S. Census spelled bad news for Hispanic girls, especially, noting that 26 percent of them do not graduate from high school, compared with 13 percent of black girls and 6.9 percent of white girls. On top of this, an Urban Institute report says that about 30 percent of immigrant children live in poverty, and that wages for immigrant men average only 68 percent of those for U.S.-born workers (*Newsweek*, p. 42). A survey by the American Management Association reported that the number of job seekers with basic skills deficiencies has steadily increased, and now stands at more than 38 percent posing "enormous challenges for organizations and, specifically, for their workplace learning and performance initiatives" (ASTD, p. 11). The public and employer outcry for more H-1B Visas (the high-tech, high-skill Visas) was heard louder and longer this year—perhaps as a reaction to the problems associated with the numerous low-skill commentaries, perhaps only as a cry for help in filling the jobs associated most closely with America's economic strength.

Although it is tempting to associate all basic skills employment problems with immigrants, unfortunately the U.S. population itself is greatly involved too. *Business Week*'s Cover Story, March 19, 2001 blasts the American system of schooling for being unequal in terms of money spent per child across states, for paying teachers

---

Sources: The 2000 ASTD Trends Report: Staying Ahead of the Winds of Change by Mark Van Buren and William Woodwell, Jr., copyright 2000, p.11. Mark Van Buren is Director of Research at ASTD; William Woodell, Jr. is an author and consultant; "How To Fix America's Schools" by William C. Symonds in *Business Week*, March 19, 2001, pp. 66–80. William C. Symonds is Manager of Boston Correspondents for *Business Week*; "Let the Huddled Masses In," Editorial in *The Economist*, March 31, 2001, pp. 15–16; "Can America Assimilate?" by Robert J. Samuelson in *Newsweek*, April 9, 2001, p. 42. Robert J. Samuelson is a regular contributor to *Newsweek*'s "Judgment Calls" column.

so poorly that "high quality" individuals shun the profession, for delivering education in outdated buildings to masses of students with generally substandard results. *Business Week* suggests ways to improve the situation so that in fact "no child is left behind," a major initiative of George W. Bush's Presidency. Major discrepancies in skills and performance are noted between poor cities and wealthy suburbs and between the technology affluent and the technology poor. Reform efforts that work, particularly those in cities, are featured. Unfortunately for employers, and for trainers, both immigrants and unskilled and undereducated U.S. citizens enter the workforce, bringing with them workplace learning challenges having not only to do with skills assessment and development, but also with assimilation attitudes. Managing and valuing diversity initiatives are changing again. The numbers are becoming overwhelming.

Freedoms, Revisited: The articles referenced here were all published prior to the terrorist attacks against American values on September 11, 2001. After September 11, there were many commentaries and warnings against the erosion of basic freedoms, especially of association, speech, the press, and of course, freedom from fear, that the attacks tended to precipitate. Civilian aircraft loaded with fuel and guided by terrorists were the perfect missiles. The institution of government itself was tested by the events themselves and their aftermaths. Our national press suggested that the press in terrorist countries purposely did not speak of American freedom and democracy, but rather assailed the American form of consumerism that drives a materialistic economy. A terrorist enemy that considered itself superior in faith and values found it easy to attack the symbols of money and might which they found so easy to hate about Americans.

The editorial in *The Economist* on March 31, 2001 comments on the attempt by so many persons all over the world to leave home in order to reach a place that promises a better life. The magazine makes an interesting point that there are compelling economic and moral arguments why more people from poor countries should be allowed to move to rich ones. The writer notes that "The world has made the movement of goods, money and ideas freer, but not, strangely, the movement of people. It is both right to give desperate people sanctuary and rewarding to welcome new citizens. History has shown that immigrants bring ideas, vigour and ambition, as well as their mere labour" (p. 15). *The Economist* notes that immigrants create jobs as well as fill them, adding to overall economic activity.

Robert J. Samuelson's article the next week in *Newsweek* (April 9, 2001) notes that assimilation is "mostly a spontaneous process, driven by the economy, popular culture, and the belief in individual opportunity" and that it has never been easy for either Americans already settled in neighborhoods here or for immigrants. He also notes that American assimilation, although allowing immigrant traditions to be retained, has historically required three things:

1. for immigrant families to adopt English as a primary language,
2. to be proud of the country's democratic principles and their American identity,
3. to embrace the work ethic of self-reliance, hard work, and moral uprightness.

These three things, Samuelson suggests, are harder and harder to accomplish with the increasingly rapid growth of immigration in the past decade. He calls for a national debate on immigration. Trainers need to be part of it.

Racism in the Workplace

Editor's Comment: The problem of racism still plagues America's workplaces, and trainers need to "think out of the box" in order to help prevent, define, and solve it. This disturbing article in *Business Week* presents facts as well as commentary on the problem.

> In an increasingly multicultural U.S., harassment of minorities is on the rise.

When Wayne A. Elliott was transferred in 1996 from a factory job to a warehouse at Lockheed Martin Corp.'s sprawling military-aircraft production facilities in Marietta, Ga., he says he found himself face to face with naked racism. Anti-black graffiti was scrawled on the restroom walls. His new white colleagues harassed him, Elliott recalls, as did his manager, who would yell at him, call him "boy," and tell him to "kiss my butt." He complained, but Elliot says the supervisor was no help. Instead, he assigned Elliott, now 46, to collecting parts to be boxed, which involves walking about 10 miles a day. Meanwhile, the eight whites in his job category sat at computer terminals and told him to get a move on—even though Elliott outranked them on the union seniority list.

The atmosphere got even uglier when Elliott and a few other blacks formed a small group in 1997 called Workers Against Discrimination, which led to the filing of two class actions. One day, he and the other two black men among the 30 warehouse workers found "back-to-Africa tickets" on their desks, he says, which said things like "Just sprinkle this dingy black dust on any sidewalk and piss on it, and, presto! Hundreds of n-----s spring up!" They reported this, but the Lockheed security officials who responded took the three victims away in their security cars as if they were the wrongdoers, he says, and interrogated them separately.

Then, one day in 1999, according to Elliott, a hangman's noose appeared near his desk.

"You're going to end up with your head in here." Elliott recalls a white co-worker threatening. Another noose appeared last November, he says. He and the other whites "hassle me all the time now, unplugging my computer so I lose work, hiding my bike or chair; it's constant," says Elliott, who gets counseling from a psychologist for the stress and says he has trouble being attentive to his two children, ages 7 and 8, when he's at home.

Lockheed spokesman Sam Grizzle says the company won't comment on any specific employee. But regarding the suits, which Lockheed is fighting, he says, "we do not tolerate, nor have we ever tolerated, harassment or discrimination of any form. We take such complaints very seriously, and we always have investigated them and taken appropriate action when needed."

The alleged incidents at Lockheed are part of an extensive pattern of charges of racial hatred in U.S. workplaces that *Business Week* investigated over a two-month period. Nearly four decades after the Civil Rights Act of 1964 gave legal equality to minorities, charges of harassment at work based on race or national origin have more than doubled, to nearly 9,000 a year, since 1990, according to the Equal Employment Opportunity Commission (charts, page 72).

> Lockheed Martin employee Wayne Elliott says he found "back-to-Africa tickets" on his desk and was called "boy" by his manager. He complained, he says, to no avail. Then came the hangman's noose.

Source: "Racism In the Workplace" by Aaron Bernstein in *Business Week*, July 30, 2001, pp. 64–67. Aaron Bernstein is a Senior Writer for *Business Week*. Reprinted with permission of *Business Week*, Copyright 2001. All rights reserved.

RISING RACIAL HARASSMENT IN THE WORKPLACE

EMPLOYEE COMPLAINTS HAVE SOARED...
Harassment charges filed with the Equal Employment Opportunity Commission

[Line graph showing RACE rising from ~3 in '91 to ~6.5 in '00, and NATIONAL ORIGIN rising from ~1 to ~2, in thousands, years '91–'00]

...AS HAVE CHARGES OF RETALIATION...
Employee charges of retaliation for complaints about racism

[Line graph rising from ~10 in '91 to ~19 in '00, in thousands]

...AND DAMAGE AWARDS ARE RISING
Awards in EEOC lawsuits involving race-based charges

[Line graph ranging from ~32 in '91 to ~62 in '00, in millions of dollars]

Data: Equal Employment Opportunity Commission

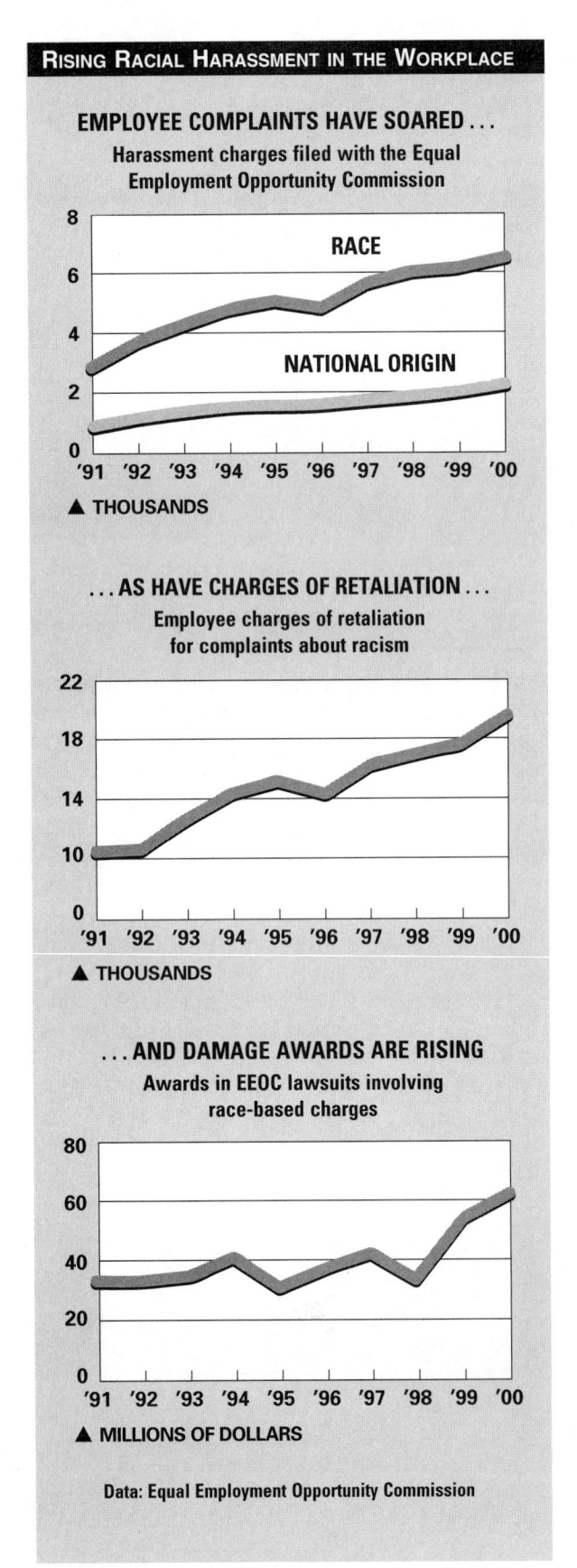

The problem is not confined to small Southern cities such as Marietta. In addition to high-profile suits at Lockheed, Boeing, and Texaco, dozens of other household names face complaints of racism in their workforce. Noose cases have been prosecuted in cosmopolitan San Francisco and in Detroit, with a black population among the largest in the nation.

It's true that minorities' share of the workforce grew over the decade, which could have led to a corresponding rise in clashes. Yet racial harassment charges have jumped by 100% since 1990, while minority employment grew by 36%. What's more, most charges involve multiple victims, so each year the cases add up to tens of thousands of workers—mostly blacks, but also Hispanics and Asians.

It's hard to reconcile such ugly episodes with an American culture that is more accepting of its increasing diversity than ever before. Today, immigrants from every ethnic and racial background flock to the U.S. There is a solid black middle class, and minorities are active in most walks of life, from academia to the nightly news. When we do think about race, it's usually to grapple with more subtle and complex issues, such as whether affirmative action is still necessary to help minorities overcome past discrimination, or whether it sometimes constitutes reverse discrimination against whites.

To some extent, the rise in harassment cases may actually reflect America's improved race relations. Because more minorities believe that society won't tolerate blatant bigotry anymore, they file EEOC charges rather than keep quiet out of despair that their complaints won't be heard, says Susan Sturm, a Columbia University law professor who studies workplace discrimination. Many cases involve allegations of harassment that endured for years.

Multimillion-dollar settlements of racial discrimination or harassment claims at such companies as Coca-Cola Co. and Boeing Co. also give victims greater hope that a remedy is available. Such suits became easier in 1991, after Congress passed a law that allowed jury trials and compensatory and punitive damages in race cases. "It's like rape, which everyone kept silent about before," says Boeing human resources chief James B. Dagnon. "Now, prominent individuals are willing to talk publicly about what happened, so there's a safer environment to speak up in."

But many experts say they are seeing a disturbing increase in incidents of harassment. Minority workers endure the oldest racial slurs in the book. They're asked if they eat "monkey meat," denigrated as inferior to whites, or find "KKK" and other intimidating graffiti on the walls at work.

Even office workers are not exempt. In May, 10 current and former black employees at Xerox Corp. offices in Houston filed harassment charges with the EEOC. One, Linda Johnson, says she has suffered racial slurs from a co-worker since 1999, when glaucoma forced her to quit the sales department and become a receptionist. Last year, a white colleague doctored a computer photo of her to make her look like a prostitute, she says. After she complained, her boss printed out the picture and hung it in his office, her charge says. "I tried to do what company procedures suggested and complain to my supervisor, then on up to human resources at headquarters," says Johnson, 47. "But they just sweep it under the rug." Xerox declined to comment on her case.

Worse yet are hangman's nooses, a potent symbol of mob lynchings in America's racial history. The EEOC has handled 25 noose cases in the past 18 months, "something that only came along every two or three years before," says Ida L. Castro, outgoing EEOC chairwoman. Management lawyers concur that racial harassment has jumped sharply. "I've seen more of these cases in the last few years than in the previous 10, and it's bad stuff," says Steve Poor, a partner at Seyfarth, Shaw, Fairweather & Geraldson, a law firm that helps companies defend harassment and discrimination suits.

Some lay the blame on blue-collar white men who think affirmative action has given minorities an unfair advantage. Their feelings may be fueled by the long-term slide in the wages of less-skilled men, which have lagged inflation since 1973. Since many whites see little evidence of discrimination anymore, the small number who harbor racist views feel more justified in lashing out at minorities, whom they perceive as getting ahead solely due to their race, says Carol M. Swain, a Vanderbilt University law professor who is writing a book about white nationalism.

Silence. Incidents of open racism at work occur below the national radar because all the parties have powerful incentives to keep it quiet. Plaintiffs' lawyers don't want employees to go public before a trial for fear of prejudicing their case in court. *BusinessWeek* spoke for more than a month with some lawyers before they agreed to let their clients talk. Even then, most workers refused to give their names, fearful of retaliation. Management and plaintiffs' lawyers alike say it takes tremendous nerve to file a suit or EEOC charges, given the likelihood that co-workers or bosses will strike back. Since 1990, the number of minorities filing charges of retaliation with the EEOC after they complained about racial mistreatment has doubled, to 20,000 a year.

Companies have an even greater desire to avoid bad publicity. Many suits end when employers settle. They routinely buy employees' silence with extra damage award money.

Because racial harassment allegations can be so embarrassing, they pose a difficult challenge for companies. Some quickly go on the offensive and take steps to change. Other employers hunker down for a fight, arguing that allegations are inaccurate or exaggerated. Northwest Airlines Corp., for example, is fighting charges made by black construction workers who found a noose last July at the airline's new terminal under construction at Detroit Metro Airport. Northwest also recently settled two noose-related suits, although it denied liability. Northwest spokeswoman Kathleen M. Peach says none of the noose incidents "rise to the level of harassment. You have to ask was it a joke at a construction site? Or was it in a cargo area where a lot of ropes are used? It's not as cut-and-dried as it seems."

Some employers dismiss nooses and slurs as harmless joking. This seems to be the view taken by Lakeside Imports Inc., New Orleans' largest Toyota Motor Corp. dealer. Last August, it signed a consent decree with the EEOC to settle charges brought by six black salesmen in its 50-person used-car department. The men said that their manager, Chris Mohrman, hit and poked them with two 3½-foot-long sticks with derogatory words on them that he called his "n----- sticks."

Lakeside brushed aside the incident, according to case depositions. Mohrman's manager at the time, a white man named David Oseng, had hired the black salesmen. When he heard what was going on, Oseng said in his deposition, he told the dealership's top brass. Oseng said the top two managers "told me they were tired of all the problems with the n-----s. And if we hired another n-----, [I] would be terminated."

Lakeside lawyer Ralph Zatzkis says the dealer didn't admit any guilt and denies that anything serious happened. He says the sticks, which the EEOC obtained by subpoena, did have writing on them, but "those weren't racial remarks." Zatzkis dismissed the episode as "horseplay." Mohrman and the black salesmen left Lakeside and couldn't be reached. Zatzkis says Lakeside's top managers declined to comment.

Frivolous harassment charges do occur, say experts, but they're rare. "It takes a lot of energy to raise a complaint, and you can make major mistakes assuming what the employees' motives are," warns Haven E. Cockerham, head of human resources at R. R. Donnelley & Sons Co., which is fighting a class action for alleged racial discrimination and harassment that included claims of whites donning KKK robes.

Consider Adelphia Communications Corp., a $2.9 billion cable-TV company based in Coudersport, Pa. In February, the EEOC filed suit on behalf of Glenford S. James, a 12-year veteran, and other black employees in the company's Miami office. A manager there racially harassed minorities "on a daily basis" after he took over in August, 1999, the suit says. The manager twice put a noose over James's door, it says. Once, says the complaint, the manager told an employee to "order monkey meat or whatever they eat" for James.

In a suit filed in June, James says that Adelphia didn't stop the problem until he complained to the EEOC in May, 2000. Then, the manager was terminated or resigned. Adelphia declined to comment. However, its brief in the EEOC suit admits that the manager displayed a noose and "made inappropriate statements of a racial nature." The brief says Adelphia "promptly and severely disciplined" the manager "as a result of his actions." The manager couldn't be reached.

> When Ted Gignilliat told what he knew about two nooses at Lockheed, he too became a target, he says. One anonymous caller told him he would "wind up on a slab, dead."

Revenge. Whites who stand up for co-workers also can run into trouble. Ted W. Gignilliat, a worker at the Marietta facility of Lockheed since 1965, says he was harassed so badly for speaking up about two nooses that he had to take a leave of absence. He says he was threatened, his truck was broken into, and he got anonymous phone calls at work and at home—one telling him he would "wind up on a slab, dead." In March, 2000, a psychologist told Gignilliat to stop work; he went on disability leave until May of this year. He now works as an alarm-room operator in the plant's fire station. "It's in the middle of the security office, with guards, but I feel they will retaliate against me again for stepping forward," says Gignilliat.

Usually, of course, minorities bear the brunt of revenge. Roosevelt Lewis, who delivers Wonder bread for an Interstate Bakeries Corp. bakery in San Francisco, says his white superiors have been making his life miserable ever since he and other blacks filed a race suit in 1998. A jury awarded them $132 million last year (later reduced by a judge to $32 million). Lewis says this only exacerbated the behavior. "They're trying to make you insubordinate, to create an excuse to fire you," charges Lewis. He says he has complained to higher-ups, but the hassling continues.

Jack N. Wiltrakis, Interstate's head of human resources, says the company has a hotline to headquarters in Kansas City but has received no complaints. "If they have a problem, it's incumbent on them to tell us," he says. Interstate, which has 34,000 workers in 64 bakeries around the U.S., has been sued for race problems in New York, Orlando, Indianapolis, and Richmond, Va. It has settled the two cases, denying liability, and is still fighting the others, including Lewis'. Wiltrakis says the suits haven't prompted Interstate to launch new policies.

In the end, racist behavior by employees lands at the door of corporate executives. They face a dilemma: If they admit there's a problem, the company is exposed to lawsuits and negative publicity. But denial only makes matters worse. Until more employers confront the rise of ugly racism head on, Americans will continue to see behavior they thought belonged to a more ignominious age.

With Michael Arndt in Chicago and bureau reports

Training's Important Role in Affirmative Action

Editor's Comment: To have or not to have Affirmative Action as a national policy initiative and what kinds of programs make sense for today's more integrated workplaces is a debate that has intensified in recent years since a California decision led the way a few years ago to make state university admission color-blind. The U.S. Labor Department has been trying to reflect the needs of persons of color and of women in the labor force with updated policies and practices. This particular issue of SHRM's *Legal Report* explains the revision to federal regulations, effective December 13, 2000.

At the heart of this revision is a reduction of the much-maligned "8 Factor Availability Analysis." Businesses receiving federal dollars, i.e., federal contractors, heretofore had to demonstrate a person's availability for work according to 8 factors of availability for women and minorities in each job group. This was tedious and paper-intensive. It has now been replaced by a "Two Factor" rule, differentiating availability by either external availability or internal availability (p. 3). External availability is to be based on the percentage of minorities and women in the "reasonable recruitment area," that is, the geographical area, from which employees are sought. Internal availability is the percentage of minorities and women who are among those "promotable, transferrable, *and trainable*" already inside a contractor's organization (Italics mine).

The words "reasonable" and "reasonably" are seen throughout the definitions and guidelines. The employer clearly has training responsibilities if he or she accepts federal dollars—that is, "appropriate training that the contractor is reasonably able to provide" (p. 3) in order for an employee to become promotable or transferrable during the Affirmative Action Program year. Getting ahead is clearly the goal of training under the new regulations, but they still leave a somewhat fuzzy understanding of exactly who is trainable and what is "reasonably able." SHRM says that this is likely to be a significant issue for discussion in months ahead. Trainers need to be aware of this debate and contribute their understandings of workplace learning and learners to it.

Source: "OFCCP's Revised 60-2 Regulations: New Wage Survey-IN, Guidance on Applicants-OUT" by Reginald E. Jones and Dara L. Dehaven in *Legal Report*, (SHRM), January–February 2001, pp. 1–4. Reginald E. Jones was a Commissioner of the U.S. Equal Employment Opportunity Commission (EEOC) from 1996–2000. He and Dara L. Dehaven are shareholders, respectively, in the Washington D.C. and Altanta, GA offices of Olgetree, Deakins, Nash, Smoak & Stewart, PC.

Learning from Informal Networks of "Girl Gangs"

Editor's Comment: The periodic newsletter, *Perspective*, published by Catalyst, reports on efforts towards and obstacles to the advancement of women in business. The January 2001 issue reported on a recent outreach to women in Canada and the United Kingdom regarding male stereotyping. The numbers are not surprising: in all three countries, male stereotyping and preconceptions of women's roles and abilities were seen by women as a major barrier to their advancement—women in the United States 52%, women in Canada 42%, and women in the UK 40% (p. 1). The women in all three countries also agreed that "exclusion from informal networks" was also a major barrier to women's advancement.

The article reproduced here provides first-hand information about how some working women are addressing the problem. Trainers can be involved in facilitating such networks of women, can provide learning resources for them, and can be a conduit for ideas and information to sources in the company that are unreachable as individuals.

Networking is a powerful way to meet people and get things done. Unfortunately, it's one of those important but not urgent things that don't always get the attention they deserve. For women in particular—who may also be running households and raising children (and who almost always shoulder most of the responsibility for those things, according to recent reality checks)—there isn't enough time to attend a formal networking meeting. And the more informal contacts one makes could be more helpful by being more specific and less guarded about giving advice and sharing information. It's easier to ask a friend about salary negotiation than to ask someone sitting across from you at a luncheon meeting.

Many women have risen to the challenge by forming their own small groups—Girl Gangs—that get together regularly in person, by phone, or via email to talk about life and career. These buddies share ideas and contacts, celebrate personal and professional successes, and help their members get more done. The power they represent is as awesome as that of any of the Powerpuff Girls on Saturday morning TV.

No less a personage than Oprah Winfrey says she relies on informal networks. In the July/August 2000 issue of her magazine, O, she writes about her "Spa Girls," a group of friends who get together to encourage each other in their diet, exercise, and personal growth programs. Because the members are all media executives, there's at least some professional networking going on during their workouts.

In this era of multitasking, Oprah isn't the only woman who is mingling her personal and professional lives with the help of an informal network of like-minded people. Given the demands faced by the average American woman juggling work, family, and life in general, an informal group offers a great way to harness the energy of different people dealing with similar situations.

Let's look at a few groups that have formed informally and that are helping their members advance professionally while providing friendship and personal support. Perhaps we'll inspire you to draw on this power for yourself or for your organization.

Source: "Girl Gangs: They Got It Goin' On" by Ann C. Logue in *Training & Development*, January 2001, pp. 24, 26–28. Ann C. Logue is principal of Freelance Communications, Chicago, IL. Reprinted with permission of *Training & Development* /ASTD, Copyright 2001. All rights reserved.

TRUE STORIES

The Corporate Manager. In a big company, one needs to network just to navigate efficiently. In fact, it's as important to network within a company as it is to network outside of it.

Daimler-Chrysler has 13,000 people working in its Auburn Hills, Michigan headquarters. Kathryn Lee, staff labor programs administrator, is proud that her company supports a Women's Network Group and provides a number of opportunities for after-hours networking, including guest speakers and presentations. But as a working mother of two young children, formal networking is a low priority for her right now.

"Being perfectly candid, I would rather spend my evenings with my family and pass on the optional business gatherings," she says. Intentionally or not, her company has provided a networking opportunity for women in the exact same circumstance.

After her second child was born, Lee started spending her lunches and breaks in Daimler-Chrysler's lactation room, where she met a lot of other women.

"You could spot us a mile away," she says, "with the sweater or suit jacket to cover up leaks and the oversized Pump-N-Style bag. Since we were all on a schedule, we got to know each other pretty well. It felt like we were in a secret club."

In part because they didn't work together, these women would use their pumping sessions to share ideas for work as well as to talk about kids. Lee credits the group for helping her stick to nursing for a year, which isn't easy. She says she's also grateful for the opportunity to meet others in her company without taking extra time to attend meetings after work.

"I learned which areas in the company have great bosses, which departments have a lot of international travel, and other information that I can use on my job," she says. And her companion nursing mothers formed a cross-departmental network as strong as any within the company.

The Academic. Universities are hardly free from the political and career-management demands of corporate life. Marita Golden is a writer and professor in the M.F.A. Graduate Creative Writing Program at Virginia Commonwealth University in Richmond. She often meets with a group of other African American women teaching at colleges in the Washington, D.C. area.

"The group has helped us feel that we are supported in the trenches, even though we're not all at the same university," she says. "It's very good to know that you're not alone and that your experiences are valid."

Golden believes these groups are vitally important. "Even in a university, there are very few situations where we get together to talk about what we are doing creatively," she says.

The Women

Nina Adams
Adams-i-Solutions
3952 Western Avenue
Western Springs, IL 60558
ninaa@adamsisolutions.com

Lisa-Ann Barnes
Iree Tec
956 S. Bartlett Road, Suite 255
Bartlett, IL 60103

Betsy Beaumon
636 Madrone Avenue
Sunnyvale, CA 94086
Bbeaumon@ix.netcom.com

Marita Golden
11506 Tommy Court
Mitchellville, MD 20721

Kathryn Lee
2088 Franklin
Berkley, MI 48072
Kll2@daimlerchrysler.com

Angela Renfroe
Kirshenbaum Bond & Partners
145 6th Avenue
New York, NY 10013
arenfroe@kb.com

Liz Ryan
Ucentric Systems
6160 N. Cicero Avenue, 5th Floor
Chicago, IL 60646
lizryan@flash.net

The Girl Gangs in Your Company

Here are some suggestions for institutionalizing several aspects of informal networking.

There are many great ideas and good work being done within informal networks in your organization. Just be aware of the risks as well as the opportunities. After all, some of these groups are forming because people don't feel comfortable where they work.

Kirshenbaum Bond & Partners, a New York-based advertising agency, has a working mothers group that meets regularly to discuss various relevant issues. Angela Renfroe, the human resources manager who runs the group, has a few tips. The first is, once again, use technology.

"Here, the culture is that we communicate through email," says Renfroe. "I've set up an email address book for the working mothers, and they use it for referrals, tips, and support."

Renfroe also found that the members preferred holding meetings onsite rather than offsite, in part because they didn't have time for long lunches.

The support of senior management in setting up the group and listening to its suggestions has made the group powerful. Besides such relatively simple matters as getting a lactation room set up, the group asked for flextime.

"We were able to do it in accounting," says Renfroe.

Nina Adams, a consultant who helps organizations use technology to improve performance, is a big believer in the use of informal networking to grow organizations. One of the things she does is help companies use their intranets to create peer-networking opportunities. She points to a large bank as an example.

"The kinds of problems a teller supervisor in Chicago has might be the same as those of a teller supervisor in Los Angeles. If a bank were to set up an [informal network] of teller supervisors, they could use email or Web meetings to share information and learn new skills."

That, Adams believes, could lead to increased power within the organization. Maybe the network develops list of FAQs for supervisors that gets on the company's intranet. Then, the network members are affecting policy and could be asked to work on larger assignments, such as best practices."

You would think that any organization might want to use informal networks to create positive change from within rather than have people pooling resources to get new jobs elsewhere. But that isn't always the case. One interviewee, who asked that neither she nor her company be identified, told this story:

> **You would think that any organization might want to use informal networks to create positive change.**

When she was working for a large consulting firm, women within each department tended to meet regularly for lunch to talk about work and to share ideas. One year, the annual promotion list came out and no women in the firm were on it. When people started asking around, it turned out that many women throughout the firm had similar issues that had been discussed informally. Several decided to form a formal group to write a letter to senior management in the hope of making changes.

"Once it became formal, it was viewed as a bad thing politically to be involved in," she says. Instead of becoming agents for positive change, the women involved were considered to be whiners and complainers, and almost all of them left the firm within two years.

In Golden's experience, an informal group gives members a better chance to talk about their research or their articles in progress than in an organized faculty forum, which often degenerates into discussions about students, grading, and university policies. Her group finds that exchanging ideas informally leads to better formal academic work in the long run. They also enjoy discussing their lives in general with colleagues who have become friends.

"One woman in the group was a grandmother who provided great wisdom about life that we came to rely on," says Golden.

That powerful combination of the personal and the professional is one reason that members come to rely on their girl gangs.

The Entrepreneur. Betsy Beaumon is an electrical engineer by training who worked for Lam Research and Cisco Systems before starting an Internet company, selling it, and then joining another startup as a vice president. In fact, if she weren't a woman, she'd be the very stereotype of the young Silicon Valley executive.

Beaumon is part of a girl gang that has been a source of great camaraderie and professional support as she has moved up in her career. The group formed years ago, when she linked up with five other women who were going to the same trade shows "even though we lived only 10 miles apart. We were just too busy."

The group gets together regularly to help each other navigate the ever-turbulent waters of high technology. The members communicate almost daily by email. "It's the same kind of things guys do," Beaumon says. "We even get together and slam down a goodly number of cosmopolitans when the opportunity arises."

Though their meetings are generally social, their discussions are not. Among other things, Beaumon says the group has exchanged leads on office space and phone systems as well as shared advice on cultural issues within startups and technology companies.

"It's an interesting dynamic when the group is together," she says, "and it's helpful to have someone you can bounce ideas off of and explain how things work. With my current job at a startup, it was great to have friends who knew how to negotiate stock options and salaries for a high-level position."

Although the economy is changing quickly, the shared strengths of Beaumon's girl gang let the members view the change as a fabulous opportunity.

THE EMAIL LIST

It's relatively easy to form a girl gang if you're running into like-minded people in the course of your day. But what if you aren't?

That was one of the problems facing Liz Ryan, co-founder and vice president of Ucentric Systems. She needed to hire a lot of technical people for her company and hoped for a good gender balance among the new employees.

"I thought, I want to meet these women. Where are they?"

How to Form Your Own Girl Gang

Chances are, you know people with whom you can share ideas and insight. But how can you harness that energy? Here are a few ideas to get you started.

First, there is no substitute for taking charge, whether your group ultimately becomes structured or informal. That's how Marita Golden launched her group. While she was teaching at George Mason University, other African American women who were teaching there kept telling her that they should get together for lunch someday.

"Finally, I just put my foot down and said, 'Hey, we're having a potluck at my house this Sunday.'"

If you have friends and colleagues with similar good intentions, maybe it's time to pick a date and invite everyone over. To make it easier, you can use an online invitation service like Yahoo! Invites (invites.yahoo.com) or evite (www.evite.com).

You can use technology other ways. Liz Ryan turned to Topica, an email list-management service (www.topica.com), when she started ChicWit. Topica lets people organize and operate their own email lists. It's one way to build informal contacts over a wide group of people, such as alums from your school, former coworkers, and people who work in the same profession in your town. Who knows? Someone may have already set up a list that's appropriate for you. To find out, check Topica.

Last, if you have a specific goal, such as changing your job or starting a fitness program, you may want to look at the ground rules that Oprah Winfrey established with her Spa Girls. She recommends creating a routine for meetings and keeping a record of members' progress, which may be what you need to do to reach your goal. Her Website has some information on how to get organized (www.oprah.com/spagirl/spagirl_landing.html).

Last July, Ryan started the Chicago Women in Technology—aptly shortened to ChicWit—email list as a virtual version of a traditional networking group. It also quickly took on characteristics of an informal group as many subscribers use the list for help with nonprofessional aspects of their life. Along with job listings and announcements for business events, there are also frequent requests for recommendations for nannies, financial planners, and even hairdressers. Some subscribers have even used it to form their own version of Oprah's Spa Girls.

"People trust the members to help them," says Ryan. By getting help with some of the personal aspects of their lives, the list members can put more energy into their careers.

ChicWit spread quickly. "I told a couple of friends, and they told a few more," says Ryan, until there were more than 1,600 subscribers. They, including Ryan, almost immediately saw a need for similar lists in other cities.

"I started MassWit when Ucentric moved to Boston and I had to hire people there," Ryan says. When that list also took off, she took the list global. There are currently 29 local lists in the United States, Canada, and Australia, with more being added wherever there are women in technology looking to meet others. The email girl gang now has a formal name, WorldWit (www.worldwit.org).

THE POWER OF THE GIRL GANG

Networks don't have to involve monthly dress-up luncheon meetings at downtown hotels. There are people you know—or can find—who may have ideas for helping you run your business and your life better. By forming your own girl gang, you can draw on possibilities to make all of the members more powerful.

How do I know these networks exist? When I got the story assignment, I sent out two emails—one to my own girl gang of friends, relatives, and acquaintances and one to the ChicWit email list, which I subscribe to because I write a lot of Web content. Every anecdote, every expert, every person mentioned in this article came from those two messages. If my gang is that good, yours can be, too.

How and Why to Be Your Own Mentor

Editor's Comment: "Historic and current discrimination on the basis of gender in determining compensation and promotions is a significant factor in the pay gap between men and women." This is the conclusion reported by a *Working Women* magazine study in the *Human Resources Report* of the Bureau of National Affairs (BNA), September 3, 2001 (p. 937). As part of this report, the BNA listed current compensation figures for men and for women in a variety of occupations, for example:

Accounting manager:	male $ 75,592	female $ 68,040
Advertising CEO	male $ 257,000	female $ 188,000
Architect	male $ 56,300	female $ 40,150
Banking Sr. Operations Officer	male $ 105,800	female $ 70,500

and so on. The conclusion is that there remains about a 24 percent discrepancy in pay between males and females, and this has not changed in a decade (p. 937). Numerous studies, including one by Catalyst, a non-profit agency working to advance women in business, in August 2001, reported during the year past on how women are doing in various businesses and with workplace prejudices and attitudes that present a barrier to advancement. This particular issue of the Catalyst newsletter, *Perspective*, reported on the barriers women in the financial services industry encounter. Among the important findings is the statistic that "only 18 percent of women report that women's opportunities to advance to senior management in their firms have increased greatly over the past five years, compared to 50 percent of men who believe this" (*Women In Financial Services Fact Sheet*). These data were based on surveys of more than 2,300 women and men employed at seven leading securities firms, with a 38 percent return rate.

In the July 25, 2001 issue, *The Wall Street Journal* ran a lead article on page 1 of the "Marketplace" section written by Staff Reporter Ronald Alsop with the title, "Business Schools Struggle to Add More Female Students to Bottom Line." Mr. Alsop profiled several leading universities offering MBA programs, indicating their nearly universal difficulty with recruiting, enrolling, and keeping women students. At Chicago, for example, the number of full-time female MBA students is expected to drop to 23 percent from 27 percent a decade ago; Stanford expects female enrollment to drop to 38 percent this year from last year's 41 percent. Southern Methodist University, Duke, and Dartmouth all report fewer female MBA students this year than last year. The article suggest that the numbers problem could be a structural problem in requirements and recruiting, not only the "fear of math and muggers" that some admissions personnel say is responsible for the falling numbers.

It is within the context of these briefs from various sources that we suggest that you read *Be Your Own Mentor* by Sheila Wellington.

The book takes off from the premise that most high-powered, high-paid, successful men have had mentors and that women have not. Women mentors are hard to find, as evidence that only 2 women lead Fortune 500 companies. There simply are too few (two) women CEOs to mentor all the women who'd like to be mentored in business life today. Therefore, as the book's title suggests: *"Be Your Own Mentor."* This book and Catalyst hope to give you the tools and encouragement to do just this. When men are asked how they measure success, they typically answer, "Money, power,

---

Source: Be Your Own Mentor by Sheila Wellington and Catalyst, with Betty Spence New York: Random House, 2001. 301 pages, $25.95. Sheila Wellington has been President of Catalyst since 1993. Prior to this, she was Secretary of Yale University, the first woman to hold that post. Catalyst is a non-profit research and advisory organization that works to advance women in business. It is headquartered in New York City.

and position;" women answer the same question by whether or not they "make a difference" (p. 41). Some of the chapter titles include, "Wise Up," "Style Matters," "Become Known," "Making Your Life Work," "Conduits to Top Leadership," and "Wisdom from the Pioneers." This is not just a book of disheartening statistics; it is a helpful set of guidelines for women on the move. Men, especially men in the training business, will find it helpful too as they help devise programs to help women contribute the most they can and be rewarded for their contributions.

The book addresses common problems head-on, and this makes it especially good. For example, Chapter 3, "Get-Ahead Basics," begins with a comment from Cathleen Black, President of Hearst Magazines. She says, simply, "Meet the Challenge." She says that you can't expect to get into The Old Boys' Network, or to have no backlash against your increased visibility. So forget it; and don't complain. Meet the challenge with tools and a winning strategy. The book goes on to provide axioms for winning behavior—things that a woman can do to manage herself as she goes forward to break that glass ceiling.

Scattered throughout the book are comments and tips from "the pioneers," people like Cathleen Black who tackle specific problems and issues. Axioms follow these gems from the pioneers. The last half of the book deals with being a mentor and finding a mentor, two teaching and learning techniques that trainers know have worked throughout history. Trainers will find a lot in here on which to base focus groups and other structured discussion groups in an effort to learn about the needs of today's working women.

3. Technology and Learning Communities

Dealing with Learner Resistance: Lessons from the Internal Revenue Service (IRS)

Editor's Comment: The common question plaguing trainers, especially those who are trying to move their workforces into more online learning, is, "If we build it, will they come?" There's no question that computer and Internet technology make possible all sorts of wonderful setups for learning; and the business press is full of examples, pronouncements about what works and what doesn't, and stories of real people learning at work. We've heard again and again to let learners be creative online, to present real work-related problems for them to solve, to make online learning game-like or competitive, and to engage learners with each other online if we want them to stay.

We also see articles about the barriers online learners find in the technology and the process, and we hear about the high dropout rate for online learners. The e-mail newsletters from numerous sources in the training community are a particularly good source of this kind of information. The June 5, 2001 issue of *TDFeNet*, online newsletter of vnulearning has a section on "Drop-out Rick Factors." Rosemarie Menager-Beeley, a professor of computer technology and psychology at Foothill College in Los Altos, CA suggests eight factors, any one of which can cause a student to drop out of online learning. Along with the usual ones we often see of low interest and low utility, she also identifies the psychological factors of "low self-efficacy," in which students believe they won't do well, and "overconfidence," in which they assume that this learning experience online will take no time at all (p. 3). We often see references to Howard Gardner and his Theory of Multiple Intelligences and the flood of literature on learning styles that followed it, Daniel Goleman and Emotional Intelligence, and Abraham Maslow and the Hierarchy of Human Needs. Trainers and learning specialists are clearly concerned with the processes of online learning and the needs of online learners as we try to fit what we know of educational psychology with a new way of working.

Against this brief background, we reprint Patricia McCormick's article about her experience at the Internal Revenue Service (IRS).

INTRODUCTION

The IRS and the Individual Information Technology Institute

The Individual Information Technology Institute of the Internal Revenue Service was founded in 1987 with the original mission of providing UNIX administration and C programming instruction by distance learning methods, primarily mentored self-study using remote login to our UNIX machine, telephone support, fax, and e-mail. With the advent of networked desktop computers and Intranet information systems, we assumed responsibility for end-user computer skills training and expanded our delivery methods to include web-based training, multimedia courses on CD-ROM, and books and job aids downloadable from our web site. Today we provide over 600 computer skills courses to an audience of over 100,000 IRS employees and our newest expansion is to offer our courses to

---

Source: "Dealing with Learner Resistance to Technology-Delivered Training" by Patricia McCormick in *Journal of Interactive Instruction Development*, Winter 01, pp. 33–38. Patricia McCormick is a Project Leader for the Internal Revenue Service School of Information Technology, Austin, TX. Reprinted with permission of the *Journal of Interactive Instruction Development*, copyright 2001. All rights reserved.

another 40,000 employees from other Treasury agencies. The IRS population includes employees dispersed over large geographical areas, all possible work shifts, seasonal workers, telecommuters, people in travel status working from their hotel rooms, and employees with reasonable accommodation needs under the Americans with Disabilities Act.

Encountering Learner Resistance

The IITI had built an attractive and useful web site and we waited for the students to come. In one sense, it was very successful. Our enrollment numbers climbed steadily and we were serving more customers than ever before. In another sense, though, we were not as successful as we had hoped. Even though we had intended to support group study, as well as individual study, we found that a high percentage of our customers were using the self-study and distance learning products in a traditional classroom setting. For true self-study and distance learning, we were seeing the same group of enthusiasts over and over as customers.

Most of the advice we found on selling distance learning internally did not apply to the problems we were observing. For example, many sources recommend a cost-benefit analysis. That's an important tool, but it addresses the wrong level of resistance for our problem. Our executive levels had already made the decision to fund us based on both cost and logistics. While students and their immediate managers take seriously their contribution to IRS budget management, the immediate decision of which type of training to request was not directly connected to the overall budget. Both types of training were already paid for at the agency level and generally, neither came out of the local office budget which was the immediate concern of the student and the supervisor. We did share with them the cost-benefit analysis and when we multiplied the impact of their training preference times 100,000 employees, they did understand why a different type of training was offered. But the budget impact was still remote from their immediate concern.

Sometimes, local offices do have a small budget for meeting special training needs. We would frequently hear the question of how much do these self-study courses cost my office if we use them instead of purchasing training from outside sources. When we explained that our courses were already paid for and there would be no charge to their local office budget, frequently the manager and student would change their preference from classroom to self-study or distance learning. Then the cost-benefit decision had an immediate impact on their level of concerns.

What Caused Learner Resistance?

If the cost-benefit analysis was not the cause of the resistance, what was the cause? Actually, there were several causes and no one cause applied to every person or group in the IRS.

General Resistance to All New Technology

Resistance to technology-delivered training, for many people, is a symptom of resistance to all changing technology. A lot of people don't like computers and don't want to have to learn a new word processor. And they especially don't want to have to learn a new word processor every two or three years. Students have no control over the speed of changing technology or the adoption of new technology in their work environment. They do have control over their interactions with technology skills training. The reaction is similar to what happens in classroom training when students may display a hostile reaction to the instructor as a symbol of management.

Having to Learn the Interface

In addition, technology-delivered training adds its own new skill set to the other new skills the student needs to master. There is no standard interface across libraries leased from different vendors so the student may face a confusing set of different procedures for operating the course with little available guidance on how to generalize rules that apply across-the-board to course operation.

Increased Student Responsibility

Learning how to learn differently requires other changes in the student's behavior, as well. Technology-delivered training generally demands that the student take responsibility for his or her learning in a way that more traditional methods do not require. In an environment such as ours, traditional training was directed from higher levels of the organization. Groups of students were led by their instructor through pre-determined topics and objectives, scheduled to begin and proceed at set times, and they were told when they were done. Documentation was the responsibility of the instructor and the training administrator.

By contrast, technology-based training is usually self-paced and in our implementation, is self-directed. Students determine what topics they need, either for job performance or for personal growth. Training is available continuously for the students to fit into their own schedules. Students determine for themselves when they are done, which may be when they have learned what they needed rather than when they have reached the end. Students initiate their registrations and take action to update their status to Complete when they have finished with the course, managing their own documentation.

In addition, they still have to take responsibility for learning and do so without the constant reassurance from the teacher that they must be learning because they are physically in the classroom. Students must decide independently whether they are learning, whether they need to review more, or whether they need to ask a question of the distance learning coach, who is not physically present to remind them to question. Technology-delivered learning places a much greater load of responsibility on the individual student. We find a small percentage of employees who are ready for that responsibility and assume it eagerly. Most of these are people who have always done a lot of independent reading and self-directed study. Most students are not ready for the increased responsibility of managing their own learning. They need to be taught how to take that responsibility in addition to whatever computer skill they are being taught.

Personality and Preferred Learning Style

Students also differ in personality or preferred learning style. Practice exercises, to support learning by doing, are built into all of our courses and encourage students to practice hands-on more with our courses than they usually do in a classroom environment. Before practice, information gathering is a necessary learning step. Those who learn primarily from reading seem to be the minority. Some need to question. Others need to listen or to watch a demonstration. Many need to talk about what they are learning, a method of making knowledge active that has been largely overlooked. For the majority, one or more of the social aspects of the experience makes a major contribution to learning success. At best, technology-derived training alters the social experience. At worst, it is completely lacking in the social pathways needed to support best-quality learning for most students unless we specifically address that need.

The Virtual Office Experience

The emergence of the virtual office adds another aspect to the problem of learning and socialization. At the IRS, we have always had a large number of field employees who worked away from the office, visiting taxpayers on site. For these employees, classroom training represents a rare opportunity to network with their peers and share experiences with other people who understand their situation. They are reluctant to give up a networking opportunity by accepting a different type of training.

Strategies for Dealing with Learner Resistance

With this understanding of some of the underlying causes for learner resistance to technology-delivered training, we can consider and evaluate strategies for overcoming the resistance. What worked and what did not work as well surprised us in the Individual Information Technology Institute. All strategies worked for reaching some students. While less effective strategies may have only succeeded with a small minority of students, those strategies were still important for some students.

Personal Relationship with Students

The most effective strategy for overcoming learner resistance turned out to be our personal relationship with our students, which may seem a little paradoxical for a distance-learning organization. Mentored self-study had been our first teaching method when we began in 1987. Over the years, using the telephone and e-mail, we had developed strong and ongoing relationships with the small group of students taking our courses in UNIX and C programming. The coaching process was time-intensive, though, and we knew we could not deliver the same level of interaction to a much larger group of students as our curriculum grew.

On the other hand, we also knew we were implementing new technology with our expanded course offerings and people would need help to get started. The subject matter for most of the new courses was less demanding than our UNIX curriculum. Rather than assigning a subject matter expert to be responsible for each student's progress, we established a help phone number and took turns answering it. Students generally only needed help accessing their first course. Then they would call occasionally with questions about enrollment procedures or what other course topics were available. As skill in using the Intranet became more widespread, many students only needed the reassurance that someone was really there on the help line in case they did need help.

We discovered that a modest amount of personal interaction could be leveraged into an atmosphere of community. Adding to the web page short video portraits in which each of us introduced ourselves gave our students an opportunity to associate a face with the voice on the phone and enhanced the familiarity of the relationship. Speaking with students one at a time kept us aware of each student as an individual person in a way that is difficult to achieve in a classroom group, which became an additional advantage.

Reasonable Accommodation

Meeting each student's individual needs with technology-based training is a powerful tool for gaining acceptance. Yet, the possibilities are frequently overlooked. Reasonable accommodation needs are different for each person and can be dealt with more easily in one-on-one sessions than in group sessions which, of necessity, focus on the needs of the majority of the group. Many people assume that reasonable accommodation is not possible with technology-driven training. In fact, IITI has discovered that reasonable accommodation can be incorporated and we are always working with our vendors to develop new strategies. Electronic books are very adaptable. If the course uses real software for practice exercises, the student can use whatever adaptive solutions he or she uses for production work. Multimedia courses that offer a choice of text, audio, or video are also adaptable to a variety of reasonable accommodation needs. The vendors that offer those choices originally designed the courses to accommodate different Internet bandwidth limitations; they were surprised when we pointed out that the same technical solutions were suitable for meeting reasonable accommodation needs and should be marketed that way. In addition, students working individually are relieved of the pressure of needing to keep up with the rest of the class.

The Institute purchases a variety of types of courses for all popular topics and tries to offer some alternatives even for less-used topics. In this way, we are able to meet other personal needs in addition to reasonable accommodation. We offer courses suitable for different learning styles, for different levels of equipment availability, for unusual locations (hotel rooms, telecommuting workplaces, home), and for different levels of knowledge. This is less expensive than it seems because one product may meet a variety of different needs for flexibility. For example, an electronic book with practice exercises using the student's own software may meet the needs of students who prefer reading, students who need to travel with their course, students with slow Internet connections, and students who need an in-depth course, as well as students who use adaptive equipment for people with visual impairments.

Just-in-Time Training and Logistical Accommodation

Another sort of personal need that we are able to meet with our courses involves timing and logistics problems. An immediate need to learn new software stimulates interest, particularly during our year 2000 equipment updates when many people were converted from older DOS-based computers to Windows-based machines that needed radically different user skills. The fact that we were able to offer training immediately, sometimes the same day their new machines were installed, meant we could help them get started working in the new environment with minimal work-stoppage time. In many cases, the next available classroom training would have been several months later and in a distant city. Outsourced training was usually just as expensive and inconvenient as the next available internal class. Employees would also have had to change their shifts temporarily to accommodate training. If all employees in an office needed to learn new software at the same time, the office would be unable to operate with all employees in training. By contrast, courses from the IITI were available on all shifts at the employee's location and could be integrated with the office's regular work schedule. Faced with temporary shift changes and workload management problems, learners would choose to try our courses even if their initial preference was for classroom training.

The Value of Hybrid Courses

In accommodating employees' learning styles, we discovered that delivery methods are flexible. Some work groups like to re-arrange the cubicle walls so that several employees can work on their courses together in a manner that might be called group self-study. Often, one employee has better computer skills than the rest and can assist the others until they learn how to use technology-delivered training. Other groups place access to the courses on machines in computer-equipped classrooms or in the Career Management and Learning Center. An on-site facilitator may be available in addition to our telephone facilitators standing by. Students may work on their courses away from the demands of their work environment, but with some social support. After experiencing their first few courses in this type of supported environment, students frequently move on to true self-study when it is logistically more convenient.

We also have had success combining an orientation to distance-learning resources with various classroom events. Our e-mail conversion included extensive orientation sessions to the new e-mail system and IITI was able to establish a partnership with the conversion team to include an orientation to our courses in the same sessions. Of course, we had available a number of courses on the new e-mail system so the distance-learning presentation was relevant to the topic of the main orientation. In other instances, local instructors presented an introduction to new software and included a lesson on using IITI distance learning courses for continuation of training. Whenever we make a presentation to management or to field education employees, we include an orientation to our products and services. The result of all of these hybrids of training delivery is to teach employees how to use technology-based training in smaller steps and to make the change less intimidating.

Acknowledging the Continued Need for Other Types of Training

Advocates of technology-based training are enthusiastic about the possibilities. Unfortunately, our enthusiasm is sometimes perceived as an attempt to force acceptance of our methods whether they are appropriate for the need or not. We have re-phrased our message to suggest that technology-based training should be used only when it is most appropriate in order to make classroom training both more available and more effective when classroom is the appropriate answer. Technology-based training is ideal for learning the basic vocabulary and concepts of a subject before attending a class on advanced material. When networking, peer interaction, or the practice of interpersonal skills is an essential part of the training, technology-based training is less effective. Using technology-based training for basic concepts leaves more resources available for valuable classroom time, and using technology to deliver computer skills training leaves more resources available for classroom taxation training. By acknowledging that classroom training should be used and should be more available for these types of needs, we gained more acceptance for the use of technology-delivered training when it is most appropriate.

Less Effective Strategies

Our vision of a world where employees would access training continuously as they needed it and would learn in a variety of ways proved difficult to communicate. Many employees may need to experience this change in order to understand the possibilities. We found that our own personalities and preferred learning styles were different from the majority of our customers. We could not simply recommend training solutions that worked for us. We needed to learn to look at the possibilities through our customers' world view and recommend the right training solutions for them.

The words "anywhere" and "any time" are frequently used to describe the benefits of technology-based training. We found this message achieved especially mixed results. Employees on odd shifts, in remote locations, or with reasonable accommodation needs responded very favorably to this idea. Many of the seasonal employees responded favorably, seeing it as a job benefit that helped them upgrade their employability. The majority of employees, though, interpreted the words as meaning that management would demand that they do job-related training on their own time. In some cases, the suspicion was correct. In other cases, the employee wanted to use work time for self-development that should properly be done after hours. We have a continuing need to keep educating both managers and employees on the rules for making an appropriate decision on training time in our organization. In other instances, the employee's work area is not a conducive environment for learning and they need to have access to a computer in a quiet training area. When employees are assured of fairness in the allocation of time and space, they are much more willing to accept technology-based training.

Finally, as mentioned previously, cost-benefit analysis is an organizational issue, but it is not a personal issue for learners. In some instances, individual learners who wanted training selected our courses because they believed their managers would appreciate the cost-benefit ratio. However, the business case did not address the learner's emotional resistance to technology-based training.

CONCLUSION

Personal is the key word, in several respects, to overcoming learner resistance to technology-delivered training. Students' concerns are individual and personal. Their personalities and learning styles influence reactions to training. The most effective strategies for overcoming learner resistance involve flexibly addressing each student's personal needs and maintaining a personal support relationship with each student. By using phone and e-mail availability, a manageable level of individual support greatly increases the acceptance of new training technologies and students can be encouraged to become more independent learners at a pace that is more comfortable for them.

What Napster Did for E-Learning

Editor's Comment: The year 2001 began with a huge worry in much of the Internet community that Napster might be dead. Napster users, according to *The Economist*, February 17, 2001, "constitute the largest community of music-lovers on earth." Napster claimed at that point to have 50 million registered users, many of whom would be willing to pay a fee, after all, for the music swapping services heretofore made available by Napster for free, according to surveys (p. 62). Fights about copyright infringement and piracy made headlines throughout the winter months.

What's interesting about the Napster model is the enthusiasm of its users for Napster's huge base of information and the strength of its network. E-learning specialists are rubbing their hands in glee that just maybe here's a model for learning that could be adapted to a learning situation—a need for knowledge or skills, similar to a need for a certain kind of music.

Ray Ozzie, creator of Lotus Notes and founder of Groove Networks, Inc. likens this kind of need to jamming—people who want and need to get together to improvise and to make music together. Ozzie was interviewed in the May 2001 issue of *Fast Company*. In this interview, he describes his software product, Groove, as one that, like Napster, circumvents centralized computer infrastructure and allows PCs to talk directly with each other (p. 194). The e-learning community needs infrastructure and interaction models that excite learners and appeal to their needs for community-building—especially the kind of community-building that's built on improvisation.

The article reprinted here addresses many of the issues in peer to peer e-learning models and the needs of learners within it.

> Peer to Peer Networking is a new technology term, but it has been the core of informal learning throughout our organization for hundreds of years. When an employee needs to know how to do something, they often look out at the workers around them and select someone to provide coaching, assistance, tutoring or even performance tools. They will pick someone with a reputation for good advice and good communication. This transaction will normally happen without any manager's authorization and it will not show up in a Training Management System. Good knowledge workers have networks that may span the globe and include colleagues that are outside the organization, even at their competitors. Simply, this is a non-virtual equivalent of the hottest term in e-Business... Peer to Peer (P2P) Networking.

My cover story this month is dedicated to the concept of Peer to Peer Learning. The Peer to Peer story was vaulted into the business conversation by the success and infamy of Napster (www.napster.com). Hundreds of thousands of people creating an informal network to share each other's music files. (For the purpose of this conversation, let's put aside the issues of copyright law and intellectual property. These will be played out in the courts and marketplace.)

Napster and similar P2P technologies like Gnutella have unleashed a simple model. People want to identify other people that share an interest and may have useful or desirable content. P2P assumes a noncentralized model of sharing this information. If you and I agree to swap access, you can have a copy of my files that I have designated for sharing. The P2P model often includes a community or rating

---

Source: "Peer to Peer e-Learning Models" by Elliott Masie in *Learning Decisions Interactive Newsletter*, November/December 2000, pp. 1–3. Elliott Masie is CEO of The MASIE Center, Saratoga Springs, NY and Editor of *Learning Decisions Interactive Newsletter*. Reprinted with permission of The MASIE Center, copyright 2000. All rights reserved.

system to determine the quality or context of the content and even the speed to which I can access the file.

Let's apply this model to e-Learning. Right now, most of e-Learning is still shaped by the centralized content creation and distribution system. An organization creates or rents content that they believe their workers will value and sets up a centralized distribution and tracking system. If a learner wants to learn how to configure a web server, they choose from one of the authorized courses and have an approved online learning experience.

In a P2P Learning model, the worker needing to learn how to configure a web server might search a network of internal techies, a larger world wide network of network professionals and/or a network of every employee and channel customer within their organization. The search would look for content (from a simple text file to a deeply structured e-Learning experience). In addition, the worker may have access to how valuable other network members have found each contributor. If Bob has a lot of content on his machine... yet most people find it out of date or poorly structured, the ratings would shift him down the totem pole. On the other hand, if Karen, or even the group that Karen works in, has great content that is well communicated, it would move to the top.

The P2P Learning model assumes a shift in how content is provided for others to use. Traditionally, the learning or training function designates the best content to use. Or, even with a Groupware product, the contributor has to believe that others would want to use their content, as they selectively contribute to a knowledge base. In P2P, the value of content is determined by the learner rather than the contributor or a centralized function.

We can push the P2P Learning model a bit further with a few examples of future models:

- **P2P Digital Collaboration:** I might locate a person that had content relevant to a current assignment. Yet, the greatest value would not be the text files on their drives, but rather the ability to have a digital collaboration moment with them. I would use their content to determine expertise but use a conversation with them as the information delivery process. In other words, their published content forms a resume of what they might be able to share dynamically with others. For example, I might keep a simple booklist on my PC, which includes books that I have read and am currently reading. Another worker would be able to guess at my interests from that file.

- **P2P Content Structuring:** Random words in text files will not suffice for P2P Learning. We will start to see the use of templates to help structure or even "Meta-Tag" content so that it can be useful to others within the organization. These tags might contain information about the date of the content, the problem that was being addressed, the usage rights of the content and even what happened as a result. For example, a salesperson might have all of their PowerPoint presentations available on a P2P network. The meta-tag information would provide insight into whether the presentation was successful and if the content is still valid.

- **P2P Annotations:** Sometimes, the most valuable P2P Learning content might merely be an annotation of a published resource. Do you remember buying a used text book in college? If you were lucky, the previous owner had highlighted or underlined the content of the book. If you were unlucky, the annotations were made by someone who received a D or F in the course. But, if you could trust the source, the annotations, in the form of notes or underlining, might be more valuable than the core textbook. In P2P Learning, we will see a dramatic rise in annotations.

- **P2P Media Capture:** As we add video and audio to our network capabilities, more and more knowledge will be captured in real time. For example, at the new MASIE Center e-Lab, we are building video and audio capture into every meeting space. Meetings will be captured and Meta-Tagged, so anyone can replay segments of a session and find value and context from content that was the result of a live event. We are predicting on-going debriefing that key contributors will do as they return from sales calls, critical meetings and projects, spontaneously sharing knowledge through talking, rather than processing it through a typed extraction. We know that informal Peer to Peer learning is almost entirely verbal and visual and we see P2P Learning assisted by technology flowing in the same direction. It fits us as a species and delivers the knowledge "story" more directly.

- **P2P Cumulative Content:** Each time a person takes an e-Learning course, there is new perspective. Sometimes this is found in a threaded discussion, but most courses are built and "locked" for some period of time. P2P Learning might shift our model towards a continuous improvement and contribution process... harnessing the value perspectives and knowledge of each subsequent learner. For example, the modules that are found to be most valuable might flow to the top of the screen... the ones that are found to be the most confusing might be allocated for correction and updating by the network members or a course owner.

In the next 12 months, you will see the P2P Learning model explode on to the e-Learning scene. It will extend the concept of community from a defined community of practice to a wider community of common interests. You will see new technologies, content development models and business models pop on to the e-Learning radar screen. In order to make P2P work, the field will need to tackle a number of key issues:

- **Quality of Content:** With access to thousands of learning resources, how does the community provide dynamic indicators of value? How does the learner decide which of three dozen resources to use? And, what is the role of an instructional design perspective in valuing the ease of learning of varied content?

- **Content Ownership Issues:** Who owns the content? Will workers want their peers to have access to content? If an employee leaves the organization, then who maintains that collection of content? How do we deal with the intellectual property issues when a network of learners modifies an externally purchased course?

- **Business Model:** Who will pay for all of this? How will we blend externally purchased content with internally purchased content?

- **Culture Issues:** What organizational culture issues have to be addressed as P2P Learning is introduced? Will there be a generational divide in comfort of operating with P2P? Will our bosses evaluate us for contributing to the P2P Learning Network?

- **Technology Issues:** What will be the search engines? How will we tag information? How will new and highly useful information rise above the mass collection? Will P2P Learning work with a wide range of wireless and mobile devices from cell phones to handhelds?

The MASIE Center is deeply intrigued with the power of P2P. Watch this phenomenon carefully in the months ahead as we investigate the role of P2P Learning and the emergence of products and services in this category.

How to Facilitate Online Communities

Editor's Comment: This article tells the stories of three different kinds of companies and how they established online communities: Ace Hardware, Cisco Systems, and Royal Dutch/Shell. As in real-live face to face communities, the secret to participation seems to be convincing people that they are welcome, and even should be, in a certain group. Selling more paint, installing more routers, and finding more oil ultimately are important goals too; but in the process, the intermediate goals of creating knowledge or delivering it to those who need it to do their jobs are the challenges of online communities.

It was just a local inspiration, one of those good ideas that small-business owners come up with every day. Tom Green, an Ace Hardware commercial dealer in Pittsburg, Calif., wanted to attract corporate customers, so he gave away a few cans of paint in a promotion aimed at local businesses. Green's effort brought in some new sales, but more important, he wrote up the experience on a message board that Ace Hardware had set up for its 300 dealers. Suddenly his local success became a hot tip broadcast to his fraternity of Ace franchisees. A dealer in Fitchburg, Mass., tried it and won new business from a major hotel and convention center. Another dealer in Bulkhead, Ariz., did the same and landed a multimillion-dollar supply contract.

Ace's win may sound like a fairy tale to managers who are more accustomed to frustration than success when it comes to sharing knowledge within a company or with customers, contractors, and suppliers. Yet companies as diverse as Cisco Systems, Royal Dutch/Shell Group, and VA Linux are discovering that experiences like Ace's aren't difficult to replicate. Message board technology—combined with creative incentives to spark participation—is quickly gaining recognition as an inexpensive way to speed up problem solving, spread good ideas, and lower the cost of customer service. The Yankee Group estimates that businesses spent $300 million in the past three years building online "communities," which is industry jargon for a group of people with similar interests who use messaging technology, such as chat and message boards, to stay in touch online.

For Ace, the payback came fast. The firm started its professional boards in August 1998 as an experiment intended to reduce costs associated with mailing out weekly newsletters and answering phone queries from franchise owners. That strategy worked, says Tina Lopotko, the head of Ace's commercial industrial unit. Her initial investment in message board software from eShare Communications and online consulting services from Participate.com pays for itself by saving her $24,000 in annual printing and mailing costs alone. To find answers to questions today, franchise owners are more likely to go to the message boards and chat at www.acehardware-acenet.com (sorry, it's password protected) than call a live customer support line, saving Ace an additional $50,000 a year. Ace's experience concurs with a McKinsey study published last year that estimated that message boards and chat rooms where business customers exchange information can cut customer support costs by 25 percent. Ace's unan-

> Businesses are embracing the humble message board to speed up problem solving and share ideas.

Source: "Talk Is Cheap. And Good for Sales Too." By Brian Caulfield in *www.ecompany.com*, April 2001, pp. 114-116. Brian Caulfield is a Staff Writer for *www.ecompany.com*. Reprinted with permission from *www.ecompany.com*, copyright 2001. All rights reserved.

Six Rules for Successful Communities

Web forums with a clear purpose—like those at Ace and Shell—are the ones most likely to prosper. Here's what you need to know.

- Define your goals. Are you looking to boost sales? Wring new information from your users? Lower the costs of customer service? Online communities falter when they are poorly defined. Decide what you want from your community before you put it together.

- Start simple. Don't sabotage yourself by splitting your online community into too many different chat groups early on. If you don't have a critical mass of participants, your forums will quickly turn into virtual ghost towns.

- Don't put marketing in charge. While the marketing department may be great at promoting your site and products, your users need substantive dialogue, not marketing pitches. Put your customers or employees in touch with the people they value most.

- Allow users to express their points of view. Controversial or daring ideas often spark great discussions. Don't let it get out of hand, though, and define the limits clearly in a statement of online conduct. Professional sites need to maintain some decorum.

- Answer posts within 24 hours. Make sure users get responses to their participation within 24 hours, or sooner if possible. You'll need a robust and well-populated community to achieve this. If you're just starting out, you may want to have a staffer check in on the boards once or twice a day. Or consider hiring an outsourcer such as Participation.com or PeopleLink to do it for you.

- Reward your posters. Keep track of who provides valuable information, such as answers to questions other members have posted. Then reward them. Ace gives out free hats and shirts to users who answer questions. SourceForge allows users to rate one another's skills and posts the results.

ticipated bonus is that the boards also serve as a clearinghouse for ideas among its dealers, not just the word from headquarters.

Cisco, an entirely different sort of hardware vendor, nonetheless tells a very similar story. It is enormously expensive for Cisco to provide individual service to each of the tens of thousands of networking consultants who work with Cisco's products; so the company is experimenting with an online community, called the Networking Professionals Connection, where its customers can help each other or drop in on live chats with Cisco's experts. After just eight months, Byron Henderson, a director of marketing at Cisco, says, "The site's proved an effective way to transfer information about technologies and products more quickly. It also gives our internal product teams an ear to the ground." Expert chats have become one of the biggest draws on the site, he says, and to date about 1,000 consultants have signed up.

Energy giant Royal Dutch/Shell Group is using the same community concept to make better use of in-house knowledge. It signed up 10,000 engineers on Shell's far-flung teams to use message board and chat software from SiteScape, of Maynard, Mass., for what it calls "communities of practices"—basically groups of professionals tackling similar problems. Shell says ideas exchanged on the system saved the company $200 million in 2000 alone. And in but one example, communication on the message boards also led to roughly $5 million in new revenue when engineering teams in Europe and the Far East helped a crew in Africa solve a problem they had already addressed. "These kinds of examples pop up over and over again," says Arjan van Unnik, of Shell International Exploration and Production. Shell spends about $3 million to $4 million annually on its online communities. "You'll find many companies

> Shell says ideas exchanged on its message boards saved the energy giant $200 million in 2000.

Essential Tools for Community Sites

Dozens of software packages and hosted services have sprung up, all competing to help businesses start online communities. Consultants such as Participate.com and PeopleLink will even run communities on a company's behalf. Here are some of the best options.

COMPANY	PRODUCTS	PRICE	CUSTOMERS
Coolboard www.coolboard.com	Hosts free basic message boards for small businesses and hobbyists; a deluxe offering has traffic-analysis tools that give detailed information on board usage.	Basic, ad-supported service is free; deluxe offering is $2,000 and up a month	14, including Alibris and Careerbuilder.com
eRoom Technology www.eroom.com	Provides virtual war rooms where professional teams can collaborate on projects through message boards, document sharing, and more. Will appeal to businesses looking for lots of features.	Software is $10,000 per server, plus $200 per user	475, including Compaq, Ford, and Pfizer
Infopop www.infopop.com	Infopop's Ultimate Bulletin Board software does just one thing—message boards—but it does it very well. Deluxe hosted service gives detailed break-downs of board usage.	Software is $500 and up per year; hosted service is $2,750 and up per month	About 20,000, including eBay, Hewlett-Packard, and Playboy.com
Multex.com www.multex.com	Multex's BuzzPower software offers message boards, chat, calendars, polls, and e-mail digests. A pricey hosted version gives detailed usage statistics.	Software is $9,500 and up; hosted service costs $6,000-plus per month and $25,000 for setup	More than 100, including Encyclopaedia Brittannica and VerticalNet
Participate.com www.participate.com	You want it, you got it: hosting, consulting, training, marketing, and even moderators who can keep discussions jumping. But all this service doesn't come cheap.	$25,000 and up per month (or at least that's what the proverbial rate card says)	50, including Ace Hardware, Cisco Systems, and MSN
PeopleLink www.peoplelink.com	Will set up, host, and manage online forums for big businesses running their own software. Not for small-fry operations.	Services are $8,000 and up per month	35, including Oracle and Viacom
SiteScape www.sitescape.com	Software for document sharing, whiteboards, message boards, and the like. Also offers a hosting option at a price palatable to small-business customers.	Software is $7,000 and up; hosted service costs $15 per user per month	More than 1,500, including EDS, Royal Dutch/Shell Group, and 3Com

working on a global scale with people in many locales focused on local problems."

Software engineers, who used message boards long before the Internet was popularized, may have taken the business community idea furthest of all—into the realm of actual product development. SourceForge, an online community for open-source developers set up by software developer VA Linux, of Fremont, Calif., has approximately 115,000 registered users working on more than 5,000 projects, according to John T. Hall, vice president for strategy and development at VA Linux. Recently the site's users—most of whom have never met each other in person—cranked out eight complete open-source software projects in a single day by using SourceForge to exchange messages, update one another on bugs, share code, and, ultimately, distribute the software to the public. All of this software is given away for free, but VA Linux benefits by being able to incorporate it into its commercial products.

Getting an online community started can be as easy as installing message board software on your company's servers or contracting with an outsourcer to host the software for you. Software prices range from free to $10,000 or more a year. If you choose to set up your own boards, software packages from eRoom Technology, Infopop, Multex.com, and SiteScape include message board tools and a wide range of other capabilities. For an experienced techie, setting up a bulletin board might take an afternoon. Making it look pretty and integrating it with your existing website could take a few days longer. You'll also need to invest in a server and Net connection to handle traffic to the boards. For those who want to leave the technical headaches to someone else, companies such as Coolboard, eRoom Technology, Infopop, and PeopleLink can set up and host the community site for you. This will cost some serious money—usually in the range of $2,000 to $6,000 a month—but may well be worth it if you're short on technical resources. (For more information, see "Essential Tools for Community Sites," below.)

Setting up the technology is one thing, but breathing life into it is a lot tougher. For every case where online communities worked wonders for a business, there are many more cases of failure. The key to reaping benefits like cost savings and new business is to attract participation. Consultants such as PeopleLink, of Santa Monica, Calif., and Chicago-based Participate.com help companies figure out a strategy and build that critical audience. They arrange programming (like live exchanges with experts) and promote the community to its target audience for fees that range well into tens of thousands of dollars a year.

Participate.com worked with Ace to get the hardware chain's community rolling. Among Participate's tactics: Its staff visited Ace dealers to show them how the site worked and sent weekly faxes about activity on the boards to encourage the dealers to join in. Ace has been able to get 30 percent of its 300 dealers to log on at least once a week, and virtually all of them visit once a month.

The golden rule is obvious: If the community delivers to its audience useful knowledge and insight—like how to sell more paint, find more oil, or use the right router—the rest will take care of itself.

4. The New Bottom Line

Faster, Cheaper, Smarter: How Rockwell Collins Reinvented Its Training

Editor's Comment: 17,500 employees in 26 locations around the world all trained in Cedar Rapids, Iowa. 1,400 courses, more than three-quarters of which had been taught only once. These are some of the numbers that shocked a new training manager at Rockwell-Collins into shaking things up. This is the outline of how a new approach to training and learning focused on business units and business goals, not on numbers of courses in the catalog or butts in chairs. Cliff Purington's 6 points are right for the times in which we live, times that link training to the rapidly changing needs of business.

When Cliff Purington arrived in 1998 as manager of learning and development at Rockwell Collins, a manufacturer of communication and aviation electronics, he checked into the company's training-history database. "I thought it would be rich with core competencies, and all I had to do was find the repeat courses to see what they were," he says.

But only 22 percent of the 1,400 individually titled classes had been repeated. Most of the course materials, developed in-house at a cost of $120 million, were unused. "We're not talking small change," Purington says. "It also told me that we didn't have a good connection back to the business, or a good needs analysis to see if training really was the issue."

He said the situation was not unusual for a large organization. "It was one of these cases where the folks in training were getting calls from line management, requesting very specific training." Often, he said, training wasn't really the fix that was needed. It might have been unclear roles and responsibilities or any number of other problems. But managers tended to identify training as the solution, even if it really wasn't. Since then, Purington has put in place a new cost-saving, business-driven learning strategy, based on six objectives:

- Link learning directly to business objectives. The training staff's job now is to work with the business groups to evaluate their training needs, make sure they're tied with the company's business objectives, and, if training is the solution or would be of benefit, work with outside vendors to develop training programs.

- Locate classes close to the work environment to provide students with easier access. When Purington began working at Rockwell Collins, all training for the company's 17,500 employees, who work at 26 locations around the world, was done in classrooms at the company's headquarters in Cedar Rapids, Iowa. The result was a lot of expensive travel and layer upon layer of scheduling difficulties.

- Make learning accessible worldwide, 24 hours a day, seven days a week.

- Deliver the highest quality learning.

Source: "Faster, Cheaper, Smarter: How Rockwell Collins Reinvented Its Training" within the article "Training Proves Its Worth" by Carol Lachnit in *Workforce*, September 2001, p. 55. Carol Lachnit is Managing Editor of *Workforce* magazine. Reprinted with permission of *Workforce* magazine, copyright 2001. All rights reserved.

- Reduce the cost of training by 40 percent.
- Increase available curriculum by 40 percent.

An example of a business-driven program that provides more learning in a more accessible form at lower cost is the course the company offers to engineers in electromagnetic interference. Previously, when courses were held only in Cedar Rapids, it would have taken 13 years to train all the engineers who needed the information, Purington says. Working with outside vendors, Purington and his staff created a Web-based course that delivered in 9 hours what took 22 hours to present in a classroom. "It has more content, and it's available 24/7 in the work environment, because it's online," he says.

Now, in the second year of the three-year learning-program overhaul, 80 percent of the company's training is available in alternative formats, including the Web and CD-ROMs. There are 450 online courses, such as ethics training, data processing, computer programming, diversity, and interpersonal skills, an increase since 1998 of 250 percent. There are still 50 courses taught in the classroom, all complex engineering classes in which student-instructor interaction is crucial. In the first year of the new learning program, the company saved $6.37 million in training costs—or 38 percent. This year, it's on target to save $6.79 million—or 39 percent.

For all of these accomplishments, can Purington show a direct line between the revamped training programs and Rockwell Collins's profitability? He doesn't measure training success that way. It's very hard to prove, and it's a defensive posture, he says.

"If you're on the back end of the process, which most training organizations are, you spend too much time trying to justify your existence. If you're on the front end, tied in to the business groups, and they know who you are and what you're doing, you don't have to do that. I don't have to justify the objectives I defined. The organization told me that's what they wanted, and that's what I provided."

An example of delivering what the business needs is the development of short courses called Quicklearns. The business groups were concerned about the loss of what Purington calls "tribal knowledge"—information that resides in the head of someone who has done a job for 40 years and vanishes when the employee retires. Quicklearns, classes of 20 minutes or less (the average adult's attention span), have a turnaround time from order to completion of 12 hours, and cost no more than $2,000.

"I'm delivering 150 of those this year," Purington says. The programs, produced by the Performance Engineering Group, based in Santa Barbara, California, begin with an expert in the procedure demonstrating the process that's going to be taught—how to clean a clean room, for instance. The producers create a storyboard that outlines what will be shown. There's a dry run, and then the process is filmed with a digital camera. The lesson is placed in an electronic template with text and questions for self-checking, and stored on a CD-ROM. The subjects of the 75 or so programs that the company has created include how to use an electronic microscope and how to choose and clean a soldering head. Two student groups, one trained via CD-ROM and the other trained by a classroom instructor, received virtually identical scores after being tested for their proficiency in clean-room techniques.

Here is Purington's formula for training success: "Get connected to the business groups as quickly as possible. Service the people you're there to service. Find out their needs, and how best you can deliver. Develop rapport and trust with the business groups, and then deliver what you say you're going to deliver. That's how you keep your budget from being cut."

Results-Oriented Customer Service Training

Editor's Comment: The TV and magazine images were so clear after September 11, 2001—businesses in New York City, lower Manhattan, that were destroyed by the terrorist attack on the World Trade Center and that were served by destroyed infrastructure set up shop across the river or in neighboring states in just a few hours after the attack, and Wall Street markets were in business on Wall Street just one week after the devastation. The message was clear: we are in business to serve our customers. The President and public officials urged people to get back to work and to refrain from short-term thinking. *The Wall Street Journal*, in an editorial, "Among the Missing," on October 14, 2001, p. 12 urged Americans to think about the "chance interconnections, as well as the necessary relations, that make a place like the World Trade Center function."

Dell Computer is among the lucky technology companies and is shipping 25,000 computers to one of its major customers, Morgan Stanley Dean Witter, a former occupant of the World Trade Center (*Business Week*, October 22, 2001, p. 16). Other companies and other customers have not fared so well, however, and the slowing economy before September 11 added to the effects of uncertainty and loss of New York workplaces. An interview by Ann Curry of NBC News on October 23, 2001 of the Deputy Editor of *TV Guide Magazine* focused on New York as a center of broadcasting, and an industry particularly sensitive to its customers, the millions of TV viewers in the United States and abroad. The point was made that TV's customers this fall season had no interest in "phony peril or contrived reality" after living through 9/11, and that the broadcasters were ready for considerable less customer interest in "Survivor 3," "Temptation Island," and other shows of similar ilk. Customers clearly matter in New York and elsewhere in this interconnected world.

This article by Brenda Paik Sunoo profiles several companies in terms of customer needs, a relationship group of great importance. The question to be answered is, "Can training help employees create new opportunities for customers?"

The scenario has a familiar ring: A frustrated buyer of computer products files a complaint online. His posting says, "TigerDirect.com has consistently refused to respond to my faxes, e-mails, and calls about this malfunctioning motherboard and CPU bundle. I have purchased many items from them in the past, and they are becoming less responsive to me when I have a problem. They take the customer's money but don't support their own product."

Never mind that the motherboard was purchased online. A new Web site called eComplaints.com provides a free online forum for customers to air complaints about *any* company's products or services. It could be a clothing retailer, manufacturer, financial institution, home-gardening company, hospital, or even your neighborhood gas station. At the same time, eComplaints.com gives the companies a chance to respond to the customers' concerns and purchase statistical information from the site in order to identify and remedy trouble spots. Interestingly, 6 out of the top 10 companies receiving online complaints on this particular Web site were airlines, among them American and United.

Roger H. Nunley, managing director of Atlanta-based Customer Care Institute, says American consumers are more knowledgeable and have higher expectations than most other people. When a company improves its service delivery, the satisfaction bar is raised.

Why the fuss? According to the American Customer Satisfaction Index—compiled by the University of Michigan—customer satisfaction

---

Source: "Results-Oriented Customer Service Training" by Brenda Paik Sunoo in *Workforce*, May 2001, pp. 84, 86, 88, 90. Brenda Paik Sunoo is a freelance writer based in Irvine, CA. Reprinted with permission of *Workforce*, copyright 2001. All rights reserved.

> Whatever method or innovation you choose, your customer-service training should be aligned with your company's own policies, procedures, and culture.

has dropped since 1994 in nearly every sector of the economy.

In many grocery chains, for example, the tongue-in-cheek phrase "customer checkout" has come to exemplify the unsettling trend of poor customer service. It means, of course, that customers won't be checking back in at the store.

Customer service training begins with *how* an employer screens candidates for hire, and *not only* during employee orientation, says a spokesman at Reid Systems, a Chicago-based developer of automated applicant-screening tools. In conjunction with several large North American grocery chains, Reid recently studied thousands of job applicant responses to pre-employment assessment questions on customer service. The study then examined the service-oriented questions and found that:

- 45 percent said they believe that customers should be told when they are wrong.
- 46 percent said customers have to follow the rules if they are going to help them.
- 34 percent said they would prefer to work behind the scenes, rather than with customers.
- 13 percent said they believe that if customers don't ask for help, they don't need it.
- 10 percent said they do not feel it is necessary to help a customer if the request falls outside their area of responsibility.
- 6 percent said they have repeatedly argued with customers and coworkers in recent jobs.

Is it any wonder that customer-service training—especially with a new generation of workers—is taking on greater importance? According to the American Society for Training and Development, in Alexandria, Virginia, service providers spent an average of $833 in education per employee in 1997, the most recent year that figures were available. This is nearly 30 percent higher than the national average for all industries.

There was a time when customer service meant hiring an individual to sit behind a complaint desk. Today, customer-service training is more comprehensive. It requires that employers hire the right employees, create a customer-service culture, view customers as high-maintenance "guests," and train employees on select technologies—without sacrificing the human touch. Gulf Breeze Hospital, Wild Oats Markets, and the PPL Corporation are examples of small, medium, and large companies, respectively, that are moving away from handling complaints to proactively anticipating customer needs—before trouble begins.

Remember, whatever method or innovation you choose, your customer-service training should be aligned with your company's own policies, procedures, and culture.

SMALL COMPANY
Promote Accountability in Your Customer-Service Team
Name: Gulf Breeze Hospital
Location: Gulf Breeze, Florida
Type of business: Hospital
Number of employees: 280

Gulf Breeze Hospital is an acute-care facility with 60 licensed beds. It opened in June 1985, following five years of research, planning, and construction.

Longtime administrator Dick Fulford says that the first step toward achieving exceptional standards was to assemble a first-class team of customer-service-oriented managers and staff. It's what he refers to as his Dream Team.

Members of the staff were trained early on to make three major pledges to ensure better customer service. It all begins with a positive attitude, he says.

- Never say, "It's not my job."
- Reduce and eliminate hassles.
- Provide personalized professional care.

Fulford says that every person working at the hospital has the opportunity to make a customer's interaction exceptional. Applicants are immediately told that if they can't make this commitment, they will probably not fit in with Gulf Breeze Hospital culture.

Once hired, team participants are encouraged to submit "bright ideas," a training mechanism to foster creative customer-service thinking on the teams. Various forms of recognition are utilized to keep the staff thinking and challenging existing procedures and policies. Rewards such as meal tickets, mentions in the hospital newsletter, written acknowledgment, and notation in performance evaluations reinforce the hospital's customer-service goals.

Ideas that require fine-tuning often are turned over to the Gulf Breeze Hospital Satisfaction Team, Fulford says. Hospital staff members representing various departments have volunteered to serve on this specialized team to address patient, physician, and employee satisfaction issues. To reinforce the ideas that emerge, a subgroup produces a newsletter called "Breeze Way." In this way, employees also are trained to market their successes.

Every month, the publication features the Baptist Health Care Standards of Performance. The standards, says Fulford, are specific behaviors that employees are required to practice while on duty, such as a positive attitude, good appearance and communication, and commitment to coworkers.

Scripts are provided to employees. Gulf Breeze Hospital employees receive booklets that describe the hospital's code of conduct. For example, they are advised to say, "May I help you? I have the time."

"This last part is very important to say. There's so much rush, rush in the health-care industry," Fulford says.

Employees are empowered to please their customers in many ways. Any employee can open the hospital gift shop and spend up to $250 to replace a patient's lost belongings or to buy flowers for a patient with a complaint. Nurses carry wireless phones so doctors can contact them without paging over a noisy intercom.

In the are of customer-service accountability, Gulf Breeze took a major step in January 1996. It joined the ranks of facilities surveyed by Press, Ganey Associates, Inc., of South Bend, Indiana. By submitting to the rigor of competition, the hospital has trained its employees to measure its performance by industry standards, Fulford says. Press, Ganey Associates processes more than 4 million surveys annually for more than 1,400 clients. The firm provides more than 20 different measurement instruments and reports and conducts surveys for health-care clients in 47 states. Its Web site reports that it has been selected by 74 major health-care systems as their satisfaction measurement provider.

During the first quarter of each year, clients submit their quality-improvement experiences for its Success Story Contest. The top six facilities from each year are invited to present their stories at the firm's annual client conference.

The first Press, Ganey Associates report was received in late May 1996, and Gulf Breeze Hospital earned an overall score of 95.7. Gulf Breeze ranked tops in patient satisfaction compared to more than 600 other hospitals nationwide.

Only a year before, the hospital had been ranked close to the bottom in national surveys. Its turnaround is a national customer-service model. Last year, the hospital ranked among the top 2 percent in customer-service surveys. Its market share reportedly jumped by 4 percentage points, and it generated $4.5 million in additional revenue in 1999 while reducing costs by $3.5 million.

"Doctors love to come to Gulf Breeze," Fulford says. "The perception is that the patient is going to be satisfied."

MEDIUM COMPANY
Treat Customers as Guests
Name: Wild Oats Markets, Inc.
Location: Boulder, Colorado
Type of business: Chain of natural foods markets
Number of employees: 7,500

In 1987, a husband-and-wife team, Mike Gilliland and Libby Cook, opened their first vegetarian health food store in Boulder, Colorado. In 13 years, Wild Oats Markets has grown into a natural-foods supermarket chain in North America,

Needs of Learners

with 110 stores in 22 states and British Columbia. The company now operates its stores under a family of trade names, including Wild Oats Community Markets, Alfalfa's Markets, Capers Markets, Oasis Fine Foods, and Sunshine Grocery.

Wild Oats Markets attracts two types of customers, says Cynthia Baxter, vice president of training and development. First are the traditionalists—those who have purchased and eaten organic foods for years. They're the ones who shudder at the thought of shopping at conventional grocery stores. The other major customers are those she describes as "trial people." They are interested in organic foods but are not necessarily avid fans of wheat germ, hummus, or alfalfa sprouts. "They like the taste and quality of many of our products and the convenience of our deli," Baxter says. "They're willing to give us a trial. If we take good care of them, they'll come back."

Wild Oats Markets, she says, always has been committed to customer-service training. In the past, however, it's been hit or miss. Employees were given basic customer-service orientation on how to smile, be polite, and assist and direct shoppers to the right aisles. But these days, customers have numerous questions about health products they know nothing about: "What are homeopathic remedies for sinusitis?" "What harmful ingredients should I avoid in a shampoo?" "What is the difference between tempeh and tofu?"

Knowing that its trial customers are seeking new information, Wild Oats Markets considers and treats its clientele as special "guests." "Our founder and former CEO Mike Gilliland is very community-oriented. His point of view is that people who come to our store are our friends. We need to help them make choices when it comes to the food they're eating and to the homeopathic remedies," Baxter says.

One of her main customer-service training goals, therefore, is to enable employees to be knowledgeable about the store's products. In preparation for the grand opening of a flagship store in Irvine, California, managers and employees underwent a two-hour orientation. Not only were they introduced to the history of Wild Oats Markets, but they also role-played various problem-solving situations.

> When employees are unable to answer a guest's questions, they refer the customer to the store's "concierge."

In the past, health foods customers knew their store clerks, Baxter says. They could depend on their knowledge of organic food products and homeopathic remedies. With Generation X employees, customer-service training has included not only the basics of social greetings but also an introduction to myriad new food products. New employees were encouraged to read about various health products and taste as many food samples as possible.

"We're not able to get people who are as passionate about health foods as in the past," Baxter says. "We have to take our [new, young] employees and make them passionate about natural foods and our guests."

When employees are unable to answer a guest's questions, they refer the customer to the store's "concierge." This newly created position was first tested in the Irvine store, which opened in March. Sue Fruhwirth was hired for the position. She says the company founder and store director have given her great leeway in developing her job description.

Many customers come to her with specific questions about product ingredients, she says. Others want to know, for example, when and if the store will sponsor classes on solar energy. If a customer has a complaint about a product or service, she often handles those issues as well. "I basically can do anything that improves customer satisfaction," she says, "even if it means driving to one of our other stores to pick up a special product."

In order to train for her unique position, Fruhwirth has worked in every store department. A former employee at the Wild Oats Community Market in Laguna Beach, California, she knows her produce, meats, baked goods, and deli foods and is familiar with the products in the store's natural living aisles.

"I work closely with the managers of every department. So when I spot customer trends, I can alert them early on," she says.

At Wild Oats Markets, guests rule—and graze.

LARGE COMPANY
Use Technology as a Tool, Not a Replacement
Name: PPL Corporation
Location: Allentown, Pennsylvania
Type of business: Energy services
Number of employees: 12,000

PPL Corporation is a *Fortune* 500 company that markets wholesale or retail energy in 42 states and Canada. It also delivers energy to nearly 6 million customers in the United States, United Kingdom, and Latin America.

About half of PPL's workforce use computers to conduct their jobs, according to Denis Esslinger, Help Center supervisor in the Information Services Department. Considering that large number, anything can go wrong. An employee could have problems preparing a spreadsheet, creating a PowerPoint presentation, writing a report to meet safety regulations, or simply connecting a laptop to a home office. PPL thus created a Help Center, a team of 30 "analysts" who provide all of the computer support for these 6,000 employees.

"Last year, they received 90,000 calls at the Help Center," Esslinger says. This special team was expected to resolve 70 percent of the problems on the first contact. But the problem was that new members of the team weren't properly trained.

In order to improve and accelerate their customer-service practices, PPL worked with Raleigh, North Carolina-based Productivity Point International (PPI)—one of its strategic alliance partners. Previously, new team members had been trained by shadowing experienced consultants and receiving support material as needed.

> "We not only solved computer problems but exceeded our customers' expectations of our service."

This method presented several problems, Esslinger says:

- There was no consistent and qualitative message from the Help Center.
- Training was too informal.
- Resources were not centralized, and instructions were hard to find.
- Previous training did not lead to a new analyst's self-directed action.

PPI designed a customer-service training program for the 30-member team that included instructor-led training with mentors, Web-based self-study, and on-the-job practice. While the training was specifically designed for new employees, it was delivered to the entire Help Center team.

The one-week training program produced positive results. New Help Center analysts were productive in half the time previously required to get them up to speed. And they were able to resolve the required 70 percent of customer problems during the first call.

"I found the blended solution to be very innovative," Esslinger says. "We not only solved computer problems but exceeded our customers' expectations of our service."

Clearly, in all three examples—Gulf Breeze Hospital, Wild Oats Markets, and PPL Corporation—a company's customer-service practice may be an employer's best competitive edge.

[workforce.com] For more info on:

Customer-Service Issues
Read other *Workforce* stories on different aspects of customer service, including a look at how New York overhauled its civil-service system to serve its customers. Just type customer service into the search box at workforce.com

Wellness at DaimlerChrysler

Editor's Comment: Changing the program to meet employees' needs, not changing employees to meet our needs. That's quite a statement from a training program manager in a big company in these days of alignment, common vision, and other concepts that attempt to get all employees focused on the corporate mission meeting the corporate needs. DaimlerChrysler looked at its workforce quite differently, and in the process garnered a prestigious "Optimas Award" given by *Workforce* magazine as one of the 10 finest companies in the country. They got the "Partnership Award" for the efforts of both labor and management together in creating a health and wellness program for 90,000 employees.

DaimlerChrysler, like so many companies in years 2001 and 2002 is faced with layoffs, before and after September 11, 2001. Throughout 2001, the business press has been reporting layoffs, amounting to the hundreds of thousands, in businesses of all sorts. *The Economist*, March 31, 2001 reported that "this is the first big redundancy wave to affect mainly 'knowledge workers,' rather than manufacturing employees." The magazine reports that Nortel and Intel, for example, use a ranking system similar to the bell curve, in which the lowest-ranked individuals are asked to leave— "ranking and spanking" or "the hell curve" as employees fondly call the system (p. 57). Even temps and contract workers are at risk during these days, as *The Wall Street Journal* reports on March 27, 2001. A "Work Week" brief quotes the Bureau of Labor Statistics which said that the unemployment claims filed by temp workers were up 29 percent from last year at the same time, and gave the example of Compaq Computer Corp. who announced that 15 percent of its 24,500 contract workers would be cut (p. 1). Jobs lost in New York City by the attack on the World Trade Center represent an $11 billion lost of human capital according to *Business Week* magazine, October 22, 2001, p. 102.

The stress and dislocation felt by many employees in these situations often is addressed by counselors brought in at the time of crisis. DaimlerChrysler took a different view, that of ongoing prevention and wellness programs. Jennifer Hutchins' article describes the program at DaimlerChrysler.

In an agreeable alliance between labor, management, and suppliers, the DaimlerChrysler/UAW National Wellness Program is soothing traditional tensions between unions and employers. "It's truly a partnership," says Teresa Bartlett, senior manager of disability and medical health-care programs for Daimler Chrysler Corporation. "We've never encountered disagreement at all."

The 15-year-old program is a negotiated benefit between DaimlerChrysler and the autoworkers' union, UAW. DaimlerChrysler and the union work with third-party providers to make health-promotion and prevention initiatives available to more than 90,000 employees at 35 major locations nationwide. The availability of programs and number of on-site coordinators depend on the site's employee population and size. The extensive program has endured Chrysler's 1998 merger with Daimler-Benz and other major organizational and industry changes. The corporation faces yet another challenging era following the announcement that it will chop 26,000 Chrysler jobs, including several thousand in the United States. Through it all, wellness continues to be a part of life at DaimlerChrysler.

"It's been a very good partnership and has been beneficial for our [union] members as well as DaimlerChrysler," says Kenneth Young, coordinator of the DaimlerChrysler/UAW benefits program. "People in the plants are appreciative

---

Source: "Labor and Management Build a Prescription for Health" by Jennifer Hutchins in *Workforce*, March 2001, pp. 50–52. Jennifer Hutchins is a freelance writer based in Rochester, NY. Reprinted with permission of *Workforce*, copyright 2001. All rights reserved.

of the programs they put on." Young has represented union interests in the program since its inception and was instrumental in its development. He says the program not only is helpful in maintaining employee health, but also has on occasion targeted and addressed a serious health risk in an employee.

At the core of the collaboration is the Wellness Advisory Council. The council meets quarterly, and is usually composed of six representatives who gather at DaimlerChrysler's headquarters in Auburn Hills, Michigan. "We are truly a team," says Bartlett. "All of the partners come together and report what's going on, how many people participated, what types of road blocks were faced, and so on. We strategize about where we should target the programs."

All U.S. locations with at least 500 employees have contracts with on-site health and fitness business partners. These coordinators spend their days in offices and warehouses and on factory floors encouraging employees to take part in health activities and gauging health concerns. The StayWell Company manages programs at 26 DaimlerChrysler locations and has 60 onsite coordinators working full-time.

The American Institute of Preventive Medicine manages the wellness program at seven sites. "We believe in empowering employees to make better health-care decisions," says Don R. Powell of AIPM. "We feel that people need to learn skills, which goes along with education. It's also important to motivate people, whether through incentives, positive reinforcement, or support groups."

The DaimlerChrysler/UAW National Wellness program won the 2000 C. Everett Koop National Health Award and has also won 29 gold-medal awards from the Wellness Councils of America (WELCOA).

The program's success is measured through health-risk assessments, employee satisfaction surveys, and outside research. Evaluation results make a strong case to all members of the team—labor, management, and suppliers. "You've got research that validates that the program does a lot of things," says Joan Bassing, national program director for StayWell Health Management. "It helps people stay healthy and come to their jobs day in and day out."

The program covers a large, geographically spread-out population. It is imperative for site coordinators to maintain strong ties with one another and with headquarters. "One thing that's a challenge for the field sites is communication," says Ed Gonzalez, program manager for StayWell. "We address that challenge very well. We try to make sure that each individual person feels like part of the bigger picture."

Awareness, education, maintenance, and assessment make up the main components of the program. The Advisory Council develops and upholds guidelines, while allowing for flexibility to meet individual employees' health needs. Each site coordinator then works closely with employees to tailor the programs. Activities cover areas such as nutrition, exercise, injury prevention, mental health, driver safety, and smoking cessation. Employees voluntarily attend one-time workshops, multi-session seminars, individual counseling, and self-directed exercises. They can also participate in maintenance strategies, including blood screenings, awareness campaigns, incentive programs, and follow-up. Some sites also offer health-oriented amenities, such as workout facilities and videos and literature for employees to take home.

StayWell's NextSteps™ Focused Interventions is a lifestyle risk counseling program that provides assistance via telephone and mail. If an employee is trying to lose weight, for example, he can partake in telephone counseling sessions while he works toward his goal. On average, DaimlerChrysler participants in NextSteps lowered their health risks by 12 percent, whereas non-participants increased their health risks by 2 percent. Program administrators stress that all activities focus on prevention and health promotion and are not meant to replace a doctor's care.

A major success of the program is its ability to cater to different work schedules and job types. At a site where workers do a lot of heavy lifting, for example, StayWell holds seminars on preventing back injury and workshops to strengthen back muscles. In a white-collar setting, activities might focus on eyestrain or coping with stress. "We are not changing the employees so they can meet our needs, but changing our program so that we can meet the employees' needs," Gonzalez says.

Employee delegates volunteer to spread the word in their departments by distributing promotional material and talking with colleagues. Some employees attend almost all the activities, while others choose to participate only in those that interest them specifically. Family members,

> "Just in terms of direct medical costs, the program pays for itself."

retirees, and contract workers are also encouraged to participate.

The DaimlerChrysler/UAW program has raised the bar in corporate wellness. In the 1980s it introduced the concept of tailoring programs to high-risk groups. Today, that method has become the standard in worksite wellness.

The Wellness Advisory Council ensures that the programs meet employees' current needs, no matter what factors might affect their health. Most recently, the corporation has faced well-publicized performance problems. "We try to be sensitive to what's going on with the world of our customers," says Bassing. "For example, with the merger there was a lot of uncertainty, and we were able to increase the number of classes in resiliency, stress management, and how to deal with ambiguity."

Outcomes are measured in lower health risks, participation, and employee satisfaction. In 1999, 36 percent of employees participated in health-risk appraisals and an even higher percentage attended the seminars. Surveys show that 95 percent of employees who participate are satisfied. In 1999, appraisal data showed that 4,184 white-collar participants had significantly lowered their health risks. Driving-habits risk decreased 42 percent, smoking risk decreased 27 percent, high-risk alcohol consumption decreased 39 percent, and mental-health risk decreased 20 percent.

Research also validates a financial return on investment. The Health Care Financing Administration predicts that by 2002, national health expenditures will total $2.1 trillion. Effective wellness programs have been shown to contain health-care costs, reduce absenteeism, and improve employee health. Researchers at the University of Rochester studied data from the program from 1997. They found that employees who completed one, two, or three health-risk assessments had, on average, lower health-care costs of $112.89, $152.29, and $134.22, respectively. Over time, the differences in health-care costs between participants and non-participants have ranged between $5 and $16 per employee, per month.

"Just in terms of direct medical costs, the program pays for itself," says Bassing. "That helps management say, 'We're not losing money on this program. Let's find someplace else to cut costs.' We respond just like other vendors in finding ways to cut costs and to streamline."

The wellness program underwent extensive measurement for the C. Everett Koop Award. It met high standards as a quality, cost-effective program to help employees to improve their health and become wise health-care consumers. "We have a goal this year to enhance our measurements even further and hone them better," says Bartlett. "The wellness industry is hungry for data to prove whether or not tools are effective, and programs work."

On That Fateful Day, Two Airlines Faced Their Darkest Scenario

Editor's Comment: The attacks on September 11, 2001 left at least 5,000 persons missing and presumed dead in New York City and nearly 1,000 at the Pentagon in Washington, DC and in the field in Shanksville, PA. Two reporters from *The Wall Street Journal* pieced together this gripping account of what began as a normal business day for airlines operations employees at American Airlines and United Airlines. Their account underscores the needs of employees like these, under stress, for continuous training in problem solving, decision making, communication, stress management, and skills development and practice. This story of ordinary people in an extraordinary situation should be part of every employee's orientation training.

Across America, skies were clear, a beautiful day for flying everywhere but in Atlanta, where low clouds draped a summery landscape.

Early in the business day, American Airlines and United Airlines each had more than 100 flights in the air, a fraction of the more than 2,000 flights they had scheduled. Their top executives were digging through paperwork, meeting with other managers and answering e-mail from home.

Then, at 7:27 A.M. CDT, Craig Marquis got a mind-boggling emergency phone call.

Mr. Marquis, manager-on-duty at American's sprawling System Operations Control center in Fort Worth, Texas, heard a reservations supervisor explain that an airborne flight attendant, hysterical with fear, was on the phone and needed to talk to the operations center. In the background, Mr. Marquis could hear the flight attendant shrieking and gasping for air.

"She said two flight attendants had been stabbed, one was on oxygen. A passenger had his throat slashed and looked dead, and they had gotten into the cockpit," Mr. Marquis recalls.

The Unthinkable Unfolds

In 22 years at American's operations center, Mr. Marquis has made split-second, multimillion-dollar decisions to cancel flights during storms, separate threats from hoaxes and set in motion the airline's response to a crash. But none of that could have prepared him for the morning of Sept. 11, when all he and other American and United Airlines officials could do was listen and watch as the system they control spun gruesomely out of control.

"I felt so helpless," says Mr. Marquis. "I was along for the ride."

A little more than 20 minutes later, inside United's System Operations Control center in suburban Chicago, Rich "Doc" Miles, the SOC duty manager, received equally startling news: air-traffic controllers had lost contact with United Flight 175 from Boston's Logan Airport, and a flight attendant on that plane had called in word that the plane had been hijacked.

The televised events of Sept. 11 are etched on the world's memory. But this is the story, recalled in detail in extensive interviews with senior executives and front-line managers, of

---

Source: "Flying Blind: On That Fateful Day, Two Airlines Faced Their Darkest Scenario" by Scott McCartney and Susan Carey in *The Wall Street Journal*, October 15, 2001, pp. 1, A6. Scott McCartney and Susan Carey are Staff Reporters of *The Wall Street Journal*. Reprinted with permission of *The Wall Street Journal*, copyright 2001. All rights reserved.

what happened that day inside the command centers of American and United, each of which lost two jets to the terrorist attacks. It was there that normally unflappable aviation experts first started to unravel the puzzle of horror that at first seemed too diabolical to be real. Hijackers were supposed to coerce pilots to land someplace that the hijackers wanted to go. Never had hijackers murdered pilots, taken control of planes and used them as giant suicide missiles.

Jim Goodwin, United's chairman and chief executive, knew instantly that the ramifications went well beyond his airline and American. "The enormity of this is going to change everyone's life profoundly," he recalls thinking to himself.

Losing Contact

As American and United lost communications, one by one, with a total of four hijacked planes, confusion set in. Managers couldn't tell right away which particular plane had been ensnared in the catastrophes that unfolded on TV sets all around them. There was an unprecedented flurry of intercompany calls; even the two chief executives spoke by phone.

Quickly, people at the football-field-sized command centers began executing the biggest shutdown in commercial aviation's 80-year history, orders that pre-empted even the Federal Aviation Administration's grounding of planes and may have prevented other hijackings. Beyond that, UAL Corp.'s United and AMR Corp.'s American also had to attend to victims' relatives, secure hundreds of stranded airplanes and accommodate tens of thousands of stranded passengers and crew.

"I remember thinking, I'm in one of those B-movies, with a script so bizarre no one would believe it. It cannot be happening," says Donald J. Carty, American's chairman and chief executive officer.

Sitting in the middle of a horseshoe of desks surrounded by screens, phones and computers when his hotline began blinking, Mr. Marquis didn't have time to imagine the unimaginable that was about to take place. Calm and quick-thinking, he told others in the operations center of the call he'd just received from a woman who identified herself as Betty Ong, an attendant aboard Flight 11, a Boeing 767 widebody that had left Boston 30 minutes earlier. Fearing a hoax, he called up her personnel record and asked her to verify her employee number and nickname.

She did. This was real.

"Is there a doctor on board?" Mr. Marquis remembers asking.

"No. No doctor," Ms. Ong said.

The plane had been headed to Los Angeles, but it turned south over Albany, N.Y., and began flying erratically, most likely when hijackers were killing the plane's two pilots. FAA air-traffic controllers told American's operation center that they could hear arguing over the plane's radio. Ms. Ong, screaming but still coherent, said the four hijackers had come from first-class seats 2A, 2B, 9A and 9B. The fatally injured passenger was in 10B. The hijackers had hit people with some sort of spray that made her eyes burn. She was having trouble breathing. Mr. Marquis recalls her saying

"Is the plane descending?" Mr. Marquis asked.

"We're starting to descend," Ms. Ong said. "We're starting to descend."

Neither air-traffic controllers nor American's dispatchers could get any response to frantic voice and text messages to the cockpit. Hijackers had turned off the plane's transponder, which identifies an airplane among hundreds of other blips on a radar, but Mr. Marquis had an aide tell the FAA that American had confirmed a hijacking.

"They're going to New York!" Mr. Marquis remembers shouting out. "Call Newark and JFK and tell them to expect a hijacking," he ordered, assuming the hijackers would land the plane. "In my wildest dreams, I was not thinking the plane was going to run into a building." Mr. Marquis says.

A Shocking Announcement

Even as the line to Flight 11 was still open, American's executives were rushing to the operations center to deal with the crisis. Gerard Arpey, American's executive vice president of operations, had been in Boston the day before for his grandmother's funeral, and had arrived at his desk in Fort Worth at 7:15 A.M. CDT to work through a pile of issues that needed attention. The 43-year-old executive called American's operations center to say he couldn't participate in the daily 7:45 A.M. system-wide operations call.

Joe Bertapelle, the manager at American's operations center, told him of Ms. Ong's phone call that had just come in. Mr. Arpey slumped back in his chair and sat stunned for 30 seconds. "Something inside me said this had the ring of truth to it," Mr. Arpey recalls. He called the office of Mr. Carty, who was at home answering e-mails, then hurried to the operations center a few miles west.

As he walked in, he was met immediately by Mr. Bertapelle and Craig Parfitt, manager of American's dispatch operations, a 29-year American veteran nicknamed "Ice Man" for his even keel. Mr. Marquis had confirmed the hijacking, they told Mr. Arpey, and they had to open American's crisis command center, a room perched one floor up in the operations center that is used in the event of crashes, military troop movements and other emergencies.

A page went out to American's top executives and operations personnel: "Confirmed hijacking Flight 11." The regular 7:45 CDT conference call started, but was almost immediately interrupted: "Gentlemen, I have some information here I need to relay," Mr. Bertapelle announced.

The FAA had tagged the radar blip that Flight 11 had become, and it was now isolated on an Aircraft Situation Display, a screen that pictures airplanes based on FAA radar. All eyes watched as the plane headed south. On the screen, the plane showed a squiggly line after its turn near Albany, then it straightened. "All we knew for sure was that he's not going to LAX," said Mr. Bertapelle.

Big centers deal almost daily with unusual events, from bomb scares to blizzards to unruly passengers, and they hold frequent crisis drills. In those few minutes of uncertainty, American's operations experts were trying to anticipate the plane's next move. But they were in new territory here.

At 7:48 A.M. CDT, the radar image stopped moving and showed Flight 11 "frozen" over New York. A blink more, the plane simply vanished from the screen.

Three minutes later, a ramp supervisor at Kennedy airport in New York called to say a plane had flown into a World Trade Center tower. Someone shouted to turn on CNN but the workers realized they didn't get CNN, so they switched to ABC.

Mr. Arpey was on the phone with Mr. Carty. "The press is reporting an airplane hit the World Trade Center. Is that our plane?" Mr. Carty remembers asking.

"I don't know, Don. We confirmed it was hijacked, and was headed south from Boston," Mr. Arpey told him.

Mr. Carty had a bad feeling that it was indeed his plane that had hit the north tower. But when his wife asked him point blank, he replied: "No, it couldn't be... In my brain, I knew. But I couldn't say it," Mr. Carty recalls.

Tension in Chicago

Outside Chicago, at United's SOC, Mike Barber, the duty manager, had his eye on two large new screens that happened to be tuned to CNN. "My God, the World Trade Center's on fire," Mr. Barber remembers blurting out.

Bill Roy, United's SOC director, wheeled to look at the pictures. "It looks like a small airplane," he said to the others. "Maybe they veered off the La Guardia flight path?" But within minutes, United got a call from the FAA saying it was an American Airlines jet.

Mr. Roy called over to the adjacent headquarters building, where Mr. Goodwin, United's chairman and chief executive, was having his morning session with senior officers. Today, he was sitting with Andy Studdert, 45, the chief operating officer; Rono Dutta, United's president, and three or four others.

Maryann Irving, Mr. Studdert's secretary, took Mr. Roy's call and ran to Mr. Goodwin's second-floor office, knocked and burst into the room. "Andy," she said, "Call the SOC. An American plane just went into the World Trade Center."

Mr. Goodwin remembers thinking, "This is rather bizarre," and flipped on the TV.

Mr. Studdert, a former banker who joined United only six years ago, ran across the bridge between the two buildings and entered the SOC, thinking about American: "My God, what they are going to go through?" Upon reaching the command post, he barked out, "Confirm—American into World Trade Center."

A manager at the post had other news: "Boss, we've lost contact with one of our airplanes."

A few minutes later, Doc Miles, the SOC shift manager, received a call from United's maintenance center in San Francisco that is set up to take in-flight calls from flight attendants about broken items in the cabin that need repairs. The mechanic had heard from a female flight attendant on Flight 175, who had said, "Oh my God, the crew has been killed, a flight attendant has been stabbed. We've been hijacked." Then, the line from the plane went dead.

"No, the information we're getting is that it was an American 757," Mr. Miles recalls protesting.

The mechanic insisted, "No, we got a call from a flight attendant on 175."

The dispatcher monitoring Flight 175, a Boeing 767 from Boston to Los Angeles, sent messages by radio and to the cockpit computer, and got no response. At 8:03 CDT, the group—now assembling in the crisis room off the SOC under Mr. Studdert's command—watched as a large, dark jet slammed into the second tower of the World Trade Center.

While United was trying to understand what happened to Flight 175, American's operations experts received a call from the FAA saying that a second American plane, Flight 77 out of Washington-Dulles, had turned off its transponder and turned around. Controllers had lost radio communications with the plane. Without hearing from anyone on the plane, American didn't know its location.

That raised the disaster to a whole new level. Mr. Arpey looked across the crisis room at Ralph Richardi, a vice president in charge of operations planning, and saw his eyes widen in horror. "That was the first time we realized this was something other than a hijacking," Mr. Richardi says.

Mr. Arpey instantly gave an order to ground every American plane in the Northeast that hadn't yet taken off. Within minutes, American got word that United also had an airliner missing and out of contact.

The minute we heard that, we all agreed we needed to ground-stop the whole airline," Mr. Arpey said. At 8:15 A.M. CDT, the order went out on the command center's loudspeaker: No new takeoffs. The decision, though it clearly would lead to monstrous logistical headaches, could save lives. "I never sensed any fear or panic. We were too shell-shocked," says Mr. Arpey.

Meanwhile, United was making similar decisions. Mr. Studdert ordered all international flights frozen on the ground at 8:20. Ten minutes later, United began diverting its domestic flights and putting them on the ground.

Just as these orders were being given, the American command center heard television reports of a plane hitting the south tower of the trade center. Many in the room instantly assumed it was American Flight 777, the missing plane from Washington.

"How did 77 get to New York and we didn't know it?" Mr. Bertapelle recalls shouting.

Mr. Arpey looked at Mr. Carty, who had just arrived. "I said, 'I think we better get everything on the deck and shut down the whole airline.'"

Mr. Carty replied: "Do it."

Bringing Them Down Quickly

American ordered planes to land at the nearest suitable airport. It activated crash teams to deal with the accident and the families of passengers and began beefing up security at American's headquarters and major stations. Mr. Carty called his counterpart at United, Mr. Goodwin. Each man told the other he thought he had a second missing plane. "We focused entirely on what was transpiring—the physical takeover of our planes," recalls Mr. Goodwin.

Mr. Carty and Mr. Goodwin also were talking on the phone with Secretary of Transportation Norman Mineta, who was in a government command bunker with Vice President Dick Cheney. Mr. Carty told Mr. Mineta that American was ordering all 162 of its planes out of the sky; United already had ordered its 122 planes down, too. About five minutes later, the FAA shut down the skies over the U.S. completely to all but military aircraft.

At 8:45 a.m. CDT, American lost contact with a third flight, a Boston-to-Seattle trip. Everyone in the room was convinced it was a third hijacking. But it turned out to be a radio glitch, and the panic ended when radio contact was restored in 10 minutes.

Soon, reports began pouring in that a plane had crashed into the Pentagon. Maybe it was the missing United plane? American still believed its Flight 77 had gone into the second World Trade Center tower. The command center ordered a plane readied to take crisis response teams to New York to assist investigators and relatives of passengers.

Capt. Ed Soliday, United's vice president of safety and security, talked to AMR Vice Chairman Bob Baker trying to sort out the confusion. "We did not want to mislead families and loved ones," said Capt. Soliday. "American was really pressing us. They thought our airplane had crashed in Washington, and that both their planes had crashed at the World Trade Center. We weren't sure." Finally, he and Mr. Baker agreed the government should make the final confirmation.

Mr. Carty recalls quizzing Mr. Mineta for confirmation of which plane had hit the Pentagon. "I was frustrated. I remember saying, 'For God's sake, it's in the Pentagon. Can't somebody go look at it and see whose plane it is?'"

"They have," Mr. Mineta responded, according to Mr. Carty's recollection. The problem, Mr. Mineta told him: "You can't tell."

At about 8:30 CDT, air-traffic controllers and United lost contact with United Flight 93, a 757 bound from Newark to San Francisco. The dispatcher who had handled Flight 175 had been sending messages to all 13 of his assigned flights that were airborne, instructing them to land at the nearest United station because of two World Trade Center crashes. One flight didn't answer: Flight 93.

The dispatcher, a 42-year veteran of United still so shaken by the tragedy he asked that his name not be used, kept firing messages, but there was no response.

In the United crisis center, managers isolated Flight 93 on the big Aircraft Situation Display screen. The plane had made a wide U-turn over Ohio and seemed to be heading toward Washington. Everyone in the room by now knew that a flight attendant on board had called the mechanics desk to report that one hijacker had a bomb strapped on and another was holding a knife on the crew. There also were reports that passengers were calling their families from cell phones and seatback air phones.

"This was worse because we watched it until the end of the radar track. . . and then, poof," says Mr. Roy, director of system operations control. "We didn't have time to cry." That was at 9:03 A.M. CDT.

After Flight 93 crashed, Mr. Studdert dispatched Pete McDonald, United's senior vice president of airport services, to Pennsylvania. Mr. McDonald had himself been in the air on a flight that was diverted from Washington's National Airport to Dulles. Because the no-fly order made flying to the crash site uncertain, Mr. McDonald recruited 40 United volunteers at Dulles, all trained in humanitarian relief duties, rounded up eight vans and cars, and set off at noon. In Pennsylvania, two state trooper squad cars met the caravan to give it a speedy escort.

After reaching the site, Mr. McDonald went up in a helicopter to take a look and all he could see was "very small pieces" of debris, since the plane itself was deep in the trench it created when it crashed.

With each twist and turn, airline officials also had the grisly task of trying to understand who was on board and who the hijackers were. Early on, American officials pulled up computerized passenger lists from Flights 11 and 77. With seat numbers from flight attendant's call, they quickly identified suspects. United, working with the FBI, did the same. Other Middle Eastern names jumped out, and as calls poured in from worried relatives, they quickly realized that they hadn't gotten calls for those very passengers.

The tally: 19 hijackers, 213 passengers, eight pilots and 25 flight attendants.

'Biting Our Nails'

Within two hours, all of United's and American's domestic flights were on the ground and accounted for. Late in the afternoon, however, United still had some planes over the Pacific. These were nerve-wracking times. United said it had to press hard on Canadian authorities and even Alaskan airport officials who initially refused to let the planes land. "Until we got the last airplanes on the ground, we were biting our fingers," CEO Mr. Goodwin recalls. "By then, we were spooked. Every time we got an unusual communication from an airplane, we thought, 'my God, is there another one?'"

Once all planes were safely on the ground, the airlines sat stunned at the logistical quagmire before them. They would have to figure out where each of their hundreds of planes were and how to get tens of thousands of stranded passengers back to their destinations.

They had to instantly create new security procedures. The days would turn into a blur of conference calls to regulators. Plans constantly changed. There was no time to go home and watch TV reports, no time to reflect.

For many in the command center that day, grief was delayed for days, if not weeks, by the workload. "Some of the reality of what happened both to our country and our company didn't set in until much later," says Mr. Arpey, who stayed in the crisis center all through the night.

Mr. Studdert, Mr. Arpey's counterpart at United, got a call three days after the terrorist attacks from an old friend. "How you doing, kid?" the friend asked. "There is no kid left in me anymore," Mr. Studdert replied. "I'll never be the same person. We'll never be the same company or the same country."

For most, going home brought the first real emotional shock. "It hit me when I first looked in my kids faces," pictures of shock and sorrow, says Kyle Phelps, manager of administration for the operations center and a 27-year veteran with American.

Mr. Parfitt, the "Ice Man," says it didn't hit him until much later, when he began to realize that his son in the Army might be headed to war. "The grief for the people on the airplanes, for the crews, for the people of New York in the World Trade Center is all-encompassing," Mr. Parfitt says.

Mr. Bertapelle says that when he is home now he craves the Comedy Channel, hungry for a laugh. On the Friday after the hijacking, Mr. Carty came on American's intercom system, piped through its headquarters, operations center, flight academy and other facilities, to observe a moment of silence. "That's the first time I remember just stopping to think about it," Mr. Bertapelle said. "Any moment of silence is hell."

Some now are angry. Others say their emotions are frozen much like the radar image of the plane flying over New York, only to disappear.

Mr. Marquis, who talked with flight attendant Betty Ong, says he's met twice with a psychologist. He hasn't had a real night of sleep since. "It's still like a dream," he says. "I've been through lots of stuff before, but nothing like this."

The United dispatcher who handled both Flight 175 and Flight 93 stayed at his post on Sept. 11 and helped the remaining planes under his watch land. Then, he says, "I went home and got drunk," after running several red lights in the stress of the moment. He took three days off and availed himself of a company counselor. When the counselor said, "It's OK to cry, I broke down" the man says.

It's been touch and go since. The dispatcher says he won't watch TV. "My wife had a dream she was seated on an airplane with her wrists bound, along with all the other passengers," he says, weeping. "The hijackers were walking down the aisle, slashing throats."

The dispatcher, who has worked some days and taken off some, says he takes solace in talking to colleagues who have lost friends in wartime. "When we're busy, I like it," he says. But then he is reminded again of what happened, like when a United pilot recently told him, "Your name is all over this airline," as word spread of who handled both doomed flights.

The man wept again in the interview. "Something inside me died," he said.

The State of the Union, September 20, 2001

Editor's Comment: Yes, Americans were asking "Why do they hate us?" and "What is expected of us?" In this well-received and unusual "State of the Union" speech to Congress and the American people, President George W. Bush gave some answers to these questions, and more. We reprint the speech here in its entirety.

Mr. Speaker, Mr. President Pro Tempore, members of Congress, and fellow Americans:

In the normal course of events, Presidents come to this chamber to report on the state of the Union. Tonight, no such report is needed. It has already been delivered by the American people.

We have seen it in the courage of passengers, who rushed terrorists to save others on the ground—passengers like an exceptional man named Todd Beamer. And would you please help me to welcome his wife, Lisa Beamer, here tonight. *(Applause.)*

We have seen the state of our Union in the endurance of rescuers, working past exhaustion. We have seen the unfurling of flags, the lighting of candles, the giving of blood, the saying of prayers—in English, Hebrew, and Arabic. We have seen the decency of a loving and giving people who have made the grief of strangers their own.

My fellow citizens, for the last nine days, the entire world has seen for itself the state of our Union—and it is strong. *(Applause.)*

Tonight we are a country awakened to danger and called to defend freedom. Our grief has turned to anger, and anger to resolution. Whether we bring our enemies to justice, or bring justice to our enemies, justice will be done. *(Applause.)*

I thank the Congress for its leadership at such an important time. All of America was touched on the evening of the tragedy to see Republicans and Democrats joined together on the steps of this Capitol, singing "God Bless America." And you did more than sing; you acted, by delivering $40 billion to rebuild our communities and meet the needs of our military.

Speaker Hastert, Minority Leader Gephardt, Majority Leader Daschle and Senator Lott, I thank you for your friendship, for your leadership and for your service to our country. *(Applause.)*

And on behalf of the American people, I thank the world for its outpouring of support. America will never forget the sounds of our National Anthem playing at Buckingham Palace, on the streets of Paris, and at Berlin's Brandenburg Gate.

We will not forget South Korean children gathering to pray outside our embassy in Seoul, or the prayers of sympathy offered at a mosque in Cairo. We will not forget moments of silence and days of mourning in Australia and Africa and Latin America.

Nor will we forget the citizens of 80 other nations who died with our own: dozens of Pakistanis; more than 130 Israelis; more than 250 citizens of India; men and women from El Salvador, Iran, Mexico and Japan; and hundreds of British citizens. America has no truer friend than Great Britain. *(Applause.)* Once again, we are joined together in a great cause—so honored the British Prime Minister has crossed an ocean to show his unity of purpose with America. Thank you for coming, friend. *(Applause.)*

On September 11th, enemies of freedom committed an act of war against our country. Americans have known wars—but for the past 136 years, they have been wars on foreign soil, except for one Sunday in 1941. Americans have known the casualties of war—but not at the center of a great city on a peaceful morning.

Source: "Address to a Joint Session of Congress and the American People" at The United States Capitol, Washington, DC by President George W. Bush, September 20, 2001, 9:00 P.M. Public information download from the White House website, in accordance with guidelines from the White House Office of Media Affairs.

Americans have known surprise attacks—but never before on thousands of civilians. All of this was brought upon us in a single day—and night fell on a different world, a world where freedom itself is under attack.

Americans have many questions tonight. Americans are asking: Who attacked our country? The evidence we have gathered all points to a collection of loosely affiliated terrorist organizations known as al Qaeda. They are the same murderers indicted for bombing American embassies in Tanzania and Kenya, and responsible for bombing the USS Cole.

Al Qaeda is to terror what the mafia is to crime. But its goal is not making money; its goal is remaking the world—and imposing its radical beliefs on people everywhere.

The terrorists practice a fringe form of Islamic extremism that has been rejected by Muslim scholars and the vast majority of Muslim clerics—a fringe movement that perverts the peaceful teachings of Islam. The terrorists' directive commands them to kill Christians and Jews, to kill all Americans, and make no distinction among military and civilians, including women and children.

This group and its leader—a person named Osama bin Laden—are linked to many other organizations in different countries, including the Egyptian Islamic Jihad and the Islamic Movement of Uzbekistan. There are thousands of these terrorists in more than 60 countries. They are recruited from their own nations and neighborhoods and brought to camps in places like Afghanistan, where they are trained in the tactics of terror. They are sent back to their homes or sent to hide in countries around the world to plot evil and destruction.

The leadership of al Qaeda has great influence in Afghanistan and supports the Taliban regime in controlling most of that country. In Afghanistan, we see al Qaeda's vision for the world.

Afghanistan's people have been brutalized—many are starving and many have fled. Women are not allowed to attend school. You can be jailed for owning a television. Religion can be practiced only as their leaders dictate. A man can be jailed in Afghanistan if his beard is not long enough.

The United States respects the people of Afghanistan—after all, we are currently its largest source of humanitarian aid—but we condemn the Taliban regime. *(Applause.)* It is not only repressing its own people, it is threatening people everywhere by sponsoring and sheltering and supplying terrorists. By aiding and abetting murder, the Taliban regime is committing murder.

And tonight, the United States of America makes the following demands on the Taliban: Deliver to the United States authorities all the leaders of al Qaeda who hide in your land. *(Applause.)* Release all foreign nationals, including American citizens, you have unjustly imprisoned. Protect foreign journalists, diplomats and aid workers in your country. Close immediately and permanently every terrorist training camp in Afghanistan, and hand over every terrorist, and every person in their support structure, to appropriate authorities. *(Applause.)* Give the United States full access to terrorist training camps, so we can make sure they are no longer operating.

These demands are not open to negotiation or discussion. *(Applause.)* The Taliban must act, and act immediately. They will hand over the terrorists, or they will share in their fate.

I also want to speak tonight directly to Muslims throughout the world. We respect your faith. It's practiced freely by many millions of Americans, and by millions more in countries that America counts as friends. Its teachings are good and peaceful, and those who commit evil in the name of Allah blaspheme the name of Allah. *(Applause.)* The terrorists are traitors to their own faith, trying, in effect, to hijack Islam itself. The enemy of America is not our many Muslim friends; it is not our many Arab friends. Our enemy is a radical network of terrorists, and every government that supports them. *(Applause.)*

Our war on terror begins with Al Qaeda, but it does not end there. It will not end until every terrorist group of global reach has been found, stopped and defeated. *(Applause.)*

Americans are asking, why do they hate us? They hate what we see right here in this chamber—a democratically elected government. Their leaders are self-appointed. They hate our freedoms—our freedom of religion, our freedom of speech, our freedom to vote and assemble and disagree with each other.

They want to overthrow existing governments in many Muslim countries, such as Egypt, Saudi Arabia, and Jordan. They want to drive Israel out of the Middle East. They want to drive Christians and Jews out of vast regions of Asia and Africa.

These terrorists kill not merely to end lives, but to disrupt and end a way of life. With every atrocity, they hope that America grows fearful, retreating from the world and forsaking our friends. They stand against us, because we stand in their way.

We are not deceived by their pretenses to piety. We have seen their kind before. They are the heirs of all the murderous ideologies of the 20th century. By sacrificing human life to serve their radical visions—by abandoning every value except the will to power—they follow in the path of fascism, and Nazism, and totalitarianism. And they will follow that path all the way, to where it ends: in history's unmarked grave of discarded lies. *(Applause.)*

Americans are asking: How will we fight and win this war? We will direct every resource at our command—every means of diplomacy, every tool of intelligence, every instrument of law enforcement, every financial influence, and every necessary weapon of war—to the disruption and to the defeat of the global terror network.

This war will not be like the war against Iraq a decade ago, with a decisive liberation of territory and a swift conclusion. It will not look like the air war above Kosovo two years ago, where no ground troops were used and not a single American was lost in combat.

Our response involves far more than instant retaliation and isolated strikes. Americans should not expect one battle, but a lengthy campaign, unlike any other we have ever seen. It may include dramatic strikes, visible on TV, and covert operations, secret even in success. We will starve terrorists of funding, turn them one against another, drive them from place to place, until there is no refuge or no rest. And we will pursue nations that provide aid or safe haven to terrorism. Every nation, in every region, now has a decision to make. Either you are with us, or you are with the terrorists. *(Applause.)* From this day forward, any nation that continues to harbor or support terrorism will be regarded by the United States as a hostile regime.

Our nation has been put on notice: We are not immune from attack. We will take defensive measures against terrorism to protect Americans. Today, dozens of federal departments and agencies, as well as state and local governments, have responsibilities affecting homeland security. These efforts must be coordinated at the highest level. So tonight I announce the creation of a Cabinet-level position reporting directly to me—the Office of Homeland Security.

And tonight I also announce a distinguished American to lead this effort, to strengthen American security: a military veteran, an effective governor, a true patriot, a trusted friend—Pennsylvania's Tom Ridge. *(Applause.)* He will lead, oversee and coordinate a comprehensive national strategy to safeguard our country against terrorism, and respond to any attacks that may come.

These measures are essential. But the only way to defeat terrorism as a threat to our way of life is to stop it, eliminate it, and destroy it where it grows. *(Applause.)*

Many will be involved in this effort, from FBI agents to intelligence operatives to the reservists we have called to active duty. All deserve our thanks, and all have our prayers. And tonight, a few miles from the damaged Pentagon, I have a message for our military: Be ready. I've called the Armed Forces to alert, and there is a reason. The hour is coming when America will act, and you will make us proud. *(Applause.)*

This is not, however, just America's fight. And what is at stake is not just America's freedom. This is the world's fight. This is civilization's fight. This is the fight of all who believe in progress and pluralism, tolerance and freedom.

We ask every nation to join us. We will ask, and we will need, the help of police forces, intelligence services, and banking systems around the world. The United States is grateful that many nations and many international organizations have already responded—with sympathy and support. Nations from Latin America, to Asia, to Africa, to Europe, to the Islamic world. Perhaps the NATO Charter reflects best the attitude of the world: An attack on one is an attack on all.

The civilized world is rallying to America's side. They understand that if this terror goes unpunished, their own cities, their own citizens may be next. Terror, unanswered, can not only bring down buildings, it can threaten the stability of legitimate governments. And you know what—we're not going to allow it. *(Applause.)*

Americans are asking: What is expected of us? I ask you to live your lives, and hug your children. I know many citizens have fears tonight, and I ask you to be calm and resolute, even in the face of a continuing threat.

I ask you to uphold the values of America, and remember why so many have come here. We are in a fight for our principles, and our first responsibility is to live by them. No one should be singled out for unfair treatment or unkind words because of their ethnic background or religious faith. *(Applause.)*

I ask you to continue to support the victims of this tragedy with your contributions. Those who want to give can go to a central source of information, libertyunites.org, to find the names of groups providing direct help in New York, Pennsylvania, and Virginia.

The thousands of FBI agents who are now at work in this investigation may need your cooperation, and I ask you to give it.

I ask for your patience, with the delays and inconveniences that may accompany tighter security; and for your patience in what will be a long struggle.

I ask your continued participation and confidence in the American economy. Terrorists attacked a symbol of American prosperity. They did not touch its source. America is successful because of the hard work, and creativity, and enterprise of our people. These were the true strengths of our economy before September 11th, and they are our strengths today. *(Applause.)*

And, finally, please continue praying for the victims of terror and their families, for those in uniform, and for our great country. Prayer has comforted us in sorrow, and will help strengthen us for the journey ahead.

Tonight I thank my fellow Americans for what you have already done and for what you will do. And ladies and gentlemen of the Congress, I thank you, their representatives, for what you have already done and for what we will do together.

Tonight, we face new and sudden national challenges. We will come together to improve air safety, to dramatically expand the number of air marshals on domestic flights, and take new measures to prevent hijacking. We will come together to promote stability and keep our airlines flying, with direct assistance during this emergency. *(Applause.)*

We will come together to give law enforcement the additional tools it needs to track down terror here at home. *(Applause.)* We will come together to strengthen our intelligence capabilities to know the plans of terrorists before they act, and find them before they strike. *(Applause.)*

We will come together to take active steps that strengthen America's economy, and put our people back to work.

Tonight we welcome two leaders who embody the extraordinary spirit of all New Yorkers: Governor George Pataki, and Mayor Rudolph Giuliani. *(Applause.)* As a symbol of America's resolve, my administration will work with Congress, and these two leaders, to show the world that we will rebuild New York City. *(Applause.)*

After all that has just passed—all the lives taken, and all the possibilities and hopes that died with them—it is natural to wonder if America's future is one of fear. Some speak of an age of terror. I know there are struggles ahead, and dangers to face. But this country will define our times, not be defined by them. As long as the United States of America is determined and strong, this will not be an age of terror; this will be an age of liberty, here and across the world. *(Applause.)*

Great harm has been done to us. We have suffered great loss. And in our grief and anger we have found our mission and our moment. Freedom and fear are at war. The advance of human freedom—the great achievement of our time, and the great hope of every time—now depends on us. Our nation—this generation—will lift a dark threat of violence from our people and our future. We will rally the world to this cause by our efforts, by our courage. We will not tire, we will not falter, and we will not fail. *(Applause.)*

It is my hope that in the months and years ahead, life will return almost to normal. We'll go back to our lives and routines, and that is good. Even grief recedes with time and grace. But our resolve must not pass. Each of us will remember what happened that day, and to whom it happened. We'll remember the moment the news came—where we were and what we were doing. Some will remember an image of a fire, or a story of rescue. Some will carry memories of a face and a voice gone forever.

And I will carry this: It is the police shield of a man named George Howard, who died at the World Trade Center trying to save others. It was given to me by his mom, Arlene, as a proud memorial to her son. This is my reminder of lives that ended, and a task that does not end. *(Applause.)*

I will not forget this wound to our country or those who inflicted it. I will not yield; I will not rest; I will not relent in waging this struggle for freedom and security for the American people.

The course of this conflict is not known, yet its outcome is certain. Freedom and fear, justice and cruelty, have always been at war, and we know that God is not neutral between them. *(Applause.)*

Fellow citizens, we'll meet violence with patient justice—assured of the rightness of our cause, and confident of the victories to come. In all that lies before us, may God grant us wisdom, and may He watch over the United States of America.

Thank you. *(Applause.)*

SECTION 3

Training Program Design

1. **ISD Reborn** 121
   Instructional Design Strategies and Considerations.................................121
   Begin with Projects 124
   Out with the Old: Is It Time to Rethink Instructional Design?...................127
   Liemandt's Feedback for and from New Hires and Customers 131

2. **Big Design Issues in E-Learning** 139
   A Project Manager's Advice: Plan and Communicate................................139
   Mission E-Possible: The Cisco E-Learning Story 140
   Learners Want More Than Technology 149
   E-Learning for Free Agents 152

3. **E-Learning Design Nuts and Bolts** 154
   How Online Course Management Systems Affect the Course...................154
   Shell's Formula for Blending Training Fuels Optimum Learning at Minimum Cost...157
   Knowledge Sharing Using a Knowledge Base..159

4. **Lonesome Online** 161
   Challenge for Designers: The Social Dimensions of Learning 161
   Strategies to Prevent Online Attrition 164
   Know Stuff Versus Do Stuff 167

INTRODUCTION TO TRAINING PROGRAM DESIGN: SECTION 3

Section 3 of *Training & Development Yearbook 2002* reviews four basic design issues in the design of training programs. These four are organized into four subsections. Sub-section 1, "ISD Reborn," includes representative entries illustrating ideas for expanding or redirecting the designer's classic Instructional System Design, now approximately fifty years old. Sub-section 2, "Big Design Issues in E-Learning," includes entries that address the big design issues in e-learning, especially as it is being pushed to incorporate the classroom or other face-to-face interactions. Sub-section 3, "E-Learning Design Nuts and Bolts," deals with issues about the particular design of parts of e-learning and reflects the need for development return on investment. Sub-section 4, "Lonesome Online," takes on the challenges of designing online courses that meet learners' needs for interactivity.

ISD Reborn

For at least a decade, the familiar and successful Instructional System Design (ISD) process with its checks and balances and system orientation has been tampered with in the name of progress. Consultants, professors, and corporate learning leaders have all been playing around with different models for design, and often have been publishing the results of their efforts in the name of ISD evolution. The motivation for systems recreation is often an e-learning effort; often it is simply a return-on-investment driver. The motivation also for many organizations is to be there first with the right combination of substance and style that American businesses love to support and fund. New models of ISD often feature different kinds of needs analysis, focusing more heavily on the cognitive and problem-solving needs of individuals as well as of organizations. Constructivist principles of building knowledge are popular, rather than the somewhat linear conceptualization of traditional ISD. A typical article about reconceptualization of ISD is that found in *Educational Technology*, March–April 2001, p. 16, using these terms: "We employ an adaptive ISD approach to draw on the sociocultural theory and constructivist perspectives in conceptualizing the design and assessment of learner-centered sites."

Since most of e-learning involves an advanced level of student capability and intuition about software and hardware, the role of the learning support and technical support personnel is given more prominence in newer representations of ISD. Structure of content and information processing are important in newer ways. This year especially we've seen a number of references to the overuse of PowerPoint slides, and the notion that just because it's available and easy, doesn't mean it's right for the job. In fact, Allison Rossett, needs assessment guru, is presenting a pre-conference workshop at Elliott Masie's TechLearn 2001 October conference in Orlando, FL with the catchy title, "Beyond Multimediocrity: A Tour of Instructional Design Basics." John Magruder, President of 4D Productions, Inc., Tampa, FL in *ONLINE LEARNING NEWS*, August 30, 2001, pp.1–3 cautioned the e-newsletter's online readers to be careful when putting a paper course onto the Web; it's not just a matter of keyboarding the text into a Website and throwing in some animation and video. Magruder also cautions project managers to "fight 'feature creep'" of last minute design changes that typically delay a training design project. Assuring quality of finished designs is becoming a business in itself, and is a natural spinoff of new approaches to ISD. Businesses, colleges, and consulting agencies are all getting into the act of certification. ASTD itself began a certification initiative, the "e-learning course certification (eCC)" program by which it gives a stamp of approval to courses developed by third parties—consultancies, businesses, colleges, other publishers. ASTD's fees are charged to course publishers at the following rate: $1,500 for up to two hours of instruction; $3,000 for two – six hours of instruction, and so on. Many consultancies are developing courses according to the federal government's SCORM standards. Universities offering online degrees are wrestling with how and how much to charge students and to pay faculties, and whether or not online students should ever be integrated with face-to-face students in classrooms. *US News & World Report*, April 9, 2001, p. 67 reported that being a part-time online student is seldom a bargain, using University of California-Berkeley's Haas School of Business as an example. Haas charges part-timers $64,000 and full-timers $21,000 for an online MBA. A *Yahoo! News* brief on August 15, 2001 noted that college graduates earn 81 percent more than those with only high school diplomas (Leslie Gervirtz, *Reuters*), so the universities seem to be taking a prudent risk in their pricing structure. Clearly there's money to be made in e-learning, after the instructional design issues, and ISD itself, are debated and settled.

Big Design Issues in E-Learning

These next two sub-sections look at the specific issues of design in e-learning, one section from the point of view of the big issues, and the other section from the perspective of the nuts and bolts issues that face instructional designers.

One of the big issues is the involvement of customers in company-developed e-learning. The hardware and software seem simple enough to share with customers, but companies are experimenting with what kind and how much of e-learning courseware the customer should be able to access, and what kind and how much of a company's technical support personnel and systems should be available to customers. How should the "customer learning system" integrate with the "employee learning system"?

Do e-learning courses need to be designed differently for customers than they do for employees? And if so, is the design cost duplication worth it? Estimates vary from 250:1 to 400:1; that is, it takes 250 hours of development time for every 1 hour of e-learning (or 400 hours to 1 hour), not including project management, creating graphics, writing scripts, gathering content, quality testing, and other tasks preliminary to putting an e-learning course together in its final format (*TDFeNet*, online newsletter, October 10, 2001, pp. 1–3).

The other major big design issue is the issue of perspective and metaphor. Like the redefinition of ISD, there seems to be an attempt to redefine the classroom. No one seems yet to be willing to give up the strengths of classroom learning, in spite of its cost and sometimes inefficiency in terms of learning. However, there seems to be a need for the field to re-think what learning is all about, and to re-define what learners like about the classroom and give it a new name. Playing around in an instructional Website is not the same as wandering through a library, although both experiences might be learning. The problem seems to be that the metaphors of "the course" are not quite appropriate for e-learning experiences. Designers run into trouble when they use one for the other. Designers and learners both are beginning to speak out about this. E-learners want community, but not necessarily the impersonal community of a college lecture hall. They want appropriate cognitive content online, with e-coaches or e-labs easily available for problem-solving assistance. Designers and learners want an online learning process that works.

E-Learning Design Nuts and Bolts

The training magazines and online newsletters during 2001 have been full of talk about the design details—threaded discussion versus chat, e-mail that supports a learning objective, best use of synchronous learning opportunities, asynchronous training that isn't boring, the size and character of a learning object, shared and reusable resources, downlinks and bandwidth, among many other "nuts and bolts" of training design. *E-Learning* magazine, April 2001, pp. 34–35, featured a short column about e-learning in the National Guard. After wowing the reader with the number of 500,000 potential Guard e-learning soldier students, the article tells of the phased-in schedule for putting courses online, beginning with 1,200 asynchronous courses including information technology training, human resources and soft skills, and job performance improvement. These were followed by 25 courses focusing on National Guard job-specific skills. Over the next five years, 90 more courses that currently require some residency will be put online, reducing the cost of classroom training significantly and reaching a much broader skilled and geographically dispersed learner base. The National Guard, as others, made a design decision early about which courses were appropriate to put online.

Course designers are talking about re-using navigation bars, backgrounds, tables of contents, certain step-by-step procedures, key chunks of information, certain graphics, to name just a few. Interactivity, usability, connectivity, collaboration, exploration, multisensory, simulation—these are just a few of the new terms and concepts instructional designers deal with in developing e-learning. Tagging, indexing, searching, and repositing are all management terms given a new meaning with online learning. Designers get involved in this part of e-learning design too; and like the issue of classroom metaphors, designers have to deal with appropriate management metaphors for e-courses and e-curriculums.

Lonesome Online

The October 2001 issue of *Workforce* magazine ran a major article called "Why Online Learners Drop Out." Numerous training publications from the beginning of the year have carried similar articles. From the beginning of online learning, studies of "completers-leavers" have pondered the same question.

Most people who try to analyze the situation or offer suggestions as to why the dropout rate averages 10 to 20 percent higher than for face to face courses (*Workforce*, October 2001, p. 53) conclude that one very big emotional reason plays a major part in the statistics. That is the fact that it is lonely online. In this final subsection of Section 3, "Training Program Design," we reprint three articles that look at this subject from different points of view.

1. ISD Reborn

Instructional Design Strategies and Considerations

Editor's Comment: We excerpt here the final portion of a long article in one of the journals of the Learning Technology Institute (LTI). The author is concerned with "information literacy" and the barriers that have an impact on adult learning. This final section of Mr. Amidon's work focuses on design strategies. Although these instructional design strategies were written to apply to learning by computer, the concept of preventing or removing barriers to learning through instructional design applies to all kinds of intentionally designed learning opportunities.

In this section we will look at various design strategies and considerations which, when incorporated in the instructional material, will help minimize the impact of barriers to adult learning, information literacy, and lifelong learning.

Anchor all learning activities to a larger task. Adults need to be able to integrate new ideas with what they already know and see how this new insight relates to the big picture of what they are working towards. This will help them retain and use the new information (Zemke, 1984).

Support the learner in developing ownership of the task. The focus of technology training should not be limited to the mastery of isolated procedures, but rather should help workers develop an understanding of what they are doing and why they are doing it. This increased understanding will foster buy-in by the learner.

Design an authentic task. Treat the adult learner with respect. Adults are relevancy-oriented. Avoid any content that is insignificant, annoying, or degrading.

Design the task to reflect the complexity of the environment the learner will face. Adults are practical. Focus on the aspects of the lesson that are most useful to the learner in his job and present it at an appropriate level of difficulty.

Self pacing. Adults prefer to be self-directed, work at their own pace, and control start and stop times (Zemke, 1984). For older learners, extra time should be factored in for the completion of tasks (extend time for exams to time and a half). As people read at different rates, do not display information that disappears after a short time that can't be retrieved (Kilby, 1999).

Instructional objectives stated initially to the learner. Adults are goal-oriented. For optimal success, the adult learner needs to understand what he is supposed to learn in each area. This can be accomplished by stating realistic goals at the beginning of each section. This, balanced by identified measurable samples of behavior, will tell the learner when he has mastered a particular skill. Most importantly, set realistic goals and ensure the learner understands the purpose of the task.

Abandon linear thinking and design by letting the learner select his/her own path of learning and/or inquiry. Page-turners can be boring. Include interaction, variety, and perhaps even some surprises to keep the learner's attention and interest. Navigation and the ability to

Source: "Designing Interactive Multimedia Instruction to Enable and Enhance Information Literacy" by Leslie E. Amidon in *Journal of Interactive Instruction Development*, Spring 2001, pp. 30–32. Leslie E. Amidon is a Senior Analyst and Interactive Multimedia Instructional Designer for MCR Federal, Inc., a company of AT&T. Excerpt reprinted with permission of *Journal of Interactive Instruction Development*. Copyright 2001. All rights reserved.

know where you are within the program are very important.

Privacy and comfort. Learning is most likely to be effective when it is conducted in a comfortable learning atmosphere free from noise and distraction. This can be accomplished by selecting appropriate furniture, the use of headphones, and the use of proper lighting and environmental controls.

Individualized attention/instruction. Individualized instruction is easier using computers since materials and presentation formats can be customized to suit different learning styles, interests, and/or workplace needs. (Lovell, 1999). Use a variety of techniques. People learn in a variety of ways (visual, textual, verbal, etc.). Pay particular attention to each activity to ensure learners with different learning styles will benefit equally (Kilby, 1999).

Small steps. Avoid information overload. Much effort must be placed on "chunking" the information, culling it down to the essential and presenting it in discrete informational units. This establishes a more immediate sense of accomplishment.

Active learning through frequent student interaction. Engage the learner. Some learners find that their motivation is sustained because of engaging and interesting interaction made possible through the use of computers (Lovell, 1999). Keep in mind that your design goal should be to encourage intellectual interaction, not simply to include lots of click areas (Kilby, 1999). Some examples of the types of interactivity which can be included are:

- *Browsing*—Content exploration
- *Branching*—Moving to a different point in the curriculum based on some action (survey questions of test results)
- *Help*—Help button or virtual tutor during practice activities
- *Practice*—Interactive practice activities
- *Coaching*—Practice activities with immediate answer judging and feedback
- *Printing*—Lesson content can be printed allowing the learner to take materials on temporary assignments away from the home unit or compile personal study material directly from the course.

Immediate reinforcement/feedback. Avoid being judgmental. Meaningful feedback to user actions reinforces a concept and hardens the foundation for further learning. Be careful not to set the user up to fail by using emotional colors such as red or phrases such as "No, stupid. Bad choice." to indicate incorrect responses. (Kilby, 1999). In contrast, offer positive feedback often. However, don't overdo it or it will become ineffective.

Opportunity for repetition. Provide exercises that can be repeated until mastery has been achieved. Ensure more than one type of exercise is available to aid in understanding of the course material (McNeely, 1991).

Use of multimedia. Never use multimedia elements in your courseware just because you can. Ensure that you choose your media types based upon the learning objectives. You are more likely to produce an impressive product by making rational choices of media types. This is especially true when downloading or taking courses over the Internet. Long download times of insignificant information can be very annoying (Kilby, 1999). Be aware, the glitziest technology is rarely the most appropriate or most effective choice to use in support of adult learning (Stites, 1998; NCAL 1999). Although not a panacea, the images, video and sounds available via technology are of particular help to those adult learners who do not possess basic communication skills (Lovell, 1999).

Test courseware on real users. Avoid creating barriers to effective learning by testing your designs on real users. Thorough testing of courseware prior to release helps maintain your professional credibility.

Ease of Use. Learners will be more productive if the courseware is well liked, easy to learn, and contains the right functions (Nelson, 2000). Indicators of ease of use include the presence of effective helps, a high degree of user friendliness and user control. These indicators are especially important concerns for adult learners with low-level language, literacy, and numeracy skills (Stites, 1998).

Readability versus irritability. Since it is neither easy nor necessarily pleasant to read from a computer monitor, readability is an important factor. The educational material should be presented in small chunks of information. Sentences should be short, as well as paragraphs.

Also, people get irritated when having to scroll through reams of material.

Screen Design. Screen design should be uncluttered and standardized to provide unambiguous navigational symbology, and thus increase readability and reduce learner confusion. This can be accomplished through the development of standardized templates. These templates reduce development time, and increase standardization of the look and feel of the program. Avoid complex graphical user interfaces (GUI). Stick to a constant location and function for all controls, buttons, navigation, etc. limited to only those items needed.

REFERENCES

Kilby, Tim (1999). *Rules for Good Web-Based Training Design.* (http://www.filename.com/wbt/pages/rules.htm)

Lovell, Mary. (1999). *Instructional Technology.* (http://www.ed.gov/offices/OVAE/AdultEd/InfoBoard/f-18html) Washington D.C: Office of Vocational and Adult Education, Division of Adult Education and Literacy.

McNeely, E. (1991). "Computer assisted instruction and the older adult learner." *Educational Gerontology.* 17(3) 229-237.

Nelson, Mark R. (2000). "We have the information you want, but getting it will cost you: Being held hostage by information overload." *Crossroads.* (http://info.acm.org/crossroads/xrds1-1/mnelson.html).

Stites, Regie. (1998). *Assessing Lifelong Learning Technology: A Guide for Choosing and Using Technology for Adult Learning (NCAL Report No. PG98-01).* Philadelphia: International Literacy Institute, National Center on Adult Literacy, Graduate School of Education, University of Pennsylvania.

Zemke, Ron and Susan. (1984). "30 things we know for sure about adult learning." *Innovation Abstracts.* National Institute for Staff and Organizational Development. Vol. VI, No. 8.

Begin with Projects

Editor's Comment: In this interview with Tamar Elkeles, a manager/designer on the front lines at QUALCOMM, editor Tammy Galvin probes just what it is that motivates and enables Elkeles to create a learning organization. In this "In Person" feature of *TRAINING Magazine*, there are numerous helpful, practical ideas from one who's tried them. Among other things, Elkeles encourages managers and instructional designers to move beyond skill development and facilitating personal growth into more strategic areas of the business like marketing and communication. One of the ways to do this is to view instructional design as a "project," and apply standards and processes of project management to instructional design work.

INTERVIEW WITH TAMAR ELKELES: VICE PRESIDENT OF LEARNING, QUALCOMM

Fresh out of graduate school, a master's degree in hand, Tamar Elkeles joined QUALCOMM to create a training and employee development department for the then 7-year-old company. A daunting task, indeed, especially for a doctorate student intern making just $9 an hour.

The year was 1992, and QUALCOMM's employee base was 700 and growing—adding upwards of 100 workers a week. Sustaining that growth, as well as the entrepreneurial spirit upon which the company was founded, demanded a multitasking, highly energetic individual capable of harnessing the current and future influx of human capital. And that's exactly what QUALCOMM found in Elkeles, who is aptly described as an "espresso bean" by her employees and professional peers alike.

One need only speak with her for a few minutes or peruse her resume to fully understand that label. Rapidly firing off what sounds like hundreds of words a second in an almost lyrical tone, Elkeles exudes a definite passion for all things learning. And she has definitely accomplished a great deal in the last 10 years. The one-person employee development department she spearheaded as an intern is now the Learning Center, staffed with 30 "learning specialists," who, under her tutelage, serve more than 7,000 QUALCOMM employees.

Unlike many companies that in recent years have jumped on the "learning, not training" bandwagon, QUALCOMM's employee development initiatives have always been learner-centric, says Elkeles. "Throughout the early '90s, much of my initial time and energy was spent identifying, creating and implementing not only the skill-building and culture-maintaining programs needed, but also assessing the various learning styles and preferences of our employees."

What she learned in those assessments and climate surveys came as no surprise. QUALCOMM has a highly educated employee base with a large concentration of engineers who don't like attending classroom sessions. Given the company's rapid growth, employees also don't like to take time away from their jobs to attend classes. Rather, they want to maximize their time by learning from true experts, and they want multiple options for learning the material.

Consequently, when most companies were embracing CD-ROMs and classrooms as preferred delivery methods, Elkeles entered the fledgling e-learning game in 1995 by building an "online training network," which, by today's standards, would be aptly described as a cross between

---

Source: "Tamar Elkeles: Vice President of Learning, QUALCOMM" by Tammy Galvin in *TRAINING Magazine*, May 2001, pp. 44, 46, 48. Tammy Galvin is Editor of *TRAINING Magazine*. Reprinted with permission of *TRAINING Magazine*. Copyright 2001. All rights reserved.

> "If you take away all of the fluff of the information, like, 'this is how you plan a project,' and begin with actual projects being worked on, you get a lot further, a lot faster."

a learning management system and a virtual university.

Elkeles supplemented every classroom program with online components, or tools, which range from job aides to pre- and post-class assignments; online resources such as checksheets and assessments to a list of reference books, videos, and the like. In recent years, she added online courses, several of which were created in-house, along with about 250 courses from SmartForce.

"At QUALCOMM we value diversity, we value differences, and that includes learning styles," Elkeles says. "So we want to make sure that every program or topic we offer has multiple delivery choices—classroom, online, online tools/job aides and reference materials like books and videos. So more often than not, an employee will see all four methods, or a combination thereof, listed for a given topic."

So successful has the program become that, over the years, other companies have approached QUALCOMM wanting to buy the "product." Elkeles' response: "We don't sell training."

Nor has Elkeles' intent ever been to put all classroom programs online. Rather, as Elkeles likes to put it: "We adhere to the philosophy that information goes online; interaction is reserved for the classroom. We spend a lot of time with our instructors to make sure that each class is focused on three things: experential learning and behavioral modeling, interaction with an expert and interaction with other employees." This approach, she adds, has definitely changed the classroom environment.

"We've been able to chunk classes down to one or two hours," she explains. "If you take away all of the fluff of the information, like, 'this is how you plan a project,' and begin with *actual* projects being worked on, you get a lot further, a lot faster, and the actual skills transfer from concept to implementation is far more immediate because it's happening in the classroom environment."

If people want more information, adds Elkeles, they know to go online. "Likewise," she says, "they know that classrooms at QUALCOMM are not reserved for someone talking at them, and they know that every single class will have an online component to it."

Interestingly enough, about 98 percent of the classroom instructors are outsourced, despite having several learning specialists on staff with strictly ISD backgrounds. The reason, Elkeles says, is quite simple. "Our employee base is highly educated. In fact, one in every 10 engineers has grad work or a PhD. They want, no, demand *the* expert . . . the best in the field, the person who wrote the book. If we have the same instructors delivering each and every topic in a classroom setting, this dilutes the perceived value."

Consequently, over the years Elkeles has developed a roster of about 30 trainers who specialize in different employee development areas. "Before an instructor begins to work with us we sit them down, show them a video and discuss what it's like to work here," she explains. "We hand out QUALCOMM materials, including an acronym list, and we customize all of their off-the-shelf content for our workforce."

STRATEGIC ALIGNMENT

Back in 1992 when Elkeles joined QUALCOMM, she was already making presentations to upper management about the need to create a "learning organization," along the lines of Peter Senge's best-selling book, *The Fifth Discipline*. Undoubtedly, her "online training network," brainchild was a first step. Step two came about three years ago, in what Elkeles refers to as a "convergence of information and learning," and the final step came in January 2000 when she championed division and individual development plans (see "Top 50 Training Organizations," *Training*, March, page 60).

"The traditional training/HR role in any organization can be extremely strategic—if you make it that way," stresses Elkeles. "At QUALCOMM, our department is heavily linked to management as well as employees. Still, our top role to fill is that of employee advocate. And in that advocacy role, we must drive organizational climate, or culture. If a department or division wants to have a certain message go out, or a certain set of skills, they come to us and discuss ways to create that message or skill set within the employee base."

But it's not quite as simple as Elkeles puts it. Aside from her department's role in designing, implementing and tracking courses as well as divisional and personal development plans, the Learning Center also is responsible for all internal communications. Enter the "convergence of information and training," an absolutely critical—but seldom required—role for training departments to fulfill.

"Most companies have a corporate communications department that is primarily responsible for external communications, and secondarily for internal," she explains. "But those people don't place as much of a priority on communicating to employees and being an employee advocate."

About three years ago, QUALCOMM's management team selected the Learning Center as an internal communications hub because "we have a very informational focus, we are experts in delivering knowledge to people, and we're constantly communicating with them in classrooms, online and via the Learning Center Web site," Elkeles says. "The site enables people to go to that one spot to get all kinds of information. So we had a lot of discussions about employee advocacy, and the Learning Center has really become the place where culture, organizational climate, information and learning are all housed."

Hence, the role of QUALCOMM's learning specialists includes information conduits. And for Elkeles, this has meant transforming her employees' jobs to ensure that they can either help with communicating a management message, or they can help by putting together a program.

"In the end, it's all about curriculum design, ISD and how you deliver the right information to the right people," Elkeles says. "Whether it's a skill or it's just information, the responsibility is ours. And so it has become a natural progression for us to be the employee advocates."

It also places the Learning Center in a strategic place in the organization. "We're in at the very beginning of planning any organizational change initiative or announcement that's coming out," says Elkeles. "So it allows us, from a training perspective, to get a jumpstart on determining what skills people are going to

> "Our role is to provide that larger context for people about why things are happening to them, to the organization, to the department."

need to go through that transformation. And it allows us to have immediate resources available for the employee base the day an announcement is made."

It's evident that Elkeles is a big believer in information sharing, not just of the latest whizbang time management program, but of any information that remotely plays a part in someone's personal development, or as she says "need- and good-to-know" reservoir.

As part of that reservoir, Elkeles initiated the QUALCOMM Daily News Web site, which her department updates daily. Like most internal communication efforts, the QUALCOMM Daily News includes an employee recognition "Wall of Fame" and company happenings. But Elkeles and her team take the information sharing a step further by including specific data on QUALCOMM's competitors, market conditions and general business or economic stories. Given the fact that QUALCOMM's core business is really research and development (or as Elkeles puts it: "We're in the business of selling knowledge, ideas and intellectual property."), it's vitally important for employees at every level to understand what's going on in the marketplace and in the industry.

"Part of the reason why we do that from an organizational learning standpoint," she says, "is because when we make an organizational change, people can't believe—*truly believe*—in the organization if they don't understand the larger context. Our role is to provide that larger context for people about why things are happening to them, to the organization, to the department. Why are we entering that market? Why are there staff changes? Why did we acquire that company? It's our job to supply all that information—before the questions are asked." Basically, it all boils down to what Elkeles calls "strategic places of impact."

"Overall, from a training organization perspective, the key thing is to find strategic places of impact," Elkeles urges. "And part of what we found is that those places of impact are centered around providing people with information. If you have information, you can increase your performance; if you have training, you can increase your performance. And so, this blending of training and information *has* to happen if you're truly invested in trying to improve employee performance."

For Elkeles, creating a true learning organization can't happen if traditional training departments remain solely focused on personal development. "Most traditional training departments don't really tackle the organizational learning concept," she explains. "They're primarily focused on the actual skill development alone, and that's disappointing because it can, and should be, so much more. You have a much greater chance of succeeding when you are managing both aspects. As the future of learning continues to evolve, our challenge is to continually evolve along with it."

Out with the Old: Is It Time to Rethink Instructional Design?

Editor's Comment: Learners these days are demanding all kinds of interaction to facilitate their learning, whether online or in class. Rod Sims is the creator of the "13 D Model" which uses graphic images to represent maximum points of influence on interactivity and development products. Sims is a professor of Instructional Technology at Deakin University in Melbourne, Australia. His model, comments by Diane Gayeski, professor at Ithaca College, NY, and the thoughts of Patti Shank, familiar U.S. writer, consultant, and faculty member at University of Colorado, Denver, are presented here.

What's wrong with my perfectly good Nehru jacket from the 1960s? For that matter, what's wrong with designing courses as if we're living in 1955? Many people believe the rules of good instructional design remain valid no matter how much time passes. But is it really true that instructional design is a rule that shouldn't change? And how does technology challenge traditional assumptions about the instructional systems design (ISD) model we grew up with?

Some folks see the Internet as just another tool for delivering information, like transparencies or those cool wall-sized sticky notes. But I think it's a bit more complex than that. Rod Sims, professor of instructional technology at Deakin University in Melbourne, Australia, argues that technology changes everything. In an article published in the winter 1997 issue of the *Australian Journal of Educational Technology* (http://cleo.murdoch.edu.au/ajet/ajet13/wi97p68.html), he warns that the poor online courses we're seeing today may be a result of faulty assumptions about instructional design.

The traditional ISD model is a linear, reliable and highly sequential approach to developing instructional materials. "The problem, though, is that the prescriptive nature of this process can result in technically correct structures which spotlight content rather than interaction," Sims says.

He's right. I've known instructional designers whose courses were, to put it nicely, uninspiring. They followed all the correct instructional design steps, but their courses still lacked soul. I've also seen courses developed without the aid

---

Source: "Out with the Old: Is It Time to Rethink Instructional Design?" Humble Opinion column by Patti Shank in *OnlineLearning* magazine, September 2001, pp. 64, 66, 68, 70. Patti Shank is an instructional technology consultant and faculty member at the University of Colorado in Denver. Reprinted with permission of *OnlineLearning* magazine. Copyright 2001. All rights reserved.

of an instructional designer that were magical. Clearly, instructional design, while helpful, isn't the be-all and end-all.

Technology opens up new possibilities for course design, Sims says, but people often use it to imitate traditional instructional techniques. "Is technology simply a means to replicate face-to-face human interaction or is this a new medium for communication which requires alternative methods of design?" he asks. "Traditional instructional design doesn't help us ask the right questions."

I couldn't agree more. In my mind, here's the question we should be asking: How can we use technology to go above and beyond what traditional face-to-face instruction can do? For instance, in a classroom course that starts at 2 P.M. and ends at 4 P.M., the discussion has to end at 4 P.M. With technology, the dialogue doesn't need to stop at a predetermined time; threaded discussions can last as long as people remain interested in the topic. In that same two-hour classroom course, it would be pretty tough to get every student involved in the discussion, but technology allows everyone to participate.

Diane Gayeski, a professor at Ithaca College in Ithaca, N.Y., points out that contrary to what many people think, instructional design does not help you select the best teaching strategies. "To select good instructional strategies," she says, "course designers need to understand learning theories, models for media selection, learning styles, etc., rather than simply relying on ISD."

IN WITH THE NEW

If traditional ISD isn't the whole answer, then what is? Perhaps some new ways of thinking can help us better harness technology to help people learn. Sims says we need to first look at our assumptions about using technology for learning and see whether they help or hinder our efforts. Here's what Sims says about these assumptions:

Assumption 1: Technology makes learning more effective. It's true that technology can allow us to individualize instruction and imitate reality. But ISD models provide little guidance in doing this.

Assumption 2: Traditional teacher-student interactions must be maintained in online learning. Should the relationship between teacher and student be the same in an online course as it is in the classroom? Lecturing, for instance, is one way instructors teach in a classroom. Does this work with technology? Not necessarily. Think about taking the transcript of a lecture and dumping it online . . . zzzzzz. So how might we present information online without doing a text dump? One way might be to allow students to work together on developing and evaluating the content. Sure, it's a challenge to come up with these new alternatives, but they open up endless possibilities for helping folks learn.

Assumption 3: Online learning will cater to differences in learning styles. Even though it's possible to develop online courses that respond to learners' individual needs, it isn't easy. And for that reason, few course developers are doing it. Sims says we need to know more about how people interact with technology before we understand how to make adaptive learning work.

Assumption 4: Instructional design will improve course quality. The traditional ISD model was designed for face-to-face instruction. Instructional design for technology-delivered learning will likely be replaced by more flexible approaches.

ISD OF THE FUTURE

In order to leave some of the old assumptions behind, we need to consider new instructional design processes specifically for technology-delivered learning. These approaches should take into account what we know and what we're learning about how people best interact with technology.

What kinds of models might we adopt for designing online courses—especially in a business environment in which it's critical to be able to respond rapidly to new learning needs? Some emerging ways to think about instructional design include:

Adoption analysis. Part of any instructional design process involves gathering information to help you create a good product. John Farquhar and Daniel Surry, in "Adoption Analysis: An Additional Tool for Instructional Developers" (1994, *Education and Training Technology Interna-*

tional), say we don't go far enough when we do that. We often neglect to pinpoint individual and organizational factors that influence people's acceptance of this new delivery method. For example, do users have the necessary skills to take the course? Do they see its benefits? Who will support and maintain the online learning initiative? These "adoption" factors are critical to the success of technology-based learning.

Rapid design and prototyping. Gayeski describes a simple model for designing instruction in this day and age. Her four-step approach mirrors the way I generally work with clients on Web-based learning projects: analyze, prototype, evaluate, tweak. The analysis phase is where you gather information about the organization, the learners and their needs. Then you develop a prototype and evaluate it to see if you're on the right track. Information gathered from a series of evaluations helps you tweak the course until it's right.

You may wonder if you can lop off the first step—the analysis—to shorten up the process. Not so fast! I have loads of sad stories about companies that passed over the first step in order to save time. The end result: wasted time and money, not to mention people looking for new jobs. It doesn't have to take a lot of time to analyze, but it's one of the most important things you can do to make sure your learning experiences work.

13D. Sims recommends a model for designing interactive instruction that I find intriguing and useful. He calls it interactive instruction influence development (13D). In this model, activities have varying amounts of influence at different times in the development of technology-based learning. The structure of the 13D model is different from the traditional linear instructional design model, but it uses most of the same components. An emphasis on prototyping is also incorporated, just like in Gayeski's model.

Here's how 13D works. Deliverables (in the left-hand column of the diagram below) show four steps you go through as you develop technology-based learning. The first step is to develop a proposal in order to get the resources you need. Next, you develop a prototype and (after getting feedback) move into development. Finally, you package the finished product for delivery to the learner.

Now move on to the Techniques column. Each of the techniques (or activities) is important throughout the project, but the peak of the triangle represents the point at which each technique is most important. In other words, the triangle shape mirrors each technique's increasing or decreasing impact during development. For instance, research is most influential at the proposal and prototyping phases (that's where the peak of the triangle is), but starts to decline after that. Evaluation is equally influential in each stage of the process, which is why it's represented by a rectangle.

The next column represents the skills you need in order to develop technology-based courseware. Instructional design skills have been split into those needed by the learning specialist and the interactive architect. Learning specialists use their knowledge of how people learn and how technology affects learning to

THE INTERACTIVE INSTRUCTION INFLUENCE DEVELOPMENT (13D) MODEL		
DELIVERABLES	**TECHNIQUES**	**SKILLS**
Proposal / Prototype / Produce / Package	Research, Plan, Develop, Deliver, Evaluate	Learning Specialist, Interactive Architect, Graphics & Media, Software Developer, Comms Technician, Content Specialist, Project Control

select appropriate instructional strategies. They make sure learning experiences have the "soul" I was talking about earlier. Interactive architects select the best media to accomplish the tasks established by the learning specialist.

Again, the peak of the triangle shows where each skill is most important. For example, the skills of the learning specialist and the interactive architect are critical up front, as the project is conceptualized and designed. The software developers' skills become critical later, as they bring to life what the instructional designers have dreamed up.

The main point behind the 13D model is that it doesn't make sense to identify how technology can replicate the face-to-face classroom. Instead, we need to see what technology allows us to do well and design toward that end.

MOVING FORWARD

As Jimmy Buffet so eloquently said, "It's these changes in latitudes, changes in attitudes. Nothing remains quite the same . . . If we couldn't laugh, we would all go insane."

I'm pretty sure he wasn't thinking about e-learning when he wrote that song, but his words ring true. Technology and the business environment have radically changed, and it makes sense to re-evaluate our design methods as well—or we might just go insane.

More on Instructional Design

If you're hungry for some new perspectives on instructional design, you may want to check out the following links:

- *www.thiagi.com/rid.html*—Sivasailam "Thiagi" Thiagarajan's online resources on rapid prototyping
- *http://cleo.murdoch.edu.au/ajet/ajet13/wi97 p68.html*—article in the *Australian Journal of Educational Technology*, written by Rod Sims, professor of instructional technology at Deakin University in Melbourne, Australia

In addition, two books I recommend are:

- *Designing Web-Based Training*, William Horton (John Wiley and Sons, 2000)
- *The Web Learning Fieldbook: Using the World Wide Web to Build Workplace Learning Environments*, Valerie Beer (Jossey-Bass/Pfeiffer, 2000)

Liemandt's Feedback for and from New Hires and Customers

Editor's Comment: "The first of a potent new type of Internet tool—an L2L (for leader-to-leader) application." New type of tool? What does this say for instructional designers who pride themselves in using a model that has had built-in feedback at all development points for decades? What about our historically proven experience with feedback? A closer look at Trilogy University (TU) and CEO Joe Liemandt's "Teachable Point of View (TPOV)" is instructive.

Through his teaching and learning software Liemandt challenges new hires to contribute ideas for improvement immediately upon joining a company. At Trilogy University, a new hire learns essential skills as well as the company culture, and is drawn into both learning and crafting the company vision. For example, one computer screen contains a survey (choice of 1–10) of items like these: "Overall, how do you rate this Vision?," "Is your Business Unit in alignment with this Vision?," "Do your goals support this Vision?". Immediate feedback on the survey items is given to participants. Many opportunities, both online and face to face, are provided for new hires to contribute their points of view and initiate projects in support of corporate goals. Corporate leaders dedicate time and resources to TU's "boot camp" program for new hires. Leimandt's idea is that the learning context must support a "virtuous teaching cycle" in which everyone learns from everyone else. Several companies are using the concept of feedback software and "L2L" to both teach and learn from customers.

Corporate boot camps. We've all heard about them. Many of us have lived through them. In my case, I've even invented a number of them. It's fair to say that, while some achieve their goals better than others, they're all pretty much the same. They typically focus on knowledge transfer–informing new hires, for instance, about the company's products and markets and how to access key resources in the organization. The best ones, like those at GE and Ford, do this by having the recruits work on real business problems, where intense teamwork is required to meet tight deadlines (a technique I've described elsewhere as "compressed action learning"). I've studied them all. I thought I'd seen it all.

But then I saw Trilogy University. It was 1998, and I was traveling around the country, studying corporate universities as part of a benchmarking research project on action learning. Within days of my arrival, I knew Trilogy University was a breed apart—in fact, my definition of best practice shot out to the horizon line. I've spent hundreds of hours since then at TU, documenting its unconventional approach—and its phenomenal results. (It should be stated, by way of full disclosure, that I briefly consulted to Trilogy last year on the matter of its reorganization. But my relationship to the company and its university at this point is purely as an observer.)

Modeled after Marine Corps basic training, a corporate boot camp is designed to push new recruits to their limits. Each day offers some nearly insurmountable challenge, and the reward for overcoming it is an even harder one the next day. It's intense and intimidating, but people emerge on the other end of the program highly confident that they are prepared for anything. They also come away with deep bonds to their fellow recruits and strong ties to the organization.

Source: "Trilogy University Goes Virtual" HRB AT LARGE article "No Ordinary Boot Camp" by Noel M. Tichy in *Harvard Business Review*, April 2001, pp. 65–70. Article reprinted with permission from *Harvard Business Review*. Copyright 2001 by the Harvard Business School Publishing Corporation. All rights reserved.

Those two goals—preparedness and bonding—are usually the whole focus of a boot camp, and achieving them is worth a great deal. That's why so many of the top-performing companies put their faith in such programs. In the mid-1980s, I ran General Electric's Crotonville leadership development center, where I led the development of its Corporate Entry Leadership Conference, a three-day program in which new hires learn about GE's strategy, its culture, and a bit about themselves. "Old man Watson" at IBM ran them, as did Ross Perot when he founded EDS, as does Andy Grove at Intel. And for years, the commercial banks have run their commercial-lending boot camps for college hires. In the past decade, consulting firms and service organizations have dramatically increased their investments in boot camps for new recruits. Accounting giant Arthur Andersen, for instance, has a 700-bed facility in St. Charles, Illinois, which runs at capacity year-round. Many old-line industrials have also set them up because they realize that energizing new hires and engaging them in the culture is just as critical as making sure they have the technical skills to do their specific jobs.

The interesting thing about Trilogy University is that it achieves those goals and more. Much more. It also serves as the company's primary R&D engine and as its way of developing its next generation of leadership. It even succeeds as the impetus and incubator for Trilogy's strategic thinking. How can it do all that? By now, it almost couldn't fail to, thanks to a virtuous cycle that was established early and continues to gain momentum. In the simplest terms, these things happen at TU because top leadership is on the scene and deeply engaged in it—and top leadership stays on the scene and deeply engaged in TU because these essential activities are happening there.

WELCOME TO TRILOGY

Trilogy University is the orientation program of Austin, Texas-based Trilogy, designed to turn the company's raw recruits—hired straight off the campuses of MIT, Stanford, U. Michigan, and the like—into highly productive contributors. Started in 1995, it is the brainchild of Trilogy's president and CEO, Joe Liemandt, and its vice president of marketing, John Price.

The company has a pressing need for new-employee orientation because its growth has been extremely rapid, and the biggest drag on growth has been the difficulty of recruiting and bringing new talent up to speed. Trilogy started fast out of the gate in 1989 when Liemandt nailed a market opportunity to create "configuration software" for large manufacturers like Hewlett-Packard and Boeing. The products these companies sell have innumerable variants, as alternative components are assembled to suit each buyer's highly specific preferences. Trilogy's software solves a huge problem traditionally faced in the selling process by allowing a salesperson with a laptop to translate a customer's needs into a workable specification. The software spots where components are incompatible, for instance, or where one part requires another, and it configures a system that will work. Then—and this is really important to those salespeople—it produces an accurate price quote on the spot.

Trilogy's breakthrough allowed it to do something most small software companies only dream of: sign up brand-name accounts like Hewlett-Packard while the product was still in its infancy. Since then, Trilogy has expanded on its original offering to launch e-commerce applications for both the buying and selling of products, and its revenues have grown to about $200 million. Along the way, its employee base has grown 35% annually. In 2000, the company brought 450 new hires into an existing organization of 1,000.

Joe Liemandt realized early on that, as each influx of new hires came through the doors, the company needed to equip them with not only the skills required for their jobs but also the vision and values with which they should align their work. But because each new group represented a fair proportion of the whole organization, assimilation wasn't going to happen in some natural, organic way. It would have to be deliberately managed. Having to compress a great deal of learning and acculturation into a short time frame, Liemandt decided he needed a boot camp.

THREE HIGH-PRESSURE MONTHS

"The first day, Joe walks in. And, like, his very few first words are, 'You're going to be the

Training Program Design 133

> One particular innovation coming out of Trilogy University strikes me as a perfect encapsulation of all that goes on there. It's a software application called Leadership.com, conceived by a TU project team in the winter of 1999.
>
> That team, freshly inspired by CEO Joe Liemandt's vision and energy, decided the word wasn't getting out far enough. It was great to have Joe presenting his most current point of view to the newest hires, but wouldn't the impact be greater if the whole organization could be hearing it too? With that in mind, they developed an Internet platform for Liemandt to post his "teachable point of view" and get feedback. That quickly expanded into Leadership.com, a multimedia platform for sharing, responding to, and holding discussions about ideas. Moreover, it isn't just Joe broadcasting those ideas. At this point, more than 200 Trilogians have posted video clips in which they offer their own takes on the vision, values, and goals of the company, their business unit, their department, or just themselves. Every individual coming out of Trilogy University can now be seen on Leadership.com explaining what they think the company is all about and how they are going to help it. It's a requirement for graduation.
>
> What's really powerful about Leadership.com, though, are the feedback people get and the thinking inspired by the exchange. Accompanying each video is a bulleted outline of its main points. There are mechanisms for viewers to numerically evaluate each presentation for both delivery and content, public forums where anyone in the company can discuss the issues raised—or not raised—in the presentations, and scorecards that show up-to-the-minute voting results. The system causes people at all levels to engage with the strategy of the company and brings TU's virtuous teaching cycle out to the broader organization.
>
> Trilogy has been so well served by Leadership.com that it decided recently to turn it into a product for sale to others. Early customers include Percepta, Ford's joint venture in customer relationship management with TeleTech. I'm hoping it will be just the first of a potent new type of Internet tool—an "L2L" (for leader-to-leader) application.
>
> So, consider: a group of new hires hits the ground running and creates a successful product innovation—one that helps develop leadership talent and serves as a force for positive change in the organization. Could this have happened anywhere but at Trilogy University?

future of Trilogy—the company is relying on you—and everybody's waiting on you.'"

The speaker is Vince Mallet, a computer science master's grad who was wearing a Java T-shirt, his long hair in a neat ponytail, and a broad grin as he recently gave me the student's view of TU. Liemandt's message was apparently hitting home. Mallet told me, "I just want to go out in the company and be able to have that impact." It would be a tough several weeks before he got that chance.

Trilogy University is run twice a year. In the summer, it currently includes 170 to 200 hires, and in the winter about 60, all coming straight from campus. A class typically has a sprinkling of freshly minted master's and PhDs, and a fair number of liberal arts majors, but it's mostly drawn from undergraduate computer science departments. The program generally lasts 12 weeks. It's structured to take students through a well-thought-out process to develop skills, relationships, and values, which they then apply in intense R&D projects before they're ultimately introduced as a positive new force into the rest of the organization.

Month One. When you arrive at Trilogy University, you are assigned to a section and to an instruction track. Your section, a group of about 20, is your social group for the duration of TU. You share a section leader (an experienced person from Trilogy who serves as a mentor) and virtually all of your time with these people. Tracks are designed to be microcosms of future work life at Trilogy. For example, as a future developer or consultant, you might learn about technologies like XML and JSP one week by building a customizable sales analysis Web site for a fictional company. The technical challenges in such exercises closely mimic real customer engagements, but the time frames are dramatically compressed. The assignments pile up week after week for the first month, each one successively more challenging than the last.

During that time, you're being constantly measured and evaluated, as assignment grades and comments are entered into a database monitoring your progress. The functional training is so intense it would be easy to assume that it is the most important goal of TU. But Allan Drummond, the Trilogy vice president who runs TU, says that's not the case. "If people don't learn Java in TU, I don't care. They're very bright—they can pick up what they need. But if they don't develop nearly unbreakable bonds with fellow TUers, if they don't learn to prioritize and make smart decisions, if they don't leave charged up, then TU is a failure."

The goals Drummond is emphasizing are the focus of the sections. Unlike tracks, sections continue past the first month. In a sense, they last for life. Effectiveness at Trilogy depends on having trusting relationships with coworkers, and sections are designed to prime that process. That's why, Vince Mallet explained to me, "on the second day, we were all asked to tell the most significant emotional experience of our lives." Vince says some of the students' first reactions were cynical: "Yeah, we're going to tell stories about us. Whatever." But the technique worked its magic as people began to talk and listen. Before long, he says, "some people were crying; some people were making other people cry. And I thought, whoa—this is totally unusual." People were getting deeply acquainted, not incidentally but intentionally. The individuals in each section represent a cross section of functions; upon graduation from TU, the students will disperse to all corners of Trilogy, and the trust and bonds they develop will form horizontal networks linking them to people throughout the company for the rest of their careers.

Beyond developing skills and relationships, month one of Trilogy University also begins to instill values. Humility is one of the values Liemandt wants to see, and that's one reason the tracks deliberately stretch students beyond the point of failure. Other values are introduced through what people at Trilogy refer to as "big talks," which Liemandt or other Trilogy stars have with the whole TU class, usually in a Socratic style, and which are further discussed and debated in sections. Students learn early that Trilogy values creativity, innovation, and

> In his senior year at Stanford, Liemandt dropped out and dedicated himself full-time to founding Trilogy. At least one very accomplished businessman, a former GE senior executive (who also happened to be his father), told him: "You're a moron."

being a force for positive change in the workplace. They learn that Trilogy wants to see teamwork and a strong belief that success means solving the customer's problem. More than anything, they learn that Trilogy values risk taking. Along with the skills and relationships forged in month one, these values will be sorely tested in month two.

Month Two. Month two is TU project month. This is when the TUers, most of them 22 years old and employees for all of a month, take on the responsibility of inventing the company's future. "We tell them that, in order for the company to survive, they have to come up with a frame-breaking great new business idea," says Liemandt. "And they believe it because I really believe it."

Liemandt's learned, he says, "the hard way" that taking risks and suffering the consequences is a crucial part of any business. When he decided to launch Trilogy, he was in his senior year at Stanford. Rather than miss what might be a narrow window of opportunity, he decided to drop out and dedicate himself full-time to it. At least one very accomplished businessman, a former GE senior executive (who also happened to be his father), told him: "You're a moron."

The TU project is Liemandt's way of giving new recruits his own experience all over again. In teams of three to five people, they have to come up with an idea, create a business model for it, build the product, and develop the marketing plan. In trying to launch bold new ideas in a hyperaccelerated time frame, they gain a deep appreciation of the need to set priorities, evaluate probabilities, and measure results. Mind you, these projects are not hypothetical—they're the real thing. But even more important, when each team presents its innovation, Liemandt is there, deciding whether or not to put up the money to launch it. It's exhausting but it's also energizing, because Trilogy's best and most senior people are in the mix. New employees know they're getting noticed and that their ideas have a chance of being taken up.

How big is that chance? About 15% of the projects survive beyond the month that's allocated to them in TU. It's that humility thing again. Drummond describes the reaction of recruits who think their ideas are brilliant but then see them fail. "They're like, 'We stink. Not near good enough.' Actually, we never want that feeling to end. Because the minute you get arrogant, someone comes and beats you."

At the same time, the seriousness with which Liemandt and all the rest of Trilogy take the projects builds confidence. "We encourage them to go for the fence with their ideas and, while we don't reward failure around here, we don't punish them for it either," says Liemandt. "So, when people leave TU, most of them are thinking, 'I know I can make a difference, and I am not afraid to try'—which is exactly what we want them to think."

Month Three. Month three at Trilogy University is all about finding your place and having a broader impact in the larger organization. A few students continue with their TU projects, but most move on to "graduation projects," which generally are assignments within the various Trilogy business units. People leave TU on a rolling basis as they find sponsors out in the company who are willing to take them on.

The graduation process is a meeting between the graduate, the new manager, and the section leader. Before the meeting, each has been asked to evaluate the TUer on his or her various abilities. At the meeting, the three of them discuss the evaluation to resolve disagreements. "We don't just want understanding; we want agreement," Drummond says. "On all of the rankings where there is a disparity, they have to reach an agreement." The TUers have also written lists of objectives and their thoughts on how they want their careers to unfold. The manager responds to these with a list of specific goals that the TUer must agree to. Typically, the manager will set three to five yearlong goals

> It's the rare TU graduate who can't find a home within Trilogy because, clearly, Trilogy University succeeds at the basics of basic training.

> What a contrast with typical practice, which assigns orientation duty to the staff the business can most easily spare. At Trilogy University, believe it or not, it's an honor to be asked to instruct.

that include a skill development goal, a mainline execution goal, and an organizational development goal. In addition, the manager creates another plan focused on creating the job assignments and coaching opportunities that will help the TUer reach his or her longer-term career goals.

"We want everyone here to be a star. We won't graduate TUers until they have found positions they want and where the new manager will take responsibility for helping them become a star," explains former TU head Danielle Rios. The TU faculty sometimes help persuade managers who are reluctant to take a risk, but a TUer who ultimately can't find a sponsor is out of the company.

It's the rare TU graduate who can't find a home within Trilogy because, clearly, Trilogy University succeeds at the basics of basic training. Graduates emerge from it prepared—by their skills, their relationships, and their values—to hit the ground running. But what really sets this boot camp apart from others I know is that it contributes much more to Trilogy than that. First, thanks to the energy and attention devoted to the TU projects, TU has become the company's primary research and development engine. Second, it has become the setting for Trilogy's leadership development. Third, it provides a great context and impetus for management to revisit and communicate strategic direction. And fourth, it serves as a constant source of organizational renewal and transformation.

A NEW-PRODUCT PIPELINE

Liemandt recalls the day in 1997 when a TU project team of six kids pitched the idea for selling cars on the Internet. At the time, e-commerce was still pretty much virgin territory. EBay was not alive yet. Amazon was a start-up. Liemandt told them their idea was one of the dumbest he had ever heard. They clearly didn't understand the automotive industry, franchise laws, and how dealers would prevent this from happening. And they were totally naïve to think people would spend that kind of money over the Internet.

The team thought Liemandt was the one who was missing something, so they decided to prove him wrong. They went ahead and developed CarOrder.com, lined up struggling dealers who were willing to cooperate, and—lo and behold—started racking up sales. Today, one of Trilogy's most talked-about businesses is its global alliance with Ford. Without the consumer-side technology, experience, and credibility Trilogy developed from that TU project—the CarOrder.com Web site won *PC Magazine*'s 2000 Editors' Choice for Best Car-Buying Site—the Ford relationship would not have happened. Liemandt, who first designed TU projects purely as a learning exercise, has come to see them as his biggest source of strategic innovation.

It makes perfect sense, if you think about it. Playing the role of the venture capitalist, Liemandt is wholly focused on the merits of the ideas as business propositions. And because he and other senior managers are paying attention, the students are truly giving their all on these projects.

Meanwhile, the intensity of the bonds between teammates helps ensure that deep collaboration is taking place among them, leading to higher creativity. And the fact that these are new hires straight out of college means their ideas are less likely to be constrained by past practices—at TU or anywhere else.

For all these reasons, R&D gets done at Trilogy and gets done well. Since 1995, TU projects have produced revenues of $25 million and have formed the basis for $100 million in new business for the company.

A recent TU class, for example, developed Fast Cycle Time, an Internet-time delivery methodology now being used by more than 20 of Trilogy's customers. In late 1999, several TUers created a Web site called IveBeen Good.com, which enabled shoppers to put products from popular retail sites like Amazon or ShopNow directly into a single shopping cart, which IveBeenGood hosted. Only nine months after its creation, a refined version of this universal shopping-cart technology, renamed UberWorks and still run by TUers, was sold to Network Commerce for $13 million. The initial investment was $2 million.

THE NEXT GENERATION OF LEADERS

TU also succeeds as a proving ground for developing the next generation of leadership at Trilogy. I've mentioned that the section leaders are experienced people. What I haven't said yet is that these are the best and brightest technical stars Trilogy has to offer—and that they dedicate themselves 100% to TU for three months at a time. Trilogy's chief scientist, David Franke, for example, was a section leader in 1999. So was Scott Snyder, Trilogy's vice president of development, who in summer 2000 asked for a turn as a section leader before he moved over to help grow Trilogy's European operations.

This is an extraordinary investment, to be sure. But consider the payback. In the hothouse of TU, and under the direct eye of Liemandt, these technical people are learning and testing out the essential skills they need to be effective leaders: inspiring others, mentoring talent, evaluating performance, communicating vision and strategy, and more. During their three months at TU, they are not only exposed to Liemandt's latest ideas about the direction of the company, they're also engaged with him as partners in developing and implementing those ideas. In the process, they are transformed from being members of the "old Trilogy" into dedicated change agents participating in its next round of transformation.

Again, it makes perfect sense. But what a contrast with typical practice, which assigns orientation duty to the staff the business can most easily spare or outsources it to consultants and professional trainers. At Trilogy University, believe it or not, it's an honor to be asked to instruct. Trilogians know this is the fast-track experience they need to move up in the company. A case in point is Ben Zaniello, a leading product manager in Trilogy's financial services practice, who actually declined a promotion in 2000, opting instead to become a section leader. "I felt that to really drive our financial service offerings forward into places like on-line wealth management," Zaniello says, "section leading was a better opportunity for growth and for really innovating."

CLARITY ON STRATEGY

Another benefit was at first unexpected but is now a crucial piece of TU's contribution to Trilogy's success: twice a year, Liemandt and other Trilogy leaders must decide what they want to teach and how they want to focus the new class of hires.

For any leader, regardless of whether he or she is ever in a classroom setting, having what I call a "teachable point of view" is crucial. This is essentially a clear idea about where the company (or organization or team) needs to go, a general understanding about how it's going to get there, and the ability to explain it in a way that inspires others. Leaders' TPOVs must be firm and clear, but they must also constantly evolve to take new conditions into account. What TU does for Liemandt and other Trilogy leaders is to compel them to update their TPOVs at least twice a year. As a result, Joe and the senior leadership are continually challenged and given candid feedback that helps them improve the way they craft and share their vision. TU is the impetus and the process for improving Liemandt and his senior people as leaders.

ORGANIZATIONAL TRANSFORMATION

There's at least one more thing TU contributes to Trilogy that a typical boot camp does not—and it may be the most important thing of all. It serves as a force for organizational renewal and transformation. Traditionally, orientation programs are designed to teach newcomers to fit into the existing organization. But TU sees its fresh hires as its best chance to change the company. "With each TU class, we have the opportunity to create in the minds of 60 or 160 new people the vision of Trilogy not as it is but as we would like it to be," says Drummond. "We make sure that they bond into a strong trust network among themselves and with the leaders who mentor them in TU, which gives them confidence. Then we send them out into the company, where they have the critical mass to make a real impact."

This, in fact, was the goal that led to Trilogy University in the first place. As Liemandt tells it now, he was concerned in 1994 that the new people coming in might have their eyes on a

> Traditionally, orientation programs are designed to teach newcomers to fit into the existing organization. But TU sees its fresh hires as its best chance to change the company.

rather short-term prize. The company was a one-trick pony; it had a very hot product, and a quick sale or an IPO could have paid off handsomely. Liemandt had already spotted that kind of perspective in some of his colleagues, and he didn't like it. He was in it for the long haul, and he wanted an organization devoted to building, as it says in the company's motto, "the next great software company." So that's when he decided to gather together a team of new hires, isolate them from the legacy organization, and spend three months helping them get the religion.

This is a big part of why the TUers' entry into the company is so carefully orchestrated. In the first few weeks of TU, they're highly isolated from the rest of the company. As the weeks go by, the amount of contact increases. By the third month, they're ready to venture out into the company, while retaining their home base and their support network back in TU.

"I and most of Trilogy don't think of TU as a training program. It is a transformational experience," Drummond says. It transforms the TUers, it transforms Liemandt and other Trilogy leaders, and, ultimately, it transforms the company.

THE VIRTUOUS TEACHING CYCLE

Of everything I've seen at Trilogy University, I'm most impressed with the power of the virtuous teaching cycle it has put in motion. The leaders of the organization are learning from the recruits as the recruits are learning from the leaders. Each element in place here—new-hire training, product innovation, leadership development, and the rest—fuels the others. It's not just that all these things get done at Trilogy University. It's that all of them get done better than they would otherwise.

Now stop and read that last sentence again, because it's big. *It's all done better.*

New hires learn faster because they are working on real projects, with guidance from the best managerial talent in the company and with the full knowledge that their efforts are not going unnoticed. Leaders in training learn more because they have real leadership responsibilities and must engage thoughtfully with the vision and strategy of the company. Even R&D pays off better because people with unconstrained perspectives are brainstorming ideas just as they are internalizing that vision and strategy. The commitment and personal involvement of the CEO keeps the cycle in motion. He serves as a role model for it and demands it of everyone else.

SO WHY DOESN'T EVERYONE DO THIS?

I'll say it again for emphasis: what I have observed at Trilogy University is completely different from what I've seen in other corporate training programs—even in other boot camps. So why is that? Why didn't someone like Jack Welch think this up? For that matter, why didn't *I*?

In Jack's defense and mine, I'll point out that this revolutionary model was also an evolutionary one—and arose from a particular circumstance that few companies share. Back in 1994, Trilogy was a very small company hiring so many people at once that the incoming group had the power to make a needed shift in the culture. Under those circumstances, to claim that new-employee orientation is the best use of a CEO's time—even three months of his time—is not such a stretch. But how many places does this describe? At this point, not even Trilogy.

Happily, TU evolved by adding other elements so important to the company's future that it remains the best use of senior management's time. In fact, at this point, the cycle is so powerful it's hard to imagine it breaking down. And the evolution continues: starting in 2001, Liemandt has decided to bring customers into the process. Selected customers can sponsor a TU session, sending their own executives to the program, which would then focus on a set of their key business challenges. Trilogy will get invaluable executive exposure for its R&D efforts and its leadership development process.

> What I have observed at Trilogy University is completely different from what I've seen in other corporate training programs.

The customer will get several man-years of innovation time—and a potential breakthrough. The point is, this isn't a case of taking top people out of the action. This *is* the action.

The challenge for other companies, then, is to set this kind of virtuous cycle in motion given their larger scale and established processes. Most will have to overcome a lot of inertia; some will even have to reverse a cycle that's going in the opposite direction.

That's not an easy task, and along the way the most dedicated reformer will constantly run up against some predictable objections: It's too expensive. We can't take our best people off the line. We can't leave innovation up to kids. We can't trust them not to train on our dime, then take their skills elsewhere. Excuses, excuses.

I'm not saying there aren't legitimate reasons that a full-blown TU-style boot camp might not be for you. Maybe most of your new hires don't come straight from campus and simply can't deal with the intense work-life imbalance of a boot camp. Maybe you're not in a hot enough business—like pre-IPO software—to attract the kind of talent that could dream up your next big hit (although Liemandt would certainly counter that the best way to attract talent is to offer this kind of opportunity). There may be more reasons that TU can't be replicated everywhere. But it seems clear that many other companies can do this—and could reap the same results. What has held the rest of us back, I hope, is not that we couldn't use this model but that we have not yet imagined it, and we have not yet seen it succeed.

We've discovered it now, and it seems to work. Now it's up to other leaders to imagine it in their own organizations. More than anything, making it succeed will require top management on the scene, truly committed to learning as a two-way street. Without those people and that attitude, no orientation program will get much respect or have much impact. With them, the impact can go far, *far* beyond the goals of simple orientation. That's what has happened at Trilogy.

2. Big Design Issues in E-Learning

A Project Manager's Advice: Plan and Communicate

Editor's Comment: The next four entries in this Section 3, "Training Program Design," are all concerned with big design issues in e-learning. Each entry represents many others of similar focus. The year 2002 will see a narrowing of the focus of many of the philosophical and mega-type points of view so characteristic of year 2001. This brief report in VNU's *ONLINE LEARNING REVIEWS* e-mail newsletter tackles the big issues of planning and communication as he suggests some specifics of good project management to make development of an instructional project possible.

YOUR PRIORITIES: ANALYSIS AND DESIGN

Analysis and design should get one-third of your total e-learning project time.

That was the advice from e-learning project manager Michael Horn as he spoke to about 45 participants in a Tuesday session on project management at OnLine Learning 2001 Asia in Singapore.

Horn is project director with Click2learn Inc. of Bellevue, Washington. Here are some of his pointers:

- Do a careful up-front analysis. More time up front helps you avoid missteps later in a project.

- Create a prototype. Horn said many people can't envision e-learning without one. "It's like me trying to visualize what my haircut is going to look like," quipped Horn. "I can't do it."

- Scale. Some companies need only a few hours of e-learning. Others need hundreds of hours. Process and tools must "allow us to do both of those things," said Horn.

- Provide an "expert button." Learners like the opportunity to click a button that lets them e-mail questions to experts, said Horn.

- Be flexible. Your process must accommodate changes as you go.

- Be organized. Project manager, lead instructional designer, lead programmer, and lead graphic designer—that's the basic team at Click2learn. On big projects, additional team members report to those basic four.

- E-learning project managers often outsource media such as video and audio. Instructional design tends to stay in-house, where the right subject-matter experts are likely at hand.

Source: "Your Priorities: Analysis and Design" report from Online Learning 2001 Asia Conference in Singapore, in *ONLINE LEARNING REVIEWS* e-mail newsletter, May 17, 2001, pp. 5–6. (*www.vnulearning.com*) Reprinted with permission of VNU Business Media, 50 South 9th St., Minneapolis, MN. Copyright 2001. All rights reserved.

Programming takes about 30% of a project's time—a share that Click2learn is trying to reduce because programming is expensive.

Instructional design takes 29% of a project's time, said Horn. Another 15% of a project's time goes to project management. Click2learn gathered the information from projects over several years.

Topping the list of reasons why projects fail, said Horn, are poor planning and poor communication.

Mission E-Possible: The Cisco E-Learning Story

Editor's Comment: Instructional designers wonder if there is a kind of knowledge-based strategic learning that is possible only with e-learning. This article, a study of Cisco's e-learning operation, explores this question. It begins with a statement that CEO John Chambers says "learning is a strategic priority for his company and important to the world economy." ASTD's Pat Galagan explores the ideas and solutions of Cisco's Learning Solutions Group in the article reprinted here, and brings these high-level concepts into low-level reality. This is a practical and helpful article about how to design an e-learning organization.

Cisco CEO John Chambers has done for training what trainers have long said they most wanted: Chambers declared publicly that learning is a strategic priority for his company and important to the world economy. But there's a catch. He's not talking about the kind of training that most practitioners have in mind when they seek top-level corporate support. Chambers is endorsing the fast-moving, results-oriented learning that is only possible with e-learning.

But why e-learning rather than another thriving Internet application such as e-commerce or e-health? Either one would drive network traffic and thus help Cisco sell more routers and switches.

"I love e-learning because it makes employees more productive, and it's available anytime, anywhere," says Chambers. "Although I think it will take three to four years for e-learning to make as much of an impact as e-commerce or virtual close (closing a company's financial books online), I truly believe that it will change the way schools and universities teach, the way students learn, and the way businesses keep employees up-to-date with the skills and information for this fast-changing Internet economy.

"Not only that, e-learning increases network traffic. And as the CEO of a networking company, I can only be happy about that."

So, what's it like to be a trainer in a company whose chairman has become spokesperson-in-chief for e-learning, declaring far and wide that it's the "next killer app for the Internet" and that its use will "make email look like a rounding error"? Chambers has planted a flag. What about the people who must supply the wind to make it fly at Cisco?

The epicenter for e-learning at Cisco is the Internet Learning Solutions Group. Although it's one of almost 30 training groups in the company (and not the first or the only one to introduce e-learning), it's the proving ground for e-learning as a business strategy that can be applied across the company—in business-speak, "an integrated solution."

"There are solid reasons that Cisco cares deeply about e-learning," says Mike Metz, direc-

---

Source: "Mission E-Possible: The Cisco E-Learning Story" by Patricia A. Galagan in *Training & Development*, February 2001, pp. 46–56. Patricia A. Galagan is Editor-In-Chief of ASTD's Magazine Group. Reprinted with permission of ASTD. Copyright 2001. All rights reserved.

tor of marketing for the Internet Learning Solutions Group.

The first is obvious: The more people learning online, the more networking gear Cisco can sell. The second is that Cisco has big plans for growth and, consequently, has big learning needs. In 12 years, it has become an $18 billion company; in the next four years, it intends to grow to a $50 billion company.

That kind of growth will require Cisco to have a workforce of more than 50,000 employees, a 40 percent jump from today. Data from IDC, a firm that tracks and predicts information technology trends, shows that by 2003, the demand for IT networking professionals will exceed the supply, a shortfall that could leave Cisco and other Internet-related companies ambushed at the skills gap.

"We really believe that our e-learning programs are a more effective way to grow skills in high volume in a shorter time than in the past," says Metz. "It's a fundamental strategic imperative for us to train more people to plan, design, and install the Internet infrastructure that we're building."

MAKING IT HAPPEN

It's one thing to strategize, another to implement, and nowhere is that more true than with e-learning. The technology is expensive, the pace is fast, and the required mind shifts can be daunting. When training is pushed to a companywide strategic level, the key decision makers are not likely to be training traditionalists.

Enter Tom Kelly, the Harley-riding, poetry-writing, bonsai-growing ex-Marine in charge of the Internet Learning Solutions Group. Kelly has 20-plus years in the training trenches. But, when it comes to e-learning, he's not afraid to attack some sacred cows. "Putting trainers in charge of e-learning is like putting postal workers in charge of e-mail," he says.

When Chambers declared that Cisco would be the leader in e-learning, its own training operations were, to be blunt, a bit of a mess.

"Three years ago, when I joined Cisco, training was an irrelevant backwater," says Kelly. "Training was fragmented, unsupported, and unsuccessful. The gag was, 'Friends don't let friends work at Cisco training.'"

> "We really believe that our e-learning programs are a more effective way to grow skills in high volume in a shorter time than in the past."
> —Mike Metz
> Director of Internet Learning Solutions Group

"It was an interesting dynamic," says Metz, who wasn't on board at the time but who has heard stories. "There were e-learning skunk works around the company, but nothing was coordinated. And then comes this top-down directive."

"Chambers fired the gun," says Kelly. "The mission facing us was, 'Make it exemplary, and make it serve thousands.'"

The Internet Learning Solutions Group is the largest and most centralized training organization within Cisco, with about 165 staff supplemented by contractors as needed. To answer Chambers's challenge, the ILSG and other e-learning stakeholders across the company came together to form the Cisco E-Learning Business Council, sponsored by HR executive Barbara Beck, head of corporate marketing Keith Fox, and Doug Allred, the executive in charge of customer advocacy. The mission of the council, and therefore of the ILSG, is "to implement an integrated e-learning solution across Cisco."

The council's first task was to uncover all of the e-learning activities in the training underground and then to create processes and standards they could share. Simultaneously, IT began to provide tools for integrating e-learning across Cisco—everything from virtual classrooms to video server technology to templates for content development.

"By no means is everything integrated yet," says Metz, "but at least we're headed in that direction."

In addition to its mission to integrate e-learning across Cisco, the Internet Learning Solutions Group provides e-learning to three audiences: the 10,000 systems engineers and account managers who make up Cisco's field salesforce, the employees of the 40,000 channel partners who resell Cisco products, and hundreds of thousands of end-user customers. Rapid learning for those audiences is considered key to Cisco's growth strategy.

> "Putting trainers in charge of e-learning is like putting postal workers in charge of email."
>
> —Tom Kelley
> Vice President Internet
> Learning Solutions
> Group

The ILSG's first move was to create a learning portal containing all of the learning resources that the company had for systems engineers and account managers in the field.

"The head of worldwide sales challenged us not to create more training," says Metz, "but first to aggregate, organize, and rationalize the resources that already existed but that nobody could find."

Called the Field E-Learning Connection, the portal puts learners in touch with more than 8,000 learning resources, including online learning, live class schedules, white papers, PowerPoint presentations, recommended books and videos, and more. It's organized around a set of learning roadmaps covering the jobs of every person in the field organization. About 95 percent of Cisco's 10,000 salespeople have logged on since the Field E-Learning Connection was launched in August 1999.

Diane Bauer is senior manager for e-learning marketing in the Internet Learning Solutions Group. With a beeper, a phone, and a security card clipped to her belt, Bauer accessorizes like a California dot.commie. Her outfit the day of our interview is navy pinstripes, but it's about three generations from being a suit. Over the back of her chair is a baseball jacket.

A veteran of two and a half years at Cisco, Bauer was brought in to manage field training when it was still staunchly instructor-led. "At that time, the field executive team wasn't convinced that anyone could learn anything over the Internet," she says.

Bauer arrived at the peak of the training problem. Salespeople and systems engineers were struggling to keep up with new products and technologies. The salesforce, a group of product sellers who "knew their feeds and speeds," were being groomed as solutions providers. And the systems engineers were making the transition from generalists to specialists. Their learning needs were huge.

"There was no standardized way to develop engineers. It was typical to start writing a course for them, only to find there were nine other courses just like it in other parts of the company. Everything we were doing was not meeting their needs," says Bauer.

The field executives were clear about what they wanted from training, says Bauer. They wanted to solve the problems that had plagued classroom training regarding timeliness, relevance, worldwide accessibility, and learner accountability for results. The field executives also wanted to endorse the content and design of all of the training created for their groups.

"And did I mention that they wanted 12 new curriculums rolled out in seven months?" adds Bauer.

"Some people said it was impossible, but that didn't stop us," she says. Following a common Cisco practice when given a mandate but little staff or funds, the ILSG built a virtual e-learning organization made up of people from all over the company. Once they got organized, the group built and rolled out the Field E-Learning Connection in less than five months.

"To make the training relevant and timely, we knew it had to be modular," says Bauer. "That, plus the requirement that it had to be accessible around the world, meant our solution had to be built on the Internet." Subject matter experts and curriculum designers created roadmaps outlining the competencies for each job in the field—everything from sales to systems engineering to account management.

To help the systems engineers become specialists, the number of learning tracks went from three to 29. "We were having trouble scaling the curriculum model to meet the number of new job requirements. Moving to the concept of roadmaps aligned with job skills and then plugging in resources or building them led naturally to the use of reusable learning objects," says Bauer.

Once the field executives endorsed the curriculum plan, the ILSG started building the infrastructure for a learning portal. But then they had to decide what learning resources to put into the portal, and a small war broke out among the trainers over the question, *What is training and what isn't?*

That a purely philosophical quibble could nearly derail a major training initiative lies at the heart of why trainers are often not asked to

Training Program Design

develop e-learning. Imagine the irony of spending 18 months demonstrating to top management that an e-learning orientation is a huge strategic advantage and having your CEO publicly endorse e-learning, only to have your training staff dig in their heels over conceptual purity. As Cisco trainers debated the What is training? Issue with the zeal of theologians arguing over what's necessary for salvation, Tom Kelly came to a quick decision: He shut down the strict constructionists.

"Our message was, 'That's caca.' E-learning is about information, communication, education, *and* training. That's a huge message that people don't hear often or well," says Kelly.

"Regardless of how trainers categorize training and education," Kelly adds, "the learner only wants the skill and knowledge to do a better job or answer the next question from a customer. So here at Cisco, we view it all as content.

"The important thing is to have good content out there. Does it have to be instructionally sound? Some of it should be. Does *all* of it have to be? No. Does that diminish its value? No, not to the learner. Only to those of us who wander around with our master's or Ph.D.s in instructional design."

Predictably, some trainers moved on to other business units. The team that remained forged ahead with a new kind of training unit. They spent little time designing and delivering training and more time putting training and communication tools in front of subject matter experts. They also worked hard to market e-learning and its benefits, and to develop processes for getting the learning out as fast as possible. Instead of building learning tools and systems, they bought them readymade and worked with IT to integrate them into Cisco networks and systems.

MEASURING SUCCESS

The Internet Learning Solutions Group found that the shift to e-learning changed their measures of success.

"Reaching competency quickly is what counts now—not the thickness of the book, the length of the class, or the number of people in the seats," says Bauer. On the road to competency, a person may have formal training, do

---

Q&A With John Chambers

Q: By being the first CEO of a major company to publicly predict the future of e-learning, you've influenced many other business leaders to think of it in a new light. How did you come to the position you hold? Who or what persuaded you to take such a bold public stand on a relatively untried phenomenon?

A: There are two global equalizers in life—the Internet and education. Although the United States has one of the best university programs in the world, education at the K-12 level is broken. I believe that if we don't fix that for our children, the competitive advantage that the United States enjoys today could change. The jobs of the future are going to go to the best-educated workforce, no matter where that workforce is. Leaders around the world get that and that the Internet is going to be key to survival, including Tony Blair of the United Kingdom, Jiang Zemin of China, and Lee Tung-hui of Taiwan.

Given that, I think we need to do what's best for the next generation. E-learning helps eliminate barriers of time, distance, and socioeconomic status, so individuals are empowered to take charge of their own lifelong learning.

Q: What's your view of the contribution of e-learning to Cisco's success as a business?

A: How many times have you sat in a 40-hour class waiting for the two hours of information you wanted to hear? E-learning is a productivity tool that not only gives students personalized learning or the information to meet their needs, but also allows for assessment and accountability.

---

private study, read a white paper, listen to a seminar, or attend an event. Bauer continues, "The point is, did they come out competent, sooner rather than later?"

Once the team had built the Web-enabled roadmaps and started to add learning resources, it could figure out what else the site needed, such as security or search capability.

> "Reaching competency quickly is what counts now."
>
> —Diane Bauer
> Senior Manager
> E-Learning Marketing

"If it existed, we said paint it blue and call is *available*; if it didn't exist, paint it white and call it *not built*. That let the user community see that even if we hadn't built everything, we had a plan. A person could mouse over the white boxes on the site to see when something was coming."

One of the requirements set for the e-learning program was accessibility. It had to be easy and quick to use. Putting it on the Cisco intranet helped solve the accessibility problem; introducing choice helped shorten learning time. If a learning objective was to be able to explain the function of firewalls, list the types of firewalls, and demonstrate firewall configurations, the site could give users the choice of viewing a video, attending a class, reading the firewall primer, or taking part in a collaborative event. At the end, the system tested the user's knowledge of firewalls as prescribed in the learning objective.

The site contains an assessment engine that is built into the competency roadmaps. At first, it provided only pre- and post-learning assessments, but now assessment questions appear throughout a module. The assessment software can direct a user back to certain material if necessary, making the assessment more of a learning aid and less of a smart-o-meter.

Some of the e-learning is assessed with the help of live mentors who observe learners' new skills in action, for example on a sales call. The goal is to have online mentors—experts around the globe—available 24 hours a day. The site also offers a storehouse of CBT and interactive multimedia instruction that the e-learning team broke into modules, tagged, and put into an LMS. The LMS tracks their use and wraps in assessment as needed.

The site also provides online access to Cisco's equipment labs so that a learner can connect from a browser to a rack of Cisco equipment, open an interactive training session, and try configuring a switch or a router before doing it at a customer's site. The company saves the cost of sending systems engineers to remote classroom labs, and the systems people gain control over when and where they test out on live equipment.

All of those options for learners—round-the-clock access, lots of choice in how to reach a learning objective, and plenty of feedback—promote a state of continual learning for which the learner, not the instructor, takes responsibility.

"We're breaking down the notion that learning is an event-only model," says Bauer. The flip side is a whole new way of working for the trainer. "When you move from static, event-based learning to e-learning, you're never done. You have to keep your content fresh and continually improve your site. You're just like a dot.com."

E-learning startups tend to follow a learning curve, Bauer notes. The first phase is about Web-enabling your content: Just get some courses on the Web, organize them by communities, and offer them through a portal. Next, modularize the content into database objects. Then put content development tools in front of subject matter experts and have the system alert them when their content is aging.

The second phase is about performance. That's where e-learning begins to tie content to performance and measure results more explicitly. Some questions to ask: Are we mapping learning objects to competencies? Are we measuring learners' competency before, during, and after learning?

The next step for the site is a state called learner-centricity. "Instead of having to follow learning roadmaps, users will have customized learning pushed to them as needed," explains Bauer. In addition, the system will be smart enough to know a user's connectivity requirements (how much bandwidth is available), performance needs, and preferred learning style. Indeed, the system will grow smarter about a user with each subsequent log-on, enabling the site to dish up ever-more relevant learning snippets.

"We want to be there within three years," says Bauer.

For now, the ISLG is working on more dynamic roadmaps, better search capabilities, improved assessment, and stronger reporting capabilities. That last improvement will enable the site software to report to managers the skill and knowledge levels of the technical salesforce, relative to new strategies. Indirectly, it is a predictor of hiring and training needs.

"One of the most challenging things we face on the road to customization is mobilizing thousands of content contributors without creating chaos," says Bauer. "We're requiring content providers to tag their data by such categories as type, form, audience, origin, language, author's ID, start and end dates, and so forth."

AGAIN, BUT FASTER

The Field E-Learning Connection had barely launched when the Internet Learning Solutions Group turned its attention to its second customer segment—the 40,000 companies that resell Cisco networking gear. Spread over 132 countries, this audience numbers more than 200,000 people who need to keep up with Cisco products and obtain certification in their use.

The Field E-Learning Connection was all built internally and took seven months from concept to launch. John Chambers didn't think that was fast enough, so for the Partner E-Learning Connection, the ISLG leaned heavily on vendors and got it running in three months—just in time for the worldwide Cisco partner summit in Las Vegas, at which Chambers made his now-famous prediction about e-learning.

Lessons and shortcuts from the field program helped ISLG produce a learning portal that was more personalized than its first one. "When you sign on," says Metz, "it knows who you are, what company you're with, what market you serve, and what geography your company works in. Already, it can push information to users."

The partner site builders, numbering about 100 people, worked in teams covering site development, technology, marketing, content, and prototypes. "We were on such a short timeline that turf wars never had time to develop," says Lisa Baumert, senior manager of the partner site.

As with the field site, the partner connection team made sure it had leadership and stakeholder support from the start, says Baumert. "Cisco people and channel partners from many

> "Our goal is to provide very personalized learning tailored to each user's experience and learning objectives."
> —Lisa Baumert
> Senior Manager
> Partner E-Learning Connection

countries were part of our extended development and pilot teams." Weekly conference calls and access to the site prototype kept them involved. "Getting their buy-in along the way meant that at launch time we had global support."

The portal offers many kinds of learning opportunities, including Web-based courses, interactive multimedia, streaming video, video-on-demand, simulations, audio-on-demand, and more. "We can offer users choices in how to access content depending on how they learn best," says Baumert.

"Our goal," she continues, "is to provide very personalized learning tailored to each user's experience and learning objectives. Eventually, the site will be able to prescribe just those parts of a curriculum that would benefit someone most given their experience. In our decisions about features, functionality, and content, we kept coming back to the user."

Since the Partner E-Learning Connection launched in March 2000, about 30 percent of Cisco's partner companies have logged on. So far, the top countries accessing the site include the United States, the United Kingdom, China, Germany, and Australia. However, reports have tracked individuals from 132 different countries logging on, adds Baumert, "indicating its global appeal."

For the moment, the site language is English, "but we're working with our local offices to translate some courses into Chinese, Korean, Spanish, and Portuguese," says Baumert. "In Asia, localization is more important for the sales content than for the technical content. We're still figuring out how to prioritize the localization effort."

The Partner E-Learning Connection resides outside of the Cisco firewall and thus presents some unique technical challenges. Its users around the globe have varying types of Inter-

Switched On

Glen Tapley is a trainer who made the switch to e-learning. One month after he was hired by Cisco as an instructor, the word went out that his training unit "was no longer in the instruction business." Tapley had joined Cisco just as it was getting serious about e-learning.

Burned out by a previous instructor job that kept him on the road 80 percent of the time, he was ready for a change. "My kids would cry on the way to the airport when I headed out for another week away from home.

Now, Tapley is a technical education consultant in Cisco's Internet Learning Solutions Group, a job he sees as having advantages over his previous role as a full-time classroom instructor.

"E-learning doesn't require skills I didn't already have, but it takes more flexibility of thought to apply the things I used to do to this new arena," says Tapley. It's also easier to get set up to do online instruction. "Instead of going to a hotel meeting room with tons of equipment, I just need a couple of PCs and an Internet connection."

Tapley admits that for an instructor, there are downsides to e-learning in its current state. "A lot of old-time trainers moved on to other business units (when e-learning became a priority) because they wanted more platform time. I understand their choice. There's a satisfaction you get from seeing the light go on in someone's eyes when they understand a complex topic. The instructor doesn't get that satisfaction from e-learning."

But Tapley is confident that e-learning will change and improve so that the excitement of the classroom becomes part of the e-learning experience.

"In the meantime," he says, "there's plenty of encouragement at Cisco to figure out how to make e-learning better."

---

net access and unequal amounts of bandwidth. "Access speed is an issue for countries outside the United States," says Baumert, "but also for people in the United States who are logging on to the site from a slow modem at home."

Because e-learning is a relatively new phenomenon for many of Cisco's channel partners, there is a need to market its benefits and promote its use. Baumert advises having a marketing plan to drive awareness and send people to the site.

Baumert is clearly jazzed about working on an e-learning project of this scale. "It's an Internet application that will grow. It's an exciting mix of technology and content, and it can help solve business problems. So, I'm excited to come to work every day."

ROCKY ROAD

All is not smooth on the road to e-learning, even at Cisco, where conditions make it likely to prosper. The ILSG must continually prove that e-learning works and why.

"Everyone wants to know how much you save with e-learning," says Metz, "but the important discussion is what are the things you can do once you have the infrastructure installed that you simply couldn't do in the old model."

Cisco acquires a new partner company on average once every two-and-a-half weeks. Before the Field E-learning Connection established a primary source for learning, account managers had to consult hundreds of internal Web sites and wade through piles of email to keep up with acquisitions information. Now the acquisitions page on the Field E-Learning Connection has one of the highest hit rates of any page on the portal.

Before the Field E-Learning Connection existed, salespeople spent days in training away from their customers, peers, and managers, so online learning was a pretty obvious benefit from a time standpoint. But to test how e-learning would work compared to classroom training, the field e-learning team studied 200 resellers taking a certification course. Half attended live classes and labs and took part in

Lessons From a Leader

Presuming top-level support and a good technology infrastructure, here's how to launch an e-learning program.

❑ Select a target audience whose learning has obvious strategic value to the company. Sales and service employees are a good bet. So are customers.

❑ If your e-learning mandate comes without a big staff and a budget, build a virtual e-learning team from all across the company. You'll need this anyway to install your e-learning on existing IT systems and to get the bosses of your target audience to support e-learning.

❑ Take yourself off the stage. Be prepared to let others (nontrainers) have the final say on training design. Give subject matter experts the tools to create good content. Make them accountable for content timeliness and learners responsible for becoming competent.

❑ To whatever results you are measuring, be sure to add time to competence. E-learning is about nothing so much as it's about speed.

❑ Start fast and get faster. Use such time-savers as templates and reusable learning objects to make subsequent versions of e-learning happen faster. Remember that e-learning is not an event but a continuous process.

❑ Don't build everything yourself. That's what vendors and partners are for.

❑ Market your e-learning effort inside and outside of the company. Anything as new as e-learning needs to be explained early and often.

❑ Don't get sucked into public debates about whether e-learning is real learning or whether information is a learning resource. Although those topics may keep you up at night, airing them at work makes you seem out of touch with real business issues.

---

study groups. The other half took their training online and used remote labs and online discussion groups. All were tested at the end: The e-learners had a 10 percent better pass rate than the classroom learners.

"The real benefit," adds Metz, "came in the opportunity savings. The classroom learners were out of pocket for a week, away from customers and co-workers. The online learners fit their learning into the valleys of their schedules and experienced little or no hit to business productivity."

There have been substantial savings from e-learning programs at Cisco, especially in manufacturing, the site of one of the most aggressive skunk works. Assembly line workers haven't seen a classroom since 1999; they have access to e-learning right on the factory floor. The result was savings of $1 million per quarter in improved process, and an 80 percent increase in speed to competence.

Another e-learning coup for that unit involved training for ISO 9000 registration. For its initial registration three years earlier, Cisco budgeted $1.4 million for classroom training. In late 1999, it spent less than $20,000 for the training delivered online, with better results measured as fewer inconsistencies with ISO standards. And while the ISO readiness program achieved 100 percent participation across a user community of 6,000 manufacturing and customer service employees, internal e-learning implementation took only four weeks from concept to global execution.

"People like to argue that e-learning isn't as effective as the classroom," says Tom Kelly, "but how effective *is* the classroom? Most of us know that classroom teaching produces about a 25 percent retention rate in the first 10 days, with a decline in skill if you don't use it.

"Tests we've done show equal or better retention with e-learning, mostly because it's targeted at what a person needs to know when they need to know it. Spend 40 hours in a classroom and how many hours of good content will there be that are applicable to you? Not many."

Classroom training's biggest benefit is human interaction, says Kelly, "and none of that happens while the instructor is talking. The benefits of informal learning through interaction give us a way to talk about how to improve e-learning. The big question is how to get human interaction in the e-learning process.

"Cost is the only argument managers will listen to. But it's not right to do e-learning if it's cost-effective but not learning-effective."

Kelly likes to argue that training and its costs should be part of product development, not an afterthought. "Until we make products that don't require any training, training is a product cost just like documentation or packaging the product in a box." To make his point, Kelly ended the practice of having ILSG develop product training.

As a result, more business units budgeted training dollars in 2000 than in past years. Some hired additional professional staff, anticipating that they'd have to pull people out periodically to do training or to create training materials. "It's a recognition that dollars have to be spent on training," says Kelly.

Proving that e-learning saves money and delivers real learning is almost easy compared to another challenge that crops up in companies making major shifts from the classroom to the Internet: making learning time a respected part of a job.

"If you're sitting at your desk going through an interactive exercise or watching a video or, God forbid, reading a book, people think you're not really working," says Kelly. "You're open to Anyone Who Comes Along With a Problem."

At Cisco, a land of cubicles, people who are taking part in an online class can put up yellow police tape to signal that they're busy learning. "We're trying to get across that learning is a valued part of a job," says Kelly.

Another significant problem facing e-learning, says Kelly, is that there are no widely used industry standards for the tools on the market, and so the tools don't work together—no matter what their creators claim. "Eight years ago, you couldn't send email between different systems even if you were in the same company. That's about where we are in e-learning today."

Kelly doesn't believe that e-learning will change the way people learn. "People will always learn through their senses and by using their bodies, their hands, and their feet. What e-learning changes is the way people teach. I see that trainers have a choice about e-learning: Take a risk and try something new, or go somewhere else where their old skills still have value and there's no need to change."

Kelly's personal hope for e-learning is that it will serve a higher purpose than just training the next salesperson or the next customer in a cheaper way. He hopes it becomes the tool that brings the best teachers in the world, the best lesson plans, and the most enthusiasm for learning to the students who want it, anywhere in the world.

"My hope is that e-learning expands their horizons and gives them the skills to achieve a brighter future."

Training Program Design

Learners Want More Than Technology

Editor's Comment: The article reprinted here is a research summary of a study by The MASIE Center and ASTD during the second half of year 2000. This workplace study looked at the factors that influence learners to accept and use e-learning to solve workplace problems. One important finding of the study was that a low initial acceptance level, in this case about 6 out of 10 employees who were offered the e-learning course, had a strong effect on learner satisfaction. The learner's initial experience with the learning technology was very important, helping to define larger issues of motivation, incentives, and instructional design of the technology components of the learning experience. More information about the survey results is found online at *www.LearningDecisions.com*.

The MASIE Center and ASTD studied the factors that influence learners to accept and use e-learning in the workplace during May–October 2000.

All the e-Learning in the world will not make a difference to employee development or workforce productivity, if learners do not "show up" to take the on-line training options. This study looked at the practices that organizations can deploy to increase the likelihood of actual learner participation in an on-line course.

Most trainers and managers inherently know that just making e-learning technology available will have no significant effect on employee development or workforce productivity. Employees may need to be motivated to take advantage of e-learning opportunities.

The study surveyed nearly 30 courses at 16 companies and over 700 learners to analyze the relationship between organizational efforts to market and motivate learner participation and actual satisfaction with technology as a means of providing learning.

The first phase of the study gathered information on all of the courses from the training functions of the companies. The information was used to assess the impact of the context of the e-learning offer on acceptance rates. Specifically, the study sought to understand why some learners begin e-learning courses and others do not. Because the context of any offer is complex and varied, the study examines the impact of three particularly important features of the context: Marketing, Support, and Incentives.

The second part of the study assessed the factors influencing acceptance from the learner's perspective for nine of the courses from the first part of the study. Data were collected from employees who received an invitation from their firm to participate in one of the courses. The information was used to differentiate the learners who accepted the offer from those employees who did not.

In general, the results revealed that the most successful e-learning course are those that are well advertised and championed, and those for which ample completion time and support are provided during work hours.

DRIVERS OF E-LEARNING ACCEPTANCE

The study confirmed that many e-learning courses are unable to attract all the learners to whom they are offered. Overall, there was a 58% participation or "start" rate across all courses. In other words, on average 6 out of every 10 employees who were offered an e-learning course actually started the course. The average start rate for courses where participation was voluntary was 32%, significantly

---

Source: "e-Learning Study: If We Build It, Will They Come?" by Elliott Masie in *LearningDecisions Interactive Newsletter*, May 2001, pp.4–5. Reprinted with permission of *LearningDecisions Interactive Newsletter*. Copyright 2001. All rights reserved.

lower than mandatory courses. However, mandatory courses were far from perfect as well, averaging only a 69% start rate.

MARKETING

Face-to-face conversations and targeted email messages were the most common means by which learners reported hearing about e-learning courses. Companies are more likely to rely on traditional methods, such as face-to-face conversations or print media, when the course was required. For instance, internal memos were utilized 10% more in cases where courses were mandatory.

Only 60% of learners reported that the course was well advertised. It is therefore critical for organizations to be intentional and varied in their marketing activities aimed at learner participation in an e-learning course.

SUPPORT

Although marketing and promotion efforts appeared to be the crucial factor in prompting learners to begin the courses in the study, they were not always likely to engage in the portions of these courses delivered via technology. Rather it was the amount of support learners received that actually increased their willingness to begin the technology-delivered portions. The level to which learners feel they are supported was one of the primary indicators regarding their participation in e-learning.

The results of the study revealed most e-learners felt supported by the technology and by technical and subject matter experts (SMEs), with levels of satisfaction ranging from 84% to 73%. However, opportunity remains for stronger manager and co-worker support in providing learners with enough time to take the course as well as the encouragement to see it through.

INCENTIVES

Most incentives offered did not increase participation in voluntary courses. Over 75% of e-learners reported that taking the course did not increase the likelihood of a promotion nor did failure to participate decrease the possibility of losing their jobs. In addition, over 80% did not feel that taking the course would affect the benefits they would receive.

Learners are driven most by their own intrinsic motivation and personal development plans—not by external factors. Only 12% and 22%, respectively, received financial or nonfinancial incentives to take the course. 79% and 77%, respectively, believed the skills and knowledge they gained would be useful in or outside the organization.

DRIVERS OF E-LEARNING SATISFACTION

In addition to looking at the factors that influence acceptance of e-learning, the study also examined the factors that produced satisfying learning experiences for those who took the courses.

Study results indicate that learners were able to benefit from their e-learning experiences, with 84% willing to take a similar course in the future and 72% indicating that they had a positive experience. However, only 51% felt that they had learned more rapidly than they would have on the job, and roughly 58% did not get adequate interaction with either instructors or other students. The lack of collaboration is one factor that potentially leads to dissatisfaction.

The amount of support learners received while taking the technology-delivered portions of the courses also played a key role in their level of satisfaction. Again, learners found the support provided by the technical staff and subject matter experts to be especially important.

TECHNOLOGY

With 80% of learners indicating that they were satisfied with the technology used for the course, it can be concluded that the technologies used to provide an e-learning course is an important factor for satisfaction. However, it must be understood that technology alone is not a valid predictor of learner satisfaction, but is rather just one component of the offer and support structure.

The impact of technology on learner satisfaction is greatly colored by the learner's previous experiences with e-learning. Learners who reported having negative experiences with e-learning previously were significantly less satisfied with their current e-learning experience. This finding underscores the importance of learner's initial experiences with e-learning.

LOCATION AND TIMING OF EVENT

Where and when learners are engaged in e-learning courses was shown to affect their level of satisfaction. The study revealed that 86% of e-learners in mandatory courses took the technology part of the course at work, either at their desk, in a shared workplace, or at an onsite training center. Learners who took courses while on the road or at a customer's site were significantly less satisfied with their e-learning experience.

When learners were asked about their preferred time, 76% stated they preferred to take e-learning during working hours. This is attributed to the fact that many learners do not want the technology training to disrupt their personal life, as today's workforce is always striving to maintain a good work-life balance. Employers that provide their mandatory training during work hours will find they have a more satisfied workforce.

RECOMMENDATIONS

Interest in e-learning has grown rapidly in recent years. Many organizations have begun taking steps along the e-learning journey. The question many of them face is whether their learners are on the journey with them. Organizations cannot rely on the technology itself to drive interest, acceptance or satisfaction with e-learning. This study has revealed that while companies can indeed view e-learning as an efficient new means for educating employees, the context in which this learning is offered must be carefully considered and managed.

In order to increase e-learning participation and satisfaction, it is recommended that organizations:

- Use intentional, dynamic, and continuous marketing activities, including traditional marketing methods, such as face-to-face discussions and print advertising.
- Provide the time and space to learn on company time.
- Create a learning culture that encourages and appreciates e-learning.
- Develop an environment where peer support is widespread.
- Ensure that frustration with e-learning technology is not a barrier to successful e-learning.
- Develop incentives beyond candy bars and meaningless certificates, which provide valuable benefits like career advancement and peer recognition.
- Continue to implement and develop synchronous, collaborative courses that fuel the learner's fundamental desire for interaction while more closely simulating the classroom experience.
- Blend e-learning with other complementary forms of instruction to attract those who may be uncomfortable with learning via technology.

E-Learning for Free Agents

Editor's Comment: During year 2001, the business press seemed not to know whether or not we are a nation of free agents. The year seemed to start out that way; then came the dot.com collapse, more mergers, acquisitions, and layoffs; and then the September 11 attack on The World Trade Center and The Pentagon, and the crash in Pennsylvania, leaving nerves jangled and workers uncertain about workplaces. The twin urges to seek community and meaningful personal contact and to retreat to working at home were both in the forefront of workers' behavior. Daniel H. Pink's book, *Free Agent Nation*, arrived on the scene early in the year, to mixed reviews.

Perhaps *Free Agent Nation* tries too hard to be seen as a trend-setter, with catchy trendy terms and slogans that define the years ahead. For example, author Daniel Pink uses the term "mamapreneurs" to identify the work-at-home mothers with young children running around, blurring the distinctions between work and home (p. 192). Pink says that today's and tomorrow's workers don't talk about "balancing" work and home; they talk about "blending" work and home—"some antibiotics and some echinacea." Pink says that the family business is the natural form of work and workplace throughout American history and in fact, is the "dominant world model" (p. 193).

He coins the phrase, "My Size Fits Me" as an approach to life and work (p. 188). This concept defines the four key values of the free agent work ethic:

- having freedom
- being authentic
- putting yourself on the line
- defining your own success (Chapter 4, pp. 65ff).

His book mostly follows this train of thought, which might have been more acceptable if the dot.com crash had not occurred and the 9/11 attacks not happened. Given the state of American workers at the beginning of year 2002, one is tempted to say that the "Me" generation is gone, and that workers have demonstrated that they need to and want to work together in all sorts of collaborative endeavors. In his somewhat fragile attempt to be the anti-organization man, he does, however, make some points about learning, skills, and talent that appeal to newer realities of work and workers.

One key point that seems to be right on target is that in the free agent nation, "an experienced brain is an asset," and that an "ailing back" is not necessarily a liability (p. 239). Free agent talent and skills will depend on Internet access and a network of smart colleagues, no matter what age worker from teenager to "e-tirees"—men and women in their 60s and 70s living in "e-communities" (pp. 233ff.). He cites many statistics, among them that in San Diego County, 8 percent of high school students already run their own online businesses (p. 254), and that by year 2003, 40 percent of households of persons age 55–65 will be online—and probably working online (p. 236).

The point is that whoever has the skills and talents that are in demand by employers has the bargaining power for money, prestige, and a satisfying work life ("My Size Fits Me"). E-learning for free agents is necessarily me-based, and primarily just-in-time and just-enough to ensure freedom and define one's own success.

His Chapter 15 is a sobering account of the failures of public education. His title is "School's

---

Source: Free Agent Nation by Daniel H. Pink. New York: Warner Books, Inc., 2001. 356 pages, $24.95. Daniel H. Pink is a free agent writer who lives in Washington DC. His articles have appeared in *Fast Company, The New York Times, The Washington Post, New Republic, Salon,* and others. He was a speech writer for former Vice-President Al Gore.

Out: Free Agency and the Future of Education," a pointed attack on the "organization man" system that has yielded an education system out of synch with what free agents really need to know. Pink says that our schools "are awash in a rising tide of irrelevancy," not only of mediocrity (p. 246). His hope is that the ever-growing home-schooling challenges to the "organization man" system and the alternative high school model together will become the foundation for free agent adults, as workers in year 2002 and beyond become "unschooled" (pp. 247ff).

Daniel H. Pink's book is provocative, full of catchy descriptive words and phrases, one picture of work and life in the 21st century, and probably right about many important things.

3. E-Learning Nuts and Bolts

How Online Course Management Systems Affect the Course

Editor's Comment: This is a story told by two faculty members at George Mason University who designed and taught a Business Writing course online. It is especially instructive to readers in a similar situation because these are *teachers,* and the story has lessons—lessons about lessons.

DESCRIPTIVE MATERIAL

In effect, the main "text" for the course was the WebCT site. It contained the syllabus, a schedule, a grade book, descriptions of all assignments (including rationale, directions, and on-line submission procedures), model assignments, and hyperlinks to readings, as well as on-line databases and optional resource materials.

No paper system could possibly provide so much learning support on a 24/7 basis and also allow us to update, revise, and add to the course material to meet emerging class needs.

We discovered that WebCT's ability to warehouse a great deal of learning relevant materials had both positive and negative consequences. As suggested above, the positive side can be simply stated: the site contained everything that skillful, committed, and independent students needed to support their learning activities. But not all of our classes were populated by such students. More than a few did not read the instructions carefully or thoughtfully; did not look, for example, at model assignments; did not bother to follow links to the resources that could have facilitated their work.

Rather than blame the students for their deficiencies, we realized that we needed to design future Web based courses in a way that anticipates a wide range in user performance. In this regard, developing on-line course material is like developing software: users reveal the bugs that successive versions eliminate. We learned, for example, that the WebCT "paths" provide a great way to index and compartmentalize the diverse materials associated with a given assignment. But some students just didn't bother to drill down into the material and thus didn't have the resources they needed to perform as we hoped they would. We also learned that what we regarded as clearly described assignments (in one case a "progress report") could convey different meanings to different students. Although we provided a fair amount of detail in the description of the assignment, it is clear that many students never gained a clear enough understanding of the aims and intent of a progress report.

Source: "How On-Line Course Management Systems Affect the Course" by Joel Foreman and Sharon Widmayer in *Journal of Interactive Instruction Development*, Fall 2000, pp. 16–18. Joel Foreman is an Associate Professor of English and Social and Organizational Learning at George Mason University. Sharon Widmayer is a Faculty Support Specialist at George Mason University, specializing in Instructional Technology and Instructional Design. She also teaches in the English Department and in the Graduate School of Education at George Mason University. The article is reprinted with permission of the *Journal of Interactive Instruction Development*. Copyright 2000. All rights reserved.

The general prescription we can make is that written materials need to be as clear and detailed as possible. But this is easier said than done. What seems clear to us may not seem clear to students. A lot of detail may be too much for students who don't like to read or are inattentive. Given these circumstances, it is desirable to have a couple of student users at various levels test assignments before they are actually deployed during a regular semester. There's no other way to be certain in advance that materials will be read as we hope and intend, or even read at all.

Our adherence to the ideal of student-centered instruction was severely challenged, for example, by students who did not read the model essays posted to guide their written efforts in similar genres. Such students need more scaffolding in the form of linked interactive quizzes (a WebCT feature) that check their comprehension of various materials. We have also considered adding discussion questions to which students must respond in WebCT's asynchronous discussion database. However, the quizzes are automatically graded and require minimal instructor supervision whereas a set of student responses in an on-line discussion board demands a direct review by the instructor, which could be very time consuming. Another technique (one that integrates course learning goals with our need to confirm that students are carefully reading course materials) is a meta-set of writing assignments in which students critique the model essays and/or write their own version of the instructions for a given task

FILE EXCHANGE AND COMMENTING ON STUDENT DOCUMENTS

A major challenge when teaching with technology, especially when teaching totally on-line, is how to manage the workflow: what's the most efficient way for students to forward documents for instructor review and then get them back for revision?

In both the f2f and on-line courses, we used WebCT's mail and file attachment function as our routing system. We avoided using regular email accounts because many students use George Mason University's antiquated Unix mail system (Pine) with its overly complicated file transfer system. It was easier to have students load their files in WebCT and use its mail system to signal a pick up.

All files had to be produced in Word because its comment insertion function provided an excellent way for us to embed commentary in student work. We archived the annotated drafts and then (using Word's "arrange" feature) compared the original draft and the revision in order to determine how precisely the student was responding to instructor feedback.

While as a whole our routing and feedback systems worked well, we did find that uploading and downloading a whole set of files takes up a significant amount of time. With a distance course, there really is no preferable alternative, but with an f2f course (as one of us learned) there is a great temptation to revert back to paper. As long as students show up for class, paper documents are effortless to exchange and handwriting marginal commentary is faster and easier for an instructor who cannot invest the time required to learn how to use Word's annotation systems efficiently.

MANAGING PEER REVIEW

In pursuit of a more student-centered approach to revision, we designed a peer review process for two of the major writing assignments. In some face-to-face sections, peer review activities were done in class, where it was easy to coordinate who was reading whose paper and to make sure everyone received appropriate feedback. However, managing this process (or any group process) at a distance introduces complications that have to do with the scheduling and coordination of student activity. First, students need to have unambiguous and clear instructions about what to do and when. In this case, they worked in 4 person teams with each team member responsible for reviewing the work of the others. Thus each student produced 3 reviews and received 3 reviews of her work. For a class of 20 people, that's 60 reviews that need to be properly posted and made easily accessible for readers. To keep things straight we used WebCT's asynchronous discussion database ("bulletins"). We set up limited members-only "forums" for each team. In these spaces each team member attached a file with the document to be reviewed. Students downloaded the files, read the documents, and then posted their reviews in their team forums. WebCT's document management tools, which excel in this area, allowed us to search for and isolate all the reviews written by an individual student. Using the "compile" feature, we could then combine the reviews in a single document for a quick assessment.

RUBRICS

Assessment rubrics were designed for this course in order to make sure that students received clear, detailed feedback from the instructor, especially considering the fact that in the on-line version of this course, this feedback represented the primary interaction with the instructor. Despite this attention to detail, we still found that at points the assignment criteria did not match the assignment learning goals. In addition, in future semesters, a better effort to train students to use the rubrics to guide their writing is needed, as some students neglected to read the rubrics and use the rubrics to gage what was expected of them. One strategy for doing so is to add some sort of self-assessment into the writing process that students complete before turning in their assignments.

DESIGNING LESSONS FOR F2F

Given the constrained communication systems that are the norm for distance learning (i.e., limited opportunities for either oral or synchronous dialogue), we spent 99% of our course design effort devising strategies that would work well for students working independently with little interaction from the teacher. As noted, a great deal of time was spent writing clear directions to assignments, providing models and explanations, devising methods to give students sufficient feedback on their work, and imagining how WebCT's functions could support our pedagogical goals.

As a result, we paid little attention to activities to be done in class. This myopia did not become apparent until we were about to teach our f2f classes. Then the hustle began to create material for in-class lessons or to adapt for a classroom environment material that had been designed with independent work in mind. One of us solved the problem by scheduling an f2f section in a computer lab. This wasn't possible for the other, who had to print and duplicate for distribution paper copies of our carefully crafted on-line materials. In addition, as the WebCT course space contained critical links to on-line databases and resource web sites, the f2f students that met in a computer-less room were severely constrained. Specifically, they did not have the opportunity to discuss these web-based materials during class time and were not able to practice useful research activities, like learning how to search for business articles on line.

In the future, we would like to make sure that face-to-face sections of web supported courses meet in a lab so that they always have access to all class material. Otherwise, many of the benefits of web support are lost.

CONCLUSION

We are both committed to the continued use of the course management system for our classes—in part because we believe such systems are the inevitable future of education. What we have learned, though, is that these systems introduce a whole new set of uncertainties into course design. Many of the elements and tactics we take for granted in the paper based and f2f classes become necessary opportunities for experimentation as we attempt to fashion instructional programs that have predictable results. Perhaps more than ever, it is critical to pay attention to our users (the students) and the problems they encounter attempting to follow our directives. With that valuable knowledge in hand, we can build better programs and maybe even develop a stable body of best pedagogical practices for digital instruction.

Shell's Formula for Blending Training Fuels Optimum Learning at Minimum Cost

Editor's Comment: The notions of de-construct and re-construct play a major role in Shell's saving training money as well as building useful learning experiences. This article tells how Shell does it by designing, choosing, and blending.

We face the same challenge as many large global organizations—how to maximize learning effectiveness while minimizing learning costs. At Shell Corporation, we have developed a methodology we believe will help solve this problem.

Beyond purchasing programs, paying for trainers and incurring huge travel expenses, the most costly aspect of traditional training is time away from work. Our solution is to find ways to bring the learning to the participants, rather than bringing participants to the learning, through our new Shell Open University.

During many years of providing professional learning, our central learning center in Holland developed more than 4,300 hours of learning material. We want to reuse as much of that material as possible in our new effort to bring learning to participants in a supportive learning environment that uses the latest technologies and research, while keeping costs to a minimum. We also needed to be sure that all learning was applicable to current business needs.

REDESIGNING COURSE MATERIAL FOR TODAY'S TECHNOLOGY

Our Learning Review Process has two phases: de-construct and re-construct. In the de-construct phrase, we developed definitions and terminology for the new learning process. Then we broke down existing learning material into topics. We identified gaps or overlaps to decide what could be shelved and where new modules needed to be developed.

In the re-construct phase we looked at ways to be sure the training is differentiated (Shell specific). Key elements in rebuilding the training were content, context, and conduct.

Most existing *content* was generic and introductory level. We had to decide whether modules should be used as is, reworked in-house, or purchased through a contractor or off-the-shelf.

The *context*, or positioning, is key to a differentiated product. The learning has to cover the competencies our business requires. Applying scenarios that reflect Shell business data and past projects makes the learning process more effective.

How the learning is *conducted* by our training staff or other Shell subject matter experts can affect its value. Choosing the appropriate format and involving facilitators with real Shell business experiences makes the training relevant to current work situations.

BLENDING LEARNING FOR BEST RESULTS

After the de-construct and re-construct phases, our attention is directed to blending the learning components for best results. We determined e-learning would be most effective when blended with the human element and provided within a framework of skills portfolios, personal development plans, and electronic tracking.

Source: "Shell's Formula for Blending Training Fuels Optimum Learning at Minimum Cost" by Regy Loknes in *Learning Decisions Interactive Newsletter*, April 2001, p. 8. Regy Loknes is Senior Learning and Development Advisor at Shell. Reprinted with permission of *Learning Decisions Interactive Newsletter* published by The MASIE Center. Copyright 2001. All rights reserved.

> **Definitions for Redesigning Course Material**
>
> *Learning Nugget:* 15–45 minute building block, stand-alone, self-assessed, any media, can be taken by anyone, anywhere, at anytime
>
> *Module:* a combination of nuggets that includes tutor support, more formal assessment, and individual assignments or job-tasks, taken by individuals, any time, anywhere
>
> *Topic*—logical grouping of modules according to subject matter
>
> *Certificate Program*—combination of nuggets and modules, taken from various topics, designed to be followed synchronously by groups of people

Our blended learning model is based on several imperatives. All learning is tied to competency frameworks. Fixed learning (fixed in time, location, and content) is blended with flexible learning (on demand, anywhere, customized). Finally, existing classroom and distance learning is blended with new e-learning and collaboration tools and network access.

At the module and certificate program level, blending the best attributes of several delivery mechanisms provides stimulating, effective learning experiences. These include pre-study work, classroom events (virtual or face-to-face), group assignments, on-line tutoring, Webcasts virtual classroom and field trips. The caveat here is to be sure the technology is used because it supports the learning process, not because it's available.

The blending formula depends on the subject and the audience. Our learners will use the global Shell intranet. Participants will be able to link in questions, get real work assignments and benefit from an on-line tutor who supplies exercises to do in their operating companies, wherever they are. This system enables peer-to-peer learning of the best kind.

After extensive benchmarking, we are pleased to find that current trends confirm the success potential of our work. With our nugget and module approach, learners gain just enough. The learning is "just in time," but not "just in case."

Knowledge Sharing Using a Knowledge Base

Editor's Comment: Extendable, adaptable, and flexible elements of knowledge needed to be available to product developers, sales persons, and learners of all sorts at ACI Worldwide. This company calls them "knowledge objects" and in this short article tells how they are defined and how the company developed them in-house.

ACI Worldwide is a leading global provider of electronic payments software and services for financial institutions, retail and healthcare organizations. Examples of our products include online transaction processing systems that run Automated Teller Machine (ATM) and Point of Sale (POS) systems. At least twenty billion times a year, ACI Worldwide software processes these transactions, powering the world's online payment systems.

THE CHALLENGE

Like many other companies and organizations, our knowledge content exists in many forms and is often difficult to share and access, especially on a global scale. Our knowledge content typically involves multiple, disparate knowledge repositories consisting of product information, documentation, and learning content in document formats such as Microsoft Word, PowerPoint, Adobe FrameMaker and HTML. To make knowledge sharing simpler and more efficient, we needed a way to organize and access our knowledge so that we could quickly and easily use a single source of content for a variety of purposes.

THE CONCEPT

ACI has developed a knowledge delivery solution that replaces some of the content repositories with a single knowledge base implementation. This knowledge base is represented in a universal document format (e.g., HTML) and shared globally with multiple product delivery channels.

In the first phase of the project, we targeted only learning and product documentation content for a single product. As a pilot project, it was important that our initial "radar screen" not be too large. Future phases may include additional knowledge types and other products.

Several factors influenced our decision to create our own knowledge base implementation. First, the implementation had to be deliverable using our existing web-based technologies. Our company already had a corporate intranet and the associated Web development tools. Second, we already possessed the skill-set necessary to design the knowledge base and build the Web server applications that would power it. Third, although we may have been able to acquire a similar solution from a Learning Management System (LMS) or Content Management System (CMS) vendor, our budget did not allow for a large expenditure. Additionally, our solution needed to be extendable, adaptable, and flexible so that other product support groups might eventually use it.

HOW IT WORKS

Our implementation of a knowledge base is comprised of organized knowledge objects. Knowledge objects are individual "chunks" of knowledge, classified according to their type. For example, *glossary*, *course*, *lesson*, and *quiz* are

---

Source: "Knowledge Sharing Using a Knowledge Base" by David Teal in *Learning Decisions Interactive Newsletter*, August 2001, p. 7. David Teal is a Senior Instructional Designer at ACI Worldwide. Article reprinted with permission from *Learning Decisions Interactive Newsletter*, a publication of The MASIE Center. Copyright 2001. All rights reserved.

knowledge object types used to represent components of learning content. The course *Business Overview* is an instance of a *course* knowledge object. The lesson *Examples of Implementations* is an instance of a *lesson* knowledge object.

To enable knowledge sharing courses are constructed of many knowledge object types other than *course, lesson, glossary,* and *quiz.* A course author might want to include other knowledge object types such as *topic* and *message flow*. So, the course content is a representation, not a copy, of the content contained in the knowledge base.

Technical writers and instructional designers share the responsibility of creating knowledge objects. This is an enormous benefit to our work group. We now have the ability to create content once, and use it for multiple purposes. Instructional designers blend knowledge objects to create courses and learning that can be facilitated synchronously or delivered asynchronously.

THE DETAILS

We use an authoring tool to develop product documentation and learning content. We chose a tool that supports content templates so we could build templates for each type of knowledge object (ex. course, lesson, glossary, and quiz). So as new lessons or quizzes are created, it frees the content authors from formatting and styling much of the content. Sections of the content templates are defined as editable regions while other sections are defined as non-editable regions. Hundreds of knowledge objects now exist.

4. Lonesome Online

Challenge for Designers: The Social Dimensions of Learning

Editor's Comment: Throughout the year 2001, training magazines, articles, newsletters, and journals have addressed the topic of online learning's need for built-in interactivity. Publications say that "f2f" (face to face) must be designed into learning activities along with any kind of e-learning delivery system. The MASIE Center itself talks about a "continuum" of online content, ranging from "rapid" through "templated" to "interactive." An article by Karen Frankola in *Workforce* magazine, October 2001, comments that the ratio should be 1 to 4: one hour of live training for every four hours of online self-paced learning (p. 58), and that "high dropout rates are e-learning's embarrassing secret" (p. 53). The social aspects of learning are on many designers' minds as year 2002 begins. Here's one man's opinion on "L-Learning" (Lonely Learning). Note the word "intentional" in the second paragraph. This is where good instructional design begins.

> "I love the idea of learning anytime and anywhere. But, when I took my first course on-line, I found myself feeling lonely! I was surprised by my reaction, since I am fairly quiet and rarely ask a lot of questions in class. What's happening?"
> —Signed, Lonely in e-Learning Land

The greatest strength of e-Learning, the empowerment of anytime, anywhere, learner defined access to training, can actually backfire by unintentionally creating L-Learning, or what I call Lonely Learning. If we "steal" the social dimension of learning from the learner, we may be taking a big step backwards in the knowledge food chain and decreasing the appeal and potential acceptance of e-Learning.

The MASIE Center believes that e-Learning can be designed and deployed in ways that will dramatically INCREASE the social dimensions of a training experience. But it must be intentional, as the simpler approach to on-line instructional design often leads to learner isolation, even when "community" activities are offered within the on-line course.

Let's start with a traditional classroom offering to better understand which social elements are in operation. A worker enrolls for a two-day class on a technical topic. Let's be a fly on the wall and track their social interactions surrounding the course:

• Their manager may have a conversation with them leading up to the decision or approval to attend the class. This chat will probably include a discussion of the content of the course and touch on how the worker will use the knowledge on the job. This face time with their manager on a "development" topic is often a key moment in their career development.

• The learner will probably have a series of conversations with peers about their attendance at the class. They may focus more on the loca-

---

Source: "Is e-Learning Lonely Learning?" by Elliott Masie in *Learning Decisions Interactive Newsletter*, January 2001, pp. 1–3. Elliott Masie is CEO of The MASIE Center, Editor of *Learning Decisions Interactive Newsletter*, and e-learning guru-in-chief of The MASIE Center. Article reprinted with permission of *Learning Decisions Interactive Newsletter*, a publication of The MASIE Center. Copyright 2001. All rights reserved.

tion of the course or even tourist plans if the class takes them out of town, but once again, a social dimension is added with peer awareness and interaction.

• When arriving at the class, the learner has both verbal and visual interaction with the other attendees. They will go through a compare and contrast with the other learners. What are their relative experience levels with this new technology? How are they using the technology? Are they there on a voluntary or "I was sent" basis? Some learners value the interaction with people who are doing similar tasks in other units or organizations as one of the big benefits of class participation.

• During the class, the learner gains "context" from the reactions of other learners. Are they the only one who is totally confused or bored out of their skull? The comments of other learners provide another perspective on how the new material is being received.

• The questions of other learners are key and critical to the effectiveness of a classroom experience. Only 10% of the class may actually ask a question, but they are asking on behalf of the rest of the class. The learner can sit in their seat and gain value from both the question and the answer. If they know the answer as soon as it is asked, it serves as a "cognitive rehearsal" of the newly acquired information and increases learner confidence.

• When there is a learning problem, peers are often easier to approach for clarification and remediation than the instructor, who might be busy, removed or downright confusing. Peer to peer learning is often vital, even in classrooms where there is no structured interaction.

• As the process moves from information delivery to workplace application, social interaction with colleagues back home will often move the content from theory to practice. An employee interaction back on the job provides a valuable debrief or application about "how we really do things!"

• If the learner keeps in touch with alumni from the class, that adds another, though rarely used, social interaction and benefit.

Throughout this classroom experience the social dimension of learning is operating. Now, there might be bad sides to this phenomenon as well, including peers that lower learner motivation and attendees in the class that ask distracting or confusing questions and dominate the instructional time. But, most learning that is classroom based is, by its construction, social and rarely seen as lonely.

So, how does e-Learning become L-Learning? When the learner is selecting the content on their own from a portal site; then taking a series of modules that are merely information delivery with practice; and the course design is fully isolated from social interaction . . . It MIGHT be seen as Lonely.

In some situations, if all I want to do is to learn how to create a routing table, then this scenario is exactly what I want. But, as the complexity and intensity of the learning objectives grow, I find myself, as a learner wanting more.

We believe that e-Learning can intentionally LEVERAGE social interaction—mediated through technology—to create higher effectiveness and more acceptable learning experiences. Here are specific methodologies to make e-Learning less lonely:

Contracting: The manager of an e-Learner can be MORE involved in the process using the power of the Internet. A potential learner can be asked to define their specific learning outcomes prior to registration and dialogue with their manager for consensus. A Learning Management System can be configured to trigger a series of self-assessments and dialogues between the learner and the manager. These might take place on-line or an in person dialogue could be launched by the system. In other words, the manager and the learner receive an email asking them to meet and discuss two or three items to prepare the learner for the program.

Pre-work: A learner can be assigned pre-work for an e-Learning experience that requires them to interact with other people within their organization about the topic. If a worker was about to attend a class on Java programming, they would be asked to spend 15 minutes with a current Java coder to see how the language was actually used for a business project. The results of that dialogue could be a pre-work assignment that must be completed before accessing the first module. In courses that are focused on business process or personal skills, the interactions might actually overlap from pre-work to the meat of the class. (We are seeing the use of 360 Degree Feedback in this process for several executive on-line programs.)

Team Work: The learner taking the e-Learning class can be assigned to a team of learners in other organizations and even other parts of the world, either for a group project or as a first level peer support during the process. Teams can change throughout the course depending on the progress of the learner or can be forged into active groups. In on-line MBA programs, the teams are often seen as MORE valuable to the learners than interaction with their faculty.

Peer Questions Observed: The learner can be given ongoing access to the questions (and answers) of other learners. Whether through a Frequently Asked Question (FAQ) list or a threaded discussion, learners can access the questions of others.

Relative Progress: The learner should have the ability to see how they are progressing relative to other learners in the class. This is not meant to set up direct competition, but to give a learner a context of how they are making progress. This can be created through a scoreboard or even a progress meter for the learner. They might be able to click and access other learners having trouble or chat with some of the learners who are breezing through the program.

At Work Coaching: The learner can also be provided with a person in the workplace that will serve as a coach on the content. It could be a subject matter expert, their manager or a peer in another part of the organization. This allows and encourages the learner to use the mouth and ears as well as eyes and fingers in the process of learning.

Community of Learning: In some situations, the learner might be invited into a more formal "Learning Community" with fellow learners, where there are structured and scheduled opportunities for interaction and a commitment for mutual support. These require both technology and facilitation. Just providing access to a chat room or bulletin board does not create a community of learning! It is a contracted and intentional process that can provide huge benefits that extend beyond the end of the formal course.

We are at the first stage of understanding the social dimensions of learning. Over the next several years, we will see changes in the instructional design process to better account for and leverage interaction in e-Learning programs. We will create more blended approaches that combine on-line with face to face (or phone to phone) interaction. And, we will come to recognize that learners do not want lonely learning! We must make e-Learning more social than classroom instruction!

Strategies to Prevent Online Attrition

Editor's Comment: By year's end there was a proliferation of studies of online learners telling surveyors what they wanted in order for online learning to be successful. Two themes running through all of these studies is "connection to other learners" and company-sponsored "motivation" to keep going. Mentoring, instructors on call, 24/7 technical support, certifications, prizes, and face-to-face meetings are all mentioned. Most students do not like totally online studying.

The article excerpt reprinted here focuses on designing motivation into online courses. Figure 8 is especially interesting because of the suggested rating system the open-ended questions can provide.

AFTER THE COURSE

Even when the learner completes the online course, motivational strategies can improve the transfer of training back to the workplace. Several key strategies can be particularly effective.

Celebrate Successful Completion

When the learners complete a course, special effort should be taken to congratulate them. A personalized congratulatory email from the instructor helps. Placing their name on the learning portal or in the company online newsletter may please successful graduates and motivate those who have not yet finished. In the University of Toyota course, those who completed the course became eligible to go to Los Angeles for sales-training exercises with fellow graduates.

Provide Support When the Learner Returns to the Workplace

The trainer's responsibility does not end when the learner completes the course. Tactics to foster transfer of learning in the workplace include:

- Encourage an environment of continuous learning, where new ideas are advocated and welcomed.
- Connect trainees to other successful users.
- Provide clear expectations of how learners will implement the new content at their job site, and be evaluated later. Tag those who complete the training as online learning "experts" who serve as valuable mentors to other employees who are taking the training. Such "flag and tag" procedures motivate both the learner and the employee, who now serves as a recognized online coach (Esque & McCausland, 1997).

Source: "How to Keep E-Learners from E-Scaping" by Jim Moshinski, Ph.D., in *Performance Improvement*, July 2001, pp. 33–34 excerpt from a longer article, pp. 28–35. Jim Moshinski, Ph.D., is the Accenture Professor of Human Performance at Baylor University, Waco, TX. He is also Director of the Center for Corporate E-Learning at Baylor University. Reprinted with permission of *Performance Improvement*. Copyright 2001. All rights reserved.

Reinforce the Learning

Follow-up to the training ensures that the skills or knowledge learned is not lost. One means of follow-up is communicating the key learning achievements to the learner's supervisor. This allows the supervisor to observe the application of this knowledge and reinforce its use. Periodic reinforcement acts as a reward system that acknowledges the effort required to incorporate new skills into your daily activities. Communication with the learner on a regular basis after the course helps the learner to focus on applying the content. This may take the form of a questionnaire that explores how they were able to apply the content or scheduled alumni chat sessions to discuss further courses and application.

View E-Learning as a Process, Not an Event

Most traditional instructor-led training is viewed as an event. After the class ends, the student has a tendency not to think about the material again because the training event is over. Online learning should be viewed as a process. A good e-learning course includes well-designed content for the core modules as well as complementary and supplementary material that aids learners in their day-to-day tasks at work. Moreover, coaches and virtual mentors can provide support before, during, and after a learner has completed an e-learning course using Web communications technology.

In addition, electronic performance support systems, have returned in popularity due to the just-in-time/just-enough nature of online learning. These types of systems are very effective in providing learning, assessment, and job support.

UNDERSTANDING METACOGNITION

Enough cannot be said about knowing your audience. Understanding how your particular audience learns (metacognition) and its willingness to apply new knowledge to jobs (motivation to transfer) could also provide you with information to create better e-learning experiences for them.

Examine Metacognitive Strategies

Learners bring their own interpretations of the virtual online environment and how they learn best from it. One way that performance technologists can better understand these interpretations is to examine the metacognitive strategies used by learners during an online course. Metacognition addresses how a person learns, and it varies between people. After your learners finish a course, invite them "to think how they learn." Analyzing their reflections provides important metacognitive insight about their learning process. By collecting data on these processes, you can build an evolving database that can guide the development of future online learning events. For example, perhaps your target population does better in a synchronous environment rather than an asynchronous environment (Campbell, Campbell, & Dickinson, 1996).

Determine Environmental Favorability

Motivation to transfer what was learned online to the actual workplace depends on trainees' perceptions of managerial and social support for the use of their new skills. This is referred to as environmental favorability. The learners can be asked several questions that specifically address their motivation to transfer using both open-ended and closed-end type responses (Machin & Fogarty, 1997). Once the data are collected from the trainees, appropriate statistical tools can analyze the data and perhaps uncover correlations to future performance.

Figure A provides some open-ended questions that can yield information about both the motivation to transfer and metacognitive strategies learners use. The information should make it possible to derive three ratings:

- Rating 1—The degree of motivation to see the course through to a successful end
- Rating 2—The degree to which the person has effective strategies to be successful

> **FIGURE A. QUESTIONS TO MEASURE MOTIVATION AND PRIMARY DRIVERS OF MOTIVATION**
>
> 1. Why are you enrolled in this course?
> 2. What's in it for you if you are successful in this course?
> 3. How important is it to you to complete this course?
> 4. What does "success" mean to you with respect to this course?
> 5. Have you set objectives for yourself with respect to this course? If so, what are they?
> 6. What is the probability of your completing this course?
> 7. Do you foresee any challenges or difficulties that would get in the way or make it more difficult for you to complete this course?
> 8. Is there anything you know about how to learn that you will take into account in approaching this course?
> 9. To what degree do you hope that this course will contribute to your ability to influence others more successfully in the work situations you face or are likely to face? *(power orientation)*
> 10. To what degree do you hope that this course will increase your ability to meet anticipated job challenges? *(achievement orientation)*
> 11. To what degree do you believe that working with others in the course is important to your learning? *(affiliation orientation)*

- Rating 3—The degree that each of the three primary driving levers of power, achievement, and affiliation motivate that particular student

CONCLUSIONS

Motivation, that is, the drive of the learners to start and finish a course and transfer the knowledge back to the work site, results from the intrinsic drive within the individual learner and extrinsic efforts externally supplied by the online learning environment. Online instructional designers especially need to understand how their students learn best (metacognition) and then provide a complementary external environment that interacts with those specific needs positively.

It is impossible and inadvisable to incorporate all these strategies in any one course. However, as you monitor and evaluate e-learning courses, you can determine which motivational strategies work best for your particular target population. Thus, you can slowly move from creating online courses through intuition to having some theoretical basis for design and development. By monitoring learners' responses to these techniques and developing a metacognitive approach unique to your audience, you can increase the effectiveness of online learning and make it a more effective tool in the performance improvement toolbox.

It is also important to recognize that it is not only instructional designers who can make substantial contributions to the success of learning activities. Many of these ideas can be made more effective through the involvement of those in different roles in the organization. This suggests a collaborative approach. It may fall on trainers to take the responsibility for encouraging appropriate contributions by those in other roles.

REFERENCES

Campbell, L., Campbell, B., & Dickinson, D. (1996). *Teaching and learning through multiple intelligences.* Needham Heights, MA: Simon & Schuster.

Esque, T., & McCausland, J. (1997). "Taking ownership for transfer: A management development study case." *Performance Improvement Quarterly, 10* (2), 116–133.

Machin, M., & Fogarty, G. (1997). "The effects of self-efficacy, motivation to transfer, and situational constraints on transfer intentions and transfer of training." *Performance Improvement Quarterly, 10* (2) 98–115.

Know Stuff Versus Do Stuff

Editor's Comment: ONLINE LEARNING NEWS asked readers to comment on the development of a blended learning program that featured 4 hours of self-paced Web-based training (WBT), a pair of 2-hour Webcasts, and a 2-day in-person seminar. The topic of the learning program was Corporate Leadership Skills. The question posed to readers was "How do you sequence development of these components to minimize expense?" Terence R. Traut's answer shows the evolution of classic instructional design and its flexibility in meeting the needs of learners who want not only less expense but also less loneliness. This is the newsletter staff's report of Traut's response:

Terence R. Traut (*ttraut@unlockit.com*) thinks your development sequence "depends on the overall goal of the training.

"What do you want participants in this training to be able to do differently when they've completed the program?" asks Traut, president of Entelechy Inc., a Merrimack, N.H., e-learning provider.

"In order for them to do something differently, they may need to know some things. And since this is new stuff—and fuzzy leadership stuff to boot—they need to be encouraged."

First determine what you want participants to DO, says Traut. Then determine what participants need to KNOW in order for them to do what you want them to do.

From there, it's fairly straightforward. "Assign the 'know' stuff to WBT and the 'do' stuff to the classroom," says Traut.

"Use the Webcast to reinforce the 'know' stuff and to encourage participants."

He suggests this approach:

- Teach leadership concepts and techniques on the self-paced WBT—after which learners "should be able to explain leadership concepts and how they apply in the real world," says Traut, "but we don't expect them to be able to do anything."

- Then use the Webcast to encourage and motivate participants. If you have more than 50, discussion is difficult, warns Traut, "so plan on monologue—which demands an energetic, articulate speaker with a planned script."

- Turn your two-day seminar into a workshop in which participants apply concepts they have learned. "Don't lecture and don't present," warns Traut. "OK," he relents, "maybe a brief review of concepts and techniques learned in the WBT, but very brief."

- In the two-day, in-person seminar-workshop, ask participants to brainstorm ways to respond to the leadership challenges they're facing at work. Participants then role-play those solutions and give each other feedback on the effectiveness of their skills—based on the concepts and techniques from the initial WBT.

- Finally, use the last two or three hours of the workshop to develop action plans for participants.

Source: "More Blended Learning" reader response by Terence R. Traut in *ONLINE LEARNING NEWS,* May 1, 2001, vol. 4 no. 6, pp. 4–5. Terence R. Traut is President of Entelechy Inc., Merrimack, NH. Reprinted with permission of *ONLINE LEARNING NEWS,* an online newsletter published by VNU Business Media, Minneapolis, MN. Copyright 2001. All rights reserved.

SECTION 4

Training Program Delivery

1. **Blended Delivery** 173
   Dot.Coms and Doughnuts 173
   Better Training Is Just a Click Away 175
   Face-to-Face and Online with Harvard and Stanford 180

2. **Advances in E-Learning**..181
   JIU: The Voice of Experience 181
   Success in Surprising Places 182
   New Letters: WAP and M-Learning 184
   Live E-Learning 185
   Help for Instructors 186

3. **Today's Trainer as Facilitator of Learning** 191
   What Is an e-Trainer? 191
   Surviving the "Technology Tsunami" 195
   Facilitated Mentoring: Rx for Stability and Skills 199
   Developing e-Employees Who Value Learning 201

INTRODUCTION TO TRAINING PROGRAM DELIVERY: SECTION 4

Section 4 of *Training & Development Yearbook 2002* considers three important trends this year in the delivery of training programs. We use the terms "delivery," "training," and "programs" deliberately so that you understand that this section focuses on intentionally designed courses, exercises, and learning opportunities—the historic and current responsibility of trainers and learning specialists. In Section 4 we concentrate on the implementation and facilitation, that is, the delivery, of these opportunities.

In sub-section 1, we give you a representative sample of articles that define and explain the persistent choice of classrooms, as trainers "blend" the best of the classroom with experimentation in e-learning. Sub-section 2 deals with some new ideas about e-learning and gives you articles and case studies that highlight experiences and assessments with it, notably in the delivery of e-learning. In sub-section 3, we focus on the enhanced role of the trainer as facilitator of learning in this new blended and collaborative world—a new context for learning that focuses on both the individual learner and a new collaborative environment—and the trainer's ability and responsibility to mobilize resources to mitigate the obstacles of technology and to harness its enormous potential for good. The goal in all of these delivery trends is to bring the learner closer to what needs to be learned.

Blended Delivery

I was amused and enlightened when I read an advertisement for Total Knowledge Management (TKM) training in the newsletter of consulting firm, Generation21 Learning Systems, Golden CO, April-May 2001, p.3. Gen21 has made a name for itself in the Knowledge Management business, a niche that is rather dependent on Internet capabilities, online action, and e-management concepts and skills. One might assume that e-learning is a priority here. However, the ad in the newsletter says, "you can send company representatives to attend a *live training* session at our headquarters . . ." and that the Tech Support Team would be there to answer all your questions "while you gain *hands-on experience* with the software" (italics mine). Clearly, this company still values classroom training.

Other advertisements also are interesting. Two are chosen here to illustrate the movement of bricks and mortar universities to offer some e-learning courses for credit, certifications, and towards degrees. New York University, for example, is promoting its Virtual College within its established School of Continuing and Professional Studies. The brochure is aimed at the working professional and uses terms like "brings the classroom to you" and "you dictate where, when, and how." A February 2001 letter from Harvard Business School Publishing announced the beginning of its e-learning division offering "personalized, practical, best-in-class learning to a global community of managers and leaders." The promotional letter says that programs can be accessed "in small bites at the convenience of the learner" and that its design of "online management support is transforming the way that important ideas are shared and applied in the workplace." In these cases, traditional universities are blending their course options and program administration.

On the other hand, e-learning pioneers University of Phoenix and Capella University are known to be reaching an already-working student population and focusing on e-learning exclusively (Heather Belt, *e-learning*, April 2001, p. 42). A promotional brochure from University of Phoenix targets the "working professional" and suggests that you can "complete 100 percent of your education via the Internet, with no residency" required, that learning will be in small interactive (online) groups, and that it "can be immediately applied to your career success." This year has been a year of experimentation by many universities across the country, as they target specific markets of students, develop blended learning using both classrooms and e-learning, and figure out ways to pay e-learning instructors, administer and manage their learning enterprises. We can expect a great deal more of this is year 2002.

Corporations too are experimenting. The online newsletter of Training Directors' Forum, *TDFeNet@vnulearning.com,* on July 18, 2001, p. 1, featured several cases of "Blended Learning," among them that of First Union Bank, Charlotte, NC. The bank needed to train employees in how to use a new automation tool for commercial lending. Trainers chose to use computer-based training to provide information about the system and to train the essentials of navigation and functionality. First Union's blending innovation was a concurrent "laboratory" which was instructor-led and served the purpose of "filling in the blanks" for trainees who needed more than what was delivered on the computer. A chart from Corporate University X-Change, Inc. was reprinted in an article in the February 2001 issue of *e-learning* magazine, p.31, that described a typical corporate university. In this chart, the "portion of training delivered by technology" was reported as 23 percent, a figure, obviously, that indicates blended training delivery of various sorts for the other 77 percent. Feedback from a reader in the August 2001 *Learning Decisions Interactive Newsletter*, p. 2, cautions that "for blended learning to be effective, instructors, facilitators, and trainers must take their lead from the learner—not the technology."

Advances in e-Learning

There is no doubt that the use of e-learning has increased dramatically in year 2001. Major organizations that study such trends include the U.S. Department of Education, ASTD, *TRAINING Magazine*, and International Data Corporation (IDC). For example, *ASTD's Industry Report 2001* found that in the past few years, the use of corporate intranets for training has jumped from 3.5 percent in 1996 to 40 percent in 1999; the U.S. Department of Education found that while 58 percent of 2- and 4-year colleges in the United States offered "distance learning" courses in 1998, 84 percent are expected to offer such courses in year 2002 (SHRM White Paper, "Learning On-Line: Benefits and Pitfalls of E-Learning" by Lin Grensing-Pophal, June 2001, p. 2). American colleges and universities have been notably slow in offering high quality, well-designed e-learning courses and other non-credit learning opportunities. By mid-year 2001, we saw evidence in professional journals and business magazines that this was changing, and that year 2002 promises to be one of great experimentation with e-learning design and delivery as well as with collaborative development and management among institutions. International Data Corporation (IDC) expects that by year 2003, U.S. companies will be spending $11.4 billion on e-learning technologies, courses, and services, up from $2.2billion just 3 years earlier (*www.ecompany.com* magazine, January–February 2001, p. 140). A *TRAINING Magazine* study, quoted in *www.ecompany.com*, p. 142, reported that about 40 percent of today's e-learning is based on delivery by CD-ROM, but that it is rapidly expanding onto the Internet and taking advantage of more exciting features and possibilities of the Web—streaming audio and video, interactive Flash animation, interaction with other people, and integration of Power Point slides into text. An IDC researcher reported that another trend he saw was that companies' favorite e-learning application, information technology (IT) training, in the early days of e-learning was fading, and that by 2003, IDC expected companies to be offering a full-range of business courses "from Accounting to Employee Wellness" (p. 142). Advances in year 2001 certainly support IDC's expectations.

One good source for information about advances in e-learning is the Teletraining Institute of Stillwater, OK, one of the pioneers in distance learning. The Institute publishes a periodic newsletter and has updated information on its Website, *www.teletrain.com*. The summer 2001 issue of the newsletter profiled several companies and agencies that were currently using teletraining in innovative ways (teletraining is the early name given to training over telecommunication lines and satellites; distance learning is the name preferred by colleges universities; e-learning or online learning seem to be favored by government and corporations). The Teletraining Institute has kept its name throughout the growth and advancement of the field.

This particular newsletter presented short profiles of a variety of enterprises. We highlight some of them here: Shoppers Drug Mart, Toronto, Canada uses e-learning, one-way video, and two-way interactive audio to deliver training from a Toronto studio to managers and department-level employees at stores spread out geographically; The U.S. Veterans Administration (VA) is using Web-based instruction using a variety of synchronous e-learning channels to deliver medical training to its nurses and leadership skills training for VA managers scattered throughout the U.S.; Cleveland College of Jewish Studies delivers religious training to lay leaders at synagogues throughout the country which are connected via a two-way video to the College's faculty; and The University of Arkansas at Little Rock is delivering a Master's Degree in Rehabilitative Counseling entirely on the Internet, using a combination of videostreaming, course documents, chat rooms, e-mail, tests, and online activities (all profiles on pp.1 and 2). *Training & Development Yearbook 2002* Section

4-2 uses other examples of current innovative practices illustrating the advances in e-learning that are preparing the field for even greater success in 2002. In this introduction, we simply suggest the range of interest, ideas, and experiences with current practices in training delivery.

Today's Trainer as Facilitator of Learning

The last sub-section of our section on "Training Program Delivery" deals with the trainer's classic and often-preferred role of facilitator—facilitator of learning in classrooms and groups of all sizes, facilitator of learning in one-to-one coaching and mentoring situations, and facilitator of learning in e-learning delivery. What we read about the trainer's role in this new e-learning environment generally attempts to translate or interpret the facilitation skills we mastered in face-to-face training into the new arena of virtual classrooms and learning spaces. Skills of feedback and performance support are receiving special attention as we experiment with ways to extend our function as learning leaders through new kinds of facilitation using familiar training delivery skills. In this sub-section you'll see some old facilitation skills cast in new roles.

This past year there have been many lists and articles describing the advantages and disadvantages of online learning. Embedded in most of the "disadvantages" lists is an undercurrent of facilitation needs for help with new kinds of delivery problems and hurdles. The American Society for Training and Development (ASTD)'s publication, *Performance in Practice*, ran such a list in its Spring 2001 issue (p.9). Among the disadvantages listed were technology fears, hidden or unexpected expenses in creating and maintaining learning network infrastructure, and difficulty in keeping up with new developments in learning support software.

Trainers who are involved as e-learning leaders have new roles as e-learning facilitators in addressing each of these three typical disadvantages: trainers need to be sure that technofear and computer illiteracy don't sabotage a learning program before it gets started; trainers need to facilitate both the "pre-test" of e-learning course readiness of all learners and facilitate the administrative problems associated with network infrastructure and software selection. Today's trainers need a wide and deep knowledge of information technology hardware and software, and they need to be able to make decisions about the technical aspects of training delivery for their particular learners. Trainers need to be prepared to fill in the gaps for the learners who are expecting trainers to be able to help.

In April 2001 *TRAINING Magazine* conducted a mail survey among subscribers of "Presentation Products." Along with the usual questions about overhead projectors, handouts, flipcharts, and computer-based screen shows like Astound or PowerPoint, the survey included 29 questions on presentation products that were totally computer-based. The survey grouped these 29 different presentation products into 6 categories: 1) computer hardware and peripherals, 2) conference/meeting distance learning tools, 3) display and projection, 4) media input/output equipment, 5) software and media, and 6) video equipment. At the very least, use of products in these kinds of categories requires different kinds of facilitation skills by trainers who engage in e-learning presentation.

A survey of a different kind was reported in the *Journal of Instruction Delivery Systems*, volume 14 no. 4, p. 29. This was a survey of a class of 24 students taking an online learning course for college credit. The survey was mostly about the support, personal and technical, that individual learners were receiving during the e-learning experience. Here are just a few of the results: 19 of 24 students thought that a technical training session should have been offered; 23 of 24 students had not been instructed as to the hardware requirements of the program at the time of enrollment; 15 of 24 students had trouble locating professional journals or articles in order to complete assignments; and 11 of 24 sometimes felt isolated. All of these responses indicate that training administration facilitation had been needed for this course. On the other hand, in terms of content and process, most students felt good about interaction with the instructor and with other students: 20 of 24 received timely feedback on assignments; 18 of 24 found it easy to communicate with the instructor; and 15 or 24 knew whom to call with a question or complaint about the program. And most telling of all, 17 of 24 said that this e-learning course was the only way they could have taken the course. Clearly, the interpretations of facilitation and feedback have changed for today's trainers. Today's trainers have new responsibilities regarding content and process. This section on training delivery explores these ideas.

1. Blended Delivery

Dot.Coms and Doughnuts

Editor's Comment: Early in the year 2001, the e-learning community was still reeling from the dot.com meltdown of the previous 6 months, and saw changes similar to the changes in businesses all over the country. E-learning suppliers were merging, laying off workers, scrambling for more funding, and even disappearing altogether. Stock market watchers were nervous about e-learning, and began to doubt its promise. Leaders in the field were cautioning restraint in "hyping" e-learning, demanding new and better models for creating content, and were urging trainers to listen to learners who wanted e-learning as an option among other options—not the only option for learning. Yet the leaders soldiered on. The MASIE Center's Guru-in-Chief, Elliot Masie, admitted that a few years ago he admonished a gathering of trainers to "Get Wired or Get Fired," and perhaps contributed to the bad rap that leaders were giving the classroom as they wanted to be seen as embracing the new e-learning wholeheartedly. First Quarter 2001 was typified by these kinds of ambivalent comments.

By Fourth Quarter 2001, the scene had changed. The MASIE Center, and many others, were freely using the terms "blended learning" and "blended training." Apologies for the classroom were no longer needed as companies and learning institutions were paying more attention to making classroom training better. (Elliott Masie also admitted that he loved the doughnuts!) In addition, by Fourth Quarter, e-learning had made great strides in quality and structure. Trainers began to pay more attention to their preferences for teaching styles and their learners' preferences for learning styles. Other measures for e-learning besides stock market activity were being discussed and implemented. Blended learning design and delivery became the new wave in training as trainers searched for ways to blend the best of the classroom with the best of e-learning.

We reprint here for you an excerpt from Elliott Masie's "Think Piece":

I do not believe that the classroom is dead! In fact, the more that I take e-Learning courses, the more I am drawn into a classroom for a very different type of experience. The classroom can be a great approach to learning delivery when:

- The learning activity involves discussion or live role modeling.
- The learning target is a motor skill that requires the use of equipment.
- The audience is small and it is easier and cheaper to put a subject matter expert with a learner, than to produce a digital learning module that will be used by just a few people.
- The content requires intense concentration for an extended period of time, which may not be available at the workplace.
- The event is a ritual or landmark event that will signal a major benchmark or promotion in one's work history.
- The learning activity is linked to a social objective to meet and work with colleagues or executives.

Source: TechLearn TRENDS online newsletter of The MASIE Center, www.masie.com, February 26, 2001 and September 4, 2001. Excerpt from the September 4 edition reprinted with permission of The MASIE Center, Saratoga Springs, NY. Copyright 2001. All rights reserved.

- The bulk of the content is gained from a Socratic dialogue with fellow learners.
- The subject matter is not appropriate to an on-line experience.
- As a strong learner/manager preference or a change of pace.

While there is a significant increase in the use of e-Learning and Blended Learning, we have not seen the death or demise of the classroom. There are changes afoot in the classroom world:

- Shorter duration classes.
- Use of pre-class and post-class learning via technology.
- Developing Communities of Learning or Practice surrounding the class.
- Targeting of classroom learning via Learning Management Systems.
- Use of simulation and other e-Learning resources in class.

Let us respect the role and power of the classroom, at the same time that we explore the capabilities and potential of e-Learning. Ultimately, we will drop the "e" from our dialogue and talk about the most strategic formats and technologies to support learning and performance. And the classroom will be one of them.

So, I tell you without shame, that I love to teach in the classroom. In fact, I am teaching a 3 day program starting tomorrow. I love the doughnuts (though I am eating more healthy these days), but more importantly, I respond to the magic that happens when motivated learners gather together in a room. And, I look forward to extending that magic beyond the last hour of the class with a range of powerful technologies. Long live the classroom! May it evolve as a cherished item in our training toolkit.

Better Training Is Just a Click Away

Editor's Comment: Whether or not every business will have an e-learning component depends on the "advantages of online training, in terms of economics and effectiveness," says writer Eilene Zimmerman in the January 2001 issue of *Workforce* magazine (p. 37). She quotes an e-learning consultant from KPMG Consulting, NY, who says trainers need to be reminded of the learner's perspective and need, and that they shouldn't be tempted to throw 200 courses online because it's easy to do so; and that especially, trainers need to be reminded that the learner needs "to see a goal at the end" of the training experience. Her article reprinted here cites examples from many companies who are experimenting with e-learning and classrooms, together.

When Ted Lehne, Delta Airline's manager of instructional technology, wanted to cut the time and money it took to train customer-service personnel, he turned to online training. A year later, nearly 70 percent of Delta's customer-service workforce gets annual required FAA training via the Internet.

"We get rave reviews about it," says Lehne. "It used to take an average of six to eight hours for these courses when they were paper-based; now employees can do it in an hour or less. It's more effective, too, because they are engaged in interactive activities." Course participation and test results are tracked, so Lehne and other managers can verify that employees are not only completing their training but also scoring as they should.

E-learning has also saved the airline a significant amount of money. "Training costs are a major factor for us because our workforce is dispersed across 115 airports," says Lehne. "Prior to online training, employees had to travel to one of five training centers, keeping them away from their jobs for at least a day."

> "There's no discussion anymore about whether or not this is going to happen, it's about how quickly it's going to happen."

Welcome to cyberschool, training New Millennium-style. Nearly 30 percent of all IT-related and business skill courses in the U.S. are now technology-based, according to IDC Research. It's becoming so prevalent that The American Society for Training and Development (ASTD) announced in October that it plans to develop standards for certifying Web-based training courses.

Stephen Barkley, executive vice president of Performance Learning systems, Inc., which creates Web-based training programs, says online learning is becoming common in both private and public sectors. "There's no discussion anymore about whether or not this is going to happen; it's about how quickly it's going to happen," he says.

Barkley compares e-learning and instructor-led learning to a microwave versus a conventional oven. "When the microwave first came out, everyone saw what it couldn't do. Then people figured out it could make popcorn, and it sold like wildfire," he says. "It's settled down to the point where you don't build every house

> It's no longer a question of whether the Web will be used to deliver workplace training. It's just a matter of how fast it will happen, and what blend of digital and classroom instruction is best for your employees.

Source: "Better Training Is Just a Click Away" by Eilene Zimmerman in *Workforce,* January 2001, pp. 36–42. Eilene Zimmerman is a freelance writer based in San Diego, CA. Reprinted with permission of *Workforce.* Copyright 2001. All rights reserved.

> "We think Web-based training is certainly more economical and convenient. For a small investment you can train a lot of people."

with one in it, although every house still has a conventional oven."

Whether or not every business will have an e-learning component in its training program remains to be seen. It will depend largely on the advantages of online training, in terms of economics and effectiveness.

Monte Rosen, vice president of marketing for AdvanceOnline, Inc., whose Web-based training programs focus on worker safety and HR-related issues, says the company's research shows little difference in effectiveness between online, CD-ROM, or instructor-led training. "But we think Web-based training is certainly more economical and convenient. For a small investment, you can train a lot of people. A small company might want every employee to take a sexual harassment course, but to bring in instructors would be cost-prohibitive. Doing it online is much less expensive, and you can track who took it and who didn't, how much time they spent on the courses, even see how they answered specific questions," says Rosen.

Web-based courses are often taught in conjunction—or "blended"—with instructor-led courses, which cuts down training time but still allows for hands-on demonstrations. For instance, AdvanceOnline offers a blended course in forklift safety. The course used to take eight hours; now it's an hour. "They still have to show the supervisor that they know how to use the equipment, but we give much of the rest of the information to them via the Web," says Rosen.

Barkley says Performance Learning Systems has built a number of training programs for public school teachers over the past 30 years. Historically, live instructors taught a 45-hour program. The trainers had to be trained themselves, and the program had to be field-tested

What to Consider When Moving to Web-Based Training

If you're thinking about moving some or all of your company's required training online, consider the following, says Kenneth Neal, e-learning solutions practice leader with KPMG Consulting in New York:

- Not everything is appropriate for Web-based training. For example, if you're teaching employees how to work effectively within a team or how to make presentations, you can teach the philosophy around those areas through examples and business simulations. "But the reality is, if it's a course about making presentations, the next day you need to have an instructor-led class where employees actually give presentations to the class," says Neal.

- With Web-based training, the structure should be three-step: show me, let me practice, and watch me do it. "There should be quizzes throughout a good course. Then there's the tactile portion, where you can perform business simulation or work through case studies, where you get a chance to practice what you've learned. Finally, there should be exams," says Neal.

- Find the course curriculum that suits each employee's career path, don't just offer 200 courses on a Web site. "This isn't knowledge for knowledge's sake, it's training," he says. "You want to design a curriculum for the employees so they can see a goal at the end."

- In implementing e-learning solutions for KPMG's clients. Neal has found that the biggest concerns are centered around privacy. "Ninety percent of those issues are communication-based. Employees are worried that Big Brother is looking over their shoulder. Who is going to see their quiz scores? What does a low score mean? It's all fear and uncertainty," he says. "But if you answer your employees' questions about it, at the end of the day you'll have the buy-in you need from them."

Rating E-Training with Online Surveys

It's all well and good to give e-learning a shot, but how will you know if your new Web-based approach to training is working? Ask.

In much the same way as students evaluate an instructor in a traditional course, surveys both before and after a course give companies an idea of how much students learned and where courses can be improved.

Richard Nadler, president of Perseus Development Corporation, a company that develops and markets Web survey software and services, says many of his clients give a survey before the event, to examine expectations. "They are often given a survey at the event, sometimes through a kiosk, to see how the training is going. Afterwards a survey measures everything from the quality of the course, the content, the instructor or leader if it's a distance-learning event, and the ways in which the training could be improved."

In traditional instructor-led training, by the time the paper survey was analyzed and results given back, the people who administered the training were gone, says Nadler. With online surveys, feedback is received within hours and the training can be modified quickly.

E-learning surveys vary in cost from about $180 up to $5,000, says Nadler, but for a large corporation, that's pennies. "They are so cost-effective, the value is clear."

---

and tweaked until it was right. Four years ago the company began online delivery of many of those courses.

Performance Learning Systems offers both synchronous and asynchronous online courses; asynchronous courses are taken independently, while synchronous courses are taught to a group of people online at the same time. Asynchronous courses, says Barkley, give the participant flexibility. "After you put the kids to bed, you can log on and work for an hour or so, and you get all the time you need. You can go back and review a piece if you didn't get it."

Laura Friedman, who handles the online training courses offered by the New York Institute of Finance, says the institute now offers Web-based courses to financial companies looking for a convenient, cost-effective way to train professionals online. "Right now we're three-quarters of the way through a project that involves 87 hours of online training for financial professionals. The training contains 20 different courses, from the most basic to the very complex," she says.

The flexibility of Web-based training is especially appealing to those whose schedules simply can't accommodate the block of time required for a traditional class. "Online training is much better than trying to attend a class at night when you've got two kids at home who need you and you're tired from a full day at the office," says Friedman.

Another advantage to managing training online is that it solves the problem of verifying to government agencies like the FDA or OSHA that required training has, indeed, been done. "In regulated industries especially, Web-based training is a huge boon," says Dan Bartholomew, practice leader, e-learning solutions, for KPMG Consulting. "If a regulator comes in and says, 'Show me that everyone in your pharmaceutical plant has been trained in good manufacturing principles,' you would have the electronic record of who has been trained and how they scored."

And there's more. Delivering training via the Web means companies can update course materials and examinations quickly and cheaply. Especially for the IT field—where subject matter changes overnight—updating paper training materials is enormously time-consuming and costly.

Because online training is less expensive than many instructor-led courses, it's also more accessible. Rather than limiting sexual harassment training to management, for example, you can educate every level of employee—from

---

The flexibility of Web-based training is especially appealing to those whose schedules simply can't accommodate the block of time required for a traditional class.

Case Study: How an Industrial Manufacturing Company Became an E-Trainer

The industrial manufacturing sector might not seem like particularly fertile ground for training via the Internet, but when Chesterton, a company that makes sealing devices, wanted to cut training costs, it decided to do a major portion of its sales-force training online. "We used to send out videotapes and we also had a four-week, on-site training course, but that was very expensive. Rather than waste the first week or two having all the salespeople in a class get an overview, we do it online now," says Ralph Merullo, manager of Chesterton Global Training in Winchester, Massachusetts.

For two weeks, salespeople receive an introduction and general information about Chesterton's equipment. Merullo says the students then come to the instructor-led class "warmed-up" and at relatively the same level. Before Web training, some students in the class found it too slow, while others were lost. "The Web training also helps us determine what our sales force knows and doesn't know coming into the classroom. If they've passed particular modules, then we know their general knowledge level," he says.

Chesterton decided to write its own instructional systems design software program, structured so that students are presented with information and then asked questions about it. The program can determine if they understand the course material or not, says Merullo.

"We have core competencies for salespeople, so for instance if we're teaching about a pump, first they learn what pressure is, what the flow of liquid should be, those kinds of things. Those are units, and they are combined into modules and on up the chain until you create a core," he says. "Then these students go out and train on the equipment at the plant or learn in one of our facilities. The Web-based portion gives them the cognitive skills, and the instructor-led portion reinforces that Web-based training."

Feedback from the sales force has been mixed. At first, managers who had been with the company for decades didn't want to take the courses, believing them unnecessary. Legal issues involved with those out in the field—safety and health issues especially—required field managers to take the online courses.

And because the courses can be started and stopped whenever an employee likes, nearly two-thirds of Chesterton's field managers have completed the required training.

In fact, the company's e-learning program is so successful that it's now marketed to Chesterton customers, and has inadvertently put the manufacturer in the online learning business. Chesterton sold nearly $30,000 worth of its training product in the last two years.

receptionist on up—because the training can be done at their desks.

But the picture isn't entirely rosy. A just-completed study of 10 companies by the ASTD looked at the kinds of factors that prevent people from taking technology-based training, either online or via a CD-ROM. Seven hundred employees across all sectors were surveyed.

"We found that people were less likely to take advantage of Web-based courses if the training is only offered at their desks. There are more distractions there, and people are also used to going to a classroom to learn because that's where they spent 20 years of their lives. They like to go someplace other than their cubicles. People like to go to a training center to do the learning, even if that learning is online," says Mark Van Buren, director of research at the ASTD.

The ASTD also found that courses which offer incentives motivate employees to take and finish a course, whether the incentive is a contest or a certificate of recognition. And the most well-attended courses were "blended," a combination of online and instructor-led components.

Monte Rosen of AdvanceOnline says his company gets mixed feedback when it comes to training conducted exclusively online. "Those that go through the courses like it and we get a lot of positive feedback. But the big issue is how to you get people to actually complete the courses? With a regularly scheduled course, you block it out on your calendar and you're there. With the Web, you tend to put it off longer," he says.

He recommends that managers send automatic e-mail reminders about each course and its required completion date. AdvanceOnline often holds contests—everyone who completes a course by a certain date can win a digital camera or some other prize. Anything, says Rosen, to encourage students.

Even if your employees are motivated to partake of online training, building the infrastructure needed for online delivery of course material is a substantial investment. Aside from physical facilities, companies have to provide hardware, software, project systems, and networks. In response, start-of-the-art training facilities have sprung up around the country, such as Knowledge Development Centers of Columbus, Ohio. The company's high-profile clients—such as Microsoft, Oracle, Cisco, and Sun Microsystems—teach classes for employees and customers at its 18 facilities.

For those who choose not to use outside facilities, companies like Digital Pipe Inc. in Foster City, California, will build a network for delivering content-rich, Web-based courses. Digital Pipe deploys a network layer on top of a company's existing IT network to distribute digital video.

"Most existing networks don't open up to large Internet connectivity points, and if they want to download something onto their networks—something with video—it takes a long time because video is a very large data file. We get around the bottlenecks because we know where the points of failure are," says Fabrizio Ornani, a cofounder of the company and vice president of marketing communications.

Using video, audio, and interactivity for e-learning can create a very dynamic environment, increasing retention and attention levels, says Ornani. But the majority of those interviewed for this article believe that, no matter how dynamic, online learning is a tool to be used in conjunction with a live instructor.

At the New York Institute of Finance, for example, feedback from online training programs has been positive, and the institute has tried to make it as compelling as possible, using graphics, audio, and animation. Yet Laura Friedman still feels that instructor-led courses are the most effective way to train. "In an ideal situation, you'd have 8 to 10 students during the day, after a good night's sleep, with a great instructor. But let's face it, that's pretty unlikely," she says. "And how much does that really cost to achieve?"

Face-to-Face and Online with Harvard and Stanford

Editor's Comment: The April 30, 2001 issue of *Business Week* reported that Harvard University and Stanford University were about to seal a deal to become partners in a new executive education venture that features both "face-to-face and online programs." Observers to the MBA scene report angst in the ranks of the most prestigious schools that have recently been trying various kinds of international partnerships, faculty recruiting among working professionals, and other financial incentives to refill the Ph.D. pipeline of business students ("Brain Drain at the B-Schools," *Business Week*, March 5, 2001, p. 106).

The Harvard-Stanford proposal has several dimensions that make it newsworthy, besides the approach to curriculum, giving extra meaning and depth to the blended programs it envisions. (1) The institution it proposes to create would be a for-profit venture, enabling it to operate outside regular university rules. (2) Each university has strengths in its high-level business curriculum the other does not have, making a partnership of two strong brand names combining their strengths a highly desirable market risk. (3) Non-degree executive training is a hugely competitive field, and even prestigious universities like Harvard and Stanford are feeling the pressure to beef up their programs and respond to the competition. The deliberations the Harvard and Stanford planners have been going through represent the kinds of considerations companies and agencies also go through as they assess the cultural, economic, and, of course, the basics of learning design and delivery that will best be bought by savvy students who want both face-to-face and online training delivery.

Sources: "B-Schools: When Harvard Met Stanford" by Jennifer Merritt and Mica Schneider in *Business Week*, April 30, 2001, p. 46. Also "Brain Drain at the B-Schools" by Jennifer Merritt in *Business Week*, March 5, 2001, p. 106. Jennifer Merritt is a Staff Editor of *Business Week*; Mica Schneider is an Online Editor of *Business Week*.

2. Advances in E-Learning

JIU: The Voice of Experience

Editor's Comment: In March 1999 Jones International University (JIU) was accredited by the North Central Association and thereby became the first fully accredited online university. In February of 2001, JIU became accredited by the same body to offer Master of Education degrees. JIU is a totally online degree-granting and certifying institution with no geographical campus location. JIU's success can provide useful stories of online delivery. Contact them at *www.jonesinternational.edu*.

The student body at Jones International is comprised of students from approximately 60 countries, and prides itself in having courses designed by well-known experts in their field who are practicing professionals. JIU set the standard for other online universities; a brochure from rival University of Phoenix recruiting faculty recently arrived in my mailbox, using similar "experienced, employed, professionals" as a standard. Courses begin every month and are delivered in "instructor-facilitated" modules. Classes are kept small, at 25 students or less. Faculty teach by logging on wherever they live; an "e-global library" and comprehensive online help feature are available 24 hours per day 7 days per week.

The focus in courses is interactivity including online workgroups and forums, e-mail, and collaborative skill-building interactions. The new M. Ed. Programs are: Research and Assessment, Corporate Training and Knowledge Management, Global Leadership and Administration, Library and Resource Management, Technology and Design, and a Generalist Master of Education. Eight new certificate programs have been recently added: e-Learning Research and Assessment, Corporate e-Training Management, Leading the Global Learning Organization, Library Management, e-Learning Instructional Design, e-Learning Design and Production, Facilitating Online Learning, and Creating and Managing e-Learning. The titles of the new certificate programs provide a framework for the breadth and depth of knowledge today's trainers need.

Source: "The Master of Education in e-learning: Jones International University Adds Masters and Certificate Programs" compiled by Elsa Schelin in *e-learning* magazine, April 2001, p. 120. Elsa Schelin is Associate Editor of *e-learning* magazine.

Success in Surprising Places

Editor's Comment: Families, workers at home, workers in offices, and trainers especially have been wondering this year about the best uses of the Internet. As trainers, we see the good kind of risk-taking in the name of learning, and we try to figure out what roles trainers should and can play in facilitating the new models that have been successful. This wide variety of sources referenced here illustrates some of the kinds of success stories of training in 2001.

WEB-BASED AND NETWORK-BASED LEARNING

Italian researcher, Guglielmo Trentin, makes a distinction between Web-based and Network-based learning. He further divides Web-based learning into individual learning and assisted learning; for Network-based learning he suggests the categories of collaborative learning using some on-site delivery, and reciprocal learning involving the work of communities of practice. Instructional designers and those responsible for implementation and delivery will find in his thinking some good ideas for structure and organization of today's and tomorrow's learning opportunities. His long article can be found in the March/April 2001 issue of *Educational Technology* journal, Englewood Cliffs, NJ.

LEARNING IN FLIGHT

Andie Evans in *TRAINING Magazine*, April 2001 reported on a company called Tenzing (*www.tenzing.com*) has recently completed beta-testing on an in-flight Internet service that includes Knowledge Anywhere's e-learning courses in Investment Fundamentals and Negotiations Skills. Some flights on Air Canada now provide the service. The customer support, and learning facilitation skills become very important in learning in flight, especially when data ports in the seats or software don't perform correctly. Airline flight attendants need to be trained as training support staff. As the program of "high-flying learning" takes off, Tenzing, the supplier, is paying the bill for customer service. The application is a good one, as long as the technical problems can be overcome. And who knows, maybe there's a job as "In-flight Trainer" in your future?

DELIVERY THROUGH EDUCATIONAL VIDEOGAMES

In year 2001, considerable political talk was heard about the Mexican border, migrant workers, and hemispheric economic cooperation and advancement. One very smart San Diego, CA software and Internet company, Lightspan, has found a way to serve our migrant worker children through educational software resembling videogames, playable on TV sets, not PCs. This is an illustration of being flexible in the delivery of learning opportunities, carefully choosing based on the nature of the learner and his/her

---

Sources: "The Internet in continuous education and training: Figure 4" by Guglielmo Trentin in *Educational Technology*, March/April 2001, p. 12; "This Is Your Trainer Speaking" by Andie Evans in *TRAINING Magazine*, April 2001, p. 25; "The Long and Wired Road" by Jodie Morse in *www.onmagazine*.com, p. 29; *Working Smarter With PowerPoint*, newsletters of April 24, 2001 and May 8, 2001; and "Napster: A Cool Billion" in *The Economist*, February 24, 2001, pp. 64-65; and "Notes from an E-Lecture: MIT's Web Giveaway" by Rachel Hartigan in *U.S. News & World Report*, April 16, 2001, p. 46. Guglielmo Trentin is a researcher at the *Italian National Research Council*, Genoa, Italy; Andie Evans is Editorial Assistant at *TRAINING Magazine*; Jodie Morse is a writer at *www.onmagazine.com*; and Rachel Hartigan writes for *U.S. News & World Report*. *Working Smarter with PowerPoint* is published by OneOnOne Computer Training, Addison, IL, www.oootraining.com.

context for learning, and not being blinded by the "WOW Factor" in much of e-learning. It is estimated that U.S. public schools today serve nearly 800,000 migrant students, and that they are migrant not only from nation to nation but also from school district to school district. Half of these students drop out of school. Many suffer from the "poor pitiful kid syndrome," never having the right clothes or toys.

Things change, however, when this population of students is introduced to technology; the syndrome disappears and becomes irrelevant to learning. Lightspan learning programs are designed with country-wide state testing standards in mind. The programs are interactive, requiring students to answer questions and record their answers. More than 3,000 schools in 46 states currently use Lightspan programs, especially in elementary schools in low-income neighborhoods. Programs are typically sent to the homes of low-income students who are likely to have television sets. These include many migrant children. Experiments with older migrant students focus on providing laptops and palm pilots to encourage continued learning while families relocate in seasonal work (*www.onmagazine.com*, pp. 29–30).

WORKING SMARTER WITH POWERPOINT NEWSLETTER

OneOnOne Computer Training, a Division of Mosaic Media, Inc. figured out a way to use an old technology—the periodic newsletter mailed to subscribers, three-hole punched to accumulate in a binder—to engage learners in implementing new ideas, formats, and uses for PowerPoint software, that much-used and much-maligned presentation aid that so neatly gets incorporated into so much of e-learning presentations. The newsletter is colorful, full of good graphics, and is skill-based to make using PowerPoint nearly irresistible. This is a lesson to trainers "to never throw away your boomerang," that old technologies can come back to be used again and again. PowerPoint's huge success is facilitated by this kind of newsletter. Call 800/424-8668 for subscription information, and never underestimate the power of a good newsletter.

NAPSTER'S UNIVERSAL JUKEBOX MODEL

Early this year, the music exchange company, Napster, was forced to change its business model, to the great dismay of about 64 million users of its services (*The Economist*, February 24, 2001, p. 65). The original, and highly customer-friendly, model featured "peer to peer" music exchange. I have personally been to training conferences where there was discussion about using the Napster model of peer to peer knowledge exchange to advance e-learning content acquisition. In Napster's new model, and in adapting it for e-learning, copyright laws might need to change and the structure of payment for services most certainly will change. But the original Napster peer to peer model has fueled an innovative spark in e-learning delivery systems designers, challenging trainers in new ways to find a place and a name for new kinds of facilitative support structures within these delivery systems.

MIT'S TANTALIZING ONLINE LIBRARY

The Massachusetts Institute of Technology (MIT) announced this year that within the years 2002 and 2003, the university would post the content of 500 of its courses on the Web, in a Website called *OpenCourseWare*. The difference with this MIT effort is that the content will be free, no charge to the student visitor to the Website. (Other universities have put courses online, for a fee.) MIT has chosen to direct its knowledge base and Website at people not typically in the MIT community—Third World academics, bright high school students, moms at home with small children waiting impatiently to get back to advanced study, and any others who are intellectually curious about the design and content of MIT's courses. An MIT spokesperson said that if brilliant students are attracted to MIT because of *OpenCourseWare*, then the free library idea will have been worth the expense to the university (*U.S. News & World Report*, April 16, 2001, p. 46). The project seems as much a marketing venture as an educational one; it is surely a development in e-learning that's worth watching.

New Letters: WAP and M-Learning

Editor's Comment: Conferences and commentaries in year 2001 attempted to add some new letters to the e-learning alphabet. These are M-Learning which stands for Mobile-Learning, and WAP which stands for Wireless Application Protocol. All of these new letters lead trainers forward into the world of training delivery by wireless devices.

Brandon Hall, Sunnyvale, CA has done trainers a big favor in recent years by collecting and producing numerous studies and lists of resources in e-learning. One of his new ones is "The Revolution Will Be Wireless" and he predicts that Mobile-Learning, or M-Learning will soon rival at-the-desk e-Learning. Americans love gadgets and technology and are on the move at work and at school. Mobile devices are becoming more sophisticated, with more kinds of mobile devices available. PC sales are leveling off. Look for the M-Learning trend to continue in 2002. Find this study at *www.brandon-hall.com*, or contact Brandon Hall by phone at 408/736-2335.

Lakewood/Bill Communications' online newsletter of May 17, 2001 reported on the organization's recent conference on OnLine Learning 2001 in Singapore. Conference participant Geoff Ring, a consultant with Icus Pte Ltd., described his experience with M-Learning in a course for executives developed for Insead, the international business school in Fontainebleau, France. Fourteen executives participated in the M-Learning course using telephones made by Nokia Corporation of Helsinki, Finland.

The course was designed so that 70 percent of its content was available both by phone and on the Web. Five percent of the course was available by phone only; and the other 20 percent was available on the Web only, including the typical proven-successful bulletin boards, video, content downloads, and e-mail. Coaches operated by phone only. Students apparently liked the convenience of being able to M-learn while waiting for a taxi or in an airport; but like many users of mobile devices, they didn't like reading text from the small screen (*Online Learning Reviews*, May 17, 2001, pp. 3,4).

Trainers, especially learning specialists, will need to be vigilant about how the delivery of learning through M-devices meets learners' needs, and be in close collaboration with designers of M-Learning opportunities and builders of the M-devices to deliver them. Insead/Icus Pte Ltd.'s bold experiment needs to be applauded as a prudent risk, and watched carefully as career opportunities for trainers explode along with the worldwide explosion of mobile devices.

Sources: "News and Notes from *brandon-hall.com*" online news brief, September 7, 2001; and "Hold the Phone: Can M-Learning Work?" from *Online Learning Reviews*, e-mail newsletter, May 17, 2001.

Live E-Learning

Editor's Comment: More hands-on, more real world, more just-in-time, more performance support . . . that is, more "Live" e-learning. That's what's on the horizon, according to a sidebar on p. 20 within Frank Gartland's article referenced here. More steak and less sizzle, that's what e-learners want. According to Gartland, they also want more sensory and interactive context and availability of high quality voice-over. In short, learners want e-learning technologies to better approximate or provide for living human interactions. Gartland and his company are working on just this.

In the sidebar called "Key Trends in Live E-Learning" Gartland elaborates on seven key characteristics of the next phase of e-learning. These are:

- Just-in-time content delivery
- More substance, less fluff
- Blended approach
- Full-sensory e-learning
- Collaboration
- Voice-over IP
- Better proof of Return on Investment.

Source: "Implementing Live, Interactive e-learning" by Frank Gartland in *e-learning* magazine, June 2001, p. 20. Frank Gartland is Director of live product development at KnowledgeNet, Scottsdale, AZ.

Help for Instructors

Editor's Comment: It seems logical and important that we include an article that provides real help for instructors in e-learning situations. Good training delivery now, as always, depends on both a good delivery system and a good instructor. As e-learning grows and changes, e-instructors need to grow and change too. Michelle Hutchinson's article is structured to speak directly to instructors and to offer specific suggestions for teaching success in a new environment. We reprint her article here in its entirety.

INTRODUCTION

A growing number of higher education institutions are adopting electronic instruction delivery systems to deliver instruction in an effort to supplement or replace face-to-face instruction. This presents the instructors of these courses with several challenges. In addition to being subject matter experts, increasingly instructors are expected to be masters of technology and delivery management (Adrian, 2000). Instructors need to understand and take advantage of the unique strengths of the Internet for interactivity, collaboration, and knowledge building.

DEVELOP DEFINED PEDAGOGICAL GOALS

A good place to begin in designing an effective online course is to make pedagogical decisions about the fundamental goals of the course, including such things as the instructional and personal goals of the course for all students, as well as the purpose of the course. (Schrum, 2000).

Take Advantage of Internet's Unique Strengths

Face-to-face classroom courses converted to the Web need to take advantage of the unique strengths of the Internet and to move from (a) delivering static content to identifying specific goals for students to purse, (b) accepting only one answer to accepting a diversity of outcomes, (c) representing knowledge to requesting production of knowledge, (d) evaluating at the product level to looking to the task level, (e) promoting individual efforts to working with teams, and (f) developing a single classroom experience to encouraging global communities of learning (Duchastel, 1996–1997).

Shift from Broadcast Learning to Interactive Learning

The new paradigm for learning involves a more active, collaborative, constructivist approach (Palloff & Pratt, 1998). Internet guru Don Tapscott (1998) echoed this need to shift from broadcast learning to interactive learning and identified the following paradigm shifts for instructors. They are (a) from content that is linear and sequential to content that accommodates the hypermedia strengths of the Internet, (b) from instructors providing instruction to students constructing their own knowledge and developing a keen sense of discovery, (c) from teacher-centered to learner-centered, (d) from students merely absorbing content to students learning how to learn, (e) from a one size fits all approach to content delivery to customized learning based on the individual needs of the student, (f) from school perceived as tor-

---

Source: "Strategies for Instructors Using Electronic Instruction Delivery Systems" by Michelle Hutchinson in *Journal of Instruction Delivery Systems*, volume 14 number 4, pp. 13–16. Michelle Hutchinson is President of Hutchinson Communications, specializing in e-learning and in e-docs. She is also the recipient of her local Chamber of Commerce's Entrepreneur of the Year award. Reprinted with permission of *Journal of Instruction Delivery Systems*. Copyright 2000. All rights reserved.

ture by students to students perceiving schools as fun and an opportunity for discovery, and (g) from the instructor as the transmitter to the instructor as the facilitator to learning.

Define Performance Evaluation Standards

Nguyen and Kira (2000) suggested that once the pedagogical goals are identified for the entire course, the next step is to develop the learning objectives for each segment of the course and to define the related performance standards. This includes setting the deadlines for each course activity and determining the evaluation scheme. In examining the assignments most appropriate for the course the following should be reviewed (a) how much homework should be assigned, (b) what types of assignments support the goals for the course, and (c) what is the degree of difficulty for the assignments.

Create a Learner-Centered Environment

Instructors can foster effective learning by creating a course that is learner-centered and avoid the trap of becoming too technology-focused. In embracing a Web-based delivery system it is easy for instructors to get caught up in the medium and forget the message. Some ways to create learner-centered courses are to include opportunities for student discussion (for example through real time chat), debating (for example through discussion forums), and researching (students find their own materials both on the Web and in paper) (Tapscott, 1998). Another example is to use group-based simulations as a form of role playing. Here, the instructor develops a scenario describing a difficult situation and assigns roles for the different students to assume in dealing with the situation (Alden, 1998).

Include Opportunities for Practice

Morphew (2000) advocated that experience is paramount in the constructivist learning process. Including opportunities for practice requires creativity on the part of instructors but this can stimulate thinking and facilitate meaningful learning experiences. For example, a course on distance education could have a practice component where students become instructors to other students and offer mini-courses over the Web; part way through the program the roles could be reversed to ensure all have an opportunity to be an instructor as well as a student. This opportunity to practice in a safe learning environment allows students to orchestrate the use of technology and instructional design and obtain valuable feedback from the other students from which they will build a very personal knowledge framework. Adult learners learn best through high levels of immersion and teacher-student dialog (Adrian, 2000).

Identify Barriers to Success

Monitoring student progress by keeping abreast of journal responses, paradigm statements, and assignments provides an early warning system to instructors as to the efficacy of their courses (Morphew, 2000). If students are not performing at acceptable levels, instructors should examine the entire learning process to identify the barriers hindering performance (Adrian, 2000). By examining the course content the instructor may find flaws that can be quickly fixed or segments of the course which can be redesigned (such as assignments which generate little value to the student).

DEVELOP CLEAR ORGANIZATION AND HIERARCHY OF CONTENT

Instructors should endeavor to create a clear organization and a straightforward hierarchy to course content that facilitates navigation and content retrieval. Simple devices, such as a site map, allow multiple access paths for students to quickly locate the necessary content and stay on track.

Develop an Expanded Syllabus

The syllabus should be well constructed to avoid ambiguity and present all the necessary information in one readily accessible place on the instructor's Web site. Hardy (1999) endorsed the concept of an expanded syllabus for distance learners and suggested that it include course topics, important dates and deadlines, administrative information on textbooks, expectations, grading policies, evaluation criteria, information regarding expected interactions, in addition to any of the technology-related aspects of the course, including phone numbers for troubleshooting.

Organize Discussion Threads by Topic

Jarmon (1999) recommended that discussion threads be organized by topic or other useful content divisions to facilitate flexibility in allowing students to post comments on items of interest. He further recommended that FAQs (Frequently Asked Questions) be posted on discussion threads where new information can be added easily and accessed by the entire group to reduce confusion about the course structure and instructor expectations.

EXERCISE EXCELLENT COMMUNICATIONS SKILLS

It is critical that instructors write discursively and clearly in all communications. When instructors fail to proofread emails, discussion thread comments, and feedback on assignments, typographical errors and ambiguity can easily creep in, leading to misunderstandings and confusion on the part of one or more students. Since rates of non-completion are far higher in distance education than in face-to-face classes (Schrum, 2000) instructors need to ensure their communications skills are not the reason that students leave. Communication between instructors and their students should be clear, concise and support the learning objectives (Boaz, 1999).

MAKE STUDENTS FEEL WELCOME

Begin with Introductions

It is important that electronic instructional delivery systems begin with introductions of both the instructor and the students (Palloff & Pratt, 1999). This immediately starts to build the sense of a learning community. As students share their expectations for the course, instructors have the opportunity to determine how closely students are to the same starting point.

If students do not share the same general expectations it gives the instructor an opportunity to shift the course to meet the needs of the majority of the learners (Palloff & Pratt, 1999). By getting beyond the technology and focusing on the students, instructors can humanize distance learning (Boaz, 1999).

Recognize Each Student

Palloff and Pratt (1999) strongly recommended that each student be individually welcomed and recognized by the instructor. This builds the first point of connection in the development of a learning community. For the learning process to be successful, it is imperative that students experience a strong sense of community.

Include Photographs

The literature indicates that instructors and students alike have commented positively on the importance of including photographs of the instructor and the students. Photos help instructors and students put names to faces and get to know each other on a personal level (McCormack & Jones 1998). Classes with both face-to-face and online instruction have a diminished need for this visualization but those with solely a cyberspace medium may need a photograph to humanize the process and connect the words in a discussion forum with a person (Palloff & Pratt, 1999).

Editors note: See, for example, *http://www.scis.nova.edu/~abramson*. The professor is on the home page and student photos may be linked to readily.

Build a Sense of Trust

Building a sense of trust so that students feel comfortable asking questions indicates the instructor's commitment to students for them to learn. Most instructors are familiar with the experience of knowing that if one student asks a question there is a high degree of probability that others want to ask the same question. By establishing an open, inviting, non-threatening learning environment where there is a high degree of trust, instructors bridge the distance between themselves and their students (Boaz, 1999).

FOSTER STUDENT-TO-STUDENT COLLABORATION

The Internet is an ideal medium for fostering student-to-student collaboration to improve communication and build learning communities. Working together in teams is one example of collaborative learning where two or more students join together to share insights, construct knowledge, formulate ideas, respond to others, and produce a product. This interactive experience can be more engaging for students than working alone.

Other examples of collaborative activities include students maintaining and sharing journal entries, creating a class homepage, dialoguing in discussion forums, and establishing a pro and con forum for point of view debates (Boaz, 1999). The shared whiteboard in synchronous learning systems is an excellent tool for collaborative activities such as brainstorming, diagramming solutions, outlining recommendations, expanding on themes, and summarizing outcomes (Driscoll, 1998).

PROVIDE TIMELY FEEDBACK

Feedback to students should be prompt, positive, and personal. Since it is difficult for distance learning students to gauge their progress in relation to that of others, targeted direct feedback is crucial for motivation (Boaz, 1999). It is also beneficial to allow students to provide mid-term feedback to instructors for the purposes of fine-tuning a course.

Instructors need to allocate time each day to review and respond to student's electronic mail messages. Students have reported feeling isolated and unconnected (Hill, 1997) and timely instructor feedback can minimize the effects of this.

Electronic instruction is time-consuming and requires excellent time management skills. Instructors may need to allocate as much as nineteen hours per week for managing data, responding individually to student questions by email and telephone, participating in forums, preparation of discussion questions, reviewing assigned reading, and marking student assignments (Schrum, 2000, Palloff & Pratt, 1999). Yet this timely feedback to students is an excellent student motivator.

CONDUCT EFFECTIVE EVALUATION

The instructor needs to evaluate student progress, the success of collaborative activities, participation in the discussion forums, the course materials, the instructor's Web site, the syllabus, the supplemental content (for example links to external Web sites), and the student teacher dialogue.

The Institute for Higher Education Policy reported to the Council for Higher Education Accreditation that quality assurance in distance learning is distinguished by a strong emphasis on program goals and the assessment of outcomes (Phipps, Wellman & Merisotis, 1998). Instructors should give themselves permission to go through trial and error and allow a few iterations incorporating student feedback into a course before feeling satisfied with the results (Schrum, 2000).

CONCLUSION

Instructors can take advantage of a variety of successful strategies as part of their goal to demonstrate excellence in the field of distance education. These include creating defined pedagogical goals, developing clear organization and hierarchy of content, exercising excellent communications skills, making students feel welcome, fostering student-to-student collaboration, providing timely feedback, and conducting an effective evaluation.

Web-based electronic instructional delivery systems allow instructors to build interactivity, collaboration, and knowledge building into their instructional strategies. By promoting collaborative learning in distance education, instructors create an enriching experience for students (Boaz, 1999) and knowledge building, as a learning strategy, encourages active articulation, sharing, and organizing of ideas and information into individual and group knowledge structures (Harasim, Calvert, and Groeneboer, 1997).

REFERENCES

Adrian, C. M. (2000). In Lau, L. (Ed.). Developing a Learning Environment: Applying Technology and TQM to Distance Learning. *Distance Learning Technologies: Issues, Trends and Opportunities*. Hershey, PA: Idea Group Publishing.

Alden, J. (1998). *A Trainer's Guide to Web-Based Instruction: Getting Started on Intranet- and Internet-Based Training*. Alexandria, VA: American Society for Training & Development.

Boaz, M. (1999). "Effective Methods of Communication and Student Collaboration." *Teaching at a Distance: A Handbook for Instructors*. Mission Viejo, CA: League for Innovation in the Community College and Archipelago, a Division of Harcourt Brace & Company.

Driscoll, M. (1998). *Web-Based Training: Using Technology to Design Adult Learning Experiences*. San Francisco, CA: Jossey-Bass Inc.

Duchastel, P. (1996–1997). "A Web-based Model for University Instruction." *Journal of Educational Technology Systems*. 25 (3), 221–228.

Ellis, T. J. (1999). "Translating a College Course for Delivery over the World Wide Web." *Journal of Instruction Delivery Systems*. 13 (3), 13–18.

Hardy, D. (1999). "Institutional Guidance for the Distance Learner." *Teaching at a Distance: A Handbook for Instructors*. Mission Viejo, CA: League for Innovation in the Community College and Archipelago, a Division of Harcourt Brace & Company.

Harasim, L., Calvert, T., & Groeneboer, C. (1997). In Khan, B. H. (Ed). "Virtual-U: A Web-Base System to Support Collaborative Learning." *Web-Based Instruction*. Englewood Cliffs, NJ: Educational Technology Publications, Inc.

Hill, J.R. (1997). In Khan, B. H. (Ed). "Distance Learning Environments via the World Wide Web." *Web-Based Instruction*. Englewood Cliffs, NJ: Educational Technology Publications, Inc.

Jarmon, C. (1999). "Fundamentals in Designing a Distance Learning Course: Strategies for Developing an Effective Distance Learning Experience." *Teaching at a Distance: A Handbook for Instructors*. Mission Viejo, CA: League for Innovation in the Community College and Archipelago, a Division of Harcourt Brace & Company.

McCormack, C., & Jones, D. (1998). *Building a Web-Based Education System*. New York, NY: John Wiley & Sons Inc.

Morphew, V. (2000). In Lau, L. (Ed.). "Web-Based Learning and Instruction: A Constructivist Approach." *Distance Learning Technologies: Issues, Trends and Opportunities*. Hershey, PA: Idea Group Publishing.

Palloff, R. M., & Pratt, K. (1999). *Building Learning Communities in Cyberspace: Effective Strategies for the Online Classroom*. San Francisco, CA: Jossey-Bass Inc.

Phipps, R. A., Wellman, J. V., & Merisotis, J. P. (1998). "Assuring Quality in Distance Learning." *Council for Higher Education Accreditation*. http://chea.org/Perspective/assuring.html/. Last updated April, 1998. Accessed February 4, 2000.

Schrum, L. (2000). In Lau, L. (Ed.). "Online Teaching and Learning: Essential Conditions for Success." *Distance Learning Technologies: Issues, Trends and Opportunities*. Hershey, PA: Idea Group Publishing.

Tapscott, D. (1998). *Growing Up Digital: The Rise of the Net Generation*. New York, NY: McGraw-Hill.

3. Today's Trainer as Facilitator of Learning

What Is an e-Trainer?

Editor's Comment: Is your training role that of coach? Reference librarian? Talk show host? The voice on the other end of the Help command? Performance consultant? Technology guru? Trainers ask themselves and their colleagues these kinds of questions with greater frequency and urgency as the search for definition of e-trainer roles and responsibilities changes and solidifies as the new year 2002 begins.

Perhaps the most clarion voice on the answer side of Q&A is Elliott Masie, chief at The MASIE Center, Saratoga Springs, NY. He is a master at soliciting, collecting, synthesizing, and reporting information from his nearly 50,000 networked colleagues around the world. We reprint here for you Masie's April 2001 answers to 8 important questions about what it means to be an e-trainer.

What does an e-Trainer actually do? Is their job similar to a classroom trainer, except for location? What is the ideal background for an e-Trainer? Does an e-Trainer have a dramatically different workday?

These are just a few of the questions that The MASIE Center receives every week as organizations are developing the role of an e-Trainer. This months's cover story and reader survey will focus on the characteristics of this emerging job assignment and will tackle a few of the questions and myths about e-Trainers.

What Are the Job Tasks of an e-Trainer?

There are three sides to the e-Trainer job:

- Development/Assembly
- Delivery/Facilitation
- Learner Support/Accountability

In some organizations, the e-Trainer will wear all three hats and take responsibility for every aspect of an e-Learning experience, from creation to completion. In some circumstances, the e-Trainer is only focused on the delivery of the content. And, in some situations, a whole team of people will work together to provide these stages, often supplying the learner support from a "help desk" type structure.

Does the Role of an e-Trainer Change Dramatically When Live, Synchronous Training Is Included in the e-Learning Offering?

Yes! As soon as we add a virtual classroom, a live chat, a videoconference or other live synchronous dimension to a training experience, there is a new set of responsibilities and skills. The e-Trainer has to have the technical and interpersonal skills to lead a one-to-many event using technology and they have to be able to change their teaching and support style to match the requirements of the new media. For example, a trainer working in a sophisticated virtual classroom environment may have to cope with dozens of simultaneous questions coming to them, at the same time as learners are providing feedback that the class is moving too slowly and one person from Paris is having

---

Source: "What Is an e-Trainer?" by Elliott Masie in *Learning Decisions Interactive Newsletter*, published by The MASIE Center, April 2001, pp. 1–3. Elliott Masie is President and CEO of The MASIE Center and Editor of *Learning Decisions Interactive Newsletter*. He can be reached by e-mail at *emasie@masie.com*. Reprinted with permission of The MASIE Center. Copyright 2001. All rights reserved.

trouble getting the audio portion of the session over the Web. Practice, structure, great software and a model for handling these concurrent demands are critical for the success of an e-Trainer.

Do Classroom Trainers Make Good e-Trainers?

This is the most difficult question that I have to answer! The good classroom trainer should have the instincts to be a good e-Trainer. They should understand how people learn, how to present information in an engaging and logical fashion, how to motivate learners, how to diagnose learner confusion and how to continuously improve the learning content of the class. However, will they ENJOY and THRIVE in an environment where their role and their relationships to learners change dramatically?

- The e-Trainer will not get as many chances to tell their stories. Some classroom trainers thrive on their ability to hold the attention of learners with great and often amusing stories. On-line teaching reduces learner tolerance for longer stories and pushes the trainer to a more concise delivery model.
- The e-Trainer will not get the same types of feedback. Some trainers need to see the eyes of their learners and hear their reactions. The e-Trainer will get very different and often less intense reactions from learners.
- The e-Trainer will be less of a personality force in the e-Learner event. We have noticed that alumni of e-Learning events talk less about their trainers and more about the content and learning activities. This means the e-Trainer may get less ego strokes for giving a great class.

We believe that many, many classroom trainers can be great e-Trainers. However, it does take practice and a rewiring of their expectations to thrive in this environment.

If We Don't Use Classroom Trainers, What Other Roles Might Make Good e-Trainers?

Organizations are looking in their customer support and help desk departments for candidates for e-Trainer positions. Someone who is used to a series of shorter, task-focused interactions over the phone or via email may have the temperament to be an e-Trainer. They will still need to learn how to teach and facilitate a learning event, but it may be easier than changing the skills of some classroom trainers. We have also found that some managers are natural e-Trainers and quickly blend training and employee support in a regularly scheduled virtual meeting environment.

How Much Teaching Does an e-Trainer Actually Do?

That totally depends on the synchronous/asynchronous mix of learning delivery and the availability of authored or referenced materials. Over time, we predict that the e-Trainer will deliver less formal lectures and seminars. Instead, the learner will be accessing asynchronous content and using the e-Trainer for dialogue, processing and assessment. In 2001, however, a large amount of e-Trainers are delivering virtual versions of classroom presentations.

Ironically, if you ask a good teacher when they teach the best, they rarely point to their front of the room presentations. They usually talk about their interactions with learners during, before and after class. When I taught a graduate course on training many years ago, I asked the learners on the last day to describe the most valuable tasks that I, their instructor, had done for them over the semester. Not one person selected the lectures as their first choice. They viewed the interactions, the spontaneous questions and the coaching that I had provided as my most valuable contribution. In the world of e-Learning, the trainer gets to do even more of these interventions!

What Are the Characteristics of a Great e-Trainer?

Well, we thought that we would start by looking at the characteristics of a great classroom trainer. On pages 4 and 5 of this month's newsletter, you will see the results of our survey of "memorable" classroom teachers. The data and comments of the readers pointed to these traits:

- Passionate about teaching
- Cared deeply about the learner
- High levels of knowledge
- Creative and varied in teaching techniques
- Highly accessible
- Strong standards for learning success
- Made us work hard.

Many of the same characteristics hold true for an e-Trainer. I would revise the list a bit to reflect the changed circumstances of the e-Learning world:

- Made the technology and the "distance" irrelevant
- Passionate about teaching in this format
- Cared deeply about the learner
- High levels of knowledge and/or access to knowledge resources
- Creative and varied in teaching techniques
- Highly accessible
- Created engagement, challenge and community with others
- Provided standards and feedback/assessment opportunities.

Can an e-Trainer Transmit These Characteristics Over the Web, Without Ever Meeting the Learner Face to Face?

Yes! But, it will take high degrees of internationality and creativity to make this happen. The learner basically knows how to learn in a classroom. Many of the learners that e-Trainers work with in the next two years do not know how to learn on-line. So, it is even more important for the e-Trainer to provide role models, structures and support opportunities. The e-Trainer cannot "hide" behind their email and send out an impersonal note to a learner. Instead, it is a great opportunity to be even more engaged and involved in assisting the learner to tackle new content.

If e-Trainers are not going to model themselves after classroom lecturers, then what are other metaphors and images to use?

There are a few that work for me when I am in the e-Trainer role:

- Coach: The "e-Coach" lives on the learner desktop (or email) and is rooting for their success. The Coach provides short bursts of support, feedback and even an occasional shout. The Coach often awaits the questions of the learner and sometimes pops out of nowhere to engage and challenge the learner.

- Reference Librarian: I still remember going to the library when I was in elementary school to do a project on Eskimo housing. I asked the librarian if she had any materials on igloos. She blinked for a second and went straight to a file cabinet and handed me a brochure from the Alaska History Society. I was blown away. For years, I thought that I had lucked out and found the igloo expert in the building. Later, I realized that she had a great filing system and was a good listener. The e-Trainer can learn a lot from this role model.

- Talk Show Host: When I conduct live, synchronous sessions, I slip into the talk show host mode. Virtual classes go so much better when the learner can hear multiple voices, listen to a question and answer session rather than a downloaded lecture, and pitch in with their opinion or listen to a peer's. In fact, the best talk shows these days are adding a second host, to provide even more variety.

Finally, How Does the e-Trainer Develop Their Skills?

The answer is a little like the joke, "How do I get to Carnegie Hall?" . . . "Practice, practice, practice!" In this case, there are three levels of practice that we would advise:

- Be an e-Learner: It is almost impossible to be a great e-Trainer unless you have been on the other side of the learning relationship. Find several opportunities to be an e-Learner. You will gain great appreciation for the change in pace, the compression effects and the lure of multi-tasking.

- Start with Blended Learning: Some of the lowest risk ways of starting as an e-Trainer can be found by adding an e-Learning experience to a classroom event. Do an on-line follow-up session. Provide a few weeks or months of post-class support. Or, teach one session of the class from a distance. You can focus on the teaching and technology aspects without having to build a whole new set of relationships with learners.

- Experiment, Capture and Coaching: The first few times that you are an e-Trainer, capture the entire process. Many of the tools will create a stored copy of the e-Trainer in action. Watch this by yourself and with a coach that you trust. Ask a few learners for suggestions on how to make the class more engaging and/or valuable. And, keep experimenting with style and process.

A final piece of advice: be authentic! If you are a caring and knowledgeable person, it will come across to your learners. Be authentic, admit your newness to the role, have some fun with it and let the technology evaporate. When you are talking to someone you love on the telephone, the phone starts to be invisible. In the same way, as you get more experience with your role as an e-Trainer, the technology will be a deep background to the gift that you provide to learners . . . you are a person that will help them learn something new and valuable.

Training Program Delivery

Surviving the "Technology Tsunami"

Editor's Comment: This article features four trainers with various titles who have figured out how to change, deliver successful courses, and facilitate learning opportunities for employees at their companies. Dave Zielinski's personal approach here resonates with many of us in the field who are surviving the "technology tsunami."

As more and more training professionals move into cyber-training, they're finding they can take their classroom expertise with them, and flourish. Many not only survive the technology tsunami, but emerge with new titles, marketable skills, fresh perspectives on their chosen field and confidence in their ability to manage change.

And while there are many challenges, and even the occasional career casualty, the majority of training professionals overcome these obstacles successfully. The success stories profiled here offer insight into this career migration and a little advice for others on the cusp of such a leap.

> A glimpse into the diaries of some classroom-turned-virtual instructors reveals the trials and tribulations of carving out new identities in the cyber-training world.

THE INVISIBLE TRAINER

John Geissler
Training Project Manager
OutlookSoft, Stamford, Conn.

Virtual instructors sometimes miss the richness of face-to-face interaction—the looks on students' faces after an "aha" moment, the compelling story enthusiastically received or the rush of shared debate and discovery.

But John Geissler, a 15-year veteran of classroom training, rarely gets sentimental about his past training life. At OutlookSoft—a seller of software for Web-based budgeting and performance analysis—he successfully conducts nearly all of his training online. He delivers synchronous Web-based training sessions to employees, clients and partners logging in from computers around the world.

Geissler uses Centra Software to teach those groups the ins and outs of his company's software products. Trainees log onto a Web site, where they hear streaming audio of Geissler walking them through Microsoft PowerPoint slides and observe demonstrations of software applications. This low-bandwidth delivery vehicle allows participants to "raise their hands" and pose questions via two-way voice-over IP.

> "It's easy to be on your feet for six hours a day in a classroom environment, but now, sitting in front of a computer console, I can teach in about two hours something that might have taken six hours in the classroom."

Source: "True Confessions" by Dave Zielinski in *TRAINING Magazine,* March 2001, pp. 108, 110, 112, 114, and 116. Dave Zielinski is a freelance writer from Minneapolis, MN. He is frequently featured as an author in *TRAINING Magazine.* Reprinted with permission from *TRAINING Magazine.* Copyright 2001. All rights reserved.

Of course, Webconferencing saves travel dollars and reduces trainee time away from jobs. But for Geissler, it's also a reprieve from the wear and tear on trainers' bodies and a more concentrated use of time. "It's easy to be on your feet for six hours a day in a classroom environment, but now, sitting in front of a computer console, I can teach in about two hours something that might have taken six hours in the classroom," Geissler says.

In a physical classroom, it's common for students' 10-minute breaks to drift into 20 minutes, and for lunch hours to expand to 90 minutes. That time isn't lost in a virtual classroom, which features more tightly paced and closely scripted sessions, he says. Consequently, these shorter sessions ease the issue of trainee attention span.

However, there are trade-offs and significant adjustments with this new delivery medium, Geissler concedes. "The strangest thing is not being able to see students' faces or get visual cues."

Surprisingly, Webconferencing also can require more concentrated lung power from instructors than the classroom. Geissler likens it to being a radio talk show host with visuals. "Initially, it was hard for me to talk for two hours nonstop," he explains. "In these sessions there are few breaks and you really have to be 'on' all the time."

Inflection and tone become even more important in a cyber-setting, where flat delivery can be tantamount to handing out sleeping aids. To keep trainees' attention, many organizations encourage their virtual instructors to go no longer than five or 10 minutes without a screen break or some form of interaction.

For Geissler, this means planning coursework and timing accordingly. "Most of my development time goes into choreographing the entire event, figuring out in detail what's the best time to jump into application sharing, where quizzes should come in, and at what points I can make best use of interactive tools."

A TECHNO-SKEPTIC CONVERTS

Dave Ferguson
Sales Training Project Manager
GE Global Exchange Services, Gaithersburg, Md.

After 30 years as a training professional and performance technologist, Dave Ferguson has seen plenty of new technology-delivered learning vehicles come down the pike, only to be marginalized by new innovations or misguided uses.

"I remember going to conferences when everyone had some form of black box between their PCs and monitors that LP-sized laser discs would run on, and that was the wave of the future," says Ferguson. "Now you couldn't find a training laser disc if you posted a $10,000 reward."

Given the skepticism, it's a bit surprising to find Ferguson designing technology-based training and information-sharing initiatives. But the self-proclaimed "techno-skeptic" discovered that e-learning vehicles not only reduce trainee travel costs and save time, they also create some extremely effective learning outcomes, too.

Ferguson's division was among the first in the General Electric empire to launch intranet-based product training that incorporates streaming audio and some video. His sales training

> "I need to learn things from scratch, and I didn't want an authoring tool doing something for me until I fully understood its underpinnings."

group adopted these tools to deliver basic product training and update information to the GE salesforce—one that can ill afford time away from jobs for basic or prerequisite training.

In its first use of Web technology, Ferguson's group collaborated with sales managers to create a series of informational "Product 101" pages on the corporate intranet. Designed as short overviews, the pages familiarize salespeople with key selling features, pricing structures, targeted prospects, and a competitive landscape of the products to be sold.

In another application, Ferguson worked with an external Web design firm to build interactive training that uses Macromedia Flash software to help teach a sales process to new employees with the aid of audio and animation. Quizzes or "self-checks" are included to test comprehension and provide specific feedback.

Like many traditional instructional designers who experiment with new mediums, Ferguson's initial learning curve was steep. "I heard someone at a conference say that good judgement comes from experience, and experience comes from bad judgement," Ferguson says. "We've learned plenty about how to design, update and manage online content through our own experimentation and work with external vendors."

Although the department's Web authoring tools of choice are now Macromedia's Coursebuilder and Dreamweaver, Ferguson believed it was necessary for him to learn HTML, using a well-known tutorial from the Maricopa Center for Learning and Instruction. "I need to learn things from scratch, and I didn't want an authoring tool doing something for me until I fully understood its underpinnings," Ferguson says.

While he has no need or desire to become an expert in Web-authoring software, Ferguson does recognize the value of a designer who can credibly "talk the talk" with members of project design teams.

The viability of the Web or intranets as instructional tools rests in part on making clear distinctions between skills training and information sharing, Ferguson says. The goal shouldn't be to make the most extensive use of technology-delivered instruction, but to make good decisions about how to train or inform employees effectively in varying circumstances.

"When you slap hyperlinked text up on the Web, you don't automatically have training, you have reference material, informational updates or 'brochureware,'" he says. "That's OK for the purposes of disseminating information; just don't call it skills training."

MIXING IT UP

Alicia Brown
National Director for Clinical Support
Sunbridge Healthcare Corp., Albuquerque, N.M.

For many training professionals, the prospect of hitting the road holds a certain allure. Teaching in new locales promises new faces, new cities and the suggestion of a jet-setter's life. But veteran road warriors know it doesn't take long to get too much of a good thing.

Alicia Brown is among the new virtual instructors who embrace the travel-saving benefits of cyber-training. When her employer, Sunbridge Healthcare Corp., moved to videoconferencing, it proved to be something of a lifesaver. "I thought I'd love the traveling aspect of training, until traveling was all I did for most of three years," says Brown, director of clinical support. Now she is able to reduce what had become a daunting travel schedule, as well as master distance-learning technology.

Brown delivers training via videoconferencing systems about six times a week for Sunbridge—a subsidiary of Sun Healthcare Group International. She teaches both basic nursing skills and regulatory issues to some 300 employees around the country.

"When I boot up my computer an hour before a session and there's a problem, or there are problems with ISDN lines connecting, no one's going to come running on-site to help me."

In one of Brown's typical 90-minute distance training sessions, up to 12 separate Sun facilities might take part in the videoconference. Sun uses InView Worldwide's bridging services to reach an average of two to four trainees or more at each site. To help enhance the effectiveness of each program, Brown sends copies of the presentations to each trainee before the videoconferences. She then uses a remote control fish-eye camera to zoom and auto-focus on visuals such as Microsoft PowerPoint slides and illustrations, as well as her own image.

Brown first received technology training from an internal technical support group as well as InView. And naturally, she continued to "learn lessons" from the earlier distance training sessions she conducted. Initially, for instance, she found that she kept her camera focused too long on supporting visuals. She hadn't fully grasped that distance learners need visual variety to stay engaged, as well as the humanizing touch of the instructor's image.

"If you don't mix things up after awhile, trainees will think you're not live, but on tape," she says. "So I project a different screen image at least every 10 or 15 minutes."

Then there's technology troubleshooting. Although Brown can phone internal technical support for help, there are some glitches an enterprising virtual instructor must learn to handle. "When I boot up my computer an hour before a session and there's a problem, or there are problems with ISDN lines connecting, no one's going to come running on-site to help me," she says.

Even more challenging for a virtual instructor is the choreography of sessions to ensure remote trainees stay engaged and interested. "I try to make all of my sessions interesting and humorous, but it's still difficult for participants not to feel simply 'talked to' because you can't create the same level of interactivity," Brown says. "But they still learn as well as in most comparable classroom settings according to our post-course evaluations."

To help her keep tabs on required interactivity levels, Brown recently acquired an auto scan feature, which allows her to simultaneously project the image of participants from six sites onto half her local screen (the other half shows her presentation). As the six sites pop up at different intervals, it helps her keep tabs on trainee reaction to, and comprehension of, content.

Still, Brown likes to combine her online instruction with occasional field training. "The job does become more alive and invigorating for me when I go out and train in person," she says. "You also get a better flavor of how a session is received when you're face to face. For me, it would be hard to be completely isolated and not get some chance to have that face-to-face experience."

EXITING CENTER STAGE

Doug Young
Online Facilitator and Instructional Designer
Walden Institute, Bonita Springs, Fla.

Doug Young knew he'd face adjustments in the leap from classroom trainer to facilitator of Web-delivered courses. He understood that the computer keyboard would become his new "eyes and ears," and that the physical separation from students would, in the end, create certain instructional design challenges.

Online facilitators, while no less important to the learning process, operate far more in the shadows, necessarily assuming a hidden, backstage role to guide and nudge distance learners. Knowing that, Young was still surprised at how much he initially missed the "showmanship" role of the stand-up classroom environment.

"Distance learning can be tough at first, particularly when you see firsthand how that element of your personality no longer can carry you in the online world," says Young, who conducted classroom training for 20-plus years at the Federal Law Enforcement Training Center, Glynco, Ga., and later with the U.S. Department of Energy, Albuquerque, N.M. Now, he's a part-time online facilitator and instructional designer at Florida's Walden Institute, a "training the trainer" organization that teaches online instruction skills to training professionals and college faculty.

Although most students who enroll at Walden adapt well to the online teaching environment, some who previously thrived in classroom set-

> "In this medium, students should be more engaged by the quality of the content than by the personality of the instructor. Once I realized I was no longer the center of attention, I started seeking new ways to build that interaction, which usually resulted in a better learning experience for students."

tings discover that they aren't yet prepared to give up that important part of their professional identity. "I had one person take an online instruction course from me, and he said that his key learning from the class was that he really didn't want to teach online," Young explains.

Those who stay with online facilitation often experience rewards in other ways. "Today I see my job as finding as many varied ways as possible to get students to interact more with each other and the content, and less with me," says Young. "In this medium, students should be more engaged by the quality of the content than by the personality of the instructor. Once I realized I was no longer the center of attention, I started seeking new ways to build that interaction, which usually resulted in a better learning experience for students."

Those new to facilitating online courses tend to be taken by surprise by workload issues, Young says of Walden enrollees. The time required to guide or monitor threaded discussions, post classwork summaries, answer e-mail questions, operate "virtual" office hours, grade final projects and troubleshoot technology can be demanding.

Consequently, Young gives fair warning on workload issues to his virtual instructors-in-training at Walden. As always, time invested on the front end is a function of the kind of learning experience the instructors want students to have. Young counsels eager new online instructors that it's important to pace themselves. Regardless of delivery format, he urges, "managing student expectations is still the key."

Facilitated Mentoring: Rx for Stability and Skills

Editor's Comment: Margo Murray is an experienced mentor, designer, and implementer of facilitated mentoring programs, the kind that are likely to have the best outcomes according to this article. She makes a point in her long article referenced here that only the fortunate few will find a mentor by looking on their own. She gives advice and suggestions for making facilitated mentoring as non-bureaucratic as possible. She convinces the reader that facilitated mentoring will reduce employee turnover, create career opportunities, foster appreciation of diversity, and transfer skills.

We reprint four excerpts from this article. First, we give you Margo Murray's 7 keys to a successful mentoring process. Underpinning all these is a foundation of an integrated, facilitated process linked to the present and to the future of the business. Her view is that mentoring should not be considered a separate "program," because programs are often the first target of elimination in down times and economic uncertainty. Trainers who get involved in the design, implementation, and evaluation of mentoring programs will find her bulleted lists useful.

Sources: "Energizing Employees With Mentoring: They Keep Staying, and Staying, and Staying..." by Margo Murray in *Performance Improvement*, March 2001, excerpts from pages 36, 37, and 38. She also refers to another publication of hers in part of the material we reprint here. This publication is an article, "Cross Cultural Competencies Improve With Mentoring" in *Spanish Trends Management & Leadership*, Euroletter, 25 de mayo, 1998. Margo Murray is the author of a new book, *Beyond the Myths and Magic of Mentoring: How to Facilitate an Effective Mentoring Process, 2nd Edition,* published by Jossey-Bass, San Francisco. She is a former President of the International Society for Performance Improvement (ISPI), and also received ISPI honors, Member for Life, and Outstanding Member. She can be reached at *margo@mentors-mmha.com.* Excerpts are reprinted with permission of ISPI. Copyright 2001. All rights reserved.

Keys to a Successful Mentoring Process

- Identification of need, goal, opportunity, readiness
- Planning and design
- Communication
- Matching, agreements
- Orientation/training
- Development plans = healthy relationships
- Evaluation

What Skills Are Being Mastered?

Here are examples of the types of skills being transferred today with facilitated mentoring processes in four well-known organizations. The job title of the protégé is listed along with the specific growth objectives stated in the development or mentoring action plan (Murray, 1998).

- Capital Projects Accountant—acquire trade relations experiences and purchasing skills
- Commodity Manager—improve people skills, exposure and awareness to upper management activities, courage
- Copy Center Manager—develop presentation skills using multilingual capabilities
- Electrical Design Engineer—develop finance and business proposals
- International Trade Specialist—improve drive strength, time-management skills
- Market Development Manager—strengthen sales skills; improve balance between standing up for own rights and being more flexible
- Personnel Relations Manager—improve skills with cost side; compensation and benefits
- Project Coordinator—learn structure of the organization; gain job opportunities; develop skills with project management
- Quality Program Manager—develop task-oriented approach to total quality management
- Technical Services Center Representative—prioritize career goals, articulate and quantify ministeps to take to get to the long-term goal
- Territory Representative—develop skills with handling customer visits
- Warehouse Supervisor—learn company policies and procedures

What Are the Best Practices?

Many organizations have now implemented a facilitated mentoring process and are reaping measured results. Here are some selected examples:

- Aerospace—creating a multi-skilled workforce
- Banking—decreasing time needed to master customer service skills
- Community foundation—enabling former welfare recipients to get and keep jobs
- Computer manufacture, sales, and service—crosstraining hardware and software specialists
- Courts—career guidance for both professional and support personnel
- Education—K-12, secondary, and higher education supporting study habits, degree design, and transition to the workplace
- Food product manufacture—development of management skills for multiple functions
- Hospitality—grooming candidates for hotel management

Why Implement Mentoring During Tough Times?

In today's lean (and sometimes mean!) organizations, no *program* will be supported and stay in place unless it directly supports a goal or specific needs of the organization. There are many more reasons than costly litigation to make the growth and development of people a high priority. You only need to look as far as the bottom line—and every organization has one, including nonprofits—to find a good reason to facilitate the pursuit of mastery performance.

Here are some of the reasons to implement facilitated mentoring processes during lean times:

- To make sure we are retaining the right people as we *rightsize*
- To attract and recruit people with the skills and experience tomorrow demands
- To improve retention by making our experienced and skilled people feel more valued
- To increase the likelihood that we will survive with global competition
- To improve results—profit or other—with people who are more competent, confident, experienced, and motivated
- To ensure representation of diverse groups at all levels of the organization
- To enable our people to learn to work with others with different education, ages, cultures, physical abilities, etc.
- To improve communication across functional and divisional lines

Developing E-Employees Who Value Learning

Editor's Comment: This is one of those books that puts it all in context—all the ideas, concepts, criticisms, models, tools, systems, and people of our e-culture. In typical Rosabeth Moss Kanter style, this book is full of metaphor, analysis, synthesis, stories, and research studies that define and explain a phenomenon—that of the arrival of "e-culture." Like her other books, this book is not one you read in a hurry or when you're distracted. It requires full attention. In this final entry in our Section 4, "Training Program Delivery," we include some of Dr. Kanter's ideas about how learning fits into the e-culture.

In the Introduction to *e-volve!*, Dr. Kanter makes the point that the World Wide Web is both *stimulus* for a new organizational culture (making it necessary) and *facilitator* of that same culture (making it possible). Italics are mine. She goes on to define this new organizational culture as e-culture, and describes it using many adjectives that are rooted in creativity, flexibility, innovation, and speed. She hones in on the concept of improvisation, suggesting that "E-culture is made up as you go along, involving emergent strategies in response to opportunities." She also notes the 24/7 nature of the context for both success and failure; but that mistakes are okay—it's what's next that matters. She coins the term "creative destruction," meaning that the denizens of e-culture need to be always ready for continuous, dramatic change (pp. 6, 7). My own interpretation through the eyes of a trainer is that the trainer who believes in the extraordinary range and power of facilitation will thrive in this culture, and be the conduit for learning at many levels. Of course, the trainer in e-culture must also be Web-savvy.

The four chapters in her Part Two, "The Essence of E-Effectiveness," form the foundation of the book. These are: Chapter 4, Waves of Raves: Strategy As Improvisational Theater; Chapter 5, Connecting the Dots: Nurturing Networks of Partners; Chapter 6, From Cells to Communities: Deconstructing and Reconstructing the Organization; and Chapter 7, People.

Source: e-volve! By Rosabeth Moss Kanter. Boston: Harvard Business School Press, 2001. 352 pages, $27.50. Rosabeth Moss Kanter is the Ernest L. Arbuckle Professor of Business Administration at Harvard Business School. She has been named one of the "50 Most Powerful Women in the World" by *The Times of London*, and is the author of several books.

com: Winning the Talent Wars. We focus on some ideas relevant to training in People.com: Winning the Talent Wars and in other parts of the book's Part Two.

Challenging work, compatible colleagues, flexible work hours, and attention to individual needs for learning and career development—these are what e-employees want from employers. Dr. Kanter takes these wants a level higher, calling the overarching ideas "Mastery, Membership, and Meaning" and then suggests that employees who have employers who are tuned in to these are characterized by stronger commitment and greater company loyalty (pp. 204–205). Trainers who design and deliver instruction and set up learning environments for these kinds of employees are faced with facilitating individual learning based on highly individualistic styles and just-in-time learning needs at the same time as facilitating groups, communities of practice, work teams, and networks of colleagues. And for trainers who do these divergent things, the Internet and possibilities of the Web are invaluable tools. Trainers are also challenged to create innovative options for empowerment and contribution.

This is a book about e-culture, and it deserves a place on your bookshelf because of its research base (a 785-company global survey and 300 on-site interviews), its heft, and its many insights that can be helpful to trainers as trainers take on the leadership to make their companies both "change ready" and "change adept" (p. 321).

SECTION 5

Evaluation of Training

1. **E-Learning Evaluation** 207
   Quality Standards in E-Business 207
   A New Business-Driven Learning Strategy at Rockwell Collins 209
   ROI Factors in E-Learning 211
   Siemens' Knowledge Management (KM) Metrics 213

2. **Evaluation of Learners** 214
   Performance Assessment: A Multi-Systems Approach 214
   Executive Coaching's Return on Investment 217
   The Evaluator's Role in Improved Performance 218
   Getting 360-Degree Feedback Right 223
   Quarterly Evaluation for Performance Improvement 229

3. **Tests, Measures, and Certification** 230
   The "E-learning Value Proposition" 230
   ASTD's New Certification 231
   Pre- and Post-Testing Tied to Objectives 232
   Court Rulings Favor Performance Measures 233
   Core Measures of Intellectual Capital 240
   GE's "Four Buckets" 242
   More to E-Learning Measures Than Stock Price 243

INTRODUCTION TO EVALUATION OF TRAINING: SECTION 5

Our final section of *Training & Development Yearbook 2002* is Section 5, "Evaluation of Training." Here we include evaluation of learning, since this year there has been a marked increase in the use of the words "learning," learning as a process that comes from within, and "training," a process that is designed and implemented from "outside."

We begin with 5 entries on the evaluation of e-learning, a topic of particular interest this year because of the increased use of e-learning. With more e-learning experience comes the need of companies for standards and evaluation processes that are valid as well as supportive of the company's strategic directions. E-learning evaluation has just begun to be seriously discussed as it's frequency increases in more and more companies. Our sub-section 1 addresses the key components of e-learning program evaluation.

As individual learners, we are still attending classes but are also blending classroom instruction with various kinds of e-learning. Coaching and mentoring are still important ways to teach and to learn, and performance measurement is becoming more refined. Our sub-section 2 raises some of the important issues in evaluation of learners as we learn in various ways and translate that learning to better performance on the job.

Our final sub-section, 3, is concerned with the details of the design of evaluation; namely, tests, measures, and certification. Throughout companies and associations, there is a cry to develop and use better measures for training and learning. Trainers are being asked to think differently about the value in training and learning—value that is directly linked to company success. E-learning has presented new evaluation challenges: the kinds of things we count have changed. The old "butts in seats" standard simply doesn't work anymore. We show you in this section, through examples and ideas, how to think differently and how to measure differently too.

E-Learning Evaluation

Professional publications in human resources and training implore trainers to "do a better job" of determining the dollars and cents value of their companies' intellectual assets, and document ways that these assets improve organizational performance and "how knowledge and learning drive success" (Mark Van Buren and William Woodell, Jr., *The 2000 ASTD Trends Report: Staying Ahead of the Winds of Change*, p. 20). *HR Magazine* in April 2001 suggested that a healthy dose of skepticism is needed when evaluating the return on investment (ROI) of e-learning. *ASTD*'s Van Buren, Director of Research, is quoted as saying that he's seen very few convincing ROI analyses, and cautions that e-learning development can be very expensive. Most companies believe that it's still too early to tell if e-learning has resulted in cost savings and only IBM was willing to declare its savings—$200 million saved over one year ("E-Learning: New Twist on CBT" by Bill Roberts, p. 106).

E-learning is in everyone's vocabulary this year, and the literature on it is full of issues on standards, design, implementation options, evaluation, and the need for strategic thinking before, during, and after its use. 2001 was full of stories of e-learning experience and learning from that experience. 2002 can be expected to be much more of the same. *Forbes* magazine, September 10, 2001, ran a story about Michael Milken's amassing a $1.75 billion education empire called Knowledge Universe that is largely driven by e-learning. Milken calls e-learning the Internet's next killer app (p. 64). He sees himself as a liberator of learning, building an empire of learning-related companies all dependent upon each other. With education in the U.S. consuming around $750 billion annually, he stands to profit handsomely from his learning business, seen as much greater in potential than e-commerce's first big applications of books, flowers, and CDs (p. 67). Milken's formula for prosperity is P = FT (HC + SC + RA): *Prosperity equals the product of Financial Technology times the sum of Human Capital plus Social Capital plus Real Assets* (p. 68). Others in the business are watching Milken's moves; many agree that the e-learning space is one of great opportunity ("Master of the Knowledge Universe" by Stephen P. Pizzo, pp. 664–69). We include Michael Milken's prosperity formula here to suggest that there are many ways to think about the variables in e-learning, and to encourage you to think strategically as you engage in evaluation.

Evaluation of Learners

In this sub-section we focus on the learner. Individual and organizational performance are both very much still with us, and both still in need of creative and sound standards and measures. A new emphasis on one-to-one training has increased in 2001 and can be expected to increase even further in 2002. We see this in the large numbers of coaches, particularly executive coaches, and in mentoring at all levels. Companies still use 360 degree evaluation, but are seeking ways to make its results and its processes more useful. E-learning has highlighted the need for valid measures of individual success.

Tests, Measures, and Certification

It seems like lots of people are talking evaluation, certification, and testing this year. Media reports in mid-year 2001 of the national census focused on the government's non-use of sampling techniques, the extended use of imputation, and implications of results based on the kinds of measures used (for example, "Sampling Is Taboo" by Glenn R. Simpson in *The Wall Street Journal*, August 30, 2001, p. 1). Standards of counting have been very much in our national consciousness as we approach year 2002 and implementation of programs based on this census data. The Scholastic Aptitude Test (SAT) came under fire again this year in our high schools and colleges as being irrelevant to college admission, and President Bush's advocacy of universal testing of elementary and high school students was the topic of many column inches of newspaper and magazine coverage all year. Testing and accountability were part of the national dialogue in year 2001. *Publishers Weekly* magazine, September 10, 2001, had a major article on testing and ran photographs of 26 new test preparation books, (Lucinda Dyer, "Testing, 1,2,3", pp. 34–44). This number is a far cry from the *Kaplan* review programs of only a few years ago, the only test review help then available.

Those who are deeply involved in ISO 9000 standards and certification know that the latest standards, ISO 9001:2000, have been totally revised, simplifying the former 20 system elements to just 5, one of which is "measurement, analysis, and improvement" (Scott Madison Paton, *Quality Digest*, March 2001, p. 4). ASTD began a program of e-learning course certification in June 2001. This is a quality standards program that certifies vendor-prepared e-learning courses as being of acceptable quality for learning. Expect to see effects of this certification effort in year 2002. Many vendors rushed into the design and marketing of e-learning products and services; many also became part of the dot.com meltdown early in the year. ASTD as leader and advocate for trainers saw a need through standards and certification to continue the quality assurance of the field. The work of the U.S. Defense Department in its SCORM specifications added significantly to the new work being done in the area of content specification. The DoD has collaborated with many associations and new learning consortiums to create standards for accessibility, interoperability, and distributability of content. Content, packaging, and distribution are all important. IMS Global Learning Consortium, Burlington, MA, is one of these associations, a 300-unit global body of educational institutions, businesses, and government agencies. IMS Global has developed the foundation for content packaging of a new version of Sharable Content Object Reference Model (SCORM) (sources: *www.vnuonlinelearning.com* newsletter and *www.imsproject.org*).

1. E-learning Evaluation

Quality Standards in E-Business

Editor's Comment: What quality means in the context of e-business is the topic of many articles and commentaries in various business magazines. The year 2001, which business journalists certainly seem to think was the year of General Electric's retiring Jack Welch, saw articles and book chapters about GE's well-known implementation of "Six Sigma," adapted from Motorola's pioneering efforts twenty years ago, and saw many changes to the newer ISO standards for quality processes. The issue is setting standards, the first step in developing a meaningful evaluation process; and, in this case, setting standards for e-business in all of its variations, including training.

Classic quality standards were developed decades ago for manufacturing processes and later adapted to all other business processes, including training and other human resources functions. People-intensive processes, like training, received the same scrutiny as thing-intensive processes, like manufacturing, in the development of classic quality theories over the decades since Deming and Juran. We are now faced with needing new quality standards for e-business. How we view training and the process of learning within an e-business context is the first important step in setting standards for e-learning and for the e-training that goes along with it.

The August 2001 issue of *Quality Digest* contains an important article by Robert A. Green (p. 9) in which he refers to the recent work of the *American Association for Quality (ASQ)*'s H. James Harrington and Thomas McNellis in designing and developing an E-Business Quality Management education curriculum for university students and business management professionals at several Pennsylvania universities. As Green says, the curriculum attempts to "identify the parameters of measurement that infuse the highest level of quality into every aspect of an e-business initiative."

Trainers are used to being challenged to develop training in response to business goals and customer needs, and the issue of parameters of measurement in training have been with us in the forefront of our professional life particularly since Donald Kirkpatrick identified the "Four Levels" of evaluation more than two decades ago. Setting overall standards for e-business first, and then training standards within the overall picture, is the recommended way to proceed.

One such effort in doing this is that of General Electric (GE), where CEO Jack Welch is credited with adapting and fine tuning the "Six Sigma" quality measurement program to current times. Thomas Pyzdek (p. 54), a consultant in Six Sigma, writes about GE's Green Belts, Black Belts, and Master Black Belts, and the powerful infrastructure for quality resources that GE built through this karate metaphor. According to Pyzdek, for example, the Master Black Belt's duties include communications and teaching skills that, according to the measurement system, "are as important as technical competence." A later commentary by "Anonymous" (p. 80), a GE employee, does not think as kindly of the Six Sigma implementation at GE, and complains that employees lose sight of their own gut ability to see and fix quality

---

Sources: "E-Business Quality Management Education Effort Launched" by Robert A. Green, p. 9; "The Six-Sigma Infrastructure" by Thomas Pyzdek, p. 54; and "The Emperor's New Woes, Revisited" by Anonymous, p. 80, in *Quality Digest*, August 2001. Robert A. Green and Thomas Pyzdak are quality consultants and contributing writers to *Quality Digest* magazine.

problems as they occur. He complains that 95 percent of Six Sigma at GE is "a nightmare and a total waste of time," and that it really is only a huge bureaucracy that is natural feed for journalistic hype that drives stock prices up. He suggests that "the emperor has no clothes." All three of these points of view indicate that the field of quality standards in e-business is in a high point of development; trainers need to be aware of what's going on at the standards level and to be a part of the evaluation of and participation in the standards-setting movement.

Here is the course list in Harrington and McNellis's E-Business curriculum; contact ASQ for more information at 800/248-1946 or 610/436-3337 extension 2695:

- E-Business 101: Quality for a New Age, E-Business Quality Management

- E-Business 201: E-Business Customer Relationship Management, E-Supply Chain Management and Operational Integration

- E-Business 301: E-Business Security, E-Risk Analysis and E-Legal Reviews

- E-Business 401: E-Business Project Management, and Effective Approach

- E-Business 501: E-Business Six Sigma Software Quality

- E-Business 601: Audit the E-Business Initiative for Value, Effectiveness, and Success.

A New Business-Driven Learning Strategy at Rockwell Collins

Editor's Comment: Rockwell Collins is a manufacturer of communication and aviation electronics, with headquarters in Cedar Rapids, Iowa. The following case study of one training manager's, that is, "manager of learning and development," remake of the training operation is true-to-life for many companies. Read how Cliff Purington decided that change was imperative and developed a business-driven strategy that worked. His reinvention of training was based on six objectives, the foundation of which is based on things that can be measured.

BUSINESS RESULTS

When Cliff Purington arrived in 1998 as manager of learning and development at Rockwell Collins, a manufacturer of communication and aviation electronics, he checked into the company's training-history database. "I thought it would be rich with core competencies, and all I had to do was find the repeat courses to see what they were," he says.

But only 22 percent of the 1,400 individually titled classes had been repeated. Most of the course materials, developed in-house at a cost of $120 million, were unused. "We're not talking small change," Purington says. "It also told me that we didn't have a good connection back to the business, or a good needs analysis to see if training really was the issue."

He said the situation was not unusual for a large organization. "It was one of these cases where the folks in training were getting calls from line management, requesting very specific training." Often, he said, training wasn't really the fix that was needed. It might have been unclear roles and responsibilities or any number of other problems. But managers tended to identify training as the solution, even if it really wasn't. Since then, Purington has put in place a new cost-saving, business-driven learning strategy, based on six objectives:

- **Link learning directly to business objectives.** The training staff's job now is to work with the business groups to evaluate their training needs, make sure they're tied with the company's business objectives, and, if training is the solution or would be of benefit, work with outside vendors to develop training programs.

- **Locate classes close to the work environment to provide students with easier access.** When Purington began working at Rockwell Collins, all training for the company's 17,500 employees, who work at 26 locations around the world, was done in classrooms at the company's headquarters in Cedar Rapids, Iowa. The result was a lot of expensive travel and layer upon layer of scheduling difficulties.

- **Make learning accessible worldwide, 24 hours a day, seven days a week.**

- **Deliver the highest quality training.**

- **Reduce the cost of training by 40 percent.**

- **Increase available curriculum by 40 percent.**

Source: "Faster, Cheaper, Smarter: How Rockwell Collins Reinvented Its Training" sidebar in the article "Training Proves Its Worth" by Carroll Lachnit in *Workforce*, September 2001, p. 55. Carroll Lachnit is Managing Editor of *Workforce*. Reprinted with permission of *Workforce*. Copyright 2001. All rights reserved.

An example of a business-driven program that provides more learning in a more accessible form at lower cost is the course the company offers to engineers in electromagnetic interference. Previously, when courses were held only in Cedar Rapids, it would have taken 13 years to train all the engineers who needed the information, Purington says. Working with outside vendors, Purington and his staff created a Web-based course that delivered in 9 hours what took 22 hours to present in a classroom. "It has more content, and it's available 24/7 in the work environment, because it's online," he says.

Now, in the second year of the three-year learning-program overhaul, 80 percent of the company's training is available in alternative formats, including the Web and CD-ROMs. There are 450 online courses, such as ethics training, data processing, computer programming, diversity, and interpersonal skills, an increase since 1998 of 250 percent. There are still 50 courses taught in the classroom, all complex engineering classes in which student-instructor interaction is crucial. In the first year of the new learning program, the company saved $6.37 million in training costs—or 38 percent. This year, it's on target to save $6.79 million—or 39 percent.

For all of these accomplishments, can Purington show a direct line between the revamped training programs and Rockwell Collins's profitability? He doesn't measure training success that way. It's very hard to prove, and it's a defensive posture, he says.

"If you're on the back end of the process, which most training organizations are, you spend too much time trying to justify your existence. If you're on the front end, tied in to the business groups, and they know who you are and what you're doing, you don't have to do that. I don't have to justify the objectives I defined. The organization told me that's what they wanted, and that's what I provided."

An example of delivering what the business needs is the development of short courses called Quicklearns. The business groups were concerned about the loss of what Purington calls "tribal knowledge"—information that resides in the head of someone who has done a job for 40 years and vanishes when the employee retires. Quicklearns, classes of 20 minutes or less (the average adult's attention span), have a turnaround time from order to completion of 12 hours, and cost no more than $2,000.

"I'm delivering 150 of those this year," Purington says. The programs, produced by the Performance Engineering Group, based in Santa Barbara, California, begin with an expert in the procedure demonstrating the process that's going to be taught—how to clean a clean room, for instance. The producers create a storyboard that outlines what will be shown. There's a dry run, and then the process is filmed with a digital camera. The lesson is placed in an electronic template with text and questions for self-checking, and stored on a CD-ROM. The subjects of the 75 or so programs that the company has created include how to use an electronic microscope and how to choose and clean a soldering head. Two student groups, one trained via CD-ROM and the other trained by a classroom instructor, received virtually identical scores after being tested for their proficiency in clean-room techniques.

Here is Purington's formula for training success: "Get connected to the business groups as quickly as possible. Service the people you're there to service. Find out their needs, and how best you can deliver. Develop rapport and trust with the business groups, and then deliver what you say you're going to deliver. That's how you keep your budget from being cut."

ROI Factors in E-Learning

Editor's Comment: This article can help you turn ideas into numbers—the kinds of numbers you'll need to determine e-learning's return on investment (ROI). Consultant Scott Lawson, based in Los Angeles, California presents his ideas as if you were creating a spreadsheet. He offers his own online spreadsheet templates at *www.oneanthem.com* or by phoning him at 909/626-6254. Leaders in e-learning have been issuing words of caution to carefully consider all factors before you leap into training built entirely on e-learning. Using the spreadsheet approach suggested here can be useful as you get down to the nitty-gritty of finding and dealing with the hard numbers. While trainers have generally been under the gun to prove their worth, as year 2002 begins, the pressure is on even more: at the end of third quarter, unemployment hovered around 5 percent; job cuts totaled more than 1 million; mass layoffs affected more than 40 percent more people than last year; the stock market reports looked like roller coasters all year; more than half of executives surveyed by the American Management Association said their corporate profit projections would not be met; and, at the same time, the U.S. is experiencing a labor shortage (*Workforce*, September 2001, p. 32). Numbers clearly matter in times like these.

One of the first questions HR professionals will hear when thinking aloud about e-learning and its potential savings for training programs is: "What's the return on investment?" A simple spreadsheet program can be used to work up some reliable ROI comparisons for online learning and traditional classroom training.

One method for simplified ROI is provided by Scott Lawson, founder and head of OneAnthem, an online consulting operation based in Los Angeles. OneAnthem's Web site includes Lawson's suggestions for showing how money can be saved by taking components of training traditionally provided in the classroom and converting them to e-learning.

Building an ROI Analysis. Tangible costs are the easy ones to track: hardware and software to run the training, hardware and software to write it, programming, and content development. HR should consider whether outside programmers will be needed.

> Tangible savings for online projects will be such things as distribution costs, including paper and binders, duplicating, shipping, packing; classroom and equipment overhead; and travel and trainer fees.

Intangible costs include items like administration time; ramping-up time, including finding and training instructional designers; internal PR work, including spending time with the IT department; and orientation. "These are the ones we forget when we think about how cool something is and we're trying to get people to agree," Lawson said.

Tangible savings for online projects will be such things as distribution costs, including paper and binders, duplicating, shipping, packing; classroom and equipment overhead; and travel and trainer fees.

Intangible savings will include employee travel and learning time. Although it's not an

---

Sources: "How to Illustrate Potential for Saving with Training Programs Using E-Learning" Policy & Practice column in the *Human Resources Report* of the Bureau of National Affairs (BNA), August 20, 2001, p. 920. Article reprinted with permission of the Bureau of National Affairs, Washington, DC. Copyright 2001. All rights reserved. Statistics are also quoted from "HR Takes On Tough Times" by Shari Caudron in *Workforce*, September 2001, p. 32. Shari Caudron is a Contributing Editor of *Workforce*.

> In one example a company's costs associated with e-learning dropped from $51,900 for the first year to about $16,900 annually.

absolute, Lawson said, common training wisdom holds that HR can get the same content with online learning in half the time.

There are also issues of higher productivity: Can learners find information more quickly with online learning? "Maybe there's some percentage," Lawton suggested. For example, "Every year the skills of the people increase 2 percent, so their accuracy goes up for their time to build or learn drops."

Lawson said any spreadsheet should contain the following data:

- **Cost of labor.** Show what labor costs are, down to the minute.
- **Number of users.** Obviously, the ROI will shoot up dramatically when the number of users rises. Use Lawson's "what-if" scenario: "For 50 users, this project stinks [no matter what]. If users increase to 300, more money will be made."
- **Longevity/re-use of product.** Online learning that is used three times a year eliminates travel for those three days, Lawson pointed out.
- **Time spent on training.** How long is the actual stand-up training?
- **Materials fee.** Online training might have materials associated with it such as workbooks and CD-ROMs.
- **Classroom space.** If free space is available, the cost is zero. There might be classroom costs associated with online learning as well, if space is rented so everyone can take the course together.
- **Time lost on job.** Calculate this by multiplying the number of class days times the average daily salary of the trainees.

Plugging in the Numbers. Lawson used as an example a company planning to provide three five-day online classes per year for 24 employees with an average annual salary of $35,000. Assuming that the cost of developing the project was $35,000, Lawson estimated total first-year costs of about $51,900, compared with a $48,600 annual cost of classroom training.

But after the first year, he observed, the course development costs no longer apply, dropping e-learning costs to about $16,900.

The total savings, after conducting the training for a three-year period, would be about $60,000, or an ROI of about 170 percent, according to Lawson.

Siemens' Knowledge Management (KM) Metrics

Editor's Comment: AQPC recently looked among its participant companies for examples of knowledge management measures. Like training measures, KM measures fell into stages which APQC labeled as 1) Enter and Advocate, 2) Explore and Experiment, 3) Discover and Conduct Pilots, 4) Expand and Support, and 5) Institutionalize. What APQC found was that most of participants' time was spent on stages 3 and 4, with very little time spent on stage 5. They also found that Siemens was a corporation that bucked this trend, and, in fact, had some well-developed ideas and measures for both Expand and Support (section 4) and Institutionalize (section 5). The following abstract describes the Siemens difference.

Siemens is a corporation that believes in the reality of Communities of Practice (CoP) as a structure for communication, sharing, and growth. The KM initiative based its KM metrics on the idea that one of the primary values in Knowledge Management is its ability to expand and support the communities the company had identified as important Communities. The four dimensions of its KM system are:

1. Knowledge community: the organization, community, people dimensions;
2. Knowledge marketplace: the technology involved;
3. Key KM processes: the sharing and creation that takes place; and
4. Knowledge environment which encompasses the other three.

Within this framework, Siemens measures quantity of knowledge coming into and going out of its various communities, and the amount and quality of feedback coming into and going out. Siemens has a history of assessment questionnaires that provide information periodically about both quantity and quality within its Communities of Practice. Siemens also collects information about the personal business effects of various practices and processes built upon knowledge acquisition and sharing. Siemens also has developed a "maturity" assessment in which they measure the institution of a process on a scale of from "chaotic" to "optimized."

The Siemens idea of stage 5, Institutionalize, is that all measures of this stage are defined to monitor progress and the continued evolution of the KM culture. They do not think of Knowledge Management as a "project" or an "initiative": they see it as an integral part of the business. Siemens goes so far as to require that evidence of competency in Knowledge Management is part of the employee's formal performance evaluation.

Source: "Measurement for Knowledge Management" online report of the American Productivity and Quality Center (APQC), Copyright 2001. www.apqc.org. Contributors to this report include: Cynthia Hartz of Dow Corning, Stuart Sammis of Dow Corning, Dr. Josef Hofer-Alfeis of Siemens AG, Kimberly Lopez of APQC, Cynthia Raybourn of APQC, and Jennifer Neumann Wilson of APQC.

2. Evaluation of Learners

Performance Assessment: A Multi-Systems Approach

Editor's Comment: This "White Paper" by a member of the Society for Human Resource Management (SHRM) is a good overview of current performance assessment issues, and so we reprint it first in this second sub-section of Section 5. Not only does the author, Ed Sherbert, detail a "multi-systems" approach, but he also invokes the spirit of W. Edwards Deming and Peter Drucker in an attempt to give historical perspective to the key components of today's theory and practice of performance assessment. One of the important points that Sherbert makes is that the speed of change today is rapid, affecting objective-setting and the expectations for meeting objectives. He also suggests that the process of performance assessment seems very difficult for many people.

One bit of data may be helpful in understanding some of the difficulties that attend the job of performance assessment. The June 28, 2001 publication of the SHRM-BNA Survey Number 66 indicated that the task of performance appraisal was split among departments in the survey sample, and that often the training for performance was done by persons other than those who did the appraising—54 percent in the case of management appraisal and 56 percent in the case of non-management appraisal. (Table 1, page s-7, and "Training" text, page s-8). The survey respondents represented 417 organizations from a survey mailed to BNA's survey panel and a random sample of SHRM members, a 9 percent response rate. These data and Ed Sherbert's observations suggests that trainers, and others, have work to do in envisioning and implementing performance appraisal processes that yield results for personal and organizational improvement.

PERFORMANCE ASSESSMENT: A MULTI-SYSTEMS APPROACH

In recent years, a steady tide of reorganizations, downsizing, mergers, rightsizings, reengineering and other changes has swept across organizations of all sizes, within all industries. Rather than receding, the tide is rising.

The need to change and adapt in this new world of work requires organizations, and their employees that run them, to respond to these dynamic situations. First, they must quickly and aggressively learn to do more with less. Second, they must effectively understand the expectations and priorities of their internal and external customers. This is why successful performance assessment can be so value-added in today's workplace.

Sources: "Performance Assessment: A Multi-Systems Approach" by Ed Sherbert, a SHRM White Paper accessed online at www.shrm.org/whitepapers, April 2001. Ed Sherbert holds SPHR certification from SHRM and is the Co-Founder of www.alight.com located in New York City. Copyright 2001, Society for Human Resource Management (SHRM). Reprinted with permission of the Society for Human Resource Management. All rights reserved. We also refer to the SHRM-BNA Survey Number 66, Human Resource Activities, Budgets and Staffs, 2000–2001 published in the *Bulletin to Management*, by the Bureau of National Affairs, copyright 2001, pp.s-8–s-9.

Performance assessment is probably the worst managed system in the workplace. Although top management defines it as strictly a development technique, performance assessment is infused with goals of salary justification, elimination of low performers, and the important correlations of employee behavior with actual results. These purposes are often frustrated, however, by obstacles: difficulties in gathering adequate information in the first place, keeping this information up to date, mistrust of uses to which information is put, treatment of the evaluation interview itself as a chore, and little or no performance assessment training. Why do we continue to use this process? W. Edwards Deming, a founder of the quality movement, went so far as to suggest that individually focused performance assessment is a "deadly management disease" that is killing organizations, and he recommended that performance appraisals be eliminated!

Performance assessment continues to exist because it is capable of serving an important purpose in the organization. It can be a useful way to look at corporate history and to attempt to link behavior with results. But whether it does accomplish this purpose depends on the implementation of the performance assessment system and whether or not it meets the needs of the leaders and followers in the organization. To meet these needs the system should be multi-purpose, in other words, "one size does not fit all." We keep hearing about designing a "simple" system and it will be successful. How can a simple system be successful in such a complex human environment? This paper suggests a multi-system approach to performance assessment so that leaders and followers have more flexibility in determining what system really fits their organization, what system can grow as the organization grows and expands.

First level, some would suggest that Management by Objectives (MBO) is dead. Peter Drucker, who pioneered this approach to performance assessment, was sure it would be successful as an assessment tool for many years. MBO is not dead, not in corporate American and not in the dot.com world. Today many companies use this tool, which measures the successful attainment of objectives and indicates the quality and/or quantity of performance. Its application and acceptance results, in part from its identity with commonly held personal values, especially the philosophy that rewarding people for what they accomplish is important. MBO can attain greater individual-organizational goals congruence and reduce the likelihood that managers are working in directions unrelated to the objectives and purposes of the organization.

Management by objectives is premised on the assumption that an organization's objectives for a specific period should cascade down through the organization. Although the use of goals in evaluating leaders is effective in motivating their performance, capturing all the important job dimensions in terms of output is not always possible. Change occurs so rapidly today that one should expect goals and objectives to change just as rapidly. This is the reason that using MBO alone as an assessment tool is not working but using it in conjunction with other performance assessment systems gives a more accurate picture of individual performance.

The MBO process is a series of activities taking place throughout the year. The process clarifies the job to be done, the results expected, and provides for a broad assessment of individual performance. The process usually begins in the first quarter of each year with the leader and follower agreeing upon a few significant business objectives for the year, such as sales volume, new business development, completion of specific projects, or achievement of specific goals. Good objectives are measurable; there should be no doubt about their being achieved.

Second level, a behavioral-based performance assessment system focuses on assessing a worker's behaviors. The rater is asked to assess whether an employee exhibits certain behaviors. This system is very complimentary to the MBO system. A leader can achieve all his/her objectives but leave "a bunch of dead bodies" along the way. In the behavior-based system ratings assess the value rather than the frequency of specific behaviors. The main advantage of a behavioral approach is that the performance standards are concrete. This concreteness makes behavioral instruments more legally defensible than purely objective-based systems. Behavioral scales also provide employees with specific examples of types of behaviors to engage in (and to avoid) if they want to do well in the organization. In addition, behavioral scales encourage supervisors to be specific in their performance feedback. This makes it tougher on the supervisor since he/she must document these behaviors during the performance period. Finally, both followers and leaders can be involved in the process, in fact, this kind of system lends itself to develop into a 360 degree system or any combination there of.

Behaviors should focus on the following areas: Action dimensions (does the employee act decisively or make sound decisions in a timely manner), problem solving, customer knowledge (both internal and external), innovation, flexibility, the ability to influence, good communications, integrity (shows consistency between words and actions), interpersonal skills, relationship building (does the employee see positive attributes in others and builds solid relationships that enhance other's "good points").

Leaders should have additional behavior performance criteria such as: the ability to delegate, a big picture thinker (does he/she see the overall implications of actions and ideas), goal setting, planning and self-development (does he/she invest personal time and energy in self-development and growth).

Behavioral systems are not without disadvantages. The development of behavioral scales can be very time consuming, easily taking several months. Another disadvantage of behavioral systems is their specificity. The points on behavioral scales are clear and concrete, but they are only examples of behavior a worker may exhibit. Employees may never exhibit some of these behaviors, which can cause difficulty at appraisal time. Also, significant organizational changes can invalidate behaviors.

Third level, Skill-based performance assessment is another way to enhance the MBO and behavioral-based systems. Employees acquire depth skills when they learn more about a specialized area or become an expert in a given field. They can also acquire horizontal or breadth skills when they learn more jobs or tasks within the company, and vertical skills when they acquire "self-management" abilities such as scheduling, coordinating, training and leadership. Skill-based performance has been adopted by a wide range of industries. Skill-based performance offers several advantages to the company. It creates a more flexible workforce that is not straitjacketed by job descriptions specifying work assignments for a given job title. It promotes cross training, thus preventing absenteeism and turnover from disrupting the work unit's ability to meet deadlines. It calls for fewer leaders, so management layers can be cut to produce a leaner organization. It also increases employees' control over their compensation if the system is tied to a compensation matrix.

A skill-based system begins by developing a list of specific skills or demonstrated knowledge required for a particular job. Competencies are developed by each follower in the company who knows the "hard" skills/abilities necessary to do the work. Then these competencies may be placed in four different levels of attainment. When an employee is fully proficient within one level of a competency, they may be considered for movement to the next level.

A good example is the competency profile of a Human Resources Assistant. The area of expertise is Employment. The **Basic** requirement may be an understanding of motivation principles such as the Hierarchy of Needs, Positive Reinforcement, Hygiene Theory, or Scientific Management. In the next level of employment, **Comprehensive**, the employee must know how to determine the appropriate recruitment and employment testing mechanisms. The next level may be **Advanced**. In this level of employment knowledge the employee must understand laws, policies, systems and have company knowledge to design employment processes. In the fourth level, **Expert**, the employee is recognized by peers as an expert in the employment field.

A skill-based performance system does pose some risks to the organization. It may lead to higher compensation and training costs that are not offset by greater productivity or cost savings. This can happen when many employees master many or all of the skills and then receive a higher wage. Employees who do not use the new skills they have learned may become "rusty." Attaching monetary values to skills can become a guessing game unless external comparable pay data are available. Finally, skill-based performance assessment may become part of the problem it is intended to solve (extensive bureaucracy and inflexibility) if an elaborate and time-consuming process is required to monitor and certify employee skills.

In summary, employees want to know what they are supposed to do, what's expected of them, what the standards of performance are, how they are doing, and they want advice for doing even better the next time around. It's important to remember that performance assessment is one of the most important activities for us in our work experiences. There are many ways to design a system, the key to successfully implementing a system is to be sure it is the right system or systems for that particular workplace.

Executive Coaching's Return on Investment

Editor's Comment: Having nobody to talk to, being lonely at the top, being blindsided by the position, lacking information about details, etc. are all reasons why executives say they need or want coaching. Freelance writer, Matt Bolch, uncovered some statistics about executive coaching's benefits, especially to the bottom line. Trainers have been searching for years for the right kinds of evaluation for their products (learning and improved productivity) and their processes (training, independent study, coaching, mentoring). Bloch reports that, typical of trainers as a whole, executive coaches seldom measure the impact of their coaching. He quotes a survey commissioned by Personnel Decisions International, Minneapolis, MN, that reports less than 10 percent of organizations measure the impact of executive coaching.

This is one look at executive coaching's return on investment (ROI). Sources for Matt Bloch's short report are Manchester Consulting, Jacksonville, FL; Agnes Mura, an Executive coach from Santa Monica, CA; and Paul Walker of Conexant Systems, Newport Beach, CA.

- Average ROI of executive coaching is 5.7 percent against its cost.
  Manchester Consulting

- 77 percent of executives using it report improvements in relationships with those who report directly to them.
  Manchester Consulting

- 71 percent of executives using it report improved relationships with supervisors.
  Manchester Consulting

- 67 percent of executives using it report improved relationships in teamwork.
  Manchester Consulting

- 63 percent of executives using it report improved relationships with peers.
  Manchester Consulting

- 61 percent of executives using it report an increase in job satisfaction.
  Manchester Consulting

- 53 percent of executives using it report an increase in company productivity.
  Manchester Consulting

- 48 percent of executives using it report an increase in quality and organizational strength.
  Manchester Consulting

These percentages, according to Manchester Consulting, translate into positive and calculable bottom line returns based on the value of executive salary. Agnes Mura, executive coach, suggests that qualitative measures of executive value to the organization include employee retention rates, client satisfaction, employee attitudes, and the strategic consequences of executive blind spots that result in wrong projections of all sorts. All of these can figure into the calculation of return on investment.

Source: "Return on Coaching" sidebar within the article "Proactive Coaching" by Matt Bolch in *TRAINING Magazine,* May 2001, p. 60. Matt Bolch is a freelance writer for *TRAINING Magazine.*

The Evaluator's Role in Improved Performance

Editor's Comment: Linking individual performance improvement to organizational benefits is the challenge trainers are faced with, and are the hallmarks of our present era in training, according to the author of the article reprinted here. Behaving differently on the job (classic Level III) is what training evaluators ought to be looking for when they evaluate training. Viewing evaluation as a problem and not a solution still seems to be a common mindset of trainers, according to Kathleen D. Harrell (p. 25). Elliott Masie of The MASIE Center, a technology and learning "thinktank," suggests that measuring time is the first consideration in finding return on investment. Some of the measures he suggests are: time to market, time to hire, and time to change. He advocates more strategic thinking, "aligning the budget closer to the impact zone" and cautions against using only cost reduction as a metric (p. 6). Kathleen D. Harrell's article presents a very good case for doing Level III evaluations to measure the kinds of organizational change Elliott Masie's time measures look at, as well as promotes the very positive role that the evaluator can have in an organization.

We've all heard of Level III training evaluation and most of us acknowledge that it is important, but how many of us actually practice it on a regular basis in our organizations? Relatively few. While training evaluation has been regarded as beneficial in organizations, the actual practice of thorough evaluation has been largely neglected. We are in the age of performance consulting, where we as human resources development (HRD) professionals must link training to performance improvement, and performance improvement to organizational benefits. To do this, we must first demonstrate that training is "transferred" to the job.

Unfortunately, training is often conducted without any thought of how the results will be evaluated. Training is *incomplete* without an evaluation, for evaluation is what gives training meaning. How do we know if course material is effective if we don't conduct a thorough evaluation?

According to the classic Kirkpatrick four-level model of training evaluation, when a training program is effective, trainees are satisfied (Level I), they have learned the material presented (Level II), they behave differently on the job (Level III), and the organization benefits from the training (Level IV) (Holton, 1996). According to an ASTD Benchmarking Forum, 92% of training evaluation ends at Level I; only 11% of courses are actually evaluated at Level III (ASTD, 1996, 1997).

Training evaluation provides data that should serve as a basis for enhancing the training system. These data can be used to improve the training program, increase feedback to trainers and trainees, and assess trainee skill levels. Most importantly, these data can help trainers move closer to reaching the ultimate goal of training evaluation—*improved trainee performance*. Through a thorough evaluation of training techniques, trainers can determine which training methods are most successful in

---

Sources: "Level III Training Evaluation: Considerations for Today's Organizations" by Kathleen D. Harrell in *Performance Improvement*, May/June 2001, pp. 24–27. Kathleen D. Harrell is a human resources analyst in Richmond, VA. Article is reprinted with permission from *Performance Improvement*, Copyright 2001. All rights reserved. We also refer in our Editor's Comments to an article on e-learning ROI metrics by Elliott Masie of The MASIE Center, Saratoga Springs, NY in his *Learning Decisions Interactive Newsletter* of February 2001, pp. 1–3 and 6.

achieving improved performance and, as a result, in benefiting organizations.

CURRENT PRACTICE

In recent years, organizations have shown an increased interest in training evaluation. This is possibly a function of current organizational trends. Downsizing has resulted in an enlargement of jobs; functions that were carried out by several employees are now the responsibility of one employee. Greater international competition, education reform, business re-engineering, technology development, and pressure to provide "first-time" products or services has made organizational change necessary. Organizations are experiencing a shift from training employees for training's sake to meeting the objectives of the organization. The implication of these changes for training professionals calls for a new way of looking at training evaluation.

The U.S. federal government spends $600 million to $1 billion annually on training. By comparison, state governments spend $12 billion or more annually and private companies spend $8 billion annually (Gray, Hall, Miller, & Shasky, 1997). Despite the billions of dollars spent on training, it is estimated that not more than 10% of the dollars invested in training and development actually results in a change of behavior (Haccoun & Saks, 1998). It is critical that HRD professionals make changes in the training development and evaluation processes to increase both behavior change and the cost effectiveness of training.

WHY CONDUCT LEVEL III EVALUATION?

Training evaluation can seem a tedious chore. It rarely involves social interactions, it often deals with numbers, it can lead to participants' criticisms, and it can seem to reflect that no learning took place. Some trainers prefer not to collect evaluation information, fearing that a poor evaluation will confirm that their training course is flawed.

For many, evaluation is viewed as a problem, not a solution. Evaluation is an end, not a *means* to an end. However, if change in behavior is a necessary indicator that a trainee has learned from training, and if individual change is a requirement for successful organizational change, then measuring trainee behavior change will be an essential part of future training programs.

Specifically, there are quite a few benefits that can result from Level III training evaluation. It can increase the ability of training programs to produce intended results, leading to greater credibility for trainers and a stronger commitment to training by top administrators. Through Level III evaluation, training programs can be tailored to be more efficient and effective in developing trainees' strengths and minimizing their weaknesses.

Training evaluation can be rewarding for all individuals involved by satisfying the curiosity of the trainer (e.g., was the training effective?), the training sponsors (e.g., was the training program appropriate?), and the trainee (e.g., did I grow?). Level III evaluation can, and should, lead to improved skills and new work behaviors.

LEVEL III EVALUATION IS UNPOPULAR

We cannot discuss the benefits of training evaluation without acknowledging that there are several challenges to completing successful Level III training evaluation. Level III evaluation is not common simply because it is difficult. Most training professionals admit that training evaluation is the *most* difficult part of their job. It is challenging to determine the impact training has on trainee performance, and the cost of doing effective evaluations can be high. Often trainers have limited time to collect and analyze data and to report the results. Organizations may not have professionals skilled in training evaluation development, statistics, computer programming, and research methodologies. Also, standardized instruments for data collection and programs for computerized analysis and storage of data may not be available in organizations.

Some organizations may lack a climate characterized by trust and openness, which is necessary for effective data collection. Information used in some training evaluation processes, including records of individual, group, departmental, and organizational performance may not be available either. Pretests, posttests, and interviews with trainees, supervisors, and subordinates before and after the training program can make employees feel like lab mice. As a result, employees may feel that their organization does not trust that they could attend a training program and learn.

Evaluation, therefore, bears the stigma of being intimidating. However, these are challenges that HRD professionals can and must overcome to ensure that the organizational environment is conducive to effective training evaluation.

INVOLVING EVALUATORS EARLY

The training evaluation process is more likely to be in harmony with the training program when employees or consultants responsible for training evaluation, or "training evaluators," are involved as much as possible in training development. The training evaluator should make sure that the training goals are consistent with the goals of the evaluation process.

To ensure that evaluation will be effective, training evaluators can make several decisions during the training development stage. A first consideration should be the number of times the training course will be offered. A course that is delivered once likely calls for little money or time to evaluate behavior change. However, if a course is going to be run multiple times, more time and money can be justified by the potential future positive results.

Training evaluators should also consider the cost of evaluating behavior in relation to the benefits that could result from the evaluation. If the estimated evaluation cost exceeds the potential benefits of the evaluation, evaluators should reconsider their evaluation methods and develop more cost-effective tools.

Evaluators should investigate the data-collection methods. Common instruments used in Level III training evaluation are questionnaires, attitude surveys, tests, interviews, focus groups, observations, and performance records. When developing an evaluation instrument, training evaluators must consider the instrument's validity, reliability, ease of administration, usability, and economic value. Evaluators should also determine if all data necessary for training evaluation are available in the organization.

Finally, the training evaluator should establish ways to make the purposes of the evaluation program clear to all training developers, trainees, managers, coworkers, subordinates, and upper-level administrators. This involves communicating the importance and benefits of evaluation and the rewards of assisting with evaluation.

To ensure that learning can transfer to the job, training evaluators must also assess the learning environment. First, the training evaluator, trainer, trainee, and manager must have a shared goal: the transfer of learning. Before the training, the training evaluator must make his or her expectations clear. The trainer must also identify obstacles to training transfer and anticipate strategies to overcome problems. Finally, the training evaluator must work with managers to provide ways to maintain the trainees' learned behavior at work.

SUGGESTIONS FOR PRACTICAL LEVEL III EVALUATION

Level III evaluation is designed to determine if trainees change as a result of a training experience. Traditional methods of training evaluation call for strict guidelines. In the past, training evaluators were advised to perform a systematic appraisal of on-the-job performance before and after training, to conduct follow-up interviews, to conduct a statistical analysis to compare before and after performance changes related to the training program, to conduct a post-training appraisal three months or more after the training, and to measure the behavior of a control group before and after the training course was offered. The goal of training evaluation was *proof*, not just *evidence*, of behavior change as a result of training.

Control groups, time series design, and random assignment of trainees to groups are ways to determine if trainee behavior change is a result of training. However, these traditional methods of evaluation are not always appropriate for modern organizations. Few organizations have the resources to dedicate to an extensive evaluation of each training course. Several alternative data collection and measurement methods attempt to overcome the challenge of effective evaluation in today's organizations.

Pretraining/Posttraining Evaluation

Conduct a pretraining evaluation to measure the skills the trainee has before training, and a posttraining evaluation to measure the skills the trainee has acquired through training. This evaluation can involve the trainee making a video of himself or herself to view before and after the training intervention. The trainee and training evaluator can view the video and determine the trainee's behavioral changes as a result of the training (Dixon, 1987).

Follow-up Assignment

Inform the trainees that at a specific date after training, they will receive an assignment to reinforce the use of their skills. The assignment should measure the trainee's application of information to a work situation. A case study is an especially effective way to reinforce information that the trainee may not have had an opportunity to use on the job.

Action Plan Audit

The trainee formulates a specific action plan for posttraining activities and goals. Before the end of the training program, the plans are reviewed for feasibility and appropriateness. Four to six months later, the training evaluator can audit the action plan by sending questionnaires to participants and supervisors. The audit can determine the trainee's progress toward achieving original goals (Phillips, 1991).

Simulation

Training evaluators assess participants' posttraining skill retention by observing the participants in task simulations and role plays. A task simulation can determine if a trainee possesses the skills needed to perform a task. Training evaluators observe the trainee performing necessary steps to determine if he or she can safely perform a task. In a role play, the trainee is given a role with specific instructions and, often, an ultimate goal. The trainee then decides the steps to take to achieve the goal and practices the skills in a situation with other trained role players. Trained assessors rate the trainee's performance in the exercise (Phillips, 1991).

Internal Referencing Strategy

Training evaluators compare pretraining and posttraining evaluation differences in content covered by training to the pre- and posttraining differences in content *not* covered by training. Training effectiveness is determined, therefore, when pre- and posttraining changes on content covered in training are greater than pre- and posttraining changes on content not covered in training (Haccoun & Saks, 1998).

Onsite Follow-up Visit by the Trainer

With this approach, the training evaluator can determine the trainees' perceptions of how effective the training has been. During the visit, training evaluators can observe trainees on the job and provide feedback and assistance with any difficulties. Additionally, evaluators and trainees can identify any organizational constraints to transfer of learning to the job. Trainees can also provide input for training modification.

Unobtrusive Monitoring

Employee performance data are commonly used for training evaluation. Performance data can include absenteeism, downtime, efficiency, promotions, overtime, productivity, scrap, sales, termination, customer complaints, total output, and work stoppages. These data can be analyzed for differences before and after training.

Training evaluators should wait an appropriate amount of time before conducting a Level III evaluation to allow trainees time to demonstrate learning on the job. Kirkpatrick recommends that training evaluators wait approximately three to six months, depending on the type of training delivered. Because trainees change behavior at different rates, training evaluation should also be repeated three to six months after the first phase of training evaluation (Kirkpatrick, 1994).

Furthermore, for training to be effective, trainees must desire to improve. Trainees are less likely to carry out learned behaviors if observers regard the behaviors as unimportant or do not encourage their use. Therefore, the training evaluator should remember that a poor evaluation can be attributed to negative reactions of observers rather than to ineffective training programs.

CONCLUSION

A failure to systematically evaluate behavioral change resulting from training leaves the potential for growth in training without accountability. This could led to the continuation of ineffective programs. During a time of budget cuts, a failure to demonstrate results could lead top administrators to regard training programs as unnecessary and to recommend that they be cut.

Most organizations do not evaluate training beyond Level I. However, in a time of workplace change, Level III evaluation has received increased attention. To maximize the impact of training and to be accepted as performance consultants, HRD professionals must demonstrate how training links to performance improvement. Before we do this, we must first demonstrate that our training methods result in behavior changes. Thus, it is to our advantage to invest financial and human resources into thorough Level III training evaluation.

REFERENCES

American Society for Training and Development. (1996). Benchmarking Survey. Available http://www.astd.org/virtual_community/research/bench/96stats/graph1.gif

American Society for Training and Development. (1997). Executive Survey. Available http:/www.astd.org/virtual_community/research/nhrd_executive_survey_97me.htm.

Dixon, N. (1987). Meet training's goals without reaction forms. *Personnel Journal, 66,* 108–115.

Gray, G. R., Hall, M. E., Miller, M., & Shasky, C. (1997). Training practices in state government agencies. *Public Personnel Management, 26,* 187–202.

Haccoun, R. R., & Saks, A. M. (1998). Training in the 21st century: Some lessons from the last one. *Canadian Psychology, 39,* 33–51.

Holton, E. F. (1996). The flawed four-level evaluation model. *Human Resource Development Quarterly, 7,* 5–21.

Kirkpatrick, D. L. (1994). *Evaluating training programs: The four levels.* San Francisco: Berrett-Koehler Publishers.

Phillips, J. J. (1991). *Handbook of training evaluation and measurement methods* (2nd ed.). Houston: Gulf Publishing Company.

Getting 360-Degree Feedback Right

Editor's Comment: We've been at this business of 360-Degree appraisal for about a decade. Much of it is coordinated by the Human Resources Department, and that usually means that Training gets involved. Trainers generally are responsible for at least showing employees how to do 360-Degree appraisals, and often are in charge of the appraisal process itself. The article reprinted here uncovers four paradoxes of peer appraisal, and suggests that these paradoxes are sometimes stumbling blocks to getting valid assessments. Author Maury A. Peiperl presents some ways to reconcile these paradoxes in order to get better results and make this kind of appraisal more helpful.

If a single e-mail can send the pulse racing, it's the one from human resources announcing that it's time for another round of 360-degree feedback. In and of itself, this type of appraisal isn't bad. Indeed, many businesspeople would argue that over the past decade, it has revolutionized performance management—for the better. But one aspect of 360-degree feedback consistently stymies executives: peer appraisal. More times than not, it exacerbates bureaucracy, heightens political tensions, and consumes enormous numbers of hours. No wonder so many executives wonder if peer appraisal is worth the effort.

I would argue that it is. Peer appraisal, when conducted effectively, can bolster the overall impact of 360-degree feedback and is as important as feedback from superiors and subordinates. Yet the question remains: can peer appraisal take place without negative side effects? The answer is yes—if executives understand and manage around four inherent paradoxes.

For the past ten years, my research has focused on the theory behind, and practice of, 360-degree feedback. Most recently, I studied its implementation at 17 companies varying in size—from start-ups of a few dozen people to *Fortune* 500 firms—and industry—from high-tech manufacturing to professional service firms. I was looking for answers to several questions. Under what circumstances does peer

> 360-degree feedback is all the rage in companies big and small. But it is frequently bureaucratic, politically charged, and agonizing. The good news is that by understanding four paradoxes inherent to peer appraisal, managers can take some of the pain out of the process—and get better results in.

appraisal improve performance? Why does peer appraisal work well in some cases and fail miserably in others? And finally, how can executives fashion peer appraisal programs to be less anxiety provoking and more productive for the organization?

My research produced a discomforting conclusion: peer appraisal is difficult because it has to be. Four inescapable paradoxes are embedded in the process:

- *The Paradox of Roles:* You cannot be both a peer and a judge.
- *The Paradox of Group Performance:* Focusing on individuals puts the entire group at risk.
- *The Measurement Paradox:* The easier feedback is to gather, the harder it is to apply.
- *The Paradox of Rewards:* When peer appraisal counts the most, it helps the least.

Source: "Getting 360-Degree Feedback Right" by Maury A. Peiperl in *Harvard Business Review,* January 2001, pp. 142–147. Article reprinted with permission of *Harvard Business Review.* Copyright 2001 by the Harvard Business School Publishing Corporation. All rights reserved.

Performance management isn't easy under any circumstances. But a certain clarity exists in the traditional form of performance review, when a boss evaluates a subordinate. The novelty and ambiguity of peer appraisal, on the other hand, give rise to its paradoxes. Fortunately, managers can, with some forward thinking and a deeper understanding of their dynamics, ease the discomfort. Let's consider each paradox in detail.

The Paradox of Roles

Peer appraisal begins with a simple premise: the people best suited to judge the performance of others are those who work most closely with them. In flatter organizations with looser hierarchies, bosses may no longer have all the information they need to appraise subordinates. But it doesn't necessarily follow that peers will eagerly step into the breach. They may tend to give fairly conservative feedback rather than risk straining relationships with colleagues by saying things that could be perceived negatively. Consequently, the feedback gathered from peers may be distorted, overly positive, and, in the end, unhelpful to managers and recipients.

In more than one team I studied, participants in peer appraisal routinely gave all their colleagues the highest ratings on all dimensions. When I questioned this practice, the responses revealed just how perplexing and risky, both personally and professionally, evaluating peers can be. Some people feared that providing negative feedback would damage relationships and ultimately hurt their own careers and those of their friends and colleagues. Others resisted because they preferred to give feedback informally rather than making it a matter of record. Still other employees resented peer appraisal's playing a part in a performance system that resulted in promotions for some and criticism and even punishment for others—thereby, they believed, compromising the egalitarian and supportive work environments they had tried to cultivate.

When the Paradox of Roles is at play, people are torn between being supportive colleagues or hard-nosed judges. Their natural inclination is to offer counsel and encouragement, and yet they've been asked to pass judgment on a colleague's performance. Unless this conflict is

> When the Paradox of Roles is at play, people are torn between being supportive colleagues or hard-nosed judges.

addressed early on, peer appraisal will go nowhere fast—and cause stress and resentment along the way.

The Paradox of Group Performance

Most peer appraisal programs can't reveal what makes a great group tick. Even though such evaluations are intended to gain insights into the workings of teams or groups, peer appraisal programs usually still target individual performance. In most cases, however, a focus on individuals doesn't address how most important work is done these days—that is, through flexible, project-based teams. Moreover, successful groups resent it when management tries to shift their focus or asks them to compare members with one another; in the extreme, peer appraisal may even harm close-knit and successful groups.

In one high-performing group I studied—the venture capital arm of a well-known bank—peer appraisal was roundly viewed as an annoyance of questionable utility. This group was utterly dismissive of the bank's appraisal system, even though the program was well constructed, aggressively backed by top management, and successful in other areas of the bank. The members considered themselves a highly independent group and believed they were already fully aware of their performance, both individually and in project teams. To their way of thinking, they had already created a collegial and cohesive environment that delivered extraordinary results for the company, so why couldn't the bank just leave them alone? The group's finely honed balance of status and responsibilities was threatened by the prospect of individual peer appraisals. Although they halfheartedly participated in one round of 360-degree feedback, over time they simply stopped completing the evaluation forms, thus registering their contempt for (and possibly their fear of) the program.

Low-performing groups also often greet peer appraisal unenthusiastically. At a professional services firm, I met with the partners in charge of a practice that had suffered a long, slow

Managing the "Peer" in Peer Appraisal

Most managers are still not accustomed to giving in-depth, constructive feedback. But by learning how to give feedback better—constructively, specifically, and in a timely manner—and by encouraging others to follow suit, managers themselves become the key ingredient in the peer appraisal process.

Go public with your support.
Let it be known that you value peer appraisal, and explicitly describe the benefit you and others have gained as a result of your own participation.

Be a counselor and role model.
Meet with subordinates to help them understand the assessments they receive, and engage them in discussions of the appraisals and their interpretation—without letting your own opinions dominate. Demystify the process by being open to feedback and self-improvement and by asking for input from others, including subordinates and peers.

Provide training early and often.
Allocate time and resources to help raters and recipients practice giving and receiving feedback. This is best accomplished in small groups and small doses, rather than through big, formal training programs.

Put substance before rankings.
Pay attention to and publicize results brought about through the feedback system, such as stronger links between departments, cost-saving innovations, and better information flows. Don't emphasize the success of individuals with high feedback numbers because then people may view 360-degree feedback as a popularity contest rather than a tool for improvement.

Let people know when they're not doing peer appraisal well.
Better yet, let their peers tell them. Set high expectations of your own peers and hold them to it. These skills only improve with practice, so scheduling time now and then to role-play with colleagues or trainers is worthwhile.

---

decline in profitability. They saw peer appraisal as a veiled attempt by the rest of the organization to assess blame. As a form of passive protest, this group provided few comments when evaluating one another, and when pressed to discuss results, they resisted. So great was the threat implied by peer appraisal that eventually they refused outright to discuss any feedback they had received, and the process shut down altogether. Their worries about their own failure and the company's motivations became self-fulfilling: as their willingness to discuss results diminished, so did the practice's performance.

As these cases suggest, when peer appraisal ignores group dynamics and work realities, it delivers counterproductive results. If most work is done in groups, focusing on individuals can compromise the group's performance or make a weak team's performance even worse. Rather than cultivating a sense of shared ownership and responsibility, the process can breed deep cynicism, suspicion, and an "us-against-them" mentality—the exact opposite of the values most companies espouse.

The Measurement Paradox

It seems logical that simple, objective, straightforward rating systems should generate the most useful appraisals. Number or letter grades make it easier for managers to gather, aggregate, and compare ratings across individuals and groups, and they often just *seem* like the right way to proceed (after all, most of us have been getting report cards since kindergarten). But ratings by themselves don't yield the detailed, qualitative comments and insights that can help a colleague improve performance. In fact, the simpler the measures and the fewer dimensions on which an individual is measured, the less useful the evaluation.

One media company I observed was especially proud of its performance measurement program, which involved elaborate rounds of evaluations by peers and bosses. The process culminated in a letter grade for every individual, which was then linked to group, division, and, ultimately, corporate results. Top executives were pleased with this approach because of the links it recognized within and between groups. However, many of the employees expressed frustration, not only because the process required an excessive amount of paperwork but also because the system lacked a mechanism for giving or getting detailed feedback beyond a letter grade. Employees frequently reported satisfaction with their ratings, but they complained that they lacked a clear sense of what they had done to deserve their grades and, more important, what they were doing wrong and needed to address in order to progress in their careers. "It's comforting to know I'm an A-plus," one person reported, "but where do I go from here?"

Simple ratings are not always bad, but most of the time they are not enough. Of course, qualitative feedback is more difficult and time-consuming to generate and is not as easily compared and aggregated. It can pose problems of interpretation when comments are personal or highly idiosyncratic (such as, "She is the class of the outfit"). But without specific comments, recipients are left with no information to act on and with little sense of what might help them get better at their jobs.

The Paradox of Rewards

Most people are keenly attuned to peer appraisal when it affects salary reviews and promotions. In the short term, employees may take steps to improve performance (a perpetual latecomer may start showing up on time). But most people focus virtually all their attention on reward outcomes ("Am I going to get a raise or not?"), ignoring the more constructive feedback that peer appraisal generates. Ironically, it is precisely this overlooked feedback that could help to improve performance. Most people don't deliberately ignore peer appraisal feedback, but even the most confident and successful find it hard to interpret objectively when it is part of the formal reward system. In these instances, peer appraisal poses a threat to feelings of self-worth—not to mention net worth.

Is the solution, then, to take rewards out of the equation? My research suggests that the answer is not nearly so straightforward. Consider this contradiction: in many organizations I surveyed, raters expressed reservations about providing critical feedback when they knew it would directly influence another's salary. One participant put it, "You could destroy somebody and not even know it." But when I queried recipients of peer appraisal, many reported that they weren't interested in feedback unless it "had teeth." If the results were seen as being for "HR purposes," not "business purposes," recipients were less inclined to take the process seriously; if peer feedback didn't have an impact on rewards, it often wasn't used.

With the Paradox of Rewards, managers find themselves in a catch-22. When rewards are on the line, peer appraisal may generate a lot of activity but usually delivers only short-term improvements in performance from feedback that may be conservative or incomplete. When not tied to rewards, feedback is likely to be more comprehensive (and thus potentially useful) but is not seen as important by recipients, who may delay in addressing it or ignore it altogether.

Managing Through the Paradoxes

As might be expected, these paradoxes do not have neat solutions. They are best seen not as obstacles to be overcome but as features of the appraisal landscape to be managed around or even through. The nature of a paradox isn't easily changed, but the way it is viewed can be. Indeed, one of the most significant findings from my research is the pivotal role that managers play in successful peer appraisal. My field notebooks are full of comments from participants about their managers—some commending bosses for active participation, and others condemning behavior that undermined the process. In too many organizations, I've seen peer appraisal programs sabotaged by managers who let it be known through offhand comments or their own lack of participation that peer appraisal might be well and good for everyone else, but not for them. The best managers, on the other hand, act as constructive critics, role models, and willing participants. (See the sidebar "Managing the 'Peer' in Peer Appraisal.")

My findings also suggest that managers and organizations don't spend enough time asking themselves and conveying to employees why peer appraisal is being used. The potential benefits may seem obvious at first, but when the purpose and the scope of peer appraisal are not made explicit, conflict soon takes over.

Purpose. In most cases, the purpose of peer appraisal is to provide timely and useful feed-

Evaluation of Training

> The nature of a paradox isn't easily changed, but the way it is viewed can be.

back to help individuals improve their performance. Detailed, qualitative feedback from peers accompanied by coaching and supportive counseling from a manager are essential. If participants understand the reasons for soliciting this kind of feedback, some of the tension of the Measurement Paradox can be overcome. If, however, the purpose of peer appraisal is simply to check that things are going smoothly and to head off major conflicts, a quick and dirty evaluation using only a few numbers will suffice. In one small organization that used only number ratings, the CEO regularly reviewed all feedback summaries; when any two employees' ratings of each other were unusually negative, he brought them together and helped them address their differences. This practice worked because its purpose was explicit—to catch conflicts before they turned into full-blown crises—and because the CEO's visibility actively mitigated the effects of the Measurement Paradox.

Occasionally, peer appraisal is used to improve ties between groups. In these cases, managers should focus the appraisal effort on the entire group rather than on particular members. When groups themselves realize the need for improved links, the effects of the Paradox of Group Performance may be stemmed. In one situation I witnessed, the sales and operations groups in a large financial services firm were not cooperating, and customer complaints were piling up. The manager invited members of each group to provide anonymous feedback to people in the other group. At first, the feedback was terse and critical, but when each group saw that the company was using the feedback not to reward or punish individuals but to highlight the problems between the two groups, the feedback became more extensive and constructive. Eventually, peer evaluation became a regular channel of communication to identify and resolve conflicts between these groups. In this example, peer appraisal succeeded because it first addressed the real-world conflicts that had led to unmet customer demands; only when participants became accustomed to the process was it folded into the formal reward system, thus decreasing the effects of the Paradox of Rewards.

I have also seen peer appraisal programs introduced as part of larger empowerment programs aimed at distributing authority and responsibility more broadly throughout an organization. In one manufacturing company I studied, a group of factory workers designed its own peer evaluation process. The group already performed multiple roles and functions on the factory floor and took responsibility for hiring, training, and quality control, so it also made sense for the members to take charge of evaluating one another's work. Instead of seeing conflict in the new roles, group members saw peer appraisal as a continuation of the other responsibilities they had assumed. The Paradox of Roles was barely evident.

Scope. Managers also need to be selective about how broadly peer appraisal, and 360-degree programs in general, are used. In the name of inclusion, many organizations feel compelled to roll out these programs everywhere. But democracy is overrated, at least when it comes to peer appraisal. One large financial services firm I studied had great success in solving business process issues across several front-office groups through the judicious use of peer evaluation. The process resulted in widely celebrated improvements and better relations between the front-office groups, so much so that other groups in the company wanted to join in. But when the firm introduced the same program to the additional thousand-plus employees, the program collapsed under its own weight. By trying to provide substantial, but in many cases unnecessary, feedback to all, the company compromised its ability to function.

In choosing rating criteria for peer appraisal, it's also important to remember that all jobs are not the same. A customized evaluation takes longer to develop, but as the Measurement Paradox suggests, such an investment of time and effort is crucial because inappropriate or narrowly defined criteria are difficult for peer evaluators to use and even harder for recipients to apply. Moreover, if participants detect that the system is unlikely to improve their performance or rewards, they are even less likely to actively engage in the process with their peers, as the Paradox of Rewards illustrates.

The Paradox of Group Performance will be less of an issue when the right balance is achieved between evaluating the contributions of individuals and acknowledging the interdependencies and connections within groups and across boundaries. Most organizations are notoriously bad at this, often touting teamwork and group performance while assiduously rewarding only individual outcomes. But in a few groups I studied, where the overall size of the bonus pool, for example, depended on everyone's ability to work together, the tension between individual contributions and group outcomes was kept in check. Practices like this not only diminished the effects of the Paradox of Group Performance but also dampened the effects of the Paradox of Rewards, in part because peer appraisal, while tied to rewards, was only one criterion used to decide them. This middle-ground approach to the Paradox of Rewards can work well when participants trust the integrity of the reward determination process.

In the ten years I have spent observing 360-degree feedback, I have seen a number of organizations gradually develop enough trust and confidence to make the most of peer appraisal without incurring dysfunctional consequences. These organizations recognize that 360-degree feedback systems, and peer appraisal programs in particular, are always works in progress—subject to vulnerabilities, requiring sensitivity to hidden conflicts as much as to tangible results, but nevertheless responsive to thoughtful design and purposeful change. Companies that have success with these programs tend to be open to learning and willing to experiment. They are led by executives who are direct about the expected benefits as well as the challenges and who actively demonstrate support for the process. By laying themselves open to praise and criticism from all directions and inviting others to do the same, they guide their organizations to new capacities for continuous improvement.

Quarterly Evaluation for Performance Improvement

Editor's Comment: It's all about being serious regarding behavior change. It's an evaluator's dream to have the results of evaluation actually be used. The Synygy software corporation near Philadelphia, PA is a young company that has grown fast and in a qualitative way, in large part because of its commitment to evaluation—quarterly evaluation. It practices with its own staff what it preaches to clients.

Synygy provides incentive compensation plan management software and services. Its clients include DuPont, Sun Microsystems, and Eli Lilly. It has approximately 260 employees and annual revenue of more than $20 million (p. 62). Synygy is the winner of *Workforce* magazine's 2001 Optimas Award for Vision.

Synygy argues that you don't have much chance of improving performance when it counts if you do evaluations only once per year. They believe that their system of quarterly evaluation fosters better communication and organizational growth because during the 3 months following evaluations, employees know exactly what they need to do to improve the way they do their jobs and they get to work at making those improvements.

Synygy uses the typical narrative assessment, but in addition adds a numerical scoring system to an employee's performance goals. That is, employees are rated on a scale of 1 to 5, with points given for those who accomplish tasks and reach their goals in less time than they indicated it would take. That evaluation score determines 40 percent of an employee's quarterly bonus. Superiors, peers, those who report directly, clients, and other persons with whom the employee interacts all have a chance to contribute to the evaluation. Feedback is essential and valued. Evaluation forms are provided online with coordination services included to eliminate paperwork and help supervisors and others make sense of the data. Training is provided to all employees in how to give feedback and be candid and truthful in order to improve the organization.

Source: "Frequent Employee Feedback Is Worth the Cost and Time" by Patrick J. Kiger in *Workforce*, March 2001, pp. 62–63 and 65. Patrick J. Kiger is a freelance writer based in the Washington, DC area.

3. Tests, Measures, and Certification

The "E-Learning Value Proposition"

Editor's Comment: This is the first comprehensive book on e-learning. Early in the Preface, author Marc Rosenberg makes the point that technology is a tool and not a strategy (p. xvii). His entire work here takes off from this perspective, describing the e-parts of learning and how to use them to facilitate learning, but more importantly, making the case for viewing e-learning as a strategic function of business that creates value. A subtitle is included for the book, *Strategies for Delivering Knowledge in the Digital Age,* and the book delivers on its strategic promise.

Dr. Rosenberg organizes his book into three parts: 1) "The Opportunity," which considers the business and technology drivers for changes in learning, 2) "New Approaches for E-Learning," which explores e-learning options and approaches, and 3) "Organizational Requirements for E-Learning," which focuses on the organizational, cultural, business, leadership and other factors that support or thwart e-learning. The book has several unique features including case studies from workers, managers and others, who tell their stories about their ventures into e-learning from various strategic points of view. Storytellers who narrate these "E-Learning Journeys" are Elliott Masie, Barry Arnett, Maddy Weinstein, Raymond Vigil, John McMorrow, John Cone, and Gloria Gery. Many useful tables and figures add to the narrative text. Each chapter opens with two quotes from business or cultural icons, setting the tone for the chapter. Charles Darwin, for example, is quoted at the beginning of Chapter 7, "It's not the strongest of the species who survive, nor the most intelligent, but the ones most responsive to change."

A section of part 3, Chapter 8, is especially appropriate to our discussion of standards and measures. The chapter generally deals with ways of justifying e-learning to management, but contains a great deal of useful information that can be re-crafted into standards or into measures. The author has devised a formula which he calls the "E-Learning Value Proposition." By this he means the sum of all the measurable variables in e-learning that contribute to creating value for the company. He suggests that eliminating any one of these will make e-learning's value "fall precipitously." This is how he defines the value proposition for e-learning:

E-Learning Cost Efficiency +
E-Learning Quality +
E-Learning Service +
E-Learning Speed =
E-Learning Value (p. 227).

Source: e-Learning by Marc J. Rosenberg. New York: The McGraw-Hill Companies, Inc. 2001. 343 pages, $29.95. Marc J. Rosenberg is a principal with DiamondCluster International, a strategy and technology solutions firm. He is also a former president of the International Society for Performance Improvement (ISPI) and a training executive at AT&T.

ASTD'S New Certification

Editor's Comment: As year 2002 is upon us, there is a proliferation of associations, companies, and university programs that offer certifications of various sorts. It seems that with so many standards of all kinds in rapid change, those who provide learning services are eager to establish some mechanism for assuring stability in a business world of flux. ASTD, the trainers' professional association, is one of these service providers. Its certification program began in June 2001.

ASTD's new certification commission's charge is "to develop a certification program for the instructional design, usability, and content of asynchronous Web-based and multimedia courses," that is, to develop standards for the evaluation of such programs and to issue certification to e-learning courses that meet ASTD's standards. ASTD's program liaison is Anne Blouin, who can be reached at 703/683-7253. Commission members are: Patricia Boverie, Albuquerque, NM; Ruth Clark, Phoenix, AZ; Bill Coscarelli, Carbondale, IL; Lynette Gillis, Mississauga, Ontario; William Horton, Boulder, CO; Peter Jones, New York, NY; Rich Mayer, Santa Barbara, CA; David Merrill, Logan, UT; Paul Jesukiewicz, Alexandria, VA; and Sharon Shrock, Carbondale, IL.

Certification programs always have their supporters and their detractors. Supporters view certification as a badge of honor and quality, while detractors see it as just another gimmick to make a few more bucks. Michael Rosenberg's article in *e-learning* magazine referenced here is a balanced look at the issues, the plusses and minuses, of this ASTD certification in particular.

Throughout his article, Rosenberg describes a niche market in flux. He begins by noting that his inbox is full of advertisements and communications from companies that each claim to be the best provider of e-learning services. He put that number at 50 companies in July 2001. How to sort out what is truly the best is a daunting task for an advertisement-weary training manager. How to know what services your company needs is also a daunting task. How to get rid of market clutter is one reason certification programs such as ASTD's program come to life. ASTD's certification aims to analyze the courseware developed by these 50 companies and more, who seek the stamp of approval of a prestigious national association and its commission of experts.

ASTD's commission developed an initial 30 standards, 20 of which are focused on instructional design. The remaining 10 are focused on usability. ASTD has partnered with the commercial venture, Lguide, who provides the actual product assessment. Rosenberg reports mixed reviews of acceptance and non-acceptance by e-learning publishers and providers, and also by client companies who purchase e-learning products. His research thus far indicates that smaller companies with minimal development staff benefit more from certification than do larger companies with instructional design staffs. But on balance, ASTD's certification is expected to increase the overall level of e-learning and provide some stability to an erratic and evolving industry.

Sources: "ASTD NEWS: ASTD Announces Formation of Certification Commission" by editors in *T+D*, February 2001, p. 86; and "Canned Content: Can ASTD Certification Standards Ensure Quality Off-the-Shelf Courseware?" by Michael Rosenberg in *e-learning*, July 2001, pp. 24–27. Michael Rosenberg is a contributing editor at *e-learning* magazine.

Pre- and Post-Testing Tied to Objectives

Editor's Comment: The role of testing in training is always a hot topic in training design and development. The instructional design system, ISD, which has been around for about 50 years is represented as a closed system, with the last function of it, evaluation, feeding back into its first function, analysis (ISD = analysis, design, development, implementation, and evaluation). Instructional design experts over the years have advocated pre-testing of an employee's skills to identify the gaps in his or her understanding or ability. Ideally, then, training is designed to fill those gaps, and evaluation of the gap-filling training shows the employee and the company how successful the training was and if it will readily transfer to the job. The key elements in this system are the performance objectives to be met by the employee and the alignment of the before and after testing with these objectives. Inexperienced designers or evaluators are often tempted by time pressures to skip the testing and the objective-setting, plowing ahead to create training programs that fail.

Dave Buck responds to the *Training Directors' Forum* newsletter question, "Should you pre-test?" with a thoughtful and helpful set of answers. Among the main points he makes is that pre- and post-tests must be aligned with each other as well as with the same objectives, "clearly stated learning objectives," as he says. He stresses the word "do"; that is, objectives must state what the learner should do in order to demonstrate learning. He also gives a word of caution not often heard that evaluators often assume that learners don't have certain skills, when actually they do. Pre-testing catches this good news and so prevents a waste of time, energy, and resources on designing training that's not necessary and ultimately only makes trainees grumble.

Buck also points out that the period between the pre- and post-test is a period when the learner deserves to get maximum feedback on his or her performance. Training built on the assessed performance gap, reinforced with performance feedback, is training that will be called successful.

Source: "Getting Pre- and Post-Tests in Line" question response by Dave Buck in *Training Director's Forum e-Net* online newsletter, August 1, 2001, pp. 1–3. Dave Buck is Chief Learning Officer with Visum LLC, an e-learning provider, Knoxville, TN. This newsletter, *TDFeNet* is available free, online, at www.vnulearning.com.

Court Rulings Favor Performance Measures

Editor's Comment: This is an article about variables and validity, key elements in test construction. The authors present this subject by beginning their work with examples of what they identify as "subjective testing" and the legal difficulty organizations get into when this is the only kind of testing they do. Four interesting legal cases illustrate their plea for valid test construction.

Subjective criterial continue to be used to evaluate the worth of individuals, criteria based on certain scores on tests. Students go through school making decisions about life choices based on grades derived from invalid measures. The trend carries over into adult education and training. Many businesses use evaluations to determine salary increases, promotion, and employees' career paths based on criteria as subjective as those used by teachers in schools.

Meanwhile, little or none of this evaluation is held up to the scrutiny of criterion and norm-referenced measurement principles to establish the congruence between the amount of knowledge gained and one's ability to perform better on the job. In essence, evaluation is failing people, rather than people failing evaluations.

Much has been written about Kirkpatrick's early work on the four levels of evaluation. Borg and Gall (1983), Shrock and Coscarelli (1989), Campbell and Stanley (1966), and Martuza (1977) are leaders in the field of measurement, evaluation, and testing. The model presented in this article synthesizes the work of these experts. It is based on the principle that the level of evaluation must primarily be connected to the purpose and intended use of the results of the evaluation. Applying appropriate levels of evaluation increases the accuracy of measuring the outcome.

LITIGATION DEFINES APPROPRIATE AND INAPPROPRIATE USES OF EVALUATION

The misuse of measurement criteria continues even though courts have repeatedly ruled that the skills trained and tested must be predictive of success on the job.

The Equal Employment Opportunity Commission (EEOC) guidelines conclude that "... [a company] continuing to use a test that has questionable validity increases the risk that [that company] will be found to be engaged in discriminatory practices and will be liable for back pay, awards, plaintiff's attorney's fees, loss of Federal contracts, subcontracts or grants, and the like." These guidelines are more widely applied than to merely protected groups or minorities; they have become the *de facto* standards for all employment (EEOC Guidelines, 1978).

Bureau of National Affairs (1978–1993 forward) Fair Employment Practices (FEP) case law consistently finds in favor of employees who are refused advancement based on subjective evaluation criteria. The following four cases are merely examples of the broader trend toward court rulings in favor of valid performance measures. The first case rules in favor of plaintiffs (employees). The other three cases are examples of rulings in favor of defendants (employers), where the use of evaluation was upheld because

---

Source: "Court Rulings Favor Performance Measures" by William W. Lee, Ph.D. and Diana L. Owens in *Performance Improvement*, Vol. 40 N. 4, April 2001, pp. 35–40. William W. Lee is Director of Performance Technology at American Airlines Flagship University in Fort Worth, TX, and the author of several books; Diana L. Owens is a Senior Consultant at Idea Integration, a part of Modis Professional Services, Inc. Both Lee and Owens are active members of the Dallas, TX chapter of ASTD. Article reprinted with permission of *Performance Improvement*. Copyright 2001. All rights reserved.

the tests met the requirements of "fairness" and where testing matched performance criteria.

Because these cases were heard in the United States Courts of Appeals, the rulings can be cited as persuasive precedence anywhere in the United States, even though they do not hold the weight of law outside of the district where they were decided.

LeGault v. Russo

In this case the U.S. District Court of New Hampshire found that a tool used to test prospective fire fighters had an adverse impact on women candidates. The fire department was enjoined from using the test as a requirement for hiring.

The issue claimed by the plaintiff was that a test of physical agility and an obstacle course were not content valid. The tests were based on a job analysis from a job description that was several years old. The job description described only general duties and did not break representative tasks into their component skills, assess their relevant importance, or indicate the degree of proficiency required by firefighters to perform them successfully. The national standards used for the test were several years old. The test designer testified that the test appeared to be the kind of thing that firefighters do. Fire department officials asserted that the test simulated things that normally occur. Anecdotal evidence was reported that four other municipalities used the same test (Case Number 93-365-B, Feb. 10, 1994; Vol. 64, FEP Cases, p. 170).

Evans v. City of Evanston, Illinois

In this case the U.S. District Court upheld the city of Evanston's use of a test of physical agility as part of the requirement for hiring firefighters because it had documented the need for performance in the job analysis and because the test had been administered to many incumbent firefighters.

At issue was whether a test of physical agility used to prescreen prospective firefighters discriminated against women. The city employed 106 firefighters, none of whom were women, although it had previously employed two women. The fire department began the selection process by administering a test of physical agility to all applicants. Those who failed this primary screening were given no further consideration. Those who passed the agility test took a written test. Those candidates who passed the written exam were trained at an academy used by several other municipalities.

The agility test consisted of five events administered at an advanced orientation. Candidates were required to perform job-related feats of agility. The feats were timed, as speed is an important factor in effective firefighting. Candidates were informed in advance that they would be timed.

The training officer and two firefighters, who were considered subject matter experts, designed the tests. These three attended and critiqued all fires in Evanston and kept records about the tasks performed.

The test was piloted with 832 firefighters under the age of 35 years. Performance of this group was timed. The cutoff score was set at 767 seconds, one standard deviation above the mean, for new hires. Male applicants passed the test at a rate of 90%, women at a rate of 10%. The plaintiff completed the feats in 880 seconds.

The defendant's position was upheld because the test was directly related to tasks that firefighters are required to perform and because the training office and subject matter experts did a thorough analysis of the tasks (Case Number DC NI11, Aug. 19, 1988; Vol. 47, FEP Cases, p. 1723).

Police Officers for Equal Rights v. the City of Columbus, Ohio

The U.S. Court of Appeals in this case upheld the use of a knowledge-based test when expert testimony declared that the test was valid. Validity was established through the positive correlation between the skills tested and the job performance.

At issue was a lower court ruling that found that a written test did discriminate against minority applicants. A job analysis of requirements to perform a police lieutenant's responsibilities was conducted. A written test rated those aspects of the knowledge of the job responsibilities. The test was not the only measure of ability. An "in-basket" test of decision-making ability was also administered.

The court ruled that employers could use a test to determine how candidates would perform in a training program if they could show that the training program provided before the test was job related. Another finding was that the test was sufficiently reliable to justify rank-order scoring, based on standards established in Uniform Guidelines on Employee Selection Procedures.

Expert testimony established that the examination had enough validity to yield passing grades, which showed a positive correlation with job performance because there was a sufficient spread among candidates' scores. Both the examination as a whole and its component parts were reliable, once again because a reasonable job analysis had been conducted (Case Number 90-3217, October 22, 1990; Vol. 54, FEP Cases, p. 276).

Bernard v. Gulf Oil Corporation

In this case the U.S. Court of Appeals ruled that tests are permissible for promotions if they are shown to be predictive of or correlated with elements of work behavior that comprise or are relevant to the job or jobs for which candidates are being evaluated.

At issue here were tests for promotion from the classification of unskilled labor into a craft (skilled) classification of employment. The Supreme Court had previously ruled that test validity was not sufficient if tests only prove that they are necessary to establish safe and efficient job performance. Tests must significantly correlate with important elements of work behavior that comprise or are related to the jobs for which candidates are being evaluated.

Gulf Oil had hired a consulting firm of industrial psychologists that conducted a job analysis by asking supervisors to rate 117 duties and 37 abilities in importance of performing jobs in two of the craft divisions. The test was developed based on the importance the supervisors attached to these duties and abilities. Three separate validity studies were conducted on the test at three different periods over 12 years. A high positive correlation was established between those who had the highest test scores and consistently performed better on the job and those who had the lowest test scores and consistently performed poorly on the job.

The plaintiffs argued that, since correlation was only conducted on two classifications of jobs in the company, tests rated only general cognitive abilities and not specific job duties and therefore did not consist of important elements of work behavior.

The plaintiffs failed to prove their position that the tests discriminated against minorities even though the overall case ruled in their favor. The ruling was on the basis of other elements of promotion and organizational structure practices that discriminated against minorities (Case No. 87-2033, Mar. 22, 1988; Vol. 49, FEP Cases, p. 1855).

Note the similarity between the first and second cases but the very different outcomes. Both cases involved the use of tests in selecting firefighters, and in both cases the test appeared to discriminate against women. Yet the use of the test in the latter case was upheld. The difference was that, in the Evans case, the feats of agility were based on those actually required by firefighters. In the LeGault case, the feats only appeared to be the kind that would be required to be performed. The difference between the words "actually" and "appeared" made a great deal of difference in the outcome of the case. That trend toward rulings in favor of tests that correlate directly to the job is also found in the third and fourth cases.

ETHICAL ISSUES

Beyond the legal issues of fairness to employees are the ethical issues. Employers have a responsibility to provide what employees need to be successful once they are selected and placed in a job. Prerequisites identified during the job interview and selection process have determined the employees' capabilities to begin the job. Employers must provide additional training to improve the employee's ability to complete current duties and handle assignments that require new skills. Once training is completed, employees should be confident that they can do what they were taught. Without valid measurements of their abilities, there can be no such assurances.

The amount of evaluation required of training is an interaction among three factors (Lee & Owens, 2000):

1. type of validity measurement
2. measurement variable
3. purpose of the training

Figure 1 shows the interaction of these three factors.

Figure 1. Validity Matrix

MEASUREMENT VARIABLE	PURPOSE	TYPE OF VALIDITY MEASURE					
		Low	Validity	High		Validity
		Face Validity	Content Validity	Test Item Distractor Analysis	Validity Correlation	Predictive Validity
Organizational Needs	Return on Investment					
	Improved Workforce					
	Regulatory Requirements					
	EEOC Requirements					
Individual Needs	Promotion					
	Professional Development					
	Improved Skills					
	Increased Knowledge					
	Self-Improvement					

Level of validity required ▭

Types of Validity Measurement

Validity is defined as the *confidence* with which one can state that a course or test teaches or tests what it claims. Reliability is the *consistency* with which a course or test teaches or tests what it claims to over time (Borg & Gall, 1983). Levels of validity run from low to high, low levels being the minimum required to be able to state that the course has some value in addressing the topics, and high levels affirming the value at the highest degree of confidence possible.

Face validity indicates that a course is approximately the same as any other course on the same topic. Face validity can be established simply by having a subject matter expert state that the approximation to other courses is present. Content validity certifies congruence among the objectives, the content of the training, and the test. The training must present material and test students to the level indicated by the objective. For example, if an objective indicates that the learner must only demonstrate his or her "knowledge" of a subject, a written test can be used. However, if an objective indicates that the learner must be able to "do" something at the end of the training, a performance test must be used, in which the learner demonstrates his or her ability to complete the task or activity.

Content validity can be established using a panel of judges consisting of subject matter experts who are trained in the process of matching objectives, content, or test items, or through the application of purely statistical measures.

Test item validity is subdivided between distractor analysis and correlation. Test item distractor analysis determines if test items are valid by analyzing the specific answers of those who took the test. If too many students answer a question incorrectly and are drawn to one particular wrong answer, the question is not valid. Correlation determines the strength or weakness of one particular item compared to the group test scores and the strength of the item compared to the overall score of a particular student.

Predictive validity is the highest level of validity, in which the test is shown to be effective in predicting between those who have the skills necessary to perform a certain job from those who do not. Results of students' performance followed over a long period showing consistent results demonstrate reliability.

MEASUREMENT VARIABLES

There are two measurement variables: organizational needs, which benefit the overall organization, and individual needs, which directly benefit the individual employee and, indirectly, the organization.

Training for Organizational Needs

The measures for organizational needs are as follows:

- Return on Investment (ROI)—affects the bottom line and contributes to increased profits and reduced operating costs. ROI involves having historical data on what the cost of the training was to the company (including direct and indirect overhead, salaries, development/delivery costs) and the cost of the new training. A component of ROI is the internal rate of return or break-even point, where the cost of the development of the new training is neutralized and the company begins to realize a profit.
- Improved Workforce—the overall productivity that directly affects the organization's ability to function more efficiently and effectively.
- Regulatory Requirements—industry requirements (e.g., Right to Know laws involving hazardous materials) or any other standards where employees must be "informed" of their rights, responsibilities, actions to take, and procedures to follow.
- Equal Employment Opportunity Commission (EEOC) Requirements—requirements legislated to ensure fair practices and standards in hiring and dismissing employees (due process under the law).

Training for Individual Needs

There are five elements to training that meets individual needs:

- Promotion—actual progression along a career path through the corporate hierarchical structure based on capabilities and skills
- Professional Development—continuous learning to ensure skill capabilities and readiness for progressing along a career path.
- Improved Skills—courses taken to improve performance in a certain area (e.g., running a certain piece of equipment).
- Increased Knowledge—information the student needs to learn a topic.
- Self-improvement—knowledge undertaken for enjoyment or self-edification (e.g., playing chess or home finance).

Training for Commercial Use

Training developed for commercial use has its own unique qualities and requires specific mention. Since much training targeted for commercial use is developed by training development companies who then sell it, the producer can't be certain of the use of the training product. Therefore it is imperative that commercially developed training be validated to the highest level (predictive validity) or specify the level of validity in the course documentation, and translate the level of validity into terms that explain how and what the results of training can be used for.

Using the Right Statistical Measure

Using incorrect statistical measures of validity or reliability will negate the results. The distinction between norm-referenced measures and criterion-referenced measures determines which statistical test of validity or reliability to use (Martuza, 1977). Norm referenced are those measures that demonstrate validity and reliability by predicting that one person has the same characteristics as most other individuals in the target population on which the test was "normed" (e.g., same age group, mental ability,

FIGURE 2. APPROPRIATE STATISTICAL MEASURES

TEST	PURPOSE	APPLICATION TYPE				SAMPLING
Name		Norm referenced	Criterion referenced	Correlation	Significance	
Biserial	1 continuous/ 1 dichotomy	√	√	√		Representative Sample Size
Chi-square	1 continuous/ 1 dichotomy	√	√	√		Representative Sample Size
Kendall's tau	2 continuous variables	√		√		n < 10
Kuder Richardson (KR-20)	measure of equal difficulty	√	√	√		Representative Sample Size
Mann Whitney	compare unequal groups	√	√	√		Representative Sample Size
Pearson Product Moment (Pearson r)	2 continuous variables	√		√		Representative Sample Size
Phi Coefficient (Φ)	2 true dichotomies			√		Representative Sample Size
Point-biserial	1 continuous/ 1 true dichotomy		√	√		Representative Sample Size
Rank Difference	2 continuous variables	√		√		n < 30
Analysis of Variance (ANOVA)	significance between more than 2 means	√	√		√	Representative Sample Size
t-Test	significance between 2 means	√			√	Representative Sample Size

sex). Criterion-referenced measures are those that demonstrate validity and reliability by comparing one person against a predetermined standard rather than to other people. For example, a criterion-referenced measure is one designed for a specific group trained on a certain process, procedure, system, etc. To determine whether someone is capable of performing the procedure, the individual is tested against a level of knowledge or performance that is set by the test designers based on the criticality of the job. For instance, the level of a brain surgeon performing a surgical technique would be set higher than the level set for a person who is practicing interpersonal skills. The results of not using appropriate interpersonal skills are not as critical as the results of poor performance by the brain surgeon. Figure 2 (Lee & Mamone, 1995) lists various statistical measures and explains where they can be applied.

CONCLUSION

Developing fair tests is not a simple issue. Whenever validity measures are not used or are inappropriately applied, there is a risk of the test being challenged if it is used for purposes that impact the performance or careers of individuals. If training doesn't result in some improvement, why deliver it?

So, it is not a question of whether or not to evaluate. It is, rather, a question of how much validity is required. Still, most educational institutions and training and development companies do not conduct validity studies because they do not know how or because customers view the studies as an added cost to the development of training and do not want it. Ask any company how much it costs to be sued for unfair employment practices. It is certain that the cities of Evanston, Illinois and Columbus, Ohio, appreciated the extra time it took to validate their tests and found the cost far less expensive than the alternative.

Training alone cannot be blamed for not producing the results intended or required. More companies need to include Kirkpatrick's (1994) Level 3 evaluation (changed behavior) in their performance reviews, and managers need to observe employees using what they learn from training. If transfer of knowledge to the workplace isn't happening, it is not the fault of the training; it's the failure of management to follow through. If management is not following through, the larger question is why money is being spent on the training.

Companies that outsource customized training should avoid development companies that disclaim responsibility for the product's effectiveness. They have not taken the time to determine if their training is valid and are leaving their customers open to law suits. Of course, no development company is responsible for the misuse of its products as long as the valid uses of the courses have been documented in the course materials.

Don't ask if tests should be valid, they should! But to what degree depends on the intended use. Define the purpose of the training and develop an evaluation plan accordingly. Waiting until the end of a project to decide to validate is often too late.

REFERENCES

Borg, W., & Gall, M. (1983). *Educational research: An introduction* (4th ed.). New York: Longman.

Bureau of National Affairs. (1978–1993 forward). *Bureau of national affairs employment cases.* Washington, D.C.: Bureau of National Affairs.

Campbell, D., & Stanley, J. (1966). *Experimental and quasi-experimental designs for research.* Chicago: Rand McNally.

Equal Employment Opportunity Commission, U.S. Civil Service Commission. U.S. Department of Labor & U.S. Department of Justice. (1978). *Uniform guidelines on employee selection procedures.* Washington, D.C.: *Federal Register.*

Kirkpatrick, D. (1994). *Evaluating training programs: The four levels.* San Francisco: Berrett-Kohler Publishers.

Lee, W., & Mamone, R. (1995). *The handbook of computer-based training: Assessment, design, development, and evaluation.* Englewood Cliffs, NJ: Educational Technology Publishing Co., Inc.

Lee, W., & Owens, D. (2000). *Multimedia-based instructional design for computer-based training, Web-based training, distance broadcast training.* San Francisco: Jossey-Bass/Pfeiffer.

Martuza, V. (1977). *Applying norm-referenced and criterion-referenced measurement in education.* Boston: Allyn & Bacon.

Shrock, S., & Coscarelli, W. (1989). *Criterion-referenced test development: Technical and legal guidelines for corporate training.* New York: Addison-Wesley Publishing Co.

Core Measures of Intellectual Capital

Editor's Comment: In this year of enormous economic stress and rebuilding since the terrorist attack in mid-September, America's businesses are more acutely aware than ever before of the value of their intellectual capital. However, it is not so easy to figure out what measures are the best ones. It's also hard to define those measures in terms of numbers. ASTD has given us a useful way to think about such measures and to turn them into things that can be represented in terms of numbers. In July of 2000, ASTD published an excellent report on measuring what matters (product #190016). We reprint here ASTD's list of 17 "core intellectual capital measures" together with a much longer list of "elective intellectual capital measures" and some "financial performance measures." We also include ASTD's definitions of the major sub-categories of core measures.

The core set of intellectual capital measures includes the sub-categories Human Capital, Innovation Capital, Process Capital, and Customer Capital. These definitions and lists can be of great help to trainers who need to develop learner objectives, courses, and tests around the seemingly elusive topic of intellectual capital.

Human Capital: the knowledge, skills, and competencies of people in an organization;

Innovation Capital: the capability of an organization to innovate and to create new products and services;

Process Capital: the work processes, techniques, systems, and tools of an organization; and

Customer Capital: the value of an organization's relationship with its customers.

Core Intellectual Capital Measures

Human Capital
- retention of key personnel
- ability to attract talented people
- IT literacy
- training expenditures as a percentage of payroll
- replacement costs of key personnel
- employee satisfaction
- employee commitment

Innovation Capital
- R&D expenditures
- percentage of workforce involved in innovation
- product freshness

Process Capital
- processes documented and mapped
- use of documented processes

Customer Capital
- customer satisfaction
- customer retention
- product and service quality
- average duration of customer relationship
- repeat orders

Elective Intellectual Capital Measures

Human Capital
- organizational learning
- effectiveness of learning transfer in key areas

Source: "Appendix A: ASTD's Core and Elective Intellectual Capital and Performance Measures" in *Measuring What Matters: Core Measures of Intellectual Capital* by Dr. Laurie J. Bassi and Dr. Mark Van Buren, July 2, pp. 15 and 2. Dr. Laurie J. Bassi is Director of Research at Saba; Dr. Mark Van Buren is Director of Research at ASTD. Reprinted with permission of ASTD. Copyright 2000. All rights reserved.

- management credibility
- employee wages and salaries
- educational levels—percentage of college graduates
- employee empowerment
- management experience
- time in training
- percentage of employees with X+ years of service
- empowered teams

Innovation Capital
- number of copyrights and trademarks
- number of patents used effectively
- planned obsolescence
- new opportunities exploited
- new markets development investment
- R&D productivity
- sales from products released in last five years
- research leadership
- net present value (NPV) of patents
- effectiveness of feedback mechanisms
- average age of patents
- percentage of R&D invested in product design
- number of patents pending
- number of new ideas in knowledge management database
- direct communications to customer per year

Process Capital
- strategy execution
- quality of decisions
- percentage of revenues invested in knowledge management
- percentage of company effectively engaged with customer
- IT access per employee
- strategy innovativeness
- cycle time

- IT investment per employee
- process quality (such as defects, error rates)
- time to market
- collaboration levels
- IT capacity (such as CPU)
- IT capacity per employee
- operating expense ratio
- administrative expense per total revenues

Customer Capital
- market growth
- customer needs met
- marketing effectiveness
- annual sales per customer
- market share
- average customer size (in dollars)
- five largest customers as percentage of revenues
- days spent visiting customers
- support expense per customer
- image-enhancing customers as percentage of revenues

Financial Performance Measures

Core Measures
- return on equity
- earnings per share
- growth rank in industry
- total shareholder return

Elective Measures
- market capitalization
- return-on-assets
- revenue growth
- market share
- revenue per employee
- new product sales
- value added per employee
- market value

GE'S "Four Buckets"

Editor's Comment: GE's legendary Chairman and CEO, Jack Welch, retired in Fall 2001. Among other things, he made a name for himself and his employees over the years through his active interest in training. He personally taught many courses in the corporate education center, and is well-known for instituting and implementing his "work-out" program throughout the country at GE locations during the last decades of the century. Along with his adaptation of the "Six Sigma" quality program pioneered by Motorola, his work-out program provides trainers with a model of measures for performance.

In a speech referenced in the newsletter, *Executive Excellence*, Welch was quoted as saying "ultimate, sustainable competitive advantage lies in the ability to learn, to transfer that learning across components, and to act on it quickly." He suggested in this 2000 Annual Meeting speech that in the Internet world, we need to measure new kinds of things. He grouped these new things into "Four Buckets." These are:

- **Buy**—including online measures of number of transactions, percentage of total, and dollars saved;
- **Make**—including time saved in moving information from source to user, and how much needless paperwork can be saved;
- **Sell**—including number of Web site visitors, number of sales online, percentage of sales online, number of new customers, and number of networked customer opportunities resulting from online activity; and
- **Strategic**—including number and dollars of new investments and partnerships with online companies.

These "Four Buckets" can be adapted to any company with products or services and customers.

Source: "Timeless Principles" adapted from a speech by John F. Welch in *Executive Excellence* newsletter, February 2001, pp. 3 and 4. John F. Welch is former Chairman and CEO of General Electric Company (GE).

More to E-Learning Measures Than Stock Price

Editor's Comment: The year 2001 leading into 2002 has been one of roller coaster stock valuation, and accumulation as well as loss of great wealth. Dot.com companies, where many of the e-learning supplier and vendors were, were watched carefully by those in the training and e-learning field. The survey results presented here represent 1,653 learning and training professionals who responded to a MASIE Center survey. Results were made available in March 2001.

Our survey this month points out the need for a better measure of the e-Learning Field in general and specific vendors/suppliers in particular.

The training and general press seem to be overly focused on the stock market side of the e-Learning industry. We receive a dozen press releases every day, from both public and private companies, aimed at influencing the perception of who is the leader and who will survive. More and more of the conversations that I hear at industry events are focused on the stock price, market cap, burn rate and venture capital status of the players in the field. As the respondents indicated in this month's survey, they don't really follow the news and their comments indicate that it does not give a true and accurate view of this exciting industry.

We would suggest that there are different metrics that would be far better to measure the health of the e-Learning field:

- Percentage of learners in the workforce that have successfully engaged in an e-Learning experience in the past six months.
- Total number of e-Learning experiences now available in organizations of different sizes.
- Cycle time to develop and deploy e-Learning content within diverse enterprises.
- Progress made towards implementation of e-Learning Strategies.
- Implementation of standards and percentage of content that is based on SCORM or IEEE specifications.
- Interoperability of content with varied Learning and Content Management Systems.
- Changes in public policy to recognize shift towards distance and on-line learning.
- Adoption rates of e-Learning and Digital Collaboration in the K to 12 and Higher Education Space.
- Measures of the use of e-Learning within the Supply Chain, to reach customers and suppliers, as well as employees.
- Learner Confidence Rating: Let's ask a sample of learners how confident they are that they have access to and would be able to learn a key skill on-line.
- Learner Impact Rating: Again, ask a sample of learners about their most impactful learning experience and measure how many reference an e-Learning offering.

In the same vein, we need to find better and more verifiable measures of the health and scope of varied e-Learning companies. Here are some of the due-diligence measures that would be awesome to have when considering a specific supplier:

- How many learners are totally using your product or system?

Source: "In Search of a Better Measure" by Elliott Masie in *Learning Decisions Interactive Newsletter*, March 2001, pp. 4, 5, and 7. Elliott Masie is CEO of The MASIE Center and Editor of *Learning Decisions Interactive Newsletter*. These pages are reprinted with permission of The MASIE Center, Saratoga Springs, NY. Copyright 2001. All rights reserved.

LEARNING DECISIONS

BENCHMARKING SURVEY:
"e-LEARNING AND THE STOCK MARKET: DOES IT MATTER?"

This survey takes a look at how closely training and learning professionals and their companies follow the status of e-Learning companies that are publicly traded on the stock market. 1,653 learning and training professionals that subscribe to The MASIE Center's publications provided benchmarking data during the week of March 26, 2001.

Do you track the stock prices of e-Learning companies?	No	67%
	Yes	33%

Do you personally invest in any e-Learning companies as part of a stock portfolio or 401K plan?	No	82%
	Yes	18%

If you were considering purchasing an e-Learning product for your organization, would it matter if the supplier organization was privately held or publicly traded stock?

- It does not matter — 78%
- We prefer to buy from publicly traded companies — 18%
- We prefer to buy from privately held companies — 4%

Would the current stock price of an e-Learning company have any impact on your organization's decision to do business with them?

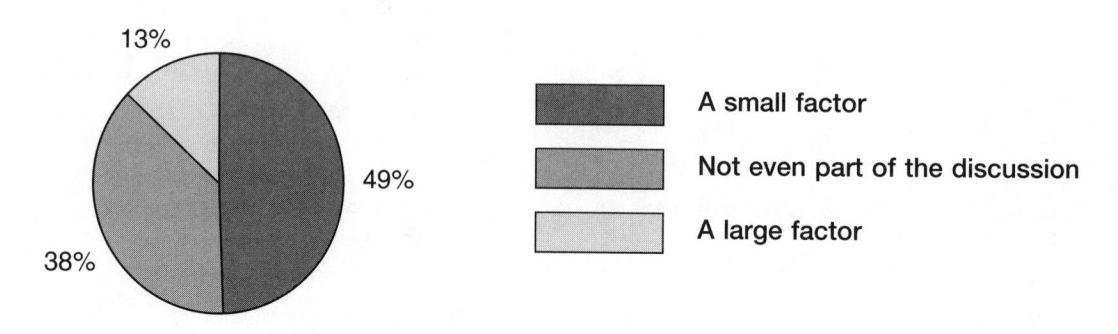

- A small factor — 49%
- Not even part of the discussion — 38%
- A large factor — 13%

Go to LearningDecisions.com for additional data and analysis

Evaluation of Training

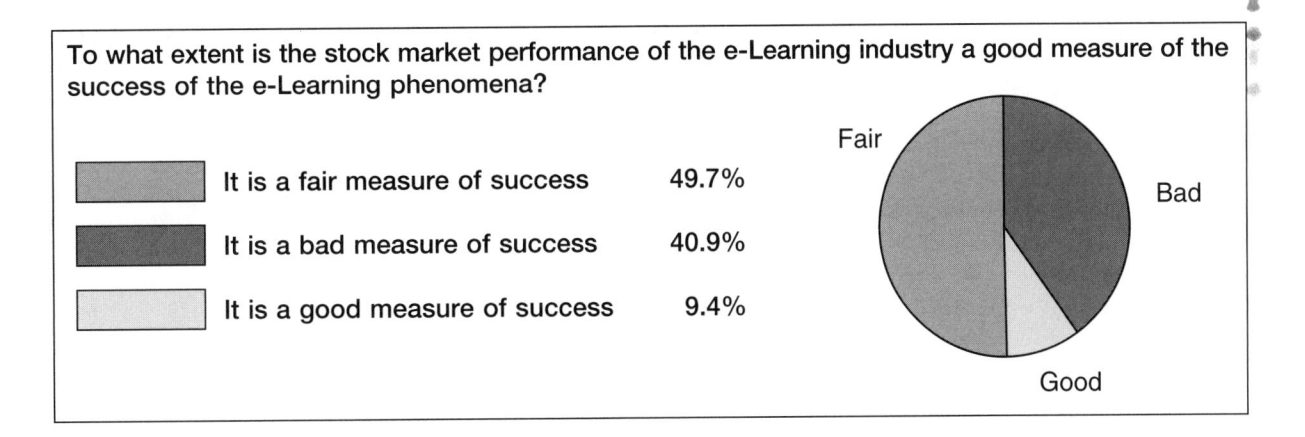

To what extent is the stock market performance of the e-Learning industry a good measure of the success of the e-Learning phenomena?

▨	It is a fair measure of success	49.7%
▨	It is a bad measure of success	40.9%
▨	It is a good measure of success	9.4%

- What is the percentage of learners that actually use the e-Learning content when offered it as part of a portal or training catalog?
- What are the types of learners that have the highest propensity to use or not use the system?
- For systems: How many actual transactions are being handled in how many companies per day or per month?
- What is the one year and two year financial strategy of the company? This would include the growth plans and the funding base.
- What percentage of the supplier's budget is used for research, support and marketing?
- If the organization were to go away (through merger or bankruptcy), what specific processes would be used to provide transition and survival of the learning investments by current customers?
- What percentage of customers are renewing, expanding or shrinking their usage patterns?

I dream about a better "Measure" of the progress of innovation and adoption of e-Learning. This dream is triggered by the conflict in what we read about e-Learning from press releases and stock market analysis and the actual stories (filled with optimism and tough challenges) when talking to real companies implementing real e-Learning solutions in the workplaces.

It is exciting to see players in the e-Learning field pursue their visions of growth and to see them get the resources they need from either bankers, venture capitalists or the stock market. But, let's not "bank" the future of this important innovation on how well a couple of stocks do in the crazy and volatile stock markets. Let's focus on the more important market site: the workplace—where learners need knowledge, skills and support every day!

SECTION 6

The Trainer's Almanac

The *Training and Development Yearbook*'s 2002 *Trainer's Almanac* brings you the most complete reference publication available today—virtually a book-within-a-book it contains essential, verified, totally up-to-date information for the training, organization development, and human resources leaders who need to make learning decisions for the calendar year 2002.

More Ways to Find Information

This *Trainer's Almanac* contains more than 1,000 references representing the broadest range of training resources in print today, presented in easy-to-find listings with descriptive information and data you'll need for making contact with each source. Website addresses are included in our organization listings, providing a way for you to check online for the latest updates. Many organizations have online listservs for their members and sometimes for the public. Many search and registration services are free, paid for by advertisers. We've included toll-free 800-numbers, fax numbers, addresses, and Websites to give you all the motivation you need to seek the resources you want. We have verified that helpful, knowledgeable, real people are at the other end of the phone call—often a telephone call is the best place to begin your information search. We want you to see *The Trainer's Almanac* as your essential starting point for shaping and enhancing your own personal knowledge base and facilitating the growth and value of your company's intellectual capital.

Again this year, we include as Section 6.8 a 13-page listing of training Websites rated and ranked by an independent source according to completeness and usefulness to trainers. We also include Web addresses of e-learning companies. We encourage you to browse through the entire *Trainer's Almanac* to get a feel for its tremendous scope, variety of resources, and fields of data.

A Representation of the Vitality of the Field

The Trainer's Almanac is designed to complement the first five narrative sections of this book which provide the current backdrop of ideas for this year's human resources programming and the business of being a professional trainer. This section, Section 6, with its eight sub-sections, contrasts with the previous five sections of text and gives you the raw resource data you'll need for the most informed training decision making for calendar year 2002.

Our choice of categories on which to focus provides you with a clear way into information and enables you to build your training operation with the extra "edge" of being able to have the whole field at hand, in one master volume. We put our decades of experience as trainers and publishers to work for you as partners in professional development.

Sections of the 2002 *The Trainer's Almanac* include:

6.1 Professional Organizations 249
6.2 Training Conferences 259
6.3 Worldwide Conference Centers 277
6.4 Training for Trainers 309
6.5 Non-Profit Organizations 347
6.6 Training Research and Reference Sources 355
6.7 Training Journals, Magazines, and Newsletters 367
6.8 Training Websites 381

6.1 Professional Organizations

We begin *The Trainer's Almanac* with an alphabetical listing of 31 professional organizations of interest to trainers. Organizations listed have updated Websites for additional information.

Membership Organizations

These are associations of professional workers with a common interest and are open to members who want to join together in like professional pursuits to advance their own professional knowledge and skills and to provide professional visibility for their organizations through their membership. In Section 6.1 we list these organizations along with current key information about the organization. Many of these organizations sponsor annual conferences open to members and to the public which we further index in Section 6.2. Non-profit organizations, which are not membership associations in the usual professional sense, are included in a separate listing, Section 6.5.

National in Scope

We have purposely included organizations that are national in scope which seek and enjoy a wide membership and which provide broad services to their members. We have checked with each professional organization listed here for their most current information. Many companies like to have their training and human resources staff join professional organizations to network and to keep up to date with changes in the field. Our Section 6.1 will give you all the guidance you need for planning the continued professionalization of your staff.

Organizations are listed alphabetically by the name of the organization, and are further indexed according to the main focus of the organization. We list 28 index terms, indicating a representation of the range of professional organizations of interest to trainers.

Index to Principal Interests of Professional Organizations

Accelerated learning
13

Adult and continuing education
1, 8, 9, 20, 23

Business and education collaboration
22, 23

Business and management skills
4, 21, 26, 27, 28

Career development
2, 3, 7, 8, 23, 24, 26

Certification of trainers
7, 9, 20, 23, 26, 30

Cooperative education programs
23, 25

Counseling
2, 24

Distance learning
10

Experiential learning
9, 13, 25, 26

Government trainers
21

Human resource management
11, 27, 30

Human resource planning
11, 21, 27

Instructional design
7, 12, 13, 17, 31

International training
3, 7, 13, 15, 22, 26, 28

Juvenile justice training
19

Knowledge management
3, 4, 7

Leadership
3, 4, 7, 11, 16, 21, 23

Literacy training
1

Manufacturing Training
23

Marketing of training
20, 31

Mentoring
7, 16, 25

Organization development
4, 11, 27, 28

Performance improvement
4, 7, 17, 23

Public sector, training in
7, 19

Sales and marketing training
5

Technology training
6, 18, 21, 29, 31

Training facilities
14

Training media
6, 21, 29

1

Name of organization:
American Association for Adult & Continuing Education (AAACE)
Contact information:
AAACE
1200 19th St., N.W., Suite 300
Washington, DC 20036
301/918-1913
www.aaace.org
Key officer:
President: Margaret Mims
Membership requirements:
Open to all interested in adult and basic education, continuing education, and lifelong learning.
Size of membership:
1,000 (includes secondary and post-secondary educators, business and labor trainers, military and government, and community-based organization leaders)
Annual dues:
$75
Publications:
Adult Learning
Adult Education Quarterly
Meetings:
Annual conference

2

Name of organization:
American Counseling Association (ACA)
(see also National Career Development Association)
Purpose/Mission Statement:
To promote public confidence and trust in the counseling profession.
Contact information:
American Counseling Association
5999 Stevenson Ave.
Alexandria, VA 22304
800/347-6647
703/823-9800
703/823-0252 (fax)
www.counseling.org
Key officer:
Executive Director: Richard Yep
Membership requirements:
Interest in the areas of counseling and human development is the primary criterion. Candidates for membership include those who work in schools, colleges, private practice, employment, and related human service settings.
Size of membership:
approximately 51,000
Annual dues:
$117 professional; $88 student
Publications:
The Journal of Counseling and Development
Counseling Today
Meetings:
Annual World Conference
Annual convention
Other benefits of membership:
Career placement, accreditation/certification programs, professional development programs, books, insurance

3

Name of organization:
American Management Association International
Purpose/Mission Statement:
AMA provides educational forums worldwide where members and their colleagues learn practical business skills and explore best practices of world-class organizations through interaction with each other and faculty practitioners. AMA's publishing program provides tools individuals use to extend learning beyond the classroom in a process of lifelong professional growth and development through education.
Contact information:
American Management Association International
1601 Broadway
New York, New York 10019–7420
212/586-8100
212/903-8329 (fax)
www.amanet.org
Key officer:
President & Chief Executive Officer: Edward Reilly
Membership requirements:
Interest in the methodology and best contemporary management practices.
Size of membership:
70,000 (includes corporations, organizations, and individuals)
Publications:
AMA publishes approximately 70 business-related books each year, plus many surveys, newsletters, management briefings, self-paced courses in print and audio, as well as videos. Its flagship publication *Management Review*, is now available to members only, online only.
Meetings:
Annual conferences
Local/regional meetings
Other benefits of membership:
Gain insights at membership briefings and programs on important issues, opportunity to advance skills with management tools provided each month by AMA, network at local & regional

Professional Organizations

meetings, special discounts on seminars, publications, CD-Roms, & other self-study tools, plus benefits of corporate membership.

4

Name of organization:
The American Productivity & Quality Center (APQC)
Purpose:
Founded in 1977, the American Productivity & Quality Center (APQC) is a tax-exempt entity supported by more than 500 member organizations of all sizes, across all industries. The mission of APQC and its service, the International Benchmarking Clearinghouse, is to help enterprises recognize when and why change is needed, manage it effectively, and achieve process and performance improvement along the way through benchmarking and best practices. APQC provides the tools, information, and support in areas such as knowledge management, measurement, customer satisfaction, benchmarking, strategic planning, competitive intelligence, leadership, call centers, and quality.
Contact information:
The American Productivity & Quality Center (APQC)
123 North Post Oak Lane, 3rd Floor
Houston, TX 77024
800/776-9676
Outside U.S. 713/681-4020
713/681-1182 (fax)
e-mail: apqcinfo@apqc.org
www.apqc.org
Key officer: Lisa Higgins, CEO
Membership requirements:
Interests in improving quality, managing change, harnessing knowledge, measuring performance, adapting best practices, and thriving in an increasingly competitive environment.
Size of membership:
more than 450 member organizations
Annual dues:
There is a one-time new-member initiation fee plus an annual fee based on the number of employees within the organization. The initiatiom fee is U.S. tax deductible. Part of the annual fee is allocated to a bank account which can be used for purchasing additional APQC products or services. Membership is for an entire organization. All employees within member organizations can take advantage of members-only resources, content, and discounts. Renewal rate $4000.
Publications:
Best-Practice Reports (results of benchmarking studies)
Passport to Success booklets
White papers, online
Conference proceedings
Meetings:
Conferences with members-only events
Open house
Regional seminars/presentations
Regional training programs
Other benefits of membership:
Membership in APQC's International Benchmarking Clearinghouse provides exclusive access to people and information, enabling you to find and adapt best practices efficiently and effectively. Clearinghouse membership gives everyone within a member organization access to knowledge and resources needed to improve productivity and quality.

5

Name of organization:
Association for Business Neuro-Linguistics Training
Purpose:
To make the latest findings from the behavioral and social sciences available to business and industry.
Contact information:
Association for Business Neuro-Linguistics Training
P.O. Box 2902
Palos Verdes, CA 90274
310/378-2666
310/378-2742 (fax)
Key officer:
Executive Director: Dr. Donald Moine
Membership requirements:
Open to sales training directors and vice-presidents of marketing and human resources
Size of membership:
2,500
Annual dues:
None
Publications:
Newsletter
Modern Persuasion Strategies: The Hidden Advantage in Selling
Unlimited Selling Power: How to Master Hypnotic Selling Skills
The Power of Story Selling
Better Than Gold
Meetings:
Quarterly meetings

6

Name of organization:
Association for Educational Communications & Technology (AECT)
Purpose:
Dedicated to the improvement of instruction through the utilization of media and technology.
Contact information:
AECT
1800 North Stonelake Dr.
Bloomington, IN 47404
812/335-7675
812/335-7678 (fax)
www.aect.org
Key officers/staff:
Executive Director: Phillip Harris
Size of membership:
7,000 members and subscribers
Annual dues:
$85 per year; additional options available
Publications:
TechTrends
Educational Technology Research and Development
Meetings:
Interactive
Annual Conference
Summer Leadership Conference
Other benefits of membership:
Low-cost insurance programs, job placement and referral services, awards program, various discounts

7

Name of organization:
ASTD (American Society for Training and Development)
Purpose:
To provide leadership to individuals, organizations, and society to achieve work-related competence, performance, and fulfillment. Part of ASTD's mission is to link people, learning, and performance.
Contact information:
ASTD
1640 King St., Box 1443
Alexandria, VA 22313
703/683-8100
703/683-8103 (fax)
703/683-1523 (customer service fax)
www.astd.org

Key officer:
  President and CEO: Tina Sung
Membership requirements:
  Interest in the field of workplace learning, training, technical training, and performance improvement.
Size of membership:
  45,000 (national and chapter)
Annual dues:
  Full Time Student $75
  Senior $75 (62 yrs or older)
  Individual membership $150
  E-Learning membership $325
Publications:
  Training & Development (monthly magazine)
  State of the Industry
  Performance in Practice newsletter
  Info-Line booklet series
  ASTD Buyer's Guide & Consultant Directory
  Learning Circuits (Web magazine)
  Human Resource Development Quarterly (Web magazine)
Meetings:
  ASTD International Conference & Exposition
  ASTD Techknowledge℠ Conference and Exposition
Other benefits of membership:
  Information Center, Member Information Exchange, TRAINET (electronic database), ASTD Online (online information service), representation in government, book service, audio cassettes and videotapes of national conferences.

8

Name of organization:
  Career Planning & Adult Development Network
Purpose:
  The Network is designed to meet the needs of human resource specialists working with adults in a variety of settings and to keep them in touch with other human resource professionals through its publications and activities.
Contact information:
  Career Planning & Adult Development Network
  4965 Sierra Rd.
  San Jose, CA 95132
    408/441-9100
    408/441-9101 (fax)
    www.careernetwork.org
Key officer:
  Richard L. Knowdell
Membership requirements:
  Interest in career planning and adult development
Size of membership:
  1,000
Annual dues:
  $49 (U.S.); $64 (foreign); these prices for pre-paid. ($10 more for invoicing)
Publications:
  Career Planning and the Adult Development Network Newsletter, bimonthly
  Career Planning and Adult Development Journal, quarterly

9

Name of organization:
  Council for Adult and Experiential Learning (CAEL)
Purpose:
  To expand lifelong learning opportunities for adults and to advance experiential learning and its assessment.
Contact information:
  CAEL
  55 East Monroe, Suite 1930
  Chicago, IL 60603
    312/499-2600
    312/499-2601 (fax)
    www.cael.org
Key officer:
  President: Pamela Tate
Membership requirements:
  Accreditation by COPA-affiliated accrediting body for institutional membership. Any individual can join as an individual member.
Size of membership:
  600
Annual dues:
  $90 (individual); $450 (organizational); institutional dues determined by enrollment ($275–$475)
  $325–450–575
Publications:
  Newsletter, 3 times per year
  Various books
Meetings:
  Annual conference
  Spring workshops
Other benefits of membership:
  Discounts on CAEL publications, conferences, institutes, workshops, and consultation services; access to membership commissions.

10

Name of organization:
  Distance Education and Training Council
Purpose:
  The Distance Education and Training Council, a voluntary association of accredited distance study institutions, was founded in 1926 to promote sound educational standards and ethical business practices within the correspondence/distance study field. The independent DETC Accrediting Commission is listed by the U.S. Dept. of Education as a "nationally recognized accrediting agency." The Accrediting Commission is also a recognized member of the Council for Higher Education Accreditation (CHEA).
Contact information:
  Distance Education and Training Council
  1601 18th St., N.W.
  Washington, DC 20009-2529
    202/234-5100
    202/332-1386 (fax)
    www.detc.org
Key officer:
  Executive Director: Michael P. Lambert
Membership requirements:
  Accreditation of correspondence/distance study is conducted by the Accrediting Commission of the DETC.
Size of membership:
  80 member institutions
Annual dues:
  Less than one percent of the institution's income, estimated at $1,300 and up.
Publications:
  DETC News
  Directory of Accredited Institutions
Meetings:
  Annual spring conference
  Other meetings and workshops periodically
Other benefits of membership:
  Training seminars, legislative information

11

Name of organization:
  The Human Resource Planning Society
Purpose:
  To increase the impact of human resource planning and management on business and organizational performance.
Contact information:
  The Human Resource Planning Society
  317 Madison Ave., Suite 1509
  New York, NY 10017
    212/490-6387
    212/682-6851 (fax)
    www.hrps.org

Professional Organizations

Key officer:
Executive Director: Walter J. Cleaver
Membership requirements:
Senior-level human resource executives
Size of membership:
3,000
Annual dues:
$250 (individual); $75 (faculty); $2,500 (corporate sponsor); $1,000 (research sponsor)
Publications:
Human Resource Planning (quarterly publication)
Membership directory (online)
Meetings:
Annual conference
Professional development workshops/Corporate sponsor forum

12

Name of organization:
Instructional Systems Association (ISA)
Purpose:
To enhance the development and success of member firms; to improve members' capability to serve their clients; and to expand the influence of the instructional systems industry.
Contact information:
ISA
4952 Warner Ave., Suite 243
Huntington Beach, CA 92649
703/730-2838
703/730-2857 (fax)
www.isaconnection.org
Key officer:
Executive Director: Pamela J. Schmidt
Membership requirements:
Membership is open to those who produce generic and custom-designed training programs and consulting services, training media and software.
Size of membership:
200; recent merge with Digital Learning Organization (DLO)
Annual dues:
Based on gross annual sales
Publications:
Intercom (newsletter, published 3 times per year)
Newswire (E-mail Newsletter)
Meetings:
Annual meeting
Fall meeting
One-day special-topic meetings
Audio conferences

13

Name of organization:
International Alliance for Learning (IAL)
Purpose:
We envision a world where everyone experiences joy and fulfillment of infinite learning. We promote and support practical implementation of accelerated learning principles.
Contact information:
IAL
P.O. Box 26175
Colorado Springs, CO 80936
800/426-2989
719/638-6153 (fax)
www.ialearn.org
Key officer:
President: Nancy Omaha Boy
Membership requirements:
None
Size of membership:
700
Annual dues:
$75 (U.S.); $90 (outside U.S.)
Publications:
Journals and newsletter online
Meetings:
Annual conference

14

Name of organization:
International Association of Conference Centers (IACC)
Purpose:
To assist members in providing the most productive meeting facilities in the world and to expand awareness of the differences between these conference facilities and other hospitality venues.
Contact information:
IACC
243 North Lindbergh Blvd.
St. Louis, MO 63141
314/993-8575
314/993-8919 (fax)
www.iacconline.org
Key officer:
Executive Vice-President: Tom Bolman
Membership requirements:
Each conference center must meet the universal criteria for membership.
Size of membership:
400 centers
Annual dues:
$850–$3675 (based on facility size)
Publications:
New Publications: A Uniform System of Accounts for Conference Centers, Trends in Conference Center Industry—North America, Compass Reports: Benchmarking the Conference Industry.
Plus the following: Annual Membership Directory, Understanding Conference Centers, A Conference Center by Design, The Conference Center Concept (brochure), online newsletter
Meetings:
Annual conference
Other benefits of membership:
Professional education, advisory services, networking, marketing, public relations, Internet

15

Name of organization:
International Federation of Training and Development Organizations (IFTDO)
Purpose:
IFTDO is a worldwide network committed to identifying, developing, and transferring knowledge, skills, and technology to enhance personal and organizational growth, human performance, productivity, and sustainable development.
Key officer:
Dr. David A. Waugh–Secretary General
Contact information:
IFTDO
1800 Duke St.
Alexandria, VA 22314
703/535-6011
703/535-6474 (fax)
www.iftdo.org
Membership requirements:
Any organization which has as a primary objective the furtherance of the science and practice of the profession of training and wishes to adopt a full voting role in the Federation may apply for full member status. This includes professional training associations, as well as multinational corporations, universities, government agencies, consulting firms, etc. Any organization wishing to be associated with the Federation but which does not want to play a full voting part may apply as an Associate Member.
Size of Membership:
150 organizations

Annual dues:
  Full members—between $300 and $900, depending on size of organization
Publications:
  IFTDO News
Meetings:
  Annual world conference

16

Name of organization:
  International Mentoring Association
Purpose:
  To provide a regular, public forum for effective mentoring, professional development activities for members, and annual conferences and workshops; to facilitate the growth of effective mentoring and the implementation and maintenance of mentoring programs; and to disseminate materials on research and practices related to effective mentoring.
Key officer:
  Penny Horne
Contact information:
  International Mentoring Association
  Conferences and Seminars Division of Continuing Education
  Western Michigan University
  1201 Oliver St.
  Kalamazoo, MI 49008-5161
    616/387-4174
    616/387-4189 (fax)
    www.mentoring-association.org
Key officers/staff:
  President: Mr. Danny Sledge
Annual dues:
  $40 (student); $65 (individual); $100 (institution)
Publications:
  The Mentoring Connection Newsletter
  Membership directory
Meetings:
  Diversity in Mentoring Annual Conference (Annual Mentoring Institutes included)

17

Name of organization:
  International Society for Performance Improvement (ISPI)
Purpose:
  To increase productivity in the workplace through the application of performance and instructional technologies.
Contact information:
  ISPI
  1400 Spring St., Ste. 260
  Silver Sprig, MD 20910
    301/587-8570
    301/587-8573 (fax)
    www.ispi.org
Key officer:
  Executive Director: Judith Hale
Membership requirements:
  None
Size of membership:
  10,000 international members and local chapters
Annual dues:
  $145 (active); $60 (student); Organizational memberships available—call for different levels of organizational membership
Publications:
  Performance Improvement Journal (10× a year)
  Performance Improvement Quarterly
  Annual membership directory
Meetings:
  Annual conference and expo
Other benefits of membership:
  Placement service, consultants resource directory, international conference, regional chapters, Performance Technology Human Institute Seminars

18

Name of organization:
  International Society for Technology in Education (ISTE)
Purpose:
  ISTE is dedicated to the improvement of all levels of education through the use of computer-based technology.
Contact information:
  ISTE
  480 Charnelton St.
  Eugene, OR 97401-2626
    800/336-5191
    541/302-3777
    541/302-3778 (fax)
    www.iste.org
Key officer:
  CEO: Ms. Leslie Conery
Size of membership:
  Members and Affiliate members 75,000
Annual dues:
  $58 (regular membership, U.S.); $35 (student members, U.S.)
Publications:
  Learning & Leading with Technology
  The Journal of Research on Technology in Education
  Special Interest Group (SIG) journals
  The Update newsletter, online plus various books and courseware packages
Meetings:
  co-sponsor of NECC Annual Conference
Other benefits of membership:
  Voting privileges, discounts on ISTE books, discounts or complimentary subscriptions to non-ISTE professional journals and magazines.

19

Name of organization:
  Juvenile Justice Trainers Association
Purpose:
  Devoted to the development and advancement of a specialized system of education and training for juvenile justice professionals. Composed primarily of staff development and training specialists, the association provides a national network for sharing information, providing technical services and developing other support mechanisms for juvenile justice trainers.
Contact information:
  Juvenile Justice Trainers Association
  930 Coddington Rd.
  Ithaca, NY 14850
    607/256-2112
    607/272-4308 (fax)
    www.jjta.org
Key President:
  Margaret Davis
Membership requirements:
  None
Size of membership:
  250
Annual dues:
  $30
Publications:
  Quarterly newsletter
Meetings:
  Semiannual conference (spring and fall)

20

Name of organization:
  LERN (Learning Resources Network)
Purpose:
  To provide information and services to organizations that offer classes for adults.

Contact information:
LERN
P.O. Box 9
River Falls, WI 54022
800/678-5376
715/426-9777
715/426-5847 (fax)
www.lern.org
Key officer:
President: William A. Draves
Membership requirements:
Organizational membership: open to organizations that offer lifelong learning programs (a tier system for organizational membership is in the works).
Size of membership:
2,500 organizational members; 6,000 members
Annual dues:
$395 (organizational membership).
Publications:
LERN magazine
Course Trends (newsletter)
Marketing Recreation Classes (newsletter)
Associations Online
Higher Education Online
Marketing Credit & Degree Programs
plus various books, pamphlets, audiotapes, videos, and software plus other newsletters
Meetings:
LERN International Conference
Regional conferences
Various seminars and institutes
Other benefits of membership:
Member networking, on-site seminars, program planner certification program, brochure critique, customized surveys, program offering analysis, consulting, LERN Internet services (chat rooms, etc.), and the LERN database.

21

Name of organization:
The MASIE Center
Purpose:
The MASIE Center is an international thinktank dedicated to exploring the intersection of learning and technology. It is both a professional organization and a commercial venture.
Contact information:
The MASIE Center
P.O. Box 397
Saratoga Springs, NY 12866
518/587-3522
518/587-3276 (fax)
www.masie.com

Key officer:
President: Elliott Masie
Membership requirements:
Interest in learning and technology.
Size of membership:
1,500
Annual dues:
$195 for *Learning Decision* newsletter subscription and Website, discounts on conferences.
Publications:
Publications written by Elliott Masie and copyrighted by The MASIE Center are posted on the Center's Website. These primarily include articles on learning and technology and TechLearn Trends newsletter. These can be copied and disseminated with attribution to The MASIE Center. A weekly letter is sent via e-mail to members.
Meetings:
Annual Fall TechLearn Conference in Orlando, FL; Summer European Conference; Singapore Symposium
Other benefits of membership:
The Center provides research, perspectives, "next generation" learning and technology solutions, new e-Labskills Training Workshops and e-learning research.

22

Name of organization:
National Association for Industry-Education Cooperation (NAIEC)
Purpose:
NAIEC is the national clearinghouse for information on industry involvement in education. The Association believes that industry has a central role to play in helping education reshape its total academic and vocational program in a coherent, systematic manner so that it is more responsive to the needs of both students (youth and adults) and employers. Therefore, the focus for the joint efforts of industry and education is continuing school improvement, preparation for work, and human resource/economic development.
Contact information:
National Association for Industry-Education Cooperation
235 Hendricks Blvd.
Buffalo, NY 14226-3304
716/834-7047
716/834-7047 (fax)
www2.Pcom.net/naiec

Key officer:
President and CEO: Dr. Donald M. Clark
Membership requirements:
None
Size of membership:
1,180
Annual dues:
$35 (individual); $45 (council/chapter); $100 (institutional); $250–$1,000 (corporate, based on net earnings)
Publications:
Industry-Education Council: A Handbook
A Guide for Evaluating Industry-Sponsored Educational Materials
NAIEC Newsletter (bimonthly)
How to Plan a Community Resources Workshop: A Handbook
Independent Education Management Audit: A System Approach
plus other books and films

23

Name of organization:
National Association of Manufacturers
Purpose:
Represents manufacturers' interest in Washington, promoting a pro-growth, pro-worker agenda.
Contact Information:
National Association of Manufacturers
1331 Pennsylvania Avenue
Washington, DC 20004
800/736-6627
202/637-3182 (fax)
www.nam.org
Key Officer:
President, Jerry Jasinowski
Membership Requirements:
Open to manufacturers and related companies
Size of Membership:
14,000, 10,000 of which are employers of 500 or fewer employees.
Annual Dues:
Depends on number of employees
Publications:
Briefing newsletter, weekly when congress is in session; *Just in Time* monthly newsletter; Washington FAXLINE
Meetings:
Manufacturers' Week March 2002, Chicago
Other Benefits of Membership:
Center for Workforce Success offering programs for recruiting,

training, and retaining skilled workers.
NAM Virtual University offering 1,000 courses online.
www.namvu.com
Benchmarking, freight alliances, global crossing, information, site selection

24

Name of organization:
National Career Development Association (a division of American Counseling Association)
Purpose:
To advance knowledge about career development and to improve career development practice.
Contact information:
National Career Development Association
4700 Reed Rd., Suite M
Columbus, OH 43220
918/663-7060
614/326-1760 (fax)
www.ncda.org
Key officer:
Executive Director: Deneen Pennington
Membership requirements:
N/A
Size of membership:
4000
Annual dues:
$45
Publications:
Career Development Quarterly
Career Development Newsletter
Adult Career Development
A Counselor's Guide to Career Assessment Instruments
The Internet: A Tool for Career Planning
Learning to Work: Experiential Activities for Teaching, Career Counseling, Career Transitions
plus other single publications and media
Online reports and surveys
Meetings:
Annual conference
Other benefits of membership:
Professional development & continuing education opportunities, special interest groups, and exciting learning and networking organization.

25

Name of organization:
National Society for Experiential Education (NSEE)
Purpose:
NSEE is a national nonprofit organization which supports schools, colleges and universities, government agencies, organizations, and businesses in helping students learn through meaningful work and service experiences. The purpose of NSEE is to assist institutions and organizations in the area of internships, cooperative education, service-learning, field studies, and other forms of experiential education.
Contact information:
NSEE
9001 Braddock Rd., Ste. 380
Springfield, VA 22151
810/803-4170
800/528-3492 (fax)
www.nsee.org
Key officer:
Executive Director: Dennis Boyd
Size of membership:
1,500
Annual dues:
$50 (student); $85 (individual); $325 (institutional); $750 (sustaining).
Publications:
Program Evaluation, Role of Service-Learning in Education Reform, Internship as Partnership: A Handbook for site supervisors, Critical Issues K-12 Service-Learning: Care Studies and Reflections. Combining Service and Learning: A Resource Book for Community and Public Service, The NSEE Quarterly
Meetings:
Annual national conference

26

Name of organization:
Ontario Society for Training and Development (OSTD)
Purpose:
The Ontario Society for Training and Development is Canada's largest training organization representing more than 1,500 training and human resources development practitioners. Established in 1946, the Association acts as an advocate for Training in the training industry, establishes and maintains professional standards, and serves its membership by providing certification, educational programs, annual conferences and publications.
Contact information:
Ontario Society for Training and Development (OSTD)
80 Richmond St. West, Suite 508
Toronto, Ontario M5H 2A4
416/367-5900
416/367-1642 (fax)
www.ostd.ca
Key officer:
Executive Director: Lynn Johnston
Membership requirements:
Interest in training and development
Size of membership:
1400
Annual dues:
$257 fee
Publications:
Canadian Learning Journal
Training Competency Architecture & Toolkit
Meetings:
Annual Conference & Trade Show
Other benefits of membership:
Professional Certification Group
Insurance Plans
Government liaison

27

Name of organization:
The Organization Development Institute
Purpose:
To promote a better understanding of and disseminate information about organization development to our members and the public. Organization development is defined as the knowledge and skill necessary to implement a program of planned change using behavioral science concepts for the purpose of building greater organizational effectiveness. A secondary effort of the Institute is to provide an up-to-date listing of resources available in the field of organization development. This includes providing information on people working or studying in the field, information on other networks and organizations in the field, and information on OD/OB

academic programs. The organization has written an International OD code of ethics for the field as well as a written statement on knowledge and skill necessary for competence in the field. Also, the organization has developed criteria for accreditation of OD/OB academic programs.
Contact information:
The Organization Development Institute
11234 Walnut Ridge Rd.
Chesterland, OH 44026
440/729-7419
http://members.aol.com/odinst
Key officer:
Dr. Donald W. Cole, RODC
Membership requirements:
Interest in organization development
Size of membership:
500
Annual dues:
$110 (regular)
Publications:
Organizations & Change (monthly)
Organization Development Journal (quarterly)
International Registry of OD Professionals & The OD Handbook (annual)
Meetings:
Annual national OD conference (annual information exchange)
Annual OD conference (world congress)
Annual international, interorganizational conference on nonviolent large systems change
Other benefits of membership:
Information on jobs and consulting assignments, publishing opportunities, Code of Ethics, traveling to places of international interest, "Outstanding OD Consultant of the Year" award, the "Outstanding Presentation by a Student" award, the "Outstanding OD Project of the Year" award, and the "Outstanding OD Article of the Year" award.

28

Name of organization:
Organization Development Network
Purpose:
To aid the growth and development of OD practitioners; to contribute to the empowerment of the OD field; to link practitioners and their work with the needs of the world.
Contact information:
Richard A. Ungerer, Executive Director
71 Valley St., Suite 301
South Orange, NJ 07079-2825
973/763-7337
973/763-7488 (fax)
www.odnetwork.org
Key officer:
Executive Director: Amy Herman
Membership requirements:
None
Size of membership:
4,000
Annual dues:
$140 (individual)—call for other membership rates
Publications:
The OD Practitioner
Education Resource Directory
Meetings:
Annual national conference
Other benefits of membership:
OD Network Job Exchange, professional liability insurance, discounted conference fees

29

Name of organization:
Society for Applied Learning Technology (SALT)
Contact information:
SALT
50 Culpeper St.
Warrenton, VA 20186
800/457-6812
540/347-0055
540/349-3169 (fax)
www.salt.org
Key officer:
President: Raymond G. Fox
Membership requirements:
None
Size of membership:
600
Annual dues:
$55
Publications:
Newsletter
Journal of Educational Technology Systems
Journal of Instruction Delivery Systems
Journal of Interactive Instruction Development
Meetings:
Annual Conference

30

Name of organization:
Society for Human Resource Management (SHRM)
Purpose:
SHRM is a 50-year-old society and is also a worldwide association of human resource professionals with approximately 470+ local chapters. SHRM provides education and information services, conferences and seminars, government and media representation, online services and publications to professionals and student members all over the world.
Contact information:
SHRM
1800 Duke St.
Alexandria, VA 22314-3499
800/283-SHRM
703/548-3440
703/836-0367 (fax)
www.shrm.org
Key officer:
President & CEO: Helen Drinan
Membership requirements:
Must be in human resource field and dues
Size of membership:
160,000
Annual dues:
$160 (national dues) plus various professional emphasis group dues
Publications:
HR Magazine (monthly)
HR News (monthly)
The SHRM Legal Report (quarterly)
Legislative Hotline
(call-in number: 703/548-3440)
Meetings:
Annual Conference
Employment Law & Legislative Conference
International Conference
Employment Management Association Conference
Workplace Diversity Conference
Leadership Conference
Other benefits of membership:
Consumer Financial Network (888/SHRM-CFN), SHRM online, Information Center, SHRM library, SHRM store (800/444-5006)

31

Name of organization:
Society for Technical Communication (STC)

Purpose:
STC is an organization dedicated to advancing the arts and sciences of technical communication. STC's work involves making technical information available and understandable to those who need it. STC also promotes the public welfare by educating its members and industry about issues concerning technical communication. Mission statement: The mission of the STC is to improve the quality and effectiveness of technical communication for audiences worldwide.

Contact information:
Society for Technical Communication (STC)
901 N. Stuart St., Suite 904
Arlington, VA 22203-1822
703/522-4114
703/522-2075 (fax)
www.stc.org

Key officer:
Executive Director: William C. Stolgitis

Size of membership:
23,000

Annual dues:
Member: $110 ($110 dues plus one-time $15 enrollment fee);
Student member: $45 (no enrollment fee)

Publications:
Technical Communication (STC's quarterly journal)
Intercom (the society's magazine)
Proceedings (contains papers presented at annual conference)
other publications include the membership directory (which includes the STC bylaws), STC's salary survey, and the society's annual report online

Meetings:
Annual conference

Other benefits of membership:
Employment information offered by many STC chapters and on STC's Internet sites, scholarships awarded to full-time undergraduate and graduate students, research grants (scientific, literary, and educational), insurance plans available at rates lower than many individual plans. Other benefits include the opportunity to network with peers and the opportunity to keep up with important developments in the field of technical communication through seminars, lectures, workshops, international symposia, and the annual conference.

6.2 Training Conferences

Conferences are one of the trainer's principal development opportunities, and, of course, there are many to choose from during the course of a year. If you plan your conference attendance passively and wait until a brochure catches your attention, you may miss opportunities or use up your conference attendance budget on an event that might not have addressed your needs. This section of *The Trainer's Almanac* solves this dilemma for you by giving you a full year's most relevant conferences at a glance both in the master calendar and in the detailed conference listings that follow it.

What Is a Conference?

As we have done in Section 6.1 with professional organizations, here, too, we have selected entries that are national in scope and open to the public. Although many conferences are designed with a particular membership organization in mind, those listed here enjoy a nationwide and often global audience and participation from exhibitors and sponsors. Most conferences have a member price, an early-bird, and a public price of admission (call sponsor for more information if prices are not listed). Some of the conferences listed here have pre- or post-conference workshops and seminars; many have expo sections and exhibit halls for vendors and service providers, book sellers and manufacturers to display their wares and mingle with conference attendees. Many conferences feature recruiters and career development sessions and other resources for professional advancement. Leadership, design, e-learning, global issues, and diversity including sexuality issues are all on conference agendas in 2002 with increasing frequency.

We have chosen conferences that reflect the broadening interests of trainers, and that are held in well-equipped conference centers that facilitate learning. Many conferences listed here regularly attract thousands of participants. We have also selected conferences that are typically annual conferences; many are the flagship conference of the sponsoring organization. Section 6.2 features 83 conferences. Contact information on each conference is provided in the actual listing for each conference.

A trend this year also has been the proliferation of vendor-provided and consulting company conferences. In this era of high-tech, service providers seem anxious to provide the high touch that "the conference" typically embodies. Universities, too, are increasingly getting into the conference business. We include a few programs in these categories to illustrate these trends. We also include some conferences whose focus is public education, as trainers become more involved in supporting schools.

Conference Calendar

Here we provide a complete "Calendar of Training Conferences," an extensive, full year's listing of conference dates by month. This calendar will help you identify which events are being held during some particular time period, and you can easily scan the cities to find conferences that will occur in locations most attractive and most convenient for you. Also, don't forget to check Websites and Internet search engines for more information. We list Web addresses here for your convenience.

Computer Training

We have intentionally chosen not to list specific commercially available hardware, software, systems, learning management systems, and other infrastructure products. We believe that these are best learned from the vendor or manufacturer who sold them to you, and suggest that you look first to them for training in how to apply and use their products. Look also to the community colleges, technical schools, and university continuing education programs for certified training in various computer products. We do, however, refer you to the Website of the Computing Technology Industry Association, which sponsors an annual International Technology Training Association (ITTA) Conference that attracts a large number of vendors of these kinds of products and features leaders in the industry: *www.itta.org*. We also refer you to section 6.8 of this yearbook for a listing of training Websites that can lead you to other computer training.

Training & Development Yearbook 2002
Trainer's Almanac 2002 Calendar of Training Conferences

Date	Location	#	Event
			January 2002
Jan. 20–22	Honolulu, HI	45	*Professional Education Conference North America* (Meeting Professionals International (MPI))
Winter	Houston, TX	31	*IAL Conference on Accelerated Learning & Teaching* (International Alliance for Learning (IAL))
Winter–Spring	Cleveland, OH	66	*Supervisory Diversity Training: Age, Gender, and Sexuality* (SENEX Counseling & Training)
			February 2002
Feb. 5–7	Las Vegas, NV	15	*ASTD TechKnowledge Conference & Exposition* (American Society for Training & Development (ASTD))
Feb. 18–29	Atlanta, GA	17	*25th Annual International TRAINING 2002 Conference & Expo* (Bill Communications/TRAINING Magazine)
Feb. 19–23	Anchorage, AK	10	*15th ASLET International Training Seminar & Law Enforcement Expo* (American Society for Law Enforcement Training (ASLET))
February	Washington, DC	4	*ACE 84th Annual Meeting* (American Council on Education (ACE))
February	Orlando, FL	64	*Winter Training Conference (also held in Spring, Summer, and Fall)* (Practical Management Inc. (PMI))
			March 2002
Mar. 22–27	New Orleans, LA	5	*ACA World Conference* (American Counseling Association (ACA))
Mar. 24–28	South Beach, FL	30	*Annual Conference* (Human Resource Planning Society (HRPS))
Mar. 26–30	Chicago, IL	13	*Annual Spring Conference & Resource Mart* (Association for Quality & Participation (AQP))
March	Chicago, IL	48	*Manufacturers' Week* (National Association of Manufacturers (NAM))
Spring	Washington, DC	74	*19th Annual Employment Law and Legislation Conference* (Society for Human Resource Management (SHRM))
Spring	Washington, DC	1	*E-Learning Conference (East)* (AdvanceStar Communications
Spring	Contact sponsor	36	*14th Annual Measuring & Maximizing 360 Degree Feedback* (International Quality & Productivity Center (IQPC))
Spring	Los Angeles, CA	46	*Milken Institute 2002 Global Conference* (Milken Institute)
			April 2002
Apr. 4–5	Fort Worth, TX	35	*Diversity In Mentoring Conference* (International Mentoring Association)
Apr. 14–16	Denver, CO	26	*Distance Education & Training Council 76th Annual Conference* (Distance Education & Training Council (DETC))
Apr. 21–24	Manama, Bahrain	34	*31st World Conference & Expo* (International Federation of Training & Development Organizations (IFTDO))
Apr. 21–25	Dallas, TX	37	*Annual Conference & Expo* (International Society for Performance Improvement (ISPI))

Apr. 24–26	San Francisco, CA	56	*NETglobal 2002: High Performance e-Learning* (NETglobal)
Apr. 24–26	Newport Beach, CA	33	*Employment Law Updates* (Institute for Applied Management & Law, Inc. (IAML))
Apr. 27–May 4	Washington, DC	8	7th Knowledge Management Conference (American Quality & Productivity Center (APQC))
April	Contact sponsor	75	*Global Conference* (Society for Human Resource Management (SHRM))
April	Contact sponsor	29	*Training World 2000* (hr events)
April	Contact sponsor	39	*Annual Spring Conference* (also *Fall Conference*) (Juvenile Justice Trainers Association (JJTA))
April	Washington, DC	52	*Quest for Excellence XVI: Official Conference of the Malcolm Baldrige National Quality Award* (National Institute of Standards and Technology Administration, U.S. Department of Commerce Baldrige National Quality Program)
April	Washington, DC	80	*2002 National Policy Forum* (United States Distance Learning Association (USDLA))
April	Cambridge, MA (2 days)	71	*Corporate Strategies for the Digital Economy* Sloan Industry Centers
April	Contact sponsor	31	*Driving the Power of E-Learning: WBT Conference & Expo* (Influent Technology Group))
April	Santa Clara, CA	58	*intranets 2002 expo: design, build, and manage your enterprise portal* (Online, Inc.)
Spring	Scottsdale, AZ	83	*Spring Roundtable* (Work in America Institute)

May 2002

May 1–3	Cape Cod, MA	27	*Burning Questions 2002* (Harvard Business School Publishing)
May 5–8	San Juan, PR	49	*2002 Annual Conference* (National Association of Workforce Development Professionals (NAWDP))
May 5–8	Nashville, TN	77	*49th Annual Conference* (Society for Technical Communication (STC))
May 19–24	Chicago, IL	60	*32nd Annual Info Exchange: What's New in OD and HRD* (Organization Development Institute (ODI))
May 20–22	Denver, CO	9	*ASQ 56th Annual Quality Congress & Exhibition* (American Society for Quality (ASQ))
May 29–31	San Diego, CA	19	*4th Annual Friends of the Center Conference* (Center for Creative Leadership (CCL))
May 30–Jn. 2	Washington, DC	53	*17th Annual National Conference* (National Multicultural Institute (NMI))
May	Washington, DC	79	*10th Annual Meeting, Briefing & Conference on Education and Training in the Global Marketplace* (United States Department of Commerce: Service Industries International Trade Association)
May	Contact sponsor	28	*HR tech 2002* (hr events)
May	New York, NY	68	*Leadership Conference* (Simmons Graduate School of Management)
Spring	California	42	*8th Annual Leadership Development Conference* (Linkage, Inc.)
Spring	California	41	*5th Annual Coaching & Mentoring Conference* Linkage, Inc. (part of the Leadershhip Development Conference)

Training Conferences 263

Spring	Menomonie, WI	82	*Annual Training Conference: e-Learning and Technologies* (University of Wisconsin-Stout; conference repeated in Fall)
Spring	Contact sponsor	21	*14th Annual Business Ethics Conference* (The Conference Board)
Spring	Contact sponsor	24	*Corporate Universities: Benchmarks for 2002* (Corporate University Xchange)

June 2002

June 2–6	New Orleans, LA	14	*International Conference & Exposition* (American Society for Training and Development (ASTD))
June 17–19	San Antonio, TX	51	*23rd National Education Computing Conference (NECC)* (National Education Computing Confernece (NECA))
June 17–19	San Antonio, TX	38	*Annual Conference* (International Society for Technology in Education (ISTE))(co-sponsor with NECC)
June 24–27	Philadelphia, PA	73	*Annual Conference & Exposition* (Society for Human Resource Development (SHRM))
June	East coast and West coast	22	*2002 E-Learning Conference* (The Conference Board)
June	New York, NY	23	*Leadership Development Conference* (The Conference Board)
June	Contact sponsor	16	*TRAINING Directors' Forum 2002* (Bill Communications/TRAINING Magazine)
June	Cleveland	67	*Gray & Gay: Issues in Organizational Diversity* (SENEX Counseling & Training)

July 2002

July 7–10	Chicago, IL	50	*Careers Across America* (National Career Development Association (NCDA))
July 22–27	Ghana, Africa	60	*22nd Annual Organization Development World Congress* (Organization Development Institute (ODI))
July 24–26	Pentagon City, DC	72	*Education Technology 2002* (Society for Applied Learning Technology (SALT))
July 26–29	Chicago, IL	12	*Summer Leadership Conference* (Association for Educational Communications and Technology (AECT))

August 2002

August	Madison, WI	81	*18th Annual Conference on Distance Teaching & Learning* (University of Wisconsin–Madison)
August	Stillwater, OK	78	*Academy 2002 Distance Learning* (Teletraining Institute)
August	Various locations; contact sponsor	70	*Leadership Development & Team Building* (SkillPath Seminars)
Summer	Dublin, Ireland	44	*E-Learning 2002 Europe* (The MASIE Center)

September 2002

September	Fort Worth, TX	20	*13th Annual International Conference on Work Teams* (Center for the Study of Work Teams, University of North Texas)

October 2002

October 1–4	Las Vegas, NV	54	*NSEE Annual National Conference* (National Society for Experiential Education (NSEE))

Oct. 17–23	Montreal, Quebec	61	*ODN Annual National Conference* (Organization Development Network (ODN))
Oct. 20–30	Las Vegas, NV	6	*Administrative Professionals Conference* (American Management Association (AMA) International)
October	Contact sponsor	63	*Systems Thinking In Action* (Pegasus Communications, Inc.)
October	Orlando, FL	44	*TechLearn 2002* (The MASIE Center)
October	Anaheim, CA	2	*E-Learning West* (AdvanceStar Communications)
Fall	Las Vegas, NV	7	*Global Human Resources Conference* (American Management Association (AMA) International)

November 2002

Nov. 6–10	Irvine, CA	18	*International Career Development Conference* (Career Planning & Adult Development Network)
Nov. 7–9	Washington, DC	25	*CAEL 2002 International Conference* (Council for Adult and Experiential Learning (CAEL))
Nov. 18–19	Toronto, Ontario	58	*Annual Conference* (Ontario Society for Training & Development (OSTD))
November	Washington, DC	47	*34th Annual Meeting* (National Alliance of Business (NAB))
November	Dallas, TX	11	*AECT National Convention & INCITE Exposition* (Association for Educational Communications & Technology AECT))
November	Orlando, FL	40	*Lifelong Learning Conference* (Learning Resources Network (LERN))
November	Contact sponsor	3	*51st Annual Adult Education Conference* (American Association for Adult & Continuing Education (AAACE))
Fall	Contact sponsor (three fall dates)	65	*Program on Negotiation for Senior Executives* Harvard University Law School
Fall	Contact sponsor	62	*2nd International Conference on Appreciative Inquiry* (Pegasus Communications, Inc.)
Fall	Contact sponsor	69	*Conference for Women* (SkillPath Seminars)

December 2002

Dec. 3–5	San Diego, CA	76	*Workplace Diversity* (Society for Human Resource Management (SHRM))
Dec. 7–11	Boston, MA	55	*NSDC Annual Conference* (National Staff Development Conference (NSDC))

Training Conferences

1

Sponsor:
Advance Star Communications
Title:
E-Learning Conference (formerly TeleCon East)
Dates:
Spring 2002
Location:
Washington, DC
Contact information:
Advance Star Communications
131 West 1st St. Box 6296
Duluth, MN 55802
800/829-3400
218/723-9122 (fax)
www.elearningexpos.com
Cost:
Contact sponsor
Exhibits:
Yes

2

Sponsor:
Advance Star Communicatons
Title:
E-Learning Conference (formerly TeleCon West)
Dates:
Fall 2002
Location:
Anaheim, CA
Contact information:
Advance Star Communications
131 West 1st St. Box 6296
Duluth, MN 55802
800/829-3400
218/723-9122 (fax)
www.elearningexpos.com
Cost:
Contact sponsor
Exhibits:
Yes

3

Sponsor:
American Association for Adult & Continuing Education (AAACE)
Title:
51st Annual Adult Education Conference
Dates:
November 2002
Location:
Contact sponsor
Contact information:
AAACE
1200 19th St., NW, Suite 300
Washington, DC 20036
301/918-1913
www.albany.edu/ace
Cost:
Regular: $250 (members)
Exhibits:
Yes

4

Sponsor:
American Council on Education
Title:
ACE 84th Annual Meeting
Dates:
February 2002
Location:
Washington, DC
Contact information:
American Council on Education
1 DuPont Circle, NW, Suite 800
Washington, DC 20036
202/939-9410
202/833-4760 (fax)
www.acenet.edu
Cost:
Contact sponsor
Exhibits:
Yes

5

Sponsor:
American Counseling Association
Title:
ACA World Conference
Dates:
March 22–27, 2002
Location:
New Orleans, LA
Contact information:
American Counseling Association
5999 Stevenson Ave.
Alexandria, VA 22304
800/347-6647
703/823-9800
703/823-0252 (fax)
www.counseling.org
Cost:
Contact sponsor
Exhibits:
Yes

6

Sponsor:
American Management Association (AMA) International
Title:
Administrative Professionals Conference
Dates:
October 20–30, 2002
Location:
Las Vegas, NV
Contact information:
American Management Assn. International
1601 Broadway
New York, NY 10019
212/586-8100
212/903-8329 (fax)
www.amanet.org
Cost:
Contact sponsor
Exhibits:
Yes

7

Sponsor:
American Management Association (AMA) International
Title:
Global Human Resources Conference
Dates:
Fall 2002
Location:
San Francisco, CA
Contact information:
American Management Association (AMA) International
1601 Broadway
New York, NY 10019-7420
212/586-8100
212/903-8329 (fax)
www.amanet.org
Cost:
Contact sponsor
Exhibits:
Yes

8

Sponsor:
American Productivity & Quality Center (APQC)
Title:
7th Knowledge Management Conference
Dates:
April 27–May 4, 2002
Location:
Washington, DC
Contact information:
APQC
123 North Post Oak Lane, Third Floor
Houston, TX 77024
800/776-9676
Outside U.S. 713/681-4020
713/681-8578 (fax)
www.apqc.org
Cost:
Contact sponsor
Exhibits:
No

9

Sponsor:
American Society for Quality (ASQ)
Title:
ASQ 56th Annual Quality Congress and Exhibition
Dates:
May 20–22, 2002
Location:
Denver, CO
Contact information:
American Society for Quality (ASQ)
Shirley Krentz
611 East Wisconsin Ave., P.O. Box 3005
Milwaukee, WI 53201-3005
800/248-1946 (customer service)
414/272-8575
414/272-1734 (fax)
www.asq.org
Cost:
Contact sponsor
Exhibits:
Yes

10

Sponsor:
American Society for Law Enforcement Training (ASLET)
Title:
15th ASLET International Training Seminar and Law Enforcement Expo
Dates:
February 19–23, 2002
Location:
Anchorage, AK
Contact information:
ASLET
121 North Court St.
Frederick, MD 21701
301/668-9466
301/668-9482 (fax)
www.ashlet.org
Cost:
For new members: $375–$450
Exhibits:
Yes

11

Sponsor:
Association for Educational Communications and Technology (AECT)
Title:
AECT International Conference
Dates:
November 2002
Location:
Dallas, TX
Contact information:
AECT
1800 North Stonelake Dr.
Bloomington, IN 47404
812/335-7675
812/335-7678 (fax)
www.aect.org
Cost:
$400
Exhibits:
Contact sponsor

12

Sponsor:
Association for Educational Communications and Technology (AECT)
Title:
Summer Leadership Conference
Dates:
July 26–29, 2002
Location:
Chicago, IL.
Contact information:
Association for Educational Communications and Technology
1800 North Stonelake Drive
Bloomington, IN 47404
812/335-7675
812/335-7678 (fax)
www.aect.org
Cost:
$495; $695 including hotel
Exhibits:
Contact sponsor

13

Sponsor:
Association for Quality and Participation (AQP)
Title:
Annual Spring Conference & Resource Mart
Dates:
March 26–30, 2002
Location:
Chicago, IL
Contact information:
Association for Quality and Participation (AQP)
2368 Victory Pkwy #200
Cincinnati, OH 45206
800/733-3310
513/381-1959
513/381-0070 (fax)
www.aqp.org
Cost:
Approximately $1,000; Contact sponsor for discount.
Exhibits:
Yes

14

Sponsor:
ASTD
Title:
International Conference and Exposition
Dates:
June 2–6, 2002
Location:
New Orleans, LA
Contact information:
ASTD
1640 King St., Box 1443
Alexandria, VA 22313
703/683-8100
703/683-8103 (fax) or
703/683-1523 (customer service fax)
www.astd.org
Cost:
Contact sponsor
Exhibits:
Yes

15

Sponsor:
ASTD
Title:
ASTD TechKnowledge^{SM} Conference & Exposition
Dates:
February 5–7, 2002
Location:
Las Vegas, NV
Contact information:
ASTD
1640 King St., Box 1443
Alexandria, VA 22313
703/683-8100
703/683-8103 (fax) or
703/683-1523 (customer service fax)
www.astd.org
Cost:
Contact sponsor
Exhibits:
Yes

16

Sponsor:
Bill Communications/ TRAINING Magazine
Title:
TRAINING Directors' Forum 2002
Dates:
June 2002
Location:
Contact sponsor
Contact information:
Bill Communications
50 South 9th Street
Minneapolis, MN 55402

Training Conferences

800/328-4329
612/333-0471
www.trainingsupersite.com
Cost:
$1,195 plus $395 for one-day pre- or post-conference workshop; golf tournament and clinic, ca $200 extra
Exhibits:
Contact sponsor

17

Sponsor:
Bill Communications/ TRAINING Magazine
Title:
25th Annual International TRAINING 2002 Conference & Expo
Dates:
February 18–20, 2002
Location:
Atlanta, GA
Contact information:
Bill Communications
50 South 9th Street
Minneapolis, MN 55402
800/328-4329
612/333-0471
www.trainingsupersite.com
Cost:
$995
Exhibits:
Yes

18

Sponsor:
Career Planning & Adult Development Network
Title:
International Career Development Conference
Dates:
November 6–10, 2002
Location:
Irvine, CA
Contact information:
Career Planning & Adult Development Network
4965 Sierra Road
San Jose, CA 95132
408/441-9100
408/441-9101 (fax)
www.careernetwork.org
Cost:
$400–$600
Exhibits:
Yes

19

Sponsor:
Center for Creative Leadership
Title:
4th Annual Friends of the Center Conference
Dates:
May 29–31, 2002
Location:
San Diego, CA
Contact information:
Center for Creative Leadership
Client Services
P.O. Box 26300
Greensboro, NC 27438
336/545-2810
336/282-3284 (fax)
www.ccl.org
Cost:
$1,000
Exhibits:
No

20

Sponsor:
Center for the Study of Work Teams
Title:
13th Annual International Conference on Work Teams
Dates:
September 2002
Location:
Fort Worth, TX
Contact information:
Center for the Study of Work Teams
University of North Texas
P.O. Box 311280
Denton, TX 76203
940/565-3096
940/565-4806 (fax)
email: www.workteams@unt.edu
Cost:
$995; Early Registration Discounted Prices available
Exhibits:
Yes

21

Sponsor:
The Conference Board
Title:
14th Annual Business Ethics Conference
Dates:
May 2002
Location:
New York, NY
Contact information:
The Conference Board
845 Third Avenue
New York, NY 10022
212/759-0900
212/980-7014 (fax)
www.conference-board.org/ethics.htm
Cost:
$1,775
Exhibits:
No

22

Sponsor:
The Conference Board
Title:
2002 E-Learning Conference
Dates:
June 2002
Location:
2 locations: one east coast; one west coast
Contact information:
The Conference Board
845 Third Avenue
New York, NY 10022
212/759-0900
212/980-7014 (fax)
www.conference-board.org
Cost:
$1,775
Exhibits:
No

23

Sponsor:
The Conference Board
Title:
Leadership Development Conference
Dates:
June 2002
Location:
New York, NY
Contact information:
The Conference Board
845 Third Avenue
New York, NY 10022
212/759-0900
212/980-7014 (fax)
www.conference-board.org
Cost:
$1,775
Exhibits:
No

24

Sponsor:
Corporate University Xchange
Title:
Corporate Universities: Benchmarks for 2002
Dates:
Spring 2002
Location:
Contact sponsor
Contact information:
Corporate University Xchange
381 Park Avenue South
New York, NY 10016

800/946-1210
212/213-8621 (fax)
www.corpu.com
Cost:
$1,395
Exhibits:
Yes

25

Sponsor:
Council for Adult & Experiential Learning (CAEL)
Title:
CAEL 2002 International Conference
Dates:
November 7–9, 2002
Location:
Washington, DC
Contact information:
CAEL
55 East Monroe
Suite 1930
Chicago, IL 60603
312/499-2600
312/499-2601 (fax)
www.cael.org
Cost:
Contact sponsor
Exhibits:
Yes

26

Sponsor:
Distance Education and Training Council
Title:
Distance Education and Training Council 76th Annual Conference
Dates:
April 14–16, 2002
Location:
Denver, CO
Contact information:
Distance Education and Training Council
1601 18th St., N.W.
Washington, DC 20009-2529
202/234-5100
202/332-1386 (fax)
www.detc.org
Cost:
Contact Ms. Tabby Stafford
202/234-5100
Exhibits:
No

27

Sponsor:
Harvard Business School Publishing
Title:
Burning Questions 2002
Dates:
May 1–3, 2002
Location:
Cape Cod, MA
Contact information:
Harvard Business School Publishing
Conference Dept, 4th Floor
60 Harvard Way
Boston, MA 02163
Cost:
Contact sponsor
Exhibits:
No

28

Sponsor:
hrevents
Title:
HR tech(TM) 2002
Dates:
May 2002
Location:
Contact sponsor
Contact information:
HRevents, LLC
150 Clove Road
PO Box 401
Little Falls, NJ 07424
800/882-8684
973/256-0205 (fax)
www.hrtechevents.com
Cost:
$1,499
Exhibits:
Contact sponsor

29

Sponsor:
hrevents
Title:
Training World(TM) 2002
Dates:
April 2002
Location:
Contact sponsor
Contact information:
HR events, LLC
150 Clove Road
PO Box 401
Little Falls, NJ 07424
800/882-8684
973/256-0205 (fax)
www.hrevents.com
Cost:
$1,499
Exhibits:
Contact sponsor

30

Sponsor:
The Human Resource Planning Society
Title:
Annual Conference
Dates:
March 24–28, 2002
Location:
South Beach, FL
Contact information:
The Human Resource Planning Society
317 Madison Ave., Suite 1509
New York, NY 10017
212/490-6387
212/682-6851 (fax)
www.hrps.org
Cost:
Contact sponsor
Exhibits:
No

31

Sponsor:
Influent Technology Group
Title:
WBT Producer Conference & Expo: Driving The Power of E-Learning
Dates:
April 2002
Location:
Contact sponsor
Contact information:
Influent Technology Group
190 North Main St.
Natick, MA 01760
888/333-9088
508/651-9532 (fax)
www.influent.com
Cost:
$1,095
Exhibits:
Yes

32

Sponsor:
International Alliance for Learning (IAL)
Title:
IAL Annual Conference on Accelerated Learning & Teaching
Dates:
Winter 2002
Location:
Houston, TX
Contact information:
IAL
P.O. Box 26175
Colorado Springs, CO 80936
800/426-2989
719/638-6153 (fax)
www.ialearn.org
Cost:
Contact sponsor: range $375–$900
Exhibits:
Yes

Training Conferences

33

Sponsor:
Institute for Applied Management & Law, Inc (IAML)
Title:
Employment Law Updates Conference
Dates:
April 24–26, 2002 (and other dates throughout the year)
Location:
Newport Beach, CA
Contact information:
Institute for Applied Management & Law, Inc. (IAML)
610 Newport Center Drive, Ste. 1060
Newport Beach, CA 92660
949/760-1700
949/760-8192
www.iaml.com
Cost:
$1,225
Exhibits:
Contact sponsor

34

Sponsor:
International Federation of Training and Development Organizations (IFTDO)
Title:
31st World Conference & Expo
Dates:
April 21–24, 2002
Location:
Manama, Bahrain
Contact information:
Dr. David A. Waugh, Secretary General
IFTDO
1800 Duke St.
Alexandria, VA 22314
703/535-6011
703/836-0367 (fax)
www.iftdo.org
Cost:
$693–$900
Exhibits:
Yes

35

Sponsor:
International Mentoring Association
Title:
Diversity in Mentoring Conference
Dates:
April 4–5, 2002
Location:
Fort Worth, TX
Contact information:
International Mentoring Association
Western Michigan University
1201 Oliver Street
Kalamazoo, MI 49008
616/387-4174
616/387-4189 (fax)
www.mentoring-association.org
Cost:
Contact sponsor
Exhibits:
No

36

Sponsor:
International Quality & Productivity Center (IQPC)
Title:
14th Annual Measuring & Maximizing 360° Feedback
Dates:
Spring 2002
Location:
Contact sponsor
Contact information:
International Quality & Productivity Center
150 Clove Rd., P.O. Box 401
Little Falls, NJ 07424
800/882-8684
973/256-0205 (fax)
www.iqpc.com
Cost:
$1,699 or $2,099 including one post-conference workshop
Exhibits:
Yes

37

Sponsor:
International Society for Performance Improvement (ISPI)
Title:
Annual Conference & Expo
Dates:
April 21–25, 2002
Location:
Dallas, TX
Contact information:
ISPI
1300 L St., NW, Suite 1250
Washington, DC 20005-4107
202/408-7969
202/408-7972 (fax)
www.ispi.org
Cost:
Contact sponsor
Exhibits:
No

38

Sponsor:
International Society for Technology in Education (ISTE)
Title:
Annual Conference (co-sponsor with NECC)
Dates:
June 17–19, 2002
Location:
San Antonio, TX
Contact information:
ISTE
480 Charnelton Street
Eugene, OR 97401
800/336-5191
541/302-3778 (fax)
www.iste.org
Cost:
$150
Exhibits:
Contact sponsor

39

Sponsor:
Juvenile Justice Trainers Assn.
Title:
Annual Spring Conference
Annual Fall Conference
(conferences co-sponsored by National Juvenile Detention Assn.)
Dates:
April 2002
October 2002
Location:
Contact sponsor
Contact information:
Juvenile Justice Trainers Assn.
430 Coddington Rd
Ithaca, NY 14850
607/256-2112
607/272-4308 (fax)
www.jjta.org
Cost:
Contact sponsor
Exhibits:
Contact sponsor

40

Sponsor:
Learning Resources Network (LERN)
Title:
Lifelong Learning Conference
Dates:
November 2002
Location:
Orlando, FL
Contact information:
LERN
P.O. Box 9
River Falls, WI 54022

800/678-5376
715/426-9777
715/426-5847 (fax)
www.lern.org
Cost:
$565
Exhibits:
Contact sponsor

41

Sponsor:
Linkage, Inc.
Title:
5th Annual Coaching & Mentoring Conference
Dates:
Spring 2002 (part of the Leadership Development Conference)
Location:
California
Contact information:
Linkage, Inc.
One Forbes Road
Lexington, MA 02421
781/862-3157
781/862-2355 (fax)
www.linkage.com
Cost:
$1195, pre- and post-conference workshops $395 extra
Exhibits:
Contact sponsor

42

Sponsor:
Linkage, Inc.
Title:
8th Annual Leadership Development Conference
Dates:
Spring 2002
Location:
California
Contact information:
Linkage, Inc.
One Forbes Road
Lexington, MA 02421
781/862-3157
781/862-2355 (fax)
www.linkage.com
Cost:
$1195; Forums $545 extra
Exhibits:
Contact sponsor

43

Sponsor:
The MASIE Center
Title:
E-Learning 2002 Europe
Dates:
Summer 2002
Location:
Dublin, Ireland
Contact information:
The MASIE Center
P.O. Box 397
Saratoga Springs, NY 12866
518/587-3522
518/587-3276
www.masie.com
Cost:
$995

44

Sponsor:
The MASIE Center
Title:
TechLearn 2002
Dates:
October 2002
Location:
Orlando, FL
Contact information:
The MASIE Center
P.O. Box 397
Saratoga Springs, NY 12866
518/587-3522
518/587-3276 (fax)
www.masie.com
Cost:
$995
Exhibits:
Yes

45

Sponsor:
Meeting Professionals International (MPI)
Title:
Professional Education Conference, North America
Dates:
January 20–22, 2002
Location:
Honolulu, HI
Contact information:
Meeting Professionals International (MPI)
4455 LBJ Frwy., Suite 1200
Dallas, TX 75244-5903
972/702-3000
972/702-3095 (fax)
www.mpiweb.org
Cost:
Contact sponsor
Exhibits:
Contact sponsor

46

Sponsor:
Milken Institute
Title:
Milken Institute 2002 Global Conference
Dates:
Spring 2002
Location:
Los Angeles, CA
Contact information:
Milken Institute
310/998-2605
www.milken-inst.org
Cost:
$1,000
Exhibits:
Contact sponsor; for corporate sponsorships phone 310/998-2632

47

Sponsor:
National Alliance of Business
Title:
34th Annual Meeting
Dates:
November 2002
Location:
Washington, DC
Contact information:
National Alliance of Business
1201 New York Avenue NW, Ste. 700
Washington, DC 20005
202/289-2888
202/289-1303 (fax)
www.nab.com
Cost:
Contact sponsor
Exhibits:
Contact sponsor

48

Sponsor:
National Association of Manufacturers
Title:
Manufacturers' Week
Dates:
March 2002
Location:
Chicago, IL
Contact information:
National Association of Manufacturers
1331 Pennsylvania Avenue
Washington, DC 20004
800/736-6627
202/637-3182
www.nam.org
Cost:
Contact sponsor
Exhibits:
Yes

49

Sponsor:
National Association of Workforce Development Professionals (NAWDP)

Training Conferences

(formerly Partnership for Training and Employment Careers)
Title:
2002 Annual Conference
Dates:
May 5–8, 2002
Location:
San Juan, P.R.
Contact information:
National Association of Workforce Development Professionals (NAWDP)
1620 I Street, NW, Suite LL (lower level) 30
Washington, DC 20006
202/887-6120
202/887-8216 (fax)
www.nawdp.org
Cost:
$445
Exhibits:
Yes

50

Sponsor:
National Career Development Association
Title:
Careers Across America
Dates:
July 7–10, 2002
Location:
Chicago, IL
Contact information:
National Career Development Assn.
4700 Reed Road, Suite M
Columbus, OH 43220
918/663-7060
614/326-1760 (fax)
www.ncda.org
Cost:
$295
Exhibits:
Contact sponsor

51

Sponsor:
National Educational Computing Association
Title:
National Education Computing Conference (focus on K-12)
Dates:
June 17–19, 2002
Location:
Chicago, IL
Contact information:
NECC/NECA
University of North Texas
Denton, TX 76203
541/201-9995
541/346-3545 (fax)
www.neccsite.org

Cost:
Contact sponsor
Exhibits:
Yes

52

Sponsor:
National Institute of Standards and Technology, Technology Administration, U.S. Department of Commerce, Baldrige National Quality Program
Title:
Quest for Excellence XIV: Official Conference of the Malcolm Baldrige National Quality Award
Dates:
April 2002
Location:
Washington, DC
Contact information:
NIST Technology Administration
U.S. Department of Commerce
Baldrige National Quality Program
Gaithersburg, MD 20899
301/975-2036
www.quality.nist.gov or 800/733-3310
www.aqp.org
Cost:
$700
Exhibits:
Contact sponsor

53

Sponsor:
National MultiCultural Institute
Title:
16th Annual National Conference
Dates:
May 30–June 2, 2002
Location:
Washington, DC
Contact information:
National MultiCultural Institute
3000 Connecticut Avenue, NW, Suite 438
Washington, DC 20008
202/483-0700
202/483-5233
www.nmci.org
Cost:
$780–$1250
Exhibits:
Yes

54

Sponsor:
National Society for Experiential Education
Title:
NSEE Annual National Conference

Dates:
October 1–4, 2002
Location:
Las Vegas, NV
Contact information:
NSEE
9001 Braddock Rd.
Springfield, VA 22151
800/803-4150
800/528-3492 (fax)
www.nsee.org
Cost:
Contact sponsor
Exhibits:
Contact sponsor

55

Sponsor:
National Staff Development Council (NSDC)
Title:
NSDC Annual Conference
Dates:
December 7–11, 2002
Location:
Boston, MA
Contact information:
National Staff Development Council (NSDC)
P.O. Box 240
Oxford, OH 45056
513/523-6029
513/523-0638 (fax)
www.nsdc.org
Cost:
Approximately $625
Exhibits:
Yes

56

Sponsor:
NETglobal
Title:
NETglobal 2002: High Performance e-Learning
Dates:
April 24–26, 2002
Location:
San Francisco, CA
Contact information:
NETglobal
1751 West Diehl Rd, 2nd floor
Naperville, IL 60563
877/561-6384
847/202-9513 (fax)
www.netg.com
Cost:
$749
Exhibits:
Contact sponsor

57

Sponsor:
Online Inc.

Title:
    intranets 2001 expo: design, build, and manage your enterprise portal
Dates:
    April 1, 2002
Location:
    Santa Clara, CA
Contact information:
    Online Inc.
    213 Danbury Road
    Wilton, CT 06897
        800/248-8466, ext 500
        203/761-1444
        www.intranets2001.com
Cost:
    $895; plus pre- and post-conference seminars at $195 each
Exhibits:
    Yes

58

Sponsor:
    Ontario Society for Training and Development (OSTD)
Title:
    Annual Conference
Dates:
    November 18–19, 2002
Location:
    Toronto, Ontario
Contact information:
    OSTD
    80 Richmond Street West, Ste. 508
    Toronto, Canada M5H 2A4
Cost:
    Contact sponsor
Exhibits:
    Yes

59

Sponsor:
    The Organization Development Institute
Title:
    22nd Annual OD World Congress
Dates:
    July 22–27, 2002
Location:
    Ghana, Africa
Contact information:
    The Organization Development Institute
    Dr. Donald W. Cole, RODC
    11234 Walnut Ridge Rd.
    Chesterland, OH 44026
        440/729-7419
        440/729-9319 (fax)
        http://members.aol.com/odinst
Cost:
    Approximately $190 (members); $250 (non-members)
Exhibits:
    Contact sponsor

60

Sponsor:
    The Organization Development Institute
Title:
    32nd Annual Information Exchange: What's New in OD and HRD (all attendees share information)
Dates:
    May 19–24, 2002
Location:
    Hickory Ridge Center
    Near Chicago, IL
Contact information:
    The Organization Development Institute
    Dr. Donald W. Cole, RODC
    11234 Walnut Ridge, Rd.
    Chesterland, OH 44026
        440/729-7419
        440/729-9319 (fax)
        http://members.aol.com/odinst
Cost:
    Approximately $190 (members); $250 (non-members)
Exhibits:
    Contact sponsor

61

Sponsor:
    Organization Development Network
Title:
    ODN Annual National Conference
Dates:
    October 17–23, 2002
Location:
    Montreal, Quebec, Canada
Contact information:
    Organization Development Network
    71 Valley St., Suite 301
    South Orange, NJ 07079-2825
        973/763-7337
        973/763-7488 (fax)
        www.odnet.org
Cost:
    Contact sponsor
Exhibits:
    Contact sponsor

62

Sponsor:
    Pegasus Communications, Inc.
Title:
    2nd International Conference on Appreciative Inquiry
Dates:
    4-day conference, including 6 pre- and post-conference workshops
    fall 2002
Location:
    Contact sponsor
Contact information:
    Pegasus Communications, Inc.
    One Moody Street
    Waltham, MA 02453
        800/272-0945
        802/862-0095
        802/864-7626 (fax)
        www.pegasuscom.com
Cost:
    $1,395 plus hotel
    $295 per 4-hour workshop, and
    $595 per 8-hour workshop
Exhibits:
    Co-sponsors: Case Western Reserve University, NTL Institute, Ai Consulting, Weatherherd School of Management, Benedictine University

63

Sponsor:
    Pegasus Communications, Inc.
Title:
    Systems Thinking in Action
Dates:
    2-day conference plus 10 pre- and post-conference sessions
    October 2002
Location:
    Contact sponsor
Contact information:
    Pegasus Communications, Inc.
    One Moody Street
    Waltham, MA 02453
        800/272-0945
        802/862-0095
        802/864-7626
        www.pegasuscom.com
Cost:
    $1,584 conference, plus hotel
    pre- and post-conference sessions $145–$2750
Exhibits:
    authors' night; coaching clinic

64

Sponsor:
    Practical Management, Inc.
Title:
    Winter Training Conference (conference held also in spring, summer, & fall)
Dates:
    February 2002
Location:
    Orlando, FL
Contact information:
    Practical Management, Inc.
    3280 West Hacienda Ave., Suite 205
    Las Vegas, NV 89118

Training Conferences

702/795-3622
800/444-9101
702/795-8339
www.practicalmgt.com
Cost:
2 days $695; 3 days $995;
4 days $1295
Exhibits:
Contact sponsor

65

Sponsor:
Program on Negotiation at Harvard Law School
Title:
Program for Senior Executives
Dates:
Fall and spring 2002
Location:
Cambridge, MA
Contact information:
Center for Management Research
55 William St., Suite 210
Wellesley, MA 02481
781/239-1111
781/239-1546 (fax)
pon.execseminars.com
Cost:
Contact sponsor
Exhibits:
No

66

Sponsor:
SENEX Counseling & Training
Title:
Supervisory Diversity Training: Age, Gender, and Sexuality
Dates:
Winter–Spring
Location:
Cleveland, OH
Contact information:
SENEX ElderCare, Counseling & Training
Fairhill Center
12200 Fairhill Road
Cleveland, OH 44120
216/421-1793
www.senexcare.com
Cost:
Contact sponsor
Exhibits:
Contact sponsor

67

Sponsor:
SENEX
Title:
Gray & Gay: Issues in Organizational Diversity (SENEX Counseling & Training)
Dates:
June
Location:
Cleveland, OH
Contact information:
SENEX ElderCare, Counseling & Training
Fairhill Center
12200 Fairhill Road
Cleveland, OH 44120
216/421-1793
www.senexcare.com
Cost:
Contact sponsor
Exhibits:
Contact sponsor

68

Sponsor:
Simmons College Graduate School of Management
Title:
Leadership Conference
Dates:
1-day conference
May 2002
Location:
New York, NY
Contact information:
Katy Bonnin
Simmons Graduate School of Management Leadership Conference
409 Commonwealth Avenue
Boston, MA 02215
800/208-4476
617/521-3880 (fax)
www.simmons.edu/leadershipconf
Cost:
$595
Exhibits:
Yes. Product information and bookstore. MBA program specifically for women.

69

Sponsor:
SkillPath Seminars
Title:
Conference for Women
Dates:
1-day conference
various dates
Location:
Various locations
Contact information:
SkillPath Seminars
6900 Squibb Road
P.O. Box 2768
Mission, KS 66201
800/873-7545
913/362-4241
www.skillpath.com
Cost:
$199
Exhibits:
No

70

Sponsor:
SkillPath Seminars
Title:
Leadership Development & Team-building
Dates:
1-day conference
various dates
Contact information:
SkillPath Seminars
6900 Squibb Road
P.O. Box 2768
Mission, KS 66201
800/873-7545
913/362-4241
www.skillpath.com
Cost:
$199
CEUs awarded for 6 contact hours
Exhibits:
No

71

Sponsor:
Sloan Industry Centers
Title:
Corporate Strategies for the Digital Economy
Dates:
2-day conference
April 2002
Location:
Cambridge, MA
Contact information:
Center for Management Research
55 William Street
Wellesley, MA 02481
781/239-1111
781/239-1546
www.execseminars.com
Cost:
$1,450 plus hotel
Exhibits:
No

72

Sponsor:
Society for Applied Learning Technology (SALT)
Title:
Education Technology 2002
Dates:
July 24–26, 2002
Location:
Pentagon City, DC

Contact information:
  SALT
  50 Culpeper St.
  Warrenton, VA 20186
    800/457-6812
    540/347-0055
    540/349-3169 (fax)
    www.salt.org
Cost:
  $700; single day $350
Exhibits:
  Contact sponsor

73

Sponsor:
  Society for Human Resource Management (SHRM)
Title:
  Annual Conference and Exposition
Dates:
  June 24–27, 2002
Location:
  Philadelphia, PA
Contact information:
  SHRM
  1800 Duke St.
  Alexandria, VA 22314
    703/548-3440
    703/836-0367 (fax)
    www.shrm.org
Cost:
  Contact sponsor
Exhibits:
  Yes

74

Sponsor:
  Society for Human Resource Management (SHRM)
Title:
  19th Annual Employment Law & Legislative Conference
Dates:
  Spring 2002
Location:
  Washington, DC
Contact information:
  SHRM
  1800 Duke St.
  Alexandria, VA 22314
    703/548-3440
    703/836-0367 (fax)
    www.shrm.org
Cost:
  Contact sponsor
Exhibits:
  No

75

Sponsor:
  Society for Human Resource Management (SHRM)
Title:
  Global Conference
Dates:
  Spring 2002
Location:
  Contact sponsor
Contact information:
  SHRM
  1800 Duke St.
  Alexandria, VA 22314
    703/548-3440
    703/836-0367 (fax)
    www.shrm.org
Cost:
  Contact sponsor
Exhibits:
  Yes

76

Sponsor:
  Society for Human Resource Management (SHRM)
Title:
  Workplace Diversity
Dates:
  December 3–5, 2002
Location:
  San Diego, CA
Contact information:
  SHRM
  1800 Duke St.
  Alexandria, VA 22314
    800/283-SHRM
    703/548-3440
    703/836-0367 (fax)
    www.shrm.org
Cost:
  Contact sponsor
Exhibits:
  Yes

77

Sponsor:
  Society for Technical Communication
Title:
  49th Annual Conference
Dates:
  May 5–8, 2002
Location:
  Nashville, TN
Contact information:
  Society for Technical Communication
  901 North Stuart St., Suite 904
  Arlington, VA 22203-1854
    703/522-4114
    703/522-2075 (fax)
    www.stc-va.org
Cost:
  $525

Exhibits:
  Contact sponsor

78

Sponsor:
  Teletraining Institute
Title:
  Academy 2002 Distance Learning
Dates:
  2 weeks
  August 2002
Location:
  Stillwater, OK
Contact information:
  Kaye White Walker
  Teletraining Institute
  1524 W. Admiral
  Stillwater, OK 74074
    405/743-3463
    800/755-2356
    www.teletrain.com
Cost:
  $3495
Exhibits:
  Contact sponsor

79

Sponsor:
  United States Department of Commerce: Service Industries, International Trade Administration
Title:
  10th Annual Meeting Briefing and Conference on Education and Training in the Global Marketplace
Dates:
  2-day Conference
  May 2002
Location:
  Washington, DC
Contact information:
  Jennifer Moll
  Office of Service Industries
  U.S. Department of Commerce
  14th Street and Constitution Ave.
  Washington, DC 20036
    202/482-1316
Cost:
  $550
Exhibits:
  Yes
  Joint sponsors: Center for Quality Assurance in International Education and National Committee for International Trade in Education

80

Sponsor:
  United States Distance Learning Association (USDLA)

Training Conferences

Title:
  2002 National Policy Forum (for corporations, universities, and public schools)
Dates:
  2-day forum
  April 2002
Location:
  Washington, DC
Contact information:
  USDLA
  140 Gould Street, Suite 200B
  Needham, MA 02494
  781/453-2389 (fax)
  www.elearningexpos.com
Cost:
  $595
Exhibits:
  Yes, in conjunction with government agencies and Advanstar e-Learning conference

81

Sponsor:
  University of Wisconsin–Madison
Title:
  18th Annual Conference on Distance Teaching and Learning
Dates:
  2-day conference
  August 2002
Location:
  Madison, WI
Contact Information:
  Dr. Christine Olgren, Conference Manager
  University of Wisconsin–Madison
  1050 University Ave.
  Room B-136
  Lathrop Hall
  Madison, WI 53706
  608/262-8530
  608-265-7848 (fax)
  www.uwex.edu/disted/conference
Cost:
  Approximately $300
Exhibits:
  Yes
  Also: Pre- and post-conference workshops at $35 each

82

Sponsor:
  University of Wisconsin–Stout
Title:
  Annual Training Conference: e-Learning and Technologies
Dates:
  One-day conference
  Spring and Fall 2001
Location:
  UW–Stout Campus, Menomonie, WI
Contact information:
  Debbie Tenorio
  College of Technology, Engineering and Management
  University of Wisconsin–Stout
  Menomonie, WI 54751
  715/232-2145
  715/232-1274 (fax)
  http://cet.uwstout.edu/epi
Cost:
  $125
Exhibits:
  Contact sponsor

83

Sponsor:
  Work in America Institute
Title:
  Spring Roundtable
Dates:
  Spring 2002
Location:
  Scottsdale, AZ
Contact information:
  Work in America Institute
  700 White Plains Rd.
  Scarsdale, NY 10583
  914/472-9600
  914/472-9606 (fax)
  www.workinamerica.org
Cost:
  $1,850
Exhibits:
  Yes

6.3 Worldwide Conference Centers

"Doing the conference" has become a favorite professional growth activity for more and more professionals at all levels. The big national conferences continue to attract record numbers of attendees, and the business of creating attractive and effective learning spaces to host the crowds is a competitive challenge. In Section 6.3 of *The Trainer's Almanac* we give you a state-by-state and international listing of conference centers, including details about accommodations, meeting facilities, and conference services.

Growth Reflects Current Trends

The continuing trend this year of outsourcing, mergers, and effects of widespread downsizing have again encouraged a booming business in training conferences. The conference experience has become a kind of "one stop shopping center" for staff who still need training and an infusion of the latest information as well as for consultants and vendors who need a venue to display and advertise their services and products. Corporate training centers, eager to bring in some more revenue and share their expertise, have now often opened their doors to the public and to other companies. The practice in recent years of benchmarking best practices, and the universal need for professionals to get together socially and exchange ideas have also spurred trainers to attend conferences. University conference centers have sought more business from corporations and agencies, independent campus-like conference centers—even mansions, historic sites, country houses, and castles—have become a conference business of their own, and hotels have continued to beef up their facilities and hired conference planning staff to provide state-of-the-art spaces and services to attract trainers and trainees. As we enter year 2002, conference trends include: more satellite links, videoconferencing, networked PCs, international phone lines, modems, data ports, ergonomic furniture, printing, food, and travel services.

A Set-up for Learning

The conference has always been an excellent vehicle for individual learning within a large group setting. Today's drive for excellence through the practice of benchmarking and the concept of lifelong learning, our appetites for travel and networking with colleagues, and the impetus of frequent flyer miles and credit card bonus points have all also helped to push us toward conference-going. With smaller corporate training department staffs and a growing proliferation of training entrepreneurs, companies have found that the conference experience can deliver a lot of bang for the training buck. Public-private partnering of all sorts and an awareness of the need to assemble the building blocks of a "learning organization" bring people together to learn from each other.

Wide Choice in Public Facilities

The International Association of Conference Centers (IACC), founded 21 years ago with 22 members, now includes more than 300 member conference facilities worldwide. You can find out more about them on IACC's Web page at *www.iacconline.org*. In our listing here, we have edited IACC's membership list to eliminate the centers that are private or for use of a single company's employees. The conference centers listed here, with permission of the International Association of Conference Centers (IACC), are from the current *Global Membership Directory*. More information about the association and about any individual center listed here is available from Steve Smith, Director of Communications, or Tom Bolman, Executive Vice President, International Association of Conference Centers (IACC), 243 North Lindbergh Blvd., St. Louis, MO 63141, telephone 314/993-8575 or on IACC's Website, *www.iacconline.org*. Conference centers in the following list are presented in alphabetical order by state, followed by conference centers in Canada, South America, Europe, Australia, Africa, and Asia. In the last year, IACC has had 6 new global centers and 26 new U.S. centers join its membership. Those listed here are open to the public. All have recreation facilities. Contact IACC or each specific center for details. Each center links from IACC's Website, *www.iacconline.org*.

ALABAMA

Auburn University Hotel and Conference Center

Address 241 South College Street, Auburn, AL 36849-5645 **Phone** (800) 2AUBURN (334) 821-8200 **Fax** (334) 844-4725

Accommodations 248 rooms (5 handicap accessible).

Meeting Facilities 16 meeting rooms with maximum capacity of 700.

Services Full-range A/V equipment; satellite uplink and downlink capabilities; computer lab; faculty expertise identification; conference management services; and complete program planning.

The Legends at Capitol Hill Conference and Golf Resort

Address 2 North Jackson Street, Montgomery, AL 36104 **Phone** (334) 223-5793 **Fax** (334) 223-5797

Accommodations 90 guest rooms, 74 single rooms, 2 8-bedroom villas.

Meeting Facilities 10 meeting rooms.

Services None listed.

ARIZONA

Sedona Center for Arts & Technology

Address Yavapai College, 4215 Arts Village Drive, Sedona, AZ 86339 **Phone** (520) 204-2691 **Fax** (520) 204-2683

Accommodations 100 guest rooms.

Meeting Facilities 10 meeting rooms.

Services Standard services.

Tempe Mission Palms Hotel and Conference Center

Address 60 E. Fifth Street, Tempe, AZ 85281 **Phone** (887) 784-1748 and (408) 894-1400 **Fax** (480) 968-7677

Accommodations 303 sleeping rooms; phones with voice mail and lines for PC usage.

Meeting Facilities 14 meeting rooms with 30,000 sq. ft. of space. Outdoor rooftop terrace with fireplace. Business center, ballroom, executive boardroom.

Services ISDN lines for video conferencing and Internet access. Wired for fiber optic; data ports in every meeting room.

YWCA of the USA Leadership Development Center

Address 9440 North 25th Avenue, Phoenix, AZ 85021 **Phone** (602) 944-0569 **Fax** (602) 997-5112

Accommodations Close to major hotels: Sheraton, Marriott, Holiday Inn, and the Wyndhams.

Meeting Facilities 52,000 sq. ft. training/conference/meeting/banquet facility with 22 meeting spaces; 2 outdoor classroom areas; 2 auditoriums; 2,500 sq. ft. fitness area with hardwood floors, mirrored wall, showers and lockers.

Services Full media services; TV studio and teleconferencing capabilities. Customized meeting packages, professional conference planners. Outdoor classrooms.

ARKANSAS

University of Arkansas Center for Continuing Education

Address 2 University Center, Fayetteville, AR 72701 **Phone** (501) 575-3604 **Fax** (501) 575-7232

Accommodations 236 rooms at adjacent Hilton Hotel.

Meeting Facilities 400-theater and 70-theater seat auditoriums; 11 conference rooms seating 650 lecture style, or 400 classroom style.

Services Professional staff meets a full range of conference/meeting needs. Complete A/V production facilities including satellite teleconferencing.

Winrock International Conference Center

Address 38 Winrock Drive, Morrilton, AR 72110 **Phone** (501) 727-5435 **Fax** (501) 727-5242

Accommodations 35 single or 40 double occupancy rooms

Meeting Facilities 4 large meeting rooms seating up to 250; 4 breakout rooms seating 10–16 persons.

Services Conference Service Department handles planning and on-site meeting coordination. Basic A/V equipment provided.

CALIFORNIA

Chaminade Executive Conference Center

Address One Chaminade Lane, Santa Cruz, CA 95065 **Phone** (800) 283-6569 **Fax** (408) 476-4798

Accommodations 152 rooms showcasing mountain and forest views; Air-conditioned rooms offer luxury accommodations including room service; 10 parlor suites with conference table and wet bar.

Meeting Facilities 12 meeting rooms (10 rooms with windows). The largest "Santa Cruz Room" is 2,600 sq. ft. A/V data control center.

Included in CMP: Standard A/V package (25" monitor and VCR, 16mm movie projector, 35 mm slide projector, overhead projector, flip chart with marker or white board with marker, podium, microphone).

New Business Center; conference concierge for on-site needs; fax/copy services; typing; telephone; messages; personal conference coordinators for planning details; professional A/V technicians on site.

Santa Cruz Room holds 20 8′ × 10′ booths. Executive Fitness Center holds 45 8′ tabletop displays.

Services Full guest services staff, concierge and free valet parking. Two phones in each room—one modem-compatible. Gift shop.

Davidson Executive Conference Center

Address 3415 S. Figueroa St., Los Angeles, CA 90089-0871 **Phone** (213) 740-5956 **Fax** (213) 740-9366 **e-mail** confrnce@usc.edu

Accommodations Rooms for up to 4,000 guests from May through August.

Meeting Facilities Newly renovated state-of-the-art center; 8 rooms with breakout capabilities, accommodating up to 400; Ergonomically designed seating with writing tables.

Services Concierge, business center with PC & Macintosh workstations, World Wide Web access, e-mail forwarding. Daily newspapers, parcel and postal services, self-parking adjacent to center. Satellite uplink, videoconferencing, credit card phone and self-fax capability, USC bookstore, gift department services.

The Hayes Mansion Conference Center

Address 200 Edenvale Ave., San Jose, CA 95136 **Phone** (408) 362-3200; (800) 420-3200 **Fax** (408) 362-2388

Accommodations 135 guest rooms and suites, work/study areas with multiple phone lines, modems, voice mail, in-room safes. Historic 1905 landmark.

Meeting Facilities 15 meeting rooms, 15,000 sq. ft. with state-of-the-art A/V, telecommunications, "help button" services.

Services Video conferencing, teleconferencing, networked computing, closed-circuit TV, secretarial services, notary public.

Kellogg West Conference Center

Address 3801 W. Temple Boulevard, Bldg. 76, Pomona, CA 91768 **Phone** (909) 869-2222 **Fax** (909) 869-4214

Accommodations 85 guest rooms, 3 suites.

Meeting Facilities 12,000 sq. ft. including auditorium seating 300. Registration desk, exhibit area, all meeting rooms have scenic views.

Services A/V on site with technical staff and complete inventory of equipment. University Speakers' bureau available. Complimentary Ontario airport shuttle. Many University resources available.

Kennolyn Conference Center

Address 8400 Glen Haven Road, Soquel, CA 95073 **Phone** (831) 479-6700 **Fax** (831) 479-6730

Accommodations 26 guest rooms; log cabins filled with antiques, down comforters, wood stoves.

Meeting Facilities 9 meeting rooms, large outdoor amphitheater. Many rooms ideal for discussion groups, set with overstuffed chairs and couches.

Services Customized personal services.

Morgan Run Resort and Club

Address 5690 Cancha de Golf, Rancho Santa Fe, CA 92091 **Phone** (858) 756-2471 **Fax** (858) 759-2196

Accommodations 89 sleeping rooms.

Meeting Facilities 6 rooms.

Services None listed.

Network Meeting Center at Techmart-Santa Clara

Address 5201 Great America Parkway, Suite 122, Santa Clara, CA 95054 **Phone** (408) 562-6111 **Fax** (408) 562-5703

Accommodations N/A (Adjacent to 500-room Westin Hotel Santa Clara).

Meeting Facilities 17 dedicated meeting rooms plus exhibit and event space.

Services Conference planning, meeting coordinators, complete A/V inventory on-site, 8-hr. chairs, videoconferencing.

PG&E Learning Center

Address 3301 Crow Canyon Road, San Ramon, CA 94583 **Phone** (510) 866-7500 **Fax** (510) 866-7378

Accommodations 119 rooms, each with a double extra long bed.

Meeting Facilities 40 rooms, totalling 27,000 sq. ft., plus a 5,300 sq. ft. conference center, breakout rooms, and a 1,700 sq. ft. auditorium. Each room has standard A/V equipment and projectors.

Services Professional meeting planners, business center, A/V specialists, phone message center, video conferencing, dry cleaning.

Resort at Squaw Creek

Address 400 Squaw Creek Road, P.O. Box 3333, Olympic Valley, CA 96146 **Phone** (800) 327-3353 **Fax** (916) 581-5407

Accommodations Luxurious mountain-view accommodations with 405 rooms including 204 suites.

Meeting Facilities 33,000-sq. ft. conf. center with 36 rooms. All rooms with multiple electrical outlets, indiv. controls for climate, sound, and 110V electricity. Rear and front screen projection. Audio conferencing. State-of-the-art A/V production capabilities.

At no charge (with CMP or CP pkg.): Standard A/V package including 25" monitor and VCR, 35 mm slide projector, overhead projector, flip chart with marker, white board with marker, podium, microphone.

Conference concierge for on-site needs; fax/copy services; typing; telephone messages; professional conference planning managers for planning details; professional A/V staff.

The Grand Sierra Ballroom has 9,525 sq. ft. of exhibit space and Squaw Peak Ballroom has 5,120 sq. ft.

Services Gift shops, room service, laundry, dry cleaning, ice machines, golf/ski tuning and pros, sports locker room. Concierge, conf. concierge, valet parking.

COLORADO

Aspen Meadows Resort Hotel

Address 845 Meadows Road, Aspen, CO 81611 **Phone** (800) 452-4240 (970) 925-4240 **Fax** (970) 544-7852

Accommodations 98 oversized guest rooms and suites.

Meeting Facilities 11,000 sq. ft., incl. state-of-the-art conference center.

Services Valet, business center, notary, complimentary airport transfers.

The Inverness Hotel & Golf Club

Address 200 Inverness Drive West, Englewood, CO 80112 **Phone** (800) 346-4891 (303) 799-5800 **Fax** (303) 799-5874

Accommodations 302 guest rooms and suites.

Meeting Facilities 33 dedicated meeting rooms, seating 10–350, with built-in A/V.

35mm slide, 16 mm film and overhead projectors; audio systems, video cassette & audio tape players.

Professional Conference Services staff, plus A/V technicians.

30,000 sq. ft. in conference wing.

Conference Services Department handles planning and on-site meeting coordination, fully-equipped A/V department and graphics studio, executive club services, complete business center.

Services Secretarial, courier, photographic and graphic design.

CONNECTICUT

Gray Conference Center University of Hartford

Address 200 Bloomfield Avenue, W. Hartford, CT 06117 **Phone** (860)

768-4996 **Fax** (860) 768-5016
e-mail gibbs@uhavax.hartford.edu

Accommodations Residence halls/apartments available, accommodating 3,200 May–August.

Meeting Facilities Executive meeting rooms, classrooms, auditoriums, banquet facilities, theater. Capacity ranging from 8–4,600.

Services 4 seminar rooms, 7 breakout rooms, 225-seat auditorium, and restaurant. Housing options available at nearby hotels during the academic year. Downlink teleconference capabilities. Other campus facilities including auditorium, theater, classrooms, meeting rooms are also available.

Hastings Hotel
A Dolce Conference Center

Address 85 Sigourney Street, Hartford, CT 06105 **Phone** (860) 727-4200 **Fax** (860) 727-4217

Accommodations 271 guest rooms and suites, each equipped with a spacious work station including dataports for Internet connectivity. 5 executive suites; 12 parlor suites.

Meeting Facilities 50 meeting rooms for 10–500 persons. Includes 28 conference rooms, 3 amphitheaters, 13 breakout rooms, 8 conference suites; 3 PC training rooms each with 15 networked computers and an instructor's station; Complete A/V and computer-based presentation equipment.

Services Skilled lighting and audio technicians, A/V production including digital editing, transcribing, typesetting, computer-generated graphics in video, slide, or hard copy formats. Desktop publishing and binding services. Fully-trained conference coordinators.

Heritage Inn,
A Dolce Conference Center

Address Heritage Road, Southbury, CT 06488 **Phone** (860) 264-8200 **Fax** (860) 264-6910

Accommodations 163 guest rooms including 5 suites.

Meeting Facilities 25 dedicated meeting rooms; 3 rear screen rooms; amphitheatre for 150; Conference Service Desk.

Services Specialty shops; shopping arcade; free parking for 200 cars.

Prudential Center for Learning & Innovation

Address Weed Avenue, Norwalk, CT 06850 **Phone** (203) 852-7300 **Fax** (203) 852-7364

Accommodations 116 king-bedded rooms with a second telephone line and closed-circuit TV.

Meeting Facilities 28 meeting rooms including 2 amphitheaters, 3,600 sq. ft. multipurpose room with 24-foot rear screen. 17 breakout rooms. Extensive A/V and computer equipment.

Services Expansive complete meeting package includes name badges, tent cards, and free parking.

DELAWARE

Conference Centers of the University of Delaware

Address 107 Clayton Hall, Newark, DE 19716 **Phone** (302) 831-2214 **Fax** (302) 831-2998

Accommodations 5–1,000 people.

Meeting Facilities 70 conference rooms, large auditorium. Three statewide locations.

Services In-house A/V equipment including satellite dish. Full-meal plans. Summer housing for 5,000 plus. Fax machine, copying, conference planners available. Free parking. Year-round housing for 38 in Virden Conference Center in Lewes, and apartment suites for 172 at Newark campus.

Hotel du Pont

Address 11th and Market Streets, Wilmington, DE 19801 **Phone** (302) 594-3107 **Fax** (302) 434-3403

Accommodations 217 guest rooms.

Meeting Facilities 30 meeting rooms.

Services N/A.

DISTRICT OF COLUMBIA

Academy for Educational Development Conference Center

Address 1825 Connecticut Avenue, NW, 8th floor, Washington, DC 20009 **Phone** (202) 884-8000 **Fax** (202) 884-8996

Accommodations Available at several nearby hotels.

Meeting Facilities Academy Hall plus 11 breakout rooms to accommodate groups of 2–300.

Services Full service day center staffed with managers in conference planning, media services, and conference services. Four translation booths with wireless headset receivers; wide range of audio/visual equipment. Three Internet stations for e-mail.

Gallaudet University Kellogg Conference Center

Address 800 Florida Ave., NE, Washington, DC 20002 **Phone** (202) 651-6000 **Fax** (202) 651-6103

Accommodations 93 accessible guest rooms, including 6 suites.

Meeting Facilities 21 meeting and breakout rooms, seating 5–150, 274-seat auditorium, exec. boardroom, tiered classroom, ballroom for groups to 400.

Services Complete conference planning services and business center. Extensive A/V, incl. multilink interactive video conferencing, full TV broadcast and online editing capabilities, satellite capabilities, Internet accessibility, on-site technicians. Total accessible facility featuring TTY telephones, visual signaling devices throughout.

FLORIDA

The Conference Center at Dodgertown

Address P.O. Box 2887, 3901 26th Street, Vero Beach, FL 32961 **Phone** (561) 569-4900 **Fax** (561) 569-9209 e-mail ladodger@iu.net

Accommodations Cluster of modern, redecorated villas with 88 rooms, including 10 executive suites and 2 pool-side cabanas.

Meeting Facilities 20 meeting rooms with multiple electrical and microphone outlets, and controls for sound and electricity. Executive Leadership Course.

At no charge: PA system, tape recorders, portable and floor microphones, A/V replacement parts, overhead, 16mm sound, 35mm slide projectors, projection screens, remote-control cords, lecterns, podiums, blackboards, easels, and tables, on-site professional conference coordinators, A/V repairmen. At a charge: CCTV equipment, name badges, opaque projectors, and 8mm sound projectors, portable stages, duplicating machines, stenographer, musicians, A/V operators, security guards.

Jackie Robinson Room has 3,000 sq. ft. of exhibit space. Holds 25 8' × 10' or 20 10' × 10' booths.

Services Newsstand, sundries, gifts, and women's/men's sportswear shops; 3 min. from local hospital.

Rear screen projectors, typewriters, truck/van, messenger service, notary public, printers, photographers, carpenters, sign painters, electricians, laborers.

Conference Center of the Americas

Address 1200 Anastasia Avenue, Coral Gables, FL 33134
Phone (305) 913-3193 **Fax** (305) 913-3120

Accommodations 400 sleeping rooms with king and/or double beds. Feather duvets. Writing desk and fax machine.

Meeting Facilities Two amphitheaters, 17 meeting rooms. High-speed Internet access, dual and rear-screen projection, built-in videoconferencing.

Services 24-hour room service. Car rental/delivery on site. Business center.

University of Florida Hotel and Conference Center

Address 1714 Southwest 34th Street, Gainesville, FL 32607
Phone (352) 378-0070
Fax (352) 378-8141

Accommodations 248 rooms in 7-story highrise; 2 phone lines per room.

Meeting Facilities 13 meeting rooms on same floor; 7,000 sq. ft. ballroom.

Services Direct Internet connection, business center, conference services desk, complete A/V inventory.

GEORGIA

Aberdeen Woods Conference Center

Address 201 Aberdeen Parkway, Peachtree City, GA 30269
Phone (770) 487-2666 **Fax** (770) 631-4096; Sales (770) 487-3029

Accommodations 233 guest rooms.

Meeting Facilities 150-seat auditorium, 59 individual meeting rooms; 40-seat and 80-seat indoor amphitheaters; all A/V equipped.

Services Conference planning, A/V staff.

Chateau Elan Resort & Conference Center

Address 100 Rue Charlemagne, Braselton, GA 30517
Phone (800) 233-WINE (770) 932-0900 **Fax** (770) 271-6005

Accommodations 276 Inn rooms, 14 spa rooms, 9 2- and 3-bedroom villas.

Meeting Facilities 25,000 sq. ft. of meeting space, including 2 ballrooms, 60-seat amphitheatre, 15 additional meeting rooms.

Services On-property transportation includes 2 24-passenger buses, 3 12-passenger vans, 4 VIP vehicles; room service; business center, AV staff, concierge, gift shop.

Emerald Pointe Resort & Conference Center

Address 7000 Holiday Road, Lake Lanier Islands, Georgia 30518
Phone (770) 945-8787 **Fax** (770) 932-8031

Accommodations 216 guest rooms, recently-rennovated suites. 30 2-bedroom lake houses.

Meeting Facilities 24 meeting rooms; 21,000 sq. ft. of flexible meeting space.

Services State-of-the-art technological support.

Emory Conference Center Hotel

Address 1615 Clifton Road, Atlanta, GA 30329 **Phone** (404) 712-6000
Fax (404) 712-6025
e-mail sales@ecch.emory.edu

Accommodations 195 deluxe guest rooms, 3 spacious suites. All guest rooms include hair dryer, coffeemaker, iron/ironing board, two-line telephone with data port & voice mail. All double-bedded rooms offer double vanity sinks with two well-lit desks; 15 ADA/accessible rooms.

Meeting Facilities 30,000 total sq. ft. of function space. 2 amphitheaters: 1 seats 200, the other seats 70. 5,400 sq. ft. ballroom; 3,000 sq. ft. Garden Courtyard, numerous additional meeting rooms.

Ergonomic chairs and hard-top writing surfaces. Advanced A/V capabilities include satellite downlink with KU and C bands, teleconferencing, multi-image projections equipment, computer data presentation, interactive video system and dedicated fiber optic phone lines.

A/V technicians, electrician, notary public.

Services Concierge, conference planning, area transportation, newsstand/gift shop, ATM, business center. Complimentary garage parking for 200.

Evergreen Conference Resort

Address P.O. Box 1363, One Lakeview Drive, Stone Mountain, GA 30086 **Phone** (770) 879-9900
Fax (770) 469-9013

Accommodations 250 guest rooms-suites.

Meeting Facilities 20 rooms; 45,209 sq. ft. of meeting and exhibit space.

Services Conference planning, secretarial, messenger, language, graphic services. Closed-circuit TV, teleconferencing, overhead viewgraph, tape recording, easels and blackboards, videotape recording, film and slide projectors, PC computers.

Hartsfield Airport Executive Conference Center

Address Airport Atrium # 300, 6000 North Terminal Pkwy., PO Box 20509, Atlanta, GA 30320
Phone (800) 713-1359 **Fax** (404) 530-4251

Accommodations No sleeping rooms. Complimentary shuttles to major airport hotels.

Meeting Facilities 24,000 sq. ft. including classrooms, press room, VIP suite, boardroom, and computer work stations.

Services Catering, conference planning staff, video conferencing, business services. Onsite airlines services, rail service, shuttles, post office, concierge.

Marietta Conference Center & Resort

Address 500 Powder Spring St., Marietta, GA 30064 **Phone** (770) 427-2500 **Fax** (770) 429-9577

Accommodations 200 guest rooms, 1 Presidential Suite, 8 parlor suites.

Meeting Facilities 20,000 total sq. ft. conf. space, 6,500 sq. ft. grand ballroom, 2 exec. boardrooms, 18 breakout rooms.

Services 24-hour business center, 2 conf. concierge desks, valet. 24-hour room service, airport shuttle.

Timber Ridge Conference Center

Address 5601 North Allen Road, Mableton, GA 30059
Phone (770) 941-2176
Fax (770) 732-1580

Accommodations 22 twins, 2 singles (barrier free).

Meeting Facilities 5 meeting rooms accommodating 15–120 people.

Services All A/V included, standard A/V package, secretarial services, including typing, photocopying, and Fax. Gift shop. Owned/operated by NW Georgia Girl Scout Council.

The Southern Conference Center

Address 188 14th Street Northeast, Atlanta, GA 30361 **Phone** (404) 892-6000 **Fax** (404) 876-3276

Accommodations 467 guest rooms.

Meeting Facilities 25 meeting rooms; 7,600 sq. ft. total meeting space.

Services Standard conference services.

Wyndham Peachtree Executive Conference Center

Address 2443 State Hwy. 54 West, Peachtree City, GA 30269
Phone (770) 487-2000
Fax (770) 487-4428

Accommodations 250 contemporary conference center guest rooms and 6 suites. All rooms are soundproof and have air conditioning control, color TV, balconies and direct-dial phones. In-room coffeemakers, iron and ironing board.

Meeting Facilities 24 meeting rooms for 10–300 people. Two ballrooms can accommodate up to 400 for banquets and 600 for receptions; all rooms have multiple electrical/microphone/phone outlets and controls for climate and sound. 200-seat amphitheater with front and rear screen projection.

Pads, pencils, direction signs available. Installed PA system, portable stages, tape recorder/player, portable and floor microphones, duplicating machines, teleconferencing facilities.

Electrician, A/V operators, notary public, graphics department.

The Peachtree Ballroom has 5,400 sq. ft. of exhibit space.

Services Conference Planning, ground transportation, airline ticketing, newsstand, gift shop, concierge. Free outdoor parking, cap. 400; full Business Center.

Stenographer, translator, photographer, entertainers.

Complete Business Center for administrative services, fax, photocopies, messenger.

ILLINOIS

Andersen Worldwide Center for Professional Education

Address 1405 North Fifth Avenue, St. Charles, IL 60174 **Phone** (630) 444-4355 **Fax** (630) 584-7212 **e-mail** pam.a.zawne@awo.com

Accommodations 1,277 sleeping rooms, including 21 suites.

Meeting Facilities 135 meeting rooms, 6 auditorium bays, and 3 amphitheaters; 27,000 sq. ft. of exhibit space.

Services 1,200 personal computers incl. 750 networked with on-site support, conference planning, TV studio, teleconferencing, business TV, interactive multimedia, Outdoor Adventure Program w/30 low/high level ropes course, on-site travel agency.

CNA2 North Conference Center

Address CNA Plaza, 2 North, Chicago, IL 60685 **Phone** (312) 822-6847 **Fax** (312) 817-3708

Accommodations Hotel rooms within walking distance.

Meeting Facilities Multi-faceted meeting rooms with built-in A/V and network capabilities. On-site A/V department.

Services Dedicated conference coordinator; conference concierge.

Doubletree Hotel North Shore Executive Meeting Center

Address 9599 Skokie Boulevard, Skokie, IL 60077 **Phone** (800) 879-4458 **Fax** (847) 679-2385

Accommodations 364 rooms. Oversized work desks with data ports, ergonomic chairs, voice mail.

Meeting Facilities 18 rooms, 10,000 sq. ft. executive board room; fiber-optic cabling, ergonomic seating, individual temperature control, soft-seating meeting rooms, state-of-the-art A/V with dedicated staff.

Services Business Center, on-site planner, two meeting coordinators, security.

Galvin Center for Continuing Education Motorola, Inc.

Address 1295 East Algonquin Road, Schaumberg, IL 60196
Phone (847) 576-8600
Fax (847) 576-8691

Accommodations Cooperative arrangements with hotels nearby.

Meeting Facilities 2 auditoriums seating 60–220; 1 large classroom seating 40–60; 18 standard classrooms seating 30; 37 breakout rooms; 4 executive conference rooms; 5 computer labs.

Services Each room equipped with 2 overhead projectors, projection system and VCR for recording and playback. Also available: satellite links, videoconferencing, cameras, slide projectors, data show. Labs include 16 IBM-ATs and 12 Macintosh computers.

Harrison Conference Center at Lake Bluff

Address Green Bay Road, Lake Bluff, IL 60044 **Phone** (847) 295-1100 **Fax** (847) 295-8792 **e-mail** lakebluff@iacc.iacconline.com

Accommodations 5-story Mediterranean-style villa comprised of 83 guest rooms. All have climate control, color TV, oversized beds, and heat lamps.

Meeting Facilities 11 meeting rooms for 2–200. All rooms have climate control, multiple electrical/microphone outlets, 110V electricity, direct truck access.

At no charge: Reel and cassette tape recorders; overhead, 16mm sound, 35mm slide projectors; portable projection screens; podiums; chairs; blackboards, on-site professional conference coordinators, A/V repairs.

For a fee: 35mm sound; Panaboard; LCD panels; opaque projectors; typewriters; duplicating machines; CCTV equipment with guest room relay capability, stenographer, musicians, A/V operators, security guards, photographer.

The "Great Hall" is 2,450 sq. ft. and can seat 200 theater style.

Services Newsstand, sundries, laundry, dry cleaning, free outdoor parking for 200 cars.

Messenger service, print shop, notary public, carpentry shop, display builder, sign painter, plumbers, electricians, locksmith, laborers.

James L. Allen Center

Address 2169 N. Campus Dr., Evanston, IL 60208 **Phone** (708) 864-9270 **Fax** (708) 491-4323

Accommodations 150 rooms (handicap accessible).

Meeting Facilities 7 rooms seating 50–230, and 38 rooms seating 10–35.

Services Full range of A/V services; computer lab and all networked PCs in conference and study rooms.

Marriott Hickory Ridge Conference Centre

Address 1195 Summerhill Drive, Lisle, IL 60532-3190 **Phone** (800) 225-4722 (708) 971-5023 **Fax** (708) 971-6939

Accommodations 376 single rooms including 50 2-room suites; handicapped and non-smoking rooms available. All have individual climate control and free cable TV.

Meeting Facilities 47 conference rooms seating 10–200, with rear-screen projection systems and closed circuit TV; majority of the rooms are wired for computer training; amphitheater for up to 90 people; board room, 3 executive meeting rooms; and 75 breakout rooms.

At no charge: Doublesize flip chart w/ markers, overhead screen and projector, 35mm slide projector, lighted podium, white boards w/ markers, paper and pencils, personal conference coordinator, A/V technicians, Business Center telephone messages, Notary Public.

For a fee: VCR with rear screen video projection, recorders, video cameras, closed-circuit TV cameras, spotlights, typewriters, PCs, fax/copy services, typing, stenographer, electricians, A/V operators, developers and speakers, simultaneous translation equipment for interpreters, signs, security, graphic arts, photographer, and shipping.

Up to 20 8' × 10' booths.

Services Executive floor, message board displayed throughout building, gift shop, laundry, dry cleaning, ice and vending machines, local shuttle. Special diet menus available. Free parking.

Entertainers. Other services upon request.

Northern Illinois University Hoffman Estates

Address 5555 Trillium Boulevard, Hoffman Estates, IL 60192 **Phone** (847) 645-3000 **Fax** (815) 753-8865 **e-mail** kgilmer@nie.edu

Accommodations Cooperative arrangements with local hotels as close as 5 mi. from the Center.

Meeting Facilities 4 executive training rooms with adjacent break service; 11 conference rooms; an auditorium seating 250 (hearing accessible); 2 networked computer laboratories; 4 breakout rooms; individual climate and lighting controls.

All rooms are equipped with ceiling-mounted VCR or video projector, overhead projector, marker boards, flip charts, presentation rail system, and projection screens. Executive rooms and auditorium include a computerized lectern system. Other equipment includes portable video/data projection, mobile computer, video camcorder, slide projector, wireless mikes, and opaque projector. All equipment is included in room rental at no additional charge.

Conference services; in-house audio/visual/computer technology staff; phone line for laptops; business desk services including fax, transparencies, photocopying, and message boards.

Services Corporate rates with selected local hotels for sleeping rooms; free parking.

Musicians, florists, recreation, ground transportation.

Oak Brook Hills Resort & Conference Center

Address 3500 Midwest Rd., Oak Brook, IL 60522-7010 **Phone** (630) 850-5555 **Fax** (630) 850-5569

Accommodations 382 elegantly appointed guest rooms including 38 suites, "business class" rooms and a concierge level with private lounge.

Meeting Facilities 35,000 sq. ft. of flexible meeting space including 140-seat amphitheater, 11 boardrooms and newly renovated Grand Ballroom.

Services Full conference planning staff, complimentary parking, concierge, full-service audiovisual, gift shop, Pro Shop, and dry cleaning.

Summit Executive Centre

Address 205 N. Michigan Avenue, Chicago, IL 60601 **Phone** (312) 938-5053 **Fax** (312) 861-0324 **e-mail** 74117.444@compuserve.com

Accommodations Connected to 3 major hotels with over a total of 3,000 guest rooms.

Meeting Facilities 20,000 square ft. with 15 rooms able to accommodate groups of 3–125 people. Dedicated computer lab with networked PCs available to accommodate groups up to 26 people.

In-house A/V staff with in-house equipment: overheads, slide projectors, flip charts, screens, VCR and monitor, cameras, LCD panels, video projectors.

Concierge to assist in access to all city amenities; professional audio visual staff; in-house caterer; business center.

Services Underground parking; in-house A/V technical support; concierge; conference planning; special rates at all adjoining hotels for sleeping rooms; team building program using the world's tallest indoor rock-climbing wall (located next door at the athletic club).

Computer rentals.

Parking; conference planning; resource center for educational programming ideas; training consultants.

INDIANA

The Marten House Hotel and Lilly Conference Center

Address 1801 West 86th St., Indianapolis, IN 46260
Phone (317) 872-4111
Fax (317) 415-5245

Accommodations 176 rooms featuring comfortable work areas, data ports.

Meeting Facilities Conference center features multi-layered state-of-the-art auditorium seating 220. Fully equipped breakout rooms. Hotel features 2 ballrooms, 2 boardrooms, 7 breakout rooms.

Services Videoconferencing, computer lab, satellite up/downlinks.

University of Notre Dame Center for Continuing Education

Address Notre Dame Avenue, P.O. Box 1008, Notre Dame, IN 46556
Phone (219) 631-6691
Fax (219) 631-8083

Accommodations 92 rooms (handicap).

Meeting Facilities 70,000 sq. ft. of meeting space available; 23 conference rooms seating 8–375.

State-of-the-art translation equipment and auditorium; most rooms equipped for audio and video recording, closed-circuit television and satellite reception and broadcasting; full audiovisual support available.

Notre Dame's Center for Continuing Education is a full-service conference center. Each conference, course or meeting is coordinated by a member of the Center's professional faculty who administers all the logistics of the program. In addition to detailed coordination by a member of the Center's professional staff, fees also include the following professional and clerical services: conference planning, marketing and evaluation; all required meeting facilities and exhibit space at the Center for Continuing Education and elsewhere on campus; advance and on-site registration, including preparation and mailing of promotional materials, confirmation of registration and preparation of name tags and rosters; full administration and accounting of program funds; secretarial support services (word processing, typing, copying, collating of handout materials); folders, maps, and other informational literature needed by program recipients.

Services Gift shop, dry cleaning, safety deposit boxes, room service, library, fax, and all University facilities and services by arrangement.

University Place Conference Center and Hotel

Address 850 West Michigan Street, Indianapolis, IN 46202-5198
Phone (800) 410-MEET (317) 274-2700 (conf. ctr.), 269-9000 (hotel) **Fax** (317) 274-3878 (conf. ctr.), 231-5168 (hotel)

Accommodations 278-room AAA 4-diamond hotel is integrated with conference center. Includes 16 suites as well as rooms for disabled. Non-smoking rooms avail. All rooms have climate control, sprinkler system, direct-dial phones, working-size desks, lounge chairs and ottomans, voice mail, computer hook-ups, TV feature movies.

Meeting Facilities 28 dedicated self-contained meeting rooms ranging from 340-seat auditorium to breakout rooms; includes two tiered meeting rooms, 2 boardrooms, and 1 ballroom.

Included in package: Overhead, and slide projectors, sound system, lectern, screens, VCRs, monitors, audio recorder, white board, easel/pads/markers, conference management and meeting support, on-site registration assistance, name tags, folders, meeting room signs.

For a fee: Total turnkey conference planning from announcement brochure to final financial statement. Special A/V services— A/V production, editing, photography, teleconferencing, technicians, audience-response system, translation facilities. Office support— photocopying, transparencies, fax, notary, desktop publishing.

Services Business Service Center with computers available. Underground 385-car parking garage, sky walk to Indiana University Medical Center, and full-time technical staff. Services center with computers available. Web: http://www.iupui.edu/it/univplac/uplac.html

Stenographer, photographer, displays, banners, locksmiths, entertainers, decorators.

MARYLAND

Belmont Conference Center

Address 6555 Belmont Woods Rd., Elkridge, MD 21075 **Phone** (410) 796-4300 **Fax** (410) 796-4565

Accommodations 21 rooms, individually decorated.

Meeting Facilities 4 rooms, 2,100 sq. ft. Spectacular views, spacious, many windows, easy access to outdoors, plenty of break space, flexible set-ups.

Services Conference coordinators, business center, transportation coordinator.

Burkshire Guest Suites and Conference Center

Address 10 West Burke Avenue, Towson, MD 21204 **Phone** (410) 324-8103 **Fax** (410) 830-3749 **e-mail** emke-n@toa.towson.edu

Accommodations 116 suites (including living/dining room and full kitchen).

Meeting Facilities 11,000 sq. ft. of meeting space, 19 meeting rooms seating 10–150.

Services Full conference planning and on-site A/V capabilities with technician services, business center, a Marriott Conference Center.

The Conference Center at Sheppard Pratt

Address 6501 North Charles Street, Baltimore, MD 21204
Phone (410) 938-3906
Fax (410) 938-4099

Accommodations N/A.

Meeting Facilities 200-seat auditorium, 5 classrooms seating 20–70 each.

Services Relaxed environment located on 100 acres of beautifully landscaped grounds. Experienced catering, A/V and conference services professionals. Full range of A/V equipment and teleconferencing capabilities.

George Meany Center for Labor Studies

Address 10,000 New Hampshire Ave., Silver Spring, MD 20903
Phone (301) 431-5417
Fax (301) 431-5411

Accommodations 115 sleeping rooms; 7 handicap accessible. Accommodations feature study desks, coffeemakers, free use of laundry room.

Meeting Facilities Attractive meeting room with ergonomic seating, in-house A/V and technical staff. 13 rooms seating 6–175 persons.

Services Campus on 47 scenic acres located 20 minutes from Washington, DC. Serves AFL-CIO union affiliates only.

The Inn & Conference Center at University of Maryland University College

Address University Boulevard at Adelphi Road, College Park, MD 20740 **Phone** (301) 985-7303
Fax (301) 985-7445

Accommodations 108 hotel rooms, 3 suites; modem compatible.

Meeting Facilities Over 32,000 square feet of meeting space. Ballroom seats 750 for banquets, beautiful auditorium for 750, Executive Board Room, 2 equipped computer labs, 29 total meeting rooms.

Motorized screens, chalkboards in majority of rooms, PCs in computer labs, tackable wall railings, teleconferencing and satellite uplink capabilities, a built-in rear-screen projection room.

Full conference services; in-house A/V; full-time Conference Coordinator; electrician.

8,200 sq. ft. ballroom available for exhibits. Ballroom concourse holds up to 20 8′ × 10's as well.

Services Newsstand with gift items, free newspaper for overnight guests, parking garage capacity 850, dry cleaning service, cable TV, Conference Planning, tape recording, videotaping, rear-screen capabilities.

Photographers, florists, decorators, golf lessons, entertainers, printers.

The Magna Center for Executive Learning

Address 901 Dual Highway, Hagerstown, MD 21740
Phone (301) 733-5566
Fax (301) 797-4286

Accommodations 210 guest rooms each with phone and dataport.

Meeting Facilities 12 meeting rooms including 4 Learning Centers with contiguous breakout areas and built-in A/V.

Services Business services provided.

Maritime Institute Conference Center

Address 5700 Hammonds Ferry Road, Linthicum Heights, MD 21090
Phone (410) 859-5700
Fax (410) 859-0942;
Telex: 87-637

Accommodations 220 guest rooms; 8 suites on 80 suburban wooded acres.

Meeting Facilities 40 meeting rooms covering 41,000 sq. ft., from 204 sq. ft. to 5,100 sq. ft; 250-seat tiered auditorium; house-owned A/V; complete A/V studio.

Services 2 free laundry rooms, dry cleaning service, Ship's Store, newsstand.

William F. Bolger Center for Leadership Development

Address 9600 Newbridge Drive, Potomac, MD 20854 **Phone** (301) 983-7000 **Fax** (301) 983-7728

Accommodations 470 rooms, including 95 new deluxe rooms and suites, cable TV, dataports.

Meeting Facilities 60 rooms with 60,000 sq. ft. Dedicated meeting rooms feature windows, business center, new furnishings. Capacity 500 persons.

Services Free nightly transportation to Bethesda, Metro, and Montgomery Mall. Complimentary computer usage and Internet access.

Wye River Conference Center at the Aspen Institute

Address P.O. Box 222, Queenstown, MD 21658 **Phone** (410) 827-7400
Fax (410) 827-9295

Accommodations 3 private houses with 86 guest rooms.

Meeting Facilities Country estate setting for groups of 5–120.

Services Business services, state-of-the-art video/teleconferencing and audio/visual equipment.

MASSACHUSETTS

Batterymarch Conference Center

Address 60 Batterymarch Street, 2nd Floor, Boston, MA 02110
Phone (617) 556-8000
Fax (617) 556-9901

Accommodations 100 guest rooms in the new Wyndham Boston Hotel, in which Batterymarch Conference Center is located.

Meeting Facilities 13 meeting rooms, 9 fully-equipped meeting rooms and 4 amphitheatres. Rooms equipped with tackable walls, white boards, presentation rails, electronic screens, ceiling-mounted video/data projectors.

Services Several-day meeting package including food and full business center services.

The Center for Executive Education at Babson College

Address Woodland Hill Drive, Babson Park (Wellesley), MA 02157
Phone (617) 239-4000
Fax (617) 239-4026
e-mail babson@iacc.iacconline.com

Accommodations Contemporary complex of low-rise buildings, including 120 rooms and 6 suites. All rooms are soundproof with climate control, direct-dial phone, color TV, and stereo.

Meeting Facilities 25 meeting rooms for 8–200. All rooms have climate control, multiple electrical and telephone outlets. Larger rooms have microphone outlets.

At no charge: Portable PA systems, cassette recorders, all microphones, A/V replacement parts, overhead and slide projectors, podiums, blackboards, easels/tables, cork boards, attendee registration.

For a fee: CCTV cameras, monitors, recorders, electrician.

Services House physician, laundry, dry cleaning, free on-site parking.

Locksmith, laborers, A/V operators, messenger, stenographer, notary, printer, photographer, carpenter, display builders, translators, painters, security, entertainers.

Fleet Conference & Training Center

Address 100 Federal Street, MS 01-02-01, Boston, MA 02110 **Phone** (617) 434-4000 **Fax** (617) 434-5626 **e-mail** bankboston@iacc.iacconline.com

Accommodations N/A.

Meeting Facilities 16 professionally designed meeting and breakout rooms including tiered meeting rooms, built-in state-of-the-art audio/visual technology, ergonomic seating and specially designed lighting systems.

At no charge: overhead projector, slide projector, screens, VCR and monitors, audio cassette and CD player, 2 flip charts.

An on-site audio/visual technician will be available to assist each instructor with all equipment questions. Printers, computer rental.

Four Points Sheraton Hotel & Conference Center

Address 1151 Boston-Providence Turnpike, Norwood, MA 02062 **Phone** (617) 769-7900 **Fax** (617) 551-3552

Accommodations 126 rooms, 2 suites, air conditioning, cable TV, facilities for physically disabled, fully sprinklered.

Meeting Facilities 30 conference rooms for 5–125 people. All have executive seating, 2 1/2 ft. x 8 ft. conference tables, dimmer lighting, white boards, built-in projection screens. Two rooms with multiple dedicated phone lines.

Services Newsstand, laundry, dry cleaning, ice and business center, free parking.

Henderson House

Address 99 Westcliff Road, Weston, MA 02193-1409 **Phone** (617) 235-4350 **Fax** (617) 235-5847 **e-mail** tpetrin@lynx.neu.edu

Accommodations Local hotels nearby.

Meeting Facilities 36-room mansion; 12 meeting rooms, seating to 100.

Services Professional conference and A/V support, complimentary standard A/V, computer projection, electronic white board, IBM/MAC compatible LCD panel; free parking on site.

John Hancock Conference Center

Address 40 Trinity Place, Boston, MA 02116 **Phone** (617) 572-7700 **Fax** (617) 572-7709

Accommodations 64 guest rooms.

Meeting Facilities 12 meeting rooms, 4 function rooms, 1,100-seat auditorium.

Services Complete A/V, incl. teleconferencing, computer-compatible projectors, on-site technicians, dedicated conference planner.

The Learning Center at Marlboro

Address 280 Locke Drive, Marlboro, MA 01752 **Phone** (508) 460-4610 **Fax** (508) 481-3451 **e-mail** nynex@iacc.iacconline.com

Accommodations Modern conference complex situated on 25 wooded acres with 226 large single rooms equipped with TV, telephone, and desk.

Meeting Facilities 40 main meeting rooms, 28 additional smaller meeting rooms; 170-seat auditorium.

At no charge: many rooms offer rear-screen projection and permanently installed 35 mm slide projectors, video and audio cassette records, voice and data lines for use with computer and quality speakers and amplifiers.

An on-site audio/visual technician will be available to assist each instructor with all equipment questions.

Services Gift shop, dry cleaning, free parking.

MIT Endicott House

Address 80 Haven Street, Dedham, MA 02026 **Phone** (617) 326-5151 **Fax** (617) 326-8702

Accommodations 50 rooms (1 handicap accessible).

Meeting Facilities 6 meeting rooms of varying size including a tiered amphitheater.

Services Standard, including 35mm, 16mm, and overhead projectors, and VCR/Monitor. Computers by arrangement.

Tufts University Conference Bureau

Address 108 Packard Ave., Medford/Boston, MA 02155 **Phone** (617) 627-3568 **Fax** (617) 627-3856 **e-mail** conferences@infonet.tufts.edu

Accommodations 600 rooms (handicap accessible). Overnight accommodations available on campus, May 22–August 13.

Meeting Facilities 35 rooms, seating 20–600.

All standard equipment including 35 mm, 16mm and overhead projectors, tape recorders, videotape equipment, PA system, blackboards and flip charts; A/V technician.

Secretarial, fax, teleconferencing, and PC or terminal hookups.

Services Specialization in English as a Second Language Program and international conferences in Boston and France. Conference planning assistance, full conference coordination.

Warren Conference Center & Inn of Northeastern University

Address 529 Chestnut St., Ashland, MA 01721 **Phone** (508) 881-1142 **Fax** (508) 881-1515

Accommodations 5 guest rooms; team-living cabins for 64.

Meeting Facilities 8 rooms, seating to 150.

Services Full A/V, business services, complete conference support.

MICHIGAN

Crystal Center at Crystal Mountain Resort

Address 12500 Crystal Mountain Drive, Thompsonville, MI 49683 **Phone** (800) 968-7686 (616) 378-2000 **Fax** (616) 378-4594 **e-mail** info@crystalmtn.com

Accommodations 210 sleeping rooms; hotel rooms, deluxe suites, 1-3 bedroom condominiums.

Meeting Facilities 6 meeting rooms with 4,800 sq. ft. of meeting space. Rear screen projection with 8' x 10' screen, ergonomic chairs, classroom tables, multilevel lighting, double drywall interior walls with quiet HVAC system.

Services Business Center, conference planning, teleconferencing, video tape recording.

Worldwide Conference Centers

Dow Leadership Development Center

Address 22 Galloway Drive, Hillsdale, MI 49242 **Phone** (517) 437-3311 **Fax** (517) 437-3240 **e-mail** jo.bates@ac.hillsdale.edu

Accommodations 32 guest rooms; conference/meeting rooms.

Meeting Facilities 11 meeting rooms accommodating up to 200.

Services VCR, overheads, 35mm, fax machines, duplication services.

Eagle Crest Conference Resort

Address 1275 South Huron Street, Ypsilanti, MI 48197 **Phone** (313) 487-0600 **Fax** (313) 484-1411

Accommodations 236 spacious guest rooms and suites with data ports and work areas. Concierge Level.

Meeting Facilities 13 conference/seminar rms., executive boardroom, computer lab. Auditorium I seats 200; Auditorium II seats 100; 9,672 sq. ft. of flexible meeting space. Satellite downlink capabilities.

Full A/V equipment with staff technicians, rear screen projection, simultaneous translation system, PC hookups in conference and seminar rooms, closed circuit TV.

PGA golf professional, full AV support, security, on-site registration assistance, office and clerical support.

58 8 × 10 booths; 9,672 sq. ft.

Services Full A/V, teleconferencing, support staff, complimentary parking, business center services, full catering and banquet services, dry cleaning and laundry services.

Fetzer Center

Address Western Michigan University, Kalamazoo, MI 49008 **Phone** (616) 387-3232 **Fax** (616) 387-5030

Accommodations N/A.

Meeting Facilities Auditorium seating 250; lecture hall seating 90; 6 conference rooms seating 10–80; video teleconferencing room seating 10–15.

Services Conference planning, all standard equipment including 35 mm, 16mm, video, overhead projectors, flip charts, as well as dual 35mm rear-screen projection, teleconferencing, video and audio recording. Computer lab.

Genoa Woods Executive Conference & Banquet Center

Address 7707 Conference Center Drive, Brighton, MI 48114 **Phone** (810) 227-4030 **Fax** (810) 227-0725

Accommodations 90 rooms, next door to Courtyard by Marriott.

Meeting Facilities In-room A/V; ergonomic chairs, windows, light-blocking curtains, sound-proof walls, supply caddy, storage closet.

Services Secretarial; business center with all amenities; tranquil, wooded location for privacy.

Haworth Inn & Conference Center

Address 225 College Ave., Holland, MI 49423 **Phone** (800) 905-9142 **Fax** (616) 395-7151

Accommodations 50 rooms, single and double occupancy. Complimentary *USA Today* newspaper.

Meeting Facilities 11 rooms, 10,000 sq. ft. Presentation boards, video conferencing, private dining room.

Services Complete A/V, gift shop, college library, fax, valet service, secretarial services.

Management Education Center Michigan State University

Address 811 West Square Lake Road, Troy, MI 48098 **Phone** (810) 879-2460 **Fax** (810) 879-6125

Accommodations 10 modern hotels within minutes of the center.

Meeting Facilities 9 rooms seating 10–400; large lobby for social functions, cocktail receptions, and product exhibits.

Services The center maintains an extensive array of A/V and computer equipment, including video/computer projection and professional sound systems.

MINNESOTA

Daniel C. Gainey Conference Center

Address Route 2, Box 1, Owatonna, MN 55060-9610 **Phone** (507) 451-7440 **Fax** (507) 451-2705 **e-mail** aesims@stthomas.edu

Accommodations 35 guest rooms (handicap accessible), on 182 acres of rolling countryside.

Meeting Facilities Executive Board Room seating 12, main conference room seating 54, five breakout rooms seating 10 each; auxiliary facility with 4 rooms accommodating 20 people each.

Services Educational resources of the University of St. Thomas; conference planning services; audio/visual equipment including interactive video capabilities.

Earle Brown Continuing Education Center

Address 1890 Buford Ave., St. Paul, MN 55108 **Phone** (612) 624-3275 **Fax** (612) 625-1948

Accommodations None.

Meeting Facilities 12 seating 10–440.

Services Computer laboratory equipped with 20 IBM PCs; Novell Netware; in-house technical staff; satellite downlink capability; 1 meeting room designed and equipped to serve as an origination point for live video teleconferences. In-house A/V. Professional staff.

The Northland Inn and Executive Conference Center

Address 7025 Northland Drive, Brooklyn Park, MN 55428 **Phone** (800) 441-6422 (612) 536-8300 **Fax** (612) 536-8790

Accommodations An all-suite executive conference center with 231 units. All suites include two work/study areas, whirlpools, color TVs and two phones.

Meeting Facilities 25 conference rooms (42,000 sq. ft.). All rooms have solid wall construction, ergonomic swivel chairs, climate controls, call buttons, projection screens, A/V feed, and multiple phone jacks.

State-of-the-art A/V equipment.

Conference concierge services, personal conference managers, A/V staff.

Services Laundry/dry cleaning, sundry shop, free parking.

Props, special transportation, carpenters, electricians, stage hands, entertainers, simultaneous translation equipment.

Oak Ridge Conference Center

Address One Oak Ridge Drive, Chaska, MN 55318 **Phone** (612) 368-3100 **Fax** (612) 368-1494

Accommodations 147 guest rooms, including handicap facilities.

Meeting Facilities 36 conference rooms (36,000 sq. ft.). All rooms have solid walls, windows, individual climate controls, multiple phone/computer jacks.

State-of-the-art A/V equipment. Complete on-site inventory.

Personal conference coordinator. Professional A/V staff.

Services Professional A/V staff, personal conference services coordinator, fax/copy service, dry cleaning, transportation.

Radisson Hotel & Conference Center Minneapolis

Address 3131 Campus Drive, Plymouth, MN 55441 **Phone** (612) 559-6600 **Fax** (612) 559-7516

Accommodations 243 rooms, 25 are jr. suites.

Meeting Facilities 32 meeting rooms. Auditorium, ballroom, boardrooms.

Services Full conference center facilities.

MISSISSIPPI

Whispering Woods Hotel & Executive Conference Center

Address 11200 E. Goodman Road, Olive Branch, MS 38654 **Phone** (601) 895-2941 **Fax** (601) 895-1590

Accommodations Modern, 4-story complex offers 181 guest rooms, including 6 suites.

Meeting Facilities 24 meeting rooms, concentrated on the first and mezzanine levels. All rooms have multiple electrical/microphone outlets and individual controls for climate.

Services Safety deposit boxes, laundry and dry cleaning. Gift shop offering gifts, books and sundry items. Free outdoor, self parking.

MISSOURI

Anheuser-Busch Conference & Sports Centre

Address One Soccer Park Rd., Fenton, MO 63026 **Phone** (314) 343-5347 **Fax** (313) 343-8340

Accommodations None listed.

Meeting Facilities 3 rooms with 4,418 sq. ft. of meeting space. Professional meeting managers. State-of-the-art A/V equipment, Sony projection systems, large screens, LCD projector (VGA Data & Video Active). Teleconferencing, on-site A/V technician.

Services Professional staff can plan theme/special events. Full service food and beverage staff.

Doubletree Hotel & Conference Center

Address 16625 Swingley Ridge Road, St. Louis, MO 63017 **Phone** (800) 222-TREE (314) 532-5000 **Fax** (314) 530-1149

Accommodations Contemporary high-rise tower with 223 guest rooms and delivery.

Meeting Facilities 15 conference rooms for 15–350, 21 breakout rooms for 4–12. All rooms have swivel chairs, flexible control lighting. Peoples Theater features stationary rear screen projection, sound booth stage, tiered SR seating for 50–150.

On-site service management, PA systems, tape recorders/players, microphones, overhead, 35mm slide projectors, 16mm sound, remote controls, screen, electronic podiums, lecterns, CCTV equipment, spotlights, duplicating machines, typewriters.

Fax, transparencies, photocopying, secretary support, message delivery, A/V technicians, computer rental, laborers, musicians.

The "Great Room" holds 30, 8 ft. × 10 ft. booths piped and draped, direct truck access.

Services Conference center service desk, club operations service desk, pro-shop rentals, concierge, valet, free outdoor parking. Express check-in/check-out and on-site car rental office.

Bus transportation, photographers, print shop, sign shop, security, translators.

Eric P. Newman Education Center—St. Louis

Address 660 S. Euclid, Campus Box 8209, St. Louis, MO 63110 **Phone** (314) 747-MEET (6338) **Fax** (314) 747-2000

Accommodations 200 rooms available at nearby hotels with wide range of amenities and prices.

Meeting Facilities 450-seat auditorium, 2 tiered seminar rooms seating 55 and 101, 10 breakout rooms and a divisible multipurpose room seating up to 168 classroom style.

Flip charts, marker boards, pointers, easels, microphones, network connections, telephones, teleconferencing, system annotating device, modem outlets, overhead, 35mm and video projectors, VCRs. All rooms have hard writing surface tables, ergonomic chairs.

Fax, transparencies, photocopying, secretarial service, security, message center and audio/visual technician on site. Satellite and interactive video teleconferencing.

Lobby, Mezzanine, Promenade exhibit areas.

Services Business Center, exceptional catering, listening assisted devices. Professional meeting planners to help with theme parties and other special needs.

Florist, photographers, printers, sign makers/decorators, computer rentals, ground transportation.

Innsbrook Resort & Conference Center

Address 1 Innsbrook Estates Drive, Wright City, MO 63390 **Phone** (314) 745-3000 **Fax** (314) 745-8855

Accommodations 100 bedrooms in 1-, 2-, or 3-bedroom condominiums overlooking 140-acre lake.

Meeting Facilities 9 meeting rooms (7,900 sq. ft.) for groups of 5–150, adjustable upholstered armchairs, additional breakout rooms, individual climate control.

Services All standard A/V equipment, fax machine, secretarial services, theme dinners and parties. Airport shuttles. Conference planners; client business office.

St. Louis Executive Conference Center at America's Center

Address 801 Convention Plaza, St. Louis, MO 63101 **Phone** (314) 342-5050 **Fax** (314) 342-5053

Accommodations One block from the Doubletree Mayfair Suites and the Holiday Inn Convention Center, two blocks from the Drury Inn-Gateway Arch. Many other excellent hotels with wide range of amenities and prices nearby.

Meeting Facilities 3 private meeting suites, each with general session room, lounge, and adjacent breakout rooms. Also, an Executive Board Room and 4 additional conference rooms. Individual climate and lighting controls.

General session rooms are equipped with microphone, modem outlets, overhead projector, 35mm, VCR and video projector, projection screens. All rooms have hard writing surface tables, ergonomic executive chairs, and phones, in addition to a presentation rail system with flip charts and marker boards.

Fax, transparencies, photocopying, secretarial service, security, message boards and audio/visual technicians on site. Satellite and interactive video teleconferencing.

Lobby, atrium and rotunda areas can be used for exhibiting. Additional space at America's Center up to 20,000 sq. ft.

Services Conference Services Desk. Professional meeting coordinators can plan theme parties, spouse activities, etc.

Florist, photographers, sign makers/decorators, computer rentals, ground transportation.

MONTANA

The Center at Salmon Lake

Address H.C. 31, Box 800 South, Seely Lake, MT 59868
Phone (888) 773-2643
Fax (406) 677-3846

Accommodations 11 suites for up to 25 people, some with fireplaces. 8,000 sq. ft. deck, satellite TV; bathrobes, slippers, hair dryers, turn-down service.

Meeting Facilities 4 rooms, 3,200 sq. ft. Executive tilt-swivel chairs, big-screen TV, casual overstuffed furniture or formal setup, huge windows.

Services Exclusive use of entire center at all times. Continuous refreshment service, business center, A/V equipment, one contact for all planning needs; airport transportation; full-service conference center for upscale retreats, strategic planning, or board of directors' meetings.

NEBRASKA

Arbor Day Farm/Lied Conference Center

Address 2700 Sylvan Road, Nebraska City, NE 68410 **Phone** (800) 546-LIED (5433) for reservations (402) 873-8733 **Fax** (402) 873-4999

Accommodations 96 guest rooms in a relaxed, warm and rustic atmosphere. Nestled on a 260-acre national historic landmark amidst apple orchards and nut trees, the facility uses wood as a source of all heating and cooling. An active recycling program produces a lesson in environmental stewardship, reflecting the philosophy of its parent organization, The National Arbor Day Foundation.

Meeting Facilities 10 conference rooms seating up to 400; 14,000 sq. ft. of meeting space with windows and distinctive natural wood themes, upholstered ergonomic chairs, computerized lighting and individual climate control.

In-house audio/visual with teleconferencing and computer network capabilities, rear screen projection.

Conference management and meeting support, registration assistance.

Services Conference planning, coordination, clerical support, teleconferencing, in-house A/V staff, environmental tours and activities available.

Clifford Hardin Nebraska Center for Continuing Education

Address University of Nebraska, 33rd and Holdrege Sts., Lincoln, NE 68583 **Phone** (402) 472-3435 **Fax** (402) 472-8207

Accommodations 96 sleeping rooms with choice of beds; complimentary continental breakfast.

Meeting Facilities 14 meeting rooms with 16,500 sq. ft. of space; tiered auditorium seating 600; complete A/V capabilities, broadcast quality TV and radio studio connections; Internet connection; large lobby for exhibits.

Services Videoconferencing, teleferencing, computer lab, satellite links, Internet access.

NEW HAMPSHIRE

New England Center A Kellogg Center

Address 15 Stafford Avenue, University of New Hampshire, Durham, NH 03824 **Phone** (603) 862-2712 **Fax** (603) 862-4351 **e-mail** bhm@hopper.unh.edu

Accommodations 115 rooms (handicap accessible), non-smoking.

Meeting Facilities 11 rooms seating 2–270.

Services Transportation services to/from airports. Complete conference center support on-site, A/V, teleconferencing via satellite. Programming support available.

NEW JERSEY

The AT&T Learning Center

Address 300 North Maple Avenue, Basking Ridge, NJ 07920
Phone (800) 288-2687
Fax (908) 953-3103

Accommodations 171 guest rooms and suites featuring easy access to voice, data, and Internet services. International parlor. Laundry services.

Meeting Facilities 24 rooms, 20,000 sq. ft., including 4,700 sq. ft. ballroom, 84-seat tiered amphitheater, advanced technology, fiber optics, interactive meeting technology, teleconferencing, rear-screen projection, tackable wall surfaces.

Services Conference concierge, business center

Chauncey Conference Center

Address Rosedale and Carter Roads, Princeton, NJ 08541 **Phone** (609) 921-3600 **Fax** (609) 683-4958

Accommodations 100 spacious guest rooms with executive-sized desks, task lighting, color TVs; most overlook the rural countryside from balconies or terraces; suites; handicap rooms.

Meeting Facilities 13 dedicated conference rooms, 1 with rear screen projection, all individually climate controlled seating up to 200; ergonomic chairs; complete computer capabilities and A/Vs including CCTV, teleconferencing, and satellite downlink. Experiential Teambuilding course.
XENO• Learning. Laurie House

Executive Retreat—a private, self-contained, restored 19th century farm house for senior-level executive groups of up to 15.

Conference Coordinator assigned to group, Conference Services desk, fax, secretarial support, transparencies, photocopying, message delivery.

Services CMP includes guest rooms, continuous refreshment breaks, meeting space, A/V services and use of recreational facilities. Collaborative Courseware^{SM} offers the most advanced training resources in strategic alliance with the leading management education providers to meeting and training professionals.

The Executive Meeting Center at the Doubletree Hotel—Somerset

Address 200 Atrium Drive, Somerset, NJ 08873 **Phone** (732) 469-2600 **Fax** (732) 509-4527

Accommodations 360 newly renovated guest rooms, including 6 deluxe suites.

Meeting Facilities 12 rooms, including 2 telephone rooms with speaker phones; 7,000 sq. ft. of meeting space.

Services Full business center; 2 self-service computer stations with print capabilities and Internet access.

Doral Forrestal at Princeton

Address 100 College Rd. East, Princeton, NJ 08540 **Phone** (609) 452-7800 **Fax** (609) 452-7883

Accommodations 291 rooms (handicapped accessible), including 10 suites.

Meeting Facilities 36 rooms seating 12–400.

Included in CMP price: monitor, VCR, flip charts, 35mm projector, overhead projector, pads/pens.

Fax, photocopying, secretarial, Business Center.

Services Fully equipped A/V department. Complete travel services, conference services, meeting planning, expanded executive services, party planning.

Conference Services handles planning and on-site meeting coordination. Audio/visual specialist on staff. In-house florist, professional catering staff, staff photographer, entertainment director.

Hamilton Park A Dolce Conference Center

Address 175 Park Avenue, Florham Park, NJ 07932 **Phone** (201) 377-2424 **Fax** (201) 377-6108

Accommodations 209 deluxe guest rooms including 13 suites.

Meeting Facilities 40 dedicated meeting rooms, 3 rear screen rooms, computer lab, teleconferencing, video taping, indiv. climate control, soundproofing, natural lighting.

Services Room service, same-day laundry and valet, free parking, local shopping.

KPMG Center for Leadership Development

Address 3 Chestnut Ridge Road, Montvale, NJ 07645 **Phone** (201) 307-7317 **Fax** (201) 307-8037

Accommodations Within walking distance of 2 major hotels.

Meeting Facilities 25,000 sq. ft., 17 meeting rooms for 2–125 people. Climate control, amphitheatre, rear screen projection, 2 computer rooms. Built-in screens. In-house audio/visual staff and equipment.

Services Professional conference coordinator and A/V technical support. On-site parking.

The Merrill Lynch Conference and Training Center

Address 900 Scudders Mill Road, Plainsboro, NJ 08536 **Phone** (800) HCC-MEET (609) 282-1000 **Fax** (609) 282-2126 **e-mail** merrilllynch@iacc.iacconline.com

Accommodations 343 guest rooms, includes 50-room Executive Center.

Meeting Facilities 34 meeting rooms, auditorium seating 316. Small breakout rooms to large classrooms, will accommodate any size group with any set-up requirements.

In-house staff provides rear screen, overheads, 35mm projectors, video cameras, monitors, phone labs, key pad response system, closed-circuit broadcast capabilities, satellite dish for downlink communications with guestroom relay capabilities; PA system, computer projector & monitors.

Personal conference planner, complete conference services staff and A/V technicians, copy services, fax services, package handling, messages, writing pads, pencils, supplies.

3,136 sq. ft. exhibit space.

Services Gift Shop with newsstand, laundry, dry cleaning, shoe shine, vending machines, on-site free parking. French and Spanish-speaking employees.

Notary, print shop, photo lab.

Sheraton Meadowlands Hotel and Conference Center

Address 2 Meadowlands Plaza, East Rutherford, NJ 07073 **Phone** (201) 896-0500 **Fax** (201) 507-2825

Accommodations 425 guest rooms, 5 with New York City skyline view. 66 Club Level rooms with private Club Lounge. All rooms with voice mail and data ports. Fully ADA compliant.

Meeting Facilities 9 meeting rooms in 4,300 sq. ft. conference center. Amphitheater, 40 executive boardrooms, 6 classrooms; 18 meeting rooms in hotel, 22,252 sq. ft.; 10 additional conference rooms; 2 ballrooms 11,520 sq. ft. and 5,200 sq. ft.

Services Full service Business Center, video conferencing packages available. New York City shuttle.

NEW YORK

Arden Conference Center: Arden House/Arden Homestead

Address Columbia University, Harriman Campus, Harriman, NY 10926 **Phone** (914) 351-4715 **Fax** (914) 351-4561 **e-mail** LisaP@tuxedo.ny.frontiercomm.net

Accommodations Total 97: Arden House (80), Arden Homestead (17).

Meeting Facilities Total 15: Arden House (12), Arden Homestead (3). Seating 6–125.

Overhead projectors, flip charts, personal computers, computer lab,

VCRs, 35mm slide projectors, computer projection.

Concierge service, conference planner, A/V computer technician on site. Graphics capability in house.

Services Laundry and dry cleaning.

North America's largest factory outlet mall nearby. Florists, barbershops, historical museums, craft village, antique shopping, outdoor sculpture museum nearby.

Faxing; duplicating; special events planning; free outdoor parking.

Beaver Hollow Conference and Training Center, NY

Address 1083 Pit Road, Java Center, NY 14082 **Phone** (800) 964-7903 (716) 457-3700 **Fax** (716) 457-9348

Accommodations 43 rooms, including 7 villa suites.

Meeting Facilities 5 rooms, seating 5–60.

Services Wide selection of A/V equipment. Ropes course, climbing wall. Experiential education facilitators on staff.

The Center for Biomedical Learning

Address 601 Elmwood Avenue, Box 307, Rochester, NY 14642 **Phone** (716) 275-6305 **Fax** (716) 756-7839

Accommodations Rooms available at several nearby hotels

Meeting Facilities Two tiered auditoriums, 242-seat and 110-seat, 100-seat multipurpose room, 4 seminar rooms, 12 breakout rooms, spectacular atrium for displays and special events, state-of-the-art technology.

Services Complete range of AV equipment, satellite links, videoconferencing, teleconferencing, audience response system, 35mm, data, video projection, business center, continuous refreshments, A/V technician on site.

Chase Conference Center (JP Morgan Chase) at Chase Manhattan Plaza

Address One Chase Manhattan Plaza, 28th Floor, New York, NY 10081 **Phone** (212) 552-5000 **Fax** (212) 552-7200

Accommodations None listed.

Meeting Facilities 44 multipurpose designed meeting rooms; 63,000 sq. ft. of meeting space.

Services A full range of audio/video and computer equipment is available. Including teleconferencing, video and audio recording/playback. Audio conferencing, digitized recording, 35 mm and overhead projectors. Podiums and dedicated control equipment. Wireless microphones. PCs with on-site technical support for standard applications and laserjet printers. Networked setup and loading of standard software available. Video and audio duplication. Internet accounts available.

Chase Conference Center (JP Morgan Chase) at 600 Fifth Avenue

Address 600 Fifth Avenue, 2nd floor, New York, NY 10020 **Phone** (212) 332-4144 **Fax** (212) 332-4143

Accommodations None listed.

Meeting Facilities 13 multipurpose designed meeting rooms ranging in size from 300 to 1,300 sq. ft. Total of 7,000 sq. ft. of meeting space.

Services Wide selection of A/V equipment including overhead projectors, CD or audio cassette playback equipment, easels and white boards, pads & pencils, videotape recording and playback, PCs, laser printers, Polycomm speakerphones, Barco projection system, limo and messenger services, conference service aides, business services desk, in-house A/V technician.

The Coleman Center

Address 810 Seventh Avenue, 23rd Floor, New York, NY 10019 **Phone** (212) 541-4600 **Fax** (212) 541-4232

Accommodations N/A. Hotel reservations at special rates.

Meeting Facilities Our only business and sole concentration of our staff are to contribute to improved meeting success. Variety of rooms to hold 10–150 attendees.

Services Extensive inventory of every type of audiovisual equipment, fax, duplicating, reproduction of handouts and collation of workbooks. Limousine service, theater tickets, messenger service. Hotel reservation at special rates.

Doral Arrowwood

Address Anderson Hill Road, Rye Brook, NY 10573 **Phone** (914) 939-5500 **Fax** (914) 939-8311

Accommodations 272 guest rooms.

Meeting Facilities 36 purpose-designed rooms, 120-seat amphitheatre.

Full A/V and technical support, computer lab.

Conference Services desk, administrative support, dedicated conference management.

Services Concierge service, valet parking, 24-hr. room service, newsstand, laundry and dry cleaning.

Project Excel, adventure-based team-building courses.

Edith Macy Conference Center

Address Chappaqua Road, Briarcliff Manor, NY 10510 **Phone** (914) 945-8098 **Fax** (914) 945-8009

Accommodations 46 rooms.

Meeting Facilities 200-seat auditorium plus 5 meeting rooms and 10 breakout areas. Steelcase highback chairs. Outdoor educational learning available.

Services A/V technician on site, full-conference planner to ensure guest satisfaction. Secretarial assistance available.

Executive Conference Center at the Sheraton New York

Address 811 Seventh Avenue, New York, NY 10019 **Phone** (212) 841-6560 **Fax** (212) 841-6445

Accommodations 1,750 rooms, corporate club rooms with fax, copier, data port, 2-line phones.

Meeting Facilities 12 conference rooms; 1 executive boardroom.

Services Videoconferencing, Internet access, conference concierges, meeting-planning offices.

Harrison Conference Center at Glen Cove

Address Dosoris Lane, Glen Cove, NY 11542 **Phone** (800) HCC-MEET (Nat'l Sales) (516) 671-6400 **Fax** (516) 671-6490 **e-mail** PGJERPEN@aol.com

Accommodations Two-story estate with 198 modern guest rooms including 4 executive suites. All rooms have air-conditioning control, color cable TV, 2 direct-dial phones, clock radio, voice mail and dataports.

Meeting Facilities 30 meeting rooms for 2–225. All have multiple electrical/microphone outlets, recessed lighting, climate controls, 110V electricity.

At no charge: Tape recorders, microphones, overhead, 16mm sound, 35mm slide projection screens, podiums, blackboards, easels (one per main meeting room), Conference coordinators.

For a fee: A/V operators, stenographers, full business center services.

The "Embassy" has 2,850 sq. ft. of exhibit space.

Services Gift shop, laundry and dry cleaning, free outdoor parking for 200 cars.

Computer rental and technical service, notary public, messenger services, print shop, photographer, carpenters, display builders, sign painters, locksmiths, laborers.

IBM Palisades Executive Conference Center

Address Route 9W, Palisades, NY 10964 **Phone** (914) 732-6000 **Fax** (914) 732-6571

Accommodations 206 guest rooms, each with IBM network station, queen-size bed, iron & board, hair dryer, bathrobe, and full amenities.

Meeting Facilities 43 meeting rooms with 47,000 sq. ft. multipurpose room. Interactive multimedia center, IBM PS/Z computer, extensive audio/visual package.

Services Business center/concierge.

Millennium Conference Center

Address 145 West 44th Street, New York, NY 10036 **Phone** (800) 317-3186 (212) 768-4400 **Fax** (212) 789-7630

Accommodations 627 luxury guest rooms, incl. 9 suites, and 72 upgraded club rooms.

Meeting Facilities 33 meeting rooms accommodating up to 125 each; 17,000 sq. ft. of exhibit space; Hudson Theatre accommodating 700.

Services Professional conference coordinators, business center, graphics center. On-site production manager.

Minnowbrook Adirondack Conference Center

Address Maple Lodge Road, Blue Mountain Lake, NY 12812 **Phone** (315) 443-4900 **Fax** (315) 443-4902

Accommodations 32 guest rooms with pine tongue-in-groove walls. Main Lodge and Greenhouse each have 10 double bedrooms. Lawn House has 4 double bedrooms. Two hillside cabins each have 4 rooms with queen-sized beds. Shared baths.

Meeting Facilities 2 meeting rooms including a 75-seat classroom. Several smaller seminar rooms for up to 56 persons.

Services Full A/V equipment, digital projection units, wired for Internet.

The Rensselaerville Institute Conference Center

Address 63 Huyck Road, PO Box 28, Rensselaerville, NY 12147 **Phone** (518) 797-5100 **Fax** (518) 797-3692

Accommodations 57 rooms in mixture of exquisite estate mansions and modern residences, all with private baths.

Meeting Facilities 10 rooms ranging from formal 180-seat auditorium to beautiful 30′ × 30′ living room in estate mansion.

Services Complete A/V and PA equipment. Personal conference planner, travel arrangements, special events coordination, secretarial, desktop publishing services.

Tarrytown House, A Dolce Conference Hotel

Address East Sunnyside Lane, Tarrytown, NY 10591 **Phone** (914) 591-8200 **Fax** (914) 591-4014

Accommodations 148 guest rooms.

Meeting Facilities 30 meeting rooms; 30,000 sq. ft. of dedicated conference space. New ballroom for up to 400 people.

Services Gift shops; free parking; same-day dry cleaning.

White Eagle Conference Center

Address P.O. Box 679, West Lake Moraine, Hamilton, NY 13346 **Phone** (800) 295-9322 (315) 824-2002 **Fax** (315) 824-6799 **e-mail** White_Eagle@iacc.iac-conline.com

Accommodations 60 private guest rooms in a rustic setting overlooking beautiful Lake Moraine, three executive suites.

Meeting Facilities 8 meeting rooms, up to 18 breakout areas; 2 stand-alone executive-training sites; theater-style seating to 200.

Services Full A/V capabilities, projectors, VCRs, cameras, monitors, recorders, fax, copiers, notary public.

NORTH CAROLINA

Conference & Education Facility, North Carolina Biotechnology Center

Address 15 T.W. Alexander Drive, P.O. Box 13547, Research Triangle Park, NC 27709 **Phone** (919) 541-9366 **Fax** (919) 990-9544 **e-mail** yvonne_patton@ncbiotech.org

Accommodations Coordinated with major hotels, 5-10 min. from facility.

Meeting Facilities 170-seat auditorium. Large multipurpose room (opens to garden) holds from 90–150 in various configurations, or exhibits.

Services Complete conference capabilities, catering, A/V services, teleconferencing.

R. David Thomas Executive Conference Center

Address One Science Drive, Durham, NC 27708 **Phone** (919) 660-6400 **Fax** (919) 660-3607 **e-mail** tmartin@mail.duke.edu

Accommodations 113 rooms including 2 suites (all guest rooms are supported by independent modem line for computer access).

Meeting Facilities 15 Thomas Center meeting rooms seating 18–75, 21 breakout rooms; 11 Fuqua School meeting rooms seating 30–450, 20 breakout rooms.

Services On-site conference planning and audio/visual technical support.

Paul J. Rizzo Conference Center

Address McLean Hall, 150 DuBose Home Lane, Chapel Hill, NC 27514
Phone (919) 913-2098
Fax (919) 913-2099

Accommodations 60 guest rooms.

Meeting Facilities 24 meeting rooms.

Services Standard conference services.

The Sanderling Inn Resort & Conference Center

Address 1461 Duck Road, Duck, NC 27949 **Phone** (800) 701-4111 (919) 261-4111 **Fax** (919) 261-1638 **e-mail** 74161.41@compuserve.com

Accommodations 87 rooms and suites, oceanfront and sound side, private balconies.

Meeting Facilities Private conference facility—meetings up to 100 people; 5 meeting rooms; breakout rooms available.

8-hr. ergo chairs; hard writing tables; tackable walls; fully controllable heating/AC/lighting; standard AV on property—other AV available on request.

Conference Concierge (if needed); fax and copying.

Services Concierge; fax and copying; private dining; theme parties.

OHIO

Dana Conference Center

Address Medical College of Ohio, P.O. Box 10008, Toledo, OH 43699 **Phone** (419) 381-4090
Fax (419) 381-4025

Accommodations 213 rooms (handicap accessible).

Meeting Facilities 19 rooms seating 10–450.

Services Teleconference equipment, CCTV, video recorders (3/4" or 1/2"), projection TV or monitors, video cameras, slide projectors, overheads, flip charts, X-ray view boxes. CD or audio cassette playback equipment, A/V technicians. Connected to the Toledo Hilton by walkway; hotel offers complimentary airport shuttle.

The David H. Ponitz Sinclair Center

Address 444 W. Third St., Dayton, OH 45402 **Phone** (937) 512-3046 **Fax** (937) 512-5164

Accommodations 100 rooms in nearby hotels.

Meeting Facilities 32 meeting rooms.

Services Contact the Center's Conference Services Manager.

The Forum Conference & Education Center, Inc.

Address 1375 East 9th Street, Cleveland, OH 44114 **Phone** (216) 241-6338 **Fax** (216) 241-2583
e-mail ForumCC@aol.com

Accommodations Adjacent to 3 full service hotels.

Meeting Facilities 12 rooms; 400-seat auditorium; 22,000 sq. ft. of meeting space.

Services Advanced A/V and video presentation capabilities, satellite downlink in all rooms, interactive video conferencing, conference planning, business services, in-room data lines.

George S. Dively Building Case Western Reserve University

Address 10900 Euclid Ave., Cleveland, OH 44106-7166
Phone (216) 368-0020
Fax (216) 368-0200
e-mail: mam56@po.cwru.edu

Accommodations Nearby quality lodging.

Meeting Facilities 6 meeting rooms seating up to 100. 7,625 sq. ft. of meeting space. First class amenities include complete catering and meal services; access to a full complement of audiovisual equipment; connections to the University's fiberoptic network and electronic distance-learning capabilities.

Services Full range of conference services. Degree and non-degree executive education programs available through the Weatherhead School of Management, Case Western Reserve University.

Kingsgate Conference Center

Address 151 Goodman Drive, Cincinnati, OH 45219
Phone (513) 487-3800
Fax (513) 487-3810

Accommodations 206 guest rooms, oversized desks, adjustable chairs, high-speed Internet connections, 2 phone lines per room.

Meeting Facilities 23 rooms, 20,000 sq. ft. including 5,355 sq. ft. ballroom accommodating 576 theater style; 396 for banquet. Two boardrooms, 2 amphitheaters, ISDN lines, A/V communications among meeting rooms and guest rooms.

Services Dedicated conference staff, A/V technicians, 24-hour business center.

Marcum Conference Center & Inn

Address Miami University, Oxford, OH 45056 **Phone** (513) 529-6911
Fax (513) 529-5700
e-mail finkll@hdgs.muohio.edu

Accommodations 92 elegantly appointed guest rooms.

Meeting Facilities 11 rooms seating 4–250, flexible set-up, complimentary audiovisual, networked computer room.

Services Free parking, laundry and dry cleaning, access to university facilities; complimentary newspapers.

The Northeast Conference Center

Address 4140 Executive Parkway, Westerville, OH 43081
Phone (614) 508-6322
Fax (614) 508-6324

Accommodations 100 guest rooms.

Meeting Facilities 14 meeting rooms.

Services Standard conference services.

Professional Education and Conference Center

Address Kent State University Stark Campus, 6000 Frank Avenue NW, Canton, OH 44720
Phone (330) 499-9600

Accommodations None.

Meeting Facilities 16 meeting rooms, corporate theatre, state-of-the-art communications, computer, and A/V technology.

Services Multimedia staff and conference center planners.

Schiff Family Conference Center

Address Xavier University, 1624 Herald Avenue, Cincinnati, OH 45207 **Phone** (513) 745-3428 **Fax** (513) 745-4307

Accommodations Non-residential.

Meeting Facilities 8 meeting rooms, 27,000 sq. ft.

Services Director of Banquet & Conference Services; Conference Assistant.

OREGON

Rock Springs Guest Ranch

Address 64201 Tyler Road, Bend, Oregon 97701 **Phone** (541) 382-1957 **Fax** (541) 382-7774

Accommodations Comfortable cabins decorated in a warm western motif nestled beneath tall ponderosa pines. Suites feature fireplaces, wet bars and separate living areas. All units have decks, private entrances and bathroom facilities. 26 guest rooms.

Meeting Facilities 4 meeting rooms; Conference center features 4,000 square feet of meeting space. Breakout areas in the main lodge.

Services The Learning Center is a full service training and development resource for improved business performance. Exclusive use of the entire facility.

PENNSYLVANIA

ACE/Eagle Lodge Conference Center & Country Club

Address Ridge Pike and Manor Road, Lafayette Hill, PA 19444 **Phone** (800) 523-3000 (610) 825-8000 **Fax** (610) 940-4344

Accommodations 120 deluxe guest rooms, including 3 Jr. suites, 6 handicap-accessible; each room has private balcony/patio, cable TV, in-room movies/games; computer hook-up, comfortable work area.

Meeting Facilities 32 dedicated meeting rooms, incl. 3 tiered amphitheaters; seating to 250. 15-station computer learning center.

Leather, ergonomic armchairs; zoned lighting, rear screen projection, built-in VCR monitors, flip charts, tackable walls, blackboards, pads/pens, microphones, overheads, podiums, individual computer rentals, other equipment on request.

Professional conference planners; PGA golf professionals, full A/V support, business concierge (faxing, typing, photocopying, messenger, reservations, etc.), security, notary public.

Services All standard A/V equipment supplied including VCR, monitor. Business concierge, bell service, social event planning, golf shop, golf lessons/clinics, recreation director. TDD equipment. Complimentary newspapers. Free parking.

The Desmond Great Valley Hotel and Conference Center

Address One Liberty Boulevard, Malvern, PA 19355 **Phone** (610) 296-9800 **Fax** (610) 889-9869

Accommodations 195 rooms (handicap accessible, non-smoking).

Meeting Facilities 16 rooms, seating up to 375; state-of-the-art amphitheater.

Services Full range of A/V, program coordinators, banquet facilities.

Gregg Conference Center at The American College

Address 270 Bryn Mawr Avenue, Bryn Mawr, PA 19010 **Phone** (215) 526-1208 **Fax** (215) 526-1156

Accommodations 50 rooms (handicap accessible).

Meeting Facilities 15 rooms seating 10–300, 25 breakout rooms, 225-seat auditorium.

Services Conference planning, in-house A/V Department, complete equipment and personalized services, teleconferencing, concierge, graphics department, video/audio recording, closed-circuit broadcast system, front and rear screen projection, 2 rooms w/multiple dedicated phone lines.

Hidden Valley Resort Conference Center

Address 1 Craighead Drive, Hidden Valley, PA 15502 **Phone** (800) 833-9308 (814) 443-8000 **Fax** (814) 443-1907

Accommodations 225 bedrooms consisting of efficiency bedrooms, parlor, and one-bedroom suites, two and three bedroom condos and townhomes, all with color cable TV, many with kitchens and fireplaces.

Meeting Facilities 21 dedicated conference rooms, expertly designed for executive comfort for up to 350; amphitheater for 100. All rooms with Vecta swivel chairs and Johnson custom work surfaces.

Portable PA systems, projection screens, remote control cords, lighted lecterns, podiums, blackboards, cork boards; tape recorders, sound mixers, rear screen, video cameras, computer monitors.

Notary public, first aid, repairmen, stenographer, electricians, A/V operators.

Services Conference center concierge, newsstand and sundry shops, free outdoor parking. Babysitting, doctors on call.

Multilingual translation, entertainment and musicians, direction signs, trucks/vans, photographer, paint shop, laborers.

Hilton Hotel and Conference Center

Address 1224 West Chester Pike #404, West Chester, PA 19382 **Phone** (610) 692-6700 **Fax** (610) 436-4149

Accommodations 175 guest rooms.

Meeting Facilities 21,000 sq. ft.

Services Airport shuttle from Scranton Airport. Conference Center opens June 2002.

Manufacturer's Association of Northwest Pennsylvania Conference Center

Address 2171 West 38th Street, Erie, PA 16508 **Phone** (800) 815-2660 **Fax** (814) 836-0819

Accommodations N/A.

Meeting Facilities 9 meeting rooms with 20,000 sq. ft. incuding 85-seat auditorium.

Services All rooms equipped with A/V capability. Conference services provided.

Penn Stater Conference Center Hotel

Address 215 Innovation Blvd., Penn State Research Park, State College, PA 16803 **Phone** (814) 863-5000 **Fax** (814) 863-5003

Accommodations 150 deluxe guest rooms; 5 suites.

Meeting Facilities 38 dedicated meeting rooms from 336–2,203 sq. ft., computer labs, forum meeting room.

Included in CMP price: Monitor, VCR, flip charts, 35 mm projector, overhead projector, pads/pens.

Fax, photocopying, secretarial, and graphics.

19,661 sq. ft. available exhibit space.

Services Conference Services handles planning and on-site meeting coordination. Audio/visual specialist on staff.

Flowers; University recreation, sports.

Gift shop, same-day dry cleaning, in-room movies.

Sheraton Park Ridge at Valley Forge

Address 480 N. Gulph Road, King of Prussia, PA 19406 **Phone** (800) 337-1801 (610) 337-1800 **Fax** (610) 337-4506

Accommodations 265 guest rooms including 19-room VIP concierge level; 1 bi-level Presidential Suite and 2 executive suites.

Meeting Facilities 14,796 square feet of meeting space. Including 24 conference rooms seating 12–600 people; 3 boardrooms; 4,864 sq. ft. ballroom.

Included in CMP price: VCR, flip charts, overhead projector, executive note pads.

Complete conference planning services available.

5,000 sq. ft. plus exhibit space.

Services Fully equipped AV department, conference planning and conference concierge.

Sugarloaf Albert M. Greenfield Conference Center

Address 9230 Germantown Avenue, Philadelphia, PA 19118 **Phone** (215) 242-9100 **Fax** (215) 242-8362

Accommodations 50 recently refurbished, well-appointed double rooms. Handicap rooms available.

Meeting Facilities 20 distinctive meeting and conference rooms for groups from 10–200 in country manor setting on 40 acres of rolling hills on this university-owned estate. Rooms are capable of a variety of arrangements and functions. Ample free parking.

Services Full-time conf. specialists assist with any and all aspects of your meeting. Full range A/V. Office support services.

The Villanova Conference Center

Address 601 Countyline Road, Radnor, PA 19087 **Phone** (610) 523-1776 **Fax** (610) 523-1779

Accommodations 58 guest rooms, each with spacious work area, phone, data line, private balcony.

Meeting Facilities 24 rooms combining early 20th century elegance with 21st century technology.

Services Conference planners, broad range of A/V services.

Wildwood Conference Center

Address One HACC Drive, Harrisburg, PA 17110-2999 **Phone** (717) 780-2678 **Fax** (717) 780-3273

Accommodations Local hotels, motels within minutes.

Meeting Facilities 9,000 sq. ft of meeting space, large dining room, state-of-the-art A/V equipment, large prefunction areas.

Services Full range, professional staff; satellite downlink in all rooms; free parking.

RHODE ISLAND

Whispering Pines Conference Center

Address University of Rhode Island, 401 Victory Highway, West Greenwich, RI 02816-9772 **Phone** (401) 397-3361 **Fax** (401) 397-6540

Accommodations 64 in double rooms (handicap accessible).

Meeting Facilities 4 rooms seating 18–100.

Services Conference and meeting planners, PA system, video cameras, flip charts, overhead projector, VCR monitors, 16-mm projectors.

SOUTH CAROLINA

Baxter M. Hood Continuing Education Center

Address 452 South Anderson Road, Rock Hill, SC 29730 **Phone** (803) 325-2888 **Fax** (803) 325-2869

Accommodations 600 rooms at hotels within 2–5 minutes drive from the facility.

Meeting Facilities 16 meeting rooms with seating for 12–1,000 people.

Services State of the art A/V equipment with professional staff. 2-way teleconferencing with satellite links. In-house capability to do graphic animation, transparencies, and slides.

TENNESSEE

Adelphia Centre at Millennium Park

Address 2001 Millennium Place, Johnson City, TN 37604 **Phone** (423) 232-2001 **Fax** (423) 232-2002

Accommodations 1,200 sleeping rooms within 5 minutes.

Meeting Facilities 15 rooms, including 2 auditoriums seating 85 and 125; 8 classrooms, 3 meeting rooms, executive lounge, boardroom.

Services Cutting-edge A/V with video and teleconferencing, satellite downlink, distance learning center, computer training room.

The Chattanoogan
(Opening April 2001)

Address 1253 South Market Street, Suite 100, Box 4, Chattanooga, TN 37402 **Phone** (423) 757-2023 **Fax** (423) 757-2025

Accommodations 202 guest rooms.

Meeting Facilities 20 meeting rooms; Conference Center features a 7,500 sq. ft. ballroom, 84 seat amphitheater, 5 general session rooms for 20–100 persons, and 12 breakout rooms.

Services Superior technology throughout including pre-wired high speed Internet access in all meeting and public spaces as well as in guest rooms. LAN capabilities; full A/V; data projection services. Full service conference concierge and Business Center.

The Fogelman Executive Center

Address University of Memphis, Memphis, TN 38152 **Phone** (901) 678-3700 **Fax** (901) 678-5329

Accommodations 51 single rooms, queen beds.

Meeting Facilities 16 meeting rooms for 12–400 including 3 auditoriums.

Services As part of the CMP: overhead projectors, flip charts, slide projectors, VCR/monitors, video cameras, PA systems, in-room A/V booths with Barco projectors, satellite downlink, van service, conference concierge, A/V technician, conference and meeting planners.

MeadowView Conference Resort

Address 1901 Meadowview Parkway, Kingsport, TN 37660 **Phone** (423) 378-0100 **Fax** (423) 378-3669

Accommodations 196 guest rooms, 73 rooms designed specifically for business travelers.

Meeting Facilities 35,000 sq. ft. convention center, 2 ballrooms (10,000 sq. ft, 4,000 sq. ft), 96-seat amphitheatre, 8 meeting rooms, 2 boardrooms.

Services Conference concierge, complete conference planning services, A/V staff. Golf professionals for tournament organization. Airport transportation.

Willis Conference Center

Address 26 Century Blvd., Nashville, TN 37214 **Phone** (615) 872-6400 **Fax** (615) 872-6429

Accommodations Adjacent to 3 full-service hotels.

Meeting Facilities A non-smoking facility with 17 rooms seating 4–100, ampitheatre with permanent tiered schoolroom seating for 175. All rooms have solid wall construction, climate controls, ergonomic chairs.

Services State-of-the-art A/V equipment, complete conference planning services, video conference equipment, flourescent and incandescent lighting.

TEXAS

American Airlines Training & Conference Center

Address 4501 Highway 360, Fort Worth, TX 76155 **Phone** (817) 967-1000 **Fax** (817) 967-4867

Accommodations 300 sleeping rooms. Single and double occupancy.

Meeting Facilities 8 amphitheaters seating 75 each (full audio/visual), 300-seat auditorium (built-in rear screen projection); 31 breakout rooms, 4 computer labs (Windows and Macintosh), 7 cabin simulators (F100, MD80, MD11, DC10, B727, B757, B767, Cargo Compartment).

Services Conference planners, support staff, audio/visual technicians, business center, airfare arrangements, full catering and banquet services, dry cleaning and laundry services, tour operations.

Del Lago Waterfront Conference Center & Resort

Address 600 Del Lago Blvd., Montgomery, TX 77356 **Phone** (800) 833-3078 **Fax** (409) 582-4918

Accommodations 488 sleeping rooms incl. 302 hi-rise tower suites and 8 penthouses, 45 golf-course cottages and 13 waterfront villas.

Meeting Facilities Over 45,000 sq. ft. of function space—all first floor, no load limit.

Services Valet, concierge.

The Executive Meeting Center

Address Doubletree Hotel—Legacy Town Center, 7120 Dallas Parkway, Plano, TX 75024 **Phone** (972) 473-6444 **Fax** (972) 473-6440

Accommodations 404 guest rooms.

Meeting Facilities 6 meeting rooms.

Services Standard conference services.

Garrett Creek Ranch Conference Center

Address Route 2, Box 235, Paradise, TX 76073 **Phone** (214) 680-8679 **Fax** (214) 690-9318

Accommodations 45 rooms.

Meeting Facilities Meeting rooms for 10–80.

Services Offers the combination of a working ranch and conference center. Complete inventory of A/V equipment, professional meeting planning services, porches with rocking chairs, personalized service.

Hilton DFW Lakes Executive Conference Center

Address 1800 Highway 26 East, DFW Airport (Dallas), TX 76051 **Phone** (817) 481-8444 **Fax** (817) 481-3160

Accommodations Two 9-story towers comprised of 400 comfortable guest rooms and 4 VIP suites. All have air-conditioning control, 26" color TV, oversized work/study area, direct-dial phone, message alert.

Meeting Facilities 40,000 sq. ft. meeting space; 40 meeting rooms for 10–500; 3 tiered amphitheaters. All have climate control.

Services Newsstand, gift shop, bookstore.

Knowledge Development Centers

Address 7301 North State Highway 161, Ste. 100 S, Irving, TX 75039 **Phone** (800) 717-6708 **Fax** (972) 910-9494

Accommodations Nearby hotels via shuttle service.

Meeting Facilities 20,000 sq. ft. of Modern "Training Suites" fully equipped with computers, networks, Internet connectivity, sound systems, ceiling-mounted projection system, support for 24 computers per room. Private lobby, catering, and phone bank for each meeting/training room.

Services On-site technical staff for computer, network, and A/V support.

Lakeway Inn A Dolce Conference Resort

Address 101 Lakeway Drive, Austin, TX 78734-4399 **Phone** (800) LAKEWAY (512) 261-6600 **Fax** (512) 261-7322

Accommodations 137 inn rooms; plus 25 villa rooms.

Meeting Facilities Austin Room with rear screen for up to 360 attendees; 9 other meeting rooms plus workshop suites.

Services Gift shop, pro shop for each golf course, conference planning, and A/V as needed.

Rough Creek Lodge Resort

Address P.O. Box 2400, Glen Rose, TX 76043 **Phone** (800) 864-4705 **Fax** (817) 571-3988

Accommodations 39 rooms, 7 suites including a presidential suite.

Meeting Facilities 4 rooms, 3,570 sq. ft. boardroom for 16; 3 meeting rooms with front/rear screen projection capabilities.

Services Guest rooms have executive desks with dataports. Business center with fax, copier. Complete in-house A/V, gift shop, personalized service.

The San Antonio Learning Center

Address 711 Navarro Street, Suite 100, San Antonio, TX 78205 **Phone** (210) 226-4600 **Fax** (210) 226-4027

Accommodations None listed.

Meeting Facilities 4 rooms, 10,000 sq. ft., 2 large computer classrooms seats 19 and 22; 2 other meeting rooms seats 20 and 80 with flexible setup.

Services 41 networked PCs and workstations; videoconferencing; multimedia presentation; Internet; satellite downlink, on-site technical and meeting planning staffs, food and beverage services.

The San Luis Resort & Conference Center

Address 5222 Seawall Blvd., Galveston, TX 77551 **Phone** (409) 744-1500 **Fax** (409) 744-7545 **e-mail** SanLuisRst@aol.com

Accommodations 244 rooms including 2 penthouse suites.

Meeting Facilities 22 meeting rooms include the 6,000 sq. ft. Argosy Ballroom and 12 dedicated conference rooms.

Services Business services include: personal computers, private offices, copy and facsimile machines. Multilingual staff.

Sheraton Austin Hotel Executive Meeting Center

Address 500 North I-35, Austin, TX 78701 **Phone** (512) 480-8181 **Fax** (512) 480-8633

Accommodations 254 guest rooms, each with voice mail and dataports.

Meeting Facilities 9 meeting rooms for 5–100 persons, each room features tackable walls, white boards, built in screens, in-room house phone, multiple floor power and data jacks, cherry conference table, meeting supply kit.

Services Business Center and staff, trained technicians.

Star Brand Ranch Executive Retreat

Address P.O. Box 660, Kaufman, TX 75142 **Phone** (214) 932-2714 **Fax** (214) 932-7606

Accommodations Comfortably appointed guest rooms with amenities, housing up to 40 double occupancy.

Meeting Facilities 3 rooms serving group up to 40; multiple breakout rooms, ergonomic chairs, climate controls.

Services A/V equipment, write-on, wipe-off, magnetic walls; conference planners; modem connections; business center with fax, copies, and transparencies at no charge.

The Woodlands Resort & Conference Center

Address 2301 N. Millbend Drive, The Woodlands, TX 77380 **Phone** (800) 433-2624 (713) 367-1100 **Fax** (713) 364-6338

Accommodations 268 guest rooms, including 79 suites.

Meeting Facilities 36 dedicated conference rooms encompassing 44,000 sq. ft. of space.

Complete in-house A/V production equipment supply and staffing is available.

Notary public, first aid, A/V repair, and conference concierge.

18,000 sq. ft. indoor exhibit space.

Services Retail shopping, airport transportation, tennis and golf professionals for tournament organization.

Printing, painting, signs, musicians, translation equipment, and other transportation.

UTAH

Snowbird Conference Center at The Cliff Lodge

Address Snowbird, UT 84092 **Phone** (800) 882-4766 (801) 742-2222 **Fax** (801) 742-3342, **Telex** (910) 240-0389

Accommodations 532-room, full-service Cliff Lodge includes deluxe bedrooms and suites, room service.

Meeting Facilities 22 rooms seating 10–900, deluxe exec. boardroom, built-in rear-screen projection in 3 sections of ballroom. Ballrooms accommodate 43 8' × 10' booths. Seasonal (June–Oct.) Event Center seats 2000.

Services Concierge, laundry, dry cleaning, day-care facility, business center.

VERMONT

Stoweflake Resort & Conference Center

Address P.O. Box 369, Stowe, VT 05672 **Phone** (800) 253-2232 (802) 253-7355 **Fax** (802) 253-4419

Accommodations Elegant Vermont countryside inn and modern townhouses offer a total of 94 guest rooms.

Meeting Facilities 10 multi-purpose meeting rooms.

Services Conference planning, gift shop, room service.

VIRGINIA

Airlie Conference Center

Address Route 605, Airlie, VA 22186 **Phone** (800) 288-9573 (703) 347-1300 **Fax** (703) 347-5957

Accommodations 160 rooms, single or double.

Meeting Facilities Conventional-style meeting rooms for up to 200 participants, other buildings for special sessions, many with fireplaces and beautiful views.

Services 3,000-acre estate in the heart of the Virginia hunt country offers a blend of retreat and meeting facilities, special events areas. Site tours are encouraged.

Donaldson Brown Hotel & Conference Center

Address Virginia Polytechnic Institute & State University, Blacksburg, VA 24061-0104 **Phone** (540) 231-8000 **Fax** (540) 231-3746 **e-mail** lisae@vt.edu

Accommodations 100 rooms (handicap accessible).

Meeting Facilities 10 rooms, seating 12–600; complete line of slide, overhead, video equipment and accessories; sound equipment, and trained technical staff.

The Founders Inn

Address 5641 Indian River Rd., Virginia Beach, VA 23464 **Phone** (800) 926-4466 (757) 424-5511 **Fax** (757) 366-5785

Accommodations 249 sleeping rooms. Elegant period decor, Georgian architecture, AAA 4-diamond rating.

Meeting Facilities 28 meeting rooms with 32,000 sq. ft. of meeting space. 70-seat amphitheater, high-speed data lines throughout.

Services Business Center, videoconferencing, teleconferencing, Internet access.

The Hotel Roanoke & Conference Center

Address 110 Shenandoah Avenue, Roanoke, VA 24016
Phone (540) 985-5900
Fax (540) 853-8290

Accommodations A 4-diamond hotel, listed in the National Register of Historic Places.

Kingsmill Resort & Conference Center

Address 1010 Kingsmill Road, Williamsburg, VA 23185
Phone (800) 482-2892 (804) 253-1703 **Fax** (804) 253-3993

Accommodations 352 guest rooms; 1-, 2-, or 3-bedroom suites in villas.

Meeting Facilities 16 meeting rooms seating 10–550.

Services Complete A/V including overhead projectors, video, monitors.

Lansdowne Resort

Address 44050 Woodridge Parkway, Leesburg, VA 20176
Phone (800) 541-4801 (703) 729-8400 **Fax** (703) 729-4096

Accommodations 305 rooms; 14 suites.

Meeting Facilities 45,000 sq. ft. of executive conference space with 25 dedicated conference rooms. Facility also includes 124-seat tiered amphitheater. All rooms have multiple electrical outlets and individual controls for climate, sound, and lighting. Rear/front screen projection. Audio conferencing. Audio and video production capabilities.

At no charge: Standard A/V package including 26" monitor and VCR, 16mm film projector, 35mm slide projector, overhead projector, flip chart, and white board with marker, podium, microphone.

At a charge: Translation equipment, camcorders, computer monitors, projectors/screens, CCTV equipment, typewriters, direction signs, name card printers, etc.

Conference concierge for on-site needs; fax/copy services, typing, phone messages, personal conference planning manager for planning details, professional A/V staff.

15,500 sq. ft. of exhibit space is available. (9,525 sq. ft. of exhibit space available in Lansdowne's ballroom.)

Services Pro Shop, sundries, valet, laundry, dry cleaning, doctor on call, free parking, massage, salon and spa services.

Stenographer, printers, photographer, carpenters, display builders, translators, painter, plumber, musicians.

Renaissance Portsmouth Hotel & Waterfront Conference Center

Address 425 Water Street, Portsmouth, VA 23704
Phone (757) 673-3000
Fax (757) 673-3030

Accommodations 249 guest rooms overlook scenic river. Oversize bathrooms.

Meeting Facilities 24,000 sq. ft. of conference space: 70-seat amphitheater, 5 meeting rooms, 2 ballrooms. Outdoor terrace, 2 waterfront boardrooms.

Services High-speed T-1 lines, on-site a/v company. Business center.

Virginia Crossings Conference Resort

Address 1000 Virginia Center Parkway, Glen Allen, VA 23060
Phone (804) 262-1010 **Fax** no number provided

Accommodations 182 guest rooms.

Meeting Facilities 25 meeting rooms; 22,700 sq. ft. total.

Services Standard conference services.

Westfields Marriott

Address 14750 Conference Center Drive, Chantilly, VA 22021
Phone (800) 635-5666 (703) 818-0400 **Fax** (703) 818-3655

Accommodations 335 guest rooms.

Meeting Facilities 40,000 sq. ft. of dedicated meeting space including 30 meeting rooms, amphitheatre.

Services Media center, full-time A/V staff, business center, simultaneous translation booths, broadcast studio.

Xerox Document University

Address P.O. Box 2000, Leesburg, VA 22075 **Phone** (703) 729-8000 **Fax** (703) 729-5382

Accommodations 800 rooms, 60 suites.

Meeting Facilities 125 rooms, seating 8–400.

Services Conference package includes meeting facilities and most services such as A/V equipment, chalkboard, easels, etc. On-site coordinators assigned to assist each group.

WASHINGTON

Bell Harbor International Conference Center

Address Pier 66, 2211 Alaskan Way, Seattle, WA 98121-1604
Phone (206) 441-6666
Fax (206) 441-6665

Accommodations Preferred arrangements available with local hotels.

Meeting Facilities 4 waterfront conference rooms, large auditorium, 5,000 sq. ft. exhibit hall.

Services Business services center, A/V support.

Hilton Seattle Airport & Conference Center

Address 17620 Pacific Highway South, Seattle, WA 98188
Phone (206) 244-4800
Fax (206) 248-4495

Skamania Lodge

Address 1131 SW Skamania Lodge Way, Stevenson, WA 98648
Phone (800) 982-9095
Fax (509) 427-2548

Accommodations 195 sleeping rooms featuring views of Columbia River Gorge or forest; 34 deluxe rooms with fireplaces.

Meeting Facilities 11 meeting rooms with 12,000 sq. ft. of meeting space. Two ballrooms totaling 11,500 sq. ft. Each is divisible into breakout space by state-of-the-art acoustical walls. Complete A/V equipment and conference services staff.

Services Forest Service information center in Hotel lobby provides directions to local points of interest including day trips to Mt. Hood and Mt. St. Helens.

Worldwide Conference Centers

WEST VIRGINIA

Summit Conference Center

Address 129 Summers Street, Charlston, WV 25301
Phone (888) 224-0515
Fax (304) 343-5114

Accommodations 3 major hotels in walking distance; shuttle service available.

Meeting Facilities 5 rooms seating 2–100 persons.

Services None listed.

WISCONSIN

Fluno Center for Executive Education

Address 675 University Avenue, Madison, WI 53706
Phone (608) 265-6084
Fax (608) 265-9470

Accommodations 100 sleeping rooms.

Meeting Facilities 18 meeting rooms.

Services Located on University of Wisconsin–Madison campus.

Minnesuing Acres

Address 8084 S. Minnesuing Acres Dr., Lake Nebagamon, WI 54849
Phone (612) 540-5205
Fax (612) 449-1150

Accommodations 40 comfortably appointed rooms, including 1 VIP suite. Private lodge situated on 100 wooded acres booked to only one group at a time—no transient business.

Meeting Facilities 4 meeting rooms with a total of 3,500 sq. ft. of meeting space. New main meeting room with state-of-the-art A/V, capable of seating 100; 3 smaller meeting rooms.

Services Transportation to and from Duluth airport at nominal charge.

University of Wisconsin Extension Conference Centers

Address 702 Langdon Street, Madison, WI 53706
Phone (608) 262-1122
Fax (608) 262-8516

Accommodations 153 guest rooms including 2 suites; handicapped accessible.

Meeting Facilities 34 rooms, seating 15–500.

Services A/V on-site with technical staff, complete inventory of equipment including CCTV, teleconference, computer lab; registration, and full conference planning services.

GLOBAL CENTERS

CANADA

The Banff Centre

Address Box 1020, Station 11, Banff, Alberta T0L 0C0 **Phone** (403) 762-6204 **Fax** (403) 762-7560

Accommodations 414 rooms, featuring a variety of types, including deluxe suites.

Meeting Facilities 60 rooms, accommodating 8–1,000.

Services Full meeting planning, off-site activities, full A/V department.

The Metropolitan Centre

Address 333 Fourth Avenue, Southwest, Calgary, Alberta, T2P 0H9
Phone (403) 266-3876
Fax (403) 233-0009

Accommodations Connected to the Westin-Calgary, with easy access to other major downtown hotels.

Meeting Facilities 8 rooms, 15,000 sq. ft. The Centre offers 5,200 sq. ft. conference hall, 250-seat tiered lecture theatre, 3 dedicated meeting rooms to accommodate a variety of set-up styles.

Services State-of-art A/V, video and teleconferencing services, satellite downlink, ISDN, fibre optics, ergonomic seating, individually climate controlled rooms, underground parking. Full-service executive catering.

Morris J. Wosk Centre for Dialogue

Address Simon Fraser University, 515 West Hastings Street, Vancouver, BC V6B 5K3 Canada
Phone (604) 291-5800
Fax (604) 291-5060

Accommodations 150 guest rooms.

Meeting Facilities 14 meeting rooms.

Services N/A.

Donald Gordon Centre

Address Queen's University, Kingston, Ontario K7L 3N6
Phone (613) 545-2221
Fax (613) 545-6624

Accommodations 75 single rooms (1 handicap).

Meeting Facilities 1 seminar room seating 100; 1 tiered lecture theater seating 50, 10 meeting/breakfast rooms seating 10–25.

Services 35mm, 16mm and overhead projectors, video recording and playback on 1/2" VHS tape, video/computer image projection available.

Eaton Hall Inn & Conference Center

Address 13990 Dufferin Street, King City, Ontario L7B 1B3
Phone (905) 833-4500 **Fax** (905) 833-1760 **e-mail** gbaker@ehalladm.senecac.on.ca

Accommodations 44 rooms, accommodating up to 67 guests in lakeside chalets or the historic Villa Fiori, a short stroll from the Hall.

Meeting Facilities 9 meeting rooms, focusing on comfort, are well-lit, climate controlled, equipped with comfortable armchairs.

Services Full range of A/V.

J. J. Wettlaufer Executive Development Center

Address Richard Ivey School of Business, 6450 Kitimat Rd., Mississauga, ON L5N 2B8, Canada
Phone (905) 819-8380
Fax (905) 819-8613

Accommodations None.

Meeting Facilities 10 rooms.

Services None.

NAV CANADA Training & Conference Centre

Address 1950 Montreal Road, Cornwall, ON K6H 6L2
Phone (613) 936-5000
Fax (613) 936-5010

Accommodations 620 sleeping rooms.

Meeting Facilities 50 meeting rooms with 50,000 sq. ft. of meeting space.

Services Business center, computer lab, interactive video, videoconferencing, teleconferencing, satellite up/down links, Internet access.

Spencer Hall

Address 551 Windermere Road, London, Ontario N5X 2T1
Phone (519) 679-4546 **Fax** (519) 645-0733

Accommodations 130 rooms (handicap accessible).

Meeting Facilities Seats 8–130.

Services Extensive A/V inventory, resident A/V technician, resident photographer, satellite conferencing.

White Oaks Conference Resort & Spa

Address 253 Taylor Road, Niagra-on-the-Lake, Ontario L0S 1J0 **Phone** (800) 263-5766 **Fax** (905) 688-2220

Accommodations 150 rooms, including luxury suites and standard rooms. Standard, king-size and double beds. Smoking and nonsmoking rooms available.

Meeting Facilities 18 meeting rooms with 15,000 sq. ft. of meeting space. Amphitheatre, grand event ballroom. Nonsmoking, new conference center added in 1998. Business center.

Services Dining, fitness, photocopying, faxing, room service, handicap accessible.

SOUTH AMERICA

World Trade Center Curacao

Address P.O. Box 6005, Piscadera Bay, Curacao **Phone** 59 9-9-636100 **Fax** 9-9-624408

Accommodations 500 hotel rooms across the street.

Meeting Facilities 11 rooms, including 325-seat auditorium and small exhibition hall.

Services Full range of A/V, conference planning, marketing services, secretarial services.

IACC EUROPE

DENMARK

Hindsgavl Slot

Address Hindsgavl Alle 7, DK 5500 Middelfart, Denmark **Phone** 45 64-41-88-00 **Fax** 64-41-88-11

Accommodations 73 rooms.

Meeting Facilities 13 rooms.

Services Conference planning, secretarial and technical services, overhead/viewgraph, tape recorder, videotape recording, film and slide projectors.

Klarskovgaard Conference Center

Address Korsoer Lystskov, DK 4220 Korsoer, Denmark **Phone** 45 53-57-23-22 **Fax** 53-57-35-41

Accommodations 104 rooms.

Meeting Facilities 24 conference rooms seating 8–200.

Services Full range, trained technicians on staff.

Pharmakon

Address 42 Milnersvej, DK 3400 Hilleroed, Denmark **Phone** 45 42-26-50-00 **Fax** 42-26-51-60

Accommodations 138 rooms.

Meeting Facilities 28 conference rooms seating 8–200.

Services Full range of A/V, computer lab with 12 networked PCs.

Scanticon Comwell Helsingor a/s

Address Norrevej 80, DK-3070 Snekkersten, Denmark **Phone** 45 42-22-03-33 **Fax** 42-22-03-99

Accommodations 149 rooms.

Meeting Facilities 33 rooms.

Services Conference planning, secretarial services, messenger service, language services, graphic services, closed-circuit TV, teleconferencing, overhead/viewgraph, tape recorder, videotape recording, film and slide projectors.

Scanticon Comwell Kolding a/s

Address Skovbrynet 1, P.O. Box 53, DK 6000 Kolding, Denmark **Phone** 45 75-50-15-55 **Fax** 75-50-15-68

Accommodations 160 rooms.

Meeting Facilities 24 rooms, seating 10–1,200.

Services Graphics workshop, conference secretariat, travel and excursion service. Overhead projectors, slide projectors, wide-screen projector, PA systems, cassette video and audio playback units, CCTV, simultaneous translation, teleconference facilities, personal computers, trained technicians on staff.

Schaeffergaarden

Address Fondet for Dansk-Norsk Samarbejde; Jaegersborg Allé 166, DK 2820 Genteofte, Denmark **Phone** 45 39-65-60-65 **Fax** 39-65-05-46 **e-mail** schaef@inet.uni-c.dk

Accommodations 74 rooms.

Meeting Facilities 1 auditorium, seating up to 130; 8 meeting rooms seating 2–50; 10 group rooms seating 2–12.

Services Overhead projectors 400/250 watt, projection screens, flip charts, video (VHS/U-Matic, Pal), LCD projector, tape recorders, special conference staff.

FRANCE

Fregate

Address Route de Bandol, R.N. 599, 83270 St. Cyr Sur Mer, France **Phone** 33 94-29-39-39 **Fax** 94-29-39-40

Accommodations 133 four-star hotel rooms, including a Presidential suite and 38 junior suites. All have outdoor terraces and views of the sea.

Meeting Facilities Seating up to 140.

Services Rear-screen SVGA projection, drop screens, video projection capabilities, PCs.

NORWAY

Klekken Hotell

Address N3500 Hønefoss, Norway **Phone** 47 32-13-22-00 **Fax** 32-13-27-93

Accommodations 116 rooms.

Meeting Facilities 27 rooms.

Services Conference planning, messenger service, all technical equipment including videotape recording.

Vettre Hotel Konferansesenter

Address Konglungveien 201, N-1392 Vettre, Norway **Phone** 47 66-90-22-11 **Fax** 66-90-28-30

Accommodations 76 rooms, 152 beds (handicap accessible).

Meeting Facilities 24 rooms, seating 6-300.

Services Full range, including overhead projector, videos and monitors, special conference staff.

SWEDEN

Best Western Hotel Riverton

Address Stora Badhasgatan 26, Göteborg, S-411-21 Sweden

Phone 46 31-750-1000
Fax 46 31-750-1001

Best Western Hotell Södra Berget

Address Box 858, S-851-24 Sundsvall, Sweden Phone 46 60-123000 Fax 60-151034

Accommodations 180 rooms.

Meeting Facilities 24 rooms, seating 10–360.

Services Full range, including overhead projector, videos, monitors.

Carlstad Conference Centre

Address Tage Erlandergatan 10, Karlstad, s-652-20, Sweden Phone 46 5422-2100 Fax 46 5422-2101

Accommodations At nearby hotels.

Meeting Facilities 25 meeting rooms seating from 6–750 people.

Services Complete inventory of equipment and services.

Engsholm Castle

Address S-153-93 Holo, Sweden Phone 46 8-55-15-51-00 Fax 55-15-50-07

Accommodations 53 single rooms.

Meeting Facilities 17 rooms.

Services Overhead, tape recorder, video VHS, slide projector. Most needs met on request.

Foresta Hotel & Conference Center

Address Box 1324, Lidingö, 18125 Sweden Phone 46 87-65-27-00 Fax 46 87-67-75-42

Accommodations 96 sleeping rooms; newly renovated large rooms and suites.

Meeting Facilities 8 meeting rooms, seating 10–400; 8 breakout rooms, seating 5–15; 600 sq. meters of exhibit space.

Services Overhead projectors, LDC, video, TV.

Hotel Strandbaden

Address Havsbadsallen, Falkenberg, S-311-42, Sweden Phone 46 346-71-49-00 Fax 46 34-61-61-11

Accommodations 135 sleeping rooms.

Meeting Facilities 7 meeting rooms plus 9 breakout rooms, each with white board, overhead projector, flip chart.

Services Conference services, business services, A/V technicians, ISDN lines, Internet connectivity.

Hotel Tylösand

Address Box 643, S-301 16 Halmstad, Sweden Phone 46 3-53-05-00 Fax 46 3-53-24-39 e-mail tylosand@info.se

Accommodations 230 rooms.

Meeting Facilities 27 rooms, seating up to 550.

Services Full range, overhead projector, videos, ISDN, monitors.

Lustikulla Konferens

Address Box 47095, S-100-74 Stockholm, Sweden Phone 46 8-744-45-40 Fax 8-19 82 85

Accommodations N.A.

Meeting Facilities 15 rooms, seating 10-225.

Services Complete inventory of equipment and services.

Nordkalotten Hotell & Konferens

Address Lulviksvägen 1, S-972-54 Luleå, Sweden Phone 46 92-08-93-50 Fax 46 92-01-99-09 e-mail info.nordkalotten@sweden-hotels.se.html

Accommodations 171 rooms, including 65 minisuites with private sauna.

Meeting Facilities 30 rooms, seating 6–345.

Services Full range, including overhead projector, videos, monitors.

Nova Park Hotel

Address Gredelbyleden, S-741-71 Uppsala/Arlanda, Sweden Phone 46 18-34-90-00 Fax 46 18-34-92-92

Accommodations 119 rooms.

Meeting Facilities 9 rooms, seating 10–125.

Services Full range, including overhead, projector, videos, monitors, computer connection, Internet (credit card terminal).

Romantik Hotel Söderköpings Brunn

Address Box 44, S-614-21 Soderkoping, Sweden Phone 46 121-10900 Fax 121-13941

Accommodations 103 rooms, including 8 suites.

Meeting Facilities 17 rooms, seating 8–200.

Services Complete inventory of equipment and services.

Rosenön Conferens Center

Address S-13054 Dalaro, Sweden Phone 46 8 501 53700 Fax 8 501 53801 e-mail rosenon@iacc.iac-conline.com

Accommodations 87 guest rooms.

Meeting Facilities 25 rooms, seating 8–120.

Services Complete inventory of equipment and services.

Selma Lagerlöf Hotel & Spa

Address Box 500, S-686-28 Sunne, Sweden Phone 46 565-166-00, SPA 565-166-21 Fax 565-166-20

Accommodations 340 rooms.

Meeting Facilities 16 conference rooms, 16 breakout rooms, seating 5–400.

Services Full range, including overhead projector, videos, monitors.

Skogshem & Wijk Conference Centers

Address Box 1213, S-181-24 Lidingo, Sweden Phone 46 8-731-42-00 Fax 8-731-42-04

Accommodations 189 rooms.

Meeting Facilities 16 rooms, seating 10–200.

Services Latest technical equipment, computer center.

Stadshotellet Eskilstuna

Address Hamngatan 9-11, Eskilstuna, S-632-20, Sweden Phone 46 1617-7800 Fax 46 1617-7811

Accommodations 213 rooms including 9 suites, 161 double rooms and 43 singles.

Meeting Facilities 25 rooms. 14 meeting rooms at various capacities including a large congress room seating 550 people, 11 meeting rooms for 2–10 people, Banquet room.

Services Catering, parking, hair dresser, dry cleaning.

Steningevik Konferens

Address Steninge allé, Märsta/Arlanda, S-195-91, Sweden **Phone** 46 8-591-231-50 **Fax** 46 8-591-127-31

Accommodations 51 sleeping rooms, all 2-bed doubles.

Meeting Facilities 14 meeting rooms seating 6–100; 8 breakout rooms.

Services Full range A/V services including overhead projector, LCD projector, video monitors, computer connections, Internet and ISDN lines.

Strand Hotell, Borgholm

Address P.O. Box 41, S-387-88 Borgholm, Sweden **Phone** 46 485-888 88 **Fax** 485-124- 27 **e-mail** strandhotell@borgholm-strand.se

Accommodations 125 rooms.

Meeting Facilities 9 rooms, seating 10–300.

Services Full range, including overhead 16mm, 35mm slide projectors, PA systems, video and audio playback units. Special conference and technical staff.

Vildmarks Hotellet

Address Kolmården S-618-93, Sweden **Phone** 46 11-15-71-00 **Fax** 46 11-39-50-84

Accommodations 213 rooms.

Meeting Facilities 10 meeting rooms.

Services N/A.

Ystads Saltsjöbad

Address Saltsjöbadsvägen 6, S-271-39 Ystad, Sweden **Phone** 46 41-11-36-30 **Fax** 46 41-15-58-35

Accommodations 108 double rooms.

Meeting Facilities 15 rooms, 1 convention hall, seating 10–325. Program for approx. 40 social activities.

Services Full range, including overhead projectors, videos, all technical facilities including ISDN.

UNITED KINGDOM

Ashridge Management College

Address Berkhamsted, HP4 1NS Hertfordshire, England **Phone** 44 1442-841027 or 841029 **Fax** 1442-841036

Accommodations 173 rooms.

Meeting Facilities 15 rooms seating 12–150; syndicate rooms.

Services Conference planning, secretarial, graphic, fixed closed-circuit TV, TV and radio studio, overhead/viewgraph, tape recorders, videotape recording, camcorders, film and slide projectors, PCs, flip charts, black or white boards.

Barnett Hill Conference & Training Centre

Address Wonersh, Guilford, Surrey GU5 ORF England **Phone** 44 1483-893361 **Fax** 44 1483-892836

Accommodations 53 rooms, contemporary and well-equipped.

Meeting Facilities 8 rooms, seating 20–70. Sophisticated conference suites equipped with state-of-the-art presentation systems, ISDN links, data projection, overhead projector, flip charts, A/V, closed-circuit TV.

Services Secretarial services, translation services. Unique outdoor, intellectually challenging exercises can test teamwork.

Barony Castle

Address Eddleston by Peebles, EH45 8QW Peeblesshire, Scotland **Phone** 01721 730395 **Fax** 01721 730275

Accommodations 78 guest rooms.

Meeting Facilities 8 rooms, 8 syndicate rooms.

Services Complete range of equipment and services.

Branksome

Address Hindhead Road, Haslemere, GU27-3PU, Surrey, England **Phone** 44 1428-664600 **Fax** 44 1428-664699

Accommodations 59 rooms.

Meeting Facilities 22 meeting rooms, 9 syndicate rooms.

Services Complete range of equipment and services.

Burleigh Court

Address Loughborough University, Loughborough, LE11-3TD Leicestershire, England **Phone** 44 1509-211515 **Fax** 1509-211508

Accommodations 118 rooms.

Meeting Facilities 20 meeting rooms.

Services Conference planning, secretarial services, language translations, closed-circuit TV, overhead/viewgraph, tape recorder, videotape recording, film and slide projectors, computer link.

24-Hour Reception fax: 44-1509-211569.

Chartridge Conference Centre

Address Chartridge Lane, Chesham, Buckinghamshire HP5 2TU, England **Phone** 44 1494-837484 **Fax** 44 1494-837305

Accommodations 57 guest rooms.

Meeting Facilities 20 modern and well-equipped meeting rooms.

Services Conference planning, secretarial services. Closed circuit TV, data projection, overhead projector, tape recorder, videotape recording, film and slide projectors. On-site conference technician.

Cranage Hall

Address Knutsford Road, Cranage, Holmes Chapel, Cheshire CW48E0, England **Phone** 44 1477-536666 **Fax** 1477-536787

Accommodations 120 double and twin ensuite rooms with T/C, TV, satellite, voicemail and tea/coffee-making facilities.

Meeting Facilities 29 rooms, seating 2–300. Largest is 3,200 sq. ft. All are air conditioned.

Services Beauty salon.

Cranfield Management Development Centre

Address Wharley End, Cranfield, Bedford MK43 OHG, United Kingdom **Phone** 44 1234-751122 **Fax** 44 1234-751707

Accommodations 186 ensuite bedrooms equipped with direct-dial telephone, modem point, tea/coffee-making facilities, ironing center, hair dryer, colour TV with radio.

Meeting Facilities 18 lecture rooms ranging from small flats to a large tiered lecture theatre seating 100, plus 38 syndicate rooms. All main meeting rooms have overhead projector, screen, TV, video, LCD projector, flip chart.

Services Full range of business and technical services.

Durdent Court

Address Tilehouse Lane, Denham, UB9-5DU Buckinghamshire, England **Phone** 44 1895-833338 **Fax** 1895-832156

Accommodations 83 rooms.

Meeting Facilities 20 rooms, seating 8–150.

Services Conference planning, secretarial services, CCTV, slide projectors, audio conferencing, data and video projection, computers, dedicated conference technicians.

Eastwood Hall Conference Centre

Address Eastwood, Nottingham, NG16 3AQ, England **Phone** 44 1773-532532 **Fax** 44 1773-532533

Accommodations 120 sleeping rooms.

Meeting Facilities 36 meeting rooms.

Services Full services; newly opened May 2000.

Elvetham Hall Ltd. Conference Centre

Address Hartley Wintney, RG27-8AR Hampshire, England **Phone** 44 1252-844871 **Fax** 1252-844161

Accommodations 72 rooms.

Meeting Facilities 17 meeting rooms.

Services Conference planning, closed-circuit TV, camcorders, overhead/viewgraph, tape recorder, videotape recording (VHS and U-matic), film and slide projectors, video/data projector. On-site technicians.

Ettington Chase Conference Centre

Address Ettington, Stratford upon Avon, CV37 7NZ Warwickshire, England **Phone** 44 1604-821666 **Fax** 1604-821596

Accommodations 113 guestrooms.

Meeting Facilities 29 meeting rooms.

Services Conference planning, secretarial services, language translators, closed-circuit TV, overhead/viewgraph, tape recorder, videotape recording, personal computers, film and slide projectors, video conferencing.

Gorse Hill

Address Gorse Hill, Hook Heath Road, Woking, GU22 Surrey, England **Phone** 44 1483-747444 **Fax** 1483-747454

Accommodations 50 rooms.

Meeting Facilities 7 meeting rooms, 10 syndicates.

Services CCTV, OHP, LCD, Barco, PCs, Lite Pro.

Harben House

Address Tickford Street, Newport Pagnell, MK16 9EY Buckinghamshire, England **Phone** 44 1908-215600 **Fax** 1908-215610

Accommodations 140 rooms.

Meeting Facilities 14 meeting rooms, 28 syndicates, theatre seating 200.

Services CCTV, OHP, LCD, Barco, PCs.

Hartsfield Manor

Address Sandy Lane, Betchworth, RH3 7AA Surrey, England **Phone** 44 1737-842821 **Fax** 1737-842965

Accommodations 50 rooms.

Meeting Facilities 7 meeting rooms, 10 syndicates, theatre seating 100.

Services CCTV, OHP, LCD, Barco, PCs.

Highfield Park

Address Heckfield, Hook, RG27 OL9 Hampshire, England **Phone** 44 118-9328-369 **Fax** 118-9326-500

Accommodations 60 rooms.

Meeting Facilities 12 meeting rooms.

Services CCTV, OHP, LCD, Barco, PCs.

Highgate House Conference Centre

Address Creaton, NN6-8NN Northamptonshire, England **Phone** 44 1604-505505 **Fax** 1604-505656

Accommodations 95 rooms.

Meeting Facilities 30 meeting rooms.

Services Conference planning, secretarial services, language translations, CCTV, LCD, ISDN, overhead/viewgraph, tape recorder, videotape recording, personal computers, film and slide projectors.

Horsley Management Centre

Address Ockham Road South, East Horsley, KT24 6DU Surrey, England **Phone** 44 1483-284211 **Fax** 44 1483-285812

Accommodations 126 rooms.

Meeting Facilities 35 meeting rooms.

Services CCTV, OHP, LCD, Barco, Lite Pro.

Horwood House

Address Little Horwood, Milton Keynes, Buckinghamshire, MK 17 OPQ England **Phone** 44 1296-722100 **Fax** 44 1296-722300

Accommodations 120 rooms, ensuite, single study with TV, voicemail, tea/coffeemaking facilities.

Meeting Facilities 29 rooms, with capacity of 2–90. Fully equipped with the latest presentation technology, including OH projector and screen, 35 mm projector, flipchart, white board. Also available: light projector, TV, video, rear screen projector.

Services None listed.

Hunton Park

Address Essex Lane, Kings Langley, WD4 8PN Hertfordshire, England **Phone** 44 1923-261511 **Fax** 1923-267537

Accommodations 60 rooms.

Meeting Facilities 6 meeting rooms, 12 syndicates.

Services CCTV, OHP, LCD, Barco, PCs.

Latimer House and Conference Center

Address Latimer, Chesham, HP5 1UD Buckinghamshire, England
Phone 44 1494-764422
Fax 1494-765704

Accommodations 135 rooms.

Meeting Facilities 20 meeting rooms.

Services CCTV, OHP, LCD, Barco, PCs, videoconferencing.

Latimer Mews Training and Conference Centre

Address Latimer, Chesham, HP5-1UD Buckinghamshire, England
Phone 44 1494-764466
Fax 1494-765891

Accommodations 53 rooms.

Meeting Facilities 4 meeting rooms, 10 syndicates.

Services CCTV, OHP, LCD, Barco, PCs.

The Mill and Old Swan Conference Centre

Address Minster Lovell, OX8 5RN Oxfordshire, England
Phone 44 01993-77441
Fax 01339-702002

Accommodations 60 guest rooms.

Meeting Facilities 5 rooms, 8 syndicates.

Services OHP, monitor and video, Barco, CCTV, PCs, 35mm projector.

Milton Hill

Address Milton Hill, Abingdon, Oxfordshire OX13-6AF, England
Phone 44 1235-831474
Fax 44 1235-825796

Accommodations 79 rooms.

Meeting Facilities 7 meeting rooms, 14 syndicate rooms.

Services Complete range of equipment and services.

The Moller Centre for Continuing Education

Address Storey's Way, CB3 ODE Cambridge, England
Phone 44 (0) 1223-465530
Fax (0) 1223-46554
e-mail jmd12@cam.ac.uk

Accommodations 70 ensuite guest rooms.

Meeting Facilities Lecture Theatre with racked seating; 14 meeting rooms ranging in size to cater for 1:1 training to 140.

Services Conference planning, overhead projectors, white boards, flip charts, slide projectors, Barco, TV/VCR sets, computer data projection, computer network facilities.

New Place Management Centre

Address Shirrell Heath, Southampton, SO32 2JH Hampshire, England
Phone 44 1329-833543
Fax 1329-833259

Accommodations 110 guest rooms.

Meeting Facilities 2 conference suites; 13 meeting rooms; 22 syndicate rooms.

Services Lite Pro, CCTV, OHP, LCD, Barco, PCs.

Radcliffe House

Address University of Warwick, CV4-7AL Coventry, Warwickshire, England Phone 44 1203-474711
Fax 1203-694282

Accommodations 154 rooms.

Meeting Facilities 11 lecture rooms; 28 syndicate rooms.

Services Conference planning, overhead projector film and slide projector, closed-circuit TV, videotape recording, tape recording, computer data projection, U-Matic recording.

Scarman House Training and Conference Centre

Address University of Warwick, Coventry, CV4-7AL Warwickshire, England Phone 44 1203-221111
Fax 1203-520362

Accommodations 200 rooms.

Meeting Facilities 52 meeting rooms.

Services Conference planning, overhead/viewgraph, film and slide projectors, closed-circuit TV, video tape recording, tape recording, computer data projection, U-matic recording.

Sedgebrook Hall

Address Pitsford Road, Chapel Brampton, NN68BD Northhampton, England Phone 44 1604-821666 Fax 1604-821596

Accommodations 102 guest rooms.

Meeting Facilities 23 meeting rooms.

Services Conference planning, secretarial services, language translators, closed-circuit TV, overhead/viewgraph, tape recorder, videotape recording, personal computers, film and slide projectors, video conferencing.

Staverton Park

Address Staverton, NN11 61T Northamptonshire, England
Phone 44 1327-302000
Fax 1327-311428

Accommodations 100 rooms.

Meeting Facilities 7 rooms, 12 syndicates.

Services CCTV, OHP, LCD.

Sundridge Park

Address Plaistow Lane, Bromley, BR1-3TP Kent, England
Phone 44 1313-3131
Fax 1313-7500

Accommodations 150 rooms.

Meeting Facilities 11 meeting rooms.

Services Conference planning, secretarial services, overhead/viewgraph, tape recorder, videotape recording, film and slide projectors.

Theobolds Park Conference Centre

Address Bulls Cross Ride, Cheshunt, Herts, EN7 5HW, England
Phone 44 1992-633375
Fax 1992-634212

Accommodations 42 guest rooms.

Meeting Facilities 15 conference rooms.

Services Full range of A/V equipment and specialist staff.

Expansion plans include 8 more conference rooms seating up to 120, and 26 additional guest rooms.

Uplands

Address Four Ashes Road, Cryers Hill, High Wycombe, HP15 6LA Buckinghamshire, England
Phone 44 1494-716473
Fax 1494-713318

Accommodations 77 rooms.

Meeting Facilities 8 meeting rooms, 10 syndicates.

Services CCTV, OHP.

Warbrook House

Address Eversley, RG27 OPL Hampshire, England
Phone 44 1189-732174
Fax 1734-730472

Accommodations 60 rooms.

Meeting Facilities 4 meeting rooms, 17 syndicates.

Services CCTV, OHP, LCD, Barco, PCs.

Worldwide Conference Centers

Wiston House

Address Steyning, West Sussex BN44 3DZ, England **Phone** 44 1903-817775 **Fax** 44 1903-816944

Accommodations 49 guest rooms.

Meeting Facilities 4 meeting rooms.

Services Conference planning, secretarial services, language translation, simultaneous translation equipment, overhead projectors, videotape recording, film and slide projectors.

Wokefield Executive Centre

Address Mortimer, Reading, RG7 3AG Berkshire, England
Phone 44 0118 9332391
Fax 0118 9333558

Accommodations 200 double ensuite guest rooms, 65 single ensuite guest rooms.

Meeting Facilities Extensive meeting rooms for 2–350, ample syndicate space.

Services Video projection, CCTV, OHP, LCD, Barco, PCs and secretarial service.

Wokefield Mansion

Address The Mansion House, Mortimer, Reading, Berkshire RG7-3AG, England **Phone** 44 1189-332391 **Fax** 44 1189-334401

Accommodations 97 rooms.

Meeting Facilities 4 meeting rooms, 14 syndicate rooms.

Services Complete range of equipment and services.

Woodside Conference & Training Centre

Address Glasshouse Lane, Kenilworth, Warwickshire CV82AL, England **Phone** 44 1926-852217 **Fax** 44 1926-859550

Accommodations 74 en-suite, well-equipped bedrooms.

Meeting Facilities 8 air-conditioned conference rooms, seating up to 85 people, with adjacent syndicates.

Services Conference planning, technical support, secretarial services, language translation, state-of-the-art A/V and presentation systems, videoconferencing, ISDN links, data projection, personal computers, outdoor team-building exercises.

IACC AUSTRALIA

Aitken Hill (BHP) Global Leadership Centre

Address Dunhelen Lane, Yuroke, Victoria 3063, Australia **Phone** 61 392-174-884 **Fax** 61 392-174-999

Accommodations 81 sleeping rooms including 10 suites and handicap accessible rooms.

Meeting Facilities 19 meeting rooms comprised of 17 syndicate rooms and 2 seminar rooms seating 100 and 300 people; rooms can be reconfigured for theatre-style seating.

Services Videoconferencing, personal computer IT support, business centre, resource facility, administrative support. Transportation services and transfers available.

Bentinck Country House

Address 1 Carlisle Street, Woodend, Victoria, 3442, Australia
Phone 61 05427-2944
Fax 054272232

Accommodations 28 rooms (24 ensuite/4 shared facility).

Meeting Facilities 2 rooms each 80 sg. mtrs.; 4 breakout rooms; office; full equipment inventory.

Services Conference planning, secretarial, messenger, and A/V services including video recording, data and video projection, and electronic whiteboard.

Blythewood Grange Conference Centre

Address CNR Morgan and Grant Streets, Sebastopol, Ballarat, Victoria, 3356, Australia
Phone 61 5335-8133
Fax 83361550

Accommodations 58 rooms.

Meeting Facilities 3 conference rooms and 9 syndicate rooms catering from 2-200 in exclusive dedicates area.

Services Full conf. planning and on-site support, secretarial, fax, copying, TV-video recording, electronic white board, direct projector, OHP including Zoom OHP, flip chart, slide projector, ergonomic furniture, climate control systems.

Campaspe House Executive Retreat

Address Goldie's Lane, Woodend, Victoria, 3442, Australia
Phone 61 354-272-273
Fax 61 534-271-049
e-mail campaspe@hitech.net.com

Accommodations 20 single rooms. Accommodates up to 34 people on a single and twin-share basis. Sole occupancy for all groups.

Meeting Facilities Main conference rooms with syndicate room and 3 breakout areas.

Services Full conference planning and on-site service. Electronic white board, OHP projectors, slide projector, video monitors, flip charts, copying, fax, climate-control systems.

Checker Resort & Conference Centre

Address 331 Mona Vale Road, Terray Hills, Victoria 2084, Australia
Phone 61 2-9450-2422 **Fax** 61 2-9450-2778

Accommodations 43 sleeping rooms.

Meeting Facilities 4 meeting rooms.

Services Standard services.

Cope Williams Conference Centre

Address PO Box 18, Romsey, Victoria 3434, Australia **Phone** 61 3-5429-5428 **Fax** 61 3-5429-5655

Accommodations 23 sleeping rooms.

Meeting Facilities 3 meeting rooms.

Services Standard services.

The Country Place Executive Resort

Address Olinda Creek Road, Kalorama, Victoria, 3186, Australia
Phone 61 03-9728-1177
Fax 03-9728-6260

Accommodations 42 elegantly appointed ensuite double rooms, including 16 twin share, accommodating up to 60.

Meeting Facilities 5 rooms, seating 10–80.

Services Secretarial support, photocopier, fax, conference planning and services, TV-video recording, electronic white board, flip charts, slide projector, ergonomic furniture, black-out facility, overhead projectors, screens, climate-control systems, high and low rope outdoor experiential learning circuit, laundry, photographer and hospitality lounge.

The Cumberland Marysville

Address 34 Murchison St., Marysville, Victoria, 3779, Australia
Phone 61 35-963-203
Fax 61 35-963-458

Accommodations 43 rooms, ensuite, with color TV, air conditioning, and heating.

Meeting Facilities 5 rooms, equipped with ergonomic chairs, electronic white boards, great lighting and garden views.

Services Full secretarial.

Deakin Management Centre

Address Deakin University, Geelong, Victoria, 3217, Australia
Phone 613 5227-3000
Fax 613 5227-3101

Accommodations 57 sleeping rooms including 30 twin share rooms and 2 facilitator suites.

Meeting Facilities 2 meeting rooms plus 7 syndicate rooms. Centre is designed for up to 100 delegates.

Services Full conference planning and secretarial services. Networked computers, laser printers, overhead projector, video, audio system/ AMP/cassette/CD player, white board, flip chart, blackout facility.

Edmund Barton Centre

Address 488 South Road, Moorabbin, Victoria, 3189, Australia
Phone 61 392-095-929 **Fax** 61 392-095-907 **e-mail** mwithers@barton.vic.edu.com.html

Accommodations 50 rooms, executive style, incl. 3 executive lounges.

Meeting Facilities 19 rooms, state-of-the-art A/V, abundance of natural light in all rooms.

Services Full catering and banquet services, free parking for 600 cars, professional conference management.

Flowerdale Estate Executive Retreat

Address Broadford-Flowerdale Road, Strath Creek, Victoria, Australia
Phone 61 3-5784-5600
Fax 61 3-5784-5699

Accommodations Large elegantly appointed double guest rooms with garden views. Fully air-conditioned. Multi-channel satellite TV. E-mail and Internet.

Meeting Facilities Air-conditioned conference rooms, quality A/V equipment, videoconferencing, high speed data transfer. Facilitator's office equipped with computer, printer, fax, copier, e-mail and Internet.

Services Full conference planning and secretarial services.

Green Gables Conference Centre

Address Gable Lane, Warburton, Victoria, 3799, Australia
Phone 61 05-966-2077
Fax 05-966-5382

Accommodations 38 ensuite rooms accommodating up to 70 people.

Meeting Facilities 4 productive conference rooms, 4 syndicate rooms, catering for 12–160 participants.

Services Full conference planning support, secretarial, fax, photocopier, TV/video, white boards, flip charts, OH projectors and screen, ergonomic furniture, climate-controlled systems.

Killara Inn

Address 480 Pacific Highway, Killara, NSW, 2071, Australia
Phone 61 02 9416-1344
Fax 61 02 9416-6347

Accommodations 39 sleeping rooms.

Meeting Facilities 5 meeting rooms, full video conferencing facilities in all rooms.

Services N/A.

Lancemore Hill Conference Center

Address Kilmore-Lancefield Rd., Kilmore, Victoria, 3764, Australia
Phone 61 57-822-009
Fax 57-822-371

Accommodations 71 ensuite rooms, sleeping capacity 130.

Meeting Facilities 4 rooms (seating to 130), 18 syndicate rooms.

Services Secretarial support, copier, fax, conf. planning, 52" monitors computer graphics and standard, vhs, pal, ntsc, u-matic 1/2 & 3/4, video cameras, overhead projectors and screens, carousel projectors.

Macquarie Graduate School of Management (MGSM)

Address Macquarie University, New South Wales, 2109, Australia
Phone 61 298-509-004 **Fax** 61 298-508-595 **e-mail** pat.mcdonald@mq.edu.au

Accommodations 40 double ensuite rooms, with queen-size beds, 2 facilitator suites available on requests. Rooms are fully serviced daily and feature individually controlled a/c and heat, hair dryers, complimentary tea and coffee-making facilities, complimentary soft drinks, ISD-STD international direct dial phones.

Meeting Facilities 33 meeting rooms in total, comprised of 21 syndicate rooms, 4 tiered theatres, 8 flat floor rooms.

Services Full A/V in meeting rooms, business centre. Guest services include laundy and dry cleaning, reading room, fully licensed bar, 24-hr. reception, TV and video hire, safety deposit, souvenir-promotional items, free parking.

Marylands Country House

Address 22 Falls Road, Marysville, Victoria, 3779, Australia
Phone 61 59-63-3204
Fax 59-633-251

Accommodations 42 double rooms accommodating up to 100 persons.

Meeting Facilities 3 main rooms with syndicate rooms available. All standard A/V and display equipment is available together with video recording facilities and computer modem connections.

Services Fax, photocopying, word processing, computer usage, laundry, event coordination, conference planning.

Monash Mt. Eliza Business School

Address Kunyung Road, Mt. Eliza, Victoria, 3930, Australia
Phone 61 392-151-100 **Fax** 61 392-875-139 **e-mail** conf@mteliza.edu.au.html

Accommodations 97 spacious single rooms.

Meeting Facilities 20 rooms, 9,160 sq. ft. Datashow and video-data projectors, slide projectors,

Worldwide Conference Centers

PAL/NTSC/VHS videos and monitors, video cameras.

Services A/V equipment and support, conference planning and administrative services. Local area network with PCs in every meeting and syndicate room, offering a wide range of applications. Secretarial support available.

Portsea Village Conference Resort

Address 3765 Point Nepean Rd., Portsea, Victoria, 3944, Australia
Phone 61 359-848-484
Fax 61 359-844-686

Accommodations 56 apartment-style accommodations with 1, 2, or 3 bedrooms. Twin share is a 2-bedroom, 2-bathroom apartment.

Meeting Facilities 2 rooms, seating 50 and 15 people. Executive lounge rooms available for small meetings.

Services CMP includes standard A/V equipment, stationery, and audio equipment.

The Shearwater Conference Centre

Address Cape Schanck Resort, Boneo Road, Cape Schanck, Victoria, 3939, Australia **Phone** 61 3-5950-8000
Fax 61 3-5950-8

Accommodations 58 rooms. Designed for today's conference market with international direct-dial phones and modem lines, TV, radio, fridge, AC, heating, private balcony with ocean view.

Meeting Facilities 8 rooms, with automated rear projectors, multimedia facilities incorporating video and slide presentation, computer display, theatre-quality sound.

Services Courtesy shuttle available, parking, full secretarial support, fax, photocopier, user-friendly technical facilities, complete in-house coordination.

Stonelea

Address Connelly's Creek Road, Acheron, 3714, Australia,
Phone 61 57-722-222
Fax 57-722-210

Accommodations 47 Boutique Australian Colonial, with ensuite, AC, mini bar and STD/ISD telephones.

Meeting Facilities 2 main conference rooms and several breakout rooms, 110 total capacity theatre style.

Services Lecterns, P.A. system, tape deck and recording facilities, electronic white board, video projection cameras, monitors, VHS/Hi-FI/VCR, slide and overhead projectors, screens, flip charts, white boards, fax, copying, secretarial services.

Vue Grand Hotel

Address 46 Hesse Street, Queenscliff, Victoria, Australia **Phone** 61 3-5258-1544 **Fax** 61 3-5258-3471

Accommodations 32 rooms, ensuite accommodations. "Old world" charm.

Meeting Facilities 4 meeting rooms with flexibility for groups from 2 to 60. Latest technical equipment.

Services Historic hotel totally renovated for corporate conferences. Standard services.

IACC JAPAN

The Tokyo Conference Center

Address 3-22-20 Iidabashi, Chiyoda-ku, Tokyo, 102-0072, Japan
Phone 81 3-3841-0791
Fax 81 3-3841-0790

Accommodations 200 rooms in nearby hotels. Reservations can be arranged.

Meeting Facilities 14 rooms, including 12 conference rooms seating 12–60; 1 boardroom, divisible large hall seating up to 900 theater style.

Services On-site A/V manager, professional conference coordinators to assist with all aspects of a meeting.

NIGERIA

The Conference & Training Centre

Address Elephant House, 16th and 17th floors, 214 Broad Street, Lagos, Nigeria, Africa
Phone 234 41-266-7329 41-264-3737 **Fax** 234 41-266-3442

Accommodations Non-residential.

Meeting Facilities 18 rooms; 18,000 sq. ft. Flexible floor arrangements. Meeting rooms for 10–15; seminar rooms for 20–25; lecture theatre seats 120.

Services Lounges, bookstore.

SINGAPORE

The Beaufort Hotel and Conference Centre

Address 2 Bukit Manis Road, Sentosa, 099891, Singapore **Phone** 65 275-0331 **Fax** 65 275-0228

Accommodations 214 guest rooms, including 4 garden villas and suites. Sizes range from 350–1600 sq. ft. View of gardens. Color TV/remote, in-room movies, minibar, in-room safe, coffee-tea making facilities, 24-hr. room service.

Meeting Facilities 12 meeting rooms, including syndicate rooms.

Services Conference concierge, conference planners, complete A/V range of equipment and services.

6.4 Training for Trainers

The latest trends in training have significantly broadened the field of opportunity for the trainer's own on-the-job training. The broader ideas of workplace learning challenge those who do training to look around for more and better opportunities to foster learning for individuals, teams, and organizations. Our representative listing also reflects the trend toward the role of instructor being done by managers, supervisors, mentors, coaches, and colleagues of all titles. It is our hope that all persons who need to function as "trainer" in today's lively workplace will find this section of *The Trainer's Almanac* particularly useful. The listing is a unique reflection of what's happening in the year 2002; Prentice Hall does not endorse any provider of services. Inclusion here in *The Trainer's Almanac* illustrates the range of services available and is meant to reflect the breadth of the field in warm-body, eyeball-to-eyeball, shoulder-to-shoulder, bricks-and-mortar training.

Our section 6.8 contains a listing of online learning opportunities with Web addresses. Our sections 3, *Training Program Design*, and 4, *Training Program Delivery*, also contain numerous references to learning opportunities other than seminars and workshops where people gather face to face.

A Representation of Current Trends

Outsourcing, again this year, has meant that training consultants and vendors of training services of all sorts are thriving as corporations, non-profits, and the government are all hiring training outsiders to do work inside. This trend alone means that training providers, especially outsiders, need to pay attention to their own professional development as businesspersons and as trainers who are aware and up on the latest changes in the field. Downsizing, of course, has worked with outsourcing to provide both a supply of independent training workers as well as a demand for services as reduced staffs continue to want and need to provide services. Trainers who are still employed full time need to be aware of and skilled in many more executive and management functions, yet competent in all of the traditional training jobs including needs assessment, instructional design and development, training presentation techniques and delivery systems, and evaluation for return on investment. Many training providers offer certification courses. Mentoring, coaching, and Web-based design and delivery skills are also required of today's trainers. Leadership training has a renewed focus this year.

Trainers, inside organizations as well as on the outside, are being both pushed and enticed by the possibilities of the performance improvement focus in human resources and organization development. The broadening of the trainer's view to encompass personal and organizational performance has opened up a host of knowledge, skill, and attitude requirements for the savvy trainer. Keeping up with the latest issues and developmental challenges in Web-based training and distance learning is also an opportunity for training for trainers. Building collaborative alliances among companies and with educational institutions is an important focus for year 2002.

And finally, facilitation skills of all sorts are required of trainers because of new ways of working in teams and in flatter and less formal organizations. The classroom is not always the delivery venue of choice, and trainers need to know more about facilitating learning online and across distances, and within different social structures with an increasingly global, multicultural, and diverse trainee population. Today's trainers also must be skilled in the management, design, and delivery of e-learning. Section 6.4's representative listing of resources for continuous learning reflects these current trends as well as indicates the field's grounding in more traditional train-the-trainer topics. Training is still in evolution, not revolution.

Our Approach to Indexing

In our approach to indexing these 164 representative training opportunities we chose 26 indexing terms or keywords that describe the major thrust of the seminar or workshop described in the listing. In some cases, an entry is indexed under more than one keyword. As you leaf through this section, you'll quickly see that the 164 seminars and workshops are listed alphabetically by the name of the vendor or company providing the service. Leafing through and scanning the section first will give you a good idea of the breadth of topics and the range of current interest. Using the index of keywords will help you with depth of coverage and focus on specific areas. You'll also see that we have indexed the 86 vendors and service provider companies by the geographic area of the headquarters office, and that we have a good representation from all four geographical areas. You'll see, too, that we have listed these vendors and service providers alphabetically in a separate listing, since in the seminar listing some providers have more than one listing for seminars or workshops. In this alphabetical listing of providers, we include Website addresses and note that some offer discounts for Web registration. Most training providers post their schedules on their Websites. Check them for dates and locations. Our indexing philosophy is to be representative, fair, and broad. Costs quoted are for one person; however, most providers offer a discount for teams.

A Focus on Public Seminars and Workshops

We have also chosen to focus on training for trainers that is open to the public. Most provider companies also offer on-site or customized training. Many offer certification programs. If this is what you want, be sure to telephone the contact number to inquire about individualized company programs. In our listing we have also deliberately not included all training offered by a particular provider. We have been selective and guided by a philosophy of being representative rather than inclusive of every seminar or program offered by a particular company. We believe we have given you enough information to whet your appetite for learning and to understand how to get in touch with a vendor for more information. We have also tried to find relevant programs throughout the country, so that our listing is truly nationwide. In addition, we cite a wide variety of training for beginning trainers as well as for those at manager and executive levels.

What you will not find here is specific training in computer software products, nor will you find programs offered by professional associations only for their members. We have also not included community college outreach programs, and although we do include some business school continuing education programs, these are not inclusive but rather are meant to encourage you to investigate further into these kinds of sources in your own local area.

We have carefully made phone calls to verify the information included here, have checked Websites, and have used information from the latest vendor brochures. We are not endorsing any company listed here. As in the purchase of any product or service, you as the buyer of a training program must choose carefully so that your objectives for learning match the product or service being offered. We have tried to include programs at varying prices and for durations of one day to several weeks. Our listing can help you comparison shop, at least. We can honestly say that we are the most truly representative, trainer-focused index of training opportunites available from any publisher. To get the most out of your search through section 6.4, we suggest that you first review the list of providers on the next four pages. Web addresses are provided for you to search complete information.

Geographic Index of Seminar and Workshop Providers

Northeast
2, 6, 7, 10, 18, 19, 20, 23, 28, 33, 34, 35, 37, 38, 41, 42, 49, 52, 53, 55, 56, 60, 68

Mid-Atlantic/South
1, 5, 14, 15, 16, 25, 27, 31, 32, 40, 48, 51, 58, 61, 70, 73, 77, 81, 82, 85

Midwest
4, 9, 12, 13, 22, 26, 36, 43, 44, 46, 54, 57, 59, 62, 67, 78, 79, 80, 83, 84, 87

West
3, 8, 11, 17, 21, 24, 29, 30, 39, 45, 47, 50, 63, 64, 65, 69, 71, 72, 74, 75, 76

1
Achieve Global, Inc.
8875 Hidden River Parkway, Ste 400
Tampa, FL 33637
800/291-2752
888/662-7692 (fax)
www.achieveglobal.com

2
American Management Association International
P.O. Box 169
Saranac Lake, NY 12983
800/262-9699
518/891-0368 (fax)
www.amanet.org/seminars

3
American Productivity & Quality Center (APQC)
123 N. Post Oak Lane
Houston, TX 77024
713/685-7227
800/776-9676
713/681-5321 (fax)
www.apqc.org

4
American Society for Quality (ASQ)
P.O. Box 3066
Milwaukee, WI 53201
800/248-1946
414/272-1734 (fax)
www.asq.org

5
ASTD
1640 King Street, Box 1443
Alexandria, VA 22313
800/628-2783
703/683-8103 (fax)
www.astd.org

6
Babson School of Executive Education
Babson Park, MA 02457
781/239-4354
781/239-5266 (fax)
www.babson.edu/see

7
Balanced Scorecard Collaborative, Inc.
55 Old Bedford Road
Lincoln, MA 01773
781/259-3737
781/259-3389 (fax)
www.bscol.com

8
Behavioral Science Technology, Inc.
417 Bryant Circle
Ojai, California 93023
800/548-5781
805/646-0328 (fax)
www.bstsolutions.com

9
The Bob Pike Group
7620 West 78th Street
Minneapolis, MN 55439
800/383-9210
952/829-0260 (fax)
www.bobpikegroup.com

10
Boston University Corporate Education Center
72 Tyng Road
Tyngsboro, MA 01879
800/288-7246
978/649-2162 (fax)
www.butrain.bu.edu

11
California Institute of Technology
Industrial Relations Center 1-90
Pasadena, CA 91125
626/395-4043
626/795-7174 (fax)
www.irc.caltech.edu

12
Capella University
222 South 9th St., Ste 2000
Minneapolis, MN 55402
612/239-8650
888/227-3552
612/337-5396 (fax)
www.capellauniversity.edu

13
Center for Accelerated Learning
1103 Wisconsin Street
Lake Geneva, WI 53147
414/248-7070
414/248-1912 (fax)
www.execpc.com/~alcenter

14
Center for Applications of Psychological Type, Inc.
2815 N.W. 13th Street, Suite 401
Gainesville, FL 32609
800/777-2278
904/378-0503 (fax)
www.info@capt.org

15
Center for Creative Leadership
One Leadership Place
P.O. Box 26300
Greensboro, NC 27438-6300
336/545-2910
336/282-3284 (fax)
www.ccl.org

16

The Center for Effective
 Performance, Inc.
2300 Peachford Road, Ste. 2000
Atlanta, GA 30338
800/558-4237
770/458-9109 (fax)
www.cep.worldwide.com

17

Center for the Study of Work
 Teams
University of North Texas
P.O. Box 311280
Denton, TX 76203
940/565-3096
940/565-4806 (fax)
www.workteams.unt.edu

18

Columbia University Teachers
 College
Center for Educational Outreach
 and Innovation
525 West 120th St., Box 132
New York, NY 10027
212/678-3987
212/678-4048 (fax)
www.tc.columbia.edu~academic/
 ceoi/

19

The Conference Board
845 Third Avenue
New York, NY 10022
212/759-0900
212/980-7014 (fax)
www.conference-board.org

20

Cornell University, School of
 Industrial and Labor Relations
Management Development and
 Human Resources Programs
16 East 34th St.
New York, NY 10016
212/340-2863
212/340-2890 (fax)
www.ilr.cornell.edu/mgmtprog

21

Corporate Coach U
PO Box 2800-331
Carefree, AZ 85377
480/595-5088
480/595-5326 (fax)
www.ccui.com

22

Crisis Prevention Institute, Inc.
3315-K North 124th Street
Brookfield, WI 53005
800/558-8976
414/783-5906 (fax)
www.crisisprevention.com

23

Dale Carnegie Training
780 Third Avenue, 22nd Floor
New York, NY 10017
800/231-5800
212/644-5532 (fax)
www.dalecarnegie.com

24

Darryl L. Sink & Associates, Inc.
60 Garden Court, Suite 101
Monterey, CA 93940
800/650-7465
831/649-3914 (fax)
www.dsink.com

25

Disney Institute
P.O. Box 10093
Lake Buena Vista, FL 32830
407/566-2645
407/828-2402 (fax)
www.disneyinstitute.com

26

Dynamic Graphics, Inc.
6000 N. Forest Park Dr.
PO Box 1901
Peoria, IL 61656
800/255-8800
309/688-5873 (fax)
www.dgusa.com

27

Eckerd College
Management Development Institute
4200 54th Avenue South
St. Petersburg, FL 33711
800/753-0444
813/864-8996 (fax)
www.eckerd.edu

28

FKA Friesen, Kaye and Associates
3448 Richmond Road
Ottawa, ON, Canada K2H8H7
800/FKA-5585
613/829-0845 (fax)
www.fka.com

29

FranklinCovey
360 West 4800 North
Provo, UT 84604
800/972-4321
801/229-1233 (fax)
www.franklincovey.com

30

The Gallup Organization
The Gallup School of
 Management
300 South 68th Street Place
Lincoln, NB 68510
800/288-8592
402/489-8700
www.gallup.com

31

Gestalt Institute of Cleveland
1588 Hazel Drive
Cleveland, OH 44106
216/421-0468
216/421-1729 (fax)
www.gestaltcleveland.org

32

Global Knowledge
P.O. Box 1039
Cary, NC 27512
800/268-7737
919/461-8600
919/461-8646 (fax)
www.globalknowledge.com

33

Goal QPC
2 Manor Parkway
Salem, NH 03079
800/643-4316
603/870-9122 (fax)
www.goalqpc.com

34

Harvard University
John F. Kennedy School of
 Government
The Leadership Education
 Program
79 JFK Street
Cambridge, MA
617/496-5920
617/495-3090 (fax)
www.ksg.harvard.edu/exceed

35

Harvard University Law School
Program on Negotiation for Senior Executives
Center for Management Research
55 William Street
Wellesley, MA 02181
781/239-1111
781/239-1546 (fax)

36

Human Synergistics International
39819 Plymouth Rd. C8020
Plymouth, MI 48170
800/622-7584
734/459-5557 (fax)
www.humansyn.com

37

Information Mapping, Inc.
41 Waverly Oaks Rd.
Waltham, MA 02154
800/463-6627
617/906-6400 (fax)
www.infomap.com

38

Innovation Associates
Acorn Park
Cambridge, MA 02140
617/498-5700
617/498-5701 (fax)
www.innovationassociates.com

39

Institute for Applied Management and Law, Inc.
610 Newport Center Drive, Ste. 1060
Newport Beach, CA 92660
949/760-1700
949/760-8192 (fax)
www.iaml.com

40

Institute for Professional Education
2200 Wilson Boulevard, Ste. 406
Arlington, VA 22201
703/527-8700
703/527-8703 (fax)
www.theipe.com

41

International Institute for Learning, Inc.
110 East 59th Street
New York, NY 10022
800/325-1533
212/755-0777 (fax)
www.iil.com

42

International Quality and Productivity Center
150 Clove Road
P.O. Box 401
Little Falls, NJ 07424
800/882-8684
201/256-0205 (fax)
www.iqpc.com

43

J&M Training & Consulting
PO Box 339
Merrill, WI 54452
888/526-3694
715/536-1638 (fax)
www.jmtrg.com

44

J.J. Keller & Associates, Inc.
3003 W. Breezewood Lane
PO Box 368
Neenah, WI 54957
800/327-6868
www.jjkeller.com/training

45

Jones International University, Ltd.
9697 East Mineral Avenue
Englewood, CO 80112
800/811-5663
303/784-8547
www.jonesinternational.edu

46

Kellogg Graduate School of Management
Northwestern University
James L. Allen Center
Evanston, IL 60208
847/467-7000
847/491-4323 (fax)
www.kellogg.nwu.edu

47

Keye Productivity Center
11221 Roe Avenue
Leawood, KS 66211-1748
800/821-3919
800/914-8879 (fax)
www.ptseminars.com

48

Otto Kroeger Associates
3605-A Chain Bridge Road
Fairfax, VA 22030-3245
703/591-6284
703/591-8338 (fax)
www.typetalk.com\oka

49

Langevin Learning Services
P.O. Box 1221, 420 Ford Street
Ogdensburg, NY 13669
800/223-2209
800/636-6869 (fax)
www.langevin.com

50

LERN (Learning Resources Network)
1550 Hayes Drive
Manhattan, KS 66502
800/678-5376
888/234-8633 (fax)
www.lern.org

51

Lessons in Leadership
Section 210
Louisville, KY 40289
800/873-3451
800/328-5644 (fax)
www.lessonsinleadership.com

52

Liberty Mutual Group
Loss Prevention, M.S. 8F
P.O. Box 140
Boston, MA 02117
800/320-7581
617/695-9216 (fax)
www.lmig.com

53

Linkage Inc.
One Forbes Road
Lexington, MA 02173
781/862-3157
781/862-2355 (fax)
www.linkageinc.com

54

Management Education Consulting Company of America (MECCA)
40 W. 919 Elodie Drive
Elburn, IL 60119
630/584-0164
630/584-0184 (fax)

55

The MASIE Center
PO Box 397
Saratoga Springs, NY 12866
518/350-2200
518/587-3276 (fax)
www.masie.com

56

Massachusetts Institute of
 Technology
The Sloan School of Management
55 William Street
Wellesley, MA 02181
781/239-1111
781/239-1546 (fax)

57

National Businesswomen's
 Leadership Association
P.O. Box 419107
Kansas City, MO 64141
800/258-7246
913/432-0824 (fax)
www.natsem.com

58

National MultiCultural Institute
3000 Connecticut Avenue, NW,
 Suite 438
Washington, DC 20008
202/483-0700
202/483-5233 (fax)
www.nmci.org/nmci/

59

National Safety Council
1121 Spring Lake Drive
Itasca, IL 60143
800/539-7468
www.nsc.org

60

nSight
10 Fawcett Street
Cambridge, MA 02138
617/354-2828
617/354-8328 (fax)
www.nSightWorks.com

61

NTL Institute
300 North Lee Street, Suite 300
Alexandria, VA 22314
800/777-5227
703/684-1256 (fax)
www.ntl.org

62

Numerof Associates
11457 Olde Cabin Road,
 Ste. 350
St. Louis, MO 63141
314/997-1587
314/997-0948 (fax)
www.nai-consulting.com

63

The Padgett-Thompson Division
 of the American Management
 Association International
P.O. Box 8297
Overland Park, KS 66208
800/255-4141
913/451-2700
800/914-8879 (fax)
www.amanet.org/seminars/public

64

Perrone-Ambrose Associates, Inc.
2 North Riverside Plaza,
 Ste. 1433
Chicago, IL 60606
800/648-0543
312/648-0622 (fax)
www.mentors2000.com

65

Practical Management
 Incorporated
3280 West Hacienda Avenue,
 Ste. 205
Las Vegas, NV 89118
800/444-9101
702/795-8339 (fax)
www.practicalmgt.com

66

Rollins College
Corporate Learning Institute
1000 Holt Avenue - 2728
Winter Park, FL 32789
800/494-4253
407/646-1503 (fax)
www.rollins.edu/cle

67

SENEX Counseling & Training
Fairhill Center
12200 Fairhill Road
Cleveland, OH 44120
216/421-1793
www.senexcare.com

68

Situation Management Systems, Inc.
195 Hanover Street
Hanover, MA 02339
617/826-4433
617/826-2863 (fax)
www.smsinc.com

69

SkillPath Seminars
6900 Squibb Rd.
PO Box 2768
Mission, KS 66201
800/873-7545
913/362-4241
www.skillpath.com

70

Society for Human Resource
 Management (SHRM)
1800 Duke Street
Alexandria, VA 22314
800/283-SHRM
703/535-6490 (fax)
www.shrm.org/seminars

71

The Sony Training Institute
3300 Zanker Road
San Jose, CA 95134
408/955-4231
408/955-5340
www.sony.com/training

72

Stanford Business School
Office of Executive Education
Stanford University
Stanford, CA 94305
650/723-3341
650/723-3950 (fax)
www-gsb.stanford.edu/eep

73

TechLink Training
P.O. Box 226
Fanwood, NJ 07023
908/789-2800
908/789-2811 (fax)
www.tltraining.com

74

TeleTraining Institute
1524 West Admiral
Stillwater, OK 74074

800/755-2356
405/744-7511 (fax)
www.teletrain.com

75

Thunderbird
The American Graduate School of International Management
15249 North 59th Avenue
Glendale, AZ 85306
602/978-7635
602/439-4851 (fax)
www.t-bird.edu

76

The Training Clinic
645 Seabreeze Drive
Seal Beach, CA 90740
800/937-4698
562/430-9603 (fax)
www.thetrainingclinic.com

77

Training Resources Group, Inc.
909 N. Washington Street, #305
Alexandria, VA 22314-1555
703/548-3535
703/836-2415 (fax)
www.trg-inc.com

78

University of Chicago
Graduate School of Business
450 N. Cityfront Plaza Drive
Chicago, IL 60611
312/464-8732
312/464-8731 (fax)
www.gsb.uchicago.edu/programs/exec-ed

79

University of Michigan
The Michigan Business School
Executive Education Center
Ann Arbor, MI 48109
734/642-3109
734/764-4267 (fax)
www.bus.umich.edu

80

University of Minnesota
Employer Education Service
430 Management and Economics Building
271-19th Avenue South
Industrial Relations Center
Minneapolis, MN 55455
800/333-3378
612/626-7747 (fax)
www.csom.umn.edu/csom/ees

81

University of Pennsylvania
Wharton Advanced Management Program
The Wharton School
255 South 38th Street
Philadelphia, PA 19104
215/898-1179
215/386-4304 (fax)
www.wharton.upenn.edu/execed/amp

82

University of Richmond
Management Institute
Special Programs Building
Richmond, VA 23173
804/289-8019

804/289-8872 (fax)
www.richmond.edu./mgmt.institute

83

University of Wisconsin–Madison
Management Institute
Grainger Hall
975 University Ave.
Madison, WI 53706
800/292-8964
800/741-7416 (fax)
800/292-8964 (program info)
608/262-4617 (fax)
www.wisc.edu/mi

84

University of Wisconsin–Stout
Technical Instructor Institutes
102 Communication Technologies Building
Menomonie, WI 54751
715/232-3289
715/836-5263 (fax)

85

Walden Institute
24311 Walden Center Drive, 3rd floor
Bonita Springs, FL 34134
800/237-6434
941/498-7821 (fax)
www.waldeninstitute.com

86

Xavier University Consulting Group
3800 Victory Parkway
Cincinnati, OH 45207
513/745-3396
513/745-4307 (fax)
www.xavierconsulting.com

Seminar and Workshop Topics TDY2002

The following listing of seminars and workshops of interest to trainers is comprehensive as well as representative of learning opportunities available in calendar year 2002 to any trainer with the interest and the funds available to attend.

In order to have been chosen for inclusion in the *Training & Development Yearbook 2002*, a seminar or workshop met some or all of the following criteria: a track record or history of being of service to a training audience; a new content focus; and a popular current leading edge topic. In addition, each provider listed has been a reputable and accessible sponsor, responsive to our inquiries about their programs. In several instances, programs delivered in a nontraditional format are also included in this listing because they are particularly interesting or timely. This year's listing of seminars again reflects the proliferation of service providers as downsized human resources employees around the country are striking out on their own to offer vendor and consulting services. New entries in 2002 also, in many instances, represent new ideas in e-learning design, leadership, Web- and technology-based delivery, and organizational and human performance. Most programs listed are given in several locations throughout the United States.

Most training providers who offer public seminars and workshops also are happy to develop custom, in-house, or on-site adaptations of their public programs listed here. Costs given here are current costs for programs open to the public; customized programs vary in cost. Costs listed are training costs only; in general, travel, food, and lodging are extra. In many cases, a toll-free telephone number is given in the listing for more information. Providers listed are prompt with faxed information in response to your request. Their fax numbers are listed for those who prefer to communicate this way. Website addresses are provided in the alphabetical listing of providers beginning on page 6.4.3. Contact information is provided for 86 different training providers, with verified, current, useful information.

The following Index is a topical index to the 164 seminars and workshops we have chosen to represent the field in year 2002.

Index to Seminar and Workshop Topics

analyzing needs
8, 13, 45, 46, 47, 61, 73, 92, 95, 102, 103, 109, 114, 115, 119, 121, 126, 140, 150, 154, 156, 165

benchmarking, quality, best practices
9, 12, 36, 39, 57, 61, 71, 102, 103, 161

business strategy
31, 32, 37, 47, 57, 77, 83, 96, 107, 125, 131, 137, 138, 141, 142, 146, 147, 148, 161

coaching, mentoring
25, 49, 53, 101, 102, 113, 117, 146

communication, documentation
33, 34, 46, 58, 72, 75, 76, 96, 111, 128, 140

conflict resolution, negotiation, problem solving, stress reduction
6, 29, 46, 47, 52, 61, 72, 99, 108, 109, 130, 143

consulting
27, 63, 81, 96, 97, 100, 115, 126

creativity, critical thinking, innovation
22, 34, 47, 50, 51, 57, 61, 71, 122, 125, 129, 148, 156

customer service, sales
1, 57, 97, 120, 125, 132

evaluation, measurement
14, 20, 40, 45, 47, 54, 62, 70, 73, 80, 85, 94, 114, 117, 119, 150, 154, 157, 164

executive education
4, 32, 37, 39, 46, 47, 72, 77, 78, 83, 88, 90, 92, 99, 110, 123, 124, 137, 138, 148, 152, 161

facilitation skills
2, 19, 22, 32, 37, 44, 45, 66, 70, 72, 87, 104, 109, 114, 122, 125, 126, 130, 131, 139, 141, 144, 151, 156

global, multicultural, and diversity issues
48, 78, 108, 123, 124, 137, 138, 152

instructional design
3, 5, 8, 23, 26, 33, 36, 42, 45, 55, 56, 74, 93, 94, 105, 106, 109, 114, 120, 121, 140, 141, 149, 153, 154, 157, 158, 162, 165

knowledge management, intellectual capital
11, 57, 58, 67, 77, 83, 84, 89, 131, 138, 141, 146, 161

leadership
19, 28, 30, 37, 38, 45, 53, 57, 65, 70, 71, 77, 79, 83, 90, 98, 102, 104, 109, 123, 124, 125, 126, 127, 131, 145, 148, 152

management and supervisory training
21, 28, 30, 45, 46, 47, 48, 49, 50, 54, 57, 60, 62, 64, 65, 70, 77, 78, 79, 82, 89, 91, 99, 105, 107, 108, 110, 116, 123, 125, 131, 141, 142, 147, 149, 150

managing the training operation
7, 17, 30, 32, 43, 48, 49, 57, 62, 69, 73, 79, 83, 85, 88, 96, 97, 112, 118, 119, 124, 145, 146, 159

organization development
18, 24, 32, 33, 45, 46, 50, 66, 67, 69, 70, 71, 72, 73, 77, 82, 83, 96, 107, 108, 124, 142, 146, 149, 152, 153, 154

performance evaluation, feedback
10, 14, 45, 60, 61, 63, 64, 65, 70, 73, 80, 85, 98, 114, 145

performance technology
13, 14, 15, 16, 17, 18, 22, 24, 31, 70, 73, 79, 86, 103

presentation skills and technologies
2, 8, 22, 23, 41, 45, 58, 74, 112, 114, 120, 122, 128, 136, 140, 143, 150, 154, 155, 156, 157, 162, 163, 164

self-directed learning, self-development
4, 28, 34, 37, 47, 50, 61, 65, 114, 115, 126, 140, 160

team development
28, 35, 60, 87, 104, 112, 116, 127, 129, 138, 139, 145, 151

technical skills
16, 33, 88, 92, 93, 106, 110, 120, 124, 128, 131, 135, 140, 150, 157, 159

web-based training, online learning, e-learning
3, 23, 33, 46, 55, 59, 67, 68, 74, 83, 84, 86, 93, 104, 106, 111, 121, 132, 133, 134, 135, 136, 163

1

Title:
Achieving Extraordinary Customer Relations
Sponsor:
AchieveGlobal, Inc.
8875 Hidden River Pkwy., Ste. 400
Tampa, FL 33637
800/291-2752
888/662-7692 (fax)
Length:
2 days
Cost:
$730
Location:
Various cities throughout the U.S.
Description:
The focus of this workshop is how to strategically manage each customer's experience; and that includes the learner as "customer." With today's emphasis on self-directed and individualized learning, this workshop's "personalized service" message is in tune with trainers' needs.

2

Title:
Tools for Trainer Excellence
Sponsor:
AchieveGlobal, Inc.
8875 Hidden River Pkwy., Ste. 400
Tampa, FL 33637
800/291-2752
888/662-7692 (fax)
Length:
3 days
Cost:
$995
Location:
Various cities throughout the U.S.
Description:
This skill-based workshop for new and experienced trainers is one of AchieveGlobal's most popular offerings. It is highly interactive and designed to turn good trainers into great trainers. The focus is on improving the speed and quality of learning with material from any source.

3

Title:
Web School 101: Demystifying Web-based Training—How to Design a Web-based Training Course
Sponsor:
American Management
Association International
P.O. Box 169
Saranac Lake, NY 12983
800/262-9699
518/891-0368 (fax)
Length:
2 days
Cost:
$1,295
Location:
Various cities throughout the U.S.
Description:
This seminar focuses on ways to adapt the latest learning strategies to Web technology.

4

Title:
Executive Effectiveness Course
Sponsor:
American Management
Association International
P.O. Box 169
Saranac Lake, NY 12983
800/262-9699
518/891-0368 (fax)
Length:
Two 4 1/2 day units
Cost:
$3,750
Location:
Various cities throughout the U.S.
Description:
The time-lapse format of this 9-day training program is one of its key features. Both units incorporate the input and support of other seminar attendees. Self-awareness and a workable plan for future action are program goals. The second unit occurs 2–6 months after the first and builds upon insights learned from experience. Throughout, the focus is on strengths and resources.

5

Title:
Instructional Design for Trainers
Sponsor:
American Management Association
International
P.O. Box 169
Saranac Lake, NY 12983
800/262-9699
518/891-0368 (fax)
Length:
3 days
Cost:
$1,645
Location:
Various cities throughout the U.S.
Description:
This seminar teaches how to create effective training programs that meet the learning needs of employees and the goals of the company. Topics include: conducting micro-needs analysis; getting top management to approve a proposal; tapping into resources; the 4-step method of training; refining a program; writing the lesson plan; designing useful and flexible leader's guides and participant manuals; preassignments and integrative post-assignments for trainee evaluation systems; how to implement a program; presentation of a program.

6

Title:
Managing Emotions in the Workplace
Sponsor:
American Management Association
International
P.O. Box 169
Saranac Lake, NY 12983
800/262-9699
518/891-0368 (fax)
Length:
2 days
Cost:
$1,395
Location:
Various cities throughout the U.S.
Description:
This seminar emphasizes self-awareness as participants learn skills to deal with difficult people and work situations.

7

Title:
Managing the Training Function
Sponsor:
American Management
Association International
P.O. Box 169
Saranac Lake, NY 12983
800/262-9699
518/891-0368 (fax)
Length:
4 1/2 days

Training for Trainers

Cost:
$2,025
Location:
Various cities throughout the U.S.
Description:
This seminar is for those who are newly responsible for a training function. Topics include: alignment with corporate goals, training budgets, outsourcing vs. internal training, partnering and forming alliances.

8

Title:
Training the Trainer
Sponsor:
American Management Association International
P.O. Box 169
Saranac Lake, NY 12983
800/262-9699
518/891-0368 (fax)
Length:
5 days
Cost:
$2,025
Location:
Various cities throughout the U.S.
Description:
Designed for trainers with less than three years' experience, this course covers the importance of training, needs analysis, setting objectives, course development, training methods, and presentation skills.

9

Title:
Applying Benchmarking Skills
Sponsor:
American Productivity & Quality Center (APQC)
123 N. Post Oak Lane
Houston, TX 77024
800/776-9676
713/681-3705 (fax)
Length:
2 days
Cost:
$995
Location:
Houston, TX; Washington, DC
Description:
This seminar focuses on a systematic process for using the findings of benchmarking studies. This and other APQC seminars are offered primarily as an adjunct to APQC's annual conference.

10

Title:
Establishing Performance Measures
Sponsor:
American Productivity & Quality Center (APQC)
123 N. Post Oak Lane
Houston, TX 77024-7797
800/776-9676
713/681-3705 (fax)
Length:
1 day
Cost:
$595
Location:
Houston, TX; Washington, DC
Description:
Individuals responsible for designing performance measures will benefit from this seminar, which offers a step-by-step facilitator's guide that shows you how to lead an in-house staff in the design and implementation of effective performance measures. As an added highlight of the seminar, you will explore the crucial role of measurement group reward systems and benchmarking.

11

Title:
Knowledge Management 101: Managing Knowledge for Results
Sponsor:
American Productivity & Quality Center (APQC)
123 N. Post Oak Lane
Houston, TX 77024-7797
800/776-9676
713/681-3705 (fax)
Length:
1 day
Cost:
$595
Location:
Houston, TX; Washington, DC
Description:
This intensive half-day session will provide participants with a strategic perspective on how to evaluate and use the principles and strategies collectively called "Knowledge Management" to add value to your bottom line, customers, and employees. Other seminars and forums on knowledge management are also available. APQC will also offer a Knowledge Management Certification in 2002.

12

Title:
Foundations in Quality Self-Directed Learning Series
Sponsor:
American Society for Quality (ASQ)
P.O. Box 3066
Milwaukee, WI 53201
800/248-1946
414/272-1734 (fax)
Length:
8 self-study modules;
600 pages of text reinforced by computer-based testing, practice, and exercises
Cost:
$345
Location:
Your home or office pc, IBM-compatible, 486 or higher 4 MEG of RAM, 8 MEG free hard disk space, Microsoft Windows 3.1 or higher
Description:
Also known as Q101. This unique quality foundations course includes 8 modules of focused study: quality standards, organizations and their functions, quality needs and overall strategic plans, customer satisfaction and focus, project management, continuous improvement, human resource management, and training and education. A demonstration program is available free of charge through the ASQ Website.

13

Title:
Analyzing Human Performance
Sponsor:
American Society for Training and Development (ASTD)
1640 King Street, Box 1443
Alexandria, VA 22313
800/628-2783
703/683-8103 (fax)
Length:
3 days
Cost:
$1,199; $1,399 (non-member)

Location:
Various universities throughout the U.S.
Description:
This seminar is part of a recently-developed ASTD Human Performance Improvement Certificate Program. Topics include: performance and cause analysis, organizational scanning, workflow/work process analysis, and ergonomic analysis. Five other related seminars listed here are offered in the Certificate Program.

14

Title:
Evaluating Performance Improvement Interventions
Sponsor:
American Society for Training and Development (ASTD)
1640 King Street, Box 1443
Alexandria, VA 22313
800/628-2783
703/683-8103 (fax)
Length:
3 days
Cost:
$1,199; $1,399 (non-member)
Location:
Various universities throughout the U.S.
Description:
This seminar is part of a recently-developed ASTD Human Performance Improvement Certificate Program. Topics include: measuring learning, behavior, and results; the value and limitations of various evaluation models; cost-benefit analysis; measuring the intangibles; and linking behavior and performance. Five other related seminars listed here are offered in the Certificate Program.

15

Title:
Human Performance Improvement in the Workplace
Sponsor:
American Society for Training and Development (ASTD)
1640 King Street, Box 1443
Alexandria, VA 22313
800/628-2783
703/683-8103 (fax)
Length:
3 days
Cost:
$1,199; $1,399 (non-member)

Location:
Various universities throughout the U.S.
Description:
This seminar is part of a recently-developed ASTD Human Performance Improvement Certificate Program. Topics include: exploring a variety of training and non-training interventions, role-specific competencies and outputs, developing a change plan for an HPI intervention, stakeholder support, and Human Performance Technology's link to systems. Five other related seminars listed here are offered in the Certificate Program.

16

Title:
Learning Technologies for Improving Performance
Sponsor:
American Society for Training and Development (ASTD)
1640 King Street, Box 1443
Alexandria, VA 22313
800/628-2783
703/683-8103 (fax)
Length:
3 days
Cost:
$1,199; $1,399 (non-member)
Location:
Various universities throughout the U.S.
Description:
This seminar is part of a recently-developed ASTD Human Performance Improvement Certificate Program. Topics include: determining appropriate technologies for your organization, justifying the move to technology, and creating a transition plan. Five other related seminars listed here are offered in the Certificate Program.

17

Title:
Selecting and Managing Performance Improvement Interventions
Sponsor:
American Society for Training and Development (ASTD)
1640 King Street, Box 1443
Alexandria, VA 22313
800/628-2783
703/683-8103 (fax)

Length:
3 days
Cost:
$1,199; $1,399 (non-member)
Location:
Various universities throughout the U.S.
Description:
This seminar is part of a recently-developed ASTD Human Performance Improvement Certificate Program. Topics include: types and examples of interventions, assessing organizational readiness, gathering support, and implementing the intervention. Five other related seminars listed here are offered in the Certificate Program.

18

Title:
Transitioning to Human Performance Improvement
Sponsor:
American Society for Training and Development (ASTD)
1640 King Street, Box 1443
Alexandria, VA 22313
800/628-2783
703/683-8103 (fax)
Length:
3 days
Cost:
$1,199; $1,399 (non-member)
Location:
Various universities throughout the U.S.
Description:
This seminar is part of a recently-developed ASTD Human Performance Improvement Certificate Program. Topics include: deciding to make the transition, organizational readiness; stakeholders, peer and management buy-in; organizing the new HPI department; keeping the change alive. Five other related seminars listed here are offered in the Certificate Program.

19

Title:
Leadership and Influence: Empowerment Through Shared Responsibility
Sponsor:
Babson School of Executive Education
Babson Park, MA 02457
781/239-4354
781/239-5266 (fax)

Length:
 5 days in May or 5 days in October, with one "Reunion" day 9–12 months later
Cost:
 $4,950 including meals, accommodations, materials plus $995 for the "Reunion" day
Location:
 Babson College's Center for Executive Education, Wellesley, MA
Description:
 This is an interactive hands-on workshop for senior managers to learn and practice effective techniques for today's "shared responsibility" workplaces. Participants learn competencies in communication, using power and influence, building commitment, dealing with conflict, developing collaboration, and teaching and coaching. A one-day followup session is optional.

20

Title:
 Building the Balanced Scorecard
Sponsor:
 Balanced Scorecard Collaborative, Inc.
 55 Old Bedford Road
 Lincoln, MA 01773
Length:
 2 days
Cost:
 $2,495
Location:
 Chicago, IL; San Francisco, CA
Description:
 This is a practical, skills-based seminar on how to develop and implement a Balanced Scorecard program. Course materials are based on more than 200 successful Balanced Scorecard programs worldwide. Strategy mapping and development of appropriate measures are key topics.

21

Title:
 Enhancing Supervisor Effectiveness in Safety
Sponsor:
 Behavioral Science Technology, Inc.
 417 Bryant Circle
 Ojai, CA 93023
 800/548-5781
 805/646-0328 (fax)
Length:
 2 days
Cost:
 $995
Location:
 Houston, TX
Description:
 This unique seminar focuses on the behavioral aspects of leadership as it applies to workforce safety. Seminar leaders include front line safety managers, training and education leaders, and psychologists. Topics include implementation planning, accountability, leadership vs. management, and where safety activities fit into the bigger corporate picture. Focus on skill-building.

22

Title:
 Creative Training Techniques
Sponsor:
 The Bob Pike Group
 7620 West 78th Street
 Minneapolis, MN 55439
 800/383-9210
 612/829-0260 (fax)
Length:
 2 days
Cost:
 $895
Location:
 Various cities throughout the U.S.
Description:
 This program is for the trainer who wants more out of training efforts, a more exciting training routine, and faster results. Participants receive a 140-page manual with charts, samples, checklists, tips, and insights. Discussion on the course covers: (1) methods for motivating adults, (2) building the "middle" of one's presentation, (3) kindergarten lessons that enhance adult learning, (4) "Ten Deadly Sins" that kill presentations, (5) incorrect ways to use audiovisuals, (6) creating personal accountability, and more.

23

Title:
 Creative Training Techniques for Web-Based Design
Sponsor:
 The Bob Pike Group
 7620 West 78th Street
 Minneapolis, MN 55439
 800/383-9210
 612/829-0260 (fax)
Length:
 2 days
Cost:
 $895
Location:
 Various cities throughout the U.S.
Description:
 This seminar explores the effective selection and redesign of current classroom courses for delivery over the Internet/Intranet in either a synchronous or an asynchronous format.

24

Title:
 The Performance Solutions Institute
Sponsor:
 The Bob Pike Group
 7620 West 78th Street
 Minneapolis, MN 55439
 800/383-9210
 952/829-0260 (fax)
Length:
 2 days, with optional add-on customized sessions
Cost:
 $895
Location:
 Minneapolis or customized on-site
Description:
 The Institute is run as a conference, with two tracks from which to choose. It is built upon master trainer, Bob Pike's, creative training techniques program expanded to encompass strategic organizational content more in line with the performance shift in training. Phone the Bob Pike Group for customization, on-site options, and group discounts.

25

Title:
 Coaching People to Work at Peak Performance
Sponsor:
 Boston University
 Corporate Education Center
 72 Tyng Road
 Tyngsboro, MA 01879
 800/288-7246
 978/649-2162 (fax)
Length:
 2 days
Cost:
 $1,095
Location:
 Various locations in the Boston, MA area

Description:
This is a skills-based workshop for anyone who needs to be a coach. Self assessment and clarification of managing, supervising, and coaching are stressed.

26
Title:
Instructional Design I and II
Sponsor:
Boston University
Corporate Education Center
72 Tyng Road
Tyngsboro, MA 01879
800/288-7246
978/649-2162 (fax)
Length:
3 days
Cost:
$1,395
Location:
Various locations in the Boston, MA area
Description:
This interactive workshop is designed to give the participant an opportunity to increase his or her abilities in developing and designing a training program either for a classroom situation or for one-on-one training. Active participation is essential for meeting training and learning objectives. Course I is a recommended prerequisite to Course II. Both courses focus on learner-focused and performance-based instructional design. The courses use a systematic instructional design methodology and provide trainees with skills for design of performance-based competency objectives.

27
Title:
Internal Consulting Skills
Sponsor:
Boston University
Corporate Education Center
72 Tyng Road
Tyngsboro, MA 01879
800/288-7246
978/649-2162 (fax)
Length:
2 days
Cost:
$1,095
Location:
Various locations in the Boston, MA area

Description:
This seminar addresses the new position many trainers are assuming, that of internal consultant. Balancing task and process, analysis skills, and communication skills for collaborative training are covered. The seminar is based on the work of Peter Block.

28
Title:
Leading & Managing Successful Teams
Sponsor:
Boston University
Corporate Education Center
72 Tyng Road
Tyngsboro, MA 01879
800/288-7246
978/649-2162 (fax)
Length:
3 days
Cost:
$1,395
Location:
Various locations in the Boston, MA area
Description:
This workshop uses the MBTI (Myers-Briggs Type Indicator) for analysis of individual styles and team dynamics. The workshop focuses on securing commitment to team, consensus-building techniques, negotiation skills, communication and leadership skills.

29
Title:
Women's Institute for Managerial Excellence
Sponsor:
Boston University
Corporate Education Center
72 Tyng Road
Tyngsboro, MA 01879
800/288-7246
978/649-2162 (fax)
Length:
3 days
Cost:
$1,395
Location:
Various locations in the Boston, MA area
Description:
This intensive and skill-focused workshop is limited to 20 participants. Motivation, conflict resolution, style assessment, interpersonal skills, and team-building are key topics.

30
Title:
Leader or Manager? It's No Longer a Choice
Sponsor:
Boston University
Corporate Education Center
72 Tyng Road
Tyngsboro, MA 01879
800/288-7246
978/649-2162 (fax)
Length:
2 days
Cost:
$1,095
Location:
Various locations in the Boston, MA area
Description:
Explore position authority versus voluntary followership. Discover new skills and better communication.

31
Title:
Integrated Strategic Planning
Sponsor:
California Institute of Technology
Industrial Relations Center 1-90
Pasadena, CA 91125
626/395-4043; 4042
626/795-7174 (fax)
Length:
2 days
Cost:
$1,695
Location:
Pasadena, CA
Description:
This program is applicable to small, medium, and large companies and to all industries manufacturing, service, distribution, and retail. It will assist companies diversifying into new markets and products as well as those consolidating their present position. Participants will build *key elements of their own strategic plans* after moving through process, strategic thinking, a case study and planning forms with both lecture and workshop activities. Trainers moving into performance management will find this a useful perspective.

32

Title:
Strategic Alliances
Sponsor:
California Institute of Technology
Industrial Relations Center 1-90
Pasadena, CA 91125
  626/395-4043; 4042
  626/795-7174 (fax)
Length:
2 days
Cost:
$1,695
Location:
Pasadena, CA
Description:
This is a skill-building executive program to help you develop a process for alliance creation and management. This is for executives who are leading change in a "partnership" world. Trainers often find themselves in this position.

33

Title:
Certificate in Teaching and Training Online
Sponsor:
Capella University
222 South 9th St., Ste. 2000
Minneapolis, MN 55402
  612/239-8650
  888/227-3552
  612/337-5396 (fax)
Length:
Certificate program averages 1 year, or 3 months per course; doctoral program averages 3–4 years
Cost:
$5,200, or $1,300 each for 4 courses; PhD Seminar residence fees: $350 Focused Seminar; $450 Two-Week Extended Seminar
Location:
Online; residence in MN; courses begin in January, April, July, and October
Description:
This online program is one of several certificate programs offered by Capella University. It is made up of 4 courses: Critical Skills for Facilitating Online Learning, Tools and Techniques for Online Learning, Strategies for Building Online Learning Communities, and Practical Applications for Online Teaching and Training. Each course can be taken separately and can be transferred into a Capella University masters degree or doctoral program. Courses may be taught in a "Directed Study" format, matching a tutor or mentor with a learner. The option of seminar extensions in residence are also provided.

34

Title:
Accelerated Learning Training Methods
Sponsor:
The Center for Accelerated Learning
1103 Wisconsin Street
Lake Geneva, WI 53147
  262/248-7070
  262/248-1912 (fax)
Length:
3 days
Cost:
$995
Location:
Various cities throughout the U.S.
Description:
This workshop teaches skills and theory of "accelerated learning" with a goal of enhanced integration of new knowledge and skill. Topics and skills include: using the whole body to learn, using imagery and mnemonics, information mapping, collaborative learning, and learning in context.

35

Title:
Using Type in Team Performance
Sponsor:
Center for Applications of
  Psychological Type, Inc.
2815 N.W. 13th Street,
  Suite 401
Gainesville, FL 32609
  800/777-2278
  904/378-0503 (fax)
Length:
2 days
Cost:
$395
Location:
Washington, D.C.;
Minneapolis, MN
Description:
This workshop is designed for professional MBTI users who wish to apply type concepts and structured team assessment techniques to their client teams, and who want a systematic way to approach the management of their own work teams. Participants learn (1) to relate type concepts to a diagnostic model, (2) to increase their predictive and explanatory capabilities in team development, and (3) to put type concepts into perspective for overall team effectiveness.

36

Title:
Benchmarks Certification Workshop
Sponsor:
Center for Creative Leadership
One Leadership Place
P.O. Box 26300
Greensboro, NC 27438-6300
  336/545-2810
  336/282-3284 (fax)
Length:
2 days
Cost:
$1,200
Location:
Greensboro, NC
Description:
To certify human resource managers, career development professionals, and consultants to give one-on-one feedback using the *Benchmarks* instrument. Participants are certified to use *Benchmarks* as either a stand-alone instrument or in conjunction with other management development programs.

37

Title:
Developing the Strategic Leader: Thinking, Acting, and Influencing
Sponsor:
Center for Creative Leadership
One Leadership Place
P.O. Box 26300
Greensboro, NC 27438-6300
  336/545-2810
  336/282-3284 (fax)
Length:
5 days
Cost:
$5,350
Location:
Colorado Springs, CO
Description:
This is a recently revamped workshop focusing on strategic skills for executive effectiveness. It features considerable one-on-one instruction and learning.

38

Title:
Leadership Development Program

Sponsor:
Center for Creative Leadership
One Leadership Place
P.O. Box 26300
Greensboro, NC 27438-6300
336/545-2810
336/282-3284 (fax)

Length:
5 days

Cost:
$5,350

Location:
Greensboro, NC; Colorado Springs, CO; San Diego, CA; Brussels, Belgium

Description:
This is the flagship workshop of the Center for Creative Leadership. Training emphasizes the practical skills and knowledge required for creative leadership and effective management. Resources of the Center's research and publishing efforts are available as guides for effective assessment, development, and practice.

39

Title:
Tools for Developing Successful Executives

Sponsor:
Center for Creative Leadership
One Leadership Place
P.O. Box 26300
Greensboro, NC 27438-6300
336/545-2810
336/282-3284 (fax)

Length:
3 days

Cost:
$2,900

Location:
Colorado Springs, CO; Greensboro, NC

Description:
The workshop is designed for human resource executives, line managers, and professionals who are responsible for establishing and operating career and executive development systems in their organizations. By evaluating a selection of assessment techniques and instruments, participants learn to design and implement career development systems. All the tools introduced during this program are research-based and free standing. Participants have the opportunity (1) to practice and evaluate using each of the tools presented and (2) to discuss applications to specific situations back home. The Center offers a *Benchmarks* Certification" option following the "Tools for Developing Executives" program at its Greensboro, San Diego, and Brussels locations. This certification allows human resource professionals to use *Benchmarks* within their own organizations. The fee for this optional certification is $1200.

40

Title:
Criterion-Referenced Instruction

Sponsor:
The Center for Effective Performance Inc.
2300 Peachford Road, Ste. 2000
Atlanta, GA 30338
800/558-4237
770/458-9109 (fax)

Length:
10 days (This self-paced workshop takes a maximum of 2 weeks to complete. Participants may attend for only one week to complete selected sections of the course.)

Cost:
$2,600

Location:
Atlanta, GA; Chicago, IL

Description:
This new edition of Robert Mager's self-paced workshop gives participants the skills to excel in a state-of-the-art training and performance improvement effort. Participants learn to: (1) reduce total training time, (2) make training results measurable, (3) use training only where it is needed, (4) guarantee that each qualified trainee reaches competence, and (5) provide substantial dollar savings in training costs. The workshop allows participants to progress at a rate comfortable to them, and apply their new skills to a course they are currently working on to use immediately back on the job.

41

Title:
Mastering the Art of Instructor-Led Training

Sponsor:
The Center for Effective Performance Inc.
2300 Peachford Road, Ste. 2000
Atlanta, GA 30338
800/558-4237
770/458-9109 (fax)

Length:
4 days

Cost:
$1,650

Location:
Atlanta, GA; Scottsdale, AZ

Description:
This four-day workshop is designed to sharpen presentation skills of both newcomers and veterans. More than 75 percent of the workshop time is devoted to practice in an environment that is positive, constructive, and non-threatening. Participants use their own course material to prepare and conduct presentations and receive constructive feedback from an expert practitioner. The workshop features a new media module.

42

Title:
Instructional Module Development

Sponsor:
The Center for Effective Performance Inc.
2300 Peachford Road, Ste. 2000
Atlanta, GA 30338
800/558-4237
770/458-9109 (fax)

Length:
10 days

Cost:
$2,700

Location:
Atlanta, GA; Chicago, IL

Description:
This program is for course writers, designers, developers, and instructors who write their own instruction. Using the prerequisite skills learned in Robert Mager's "Criterion-Referenced Instruction," participants learn to develop instructional material, speed development time, and save training costs. Using their own objectives, participants go through each step of the development process. They leave the workshop with two modules of their own instruction that have been developed and tested.

Training for Trainers

43

Title:
Training Manager Workshop
Sponsor:
The Center for Effective
  Performance Inc.
2300 Peachford Rd., Ste. 2000
Atlanta, GA 30338
  800/558-4237
  770/458-9109 (fax)
Length:
5 days
Cost:
$2,475
Location:
Orlando, FL; Dallas, TX; Vail, CO
Description:
For new or experienced training managers, Robert Mager's workshop gives participants the skills to manage a modern training function with confidence. Participants learn: (1) to recommend appropriate solutions to performance problems, (2) to review and evaluate instruction, media choices, project proposals, and vendor proposals, and (3) how to respond to, and stimulate, requests for services. The workshop is performance-based and self-paced.

44

Title:
Skilled Facilitator
Sponsor:
Center for the Study of Work Teams
University of North Texas
P.O. Box 311280
Denton, TX 76203
  940/565-3096
  940/565-4806 (fax)
Length:
5 days
Cost:
$2,395
Location:
Denton, TX
Description:
This 5-day workshop is a skill-based workshop on how to facilitate fundamental change in organizations. The workshop is based on core values and principles of the participant organizations. Preparatory reading and self-reflection are required.

45

Title:
Adult Learning and Leadership Certificate Program
Sponsor:
Columbia University
Teachers College
Center for Educational Outreach
  and Innovation
525 West 120th Street, Box 132
New York, NY 10027
  212/678-3987
  212/678-4048 (fax)
Length:
One year; 6 courses each lasting 9 weeks
Cost:
$740 per credit; $2,220 per course (times 6)
Location:
New York, NY
Description:
This is a new, comprehensive program beginning in Fall 2002. Participants will be prepared to lead a wide variety of programs focused on adult learning in corporations, associations, government agencies, and nonprofit organizations. Both classroom and Web-based coursework are required. Courses include: Leadership & Adult Learning, Intro to Adult Education, Assessing Needs and Evaluating Outcomes, Staff Development and Training, Facilitating Adult Learning, and Human Resource Development & Leadership.

46

Title:
Corporate Communication: Strategic Communication Planning and Intranet Communication Planning
Sponsor:
The Conference Board
845 Third Avenue
New York, NY 10022
  212/759-0900
  212/980-7014 (fax)
Length:
2 days
Cost:
$1,850
Location:
New York, NY
Description:
This is a 2-day intensive focus on corporate communications comprised of 2 workshops both designed to boost business performance through communication. Developing strategy, building trust, leveraging intellectual capital, and gaining employee buy-in are all topics of the day one workshop. The day two workshop includes various topics in harnessing the power of the Web to change the way people work. One of many seminars and learning opportunities. Check the Website for other listings.

47

Title:
Resilience: How to Bounce Back Stronger and Smarter
Sponsor:
Cornell University, School of
  Industrial & Labor Relations
Management Development and
  Human Resources Programs
16 East 34th St.
New York, NY 10016-4328
  212/340-2863
  212/340-2822 (fax)
Length:
2 days
Cost:
$895
Location:
New York, NY
Description:
This workshop focuses on the positive behavioral skills required to survive the trauma of job loss.

48

Title:
Managing a Diverse Workforce
Sponsor:
Cornell University, School of
  Industrial & Labor Relations
Management Development and
  Human Resources Programs
16 East 34th St.
New York, NY 10016-4328
  212/340-2863
  212/340-2822 (fax)
Length:
1 day
Cost:
$495
Location:
New York, NY; Ithaca, NY; Long Island
Description:
This is an innovative workshop on building a diversity program and making it work. Special features include a live theater presentation exploring workplace diversity issues, and keynote speakers discussing tough issues such as how to train and evaluate training, respond to backlash, demographics and

EEO/AA laws, and diversity's place in globalization efforts.

49

Title:
Manager as Coach
Sponsor:
Cornell University, School of Industrial & Labor Relations
Management Development and Human Resources Programs
16 East 34th Street
New York, NY 10016-4328
212/340-2863
212/340-2822 (fax)
Length:
2 days
Cost:
$895
Location:
New York, NY; Rochester, NY; Long Island
Description:
This workshop focuses on a coach's "Toolbox" for building a successful coaching program to motivate people, change problem behavior, and boost individual and team behavior.

50

Title:
Thinking Outside the Box: Creativity and Innovation
Sponsor:
Cornell University, School of Industrial & Labor Relations
Office of Management & Executive Education
16 E. 34th St.
New York, NY
212/340-2863
212/340-2822 (fax)
Length:
2 days
Cost:
$995
Location:
Ithaca, NY; New York, NY; Albany, NY; Long Island
Description:
This workshop focuses on discovery of the trainee's own personal creativity and features development and a Creativity Workout Plan.

51

Title:
The Coaching Clinic Train the Trainer Program
Sponsor:
Corporate Coach U
PO Box 2800-331
Carefree, AZ 85377
480/595-5088
480/595-5326
Length:
4 days
Cost:
$2,995
Location:
Various cities throughout the U.S.
Description:
The Coaching Clinic challenges participants to raise their standards for their own skills and competencies. Topics include: The 5-Step Process of Coaching, The Tool Chest of Coaching Skills, Personal Coaching Styles Inventory, Advanced Coaching Skills, and practice sessions using Case Scenarios.

52

Title:
Nonviolent Crisis Intervention
Sponsor:
Crisis Prevention Institute, Inc.
3315-K North 124th Street
Brookfield, WI 53005
800/558-8976
414/783-5787
414/783-5906 (fax)
Length:
1 or 2 days
Cost:
$295 or $545
Location:
Various cities in the U.S. and Canada
Description:
Day 1 focuses on preventing physical violence at work, nonverbal techniques for controlling disruptive behavior, dealing with fear and anxiety, and verbal crisis resolution. Day 2 includes when and how to restrain disruptive persons, staff and spectator safety, team intervention, and tension reduction after intervention. Videotapes and publications are also available. A 4-day program leading to instructor certification is also available for $995. With video included, $1,102.

53

Title:
Developing the Leader in You
Sponsor:
Dale Carnegie Training
780 Third Avenue, 22nd Floor
New York, NY 10017
800/231-5800
212/644-5532
Length:
2 days
Cost:
$1,295
Location:
Various cities throughout the U.S.
Description:
The focus of this seminar is on the differences between managing and leading. Goals are to help managers increase productivity, lift morale, and improve quality. It incorporates Dale Carnegie's proven ways to win people to your way of thinking. Empowerment, motivation, and coaching are key topics.

54

Title:
The Criterion-Referenced Testing Workshop
Sponsor:
Darryl L. Sink & Associates, Inc.
60 Garden Court, Suite 101
Monterey, CA 93940
831/649-8384
800/650-7465
831/649-3914 (fax)
Length:
2 days
Cost:
$749
Location:
Various cities throughout the U.S.
Description:
This program is for trainers, training managers, and course developers who want to design or redesign the measurement of training results. Participants practice writing all kinds of test items used to evaluate what learners need on the job. Topics include writing checklists, testing at the correct level, developing a testing plan, and issues in Web-based testing.

Training for Trainers

55

Title:
Designing Instruction for Web-Based Training
Sponsor:
Darryl L. Sink & Associates, Inc.
60 Garden Court, Suite 101
Monterey, CA 93940
800/650-7465
831/649-8384
831/649-3914 (fax)
Length:
3 days
Cost:
$1,199
Location:
Various cities throughout the U.S.
Description:
This is an intensive workshop for instructional designers, training managers, and supervisors. Participants receive over 50 job aids and a 300-page guide for use back on the job. Topics include: site maps, Web development models, navigation, active responding, types of authoring tools, domain and content types, templates and prototypes, writing Web-based instruction, creating engaging instruction, implementation strategies, usability, formative evaluation, review and feedback, and identifying and assessing business need for Web-based training.

56

Title:
The Instructional Developer Workshop
Sponsor:
Darryl L. Sink & Associates, Inc.
60 Garden Court, Suite 101
Monterey, CA 93940
831/649-8384
800/650-7465
831/649-3914 (fax)
Length:
3 days
Cost:
$999
Location:
Various cities throughout the U.S.
Description:
This course moves the learner through the basic techniques of course development, as well as through more advanced skills in instructional design. Examples include Web-based and computer-based training. Includes course-writed software.

57

Title:
The Disney Approach to Quality Service
Sponsor:
Disney Institute
P.O. Box 10093
Lake Buena Vista, FL 32830
407/566-2645
407/828-2402 (fax)
Length:
3 days
Cost:
$3,295 includes lodging and meals
Location:
Walt Disney World,
Orlando, FL
Description:
This seminar uses the Walt Disney World Resort as a "living classroom" to learn how Disney creates "magic moments" for customers. Visits to behind-the-scenes operations, presentations by Disney managers, and extensive take-home materials focus on ways to maximize delivery systems. Check the Website for other programs.

58

Title:
Advanced Design for Desktop Publishers
Sponsor:
Dynamic Graphics, Inc.
6000 N. Forest Park Drive
PO Box 1901
Peoria, IL 61656
800/255-8800
Length:
2 days
Cost:
$595
Location:
Various locations throughout the country.
Description:
This is an intermediate-level workshop of techniques and strategies to improve the quality of design decisions and desktop-published materials. Emphasis is on professional design, rather than how to use a specific program or system. Contact the provider for numerous other courses at elementary and advanced levels.

59

Title:
Hands-on Web Page Design
Sponsor:
Dynamic Graphics
6000 N. Forest Park Dr.
PO Box 1901
Peoria, IL 61656
800/255-8800
309/688-5873
Length:
3 days
Cost:
$995
Location:
Various colleges throughout the U.S.
Description:
This intermediate-level workshop includes how to build links, FTP, making transparent images, file optimization and management, creating an adaptive palette, frames, animation, and generating client-supported image maps. Check sponsor for many more skill-based graphics workshops.

60

Title:
Teamwork in Action
Sponsor:
Eckerd College
Management Development Institute
4200 54th Avenue South
St. Petersburg, FL 33711
800/753-0444
813/864-8996 (fax)
Length:
3 days
Cost:
$2,400
Location:
St. Petersburg, FL
Description:
Teamwork in Action features two powerful "feedback from colleagues" instruments. The Systematic Multiple Level Observation of Groups® (SYMLOG) enables participants to examine in detail those aspects of their behavior which enhance teamwork and those which may be interfering with it. The second instrument, the Leadership Effectiveness Analysis® 360° (LEA), allows participants to measure leadership behaviors as perceived by superiors, peers, and direct reports. The results help par-

ticipants assess their impact on others and their ability to inspire team commitment. Additional features include confidential one-on-one feedback with a professional staff member, peer learning, and action planning.

61

Title:
The 7 Habits of Highly Effective People
Sponsor:
FranklinCovey
360 West 4800 North
Provo, UT 84604
801/391-1492
801/229-1233
Length:
3 days
Cost:
$1,495
Location:
Various cities throughout the U.S.
Description:
This workshop is based on the best-selling book of the same title by Stephen R. Covey. One month prior to the workshop, anonymous feedback is gathered from supervisors, associates, peers, and those who report to you. During the workshop, you receive confidential, computerized feedback along with an Action Planning Guide.

62

Title:
Managing the Training Function
Sponsor:
FKA Friesen, Kaye and Associates
3448 Richmond Rd.
Ottawa, ON, Canada
800/FKA-5585
613/829-0845 (fax)
Length:
2 days
Cost:
$995
Location:
Various cities in the U.S.; also in Ottawa, Toronto, and Vancouver, Canada
Description:
Managing the Training Function examines the critical components necessary to ensure that training initiatives in organizations are linked to business needs, and provide measurable results. The program assesses the training function through a series of highly interactive applications, facilitated by Michael Nolan, President of Friesen, Kaye and Associates.

63

Title:
Performance Consulting Skills
Sponsor:
FKA Friesen, Kaye and Associates
3448 Richmond Rd.
Ottawa, ON, Canada
800/FKA-5585
613/829-0845 (fax)
Length:
2 days
Cost:
$995
Location:
Various cities in the U.S.; also in Ottawa and Toronto, Canada
Description:
The Performance Consulting Skills Workshop is a comprehensive program which addresses the development needs of trainers and HRD professionals. The workshop offers participants, whose roles are evolving into consultancy, the opportunity to build the skills necessary to link training and other interventions to business needs. Participants practice the concepts and skills learned in the workshop through highly interactive applications of the consulting process.

64

Title:
The Great Manager Program
Sponsor:
The Gallup Organization
The Gallup School of Management
300 South 68th Street Place
Lincoln, NB 68510
800/288-8592
402/486-6369 (fax)
Length:
4 days
Cost:
$3,500
Location:
Lincoln, NB
Description:
This highly interactive workshop is limited to 20 participants. Each participant benefits from a 360° assessment study conducted by the Gallup Organization prior to the workshop at each participant's work location. The workshop is built upon Gallup's "18 themes of excellent management" developed from 25 years of research involving executives, managers, and employees. The reality base of the workshop includes results of 40,000 executive interviews and 250,000 manager/employee interviews.

65

Title:
Leadership Institute: Leveraging Individual Talent for Organizational Excellence
Sponsor:
The Gallup Organization
The Gallup School of Management
300 South 68th Street Place
Lincoln, NB 68510
800/288-8592
402/486-6369 (fax)
Length:
5 days
Cost:
$5,000
Location:
Lincoln, NB
Description:
This intensive full week of learning begins with a social time on Sunday evening, and continues through Friday. Prior to the Institute, the Gallup research staff administers a 360° information and feedback instrument to colleagues, superiors, and direct reports of Institute participants. Enrollment is limited to 20 persons. Research conducted by The Gallup Organization is used throughout the Institute.

66

Title:
Becoming a Better Intervener
Sponsor:
Gestalt Institute of Cleveland
1588 Hazel Drive
Cleveland, OH 44106
216/421-0468
216/421-1729
Length:
7 days
Cost:
$11,800
Location:
Cleveland, OH

Description:
This was the first training program in the world to integrate Gestalt theory, System theory and Organizational Development Theory. It offers theory, concepts, methodology, tools, and techniques for intervening at the individual, two-person, group, and organization level of systems. It offers a unique Gestalt framework for developing professionals, designing interventions, and managing systems change. An interview is required as part of the admission process.

67

Title:
Data Warehouse Essentials
Sponsor:
Global Knowledge
P.O. Box 1039
Cary, NC 27512
919/461-8600
800/268-7737
919/461-8646 (fax)
Length:
3 days
Cost:
$1,695
Location:
Various cities throughout the U.S.
Description:
This is a new workshop for those interested in information sharing and knowledge management. The workshop focuses on what works and what doesn't, how to maximize the profits and value of data warehouses, and how to build a data warehouse. Tuition financing is available.

68

Title:
Web Development Fundamentals
Sponsor:
Global Knowledge
P.O. Box 1039
Cary, NC 27512
919/461-8600
919/461-8646 (fax)
Length:
3 days
Cost:
$1,695
Location:
Various cities throughout the U.S.

Description:
In this workshop, participants learn to install and configure Web servers. Topics include: Web components (clients, servers, protocols); product overviews, and various server installation and configuration options. Global Knowledge Network, Inc. is a certified Cisco, Linux, Microsoft, and UNIX trainer. Phone for extensive software, hardware, and Internet courses. Course financing is also available as a student service.

69

Title:
Project Management Techniques
Sponsor:
Goal QPC
2 Manor Pkwy.
Salem, NH 03079
800/643-4316
603/870-9122
Length:
2 days
Cost:
$795
Location:
Various cities throughout the U.S.
Description:
This workshop is for beginning project leaders and project team members at all organizational levels. Topics include: staying within budget, enhanced team participation in planning and monitoring, risk assessment, and executing a deliverable schedule. Check the sponsor for other workshops: Basic Problem Solving, Facilitation Skills, and Principles and Tools for Creativity.

70

Title:
Managing People for Maximum Performance
Sponsor:
Harvard University
John F. Kennedy School of Government
Center for Management Research
55 William Street
Wellesley, MA 02181
781/239-1111
781/239-1546 (fax)
Length:
2 days

Cost:
$1,950
Location:
Cambridge, MA
Description:
Faculty from Harvard University are presenters and facilitators in this program for executives and senior managers. Its focus is decision making and building toward long-term improvement. Topics include how and why people work, making good performance pay off, setting goals, and tracking results. Case studies on improving performance are analyzed. Part of a series of programs on leadership.

71

Title:
Promoting Innovation & Organizational Change
Sponsor:
Harvard University
John F. Kennedy School of Government
Center for Management Research
55 William Street
Wellesley, MA 02181
781/239-1111
781/239-1546 (fax)
Length:
2 days
Cost:
$1,950
Location:
Cambridge, MA
Description:
Faculty from Harvard University are presenters and facilitators in this program for executives and senior managers. The focus of the seminar is how to promote innovation that is manageable and measurable, including small improvements, major changes, and strategic breakthroughs. Topics include strategies for generating innovative alternatives, building an innovation-friendly workplace, and developing suggestion systems that rake in spontaneous creativity. Lessons from both public and private sectors are used as examples. Part of a series of programs on leadership.

72

Title:
Teaching Negotiation in the Corporation

Sponsor:
Harvard University Law School Program on Negotiation
Center for Management Research
55 William Street
Wellesley, MA 02181
781/239-1111
781/239-1546 (fax)

Length:
2½ days

Cost:
$2,250

Location:
Cambridge, MA

Description:
This seminar teaches a new negotiation process and offers the opportunity to get a behind-the-scenes view of the strategies and objectives which the faculty at the Program on Negotiation at Harvard Law School have developed for teaching that process to senior executives. The course was designed to provide strategies, tools, and techniques needed to develop the participants' own curriculum training objectives. It is part of a major program on various aspects of negotiation.

73

Title:
Charting Change Workshop

Sponsor:
Human Synergistics International
39819 Plymouth Rd. C8020
Plymouth, MI 48170
800/622-7584
734/459-5557 (fax)
International affiliates throughout the world

Length:
4½ days

Cost:
$995

Location:
Plymouth, MI

Description:
This workshop focuses on producing measurable, cost-effective improvement in individuals, groups, and organizations, especially in productivity, quality, and cultural change. Participants use sponsor-developed tools for customizing their own measurement-based systems, including how to administer and interpret assessments. The goal is performance improvement from an "inside/outside" perspective.

74

Title:
Designing Information for the Web

Sponsor:
Information Mapping, Inc.
41 Waverly Oaks Road
Waltham, MA 02154
800/463-6627
781/906-6400 (fax)

Length:
2 days

Cost:
$1,225

Location:
Various cities throughout the U.S.

Description:
This seminar focuses on the design of information and its organization for the Web and Internet. The emphasis is on accessibility and usability of information. One of several Web seminars.

75

Title:
Developing Procedures, Policies, and Documentation

Sponsor:
Information Mapping, Inc.
411 Waverly Oaks Rd.
Waltham, MA 02154
800/463-6627
781/906-6400 (fax)

Length:
3 days

Cost:
$1,395

Location:
Various cities throughout the U.S.

Description:
This seminar is for trainers, developers, and managers who need a standard approach to documentation. The program teaches how to create consistent, high-quality materials. It can be applied to a variety of types of manuals and business documentation.

76

Title:
Structuring User Documentation

Sponsor:
Information Mapping, Inc.
411 Waverly Oaks Rd.
Waltham, MA 02154
800/463-6627
781/906-6400 (fax)

Length:
3 days

Cost:
$1,395

Location:
Various cities throughout the U.S.

Description:
This seminar focuses on creating user guides for paper and online distribution.

77

Title:
Systems Thinking

Sponsor:
Innovation Associates
Acorn Park
Cambridge, MA 02140
617/498-5700
617/498-5701 (fax)

Length:
3 days

Cost:
$2,450; Team rates available

Location:
Boston, MA

Description:
This program is an in-depth introduction to the discipline of Systems Thinking. It includes a focus on leverage points and communication strategies, including system "stories" and archetypes. Other workshops can be developed for on-site presentation.

78

Title:
Employment Law Overview

Sponsor:
Institute for Applied Management and Law
610 Newport Center Drive, Ste. 1060
Newport Beach, CA 92660
949/760-1700
949/760-8192 (fax)

Length:
4½ days

Cost:
$2,125

Location:
Various cities throughout the U.S.

Description:
This seminar covers all facets of employment law, taught by employment law attorneys from leading law firms. The focus is practical, providing participants with information that can help compa-

Training for Trainers

nies avoid litigation. The first 2 days cover labor law; the second 2 days focus on employment discrimination law. The final day focuses on special issues in employee relations law. Other seminars on specific laws are also available.

79

Title:
Essentials of Human Resource Management
Sponsor:
Institute for Applied Management and Law
610 Newport Center Drive, Ste. 1060
Newport Beach, CA 92660
949/760-1700
949/760-8192 (fax)
Length:
4½ days
Cost:
$2,125
Location:
Various cities throughout the U.S.
Description:
This seminar focuses on human resource management and the law. The first half of the seminar is presented by employment law attorneys; the second half focuses on topics such as performance-based management, taking the chaos out of change, and training the trainers.

80

Title:
Designing Effective Program Evaluations
Sponsor:
Institute for Professional Education
2200 Wilson Blvd., Ste 406
Arlington, VA 22201
703/527-8700
703/527-8703 (fax)
Length:
3 days
Cost:
$1,495
Location:
Washington, DC; San Francisco, CA
Description:
This seminar is designed for program managers and others interested in assessing the efficiency, effectiveness, and responsiveness of programs and policies. The course will outline step-by-step procedures for conducting effective evaluation research utilizing examples from business, education, criminal justice, and health.

81

Title:
Improving Consulting Effectiveness
Sponsor:
Institute for Professional Education
2200 Wilson Blvd., Ste. 406
Arlington, VA 22201
703/527-8700
703/527-8703 (fax)
Length:
3 days
Cost:
$1,250
Location:
Washington, DC
Description:
This intense, pragmatic seminar enables participants to improve their overall effectiveness in consulting. The seminar provides participants with strategies and skills in four areas:
- tools to better understand the consulting role, its opportunities and limitations, and to use that understanding to design the role for maximum impact
- human relations tools to better understand the diverse people they must work with
- strategies to design effective, collaborative consulting relationships
- everyday communications skills to work more effectively, one-on-one, with all kinds of clients

82

Title:
Project Management Fundamentals
Sponsor:
International Institute for Learning, Inc.
110 East 59th Street
New York, NY 10022
800/325-1533
212/755-0777 (fax)
Length:
2 days
Cost:
$1,295
Location:
Various cities throughout the U.S.
Description:
This course provides the skills, concepts, principles, and tools that apply immediately to the job. It takes an actual project and uses it as an ongoing case throughout the course.

83

Title:
Corporate University Week
Sponsor:
International Quality & Productivity Center
150 Clove Rd.
P.O. Box 401
Little Falls, NJ 07424
800/882-8684
201/256-0205 (fax)
Length:
2 days plus pre- and post-conference workshops
Cost:
$1,699 conference only; $500 extra per workshop
Location:
Scottsdale, AZ
Description:
Based on the premise that corporate training functions will undergo dramatic growth and change in the coming years, this program focuses on the "corporate university" as the vehicle of that change. Delivered in a conference format, the program consists mostly of presentations of the experiences of various organizations with the corporate university format. Included is information about putting the corporate university online. The principal thrust of the program, however, is how to establish, organize, manage, and empower a corporate university as a focal point for an organization's training and development activity.

84

Title:
Creating & Launching Learning Portals: The Next Wave in Web-Based Distance Learning
Sponsor:
International Quality & Productivity Center
150 Clove Road
P.O. Box 401
Little Falls, NJ 07424
800/882-8684
201/256-0205 (fax)

Length:
2 days of conference; plus 2 days of workshop
Cost:
$1,699 conference only; $500 extra per workshop
Location:
Several locations; phone for specifics
Description:
This training features a panel of experts from leading companies who have been successful with online learning. Benefits of learning portals, communities of learning, pros and cons of outsourcing, and technical topics concerning software architecture, bandwidth, marketing, and financing are included.

85

Title:
Performance Measurements for Training
Sponsor:
International Quality & Productivity Center
150 Clove Road
P.O. Box 401
Little Falls, NJ 07424
800/882-8684
201/256-0205 (fax)
Length:
2 days of workshops in conjunction with a 2-day conference on the same topic
Cost:
$1,699; conference only
$500 extra per workshop
Location:
Various cities throughout the U.S.
Description:
Participants learn how to define, measure, and improve the results of training. Topics include budgeting, determining return on investment, and collaborative tracking of the impact of training. Case studies of numerous successful companies are presented in conference format; workshops supplement the conference and deal with details.

86

Title:
Web-Based Training Performance Support
Sponsor:
International Quality & Productivity Center
150 Clove Road
P.O. Box 401
Little Falls, NJ 07424
800/822-8684
201/256-0205 (fax)
Length:
2 days
Cost:
$1,699
Location:
Various cities throughout the U.S.
Description:
Participants focus on how Web-based systems support today's workers with advice, know-how, tools, references, and training exactly at the required time and place of need. The seminar deals with specific development skills, desktop learning, multimedia deployment over the Internet, and cost structures for Web-based training. Case studies are included.

87

Title:
Facilitation Skills Workshop
Sponsor:
J&M Training & Consultants
PO Box 339
Merrill, WI 54452
715/536-8144
715/536-1638 (fax)
Length:
3 days
Cost:
$825
Location:
Atlanta, GA
Description:
This workshop uses case studies and feedback from peers to focus on improvement of skills. Topics include: leadership, facilitation, active listening, content development, process development, and team development.

88

Title:
D.O.T. Safety Compliance
Sponsor:
J.J. Keller & Associates
3003 W. Breezewood Lane
PO Box 368
Neenah, WI 54957
800/327-6868
Length:
1 day
Cost:
$229
Location:
Various locations throughout the U.S.
Description:
This seminar focuses on various essentials of Department of Transportation compliance: Federal rules and regulations information, hours of service, accident prevention, insurance issues, and alcohol and drug testing.

89

Title:
Corporate Training and Knowledge Management
Sponsor:
Jones International University
9697 East Mineral Avenue
Englewood, CO 80112
800/811-5663
303/784-8547 (fax)
Length:
Average time to take all courses required for the degree is 2^1/$_2$ years; courses are 8 weeks and 12 weeks
Cost:
$850 per course
Location:
All online
Description:
This is one of six Master of e-Learning degree programs offered by Jones International University, the first fully accredited online university. Courses begin each month and are available 24/7. Students interact with instructors and other students from around the world. Contact Jones for more information. Other degrees are: Technology and Design, Global Leadership and Administration, Research and Assessment, Library and Resource Management, and e-Learning Generalist.

90

Title:
Executive Development Program
Sponsor:
J.L. Kellogg Graduate School of Management
Northwestern University
James L. Allen Center
Evanston, IL 60208
847/467-7000
847/491-4323 (fax)
Length:
20 days

Cost:
$18,000, includes food, lodging, all materials
Location:
Evanston, IL
Description:
For those with at least 10 years experience with senior management potential who want to lead or contribute to organizational change initiatives. Topics include investing and customer service in addition to global competition opportunities, interaction of various functions, improved strategic thinking and analytical skills for better decision making and problem solving. Other 3- and 4-day seminars are also available, for example: Reinventing Leadership, and Changing Strategic Direction.

91

Title:
Basic Supervision
Sponsor:
Keye Productivity Center/AMAI
11221 Roe Ave.
Leawood, KS 66211
800/821-3919
800/914-8879 (fax)
Length:
1 day
Cost:
$169
Location:
Various cities throughout the U.S.
Description:
This is one of many one-day seminars of Keye Productivity Center, affiliated with The American Management Association International. Topics include basic supervisory skills, specific skills such as coaching and counseling, how to motivate and discipline employees, effective communication, boosting productivity, and solving problems.

92

Title:
OSHA Basics of Accident Prevention and Compliance
Sponsor:
Keye Productivity Center/AMAI
11221 Roe Avenue
Leawood, KS 66211
800/821-3919
800/914-8879 (fax)
Length:
1 day

Cost:
$229
Location:
Various cities throughout the U.S.
Description:
This workshop focuses on content and techniques for creating and delivering safety training. Topics include: identifying training requirements for each worker, finding and using resources, presentation techniques, legal issues, personal protective equipment, machine operations, and confined spaces training.

93

Title:
Designing Computer-Based Training
Sponsor:
Langevin Learning Services
P.O. Box 1221, 420 Ford St.
Ogdensburg, NY 13669
800/223-2209
800/636-6869 (fax)
Length:
5 days
Cost:
$3,695
Location:
Various cities throughout the U.S.; Ottawa and Toronto, Canada
Description:
This is a practical workshop in all elements of design and production of Computer-based Training (CBT). Topics include: designing linear tutorials, designing branching tutorials, developing a structure plan, designing frames and storyboards, applying motivational techniques in lesson design, constructing pre-tests, and choosing an authoring system.

94

Title:
Instructional Design for New Designers
Sponsor:
Langevin Learning Systems
P.O. Box 1221, 420 Ford St.
Ogdensburg, NY 13669
800/223-2209
800/636-6869 (fax)
Length:
6 days
Cost:
$3,496
Location:
Various cities throughout the U.S.; Ottawa, Toronto, and Vancouver, Canada

Description:
This skills-based workshop is for those new to instructional design with no formal training in design. Major sections of the workshop include: work plans and estimating design time, learner analysis including dealing with diversity among learners, task analysis and sequencing content, how to write measurable objectives, and designing tests. A 6-month post-workshop edit service is included for all participants. An advanced workshop is also available.

95

Title:
Training Needs Analysis
Sponsor:
Langevin Learning Services
P.O. Box 1221, 420 Ford St.
Ogdensburg, NY 13669
800/223-2209
800/636-6869 (fax)
Length:
6 days
Cost:
$3,696
Location:
Various cities throughout the U.S.; Ottawa, Toronto, and Vancouver, Canada
Description:
This practical, "how to" workshop includes planning a needs analysis, data collection, data analysis, cost-benefit analysis, and dealing with politics surrounding needs analysis. Participants receive a diskette of templates to use back on the job, and receive unlimited telephone consultation for one year post-workshop.

96

Title:
Contract Training Institute
Sponsor:
LERN (Learning Resources Network)
1550 Hayes Dr.
Manhattan, KS 66502
800/678-5376
888/234-8633 (fax)
Length:
4 days
Cost:
$1,195
Location:
Minneapolis, MN

Description:
Designed for professionals who conduct programs for business and industry, this institute covers topics such as personal selling, telemarketing, direct e-mail promotions, etc. as they relate to contract training, seminars, and business courses.

97
Title:
Program Management Institute
Sponsor:
LERN (Learning Resources Network)
1550 Hayes Dr.
Manhattan, KS 66502
800/678-5376
888/234-8633 (fax)
Length:
4 days
Cost:
$745
Location:
Minneapolis, MN
Description:
In sessions led by a 4-person faculty, a maximum of 10 program managers, coordinators, and directors receive intensive training in the management of programs for adult education, continuing education, corporate training, etc.

98
Title:
Leadership Is a Choice: The Four Roles of a Leader
Sponsor:
Lessons In Leadership
Section 210
Louisville, KY 40289
800/873-3451
800/328-5644 (fax)
Length:
1 day
Cost:
$379
Location:
Various cities throughout the U.S.
Description:
This seminar presentation is by Dr. Stephen Covey, author of *Living the 7 Habits*. Among the topics are: how to build trust, how to reduce cynicism, how to keep and inspire your most talented workers, how to develop leadership and achieve new levels of performance at every organizational level.

99
Title:
Workplace Violence Prevention and Conflict Resolution
Sponsor:
Liberty Mutual Group
175 Berkeley Street, M.S.8F
P.O. Box 140
Boston, MA 02117
800/320-7581
617/695-9216 (fax)
Length:
2 days
Cost:
$500
Location:
Various cities throughout the U.S.
Description:
This seminar is designed to provide attendees with the principles and procedures for control of exposures to workplace violence. Topics include: OSHA guidelines and enforcement policy, developing a loss control program, outside workplace violence assistance, employment-related prevention measures, intruder-related prevention measures, and major types of workplace exposures and risk factors for workplace violence.

100
Title:
Consulting Skills for Human Resource Professionals
Sponsor:
Linkage, Inc.
One Forbes Rd.
Lexington, MA 02173
781/862-3157
781/862-2355 (fax)
Length:
2 days
Cost:
$1,195
Location:
Lexington, MA, and other cities throughout the U.S.
Description:
This workshop provides participants with the knowledge and skills necessary to increase their consulting role with internal clients and customers. It examines the variety of roles that consultants perform and the appropriateness and applications of each. Participants practice applying a step-by-step consulting (problem-solving) methodology which provides them with a practical tool for immediate application on the job. An advanced workshop is also available.

101
Title:
Developing a Coaching and Mentoring System
Sponsor:
Linkage, Inc.
One Forbes Rd.
Lexington, MA 02173
781/862-3157
781/862-2355 (fax)
Length:
2 days
Cost:
$1,195
Location:
Boston, MA; Chicago, IL; New York, NY; Washington, DC; Denver, CO
Description:
This workshop helps participants identify the best options for building an environment to support coaching and mentoring and use the best tools for developing the program.

102
Title:
Global Institute for Leadership Development
Sponsor:
Linkage, Inc.
One Forbes Rd.
Lexington, MA 02173
781/862-3157
781/862-2355 (fax)
Length:
5 days
Cost:
$5,595
Location:
San Diego, CA
Description:
This is an intensive institute for leadership development featuring topics in assessment, training, coaching, and benchmarking within a global needs model. The Institute's mission is "to accelerate the development of emerging leaders through focused learning around core leadership competencies, knowledge areas, and skills." The 50-hour program features more than 50 CEOs, COOs, internation-

Training for Trainers

ally known thought leaders, authors, and facilitators. An action learning model is used for work in teams during the Institute.

103

Title:
Introduction to Competency-Based Systems
Sponsor:
Linkage, Inc.
One Forbes Rd.
Lexington, MA 02173
781/862-3157
781/862-2355 (fax)
Length:
2 days
Cost:
$1,195
Location:
Boston, MA; Chicago, IL
Description:
In this program, participants learn to analyze the skills and competencies demonstrated by the top performers in their business. They get training in competency and workforce analysis that will enable them to articulate the critical development issues in their company's future, and they develop skills in interviewing, running focus groups, performing data analysis, and building models.

104

Title:
Leading Teams
Sponsor:
Linkage, Inc.
One Forbes Rd.
Lexington, MA 02173
781/862-3157
781/862-2355 (fax)
Length:
2 days
Cost:
$1,195
Location:
Boston, MA; Atlanta, GA; Chicago, IL
Description:
Results through facilitative leadership is the focus of this workshop. Topics include: how to achieve consensus, how to identify what derails teams, how to deal with special projects and virtual teams.

105

Title:
How to Build a Complete Management Training Curriculum
Sponsor:
Management Education Consulting Company of America (MECCA)
40 W. 919 Elodie Dr.
Elburn, IL 60119
630/584-0164
630/584-0184 (fax)
Length:
1 day
Cost:
$550
Location:
Various cities throughout the U.S.
Description:
This program shows trainers how to develop a "just-in-time" management training curriculum. It teaches how to properly sequence and configure management training into an integrated curriculum for new supervisors, experienced supervisors, managers of supervisors, and executives. Sample curricula from several companies are presented.

106

Title:
Skills for e-Trainers
Sponsor:
The MASIE Center, e-Lab
PO Box 397
Saratoga Springs, NY 12866
518/350-2200
518/587-3276 (fax)
Length:
3 days
Cost:
$1,795
Location:
Saratoga Springs, NY
Description:
The MASIE Center features a new 10,000 sq. ft. facility for e-learning research, training, and development. This 3-day (plus evenings) workshop includes project work, contact with remote experts, virtual teaching studios, a learning usability lab, bandwidth simulators, workplace distraction simulators, tools gallery, videocapture, feedback rooms, wireless and form factor e-learning, broadcast flash studio, workgroup rooms, strategy arena, and more.

107

Title:
System Dynamics for Senior Managers
Sponsor:
MIT
Massachusetts Institute of Technology
Sloan School of Management
55 William Street
Wellesley, MA 02181
781/239-1111
781/239-1546 (fax)
Length:
2 days
Cost:
$2,300
Location:
Wellesley, MA
Description:
For senior managers interested in a systems framework supporting high performance. Topics include: project management, integrated growth strategies, organizational change, process improvement, supply chains, competitive response, cultural conflict, system archetypes, and simulation modeling. Part of MIT's Executive Series on Management and Technology.

108

Title:
Leadership and Supervisory Skills for Women; Life Balance and Stress Reduction Solutions
Sponsor:
National Businesswomen's Leadership Association
P.O. Box 419107
Kansas City, MO 64141
800/258-7246
913/432-0824 (fax)
Length:
1 day
Cost:
$69
Location:
Numerous cities throughout the U.S.
Description:
An intensive day focused on typical problems and how to solve them. Topics include: how to lead and supervise, build teamwork and cooperation, position yourself as credible and authoritative, communicate with groups and one-to-one, handle conflict, reduce stress, and prevent burnout.

109

Title:
Training of Trainers: Developing Cultural Diversity Programs for the Workplace

Sponsor:
National MultiCultural Institute
3000 Connecticut Ave., NW, Suite 438
Washington, DC 20008
202/483-0700
202/483-5233 (fax)

Length:
4 days

Cost:
$995

Location:
Washington, DC

Description:
The purpose of this program is to enable participants to design and deliver a basic, one-day "Valuing Cultural Diversity Workshop" for the workplace. It focuses on design, facilitation skills, exercises, and lecturette material. After an introduction to several fundamental workshop components, participants have the opportunity, in small groups, to design and present a one-day workshop and to facilitate an exercise. The session combines didactic and experiential teaching techniques. This program is for experienced trainers in the government, corporate, and non-profit sectors who have participated in personal cultural awareness training, but who have limited experience in facilitating diversity workshops.

110

Title:
Supervisors' Development Program

Sponsor:
National Safety Council
1121 Spring Lake Drive
Itasca, IL 60143
800/539-7468

Length:
2 days

Cost:
$495

Location:
At various state safety council facilities throughout the U.S.

Description:
The goal of the program is to enable participants to apply safety and health education, training, and communication methods that promote safe and healthful actions by employees. Contact sponsor for additional workplace safety courses.

111

Title:
Writing for the Web

Sponsor:
n Sight
10 Fawcett Street
Cambridge, MA 02138
617/354-2828
617/354-8328 (fax)

Length:
1 day

Cost:
$354

Location:
Framingham, MA

Description:
In this workshop you will learn how to apply journalism techniques to Web writing, create and edit material for different Web audiences, establish voice and personality, and transform legacy text. Contact sponsor for other Web strategy and management courses.

112

Title:
Advanced Team Building

Sponsor:
NTL Institute
1240 N. Pitt St., Suite 100
Alexandria, VA 22314-1403
703/548-1500
703/684-1256 (fax)

Length:
7 days

Cost:
$2,000

Location:
Bethel, ME

Description:
This experiential workshop emphasizes diagnosis, instruments, application skills, and interventions with a particular focus on: roles, vision, mission, problem solving, decision making, interpersonal relations, conflict, and resistance to change. Participants (1) develop a file of team-building activities, simulations, and readings, (2) create strategies for elite team building with executives and top management groups, and (3) learn how to "sell" team building to the organization.

113

Title:
The Art of Coaching Employees

Sponsor:
NTL Institute
1240 N. Pitt St., Ste. 100
Alexandria, VA 22314-1403
703/548-1500
703/684-1256 (fax)

Length:
4 days

Cost:
$1,500

Location:
Clearwater, FL

Description:
This program is designed to help managers and other leaders develop staff through coaching and mentoring. Participants assess their styles and learn how to create an effective coaching climate.

114

Title:
Trainer Skillshop

Sponsor:
NTL Institute
1240 N. Pitt St., Suite 100
Alexandria, VA 22314-1403
703/548-1500
703/684-1256 (fax)

Length:
7 days

Cost:
$1,900

Location:
Bethel, ME

Description:
This workshop is a hands-on, skills training course for instructors and trainers who feel they have not had adequate preparation for activities like preparing course outlines and materials, giving presentations, creating a good learning climate, and evaluating other adults. This workshop helps improve participants' ability (1) to use a variety of training techniques, (2) to effectively use questioning, listening, and feedback skills, (3) to manage course time, difficult students, and difficult situations, (4) to diagnose their own strengths from peer and video feedback,

using behavioral checklists, (5) to write plans for continued self-development, and (6) to evaluate training sessions and programs.

115

Title:
Internal Consulting
Sponsor:
Numerof & Associates, Inc.
11457 Olde Cabin Rd., Ste. 350
St. Louis, MO 63141
314/997-1587
314/997-0948 (fax)
Length:
2 days
Cost:
$1,195
Location:
Various cities throughout the U.S.
Description:
This workshop focuses on consultative skill development, particularly in problem diagnosis, needs assessment, and intervention. Program attendance is limited to 15 persons. One hour of telephone consultation with staff consultants is included with the workshop fee.

116

Title:
How to Motivate, Manage, and Lead a Team
Sponsor:
The Padgett-Thompson Division of the American Management Association International
Padgett-Thompson Building
P.O. Box 8297
Overland Park, KS 66208
800/255-4141
800/914-8879 (fax)
Length:
1 day
Cost:
$179
Location:
Various cities throughout the U.S.
Description:
This program focuses on the fundamental skills needed for effective leadership and management of teams. Topics include problem analysis, elimination of obstacles, strengthening and motivational tools. Focus on "how to" throughout the seminar.

117

Title:
Setting Up Your Mentoring System
Sponsor:
Perrone-Ambrose Associates, Inc.
2 North Riverside Plaza, Ste. 1433
Chicago, IL 60606
800/648-0543
312/648-0622 (fax)
Length:
1 day
Cost:
$1,000
Location:
Alexandria, VA; Los Angeles, CA; Chicago, IL; New York, NY
Description:
The focus of this workshop is how to establish strategic goals and plans for implementing a mentoring system. Topics include how to watch mentors and mentees, and how to sustain and measure progress and results. A workshop outcome is a system "layout." Perrone-Ambrose also has a full range of job aids and mentoring books and products, and provides mentoring services. A workshop on sharpening mentoring skills is also available.

118

Title:
Managing the Training Function
Sponsor:
Practical Management Incorporated
3280 West Hacienda, Ste. 205
Las Vegas, NV 89118
800/444-9101
702/795-8339 (fax)
Length:
2 days
Cost:
$695
Location:
Various cities throughout the U.S.
Description:
This course first leads participants through the process of building a training philosophy for their organization. Next, they cover how to: (1) improve relations with line management, (2) respond to their needs, and (3) analyze training requests. Other topics include: (a) the hierarchy of objectives, (b) the strategic training plan, (c) the buy-vs.-build decision, (d) working effectively with outside resources, and (e) analyzing the training department's contribution. The workshop culminates with participants preparing their own action plan.

119

Title:
Needs Analysis, Evaluation, and Validation
Sponsor:
Practical Management Incorporated
3280 West Hacienda, Ste. 205
Las Vegas, NV 89118
800/444-9101
702/795-8339 (fax)
Length:
3 days
Cost:
$995
Location:
Various cities throughout the U.S.
Description:
This program is for trainers, training analysts, and training managers. Through a combination of participative instructional techniques and application exercises, attendees participate in the development of a training plan that combines the major training functions—from needs analysis through evaluation to the validation process.

120

Title:
Teaching Technical Topics
Sponsor:
Practical Management Incorporated
3280 West Hacienda, Ste. 205
Las Vegas, NV 89118
800/444-9101
702/795-8339 (fax)
Length:
3 days
Cost:
$995
Location:
Various cities throughout the U.S.
Description:
This program is for technical trainers or for customer service reps, supervisors, and employees with teaching duties—in particular those who teach technical subjects or sales programs. Relying heavily on practice and application, this course begins by reviewing the common failure points of technical instruction and the keys to effective training, including the use of questions, written materials, visual aids,

and ice-breakers. Participants are taught the use of objectives and lesson plans, and they practice new skills using the specifics of courses currently taught by them or those which they are preparing to teach.

121

Title:
Web-Based Training
Sponsor:
Practical Management Incorporated
3280 West Hacienda, Ste. 205
Las Vegas, NV 89118
800/444-9101
702/795-8339 (fax)
Length:
3 days
Cost:
$1,695
Location:
Various cities throughout the U.S.
Description:
This program is for individuals who use personal computers in developing and delivering training. It covers each aspect of the design of CBT, including: (1) selection of hardware options, (2) course authoring alternatives, (3) design steps, (4) lesson flow alternatives, and (5) validation. Hands-on practice is provided throughout the program. New developments in Web-based and intranet-based training are featured.

122

Title:
Beyond Train-the-Trainer
Sponsor:
Rollins College
Corporate Learning Institute
1000 Holt Avenue - 2728
Winter Park, FL 32789
800/494-4253
407/646-1503 (fax)
Length:
2 days
Cost:
$695
Location:
Winter Park, FL
Description:
An advanced workshop created by Ed Jones, master trainer, this program features limited enrollment, small group, and hands-on work. Special topics include facilitation skills, designing and using case studies, and designing creative games that encourage learning. Prerequisite to attending this workshop is at least 2 years of classroom training experience.

123

Title:
Diversity Training
Sponsor:
SENEX Counseling & Training
Fairhill Center
12200 Fairhill Road
Cleveland, OH 44120
216/421-1793
Length:
1 day
Cost:
$99 (partially funded by area agencies on aging)
Location:
Cleveland, OH
Description:
Senex Training provides diversity training that targets important human processes that allow your company to take full advantage of all of your human resources while encouraging productivity and employee satisfaction. Senex also provides continuing education credit to professionals seeking to expand their understanding of age, gender, and sexuality, especially where those identities intersect with race, class, culture, and ability.

124

Title:
Transnational Human Resources: Best Practices
Sponsor:
Institute for International Human Resources
Society for Human Resource Management (SHRM)
1800 Duke Street
Alexandria, VA 22314
800/283-SHRM
703/535-6490 (fax)
Length:
1 day
Cost:
$225
Location:
New York, NY
Description:
This seminar is jointly organized by the Institute and Fordham University's Graduate School of Business. SHRM members and Fordham Alumni receive substantial discount on tuition. Topics include: Best Practices in China, Managing the Expatriate Function, Global Compensation in a Fiercely Competitive Market, and Transnational Information Technology Recruiting.

125

Title:
The Walt Disney Approach to Leadership Excellence for HR Professionals
Sponsor:
Society for Human Resource Management (SHRM)
1800 Duke Street
Alexandria, VA 22314
800/283-SHRM
407/828-4411
703/535-6490 (fax)
Length:
4 days
Cost:
$2,995 includes lodging, meals, course materials
Location:
Orlando, FL
Description:
Especially designed for HR professionals who are middle managers and change agents. Topics include: strategies for employee involvement, accountability, organization and culture, improvement strategies, character, and the power of story. The program is focused on Disney's successful strategies and practices. Cost includes theme park admission and free use of the Park's transportation system.

126

Title:
Positive Power and Influence Program
Sponsor:
Situation Management Systems
195 Hanover Street
Hanover, MA 02339
781/826-4433
781/826-2863 (fax)
Length:
3 days
Cost:
$1,675
Location:
Various cities throughout the U.S.
Description:
This program helps participants to develop and refine skills required to influence others in a positive

Training for Trainers

and constructive manner. Mastery over several influence styles is the key to achieving effective results. Participants learn appropriate tactics to analyze situations and achieve their influence objectives.

127

Title:
Excelling as a Highly Effective Team Leader
Sponsor:
SkillPath Seminars
6900 Squibb Road
PO Box 2768
Mission, KS 66201
800/873-7545
913/362-4241 (fax)
Length:
2 days
Cost:
$399
Location:
Various cities throughout the U.S.
Description:
How to lead teams to peak performance is the goal of this workshop: How to motivate, resolve differences, gain member commitment, grant more decision-making and problem-solving authority. Contact sponsor for numerous other workshops.

128

Title:
Introduction to Video Production
Sponsor:
Sony Video Institute
3300 Zanker Road
San Jose, CA 95134
408/955-4231
408/955-5340 (fax)
Length:
4 days
Cost:
$1,600
Location:
Various cities throughout the U.S.
Description:
This program covers the elements of preproduction, production, and postproduction, as well as operational, organizational, and marketing concepts. In the 20-step approach, "Progressive Video Programming," students learn essentials of preparation and execution of "film-style" on-location taping and editing. Participants gain confidence handling equipment in actual "shooting" and "editing" exercises, using state-of-the-art video equipment. Subjects include: program design, content qualification, behavioral objectives, brainstorming, budgeting, client presentation, composition, storyboarding, scripting, shot selection, movement, audio and lighting, staging and blocking, rehearsal, talent releases, makeup, interviews, directing, post-production, graphics, logging, editing, validation, and marketing.

129

Title:
Managing Teams for Innovation and Success
Sponsor:
Stanford Business School
Office of Executive Education
Stanford University
Stanford, CA 94305
650/723-3341
650/723-3950 (fax)
Length:
1 week, February
Cost:
$6,700 including room, board, and materials
Location:
Stanford, CA
Description:
This is especially for the executive who is new to managing teams and for teams of up to six members. The focus is on how to increase organizational responsiveness and foster innovation through teams and groups.

130

Title:
Negotiation and Influence Strategies
Sponsor:
Stanford Business School
Office of Executive Education
Stanford University
Stanford, CA 94305
650/723-3341
650/723-3950 (fax)
Length:
1 week, April
Cost:
$6,700 including room, board, and materials
Location:
Stanford, CA
Description:
This is a challenging and interactive program for executives who want to improve their skills in negotiation and increase their influence. Topics include: social networks, cross-cultural influence, ethical concerns, power, and getting things done through other people.

131

Title:
Strategic Uses of Information Technology
Sponsor:
Stanford Business School
Office of Executive Education
Stanford University
Stanford, CA 94305
650/723-3341
650/723-3950 (fax)
Length:
1 week, April
Cost:
$6,700 including room, board, and materials
Location:
Stanford, CA
Description:
Sharing a wealth of expertise gained in part from Stanford's long connection to nearby Silicon Valley, this program will help executives integrate technology, operating procedures, and people into a cohesive strategy for the future. It is designed for senior managers with responsibility for the strategic direction of their companies.

132

Title:
Managing a Customer Support Help Desk
Sponsor:
TechLink Training
P.O. Box 226
Fanwood, NJ 07023
908/789-2800
908/789-2811 (fax)
Length:
2 days
Cost:
$995
Location:
Various cities throughout the U.S.
Description:
This workshop presents practical, innovative tips and techniques

for helping customers learn just-in-time what they need to do better work. Topics include selecting technology, adding value, problem solving, and change management.

133

Title:
The Academy
Sponsor:
TeleTraining Institute
1524 West Admiral
Stillwater, OK 74074
800/755-2356
405/744-7511 (fax)
Length:
10 days, 8:30 A.M.-5:00 P.M. with some evening computer labs
Cost:
$3,500
Location:
Stillwater, OK (online); adjacent to campus of Oklahoma State University
Description:
An extensive immersion course in distance education, this is the most comprehensive course offered by the Teletraining Institute. It is for educators, corporate trainers, and government instructors who are responsible for designing a course for delivery at remote sites, adapting existing training programs to a new distance education format, or implementing new techniques for interest or cost-effectiveness. Focus on video and Web-based instruction.

134

Title:
Distance Education Boot Camp
Sponsor:
TeleTraining Institute
1524 West Admiral
Stillwater, OK 74074
800/755-2356
405/744-7511 (fax)
Length:
1 day; online
Cost:
$149
Location:
from Stillwater, OK; online
Description:
This is an informational and motivational workshop focusing on the implementation and management of distance education. Topics include: designing, equipping, and operating a distance education network.

135

Title:
The TeleTrainer's Toolkit
Sponsor:
TeleTraining Institute
1524 West Admiral
Stillwater, OK 74074
800/755-2356
405/744-7511 (fax)
Length:
1 day; online
Cost:
$149
Location:
From Stillwater, OK, to any organizational site
Description:
This 2-day workshop is delivered at a distance via ISDN. Participating sites can enroll up to 30 individuals and may charge an additional participant fee. The workshop covers the basics of how to teach in this environment.

136

Title:
Train the (Tele)Trainer
Sponsor:
TeleTraining Institute
1524 West Admiral
Stillwater, OK 74074
800/755-2356
405/744-7511 (fax)
Length:
5 days
Cost:
Call for quote: includes site license and materials to train persons within the purchaser's organization
Location:
Stillwater, OK
Description:
This program is for trainers to learn how to train others within their organization to effectively design and deliver a learning program at a distance using a live, interactive, video-based medium. Student presentations to others in the program are required.

137

Title:
Globalization: Merging Strategy with Action
Sponsor:
Thunderbird
The American Graduate School of International Management
15249 North 59th Avenue
Glendale, AZ 85306
602/978-7635
602/439-4851 (fax)
Length:
6 days
Cost:
$5,200 includes lodging, meals, course materials
Location:
Glendale, AZ
Description:
This program focuses on how to combine functional areas of a business across the globe and develop a strategic plan of action to meet global goals. Participants stay at a new Executive Conference Center on campus.

138

Title:
Leadership: Leading the Global Organization
Sponsor:
Thunderbird
The American Graduate School of International Management
15249 North 59th Avenue
Glendale, AZ 85306
602/978-7635
602/439-4851 (fax)
Length:
6 days
Cost:
$5,200 includes lodging, meals, course materials
Location:
Glendale, AZ
Description:
This program is for leaders at many levels and in many positions within organizations that need help in becoming a global organization. The program focuses on how to structure a global organization, how to lead global teams, and how to meet the needs of persons working together from many cultures. Participants stay at a new Executive Conference Center on campus. Contact sponsor for similar 3-day programs.

Training for Trainers

139

Title:
Facilitation Skills for Trainers and Team Leaders
Sponsor:
The Training Clinic
645 Seabreeze Dr.
Seal Beach, CA 90740
800/937-4698
310/430-9603 (fax)
Length:
1 day
Cost:
$349
Location:
Numerous cities throughout the U.S.
Description:
A one-day workshop for classroom trainers who want to encourage group participation and for team leaders who need to help groups become productive. Major topics covered are: (1) What is facilitation? (2) facilitation skills, (3) Group dynamics and group functions, and (4) Facilitator issues.

140

Title:
How to Design Effective Training Programs
Sponsor:
The Training Clinic
645 Seabreeze Dr.
Seal Beach, CA 97040
800/937-4698
310/430-9603 (fax)
Length:
2 days
Cost:
$699
Location:
Numerous cities throughout the U.S.
Description:
This is a hands-on workshop in the theory and practice of effective training program design. The program begins with the issue of assessing training needs, including the avoidance of unnecessary training, assessment techniques, and task analysis. After reviewing the reasons for and the techniques behind developing behavioral objectives, the program proceeds to the basics of program design, including consideration of: (1) adult learning principles, (2) the selection of methods, (3) the use of case studies, (4) the use of audiovisual support, and (5) the design of handout materials. The next topic is four methods of program evaluation, and the program concludes with a survey of training applications: classroom instruction, on-the-job training, self-paced instruction, small group learning, and technical training.

141

Title:
Make Training Stick
Sponsor:
The Training Clinic
645 Seabreeze Dr.
Seal Beach, CA 90740
800/937-4698
310/430-9603 (fax)
Length:
1 day
Cost:
$349
Location:
Numerous cities throughout the U.S.
Description:
This workshop is an overview of issues in training transfer: the Trainer's Role, Manager's Role, and Trainee's Role. Skills for effective transfer from learning situation to the job are demonstrated and discussed.

142

Title:
Make New Employee Orientation a Success
Sponsor:
The Training Clinic
645 Seabreeze Dr.
Seal Beach, CA 90740
800/937-4698
310/430-9603 (fax)
Length:
1 day
Cost:
$399
Location:
Numerous cities throughout the U.S.
Description:
This workshop is based on research of the most productive orientation methods in use today. Participants learn how to design and conduct a successful orientation program—setting objectives, selecting content and methods, and evaluating the program. Some of the points covered in the workshop are: (1) the benefits of orientation, (2) how to make it more self-directed, (3) how to eliminate boredom, and (4) how to deal with new company start-ups, mergers, and other special situations. Supplemental text included at no charge.

143

Title:
Survival Skills for the New Trainer
Sponsor:
The Training Clinic
645 Seabreeze Dr.
Seal Beach, CA 90740
800/937-4698
310/430-9603 (fax)
Length:
1 day
Cost:
$349
Location:
Numerous cities throughout the U.S.
Description:
The special concerns of the new trainer are addressed in this workshop. Participants are shown how to relate to the learner—building rapport, maintaining pace, giving and getting feedback, etc. They are also taught classroom assertion skills, including (1) how to avoid manipulation, (2) how to get along with difficult people, (3) what to do when they are wrong or don't know an answer, and (4) how to act assertively without acting aggressively. Another major topic of this workshop is the new trainer's self-image and specific techniques for building confidence and projecting an image of confidence.

144

Title:
Facilitator Training Program
Sponsor:
Training Resources Group, Inc.
909 N. Washington St., #305
Alexandria, VA 22314-1555
703/548-3535
703/836-2415 (fax)
Length:
3 days

Cost:
    $995
Location:
    Alexandria, VA
Description:
    Designed for full-time trainers/facilitators or other professionals with similar responsibilities. Participants have the opportunity to design experiential sessions, write case studies and role plays, learn to facilitate group activities, practice giving and receiving feedback, develop stand-up delivery and recovery skills, and receive video-based feedback on their skills.

145

Title:
    Enhancing Leadership Performance: The Leader as Teacher
Sponsor:
    University of Chicago
    Graduate School of Business
    450 N. Cityfront Plaza Drive
    Chicago, IL 60611
        312/464-8732
        312/464-8731 (fax)
Length:
    5 days
Cost:
    $5,200
Location:
    Chicago, IL; Barcelona, Spain; Singapore
Description:
    This program uses the metaphor of theater roles and skills to explore how to become a leader-teacher. It explores both teaching and coaching, and how to create a learning environment. The program features self-assessment and peer assessment regarding power and creativity as leader-teacher.

146

Title:
    The Entrepreneurial Manager: Power and Influence in Organizations
Sponsor:
    University of Chicago
    Graduate School of Business
    450 N. Cityfront Plaza Drive
    Chicago, IL 60611
        312/464-8732
        312/464-8731 (fax)
Length:
    5 days

Cost:
    $5,200
Location:
    Chicago, IL
Description:
    This program will equip managers to effectively manage their work and relationships to be more productive in contemporary organizations. They will learn to manage cross-functional, cross-organizational relationships, develop social capital, and create and manage organizational strategic partners.

147

Title:
    Financial Analysis for Nonfinancial Managers
Sponsor:
    University of Chicago
    Graduate School of Business
    450 N. Cityfront Plaza Drive
    Chicago, IL 60611
        312/464-8732
        312/464-8731 (fax)
Length:
    5 days
Cost:
    $5,200
Location:
    Chicago, IL; Barcelona, Spain; Singapore
Description:
    This program is one of seven in the University's "Finance Series." It is particularly of interest to training directors and managers responsible for determining training's financial value to a company. Topics include: analyzing historical performance, forecasting financial performance, the firm's internal information systems, activity-based costing and management systems, profitability and strategy, and planning, control, and evaluation systems.

148

Title:
    Leading Change: Creating Transformational Competencies
Sponsor:
    University of Michigan
    The Michigan Business School
    Executive Education Center
    Ann Arbor, MI 48109
        734/763-1000
        734/764-4267 (fax)
Length:
    5 days; March and September
Cost:
    $6,200 includes hotel
Location:
    Ann Arbor, MI
Description:
    This seminar focuses on the role of leadership in change. It provides participants with tools and methods to effectively manage change initiatives. It is designed to engage the participant in the application of change methodology.

149

Title:
    Designing Employee Orientation Programs
Sponsor:
    University of Minnesota
    Employer Education Service
    321-19th Ave. South
    Industrial Relations Center
    Minneapolis, MN 55455
        800/333-3378
        612/626-7747 (fax)
Length:
    1 day
Cost:
    $315
Location:
    Minneapolis, MN
Description:
    Participants learn what to include in an orientation program, how to include it, and when to present it. They also discover ways to get others involved in and committed to the orientation process. The course is designed for anyone with orientation responsibilities who is either starting an orientation program from scratch or revising an existing program. The course covers: (1) understanding the major objectives and potential payoffs of orientation, (2) designing an orientation program that meets the needs of the organization, (3) incorporating organizational values and goals into the orientation program, (4) sharing responsibility for orientation, and (5) monitoring, evaluating, and updating the orientation process. Participants receive a notebook with checklists and other helpful information.

Training for Trainers

150

Title:
Public Sector Training and Development
Sponsor:
University of Minnesota
Employer Education Services
321-19th Ave. South
Industrial Relations Center
Minneapolis, MN 55455
  800/333-3378
  612/626-7747 (fax)
Length:
1 day
Cost:
$315
Location:
Minneapolis, MN
Description:
This program is designed for public sector personnel practitioners and managers. It is a survey course that presents an overview of the practices and theories in training and development. Topics covered include: needs assessments, skill-building methods and techniques, team building and quality of working life, training and motivating "seasoned" employees, computer-based instruction, getting a return on investment in training, retention of learning, and career and job development. Phone sponsor for other seminars in the "public sector" series.

151

Title:
The Skilled Team Facilitator Intensive Workshop
Sponsor:
University of North Texas
Center for the Study of Work Teams
P.O. Box 311280
Denton, TX 76203
  940/565-3096
  940/565-4806 (fax)
Length:
5 days
Cost:
$2,395
Location:
Chapel Hill, NC; Denton, TX
Description:
This is a skills- and values-based intensive workshop for experienced facilitators who want to upgrade their effectiveness as agents of change in working with teams. It is limited to 28 participants and requires completion of assignments prior to the workshop.

152

Title:
Wharton Advanced Management Program
Sponsor:
The Wharton School
255 South 38th Street
Philadelphia, PA 19104
  215/898-1179
  215/386-4304 (fax)
Length:
5 weeks
Cost:
$37,000 including hotel and all meals
Location:
Philadelphia, PA
Description:
This is a graduate program of standard business topics plus an arts and sciences focus. It is interactive, experiential, and features group dynamics sessions throughout. Forty different U Penn faculty provide leadership. Two-thirds of the participants come from outside the U.S. Class size is limited to around fifty participants.

153

Title:
How Adults Learn: 15 Practical Tips
Sponsor:
University of Richmond
Management Institute
Special Programs Building
Richmond, VA 23173
  804/289-8019
  804/289-8872 (fax)
Length:
1 day
Cost:
$425
Location:
Richmond, VA
Description:
Participants in this seminar gain a working understanding of Malcolm Knowles' work on "andragogy" (how adults learn), while discovering what motivates adult learners and how to do it most effectively. Participants also learn instructional techniques that work best with adult learners and how to tap their life experiences to help them relate to the material at hand. The seminar includes group involvement methods and specific tips for designing workshops for adults. The program also explicitly covers the special case of retraining the older worker.

154

Title:
Planning, Designing, and Evaluating Training Programs
Sponsors:
University of Richmond
Management Institute
Special Programs Building
Richmond, VA 23173
  804/289-8019
  804/289-8872 (fax)
Length:
2 days
Cost:
$795
Location:
Richmond, VA
Description:
Participants in this program learn: (1) three necessary components of instructional outcomes, (2) how to use the C.A.P. model for identifying instructional goals, (3) nine ways of identifying training needs, (4) ten creative points to keep in mind when designing training programs, (5) how to write measurable instructional objectives, and (6) how to design effective training strategies. Participants are encouraged to bring materials with them which they can use in designing a training program for "back home" use. Some of the other topics covered in the workshop include: giving on-the-job instruction, using handouts, effective lecture techniques, and classroom arrangements.

155

Title:
Proven Classroom Training Techniques
Sponsor:
University of Richmond
Management Institute
Special Programs Building
Richmond, VA 23173
  804/289-8019
  804/289-8872 (fax)

Length:
  2 days
Cost:
  $795
Location:
  Richmond, VA
Description:
  This workshop begins by exploring creative ideas for providing effective training inexpensively. Then the focus turns to specific platform skills: holding the group's interest, making the subject matter interesting, getting participants involved, dealing with negative learners, employing visual aids effectively, using questions, maintaining a motivational learning climate, and wrapping up the presentation. Also covered is the development and use of lesson plans. Participants make their own 10-minute presentation, which is videotaped (for them to keep) and critiqued by the instructor and fellow participants.

156

Title:
  Train-the-Trainer
Sponsor:
  University of Richmond
  Management Institute
  Special Programs Building
  Richmond, VA 23173
    804/289-8019
    804/289-8872 (fax)
Length:
  5 days
Cost:
  $1,795
Location:
  Richmond, VA
Description:
  Participants learn to (1) choose when to train and when to facilitate learning; (2) apply the 18 characteristics unique to a facilitator; (3) design a results-oriented case study for the general classroom instructor, as well as for the technical trainer; (4) plan and use a results-oriented game; (5) employ easy-to-use techniques that avoid time wasters in a training session; and (6) practice creative problem-solving techniques.

157

Title:
  Advanced Training Skills for Instructors
Sponsor:
  University of Wisconsin–Stout
  Technical Instructor Institutes
  162 Communication Technologies Building
  Menomonie, WI 54751
    715/232-1367
    715/232-5614 (fax)
Length:
  4 days
Cost:
  $1,250
Location:
  Menomonie, WI
Description:
  This institute provides a mix of theory and practice in developing effective technical presentations: (1) principles and practices which facilitate the learning process are examined; (2) help is provided in setting objectives, lesson planning, and evaluation; and (3) elements of good technical presentations are discussed. The participant's technical presentation is videotaped and professionally critiqued.

158

Title:
  Instructional System Design
Sponsor:
  University of Wisconsin–Stout
  Technical Instructor Institutes
  162 Communication Technologies Building
  Menomonie, WI 54751
    715/232-1367
    715/232-5614 (fax)
Length:
  5 days
Cost:
  $1,250
Location:
  Menomonie, WI
Description:
  This "systems approach" institute was developed for trainers who are concerned with design and implementation of total training programs—from needs analysis through evaluation. All elements of the closed-loop system approach are discussed to help participants design instruction based on job tasks their prospective students must be able to perform.

159

Title:
  Managing Technical Training
Sponsor:
  University of Wisconsin–Stout
  Technical Instructor Institutes
  162 Communication Technologies Building
  Menomonie, WI 54751
    715/232-1367
    715/232-5614 (fax)
Length:
  4 days
Cost:
  $1,250
Location:
  Menomonie, WI
Description:
  This institute is for those who are responsible for directing the work of technical instructors. The instructors discuss practical applications for managing a training department, providing a base for the process of selecting, training, and updating instructors. They also cover techniques for managing training projects that help in the crucial area of selling the training function to management.

160

Title:
  Training One-on-One Instructors
Sponsor:
  University of Wisconsin–Stout
  Technical Instructor Institutes
  162 Communication Technologies Building
  Menomonie, WI 54751
    715/232-1367
    715/232-5614 (fax)
Length:
  4 days
Cost:
  $1,250
Location:
  Menomonie, WI
Description:
  This workshop is concerned with several distinct tasks that a senior instructor may encounter. Team building, and inter-group communication techniques are discussed to help establish the effective work relationships necessary for successful training one on one. Participants gain knowledge and skill in making tough decisions regarding

Training for Trainers

training value and instructional strategies with peers and across levels as a one-on-one instructor.

161

Title:
Competitive Intelligence
Sponsor:
University of Wisconsin–Madison
Management Institute
Grainger Hall
975 University Avenue
Madison, WI 53706-1323
800/348-8964
800/741-7416 (fax)
Length:
2 days
Cost:
$1,045
Location:
Madison, WI
Description:
This workshop shows participants how to use competitive intelligence as a foundation for more profitable corporate strategies. Topics include: data collection, project staffing, features and benefits of information products.

162

Title:
Instructional Skills for New Trainers
Sponsor:
University of Wisconsin–Madison
Management Institute
Grainger Hall
975 University Ave.
Madison, WI 53706-1323
800/348-8964
800/741-7416 (fax)
Length:
3 days
Cost:
$1,095
Location:
Madison, WI
Description:
Increasing change is forcing many organizations to use internal staff—those who know a subject, concept, or process—as instructors. This program is designed for these people. An effective trainer must know how to create a learning climate, build a lesson plan, present knowledge and ideas, and evaluate a presentation. This workshop gives new trainers the opportunity to practice the skills that instructors need. It features numerous suggestions, tips, and personal counsel to improve participants' effectiveness and build their confidence as instructors. Lodging available at the new Fluno Center for Executive Education.

163

Title:
Online Instructor Program: Corporate Training Track
Sponsor:
Walden Institute for Learning and Leadership
24311 Walden Center Drive, 3rd floor
Bonita Springs, FL 34134
800/237-6434
941/498-7821 (fax)
Length:
12 weeks, online; Programs begin in June, September, March, and December.
Cost:
$995
Location:
online
Description:
This is one example of an online professional development program for trainers. This one offers "an online classroom" and "a learning community." This is considered an overview of online learning. Topics include online tools and their purposes, instructional design theory and techniques, distance-based evaluation, quality assurance in online learning, and Collaborative learning communities. Program completion results in an Online Instruction Certificate.

164

Title:
Train-the-Trainer
Sponsor:
Xavier University Consulting Group
3800 Victory Parkway
Cincinnati, OH 45207
513/745-3396
513/745-4307 (fax)
Length:
5 days
Cost:
$1,600; or 1 day $395; 2 days $745
Location:
Cincinnati, OH; Boston, MA
Description:
This is a 5-day comprehensive workshop of particular interest to new trainers. It is made up of 3 shorter workshops, each of which can be taken separately. These are: How Adults Learn, 1 day; Planning Designing, and Evaluating Training, 2 days; and Proven Classroom Training Techniques, 2 days.

6.5 Non-Profit Organizations

Organizations listed in this section hold non-profit status. These organizations conduct research, hold meetings and conferences, publish newsletters, reports and books, have online services, and provide various other customized services to trainers. They particularly represent potential partnering possibilities for businesses who want to expand their networks and collaborate with the non-profit sector.

Training-Related Services Worth Investigating

Listing these organizations here differentiates them from the professional associations in Section 6.1 who seek membership and charge dues, and from the traditional "vendor" training suppliers listed in Section 6.4. The often unique and specialized services of these non-profit organizations are frequently overlooked in other directories of training providers; we provide them here because they are an excellent source of research-based information and a complement to commercial training sources. We list 25 non-profit organizations. We include a small sample of university-based centers and institutes as well as a sample of government-funded organizations whose focus is business school partnerships. Don't overlook your local university, college, or school as a source of program collaboration.

Index to Principal Interests of Non-Profit Organizations

Accreditation programs
1, 11, 21, 22

Advancement of women
4

Career development
1, 3, 4, 8, 22

Co-operative education/job training
6, 17, 19

Conference centers
16

Distance learning
24

Diversity training
20

Higher education
2, 23

Leadership
6, 10

Literacy in the workplace
14, 17, 18

National training needs/policy
10, 12, 23, 25

Research in training/development
6, 10, 11, 13, 14, 23, 25

Team training
5, 7

Technical/computer training
6, 9, 15, 21, 22

Testing
11, 21, 22

Vocational training
6, 17, 19, 21, 22

1

Name of organization:
Accrediting Council for Continuing Education & Training

Purpose:
The Accrediting Council for Continuing Education & Training (ACCET) is a voluntary group of educational organizations affiliated for the purpose of improving continuing education and training. Through its support of an independent Accrediting Commission, the ACCET membership promulgates and sustains the Standards for Accreditation along with policies and procedures that measure and ensure educational standards of quality.

Contact information:
ACCET
1200 19th St., NW, Suite 200
Washington, DC 20036
202/955-1113
202/955-1118 (fax)
www.accet.org

Key officers/staff:
Executive Director: Roger J. Williams

Funded by:
Sustaining organizations

Publications:
Annual Accredited Schools' Directory

Seminars/conferences:
Accreditation workshop
Annual convention

2

Name of organization:
American Council on Education, Center for Adult Learning and Educational Credentials

Purpose:
An independent, non-profit organization founded in 1918, the American Council on Education is the umbrella organization for the nation's college and universities. ACE's Center for Adult Learning administers the General Educational Development (GED) and National External Diploma (EDP) testing programs, which allow adults to earn a high school credential. It also evaluates courses offered by business and industry, labor unions, associations, government agencies, and the military services and makes college credit recommendations where appropriate.

Contact information:
American Council on Education
One DuPont Circle, Suite 250
Washington, DC 20036–1193
202/939-9475
202/775-8578 (fax)
www.acenet.edu

Key officers/staff:
President: Stanley Ikenberry

Parent Organization:
American Council on Education

Funded by:
Membership dues, fees for services, federal contracts, private support

Publications:
The following ACE publications are the standard reference tools used by the majority of U.S. colleges and universities to award credit for learning attained outside the classroom:
- The National Guide to Educational Credit for Training Programs, 1998
- Guide to Educational Credit by Examination, 1996
- Guide to the Evaluation of Educational Experiences in the Armed Services, 1998

A catalog of nearly 100 other titles in the ACE/Oryx Press Series on Higher Education is available by calling 800/279-6799.

Seminars/conferences:
ACE Annual Meeting
"All of One Nation" a conference on minorities in higher education, every 2 years

Other activities:
Other ACE activities are the Business-Higher Education Forum, which provides an opportunity for interchange among corporate and academic chief executives, and the Labor-Higher Education Council, which is conducted in cooperation with the AFL-CIO.

3

Name of organization:
Career Planning & Adult Development Network

Purpose:
The Career Planning and Adult Development Network is a non-profit international organization of professionals who work with adults in career transition. The Network offers a professional certification program for Job and Career Transition Coaches, conferences, meetings, workshops, and publications.

Contact information:
Career Planning and Adult Development Network
4965 Sierra Rd.
San Jose, CA 95132
408/441-9100
408/441-9101 (fax)
www.careertrainer.com

Key officers/staff:
President: Richard Knowdell

Funded by:
Annual memberships
$49 U.S. addresses
$69 foreign addresses

Publications:
- Job search catalog
- Monthly newsletter
- Quarterly Journal

Seminars/conferences:
International Career Development Conference
California Career Conference

Other activities:
List of local area referral sources throughout the U.S.

4

Name of organization:
Catalyst

Purpose:
Catalyst is a non-profit research and advisory organization working to advance women in business and the professions. Catalyst works with corporations and professional firms to effect change for women through the workplace.

Contact information:
Catalyst
120 Wall Street
New York, NY 10005
212/514-7600
212/514-8470 (fax)
www.catalystwomen.org

Key officers/staff:
President: Sheila Wellington

Funded by:
FORTUNE 500 companies

Publications:
Perspective (newsletter)
Research Studies (check website)
Other publications available—check website for more details

Seminars/conferences:
The Catalyst Awards gala
Check website for updates on future events

Non-Profit Organizations

Other activities:
Catalyst issue specialists and senior staff members of the organization's research and advisory service teams are regularly on the road across the country, spreading the word about their research findings at many types of venues. Speakers can deliver presentations on every issue affecting working women.

5

Name of organization:
Center for Creative Leadership (CCL)
Purpose:
The Center for Creative Leadership is a non-profit educational institution offering open enrollment and custom programs. Its mission is "to advance the understanding, practice, and development of leadership for the benefit of society worldwide."
Contact information:
Center for Creative Leadership
One Leadership Place
P.O. Box 26300
Greensboro, NC 27438
336/545-2810
336/282-3284 (fax)
www.ccl.org
Key officers/staff:
President: John R. Alexander
Funded by:
Grants and donations from foundations, corporations, and individuals
Tuition, royalties, fees for services
Sales of products
Publications:
Books, reports, papers on wide variety of leadership topics
Catalogs of publications
Magazine, *Leadership in Action* magazine
Seminars/conferences:
Numerous conferences, seminars, workshops, and colloquia
Other activities:
Research, assessment instruments, simulations
Educational facilities in Brussels, Belgium; Colorado Springs, CO; San Diego, CA; and Greensboro, NC

6

Name of organization:
Center for Occupational Research and Development
Purpose:
The Center for Occupational Research and Development (CORD) is a nonprofit public service organization. CORD helps educators in schools and industry address the technical education, training, and retraining needs of workers. CORD's primary areas of operation include technical assistance for Tech Prep, school-to-work transition, and work-site learning, contextual academic curriculum development, advanced technologies curriculum development, and adult training program implementation assistance. CORD also administers the National Tech Prep Network and the National Coalition for Advanced Technology Centers.
Contact information:
Center for Occupational Research and Development (CORD)
601 Lake Air Drive
P.O. Box 21689
Waco, TX 76702–1689
800/972-2766
254/772-8972 (fax)
www.cord.org
Key officers/staff:
President & Chief Executive Officer: Daniel M. Hull
Publications:
CORD is best known for having developed applied academic course materials in mathematics, biology, chemistry, and physics. In addition to these materials, CORD publishes educational planning guides, research studies, reports, and books.
Other activities:
CORD consists of the CORD Foundation, a nonprofit educational foundation, and CORD Communications, Inc., a publishing subsidiary, to serve the needs of the educational community. The 3 organizations work together to provide quality educational materials and services for students, educators, and employers.

7

Name of organization:
Center for the Study of Work Teams
Purpose:
The Center for the Study of Work Teams is a center for research and education on collaborative work systems. Center staff and associates include faculty and graduate students from the Department of Psychology, the College of Business, College of Education, and School of Community Service. The center features corporate sponsors at annual conferences.
Contact information:
Center for the Study of Work Teams
Claims Accounting
University of North Texas
P.O. Box 310499
Denton, TX 76203
940/565-3096
940/565-4806 (fax)
www.workteams.unt.edu
Key officers/staff:
Director: Michael Beyerline
Funded by corporate sponsors and other grants.
Publications:
Proceedings from International Conference, Quarterly Newsletter, Books
Other activities:
Annual international conference, advanced concepts conference, strategies and skills for effective teaming conferences, seminars, forums, team assessment, corporate sponsors, research projects

8

Name of organization:
Clearinghouse on Adult, Career, & Vocational Education
Purpose:
ERIC/ACVE is one of 16 clearinghouses in the U.S. Department of Education-sponsored ERIC system. ERIC is a national education information service that identifies, selects, processes, and disseminates information in all areas of education. The ERIC Clearinghouse on Adult, Career, and Vocational Education covers adult and continuing education, career education, and vocational and technical education and training.
Contact information:
Clearinghouse on Adult, Career, and Vocational Education
Center on Education and Training for Employment
Ohio State University
1900 Kenny Rd.
Columbus, OH 43210–1090

800/848-4815
614/292-4353
614/292-1260 (fax)
www.ericacve.org
Key officers/staff:
Manager: Judy Wagner
Parent organization:
Center on Education and Training for Employment, The Ohio State University
Funded by:
Office of Educational Research and Improvement, U.S. Department of Education
Publications:
ERIC Digests
Trends and Issues Alerts
Practice Applications Briefs
Information brochures
Newsletter
Seminars/conferences:
Training workshops offered on a cost-recovery basis

9

Name of organization:
Computer Education Management Association (CEdMA)
Purpose:
CEdMA is an independent, nonprofit organization made up of education executives, managers and directors from companies that manufacture hardware and software products. Its goal is to shape the future for "Excellence in Education, Training, and Learning" through dialogue, shared experiences, and member networking and support.
Contact information:
CEdMA
P.O. Box 749
Scotch Plains, NJ 07076
908/322-1846
www.cedma.org
Key officers/staff:
President: Dick LaForge
Association Manager: Nancy Louis
Funded by:
Company memberships
Publications:
CEdMA Connections newsletter
CEdMA research surveys and polls
Seminars/conferences:
National Conference, spring and fall
Regional member meetings
Online seminars
Task force and special interest groups

Other activities:
Threaded discussions online, The "CEdMA Mall" of resources, searchable member database via the Web, job board.

10

Name of organization:
The Conference Board
Purpose:
The Conference Board is the world's leading business membership organization, connecting companies in more than 60 nations. Founded in 1916, the Board's twofold purpose is to improve the business enterprise system and to enhance the contribution of business to society. A not-for-profit, non-advocacy organization, The Conference Board's membership includes over 3,300 companies and other organizations worldwide in 63 countries.
Contact information:
The Conference Board
845 Third Avenue
New York, NY 10022
212/759-0900
212/980-7014
www.conference-board.org
Key officers/staff:
President, and CEO: Richard E. Cavanaugh
Funded by:
Corporate and organization associate memberships; colleges and universities
Publications:
Research reports
Conference proceedings
Across the Board, monthly magazines
Seminars/conferences:
Meetings and conferences are held weekly throughout the year. The focus for all meetings is actual business experience shared by executives, providing a superior level of networking with peers.
Other activities:
Research centers located in New York City

11

Name of organization:
Educational Testing Service (ETS)
Purpose:
Educational Testing Service (ETS) is a private, nonprofit corporation devoted to measurement and research, primarily in the field of education. Testing programs are used for school and college admission, student guidance and placement, awarding degree credit for independent or advanced learning, and continuing education.
Contact information:
Educational Testing Service
Rosedale Road, P.O. Box 6736
Princeton, NJ 08541
609/921-9000
www.ets.org
Key officers/staff:
President: Kurt Landgraf
Funded by:
Most ETS programs are conducted under contract with independent client agencies or organizations.
Publications:
Numerous publications of all sorts related to testing. Well-known trademarks of ETS include: The Graduate Record Examinations (GREs), The Praxis Series, Strategies for Teaching Critical Thinking, Worklink, and others.
Seminars/conferences:
Periodic seminars and conferences sponsored by various ETS clients and partners
Other activities:
Software, films, videos; The Center for the Assessment of Educational Progress (CAEP) is a division of ETS which administers The National Assessment of Educational Progress.

12

Name of organization:
Hudson Institute
Purpose:
Hudson Institute is a private, not-for-profit research organization founded in 1961 by the late Herman Kahn. The institute analyzes and makes recommendations about public policy for business and government executives, as well as for the public at large. It does not advocate an express ideology or political position. However, more than thirty years of work on the most important issues of the day has forged a viewpoint that embodies skepticism about the conventional wisdom, optimism about solving problems, a commitment to free institutions and individual responsibility, an appreciation of the crucial role of technol-

ogy in achieving progress, and an abiding respect for the importance of values, culture, and religion in human affairs.

Contact information:
Hudson Institute, Inc.
5395 Emerson Way
Indianapolis, IN 46226
317/545-1000
317/545-9639 (fax)
Offices also in Washington, DC; Madison, WI; San Antonio, TX; and Montreal, Canada
www.hudson.org

Key officers/staff:
President: Herbert London

Funded by:
Foundation and private gifts

Publications:
Quarterly newsletter, *Visions*
Monthly monographs
Monthly research reports
Book: *Workforce 2000* (1987)
Book: *Workforce 2020* (1997)
Healthcare 2020

13

Name of organization:
The Human Resource Planning Society

Purpose:
The Human Resource Planning Society is a not-for-profit association committed to "improving organizational performance by creating a global network of individuals who function as business partners in the application of strategic human resource management practices."

Contact information:
The Human Resource Planning Society
317 Madison Ave., Suite 1509
New York, NY 10017
212/490-6387
212/682-6851 (fax)
www.hrps.org

Key officers/staff:
Executive Director: Walter J. Cleaver

Funded by:
More than 3,300 individual members and 200 corporate and research sponsors.
$250 - individual
$2,500 - corporate
$1,000 - research

Publications:
Quarterly publication, Human Resource Planning
Price: $120

Seminars/conferences:
Annual conferences
Professional development monthly seminars

Other activities:
Corporate sponsor forum annually
Research symposium biennially

14

Name of organization:
Institute for the Study of Adult Literacy

Purpose:
The Institute for the Study of Adult Literacy's goals include (1) development and dissemination of a sound conceptual and research base in adult literacy, (2) improvement of practice, and (3) leadership and coordination of comprehensive approaches to the delivery of adult literacy services. Projects address interrelated themes, such as: workplace literacy, technology in adult literacy, intergenerational literacy, special needs populations, customized materials development, and staff development/training. The Institute is nationally recognized for its work in literacy research, development, and dissemination activities.

Contact information:
Institute for the Study of Adult Literacy
Pennsylvania State University
102 Rackley Building
University Park, PA 16802–3202
814/863-3777
814/863-6108 (fax)
www.ed.psu.edu\isal\

Key officers/staff:
Director and Professor of Education: Eunice N. Askov

Parent organization:
College on Education, The Pennsylvania State University

Funded by:
Grants and contracts

Publications:
Newsletter *The Mosaic*
Other publications available

Seminars/conferences:
Project staff presents workshops and seminars on selected topics in adult literacy via contracted services.

Other activities:
Project staff provides consulting services via contract; sponsors "America Reads" program.

15

Name of organization:
Information Technology Training Associates (ITTA)

Purpose:
ITTA's mission is to shape and support Information Technology Education for the future.

Contact information:
ITTA
4210 Spicewood Springs Road, Ste 103
Austin, TX 78759
512/502-9300
512/502-9308
www.itta.org

Key officers/staff:
Rachel Cheeseman, Executive Director

Parent organization:
CompTIA

Funded by:
Corporate and individual memberships

Publications:
Resource library for members

Seminars/conferences:
Annual IT Training Industry "Strategies" conference focus seminars held around the world.

Other activities:
Public policy statements and legislative efforts; industry standards' development; industry research.

16

Name of organization:
International Association of Conference Centers (IACC)

Purpose:
To work for quality and best practices in the conference center industry. IACC's worldwide membership meets a high-level "Universal Criteria" of 29 items regarding conference room design, business services, and hospitality.

Contact information:
IACC
243 North Lindbergh Blvd. #315
St. Louis, MO 63141
314/993-8575
314/993-8919 (fax)
www.iacconline.org

Key officers/staff:
President IACC Global Board of Directors: Jeffrey Farman
President: Wende Blumberg, IACC North America

Funded by:
  Member conference center and affiliate dues
Publications:
  Annual Directory of Member Conference Centers that includes accommodations, meeting facilities, conference services, and recreation/dining opportunities for each of 300-plus member centers.
Seminars/conferences:
  Annual Conference
  Regional meetings
Other activities:
  Professional Development Communications, Technology Initiative, IACCONLINE

17

Name of organization:
  National Alliance of Business (NAB)
Purpose:
  A business-led nonprofit organization dedicated to building a quality workforce that meets the needs of employers. This objective is met through partnerships with business and education leaders who also are committed to building an internationally competitive workforce through education reform and enhanced job training.
Contact information:
  National Alliance of Business
  1201 New York Avenue, N.W., Suite 700
  Washington, DC 20005
    202/289-2888
    202/289-1303 (fax)
    www.nab.com
Key officer:
  President & CEO: Roberts T. Jones
Funded by:
  Member dues from 5,000 members
Publications:
  WorkAmerica
  Workforce Economics Trends
  Workforce Economics Legislative Update
  Policy Notes
Seminars/Conferences:
  Annual Workforce Conferences
  Annual Founder's Awards Dinner
  Teleconferences/Town Meetings
  Focus groups/training seminars
Other activities:
  Member networking, monthly/bimonthly publications, access to database, staff resources, technological trends updates

18

Name of organization:
  National Clearinghouse for ESL Literacy Education (NCLE)
Purpose:
  The National Clearinghouse for ESL Literacy Education (NCLE), an adjunct ERIC Clearinghouse, provides information, referral, and technical assistance on literacy education for limited-English-proficient adults and out-of-school youth. As the only national clearinghouse for adult ESL literacy, NCLE primarily serves researchers, literacy instructors, and program administrators.
Contact information:
  NCLE
  Center for Applied Linguistics
  4646 40th Street, NW
  Washington, DC 20016-1859
    202/362-0700 x200
    202/362-3740 (fax)
    www.cal.org/ncle
Key officers/staff:
  Director: Miriam Burt
  Associate Director: Miriam Burt
Parent organization:
  Center for Applied Linguistics
Funded by:
  Office of Vocational and Adult Education, U.S. Dept. of Education
Publications:
  NCLE Notes newsletter (semi-annual), books, ERIC digest and annotated bibliographies, issue papers, and resource guides
Other activities:
  NCLE maintains a resource center that is open to the public and has materials on ESL and native language literacy. NCLE has produced a series of videos for staff development, documenting effective ESL and adult literacy programs. NCLE moderates a listserv for adult ESL educators, NIFL-ESL.

19

Name of organization:
  National Commission for Cooperative Education
Purpose:
  Founded in 1962, The National Commission for Cooperative Education is a non-profit higher education organization and advocacy group. NCCE's mission is to advance the concept of cooperative education as an educational strategy, integrating classroom curriculum with related work experience.
Contact information:
  National Commission for Cooperative Education
  360 Huntington Ave.
  Boston, MA 02115-5096
    617/373-3770
    617/373-3463 (fax)
    www.co-op.edu
Key officers/staff:
  President: Paul J. Stonely
Funded by:
  Corporations, foundations, and higher education institutions
Publications:
  Informational brochures
  Newsletters, booklets
Seminars/conferences:
  Annual meeting (June)
Other activities:
  Public awareness activities in collaboration with employment and educational organizations; professional outreach and training for educators and employers.

20

Name of organization:
  National MultiCultural Institute
Purpose:
  The National MultiCultural Institute's mission is to increase communication, understanding, and respect among people of different racial, ethnic, and cultural backgrounds. NMCI is a non-profit training and development and consulting organization.
Contact information:
  National MultiCultural Institute
  3000 Connecticut Ave., NW, Suite 438
  Washington, DC 20008-2556
    202/483-0700
    202/483-5233 (fax)
    www.nmci.org/nmci/
Key officers/staff:
  President: Elizabeth P. Salett
Funded by:
  Contracts, fees for service, foundation grants, and corporate and individual contributions
Publications:
  Educational materials
  Videos
  Training manuals
  Books
Seminars/conferences:
  Annual national conference
  Training courses

Non-Profit Organizations

Other activities:
Mental health counseling and referral service

21

Name of organization:
National Occupational Competency Testing Institute (NOCTI)
Purpose:
NOCTI is America's foremost developer of high-quality validated written and performance occupational competency assessments and testing materials. NOCTI's products and services are purchased by businesses, industry, educational, and government agencies. NOCTI is a not-for-profit educational consortium dedicated to facilitating development of national workforce standards.
Contact information:
National Occupational Competency Testing Institute
500 N. Bronson Avenue
Big Rapids, MI 49307
800/334-6283
616/796-4699 (fax)
www.nocti.org
Key officers/staff:
President/CEO: Ray Ryan
Funded by:
Clients who purchase assessment products and services
Publications:
Individual occupational competency assessments built around a job and task analysis which defines occupational competencies, knowledges, skills, worker traits, and attitudes.
Newsletter, *NOCTI Network*
Seminars/conferences:
National conference, biennial
Other activities:
Partnerships with diverse individuals, organizations, businesses, industries, government associations, and communities to facilitate national workforce standards and to improve the assessment of occupational competency.

22

Name of organization:
National Skill Standards Board (NSSB)
Purpose:
The NSSB is building a voluntary national system of skill standards, assessment and certification that will enhance the ability of the United States to compete effectively in a global economy. These skills are being identified by industry in full partnership with education, labor, civil rights, and community-based organizations. The standards will be based on high performance work and will be portable across industry sectors.
Contact information:
National Skill Standards Board
1441 L Street, NW, Suite 9000
Washington, DC 20005
202/254-8628
202/254-8686 (fax)
www.nssb.org
Key officers/staff:
Executive Director: Edie West
Parent organization:
U.S. Congress
Funded by:
U.S. Congress; U.S. Department of Labor, 1994 National Skill Standards Act
Publications:
Newsletter, annual report, brochures, electronic Clearinghouse of Skill Standards in academic education, occupation-specific areas, and for employability, database of certification and apprenticeship programs
Seminars/conferences:
Staff regularly functions as presenters at various national conferences of many other organizations. Check the NSSB Website for updates.
Other activities:
Partnerships with K–12 educators, vocational educators, community- and four-year colleges and job training organizations

23

Name of organization:
RAND Education
Purpose:
This institute was established: (1) to conduct research, analysis, and technical assistance that will improve policy and practice at all levels and in all sectors that provide education and training in the United States; and (2) to train policy analysts in this field of research. It has developed a comprehensive program of policy analysis in these areas: educational assessment and accountability, alternative institutional reform concepts, response to new fiscal limits, preparation for work, educational technology, and the social context of education and training. This "integrative" approach ensures that a major theme in all these areas is educational access, equity, and achievement for poor and minority students.
Contact information:
RAND Education
P.O. Box 2138
Santa Monica, CA 90407–2138
310/393-0411
310/393-4818 (fax)
www.rand.org
Key officers/staff:
Director: James Thomson
Parent organization:
RAND; Chairman: Paul H. O'Neill
Funded by:
Multiple governmental and non-governmental sources (National Science Foundation, and other foundations)
Publications:
RAND Research Review; various reports, issue papers, and policy briefs
Seminars/conferences:
Occasional conferences and seminars

24

Name of organization:
United States Distance Learning Association
Purpose:
To promote the development and application of distance learning to education and training, including K–12, higher education, continuing education, and corporate training.
Contact information:
USDLA
P.O. Box 376
Watertown, MA 02471
800/275-5162
617/924-1308 (fax)
www.usdla.org
Key officers/staff:
Executive Director: John G. Flores
Publications:
ED—Education at a Distance
Annual report on data and funding sources
Monthly newsletter
Policy forum report

Seminars/conferences:
  IDLCON—International Distance Learning Conference
Other activities:
  Summer board meeting, annual meeting

25

Name of organization:
Work in America Institute, Inc.
Purpose:
The mission of Work in America Institute is to study and promote high performance work systems that improve productivity and the quality of worklife. Founded in 1975, the Institute is a nonpartisan, multipartite organization with a board composed of corporate, labor union, government, and academic leaders. In its action-oriented research and its events, the Institute serves as a catalyst for change in the human resources practices of American corporations and unions.
Contact information:
  Work in America Institute, Inc.
  700 White Plains Road
  Scarsdale, NY 10583–5058
  914/472-9600
  914/472-9606 (fax)
  www.workinamerica.org
Key officers/staff:
  CEO/Chairman: Jerome M. Rosow
  Vice-President, Policy Studies Jill Casner-Lotto
Funded by:
  Major foundations, membership fees, sale of publications, contributions
Publications:
  National Policy Studies (e.g., *Strategic Partners for High Performance*; *New Roles for Managers*; *Training for New Technology*; *Job-Linked Literacy*); *Holding a Job, Having a Life*
  Books (e.g., *Employment Security in a Free Economy*; *The Innovative Organization*)
  Studies in Productivity
Seminars/conferences:
  10–15 Site Visits annually
  Productivity Forum Roundtables
  Network Meetings
  Training workshops
  Website training and resources

6.6 Training Research and Reference Sources

This section of *The Trainer's Almanac* lists sources of sources; that is, references listed here are tools to lead you forward into finding more sources and expanded information in each specific category presented.

Variety and Focus

Resources listed here are in many formats: books, catalogs, directories, audiotapes, videos, CD-ROMs, and online databases. Services referenced here are delivered through many formats, too: telephone, Website, diskette, multimedia, Internet communication, online subscription, referral, and consulting services.

Entries here are listed only once, although several of the entires could be listed in more than one category; for example, *ASTD's Buyer's Guide and Consultant Directory* could be listed in the categories "Training Suppliers," "Consultants," and "Online Services." We've chosen the category that made the most sense to us. However, be sure to read the individual descriptions carefully to understand the complete nature of each entry. The Websites *astd.org, brandonhall.com, masie.com*, and *trainingsupersite.com* are comprehensive training Websites and good places to begin a search for references.

Eight Categories

In this section we list 55 reference sources, including new listings for Annuals, Compendia, and Directories; and separate listings for "Handbooks" and for "Toolbooks." These references are the latest versions of the resource; all have been published within the last 5 years, most within the last 2 years. The following categories are included for the year 2002:

- Annuals, Compendia, and Directories
- Consultants and Training Suppliers
- Handbooks
- Online Services
- Seminar Databases
- Toolbooks
- Videos, Films, Audiotapes

Annuals, Compendia, and Directories

1

Title:
The ASTD Training and Performance Yearbook
Authors:
James W. Cortado and John A. Woods, Editors
Publisher:
ASTD/McGraw-Hill
ASTD Publishing Service
P.O. Box 4856
Hampden Station, Baltimore, MD 21211
703/683-8100
www.astd.org
Publication data:
2002 book, $99.95
Description:
The book consists of articles reprinted from training magazines and chapters of books by the authors. A directory of contact information is included.

2

Title:
The Census Desk Set
Type of resource:
Book set
Publisher:
Catalyst
120 Wall Street
New York, NY 10005
212/514-7600
212/514-8470 (fax)
www.catalystwomen.org
Price:
$175
Description:
This set of 2 major directories includes The *Catalyst Census of Women Board Directors of the Fortune 500* and the *2002 Catalyst Census of Women Corporate Officers and Top Earners*. The books list where the women are and tell how they got there. Company comparisons are provided. Catalyst provides many other research reports. Published every other year.

3

Title:
Directory of E-Learning Providers
Type of resource:
Online directory (updated monthly online)
Publisher:
brandon-hall.com
690 W. Freemont Ave., Ste. 10
Sunnyvale, CA 94087
408/736-2335
www.brandon-hall.com
Price:
$99
Description:
This online-only directory lists contact information for more than 600 e-learning providers. The listing categorizes providers according to service, content, and architecture. Adobe Acrobat Reader version 5.0 is required to view downloads.

4

Title:
The 2002 Higher Education Directory
Type of resource:
Book, 800 pages
Publisher:
Higher Education Publications, Inc.
6400 Arlington Blvd., Suite 648
Falls Church, VA 22042
703/532-2300
703/532-2305 (fax)
www.hepinc.com
Price:
$67
Description:
This directory is a listing of all postsecondary, degree-granting institutions that are accredited by agencies recognized by the U.S. Secretary of Education and the Council of Higher Education Accreditation. It contains information regarding tuition reimbursement, assistance, and career development.

5

Title:
Off-Site Meetings 2001/2002 Marketplace Directory: Training Meeting Facilities
Type of resource:
Directory of meeting facilities in U.S. and Canada, 75 pages
Provider:
Bill Communications
TRAINING Directories
50 South Ninth St.
Minneapolis, MN 55402
800/707-7749
612/333-0471
612/333-6526 (fax)
Price:
Free with subscription to TRAINING Magazine. $6 cost to nonsubscribers.
Description:
This directory lists approximately 350 facilities that are available for off-site training meetings. Information on each listing includes: number of meeting rooms and their capacity, number of guest rooms, whether or not they belong to the professional association IACC, audiovisual capabilities, recreation and fitness facilities, and distance to airport and other transportation and travel notes.

6

Title:
Leadership Directories, The "Yellow Books" and Leadership Library
Type of resource:
Catalog of directories, or CD-ROM, and Internet
Publisher:
Leadership Directories, Inc.
104 Fifth Avenue
New York, NY 10011
212/627-4140
212/645-0931 (fax)
www.leadershipdirectories.com
Price:
Individual directories range from $233–309; All 14 directories on CD-ROM, plus Internet subscription, $3,065 annually; print copy $2,300
Description:
14 directories of leaders in various segments of society; described as a Who's Who in leadership of the United States. Each directory features clear data in chart form in a variety of fields and includes a photo of each person listed. Directory titles include: Congressional, Federal, State, Municipal, Federal, Regional, Judicial, Corporate, Financial, News Media, Associations, Law Firms, Government Affairs, Foreign Representatives, and Nonprofit Sector. The compilation of all individual directories is called "Leadership Library."

Training Research and Reference Sources

7

Title:
Complete Games Trainers Play, vol. II
Type of resource:
Looseleaf binder
Authors:
Edward Scannell, John Newstrom, Carolyn Nilson
Publisher:
McGraw-Hill
11 West 19th Street
New York, NY 10011
800/2-McGRAW
614/759-3644 (fax)
Publication data:
1998, 724 pages, $110
Description:
This is a compendium of nearly 300 short training games and exercises to increase creativity and focus on learning. Binder format allows easy copying for class handouts. All are field tested, can be used in less than 30 minutes, and are inexpensive or free to implement. Best-selling vol. I is also available.

8

Title:
The Pfeiffer Annuals
Editor:
Elaine Beich, Consulting Editor
Publisher:
Pfeiffer & Company
8517 Production Ave.
San Diego, CA 92121-2280
800/274-4434
www.pfeiffer.com
Publication data:
2 volumes, $79.95 (paper); $169.95 (looseleaf)
Description:
Material from hundreds of authors is organized into experiential learning activities; inventories, questionnaires, and surveys; presentation and discussion resources; and theories and models in applied behavioral science. Updated annually.

9

Title:
Stern's SourceFinder®: The Master Reference to Information Resources for Leadership, Strategy, Organization, and Human Resource Management
Type of resource:
Book (1998, 815 pages) and database, 2 volume set
Publisher:
Michael Daniel Publishers
P.O. Box 3233
Culver City, CA 90231–3233
310/838-4437
310/838-2344 (fax)
Price:
$239.95 for book and hotline
Description:
This reference covers the whole field of human resource management—including training and development. Of the 46 chapters (which cover compensation, benefits, law, etc.), about one-third are related to the various aspects of human resource development. The 5,000 plus entries include books, directories, professional journals, databases, information services, associations, libraries, government agencies, and research services—among other resources. Each entry consists of the name of the item, the address and phone of its source, price, date, length, and a 25- to 50-word description. There is a subject index (with over 9,000 entries), as well as indexes for titles and authors. Update available in 2002.

10

Title:
Soundview Executive Book Summaries
Type of resource:
Periodic book reviews of current business books
Publisher:
Soundview Executive Book Summaries
10 LaCrue Avenue
Concordville, PA 19331
800/521-1227
800/453-5062 (fax)
Price:
Annual subscription, $89.50
Description:
Extensive book reviews (8 pages each) of current business books are mailed monthly to subscribers. Reviewed books may also be purchased through Soundview Executive Book summaries. A large binder is provided with tabs for easy organization into categories of interest.

11

Title:
Business References Catalog
Type of resource:
Catalog of government publications
Publisher:
U.S. Government Printing Office
Superintendent of Documents
Mail Stop SM
732 N. Capitol Street, NW
Washington, DC 20402-0003
202/512-1800
202/512-2250 (fax)
www.access.gpo.gov/su_docs/sale/prf/prf.html
Price:
Free
Description:
This is a 28-page catalog of selected references of particular interest to businesses. Large databases are represented; all publications are described; many are illustrated. A sample of titles includes: The Census Catalog and Guide (344 pages); Statistical Abstract of the United States (1,044 pages); Congressional Directory including Internet and e-mail addresses (1,193 pages); Health Information for International Travel (220 pages); Education and the Economy Report (134 pages); Defense Acquisition Deskbook on CD-ROM; and Foreign Labor Trends (60-issue subscription). Prices vary for listed publications.

Consultants and Training Providers

12

Title:
ASTD Buyer's Guide and Consultant Directory (Annual)
Type of resource:
Book (350 pages)
Publisher:
American Society for Training and Development
1640 King St., Box 1443
Alexandria, VA 22313
703/683-8100
703/683-1523 (fax)
www.astd.org
Price:
$85
Description:
This directory lists over 700 providers of training services

alphabetically with name, address, phone, and contact person. Each supplier describes its firm and its products and services in its own words, with a special notation regarding the type of media and services of subject areas in which they provide (1) consulting services, (2) off-the-shelf courseware, (3) custom-designed courseware (if any), (4) continuing education, (5) workshops/seminars, (6) equipment/supplies/furniture, and (7) training media. Some 300 subject terms are used to annotate these products and services. Suppliers are cross-indexed by geographical location, industry specialty (if any), and subject. Subjects are further annotated to indicate whether the supplier offers: computer-based materials, correspondence/home study, games/simulations, instructor-led training, printed materials, videodisc/CD-ROM, and videotape/films. The book is published every January.

13

Title:
The Consulting Exchange
Type of resource:
Referral service
Provider:
The Consulting Exchange
1770 Massachusetts Avenue
Cambridge, MA 02140
617/576-2100
800/824-4828
www.cx.com
Price:
Free to inquirer
Description:
Covering the northeastern U.S., this firm provides referrals to consultants in all fields, but especially general management consultants, computer consultants, expert witnesses, and, of course, training consultants. The user of the service is interviewed over the phone (or on-site) to determine the need, which is then compared to information maintained in a free-text database of the capabilities of the listed consulting firms and sole practitioners. Referred consultants pay a service fee.

14

Title:
Consultants and Consulting Organizations Directory, 25th Edition
Type of resource:
Book (3 volumes–4,000 pages) and database
Publisher:
Gale Research Inc.
835 Penobscot Bldg.
645 Griswold Street
Detroit, MI 48277-0748
800/877-GALE or
313/961-2242
313/961-6083 (fax)
Price:
$795 for 3-volume set
Description:
This book covers 25,000 firms in over 200 fields. The data provided on each includes: name, address, phone, fax, telex, branch offices, principals, size of staff, organizational purpose, markets/clients/regions served, and services provided. There are special notations for organizations that serve the U.S. government, that serve a particular industry, and that offer international counsel. Seminars/ workshops that might be offered by the firm are also noted. Four indexes are provided. The content of this directory is available online through "The Human Resource Information Network" and on diskette or magnetic tape. This reference is revised annually, and *New Consultants and Consulting Organizations* is issued 6 months after publication to update each year's directory. Published in August.

15

Title:
2002 Select Guide to Human Resource Executives
Type of resource:
Directory/Book and CD-ROM
Publisher:
Hunt-Scanlon Publishing Company
One East Putnam Ave.
Greenwich, CT 06830
800/477-1199
203/629-3701 (fax)
www.hunt-scanlon.com
Price:
$269
Description:
This directory lists over 23,000 human resources executives at 9,500 leading companies in the U.S. The CD-ROM features searching by 14 different criteria, including name, title, business sector, SIC code, and others. The listing includes the title "Manager Training and Development." 2002 edition available in July 2002.

Handbooks

16

Title:
The Extreme Searcher's Guide to Web Search Engines: A Handbook for the Serious Searcher, 2nd edition
Author:
Randolph Hock
Publisher:
CyberAge Books
143 Old Marlton Pike
Medford, NJ 08055
Publication data:
2001, 241 pages, $24.95
Description:
This practical handbook helps Internet users make the most of all the leading Web search tools. Features include descriptions, explanations, and "how to" information in search engines, Web directories, and meta-search tools. These are included: Alta Vista, Excite, Fast Search, Google, Hot Bot, Lycos, Northern Light, Yahoo!, Dogpile, ixquick, MetaCrawler, and ProFusion.

17

Title:
The Trainer's Handbook, Third Edition
Author:
Gary Mitchell
Publisher:
AMACOM
P.O. Box 1026
Saranac Lake, NY 12983
518/891-5510
Publication data:
1998, 428 pages, $75
Description:
This is a pragmatic, basic survey of training, written in a personal style. Chapters are titled: (1) The Function of Training, (2) The Object of Training, (3) The Structure of Training, (4) The Role of the Trainer, (5) Preparing a Needs Analysis, (6) Evaluating Your Effectiveness, (7) Researching the Subject Matter, (8) Writing the Training Program, (9) Alternatives to Writing Programs, (10) Setting the Physical Environment, (11) Aids to Training, (12) Computer-Based Training and Interactive Videodisc Instruction, (13) Setting

the Physical Environment, (14) Managing the Training Department, (15) Special Problems in Training, (16) Marketing the Training Function, (17) Negotiations and Training, and (18) Issues in Training.

18

Title:
The Cost of E-Learning Packaged Courses
Type of resource:
Handbook/Report
Provider:
brandon-hall.com
690 W. Freemont Ave., Ste. 10
Sunnyvale, CA 94087
408/736-2335
www.brandon-hall.com
Publication data:
2000, 100 pages, $300.00
Description:
How to determine company readiness, how to identify business requirements, how to determine customer needs, LMS, authoring tools, and choosing tools that match company goals.

19

Title:
E-Learning Across the Enterprise: The Benchmarking Study of Best Practices
Type of resource:
Directory/Benchmarking Study
Publisher:
brandon-hall.com
690 W. Freemont Ave., Ste. 10
Sunnyvale, CA 94087
408/736-2335
www.brandon-hall.com
Publication data:
2000, 113 pages, $1,795.00
Description:
10 domestic and foreign companies form the research base for this study: Air Canada, Cisco Systems, Dell, Ernst & Young, GTE, IBM, Rockwell Collins, Shell, Unipart, and the U.S. Navy. Information includes success stories around the business imperative, impact, leadership, tactics, models, content, and tools. Parts of the study can be purchased separately.

20

Title:
Handbook of Leadership Development
Editor/Author:
C. D. McCauley, R. Moxley, and E. Van Velsor
Publisher:
Center for Creative Leadership
One Leadership Place, P.O. Box 26300
Greensboro, NC 27438
336/286-4011
336/288-3999 (fax)
www.ccl.org
Publication data:
1998, $65
A CCL Jossey-Bass publication
Description:
As a result of almost three decades of work with thousands of leaders, the Center has refined a view of leadership development that can be simply stated: it is an ongoing process, grounded in personal development and embedded in experience, and it can be facilitated by interventions that are woven into those experiences. This handbook provides strategies and practices for people responsible for or interested in the not-so-simple task of facilitating this process. Updates and leadership research report.

21

Title:
Learning Management Systems 2001: How to Choose the Right System for Your Organization
Type of resource:
Handbook/report
Publisher:
brandon-hall.com
690 W. Freemont Ave., Ste. 10
Sunnyvale, CA 94087
408/736-2335
www.brandon-hall.com
Publication data:
2001, 500 pages, $795.00
Description:
This book will walk you through the process of selecting a Learning Management System (LMS). Topics include: how to analyze business requirements, how to develop an RFP, questions to ask vendors, how to narrow your review of vendors' systems.

22

Title:
Live E-Learning: How to Choose a System for Your Organization
Type of resource:
Handbook/report
Publisher:
brandon-hall.com
690 W. Freemont Ave., Ste. 10
Sunnyvale, CA 94087
408/736-2335
www.brandon-hall.com
Publication data:
2000, 155 pages, $345.00
Description:
Analyzes and critiques features and benefits of live e-learning tools using actual products on the market today. Focus is on informed, intelligent decision making.

23

Title:
The McGraw-Hill Handbook of Distance Learning
Authors:
Alan Chute, Burton Hancock, Melody Thompson
Type of Resource:
Book
Publisher:
McGraw-Hill
11 West 19th Street
New York, NY 10011
800/2-McGRAW
614/759-3644 (fax)
Publication data:
1998, 350 pages, $39.95
Description:
This book shows you how to get started with videoconferencing, internal online networks, satellite broadcasting, and virtual training rooms. It includes tips and guidelines regarding: technology options, costs, staffing, technical support requirements, and program development and evaluation tips.

24

Title:
Occupational Outlook Handbook 2000/2001
Editor/Author:
U.S. Department of Labor
Publisher:
U.S. Government Printing Office
Superintendent of Documents
Mail Stop M
732 N. Capitol St., N.W.
Washington, DC 20402
202/512-1800
202/512-2250 (fax)
Publication data:
560 pages, paper $49, cloth $51

Description:
This is the latest version of the classic government publication on jobs, occupations, and hiring trends. It contains detailed descriptions of more than 250 occupations—covering what the work entails, working conditions, education and training needed, earnings, job outlook, advancement potential, and related occupations. Includes 10- to 15-year projections of the labor force, economic growth, industry outlook and employment, and occupational employment. Published in February every other year.

25

Title:
Teamwork: The Team Member Handbook
Type of resource:
Employee handbooks
Publisher:
Pritchett Rummler-Brache (PRB)
5800 Granite Pkwy, Ste. 450
Plano, TX 75024
800/992-5922
972/731-1550 (fax)
www.PRBweb.com
Price:
$6.95 per book; 100 copies at $5.95 per book
Description:
This handbook is one of approximately 30 employee handbooks on various topics. Each soft-cover, 6″ x 9″ book contains approximately 30 pages of quotations and advice for dealing with work and career. Among recent titles are: Managing Sideways; Fast Growth—A Career Acceleration Strategy; Resistance-Moving Beyond Barriers to Change; The Ethics of Excellence; and After the Merger—the Authoritative Guide for Integration Success.
The handbook series is also available online for corporate licensing.

Online Services

26

Title:
ASTD Website: astd.org
Type of resource:
Website
Provider:
American Society for Training and Development (ASTD)
1640 King Street, Box 1443
Alexandria, VA 22313
703/683-8122
703/683-8103 (fax)
www.astd.org
Price:
Free
Description:
In addition to chat groups, job bank, and networking opportunities online, this service provides full Internet/www access and help guides developed specifically for trainers. The database includes training news, a training library of more than 10,000 references, policy studies, information on performance improvement and technical training, buyer's guide, and job bank. This is the most comprehensive Website for trainers. See section 6.8 of this yearbook for other sites. Chapter 4 "Training Delivery" also features Websites.

27

Title:
brandon-hall.com: Your Guide to E-Learning
Type of resource:
Website of publications, surveys, discussion groups focused on e-learning
Publisher:
brandon-hall.com
690 W. Freemont Ave., Ste. 10
Sunnyvale, CA 94087
408/736-2335
email: info@brandon-hall.com
www.brandon-hall.com
Price:
Some free information; price range for reports and books $49–$1,795.
Description:
Brandon Hall provides independent, objective information about using technology for learning and organizationl decision making. Provides frequent online publications, and some print copy, on trends, best practices, tools, and vendors. The site accepts no advertising.

28

Title:
www.masie.com
Type of resource:
Website of research and resource information

Publisher:
The MASIE Center
P.O. Box 397
Saratoga Springs, NY 12866
518/350-2200
518/587-3276
Price:
Prices range from free for TechLearn Trends online newsletter to going rates for skills training, information products, and conference services.
Description:
The MASIE Center is an international e-lab and ThinkTank dedicated to exploring the intersection of learning and technology. The Website is updated frequently and can lead you to the key questions about technology, behavior, performance, and learning.

29

Title:
TRAINET.com
Type of resource:
Website information center
Provider:
Linton Publishing Company
1011 First Street South
Hopkins, MN 55343
612/936-2288
www.trainet.com
Price:
Access is free
Description:
This Website is a complete and up-to-date training and development information center on the World Wide Web designed to offer a variety of information for the training professional.
Included are numerous databases allowing trainers to freely browse and locate resources as well as post requests to training consultants for products and services. Directories previously published as books are now available online. These include: Corporate Human Resources and Personnel Directory, Recommended Training Supplier and Consultant Directory, and Linton's Top 5,000 U.S. Industry Directory.

30

Title:
Training Newsletters Online
Type of resource:
Online and e-mail newsletters

Training Research and Reference Sources	361

Provider:
Dartnell/LRP
360 Hiatt Drive
Palm Beach Gardens, FL 83418
800/621-5463
561/622-2423
www.dartnellcorp.com
Price:
Prices vary
Description:
This is a new service of Dartnell, publisher of audios, videos, and books on sales, customer service, and teamwork. This new service is an online newsletter service, available through e-mail or on diskette. Titles include: Teamwork, From 9 to 5, Customers First, Quality 1st, Salesmanship, Effective Telephone Techniques, Communication at Work, Small Office/Home Office Solutions, Getting Along, Successful Supervisor, and others.

31

Title:
TRAINING Website: trainingsupersite.com
Type of resource:
Website of training resources
Provider:
Lakewood Publications
50 South Ninth St.
Minneapolis, MN 55402
800/707-7769
612/340-4819 (fax)
www.trainingsupersite.com
Price:
Free
Description:
This Website is a comprehensive collection of human performance and productivity resources. Key features are a commercial center called the "Training Mall" where training products and programs are sold, and a "Learning Center" through which more than 1,000 courses can be taken and conference presentations accessed. A link to the SIS seminar and conference database is available through The Learning Center. The usual books and publications of Bill Communications and Lakewood Publications are also available for purchase online.

32

Title:
TRAINSEEK.com
Type of resource:
Online product catalog and e-commerce resource

Provider:
TrainSeek.com
850 W. Lancaster Ave.,
Bryn Mawr, PA 19010
800/622-3610
610/525-2563 (fax)
www,.trainseek.com
Price:
Free online previews
Description:
This is an online catalog of training products and services, annotated and reviewed for easy comparison among vendors. Videos, CD-ROMS, and instructor-led programs are featured. Features over 300 listings of e-learning tools and systems.

33

Title:
International Academic Journals
Publisher:
MCB University Press
P.O. Box 10812
Birmingham, AL 35201
888/622-0075
205/995-1588 (fax)
www.mcb.co/uk
Type of resource:
Journals plus online database; full Internet Archive capability.
Price:
Journals range in price from $200 to $10,000
Description:
Academic journals of interest to training and development professionals are electronically enhanced to provide researchers with instant access to journal editions as far back as 1993. Archive permits interactive search by subject, type of material, and quality level. Journal titles include: Industrial & Commercial Training, Journal of European Industrial Training, Journal of Management Development, Leadership & Organization Development Journal, Training for Quality, and Training & Management Development Methods.

34

Title:
ERIC® (Educational Resources Information Center)
Provider:
U.S. Department of Education
Office of Educational Research and Improvement
ERIC ACVE/Center on Employment
1900 Kenny Road
Columbus, OH 43210-1090
800/848-4815
614/292-4353
614/292-1260 (fax)
www.cete.org
www.ericacve.org
Type of resource:
Online information service
Description:
Begun in 1966 as a project of the U.S. Dept. of Education and converted into an online database in 1972, *ERIC* houses about 700,000 records. These consist of abstracts from 800 education and education-related journals, as well as conference proceedings, papers, research materials, and other unpublished documents. The number of access points to *ERIC* is increasing. In addition, there are several access points to *ERIC* via the Internet. For instructions and a current list, call ACCESS ERIC at 800/538-3742 or send a message to askeric@ericir.syr.edu.

Seminar Databases

35

Title:
Leadership Education Resources Handbook: A Guide to Training and Development, 8th edition
Type of resource:
Book
Publisher:
Center for Creative Leadership
P.O. Box 26300
Greensboro, NC 27438-6300
336/288-7210
336/288-3999 (fax)
www.ccl.org
Price:
$49.95
Description:
Designed as a complete reference to leadership education, nearly half of this book is devoted to detailed descriptions of leadership courses and programs offered by colleges, universities, and other selected organizations. Another section of the book covers instruments, exercises, simulations, and games for leadership education. A Leadership Bibliography gives summaries of 1,000 books and journal articles, and there is also a

directory of 130 films and videos. Some 300 professionals in the field are profiled in a Resource Persons Directory, and 80 organizations (associations, institutes, foundations) are described in a Resource Organizations Directory. The final directory lists dozens of annual leadership events. Extensive detail is provided for each item in the directory, and indexes provide subject, author, name, and institutional access to all sections.

36
Title:
The 2002 Corporate University Evaluation Guide to Executive Programs

The 2002 Corporate University Guide to Management Seminars
Type of resource:
Binder manuals, 500+ pages each
Publisher:
The Corporate University Press
P.O. Box 2080, 504 N. 4th St.
Fairfield, IA 52556
800/255-1261
515/472-7105 (fax)
Price:
$295 per binder
Description:
These guides cover training seminars in the U.S. and worldwide provided by universities and independent seminar providers. Programs are categorized into approximately a dozen fields and provide evaluative comments from program participants and others. The same information is available on CD-ROM or through the webpage www.hrsoft.com. at $400 per user per year. Quantity discounts are available.

37
Title:
Bricker's International Directory: University-Based Executive Programs 2002
Type of resource:
Book
Publisher:
Peterson's Thompson Learning
202 Carnegie Center
P.O. Box 2123
Princeton, NJ 08543–2123
800/338-3282 or
609/243-9111
609/243-9150 (fax)
Price:
$395
Description:
This guide appears annually in November, presenting information on some 720 university-based executive development programs (from 92 institutions) for mid- to upper-level executives, ranging from 2 days to up to a year in length. Each program is described in at least a page, covering data such as the sponsoring organization, location, dates/duration, course objectives, key topics, methods of instruction, profile of participants, faculty, facilities, program contact, and special features offered.

38
Title:
Seminar Clearinghouse International Inc.
Type of resource:
Telephone service, database, and seminar registration service
Provider:
Seminar Clearinghouse International Inc.
P.O. Box 1757
St. Paul, MN 55101-0757
612/293-1044
612/293-0492 (fax)
800/927-0502
Price:
$55 per search; $27 each for 100 or more
Description:
Clients of this service can get information on seminars, videos/training films and consultants over the phone, or by fax. In providing this personal service, SCI draws on a number of information resources to meet a client's particular training resource need. In SCI's databases, there is information on about 29,000 seminar titles (including public and on-site seminars) comprising about 60,000 events. The most significant part of the firm's service is the database of seminar evaluations (plus instructor/ speaker evaluations) contributed by clients. SCI also offers a service, Training Information Management System, which centralizes all external seminar enrollments. SCI performs all administrative responsibilities related to attendances including enrollment, registration fee payments, tracking, reporting, and evaluating. It is a comprehensive, quality-driven system that provides organizations with the tools to manage their training costs.

39
Title:
SIS Electronic
Type of resource:
Database; CD-ROM updated every 3 months
Publisher:
Seminar Information Service, Inc.
17752 Skypark Circle, Suite 210
Irvine, CA 92714
949/261-9104
949/261-1963 (fax)
Price:
$295
Description:
This CD-ROM covers thousands of business and technical seminars. Both public and in-house programs are included. They are listed by topic (e.g. "general management: time/stress management"), then alphabetically by sponsor, then in a calendar format. Data includes a 1- to 3-sentence description, the fee, the sponsor, contact information, and the date and location. Evaluative information is available for selected seminars. Some 200,000 separate events from over 500 sponsors are tracked. Formerly published in workbook format as an annual. Also accessible on trainingsupersite.com.

40
Title:
Distance Learning Directory
Type of resource:
Book (about 225 pages in length)
6th edition, 2001
Publisher:
Virginia A. Ostendorf, Inc.
P.O. Box 2896
Littleton, CO 80161-2896
303/797-3131
303/797-3524 (fax)
Price:
$250
Description:
This directory covers scheduled live instructional programs that are delivered at a distance. The types of programs include corporate

Training Research and Reference Sources

training, medical topics, K–12, higher education, formal degree programs, continuing education, certification, etc. A wide variety of technologies are represented: audiographic programs and courses, computer conferencing, and full motion video (including satellite, microwave, fiber optics, and cable delivery). Lists vendors, products, and services.

Toolbooks

41
Title:
Collaboration Tools for E-Learning
Type of resource:
Tool Book
Publisher:
brandon-hall.com
690 W. Freemont Ave., Ste. 10
Sunnyvale, CA 94087
408/736-2335
www.brandon-hall.com
Publication Data:
2000, 86 pages, $145.00
Description:
Examples of applications, case studies, and tools of digital collaboration. Expert analysis and recommendations.

42
Title:
The Complete Guide to Teams
Author:
Human Technology Inc.
Publisher:
HRD Press
22 Amherst Rd.
Amherst, MA 01002
800/822-2801
413/253-3490 (fax)
www.hrdpress.com
Publication Data:
1999, 250 pages, $99.95
Description:
Contains over 70 tools and resources for teams including assessments, job aids, worksheets, and troubleshooting tips.

43
Title:
How to Manage Training, 2nd edition: A Guide to Design and Delivery for High Performance
Author:
Carolyn Nilson
Publisher:
AMACOM Books
P.O. Box 169
Saranac Lake, NY 12983
800/250-5308
518/891-3653
Publication Data:
1998, 304 pages, $75.00
Description:
This handbook covers the details of setting up and running a training operation. More than 100 forms and checklists, graphics, and models are presented in a looseleaf binder for easy copying and adaptation. The book includes an extensive annotated bibliography representing a historical and current view of thinkers from Deming, Bloom, Maslow, Gilbert, Gagne, Guilford to Senge, Blanchard, Kirkpatrick, Robinson, and Gery. On amazon.com's best-selling training books list.

44
Title:
2001/2002 Distance Learning Yearbook
Authors:
Karen Mantyla and John Woods
Type of resource:
Book
Publisher:
American Society for Training and Development (ASTD)
1640 King Street, Box 1443
Alexandria, VA 22313
703/683-8100
410/516-6998 (fax)
Publication data:
2001, 554 pages, $79.95
Description:
This book examines distance learning from three perspectives: the learner, the trainer, and the manager. It includes templates, checklists, and job aids for creating and managing distance learning events. Topics include interactive audio and interactive video conferencing, CBT, Internet and Intranet based training. Examples of success stories are included.

45
Title:
How to Start a Training Program: Training Is a Strategic Tool in Any Organization
Author:
Carolyn Nilson
Type of resource:
Book
Publisher:
American Society for Training and Development (ASTD)
1640 King Street, Box 1443
Alexandria, VA 22313
703/683-8100
410/516-6998 (fax)
Publication data:
1999, 231 pages, $32.00
Description:
This book is a practical guide to setting up a training program. It covers: creating a business plan, developing training standards and writing policy, setting budgets, and introducing the program in your company. It also includes designing and delivering training courses and programs, evaluating training, and focusing on performance. Numerous interviews and case studies illustrate and supplement the how-to ideas.

46
Title:
Info-line
Type of resource:
Series of booklets, each 16–20 pages, 8 1/2" × 11"
Publisher:
American Society for Training and Development (ASTD)
1640 King Street, Box 1443
Alexandria, VA 22313
800/628-2783
888/628-5329 (fax)
Price:
Annual subscription $119; single issue $10; quantity discounts
Description:
The Info-line series are single-issue/topic publications produced by training practitioners throughout the year. Currently more than 150 topics are available. Many titles are available in Spanish. The series features step-by-step guidelines, how-to tips, diagrams and illustrations, job-aids, worksheets, templates, forms, checklists, reference lists, mini-case studies of practical applications. Recent topics include: knowledge management, Group Decision Making, Learning Technologies, Successful Global Training, Selecting a Coach, Training Telecommuters,

Service Management, and many others. Info-line collections are also available at $75 each on a single topic, for example, evaluation.

47

Title:
The ASTD Media Selection Tool for Workplace Learning
Author:
Raymond J. Marx and Karen Hudson-Samuels
Type of resource:
Book and CD-ROM
Publisher:
American Society for Training and Development (ASTD)
1640 King Street, Box 1443
Alexandria, VA 22313
703/683-8100
410/516-6998 (fax)
Publication data:
1999, 158 pages, $59.95
Description:
This book and CD-ROM on media selection includes practical job aids and questionnaires to help the trainer choose the best delivery option. Customizable spreadsheets are included for cost comparison studies. Topics include: development time, development cost, equipment and facility requirements, maintenance issues, business and financial factors in media selection, and integrated delivery. References are provided to Web resources and URL links.

48

Title:
ASTD Toolkits
Author:
ASTD editors
Publisher:
American Society for Training & Developing (ASTD)
P.O. Box 4856, Hampden Station
Baltimore, MD 21211
703/683-8100
410/516-6998 (fax)
Publication data:
$59.00 each; Publication dates range from 1990–2000
Description:
This is a series of books containing samples of materials used by trainers throughout the U.S. The books have been compiled by ASTD's Information Center in response to requests for original documents, forms, and job aids in actual use by trainers. Each Toolkit contains related journal articles and a bibliography. Titles include: Lesson Plans, Needs Assessment Instruments, Project Plans, Evaluation Instruments, Job Descriptions, Mission Statements, Educational Assistance Policies, and others.

49

Title:
The Performance Consulting Toolbook
Author:
Carolyn Nilson
Type of resource:
Book
Publisher:
McGraw-Hill
11 West 19th St.
New York, NY 10011
800/2-McGRAW
614/759-3644 (fax)
Publication data:
1999, 259 pages, $39.95
Description:
This is a book of tools designed to help trainers think like performance consultants. It provides step-by-step exercises, activities, checklists, questionnaires, charts and forms for individual use in making the transition from trainer to performance consultant.

Videos, Films, Audiotapes

50

Title:
ASTD Audio and Videotapes Collection
Type of resource:
Audio/Videotapes from ASTD Conferences Catalog of tapes
Publisher:
Mobiltape Company Inc.
24730 Avenue Tibbitts,
Suite 170
Valencia, CA 91355
800/369-5718
661/295-8474 (fax)
Price:
Audiotapes: members of ASTD $13 each, plus $2.00 shipping; non-members, $16.50 each, plus $2.00 shipping; Videotapes $69.95 each, plus shipping $4.00
Description:
Mobiltape Company Inc. reproduces sessions presented by conference speakers and makes them available to members and non-members of sponsoring associations. The pricing structure and reference listed here are for current ASTD conferences. Phone Mobiltape for other conferences recorded by them.

51

Title:
InfoComm iQ Directory of Video, Computer, and Audio Visual Products
Publisher:
InfoComm Resources
505 First Av. NE
Minneapolis, MN 55413
612/676-6160
ype of resource:
Website www.infocom.org
Price:
$50
Description:
This online directory covers over 250 categories of equipment with over 2,500 products, and it includes a complete glossary. Over 400 manufacturers and 800 dealers are represented. Some of the categories include: video (presentation units, monitors, projectors, cameras, VCRs), slide/transparency viewing equipment, projection/video screens, slide projectors (silent, sound, random access), overhead and opaque projectors, filmstrip projectors and viewers, sound motion picture projectors (8mm, 16mm, 35mm), multi-image (dissolves, programmers, racks), interactive video, computer-generated graphics systems, and audio equipment (mixers, sound systems, lecterns, tape duplicators and recorders). There are illustrated and unillustrated sections of the directory. In the illustrated section, the following data is provided: suggested list price, model number, weight, capacity, features, applications, accessories, and other tech-

nical details. Free e-newsletter: infocommnewsinfo.net/

52

Title:
Marketplace Directory: Training Presentation Products
Publisher:
Bill Communications
50 South Ninth St.
Lakewood Building
Minneapolis, MN 55402
612/333-0471
Type of resource:
Magazine feature (a supplement to the November issue of *TRAINING Magazine*)
Price:
$6 cost for non-subscribers
Description:
The latest edition of this annual directory covers hundreds of suppliers of: audio, computer/multimedia, furniture/fixtures, presentation aids/packaging, slides, video, visual projection, rental equipment, services, and computer software. Each of these areas is further subdivided to get 180 product categories in all. An address, phone, and contact person are provided for each vendor.

53

Title:
The Multimedia and Videodisc Compendium
Type of resource:
Book (208 pages) 2002 edition
Publishers:
Emerging Technology Consultants, Inc.
2819 Hamline Ave. North
St. Paul, MN 55113
651/639-3973
651/639-0110 (fax)
Price:
$69.95 with index diskette
Description:
This publication covers over 5,000 titles (videodiscs, CDs, and multimedia software) from more than 350 producers. The programs included are those which are suitable for school/college and business training and healthcare purposes, and they are categorized into 24 major subject areas, including the categories of training, authoring systems, and presentation systems. Each listing includes up to a 100-word description, price, level of interactivity, audience, and producer contact information. Published in January.

54

Title:
SHRM Conference Audiotapes
Type of resource:
Audiotapes from the Annual Conference of Society for Human Resource Management (SHRM)
Publisher:
InfoMedia
12800 Garden Grove Blvd., Suite F
Garden Grove, CA 92843
800/367-9286
714/537-3244 (fax)
Price:
$10 each tape; $1.00 shipping
Description:
InfoMedia produces audiotapes directly from keynote speeches and breakout sessions. Approximately 100 tapes are available. If you buy 6 tapes, you get the 7th one free.

55

Title:
TRAINING Conference Audiotapes
Type of resource:
Audiotapes from Lakewood's Annual TRAINING Conference
Provider:
Audio Transcripts, Ltd.
3660-B Wheeler Avenue
Alexandria, VA 22304
703/370-8273
703/370-5162 (fax)
Price:
$13 each tape; $2.00 shipping
Description:
Audio Transcripts, Ltd. (ATL) produces audiotapes directly from keynote speeches and breakout sessions. Approximately 150 audiotapes are available. A complete listing is available through atltapes@aol.com.

6.7 Training Journals, Magazines, and Newsletters

Any experienced trainer is well aware that there is a flood of training publications vying for his or her attention. In a way, this whole book is a testament to the incredible volume of HRD media; and in this section of *The Trainer's Almanac* we list the journals, magazines, and newsletters that especially serve the training field. Of course, many of the popular business magazines, such as *Business Week, Fortune, Newsweek,* and *Fast Company* have articles and features of particular interest to trainers. These magazines are not listed here; these general business magazines are easy to find on newsstands and store shelves everywhere, and on the Internet. See the frontmatter pages of this book for addresses of these general business magazines and other training-focused magazines that have informed this *Training & Development Yearbook 2002*.

Content to Lead You Forward

We have compiled the key information on each publication, including a description of its editorial thrust. One of our objectives is to simply give you enough information to contact a publication that may have been difficult to find. No doubt, also, you will discover some titles in the following directory that you were unaware of, but which may well suit your needs. We can also imagine readers using these listings to prepare subscription budgets, assess the completeness of the department library, or facilitate the development of individual trainers and trainees. All prices are for subscriptions addressed to U.S. addresses; rates for foreign subscribers are higher to reflect mailing costs. If you are interested in examining a certain publication, you will find that almost all publishers offer a complimentary sample issue.

Trends this year include a surge in growth of online newsletters. Some former paper-based periodicals are now available online only and some are in transition from paper to digital format. Some online newsletters are free, others are available by subscription only. We list some of the important ones here. Check publishers' Websites to see what's new. ASTD's *Technical and Skills Training* magazine and Bill Communications' (formerly Lakewood Publications) *Training Directors Forum* newsletter are examples. AMA's *Management Review* is now a members-only publication and now only online.

Also, large management consulting companies, and some smaller ones too, are increasing their publication efforts, both online and via paper periodical newsletters, reports, and magazine-like publications. We include some of these here too. Booz-Allen & Hamilton's *Strategy and Business*, Berlitz's *Global Voice*, and Elliott Masie's *TechLearn Trends* are examples.

As the blurring of news and entertainment has confounded our TV, so the blurring of advertisement and information in our periodicals offline and online has continued to increase. The reader simply has to become more astute at recognizing these important points of view, and in many cases, you yourself must perform the function of peer review board or editor. Availability and ease of use of software to create newsletters and Websites have resulted in a proliferation of newsletters this year.

67 Publications Are Listed

We present the publications in alphabetical order by title. This is a broad representation of topics of interest to trainers, covering these content areas:

- Career development
- Computer-based training
- Communication
- Corporate universities
- Distance learning
- Diversity
- e-learning/Web-based training
- Higher education
- Instructional design
- Global/international issues
- Knowledge management
- Leadership
- Legislation
- Literacy
- Management development
- Multimedia
- Organization development
- Performance improvement
- Research in training and learning
- Teams
- Technical training
- Quality

1

Publication Title:
Across the Board
Publisher:
The Conference Board
P.O. Box 4026
Church Street Station
New York, NY 10261
212/759-0900
212/980-7014 (fax)
Issue Frequency:
10/yr.
Price:
$45
Description:
This magazine features articles that further the purpose of The Conference Board, that is, "to improve the business enterprise system and to enhance the contribution of business to society." Contributors are frequently high-profile business leaders. Content covers a wide range of current issues of concern to human resource leaders.

2

Publication Title:
The American Journal of Distance Education
Publisher:
Penn State University
College of Education
403 S. Allen St., Suite 206
University Park, PA 16801-5202
814/863-3764
814/865-5878 (fax)
www.ed.psu.edu/ACSDE
Issue Frequency:
3/yr.
Price:
$75 institutional; $45 personal
Description:
This journal's stated purpose is "to disseminate information and act as a forum for criticism and debate about research in and practice of distance education in the Americas." Defining "distance education" as "teaching-learning relationships in which the actors are geographically separated and communication between them is achieved through such media as radio and television programs, audio and video recordings, personal computers, various types of teleconferences, and correspondence texts," this journal is aimed at professional trainers, adult educators, communication specialists, and professionals in higher and continuing education and in public schools. In addition to referred articles, each issue contains a mixture of editorials, opinion pieces by readers, interviews, and reviews of books and other media.

3

Publication Title:
Bulletin to Management
Publisher:
Bureau of National Affairs (BNA)
1231 25th Street, NW
Washington, DC 20037
800/372-1033
www.bna.com
Issue Frequency:
Bi-weekly
Price:
$225
Description:
This is one of a group of newsletters that focus on developments in federal legislation, regulatory agencies, and in corporate issues around what's new in Washington. Other BNA newsletters include *Policy & Practice*, *Union Labor Report*, *HR Practitioners Guide*, and others. CD-ROM and online versions are available

4

Publication Title:
The Career Development Quarterly
Publisher:
National Career Development Association
4700 Reed Rd., Suite M
Columbus, OH 43220
888/326-1750 (toll free)
800/633-4931
614/326-1760 (fax)
Issue Frequency:
Quarterly

Price:
Free to NCDA and American Counseling Association members; non-member prices $67
Description:
Each issue of this journal includes 7–10 articles on research, theory, and practice in the field of career development. Some of the specific areas covered include career counseling, occupational resources, labor market dynamics, career education, and work and leisure. Occasionally, special issues are published, and recent topics have been "Career Development of Racial and Ethnic Minorities" and "Work and Family Issues." The objective of the journal is to foster career development through the design and use of career interventions in educational institutions, in community and government agencies, and in business and industry settings.

5

Publication Title:
Communication Briefings: Ideas That Work
Publisher:
Communication Briefing's (Wicks Information LLC)
1101 King Street, Ste. 110
Alexandria, VA 22314
800/888-2084
703/684-2136 (fax)
www.briefings.com/cb
Issue Frequency:
monthly
Price:
$89.00 year
Description:
This is one of the best "tips for action" type of publication. Up to ten bullets of information per short article (3 or 4 column inches) characterize the 8-page newsletter. Each short article is a very brief abstract of a recent book or article. Attributions do not include publication date of original source: this is a publication for mass appeal, not an academic publication.

6

Publication Title:
Corporate University Newsletter
Publisher:
Corporate University Xchange
381 Park Avenue So., Ste. 713
New York, NY 10016
212/213-2828
212/213-8621 (fax)
Issue Frequency:
6/yr.
Price:
$199/yr.; $99 for non-profit organizations
Description:
This newsletter is published and edited by Jeanne C. Meister, author of *Corporate Quality Universities: Lessons in Building a World-Class Work Force*. The newsletter addresses the corporate university concept in the broadest sense, dealing with all aspects of continuous intentional learning in the workplace. Some of the recent topics include: the results of the *Corporate University Xchange Annual Survey of 100 Corporate University Deans* on the future direction of corporate universities, a new paradigm for leadership development as reported in a research monograph from Penn State Institute for the Study of Organizational Effectiveness. *Corporate University Xchange* also publishes several research monographs on topics uncovered in *Corporate University Xchange Annual Survey*. Upcoming research monographs will examine best practice alliances between corporate universities and conventional universities and how to promote a commitment for individual employee self-development.

7

Publication Title:
Creative Training Techniques
Publisher:
Bill Communications
50 South Ninth St.
Lakewood Building
Minneapolis, MN 55402
800/707-7749
612/333-0471
612/333-6526 (fax)
Issue Frequency:
Monthly
Price:
$99 per year
Description:
Edited by experienced trainer Bob Pike, this 8-page newsletter consists of practical ideas on training that don't require major redesigns or large capital expenditures. Addressed to the stand-up trainer, *Creative Training Techniques* consists of short items on classroom techniques (e.g., ice breakers, motivation, use of audiovisuals), administration, evaluation, new products, etc. There is also a "tip of the month," a book review section, and a question-and-answer column, and a new department called "Covering Technology for Learning."

8

Publication Title:
Cultural Diversity at Work
Publisher:
The GilDeane Group
13751 Lake City Way, N.E., Suite 106
Seattle, WA 98125-3615
206/362-0336
206/363-5028 (fax)
www.diversitycentral.com
Issue Frequency:
Newsletter
Bulletin
Price:
$99/yr. (includes newsletter, bulletin, and access to interactive worldwide diversity forum and online archive)
Description:
This online newsletter, subtitled "Preparing You for Managing, Training, and Conducting Business in the Global Age," explores the fabric of cultural differences in the workplace and marketplace. Each issue seeks answers to the question, "How can diverse people work together and conduct business effectively?" Focusing on the new strategies, new skills, and new perspectives all people must acquire for a multicultural work environment, articles offer solutions from both the training and learning viewpoints. Each issue centers on a theme. Past themes include: multicultural skills for managers, diversity and cross-cultural trainers (Do they know what they're doing?), misinterpreting behavior and resolving conflict, and recruiting diverse employees. The newsletter includes practical tips and techniques for managers of diverse employees, applications of intercultural communication skills, case studies,

resource reviews, and model programs. Contributing writers include diversity and cross-cultural consultants, internal diversity managers, and international human resource managers. The *Bulletin* is a monthly listing of workshops, conferences/meetings, and related announcements on diversity/cross-cultural topics and issues.

9

Publication Title:
Educational Technology
Publisher:
Educational Technology Publishers
700 Palisade Ave.
Englewood Cliffs, NJ 07632-0564
   201/871-4007
   201/871-4009 (fax)
Issue Frequency:
6/year
Price:
$119 ($139 overseas)
Description:
This magazine deals with all aspects of the use of technology in education and training, including, but not restricted to, instructional system design, computer and video-based technologies such as interactive video, multimedia, expert systems, and artificial intelligence. The publication is directed to both the business and educational communities, and the number of articles devoted to training (as opposed to education) has risen in recent years. One unique feature of *Educational Technology* is about half of its readership is outside the U.S., and many of its articles are contributed from this international readership. The editorial content of the magazine includes: case studies/applications, essays on the state of educational technology, reports of research, reviews of products (including software), reviews of books, organizational news, news of people in the field, and a new research section. It publishes a number of special issues each year on various aspects of work in the field.

10

Publication Title:
Educational Technology Research and Development
Publisher:
Association for Educational Communications and Technology (AECT)
1800 North Stone Lake Dr., Suite 2
Bloomington, IN 47404
   812/335-7675
   812/335-7678 (fax)
Issue Frequency:
Quarterly
Price:
$75
Description:
This journal consists of referreed articles on research (in educational technology) and development (i.e., instructional development and other applications of educational technology). In addition, each issue features one or more formal book reviews, "international reviews" (profiles of educational technology applications from around the world), and "research abstracts" culled from the ERIC database.

11

Publication Title:
Educom Review
Publisher:
EDUCAUSE
1112 16th St., NW, Ste. 600
Washington, DC 20036
   202/872-4200; 303/449-4430
   202/872-4318 (fax)
Issue Frequency:
6/year
Price:
$24
Description:
Articles in this magazine focus on learning, communications, and information technology. Content generally deals with issues of concern to higher education and university students and faculty.

12

Publication Title:
e-learning
Publisher:
Advanstar Communications, Inc.
P.O. Box 6011
Duluth, MN 55806
   888/527-7008
   218/723-9417
   www.elearningmag.com
Issue Frequency:
Monthly
Price:
free
Description:
This is a general business magazine whose focus is entirely e-learning. It is self-described as a publication of "content, technology and services for corporate, government, ,and higher education."

13

Publication Title:
Executive Book Summaries
Publisher:
Soundview Executive Book Summaries
3 Pond Lane
Middlebury, VT 05753–1164
   800/521-1227
   800/453-5062 (fax)
Issue Frequency:
12/year
Price:
$89.50
Description:
This is a monthly publication of book reviews, two or three of which are extensive (6–8 pages) on featured current, high-interest books. In addition to the main selections, 6–10 additional books are highlighted with brief reviews. The editorial staff and board review approximately 100 books per month and choose the books they feature from among the latest proofs, manuscripts, and books on current management issues, including many of interest to trainers.

14

Publication Title:
Global Voice
Publisher:
Berlitz International Inc.
400 Alexander Park
Princeton, NJ 08540
   800/528-8908
   609/514-9640 (fax)
   www.berlitz.com
Issue Frequency:
Quarterly
Price:
Free
Description:
This 6-page newsletter, while a promotional tool for Berlitz language services, contains good information and case studies about a variety of language training options and situations.

15

Publication Title:
Global Workforce
Publisher:
ACC Communications
245 Fischer Ave., B-2
Costa Mesa, CA 92626
714/751-1883
714/751-4106
www.workforceonline.com
Issue Frequency:
12/year
Price:
Provided as a free supplement to *Workforce* magazine which costs $59 per year, or at a cost of $8 per issue
Description:
Global issues in the workforce are featured exclusively in this new magazine. These include: culture and language training, expatriate and dual-career spouse services, global competency development, workforce travel and communication, and more. Advertising within the magazine is geared to global needs.

16

Publication Title:
Harvard Business Review
Publisher:
Harvard Business Review
60 Harvard Way
Boston, MA 02163
800/988-0886
617/496-1029 (fax)
Issue Frequency:
6/year
Price:
$95 (1 yr)
Description:
Harvard Business Review is a publication of ideas and stories about solving business problems across a range of industries. Contributors include well-known business persons, consultants, and professors. *HBR* is often full of articles of interest to trainers and to human resources development management. Particularly popular and unique are the "Executive Summaries" of key articles, a book review section, an extensive case study with interpretations, and a Letters to the Editor section which is always worth reading.

17

Publication Title:
Harvard Management Communication Letter
Publisher:
Harvard Business School Publishing
60 Harvard Way
Boston, MA 02163
800/668-6705
www.hbsp.harvard.edu/hmcl
Issue Frequency:
Monthly
Price:
$99
Description:
This newsletter contains tools, techniques, and ideas for the articulate executive. Its contents can provide material for communication course design and other training. Tools include letters, memos, reports, e-mail, telephone, meetings, speeches, presentations, the Web. Articles are substantial, current, and attributed. Typical newsletter size is 12 pages.

18

Publication Title:
Harvard Management Update
Publisher:
Harvard Business School Publishing
60 Harvard Way
Boston, MA 02163
800/668-6705
617/496-1029 (fax)
www.hbsp.harvard.edu/hmu
Issue Frequency:
12/year, monthly
Price:
$99
Description:
Billed as a newsletter for "people with managerial responsibilities, particularly people who are still working their way toward the corner office," this newsletter is for middle managers. Negotiating, dealing with problem employees, and getting results are some of the issues addressed by contributing writers. The publication is especially appropriate for training managers and consultants.

19

Publication Title:
HR Magazine
Publisher:
Society for Human Resource Management (SHRM)
606 N. Washington St.
Alexandria, VA 22314
703/548-3440
703/836-0367 (fax)
Issue Frequency:
12/year, monthly
Price:
$70
Description:
This is the monthly magazine of SHRM, providing news and features of concern to the broad range of human resources specialists including training professionals. Regular features include benefits, recruitment, and technology, in addition to training and development. The magazine is also a good source of current information about legal issues and actions in topics such as diversity, affirmative action, and specific developments in legislation such as The Americans with Disabilities Act (ADA) and Family and Medical Leave Act.

20

Publication Title:
Human Resource Development Quarterly (HRDQ)
Publisher:
Jossey-Bass, Inc.
350 Sansome St.
San Francisco, CA 94104
800/274-4434
800/569-0043 (fax)
Issue Frequency:
Quarterly
Price:
Free online to ASTD members (www.astd.org); $57/yr. individuals; $119 libraries
Description:
Sponsored by ASTD and the Academy of Human Resource Development. Following on the premise that there is adequate discussion and exchange of the practice of HRD in the media, the focus of the journal is on theory and research—specifically the application of quantitative and qualitative methods of inquiry to HRD topics. The journal is interdisciplinary in concept, drawing on fields such as industrial psychology, economics, adult educa-

tion, organizational behavior, instructional technology, management, and human resource development, and it is "dedicated to serving the needs of researchers, senior practitioners, and academics in the field of human resource development." To stimulate healthy debate, each issue presents a featured article and an invited reaction. In addition to a selection of peer-reviewed articles, there are book, videotape, and software reviews, and a "forum" section for reader reactions and short essays.

21

Publication Title:
Human Resource Management
Publisher:
John Wiley & Sons, Inc.
605 Third Avenue
New York, NY 10158
800/825-7550
212/850-6021 (fax)
Issue Frequency:
Quarterly
Price:
$195; $125 for members of the Society for Human Resource Management (SHRM)
Description:
Described as a journal of strategy and innovation, it is co-sponsored by the University of Michigan Business School, SHRM, and John Wiley & Sons, publisher. It is a combination academic journal and report on workplace trends in human resources management, including training and learning.

22

Publication Title:
Human Resources Report (Bureau of National Affairs)
Publisher:
Bureau of National Affairs (BNA)
1231 25th St. NW
Washington DC 20037
800/372-1033
www.bna.com
Issue Frequency:
Weekly
Price:
$975
Description:
This is one of many reports in the general field of human resources and labor. The newsletter-type publications are available in print and electronic format. Archived reports are available on CD-ROM. The reports feature human resources developments from Capitol Hill, at state and federal regulatory agencies, in the courts, and inside companies across the country. Titles, in addition to the *Human Resources Report*, include *Union Labor Report*, *Bulletin to Management*, *HR Practitioners Guide*, and others.

23

Publication Title:
INFO-LINE
Publisher:
American Society for Training and Development
P.O. Box 1567
Merrifield, VA 22116
703/683-8100
703/683-1523
Issue Frequency:
Monthly
Price:
$10 single issue; $119/yr; quantity discounts
Description:
This is a series of booklets on a single training topic. Since *INFO-LINE* was introduced in 1984, over 400 topics have been covered. The content of the typical booklet covers: preliminary steps, key terms, benefits/advantages, potential implementation problems, do's and don'ts, guidelines, tips, techniques, roles/responsibilities, activities/exercises, materials, tools, evaluation standards, etc. *INFO-LINE* uses lists, diagrams, and other presentation devices extensively, and each issue includes a "job aid" and a lengthy list of references and resources (articles, books, video, and other media).

24

Publication Title:
Journal of Applied Behavioral Science
Publisher:
SAGE Publications, Inc.
2455 Teller Road
Thousand Oaks, CA 91320
805/499-9774
805/499-0871 (fax)
www.sagepub.com
Issue Frequency:
Quarterly
Price:
$66
Description:
Founded and sponsored by NTL, JABS is now in its 35th year. The academic journal focuses on the effects of evolutionary and planned change, including group dynamics, organization development, and social change.

25

Publication Title:
Journal of Career Development
Publisher:
Human Sciences Press
233 Spring St.
New York, NY 10013
212/620-8000
212/463-0742 (fax)
Issue Frequency:
Quarterly
Price:
$335 (institutional); $57 (personal)
Description:
Each issue of this journal consists of 6–8 articles on career development theory, research, and practice—with an emphasis on the impact that theory and research have on practice. Topics covered include career education, adult career development, career development of special-needs populations, career development and the family, and career and leisure. Occasionally, issues are thematic (e.g., "Evaluating Computer-Assisted Career Guidance Systems").

26

Publication Title:
Journal of European Industrial Training
Publisher:
MCB University Press North America
875 Massachusetts Ave., Suite 82
Cambridge, MA 02139
888/622-0075
www/mcb/co.uk/customer
Issue Frequency:
9/yr., plus online services
Price:
$7,429
Description:
The editorial objective of this journal is "to provide all those involved in training [and] training manage-

ment with current practice, ideas, news and research on major issues in organization development and employee education and training." The editors strive to provide a balance between the theory and practice of training, and they favor articles based on experience and evidence. Most issues include 5 or 6 major articles, though there are occasional special issues that consist of a single monograph. In addition, each regular issue includes new items, information about training products and services, and book reviews. Includes CD-ROM, online edition, and Internet chatrooms.

27

Publication Title:
Journal of Instruction Delivery Systems
Publisher:
Learning Technology Institute
50 Culpeper St.
Warrenton, VA 22186
540/347-0055
540/349-3169 (fax)
Issue Frequency:
Quarterly
Price:
$60 per year for non-members
Description:
This quarterly journal is devoted to enhancing productivity through the appropriate application of technology in education, training, and job performance. The journal's purpose is to heighten awareness of technology-based learning system capabilities, to present information on applications and issues related to technology-based learning systems, and make them accessible to all who are interested.

28

Publication Title:
Journal of Interactive Instruction Development
Publisher:
Learning Technology Institute
50 Culpeper St.
Warrenton, VA 22186
540/347-0055
540/349-3169 (fax)
Issue Frequency:
Quarterly
Price:
$60 for non-members

Description:
The object of this journal is to enhance quality, effectiveness, and productivity in the design of interactive instructional systems. It covers strategies and techniques of design, tools and templates, objective discussion of the facilities provided by different hardware and software systems, and commentary on issues related to interactive program design. The audience includes HRD professionals, software/courseware developers, designers and vendors, academic leaders, and government officials. Although a technical, scholarly publication, the journal focuses on practical approaches that can be understood by the entry-level designer.

29

Publication Title:
Journal of Organizational Excellence
Publisher:
John Wiley & Sons, Inc.
605 Third Avenue
New York, NY 10158
800/825-7550
212/850-6021 (fax)
www.wiley.com
Issue Frequency:
4 times per year
Price:
$399.00
Description:
This is an academic journal offering case studies and practical organizational research results. The focus is on realizing the value of human capital in achieving business success.

30

Publication Title:
Knowledge Management Review
Publisher:
Melcrum Publishing Ltd.
311 South Wacker Dr., Suite 4550
Chicago, IL 60606
877/226-2764
312/803-1871 (fax)
www.melcrum.com
Issue Frequency:
Bimonthly
Price:
$337

Description:
Knowledge Management Review is a publication that gives its subscribers a "one-stop" guide to the latest ideas and techniques in knowledge management. Knowledge Management Review provides its readers with corporate case studies, special reports, reviews and practitioners' insights as well as the following sections: Briefings, Q&A, Bookmarks, and a Calendar of all relevant conferences and KM events.

31

Publication Title:
Leader to Leader
Publisher:
Jossey-Bass Inc.
350 Sansome St.
San Francisco, CA 94104-9960
888/378-2537
800/605-2665 (fax)
www.jbp.com
Issue Frequency:
4/year
Price:
1 year (4 issues) $149; single issues $37.25
Description:
Leader to Leader is a quarterly report that brings leaders together to address the strategic issues we will face in the new millennium. This publication provides a forum for world-class leaders and thinkers to meet and share insights in their own words.

32

Publication Title:
Leadership & Organization Development Journal
Publisher:
MCB University Press North America
875 Massachusetts Ave., Suite 82
Cambridge, MA 02139
888/622-0075
www/mcb.co.uk
Issue Frequency:
7/yr., plus online services
Price:
$6,599
Description:
As the editors explain, this journal undertakes to "offer a sound balance between theory and practice, with articles based on experiences and evidence rather than just

philosophical encouragement." Some of the topics covered include: organizational culture, managing change, leadership issues, consultation, team building, conflict management, politics in organizations, organization development techniques, productivity, and communication. Both readers and contributors come from experienced organization development professionals in industry and the public sector, as well as in consulting firms and academia. Most issues consist of 4 or 5 major articles, plus conference reports, book reviews, article abstracts, and news of the field. Occasionally, issues are devoted to a single monograph.

33

Publication Title:
Leadership In Action
Publisher:
Jossey-Bass, Inc.
350 Sansome St.
San Francisco, CA 94104
800/274-4434
800/569-0443 (fax)
Issue Frequency:
6/yr.
Price:
$124
Description:
Formerly *Issues & Observations*. Primarily, this publication is a communication vehicle for the non-profit Center for Creative Leadership, reporting on the Center's research, publications, and seminars. In each issue, however, there is one major article, based on Center research, on some aspect of leadership or management development. These subjects are also addressed in each issue in several other shorter articles and columns that are of interest to practitioners of management and executive development. CCL's Website is www.ccl.org/publications.

34

Publication Title:
Learning Circuits
Publisher:
ASTD (American Society for Training & Development)
1640 King St., Box 1443
Alexandria, VA 22313
703/683-8100
703/683-1523 (fax)
www.learningcircuits.org
Issue Frequency:
12 issues/year; monthly
Price:
Free
Description:
This is ASTD's new (2000) Webzine. As expected it features reports of Web-based training and online learning of all sorts. It is practical in focus and has some features available to ASTD members only. A free e-mail newsletter based on *Learning Circuits* is called *Learning Circuits Express* and is available simply by signing up.

35

Publication Title:
Learning Decisions
Publisher:
The MASIE Center
P.O. Box 397
Saratoga Springs, NY 12866
800/956-2743
www.learningdecisions.com
Issue Frequency:
11/year
Price:
$195 plus online resources
Description:
This is an interactive online and print newsletter featuring issues in digital learning, presentation and analysis of issues including subscriber surveys and information sharing, research summaries product and services analyses. Subscribers receive discounts to MASIE Center conferences and events.

36

Publication Title:
The Learning Organization
Publisher:
MCB University Press North America
875 Massachusetts Ave., Suite 82
Cambridge, MA 02139
888/622-0075
www/mcb.co.uk/customer
Issue Frequency:
5/yr., plus online services
Price:
$649
Description:
Published for the first time in 1994, this journal presents articles that focus on the relationship between learning undertaken by managers as individuals and the continuous learning which occurs within organizations. This recognizes the need for organizations to harness the development activity which occurs for individuals so that the organization as a whole advances. As the economic and market conditions become more turbulent, the flexibility inherent in a learning organization will become of paramount importance. The journal publishes articles of relevance to human resource professionals, management development specialists, consultants, and individual managers who wish to grow their skills in tune with organizational requirements.

37

Publication Title:
Leverage
Publisher:
Pegasus Communications, Inc.
One Moody St.
Waltham, MA 02453
781/398-9700
781/894-7175 (fax)
www.pegasus.com
Issue Frequency:
12/yr (monthly)
Price:
$99
Description:
Leverage is designed to provide a forum for news, concepts, and sharing from the organizational learning community. Articles are written by academics, consultants, and managers in public and private corporations. A conference calendar is included. A free online newsletter is also available: *Leverage Points*.

38

Publication Title:
Managers Edge
Publisher:
Briefings Publishing Group
A Division of Financial Times Professional Inc.
1101 King St., Ste 110
Alexandria, VA 22314
703/548-3800
703/684-2136
www.briefings.com

Training Journals, Magazines, and Newsletters 375

Issue Frequency:
12/yr (monthly)
Price:
$97
Description:
The founding publisher of Managers Edge is *The Fred Pryor Report*. It is similar in concept and format to other Fred Pryor reports such as *Communication Briefings*. Articles are short. Sources do not have full attribution. Articles are actually selected abstracts and excerpts of current books and articles on management and leadership. Sources are provided for reader follow-up. Other "briefings" newsletters are also available. See Website or phone for other titles.

39

Publication Title:
Managing Employees Under FMLA & ADA
Publisher:
Clement Communications, Inc.
10 LaCrue Avenue
Concordville, PA 19331
800/345-8101
800/459-1933 (fax)
Issue Frequency:
Bi-weekly
Price:
$247
Description:
This 6-page newsletter provides strategies and techniques for dealing with The Family and Medical Leave Act (FMLA) and the Americans with Disabilities Act (ADA). Trainers will find this newsletter of use in classes to explain the FMLA and ADA to employees. Among the features in each issue are: breaking news, legislative updates, case studies, surveys, and court decisions.

40

Publication Title:
Marketing Contract Training
Publisher:
LERN
1550 Hayes Dr.
Manhattan, KS 66502
800/678-5376
888/234-8633
Issue Frequency:
12/yr (monthly)
Price:
$145

Description:
This newsletter from a non-profit lifelong learning organization is focused narrowly on the contract trainer. Articles are practical and provide specific help in marketing issues of all sorts. Internet reports and other networking services are included with the subscription.

41

Publication Title:
The Microcomputer Trainer
Publisher:
Systems Literacy, Inc.
6 Saint Lo Pl.
P.O. Box 1032
Hopatcong, NJ 07843
973/770-7762
973/770-2205 (fax)
www.systemsliteracy.com
Issue Frequency:
11/yr.
Price:
$195/yr.
Description:
Billed as providing "practical solutions and strategies for the professional responsible for building end-user skills," this newsletter presents practical, in-depth information with "tips" on everything. There is an emphasis on what successful trainers are doing, with samples of their work in the form of lists, course outlines, models, forms, illustrations, etc. Articles, case studies, and interviews report on the work of trainers in corporations, educational institutions, government, and the computer training industry, worldwide. Also available: an online newsletter, Quick Training Tips, featuring numerous trainer anecdotes. You can request free samples of both The Microcomputer Trainer and Quick Training Tips by checking the Website.

42

Publication Title:
Multimedia and Internet Training Newsletter
Publisher:
Brandon Hall, Ph.D.
690 W. Fremont Ave., Suite 10
Sunnyvale, CA 94087
408/736-2335
408/736-9425 (fax)
www.brandon-hall.com

Issue Frequency:
12/yr (monthly)
Price:
$189
Description:
This newsletter provides its readers with independent technology-based training information. You will learn about the latest industry trends and products, find out how to use technology-based training to save money and increase productivity, and read insightful editorials from industry experts. You will also have access to the following vital information:
• case studies showing viability of technology-based training
• return-on-investment studies that show how to reduce cost of training
• how to separate hype from reality using the internet and intranet for training
• instructional design for computer-based training
• interviews
• new product information
• industry trends
• program reviews
• upcoming events
• employment opportunities and more.

43

Publication Title:
Online Learning News
Publisher:
VNU Business Media
50 S. Ninth Street
Minneapolis, MN 55402
www.vnulearning.com
Issue Frequency:
Weekly
Price:
free
Description:
This is a truly interactive online newsletter with a broad base of subscribers who share questions and answers on the practice and process of e-learning. Contact information and leads for more information are always included. Well-known and experienced editorial team.

44

Publication Title:
Performance Improvement

Publisher:
  International Society for Performance Improvement
  1300 L St., NW, Suite 1250
  Washington, DC 20005
  202/408-7969
  202/408-7972 (fax)
Issue Frequency:
  Monthly except for combined May/June and November/December issues
Price:
  Included in annual membership dues of $125; $69 per year for non-members
Description:
  NSPI's official journal is dedicated to the advancement of performance science and technology. *PI* publishes practical articles, theoretical and conceptual discussions, procedural models, research reports, case studies, book and software reviews, and short essays on topics related to improving human performance.

45

Publication Title:
Performance Improvement Quarterly
Publisher:
  Learning Systems Institute
  Florida State University
  384 Hickory Wood Drive
  Crawfordville, FL 32327
  904/926-5266
  904/926-8694 (fax)
  (Subscription information from:)
  International Society for Performance Improvement
  1300 L St., NW, Suite 1250
  Washington, DC 20005–4107
  202/408-7969
  202/408-7972 (fax)
  www.ispi.org
Issue Frequency:
  Quarterly
Price:
  $50/yr. non-members; $22 students; $64 libraries
Description:
  This is a peer-reviewed journal that publishes scholarly works on performance technology, which the editors define as "a set of methods and processes for solving problems and realizing opportunities related to the performance of people." The journal's editorial content emphasizes original work involving technologies such as front-end analysis, systems thinking and strategic alignment, process redesign, design models, problem solving, and evaluation, and interventions such as motivation, mentoring, management development, reengineering, instruction, and performance support systems. Each issue includes 5–7 articles and special features: ERIC research abstracts, tables of contents from journals of interest to readers, and/or book reviews.

46

Publication Title:
People@Work
Publisher:
  Professional Training Associates, Inc.
  210 Commerce Blvd.
  Round Rock, TX 78664
  800/424-2112
  512/255-7532 (fax)
  www.hardatwork.com
Issue Frequency:
  12/year, monthly
Price:
  $72
Description:
  This is a newsletter full of a variety of short articles to help readers make "the most of your job and the people on your team." It is unique in its way of engaging the reader through quizzes, puzzles, and "what if" scenarios. With each issue, subscribers also receive a 4-page "in-depth" special report containing how-to guidance on a single topic. A recurring feature throughout the newsletter is "a bottom-line idea" or how-to tip.

47

Publication Title:
Quality Digest
Publisher:
  QCI International
  40 Declaration Dr., Ste. 100-C
  Chico, CA 95973
  530/893-4095
  530/893-0395 (fax)
Issue Frequency:
  12/year, monthly
Price:
  $59
Description:
  This magazine covers a broad range of quality issues in corporations, government, and non-profits. Articles tend to be short; advertisements are many, and provide the trainer with a good example of products available to help get the quality message out. The publication includes regular columns by A. Blanton Godfrey, Paul Scicchitano, and Ken Blanchard. Certifications and standards are common topics in most issues.

48

Publication Title:
Quality Progress
Publisher:
  American Society for Quality Control (ASQC)
  P.O. Box 3005
  Milwaukee, WI 53201-9488
  800/248-1946
  414/272-8575
Issue Frequency:
  12/year, monthly
Price:
  $60 non-members; free to members
Description:
  Quality Progress is a peer-reviewed journal with 85% of its feature articles written by quality professionals. Many of the issues addressed in the magazine deal with performance measurement and training for continuous improvement. Human resources issues associated with The Baldrige National Quality Award and ISO 9000 certification are found in many issues of the publication.

49

Publication Title:
Ragan's Positive Leadership
Publisher:
  Ragan Communications, Inc.
  316 N. Michigan Ave.
  Chicago, IL 60610
  800/878-5331
  312/960-4106 (fax)
  www.ragan.com
Issue Frequency:
  12/year

Price:
$89
Description:
The subtitle of this newsletter is "improving performance through value-centered management." Short articles are abstracts and adaptations of materials published within the last several years. Ask about other Ragan newsletters.

50

Publication Title:
Ragan's Strategic Training Report
Publisher:
Ragan Communications, Inc.
316 N. Michigan Ave.
Chicago, IL 60601
800/878-5331
312/960-4106 (fax)
www.ragan.com
Issue Frequency:
12/year, monthly
Price:
$169
Description:
This is a Ragan newsletter targeted to the training executive. It features articles on curriculum options, measurement practices, and the latest technology. It is problem-and-solution focused. Ask about other Ragan newsletters.

51

Publication Title:
Reflections: The SoL Journal
Publisher:
Reflections: The SoL Journal
222 Third St., Ste 2323
Cambridge, MA 02142
617/492-7236
617/577-1545 (fax)
www.mitpress.mit.edu/SOLJ
Issue Frequency:
Quarterly
Price:
$55
Description:
This journal from Massachusetts Institute of Technology (MIT) Press is a hybrid academic journal and magazine. It is fairly broad in scope, featuring contributions from researchers, consultants, and practitioners. It also includes poetry, photography, drawing, painting, and other types of artistic reflection. It is meant to be an eclectic, international, and intellectually diverse publication on managing knowledge, learning, and change.

52

Publication Title:
Report on Literacy Programs
Publisher:
Business Publishers, Inc.
951 Pershing Dr.
Silver Spring, MD 20910–4464
800/274-6737
301/589-5103
301/589-8493 (fax)
Issue Frequency:
25/yr.
Price:
$317 or $307 by e-mail
Description:
This 8-page newsletter is designed for those who administer adult literacy programs. It provides current intelligence on the public policy debate concerning adult literacy, as well as information about programs around the country. Another feature is notice of grants, contracts, and other funding sources. There is also notice of meetings and conferences in the literacy field, as well as details on books, reports, periodicals, curricula, software, and other resource materials on basic skills education. A special benefit to subscribers is access to a service called DocuDial that allows one to order by phone faxed copies of the full text of government studies, speeches, and other documents.

53

Publication Title:
Sloan Management Review
Publisher:
MIT Sloan School of Management
77 Massachusetts Ave., E53-416
Cambridge, MA 02139-4307
617/253-7170
617/258-9739 (fax)
Issue Frequency:
Quarterly
Price:
$89
Description:
This is an academic journal written by management academics, consultants, and practitioners and edited for professional managers. The emphasis is on general management issues, with special focus on organizational change, management of technology, and international management. Training issues associated with these topics are frequently discussed.

54

Publication Title:
Strategy and Business
Publisher:
Booz-Allen & Hamilton, Inc.
101 Park Ave.
New York, NY 10178
888/557-5550
617/723-3989 (fax)
www.strategy-business.com
Issue Frequency:
4/year
Price:
$38
Description:
This is a publication of a consulting company, launched in 1995 with a mission "to provoke readers with new ideas about business." In it are best practice reports and case studies, interviews with thought leaders, articles on strategy and competition, and research reports. Book reviews and "noteworthy quotes" are features of each issue.

55

Publication Title:
The Systems Thinker
Publisher:
Pegasus Communications, Inc.
One Moody St.
Waltham, MA 02453
800/272-0945
800/701-7083 (fax)
www.pegasus.com
Issue Frequency:
10/year
Price:
$139
Description:
This newsletter helps managers and leaders put systems thinking to work in their organizations. It introduces readers to tools and concepts of systems thinking. It is practical in focus and encourages readers to share innovative ideas and "systems stories."

56

Publication Title:
Team Leader
Publisher:
Dartnell Corporation
360 Hiatt Drive
Palm Beach Gardens, FL 33418
  800/621-5463
  561/622-2423 (fax)
  www.dartnellcorp.com
Issue Frequency:
Bi-weekly
Price:
$219 plus $17.50 shipping and handling; price reduction on multiple copies
Description:
This 4-page newsletter is one of many newsletters published by Dartnell Corporation. Like the others, it is written simply and articles are short, often in bullet-list format for easy reading. Most articles have neither attribution source nor byline of writers. It is meant to give the reader practical techniques on facilitating the work of teams. Another Dartnell newsletter on teams is *Teamwork: Manufacturing*. Check their Website for more information.

57

Publication Title:
Team Management Briefings
Publisher:
Team Management Briefings
1101 King Street, Ste 110
Alexandria, VA 22314
  800/722-9221
  703/684-2136
  www.combriefings.com
Issue Frequency:
Monthly
Price:
$99
Description:
This 8-page newsletter consists of short articles, bullet lists, checklists, and brief abstracts of recent business publications on teams. The newsletter's subtitle is "Ideas for Building the Winning, High-Performance Organization."

58

Publication Title:
TechTrends for Leaders in Education & Training
Publisher:
Association for Educational Communications and Technology (AECT)
1800 North Stone Lake Dr., Suite 2
Bloomington, IN 47404
  202/624-9731
  812/355-7675 (voice)
  812/355-7678 (fax)
  www.aect.org
Issue Frequency:
6/yr.
Price:
$50; free to AECT members
Description:
Described as being directed to "leaders in education and training," this is the official publication of the Association for Educational Communications and Technology. Although it welcomes articles "on any aspect of new technology in education and training in schools, colleges and private industry," most of the articles in this publication are by educators and for educators. All feature articles are reviewed by experts in the field before acceptance for publication. Recent issues have focused on distance learning, interactive video, CBT, CD-ROM, and hypermedia. Other features of the magazine include news of the field, interviews, abstracts from the ERIC database, descriptions of new books and software, profiles of new hardware products, and a calendar of events.

59

Publication Title:
T&D
Publisher:
American Society for Training and Development, Inc.
1640 King St., Box 1443
Alexandria, VA 22313–2043
  703/683-8100
  703/683-8103 (fax)
Issue Frequency:
Monthly
Price:
Included in dues of national ASTD members; $85/yr. to non-members
Description:
As the monthly magazine of the American Society for Training and Development, this is, by definition, the flagship publication in the industry of HRD and workplace performance. Each issue includes 12–13 in-depth feature articles with practical, how-to information—written primarily by practitioners for practitioners. Departments include: "News You Can Use" with short news items covering the trends, approaches, and happenings in the field. A special section, "@work," lists current online resources. "FaxForum" lets readers share opinions and experiences on work-related topics. "Training 101" covers the basic concepts and techniques of the profession. "Career Power" gives tips on personal and professional development. "Working Life" is a lively wrap-up of issues and anecdotes from the world of work. Other columns include reactions from readers via letter, fax, and e-mail; descriptions and contact information on new products and services; up-to-date reports on the state of technology; and "Marketplace," a one-stop shopping guide to suppliers and consultants. Global issues are often featured.

60

Publication Title:
Training Directors' Forum Newsletter (online only)
Publisher:
Bill Communications
50 South Ninth St.
Lakewood Building
Minneapolis, MN 55402
  612/333-0471
  612/333-6526 (fax)
  www.trainingsupersite.com
Issue Frequency:
Frequent updates
Price:
Free
Description:
This online newsletter is designed as a communication vehicle among training directors and other leaders of the HRD field. It is completely experience-based, and most articles are detailed and specific descriptions of "how they do it," using input from training managers and directors. The subjects covered include every aspect of the administration of the training function, plus a wide variety of training programs, projects, techniques, etc.

61

Publication Title:
TRAINING Magazine
Publisher:
Bill Communications
50 South Ninth St.
Lakewood Building
Minneapolis, MN 55402
612/333-0471
612/333-6526 (fax)
Issue Frequency:
Monthly
Price:
$78 per year
Description:
This magazine is well-known to every professional trainer. It covers the full range of training and development topics through a mix of articles written by the magazine's staff (in their characteristically lively style) and by practicing trainers, consultants, suppliers, etc. Many issues include a special editorial supplement on a particular training subject. The supplements on off-site training meetings and on presentation technologies feature a "marketplace directory" of suppliers in these areas. Then every year in October, the magazine publishes its *Industry Report*, (available separately for $35) the results of its nationwide survey of training practices: types of training being provided, who is being trained, modes of training delivery, budgets, etc. This survey also covers salaries, and the following issue (November) reports extensively on the trainer salary information that is collected. In addition, each monthly issue of *TRAINING Magazine* includes numerous short articles (on research events, training practices, etc.), letters from readers, calendars of conferences and seminars, reviews of books and films, and extensive listings of new products.

62

Publication Title:
Training Media Review
Publisher:
TMR Publications
P.O. Box 381822
Cambridge, MA 02238-1822
877/532-1838 (toll-free)
617/661-1095 (editor)
617/661-1797 (fax)
www.tmreview.com

Issue Frequency:
6/yr. plus special issues
Price:
$79 (6 bimonthly issues and online access); e-mail edition $59
Description:
This newsletter features candid reviews of training videos and multimedia software. Written by working trainers, the reviews include (1) key information about the title (producer, running time, price, supplementary materials); (2) a 200- to 1,000-word review; and (3) ratings (1 to 4 stars) on ability to hold viewer attention, acting/presenting, instructional value, production quality, value of content, portrayal and casting of women/minorities, instructional value, value for the money—and an overall rating. There are 10–12 reviews in each issue, drawn from some 200 producers monitored by the editors. Occasionally, reviews of videos on a particular subject are grouped together. Apart from the reviews, there are a variety of other features in an issue, including industry news (e.g., notes about new video releases).

63

Publication Title:
Web Content Report
Publisher:
Ragan Communications, Inc.
316 N. Michigan Ave., Ste 300
Chicago, IL 60601
800/878-5331
312/960-4105 (fax)
www.ragan.com
Issue Frequency:
12/year, monthly
Price:
$249
Description:
This newsletter reports on practical, effective ways various organizations have created Websites that keep audiences and users coming back. It is full of short real-life stories and designs for Websites that work. Issues are full of tips and contact persons at sites.

64

Publication Title:
What's Working in Human Resources

Publisher:
Progressive Business Publications
370 Technology Dr.
Malvern, PA 19355
800/220-5000
610/647-8089 (fax)
Issue Frequency:
Semimonthly except December
Price:
$299/year
Description:
This is an 8-page newsletter of short and information-rich articles. Phone numbers and specific citations are given in each article for further exploration. Performance boosters, legal issues, and case studies on difficult issues are found in most editions. "Training & Development" is a regular feature. Ask for information on other publications.

65

Publication Title:
Workforce
Publisher:
ACC Communications Inc.
245 Fischer Ave., B-2
Costa Mesa, CA 92628
714/751-1883
714/751-4106 (fax)
www.workforceonline.com
Issue Frequency:
12/year, monthly
Price:
$59/year
Description:
This magazine focuses on issues of concern to personnel managers and others such as trainers with direct responsibility for workforce development. The magazine has a particular interest in human resources issues created by implementation and changes in employment law and by changes in the composition of the workforce. Global issues are frequently featured.

66

Publication Title:
Working Smarter with Powerpoint
Publisher:
One On One Computer Training
A Division of Mosaic Media, Inc.
2055 Army Trail Road, Ste. 100
Addision, IL 60101
800/424-8668
630/628-0550 (fax)
www.oootraining.com
Issue Frequency:
Bi-weekly

Price:
$27.99
Quantity discounts available
Description:
This very practical 4-page newsletter is aimed at the everyday user of Powerpoint. It is a publication that calls itself "simply the most cost-effective training solution available." The publisher offers a free upgrade on the newsletter to reflect upgrades in your Powerpoint software.

67

Publication Title:
Working Together

Publisher:
Dartnell Corporation
360 Hiatt Drive
Palm Beach Gardens, FL 33418
800/621-5463
561/622-2423 (fax)
www.dartnellcorp.com
Issue Frequency:
Bi-weekly
Price:
$219 plus $17.50 shipping and handling; price reduction on multiple copies
Description:
This 4-page newsletter is one of many newsletters published by Dartnell Corporation. Like the others, it is written simply and the articles are short, often in bullet list format for easy reading. Some of the articles contain references to original sources, but many do not. It is meant to give the reader practical tips on building working relationships around issues of diversity, management and structural change, ethics, and behavior. Content is broader than the typical diversity publication.

6.8 Training Websites

This final section of *The Trainer's Almanac 2002* is organized in two parts, an introductory section on representative **E-Learning Web Resources**, and a concluding section on **Ratings of Training Websites**. In both parts our goal is to motivate you to seek further information, to get a feel for Website resource range and evaluation, and to provide you with organizing suggestions and ways of looking at Web resources that can help you find the right information for your needs.

For this section's database, we have culled information from various sources. Among these are listings, commentaries, and advertisements in current business periodicals and online newsletters; *TrainSeek.com*'s e-commerce Website; *LGuide.com*'s **E-Learning Industry Directory**; ASTD's Web guru, Ryann Ellis (rellis@astd.org), The MASIE Center, *MASIE.com*; *shrm.org*'s **Web Site Training Databases**; *brandon-hall.com*'s **E-Learning Vendor Directory**; and Lakewood Publications' *TrainingSupersite.com*. We make no attempt to be inclusive of all directories; the field of Website resource management is so complex that such an exercise would be futile. ASTD, for example, estimates that there are currently more than 650,000 e-Learning courses alone on the Web (**T+D** magazine, June 2001, p. 17). The *TrainSeek.com* database claims more than 1 million offerings (SHRM White Paper by Kondrasuk and Auerbach, accessed on the SHRM Website on April 17, 2001). We simply give you suggestions of ways to make sense of information and tempt you to look deeper. We also suggest that you experiment with search engines and meta-search tools. These are some that might be helpful:

AltaVista   ixquick
Dogpile   Lycos
Excite   MetaCrawler
extremesearcher.com   Northern Light
Fast Search   ProFusion
Freepint.co.uk   searchengineshowdown.com
Google   searchenginewatch.com
HotBot   Yahoo!

We caution you that information is no longer free, and that prices vary widely for directory and evaluation documents— so the bad news is that buyers must beware and be informed. We have chosen a small sample of responsible resource providers to lead you onward in your own quest. We are particularly grateful to Matt Tews of Lakewood Publications' *TrainingSupersite.com* for granting us permission to download and reprint the **Ratings of Training Websites**. E-Learning, is, after all, e-commerce, and obviously affected by market pressures and fluctuations. The good news this year is that there's been a major improvement in vendors' and organizations' ability to maintain their Websites; we encourage you to check Websites listed throughout this section for updates beyond their copyright dates as this book goes to press.

E-Learning Web Resources

Authoring Tools

Cybermax, Inc.
www.cybermax.com

Global Knowledge Network, Inc.
www.globalknowledge.com

Jenzabar
www.Jenzabar.com

Learning Stream, Inc.
www.learningstream.net

Quest 6.0
www.mentergy.com

SWIFT Author 5.0
www.Geminielearningsolutions.com

Toolbook II Instructor 8
www.click2learn.com

Trainersoft 7 Professional
www.trainersoft.com

Web Learning Studio
www.macromedia.com

Online Course Publishers

Achieve Global
www.achieveglobal.com

Digital Think
www.digitalthink.com

Element K
www.elementk.com

Harvard Business School Publishing
www.hbsp.harvard.edu 800/795-5200

Knowledge Quest
www.knowledgequest.com

Learn2.com
www.learn2.com

Netg
www.netg.com

Pearson Technology
Group Interactive
www.pearsonptg.com

Skill Soft
www.skillsoft.com

Learning Management Systems

Docent
www.docent.com

Information Mapping Inc.
www.infomap.com

KnowledgePlanet
www.knowledgeplanet.com

LeadingWay Corporation
www.leadingway.com

mGen, Inc.
www.mgen.com

MindLeaders
www.mindleaders.com

Performance Impact
www.knowledgepoint.com

RealTime 360
www.realtimeperformance.com

SkillSpace
www.skillspace.com

E-Learning Consulting

Advance Online, Inc.
www.advance.com

Brandon-Hall.com
www.brandon-hall.com

Corporate University Xchange
www.corpu.com

Eduprise
www.eduprise.com

ExpressLearning, Inc.
www.expresslearning.com

Interact Multimedia
www.interactmultimedia.com

The MASIE Center
www.masie.com

RWD Technologies
www.rwd.com

TutorPro
www.tutorpro.com

Website Databases

ASK International
www.askintl.com

America's Learning eXchange
www.alx.com

IVID Communication
www.ivid.com

L Guide
www.lguide.com

Seminar Finder
www.seminarfinder.com

SyberWorks Inc.
www.syberworks.com

THINQ
www.thinq.com

The Training Registry
www.trainingregistry.com

Trainseek
www.trainseek.com

Ratings of Training Websites

Over 250 Websites have been objectively evaluated and rated by an independent rater in this study sponsored by Lakewood Publications. This listing is a download from Lakewood's TrainingSuperSite, *www.trainingsupersite.com.*

Alphabetic Index by Category

We have chosen this listing by rank of the Web resource. Other representations of the list are available by choosing other options for viewing it on the site itself. Each item in the list here is further categorized according to the type of resource it is. The two capital letters at the beginning of each item are a key to the category of resource. These are:

BP	Books and Products Sites
CL	Commercial Sites
GA	Government Agency Sites
JN	Journals and Newsletters Sites
OR	Organization Sites
RT	Research Tools Sites
TR	Training Resources Sites
VL	Value-Added Sites

The list of Websites can be accessed and sorted through each of these categories, and downloaded by single category to focus your search more intentionally.

A-B-Cs of the Site Rating

Lakewood's Master List of Links contains no sites with a rating lower than C minus, although many "D" and "F" sites were reviewed. While some of the sites on the master list are academic and somewhat tangential to training, the vast majority are readily usable. Sites which did not function as advertised were culled from the list.

Methodology

Study Purpose

An independent research service was hired to analyze the World Wide Web and select those sites related to training, or which may prove to be (or provide links to) valuable online resources to trainers and to provide an unbiased rating system to help users get the most from the World Wide Web as a resource tool.

Study Duration
The study began in October 1996 and was completed in January 1997.

Criteria for Site Identification
No limitations were placed on the sites reviewed. None were eliminated due to competitiveness of products or services, nor included due to any special considerations.

Scope of Study
As with the criteria for site identification, no limitations were placed on site selection methods that were used. They include:

Requests for input from subscribers on three major training listservs. No indication was given that the sites were for a comparative analysis.

C/NET, PR Newswire, Z-D Press, Business Wire and other news services were monitored daily to filter out site URL information on sites which might be of potential value for the study.

Newsgroups such as NewsBytes, DejaNews, and others were combed weekly to find sites of interest.

Internet-savvy trainers were polled as to what sites they used regularly.

World Wide Web site guides (New Riders and others) were reviewed.

Searched the World Wide Web (using two browsers: Microsoft Internet Explorer and Netscape Navigator 3.0) using a variety of search engines, indices, and directories (Lycos, World Wide Web Worm, Galaxy, Infoseek, Excite, Hot Bot, Yahoo, Webcrawler, Open Text, and hosts of others).

Findings
From mid-October 1996, through January 15, 1997, 10,200 Websites out of the 600,000 plus that claimed to discuss some aspect of "training" were investigated for their value to human resource, motivation, sales, and productivity trainers.

It took very liittle time to determine "training" is a broad term encompassing weight training, baseball spring training, dog obedience, and even some mysterious aspect of hair beautification. Sites were weeded out as they slipped through the various Boolean algebraic strings used, but still several thousand site choices remained. From the remaining sites, 255 (2.5% of the original 10,200) were chosen as high-potential sites for inclusion in the study.

Undoubtedly, some sites were missed, which could have been included and others were selected, which may not have universal appeal.

Site Classification
For the purposes of the study, sites were divided into eight categories: (1) Books and Products; (2) Commercial Links; (3) Government Agencies; (4) Journals and Newsletters; (5) Organizations; (6) Research Tools; (7) Training Resources; and (8) Value-Added Links. All are described in more depth under SITE CATEGORIES and RATING SYSTEM.

Of the 255 sites selected, 12 are Books and Products, 36 are Commercial Links, 18 are Government Agencies, 25 are Journals and Newsletters, 39 are Organizations, 41 are Research Tools, 51 are Training Resources, and 32 are Value-Added Links.

Ratings
Each site has been rated according to the criteria detailed in the SITE CATEGORIES and RATING SYSTEM. Sites rated lower than a "C-" were discarded in favor of higher rated sites.

URL Transfer
The URL for each site appears in a field of the analysis tables. It is not a "live" link (selecting one will not take you to the site described). The links are provided for further research only. The analysis tables can be printed, and the individual sites can be accessed by typing them into a browser. The addresses can also be lifted directly from the table and pasted to the browser's address window, if desired.

DISCLAIMER: *These sites have been rated by an independent third-party, whose ratings do not reflect the interests or opinions of TrainingSuperSite, or of its sponsors Training Magazine and WingsNet. This analysis does not promote itself as being all-inclusive, current, nor regularly updated. Sites were rated based on content and design at the time of initial access. No attempts have been made to re-access these sites and update the ratings based on improvements, or planned enhancements (although this is being discussed).*

Training Websites

The following chart describes the site rating system:

A+	Top level site. High level of usability. Attractive. Information packed. Current.
A	Excellent site. Very usable. Appealing. Plenty of information. Good interest.
A–	Excellent site. Minor flaw or paucity of information keeps it from an A or A+.
B+	Very good site. Usable. Good information. A better-than-average site overall.
B	Good site. Usable. Good information. May be short on ambiance or content.
B–	Good site with a flaw. May have an out-of-date link. May be slow to load.
C+	Average site. May be put together a little awkwardly. Still has value.
C	Average. A take-it-or-leave-it site. Take a higher rated site if available.
C–	Ho hum. OK, but just barely. Included only if info cannot be found elsewhere.

This list of ratings of Websites in this section of *The Trainer's Almanac* is reprinted with permission from TrainingSuperSite (*www.trainingsupersite.com*) Bill Communications. Copyright 1997–1998. Website accessed August 15, 2001.

All Sites, Listed by Rank

Sites are listed by ranking (alphabetically within ranks).

BP	Amazon.com Books	http://www.amazon.com/exec/obidos/subst/index2.html	A+
VL	Argus ClearingHouse	http://www.clearinghouse.net/	A+
TR	Big Dog's HR Development Page	http://www.nwlink.com/~donclark/hrd.html	A+
TR	CMC Information Services	http://www.december.com/cmc/info/	A+
VL	Comic Strip®	http://www.unitedmedia.com/comics/	A+
VL	Dilbert Zone	http://www.unitedmedia.com/comics/dilbert/	A+
VL	Dilbert's Daily Mental Workout	http://www.unitedmedia.com/comics/dilbert/ddmw/	A+
JN	Electronic Newsstand	http://www.enews.com/	A+
RT	EZ Connect Search Directory	http://www.ezconnect.com//home.htm	A+
JN	Future Net	http://www.futurenet.co.uk/	A+
TR	Home for Intranet Planners	http://www.kensho.com/hip/	A+
RT	InfoSeek Search Engine	http://www.infoseek.com/	A+
JN	Intranet Design Magazine	http://www.innergy.com/	A+
GA	Library of Congress	http://marvel.loc.gov/	A+
RT	LISTZ Directory of E-Mail Discussion Groups	http://www.liszt.com/	A+
VL	Mercury Mail	http://www.merc.com/	A+
JN	Newsletter Library	http://pub.savvy.com/	A+
VL	Newspapers Online	http://www.newspapers.com/	A+
RT	Open Text Index	http://index.opentext.net/	A+
RT	Publicly Accessible Mailing Lists	http://www.neosoft.com/internet/paml/	A+
VL	Smart Business Super Site	http://www.smartbiz.com/	A+
GA	Superintendent of Documents	http://www.access.gpo.gov/su_docs/	A+
JN	Training Magazine	http://www.lakewoodpub.com/	A+
TR	Training Net	http://www.trainingnet.com/	A+
CL	Training Registry	http://www.tregistry.com/	A+
TR	TRDEV-L - Training and Development Home Page	http://train.ed.psu.edu/TRDEV-L	A+
CL	Ultimate Industry Connection	http://www.hardware.com/complist.html	A+
VL	URL Minder	http://www.netmind.com/URL-minder/	A+
GA	US Government Printing Office	http://www.access.gpo.gov/	A+
TR	World Economic & Business Development Resources	http://www.mecnet.org/edr/	A+
RT	World Fax Directory	http://infolab.ms.wwa.com/wtx/m_r.htm	A+
JN	+Value: MoreValue.com	http://www.gonogo.com/	A
VL	A-Word-A-Day Home Page	http://lrdc5.lrdc.pitt.edu/awad/home.html	A
OR	Academy of Human Resource Development	http://www.ahrd.org/	A

Training Websites

OR	Academy of Human Resource Development	http://www.ahrd.org/	A
RT	Access Business Online	http://www.clickit.com/touch/accbiz.htm	A
TR	Adult Education Collection at Syracuse University	http://web.syr.edu/~ancharte/resource.html	A
CL	Advanced Leadership Group	http://www.adv-leadership-grp.com/	A
RT	AltaVista Search Engine	http://www.altavista.digital.com/	A
VL	America's Job Bank	http://www.ajb.dni.us/	A
OR	American Compensation Association	http://www.ahrm.org/aca/aca.htm	A
OR	American Council on International Personnel	http://www.ahrm.org/acip/acip.htm	A
OR	American Management Association	http://www.amanet.org/	A
OR	American Productivity and Quality Center	http://www.apqc.org/	A
OR	American Society for Training and Development	http://www.astd.org/	A
OR	ASAE Online Association Directory	http://www.asaenet.org/gateway/OnlineAssocDir.html	A
CL	Ask the Expert - Bob Pike	http://www.training-info.com/expert/pike.html	A
TR	AskERIC	http://ericir.syr.edu/	A
OR	Association of Federal Technology Transfer Executives	http://www.datasync.com/	A
RT	AT&T Toll Free Internet Directory	http://www.tollfree.dir.att.net/	A
TR	Atlas Web Workshop	http://ua1vm.ua.edu/~crispen/atlas.html	A
VL	Awesome Lists	http://www.princeton.edu/~rcurtis/aee.html	A
JN	Business Week Online	http://www.businessweek.com/	A
JN	Catalog Mart	http://catalog.savvy.com/	A
GA	CDC National Aids Clearinghouse	http://cdcnac.org/	A
OR	Center for Internet-Based Training	http://www.internet-basedtraining.com/	A
CL	Center for Mgmt and Org Effectiveness	http://www.thecoach.com/	A
OR	Center for the Study of Work Teams	http://www.workteams.unt.edu/	A
CL	Change Technologies	http://www.city-net.com/changetech/	A
VL	CNBC News	http://www.cnbc.com/	A
RT	CNET Search Site	http://www.search.com/	A
VL	CNN Interactive	http://www.cnn.com/	A
JN	Communications Week	http://techweb.cmp.com/cw/cwi/	A
TR	Computer Training Network	http://www.crctraining.com/training/	A
TR	Consultant Resource Center	http://www.consultant-center.com/	A
VL	Corporate Financials Online	http://www.cfonews.com/	A
CL	Covey Leadership Center	http://www.covey.com/	A
CL	Creative Training Techniques International, Inc.	http://www.cttbobpike.com/	A
JN	Customer Service Review	http://www.csr.co.za/	A

CL	Cyber State University	http://cyberstateu.com/	A
RT	DejaNews News Group Search Engine	http://www.dejanews.com/	A
JN	Directory of Electronic Journals and Newsletters	http://arl.cni.org/scomm/edir/	A
RT	dNet Directory Central	http://www.d-net.com/	A
VL	E-Minder	http://www.netmind.com/e-minder/e-minder.html	A
RT	E-ZINE-LIST	http://www.meer.net/~johnl/e-zine-list/	A
RT	Education Index	http://www.educationindex.com/	A
JN	Educational Technology Journal	http://www.pacificrim.net/~mckenzie/	A
OR	Employee Assistance Professionals Association	http://www.ahrm.org/eapa/eapa.htm	A
CL	Excellence in Training Corporation	http://www.extrain.com/	A
RT	Excite Search Engine	http://www.excite.com/	A
JN	Fortune	http://pathfinder.com/@@D9OHhwQAq24kTKSx/fortune/	A
RT	FTP Search 3.3	http://ftpsearch.ntnu.no/	A
VL	Funny Bone Home Page	http://www.indirect.com/www/nunley/bone/index.html	A
RT	Galaxy Search Engines (Professionals)	http://www.einet.net/	A
JN	Georgia Center Quarterly	http://www.gactr.uga.edu/GCQ/gcq.html	A
JN	High Technology Careers	http://hightechcareers.com/	A
RT	HotMail - World's Free Web-Based E-Mail Site	http://www.hotmail.com/	A
TR	HR Headquarters	http://www.hrhq.com/	A
BP	HRD Press	http://www.hrdpress.com/	A
OR	Human Resource Planning Society	http://www.ahrm.org/hrps/hrps.htm	A
JN	Information Week	http://techweb.cmp.com/iw/613/	A
OR	Institute for Learning Sciences	http://www.ils.nwu.edu/	A
OR	Institute for Learning Technologies	http://www.ilt.columbia.edu/	A
OR	International Association for Information Management	http://www.ihrim.org/	A
OR	International Personnel Management Association	http://www.ipma-hr.org/	A
CL	Internet and Online Industry Sourcebook Online	http://www.internetsourcebook.com/	A
VL	Internet Business Connection	http://www.intbc.com/	A
VL	Internet Pizza Server	http://www.ecst.csuchico.edu/~pizza/	A
TR	Internet Training Center Training Links	http://world.std.com/~walthowe/tnglinks.htm	A
RT	INTERNIC Services Directory	http://ds.internic.net/	A
JN	Intranet Journal	http://www.intranetjournal.com/ijx/	A
JN	IT Training	http://www.train-net.co.uk/it/	A

JN	iWorld	http://www.iworld.com/	A
JN	Journal of Industrial Teacher Education	http://scholar.lib.vt.edu/ejournals/JITE/jite.html	A
RT	Library of Congress Search Tools	http://lcweb.loc.gov/global/search.html	A
RT	Link Star Business Directory	http://www.linkstar.com/	A
RT	Lycos Search Engine	http://www.lycos.com/	A
CL	Masie Center	http://www.masie.com	A
CL	Microsoft Office	http://www.microsoft.com/office/	A
CL	Microsoft Training & Certification	http://www.microsoft.com/train_cert/	A
GA	NASA Online Educational Resources	http://www.nasa.gov/nasa_online_education.html	A
OR	National Center on Adult Education	http://litserver.literacy.upenn.edu	A
GA	National Institute of Standards and Technology	http://www.nist.gov/	A
GA	National Performance Review	http://www.npr.gov/	A
JN	Net Smart	http://www.microsoft.com/industry/acc/pages/intra-en.htm	A
CL	NeverForget	http://www.neverforget.com/	A
VL	News.Com	http://www.news.com/	A
OR	Organization Development Network	http://www.odnet.org/	A
VL	PR Newswire	http://www.prnewswire.com/	A
OR	Professional Society for Sales and Marketing Training	http://www.smt.org/	A
JN	Quality Improvement Newsletter	http://www.ccc.govt.nz/Library/Connect/42Peters.html	A
TR	Resources for Internet Training	http://world.std.com/~walthowe/training.htm	A
TR	San Diego State University EdWeb	http://edweb.sdsu.edu/	A
VL	Science in the Headlines	http://www2.nas.edu/new/newshead.htm	A
VL	Shareware	http://www.shareware.com/	A
OR	Society for Applied Learning Technology	http://www.salt.org/	A
OR	Society for Human Resource Management	http://www.shrm.org/	A
OR	Society for Technical Communication	http://stc.org/	A
VL	Stat-USA	http://www.stat-usa.gov/	A
CL	Sterling Speakers Bureau	http://members.aol.com/speakers2u/meetings.htm	A
RT	Switchboard Business Directory	http://www.switchboard.com/	A
TR	Syllabus Web Top 40 Education Sites	http://www.syllabus.com/top40.htm	A
CL	TASL - Training and Seminar Locators	http://www.tasl.com/	A
BP	Tech Expo Product and Literature Showcase	http://www.techexpo.com/home_pg.html/	A
VL	Trade Show Central	http://www.tscentral.com/	A
VL	Trade Show Central	http://www.tscentral.com/	A
TR	TRAIN - Australian Training Information Network	http://www.opennet.net.au/partners/bvet/train/topics.htm	A

TR	Training and Development Via the Internet	http://cac.psu.edu/~cxl18/trdev/	A
TR	Training Forum Speakers Database	http://www.trainingforum.com/Speakers/index.html	A
TR	Training Net	http://www.trainingnet.com/	A
TR	Training Net Magazine	http://www.trainingnet.com/magazine/magazine.html-ssi	A
TR	Training Resource Access Center	http://trainingaccesscenter.com/	A
BP	TrainingSpace Online	http://www.trainingspace.com/	A
TR	TRDEV-L Training Summaries (Pennsylvania State Univ.)	http://cac.psu.edu/~cxl18/trdev-l/summary.html	A
VL	UPS	http://www.ups.com/	A
GA	US Department of Labor OSHA Information	http://www.osha-slc.gov/	A
GA	US Federal Government Agencies	http://www.lib.lsu.edu/gov/fedgov.html	A
TR	Walt Howe's Internet Learning Center	http://world.std.com/~walthowe/index.html	A
RT	Web Search - Computer and Communication URLs	http://www.cmpcmm.com/cc/	A
RT	Web Technology Super Site	http://www.techweb.com/	A
RT	Webcrawler Search Engine	http://www.webcrawler.com/	A
TR	Wellness on the Web	http://planet-hawaii.com/wellnet/allco2.html	A
RT	WhoWhere? Directory Search	http://www.whowhere.com/about.html	A
RT	World Pages Phone, E-Mail and Web Search	http://www.worldpages.com/	A
RT	World Post Business Research	http://www.worldpost.com/research.html	A
VL	WWW Measurements Converter	http://www.mplik.ru/~sg/transl/	A
RT	Yahoo Search Engine	http://www.yahoo.com/	A
RT	Ahoy - Home Page Finder	http://ahoy.cs.washington.edu:6060/	A–
OR	Association for Experiential Education	http://www.princeton.edu/~rcurtis/aee.html	A–
VL	Automatic Complaint Letter Generator	http://www-csag.cs.uiuc.edu/individual/pakin/complaint	A–
TR	Bill Communications	http://www.billcom.com/	A–
JN	Career Magazine	http://www.careermag.com/	A–
OR	Distance Learning Association	http://www.usdla.org/	A–
GA	Education and Training (White House)	http://www.gsa.gov/	A–
TR	Educom	http://educom.edu/	A–
OR	EdWeb Home Room	http://edweb.cnidr.org:90/resource.cntnts.html	A–
CL	Employease, Inc.	http://www.employease.com/	A–
OR	Ethics Resource Center	http://www.lmco.com/erc/	A–
CL	ExpertSpace Speakers	http://www.expertspace.com/	A–
GA	Federal Information Exchange	http://www.fie.com/	A–
CL	Help Desk Institute	http://www.tregistry.com/ttr/hdi.htm	A–
RT	ICS Ultimate Search Page	http://www.internethub.com/search.html	A–

Training Websites

BP	IIR Technology	http://www.iir.co.za/	A–
RT	Inter-Link Search Engine	http://www.nova.edu/Inter-Links/	A–
OR	International Organization for Standardization	http://www.iso.ch/	A–
CL	International Quality and Productivity Center	http://www.iqpc.com/	A–
TR	Internet Documentation and IETF Information	http://www.internic.net/ds/dspg0intdoc.html	A–
BP	Internet Training & Consulting Services	http://www.itcs.com/	A–
BP	Internet Videos	http://www.webcom.com/~ivi/	A–
RT	InterNic Directory of Directories	http://ds.internic.net/ds/dsdirofdirs.html	A–
RT	Meta Crawler Search Engine	http://metacrawler.cs.washington.edu:8080/	A–
TR	National Centre for Vocational Education Research (Aust.)	http://www.ncver.edu.au/ncver.htm	A–
CL	Networked Learning	http://www.knowab.co.uk/nl.html	A–
TR	PC Trainer's Gateway	http://www.isitraining.com/gateway.html	A–
CL	Quality Improvement Newsletter	http://www.weber.edu/QualityNews/QualityNews-0296.htm	A–
TR	Que Education & Training	http://www.mcp.com/queet/linx0311.html	A–
OR	Society of Competitive Intelligence Professionals	http://www.scip.org/	A–
CL	TCM - T&D Resource Center	http://www.tcm.com/trdev/	A–
CL	Training Consortium Vendors	http://www.trainingconsortium.com/suppliers.shtml	A–
CL	Training Express	http://www.dgl.com/te/	A–
TR	Training Forum Home Page	http://www.trainingforum.com/	A–
BP	UC Davis Information Technology Training	http://instruction.ucdavis.edu/	A–
TR	Virtual Environment Technical Training (VETT)	http://mimsy.mit.edu/	A–
RT	Virtual Multi-Search Engine	http://www.dreamscape.com/frankvad/search.multi.html	A–
TR	Vision for Human Resource Development Network	http://www.mcb.co.uk/hrn/nethome.htm	A–
TR	Visual Edge Productions	http://www.vised.com/home.htm	A–
VL	Wall Street Journal	http://www.wsj.com/	A–
TR	Web-Based-Training Information Site	http://www.multimediatraining.com/training.html	A–
TR	World Wide Web Virtual Library	http://tecfa.unige.ch/info-edu-comp.html	A–
RT	World Wide Web Worm	http://wwww.cs.colorado.edu/wwww	A–
RT	Yanoff's Internet Services List	http://www.spectracom.com/islist/	A–
OR	International Technology Education Association	http://www.iteawww.org/	B+

GA	O-Net: Organizational Information Network	http://www1.whitehouse.gov/WH/pointers/html/educ.html	B+
BP	The Learning Center	http://www.tlckinkos.com/	B+
RT	US Universities and Community Colleges	http://www.utexas.edu/world/univ/	B+
VL	Anonymous Message Server	http://sp1.berkeley.edu/anon.html	B
TR	Benchmarking Exchange	http://www.benchnet.com/	B
GA	Bureau of Labor Statistics	http://stats.bls.gov/	B
OR	Center for Advanced Technology Education	http://www.cate.ryerson.ca/	B
CL	Cheltenham Computer Training	http://www.cctglobal.com/	B
CL	ComputerPrep	http://www.computerprep.com/	B
TR	Courseware Clearinghouse	http://owrw.mrg.ab.ca/clear/	B
RT	CyberStacks	http://www.public.iastate.edu/~CYBERSTACKS/	B
JN	Educational Technology Review	http://aace.virginia.edu/AACE/pubs/etr/etr.html	B
OR	Employee Benefit & Research Institute	http://www.ebri.org/	B
VL	Federal Express	http://www.fedex.com/	B
GA	Federal Training Mall	http://www.fedworld.gov/training/	B
GA	General Services Administration	http://www.gsa.gov/	B
CL	Human Resource Sofware and CBT Library	http://www.hrpress-software.com/	B
BP	IETF/TERENA Training Materials Catalogue	http://www.trainmat.ietf.org/catalogue.html	B
TR	Interesting Listservs and Their Usage	http://www.teleport.com/~erwilson/listserv.html	B
OR	International Foundation of Employee Benefits	http://www.ifebp.org/	B
CL	International Education Services	http://www.iac.co.jp/~iesinfo/index.html	B
TR	Internet Resources	http://www.brandonu.ca/~ennsnr/Resources/	B
OR	Internet Society	http://www.isoc.org/	B
TR	Internet/Intranet Resources	http://www.mahesh.com/internet.html	B
BP	Knowledge Online	http://www.meu.edu/	B
OR	National Association of Student Personnel Administration	http://www.naspa.org/	B
TR	On the Horizon	http://sunsite.unc.edu/horizon/index.html	B
CL	Plus Style Training	http://www.es.co.nz/~meta4/	B
TR	ProEd - Clearinghouse for Training and Development	http://www.proed.com/ch/	B
OR	Rand Institute on Education and Training	http://www.ils.nwu.edu/	B
TR	Roadmaps 96 Workshop	http://www.ultranet.com/~mobius/Roadmap/	B
CL	SalesSense	http://ourworld.compuserve.com/homepages/SalesSense/	B

Training Websites

CL	Training and Education Resource Database	http://web20.mindlink.net/skillnet/training.html	B
CL	Training Broker	http://www.trainingbroker.com/	B
TR	Training Forum Associations Database	http://www.trainingforum.com/assoc.html	B
BP	Via Grafix Software and Training Products	http://www.deerfield.com/viagrafix/training/	B
OR	Vocational Evaluation and Work Adjustment Association	http://www.impactonline.org/vewaa/lists.html	B
VL	Web Employment Opportunities for Training	http://www.iweb.co.uk/DIRJT6.html	B
TR	World On-Line Internet Guide	http://toltec.lib.utk.edu/~lss/training/WebTutorial/tutor1.html	B
TR	Adult Education on the Internet-NetTutoring Group	http://www.oise.on.ca/~fkeller/AdultAid.html	B–
CL	Connect - Tom Peters	http://www.ccc.govt.nz/Library/Connect/42Peters.html	B–
JN	Human Resource Development Quarterly	http://www.jbp.com/hrdq.html	B–
CL	Learning Exchange	http://www.tcm.com/trdev/faq/index.html	B–
TR	Learning Styles	http://www.hcc.hawaii.edu/hccinfo/facdev/8.html	B–
GA	Minority Information Service (USAID)	http://www.fie.com/fedix/aid.html	B–
OR	National Association of Temporary Staffing Services	http://www.podi.com/staffing/	B–
TR	Training Stuff Training Materials and Development	http://www.ccn.cs.dal.ca/~aa068/TrainDev.html	B–
RT	World College and University Home Page Links	http://www.mit.edu:8001/people/cdemello/univ.html	B–
GA	Alabama Industrial Development Technology	http://www.aidt.edu/	C+
GA	Advanced Technologies Applied to Training Design	http://ott.sc.ist.ucf.edu/1_2/nato.htm	C
OR	NewMedia Centers	http://www.csulb.edu/gc/nmc/	C

SECTION 7

Index

A

Ace Hardware, 92–93, 95
Achievement orientation, 166
Achievement vs. relationship, and training, 34
ACI Worldwide:
   knowledge base implementation, 159–160
   and knowledge sharing, 159–160
      challenge, 159
      concept, 159
      course construction, 160
      details, 160
Adelphia Communications Corp., 74
AdvanceOnline Inc., 176, 178–179
Affiliation orientation, 166
Affirmative action, training's role in, 75
Air Canada, in-flight learning, 182
Albertsson, Candy, 49–53
Aldrich, Clark, 9
Alsop, Ronald, 81
American Airlines, and September 11 attacks, 106–111
American Association for Quality (ASQ), 207
American nursing home crisis, 15
Americans with Disabilities Act (ADA), 45
Amidon, Leslie E., 121
Anchoring learning activities to a larger task, 121
Anthrax bioterrorism, 44, 47
Arnett, Barry, 230
Arpey, Gerard, 107–109
ASTD, new certification, 231

B

Baker, Bob, 110
Barber, Mike, 108
Barkley, Stephen, 175–177
Barone, Michael, 67
Barriers to success, identifying, 187
Bartholomew, Dan, 177
Bartlett, Teresa, 103, 105
Bassi, Laurie J., 240
Bassing, Joan, 104–105
Bauer, Diane, 142–144
Baumert, Lisa, 145–146
Baxter, Cynthia, 101
Beaumon, Betsey, 79
Beck, Barbara, 141
Behavior systems, 216
Behavioral-based performance assessment, 215–216
Bender, Jonathan, 62–64
Bennis, Warren, 49–54
Bernard v. *Gulf Oil Corporation*, 235
Bernstein, Aaron, 71
Bertapelle, Joe, 108–109, 111
Black, Cathleen, 82
Blended delivery, 170–171, 173–180
   dot.coms, 173–174
   face-to-face and online programs, 180
   online training, 175–179
Blended learning, 157–158
   and e-learning, 9
   and e-trainers, 193–194
   redesign of course material, 157
      definitions for, 158
   results from, 157–158
Bloch, Matt, 217
Blouin, Anne, 231
Boverie, Patricia, 231
Branching, 122
Brown, Alicia, 197–198
Brown, Jeff, 63–64
Browsing, 122
Buck, Dave, 232
Buffet, Jimmy, 130
Bush, George W., 44, 47, 70, 112–116
Business-to-business (B2B) e-commerce, 10–13

C

Carey, Susan, 106
Carty, Donald J., 107–111
Cashman, Kevin, 49–54
Castro, Ida L., 73
Catalyst, 81
Caudron, Shari, 211
Caulfield, Brian, 92
Cavallo, Mike, 9
Centra Software, 195
Certificate program, 158
Chambers, John, 9, 10, 140–148
Chao, Elaine, 14
Cheney, Dick, 109
Chesteron, 178
ChicWit, 80
Cisco e-learning operation:
   Field E-Learning Connection, 142, 145–146,
      implementation, 141–143
   Internet Learning Solutions Group, 141, 143, 145
   learner-centricity, 144
   measuring success, 143–145
   Partner E-Learning Connection, 145–146
   problems facing e-learning, 148
   rocky road for, 146–148
   saving realized from, 147–148
   and training for ISO 9000 registration, 147
Clark, Ruth, 231
Classroom world, changes in, 174
Click2learn, 139–140
Coaching, 122
Cockerham, Haven E., 74
Color-blind society, moving toward, 67–68
Comfort, and learning, 122
Communications skills, 188
Computer-delivered training breakdown, 40
Computer-mediated teams vs. conventional teams, 28
Cone, John, 9, 230
Content delivery, and e-learning, 9
Content Management System (CMS), 159
Content validity, 236
Contracting, as social dimension of learning, 162
Cook, Libby, 100
Coolboard, 94–95
Corporate boot camps, 131–138
Coscarelli, Bill, 231
Coursebuilder (Macromedia), 197
Courseware, testing on users, 122

Creative destruction, use of term, 201–202
Creativity, among managers, 19
Crossen, M., 20
Curphy, Gordon J., 28
Curry, Ann, 98
Customer service, 99

D

Dagnon, James B., 72
DaimlerChrysler wellness program, 103–105
   components of, 104
   evaluation results, 104
   StayWell's NextSteps Focused Interventions, 104
   and tailoring of programs to high-risk groups, 105
   Wellness Advisory Council, 104–105
Decision making, 16–21
   "doing first," 18, 20–21
   "seeing first," 17–18, 20–21
   suspended thinking, 20–21
   "thinking first," 17, 19, 20
   through discussion/collage/improvisation, 18–20
Dehaven, Dara L., 75
Delivery:
   in-flight learning, 182
   Lightspan learning programs, 183
   network-based learning, 182
   OpenCourseWare (MIT), 183
   PowerPoint newsletter, 183
   through educational videogames, 182–183
   Universal Jukebox Model (Napster), 183
   Web-based learning, 182
Delivery method, 38–41
Dell Computer, 98
Delta Airlines, 175–179
Deming, W. Edwards, 215
Digital Pipe Inc., 179
Digital structures, 4, 22–24
   Learning Management Systems (LMS), 22
   supportive managers, 23–24
Discussion threads, organizing by topic, 188
Distance learning, 198–199
"Doing first," 18, 20–21
Dot.coms, 243–245
Dreamweaver, 197
Drop-out/drop-in rate, e-learning, 9
Drucker, Peter, 215
Drummond, Allan, 134, 137

E

E-business quality standards, 207–208
E-culture, 201–202
E-learning:
   for free agents, 152–153
   international, 25–26
   live, 185
   and Napster, 89–91
   ROI factors in, 211–212
   strength of, 161
E-learning acceptance, 149–151
   drivers of, 149–150
   incentives, 150
   location/timing of event, 151
   marketing, 150
   recommendations, 151
   support, 150
   technology, 150–151
E-learning advances, 171–172, 181–190
   Jones International University (JIU), 181
E-learning design issues, 119, 139–153
   Cisco e-learning operation, 140–148
      Field E-Learning Connection, 145–146
      implementation, 141–143
      measuring success, 143–145
      rocky road for, 146–148
   e-learning acceptance, 149–151
   e-learning for free agents, 152–153
   plan and communicate, 139–140
      analysis, 139
      Click2learn, 139–140
      expert button, 139
      flexibility, 139
      organization, 139
      outsourcing vs. in-house design, 139
      project failure, 140
      prototype, 139
      scale, 139
E-learning design nuts and bolts, 119–120, 154–160
   blending training, 157–158
   knowing stuff vs. doing stuff, 167
   knowledge sharing, 159–160
   online attrition, strategies to prevent, 164–166
   online course management systems, 154–156
      assessment rubrics, 156
      commenting on student documents, 155
      descriptive material, 154–155
      designing lessons for F2F, 156
      file exchange, 155
      peer review management, 155–156

E-learning evaluation, 204, 207–213
   quality standard in e-business, 207–208
   Rockwell Collins business-driven learning strategy, 209–210
   ROI factors in e-learning, 211–212
   Seimen's knowledge management (KM) metrics, 213
E-learning industry, and the stock market, 243–245
E-learning management, 2, 5–13
   e-learning pricing, 5–8
   e-learning sessions vs. classroom sessions, 8
   tips for avoiding failure, 9
E-learning pricing, 5–8
   free, 6–8
   one-time flat fee, 6–7
   pay as you go, 6–7
   payment based on time, 7–8
   per server, 6–7
   price per seat, 6–7
E-learning satisfaction, drivers of, 150
E-learning value proposition, 230
E-mail usage assessment, e-learning, 9
E-trainers, 191–194
   amount of training done by, 192
   and blended learning, 193–194
   candidates for, 192
   characteristics of, 192–193
   classroom trainers as, 192
   as coaches, 193
   experiment/capture/coaching, 194
   job tasks, 191
   as reference librarians, 193
   skill development, 193–194
   and synchronous training, 191–192
   as talk show hosts, 193
eBay, 46
eComplaints.com, 98
Educational videogames, delivery through, 182–183
Egalitarian cultures vs. hierarchical cultures, and training, 32–33
Eldercare crisis, 15
Elkeles, Tamar, 124–127
Elliott, Wayne A., 71
Enterprise resource planning, 11
Epstein, Jason, 49
eRoom Technology, 94–95
Esslinger, Denis, 102
Eureka moments, 17
Evaluation, conducting, 189

Evaluator's role in improved performance, 218–222
   action plan audit, 221
   current practice, 219
   follow-up assignment, 221
   internal referencing strategy, 221
   involving evaluators early, 220
   Level III evaluation
      purpose of, 219
      suggestions for, 220–222
      unpopularity of, 219–220
   onsite follow-up visit by trainer, 221
   pretraining/posttraining evaluation, 221
   simulations, 221
   unobtrusive monitoring, 221–222
Evans, Andie, 182
Evans v. *City of Evanston, Illinois*, 234
Everidge, Jim, 9
Executive coaching, 217
Expanded syllabus, developing, 187–188

F
Face-to-face and online programs, 180
Face validity, 236
Facilitated mentoring, 199–201
   best practices, 200
   keys to successful mentoring, 200
   skills, 200
   and tough times, 200–201
Federal Law Enforcement Training Center, 198–199
Feedback, 122, 232
   for/from new hires and customers, 131–138
   providing, 189
Ferguson, Dave, 196–197
Field E-Learning Connection, 145–146
   Cisco, 142, 145–146,
First USA Bank, 62–64
Fitzgerald, Joan, 14
Fixed learning, 158
Fleming, Alexander, 17
Fluid content delivery, and e-learning, 9
Ford Motor Company:
   action learning at, 57
   BLI 3 Flawless Execution program, 58
   business impact, generating, 60–61
   Capstone program, 58
   core programs, 57–58
   e-rooms, 58–59
   e-tools, use of, 58–59
   Experienced Leader Challenge program, 57–58, 60
   Ford Supplier/Business Leadership Initiative program, 58, 60
   Global Leadership Forum, 58
   integrating work and life, 59–60
   leader-teachers, 58
   Leadership Development Center, 58
   Leadership for Consumer-Driven, Six-Sigma, 58
   Leadership for the New Economy program, 57, 58
   New Business Leader program, 57, 58
   New Leader Impact program, 58
   new leadership DNA, 56–57
   and transformational leaders, 55–61
   transformational mindset, adopting, 56–57
Ford, William Clay Jr., 55
Foreman, Joel, 154
"Four Buckets" (General Electric), 242
Franke, David, 136
Frankola, Karen, 161
Free Agent Nation, 152–153
Free e-learning, 6–8
Friedman, Laura, 177, 179
Friedman, Stewart S., 55
Fruhwirth, Sue, 101
Fulford, Dick, 99–101

G
Galagan, Patricia A., 140
Galvin, Tammy, 124
Gartland, Frank, 185
Gayeski, Diane, 127–129
GE Global eXchange Services (GXS) (General Electric), 12–13
Geissler, John, 195–196
General Electric, 10–13
   e-business movement at, 12
   "Four Buckets," 242
   GE Global eXchange Services (GXS), 12–13
   GE Information Services (GEIS) division, 11–12
   and the Internet, 11–12
   and technology, 11
   Trading Partner Network, 12
Generation Y (Gen Y), 66
Geographically dispersed teams (GDTs), 27–31
   challenges faced by, 31
   communication, 31
   goals/objectives, 31

group effectiveness within, 28
rewards, 31
Gery, Gloria, 230
Gignilliat, Ted, 74
Gilliland, Mike, 100–101
Gillis, Lynette, 231
Ginnett, Robert C., 28
Girl gangs, 76–80
  academic, 77–79
  corporate manager, 77
  email list, 79–80
  entrepreneur, 79
  forming your own girl gang, 79
  networking, 76
  power of, 80
Global connections, 4, 25–35
  e-learning, international, 25–26
  teams, 27–31
  training across cultures, 32–35
Golden, Marita, 77–79
Goldsborough, Margaret W., 14
Goleman, Daniel, 83
Gonzalez, Ed, 104
Gordon, Jack, 45
Green, Robert A., 207
Green, Tom, 92
Grizzle, Sam, 71
Group decision support systems, 28
Gulf Breeze Hospital, 99

H

Haber, R., 19
Hall, Brandon, 184,
Hall, John T., 95
Hansen, Michael C., 27
Harrell, Kathleen D., 218
Harrington, H. James, 207–208
Hartigan, Rachel, 182
Hartley, Darin E., 5
Hartz, Cynthia, 213
Help, 122
Hierarchy of content, developing, 187–188
Hispanic workers, 45
Hispanics:
  diversity among, 68
  new broad meaning of, 67–68
Hofer-Alfeis, Josef, 213
Hogan, Paul, 49–54
Horn, Michael, 139–140
Horton, William, 231

Hughes, Richard L., 28
Hutchins, Jennifer, 103
Hutchinson, Michelle, 186

I

Icus Pte Ltd., 184
Immigration:
  basic skills challenge, 69–70
  freedoms, 70
  institutional effects of, 69–70
Improved performance, evaluator's role in, 218–222
Improvisation skits, 18, 20
IMS Global Learning Consortium, 205
In-flight learning, 182
Individualism vs. collectivism, and training, 33–34
Individualized attention/instruction, 122
InfoLines, 4
Infopop, 94–95
Insight, 17–18
Instructional objectives stated to learner, 121
Instructional System Design (ISD), 118–119, 121–138
  of the future, 128–130
  instructional design strategies/considerations, 121–123
  interactive instruction influence development (I3D), 129–130
  projects, 124–127
  rapid design and prototyping, 129
  rethinking instruction design, 127–130
  URLs, 130
Instructor help, 186–190
  barriers to success, identifying, 187
  communications skills, 188
  defined pedagogical goals, developing, 186–187
  discussion threads, organizing by topic, 188
  evaluation, conducting, 189
  expanded syllabus, developing, 187–188
  feedback, providing, 189
  hierarchy of content, developing, 187–188
  interactive learning, shift from broadcast learning to, 186–187
  and the Internet, 186
  introductions of instructor and students, 188
  learner-centered environment, creating, 187
  organization, developing, 187–188

performance evaluation standards, defining, 187
photographs, including, 188
practice, including opportunities for, 187
recognition of each student, 188
student-to-student collaborations, 189
trust, building, 188
Instructors, virtual, 195–198
Integrating learning experiences, with e-learning, 9
Intellectual capital, core measures of, 240–241
Interactive instruction influence development (I3D), 129–130
Interactivity, 122
Internal referencing strategy, 221
Internal Revenue Service (IRS):
    and Individual Information Technology Institute, 83–84
    and learner resistance, 83–88
        acknowledging the need for other types of learning, 87
        cause of, 84
        general resistance to all new technology, 84
        hybrid courses, 87
        increased student responsibility, 84–85
        just-in-time training and accommodation, 86–87
        learning the interface, 84
        personal relationship with students, 85–86
        personality and preferred learning style, 85
        reasonable accommodation, 86
        strategies for dealing with, 85
        virtual office experience, 85
International e-learning, 25–26
International educational policy, State Dept. activity in, 15
International Masters Program in Practicing Management, 18–20
Internet Learning Solutions Group, Cisco, 141, 143, 145
Interstate Bakeries Corp., 74
Introduction of instructor and students, 188
Invisible trainers, 195–196
Irving, Maryann, 108
ISD, *See* Instructional System Design (ISD)

J
James, Glenford S., 74
Jesukiewicz, Paul, 231
Job Expo, 46
Johnson, Linda, 73

Jones International University (JIU), 181
Jones, Peter, 231
Jones, Reginald E., 75

K
Kanter, Rosabeth Moss, 2, 201–202
Kaye, Beverly, 63
Keats, John, 51
Kelly, Tom, 141–143, 147–148
Kerrey, Sen. Bob, 14
Kiger, Patrick J., 62, 229
King, Stephen B., 25
Kirshenbaum Bond & Partners, 78
Knowing stuff vs. doing stuff, 167
knowledge management (KM) metrics (Siemens), 213
Knowledge objects, 159
Knowledge sharing, 159–160
Koehler, W., 17
Koon, Eustace, 25
Kossler, Michael E., 27

L
La Ferla, Ruth, 67–68
Lachnit, Carol, 96, 209–210
Lakeside Imports Inc., 73–74
Langley, A., 17
Lawson, Scott, 211–212
Leadership and culture:
    CEO in jeans/t-shirt, 65
    First USA Bank, 62–64
    Ford Motor Company, 55–61
    Generation Y, 66
    learning to learn dialogue with Warren Bennis, 49–54
    thought on leadership from Warren Bennis, 51
Leadership Development Center, Ford Motor Company, 58
Learner-centered environment, creating, 187
Learner-centricity, 144
Learner evaluation, 205, 214–229
    ASTD's new certification, 231
    evaluator's role in improved performance, 218–222
    executive coaching, 217
    peer appraisal, 223–228
    performance assessment, 214–217
    performance measures, court rulings favoring, 233–239
    quarterly evaluation of performance improvement, 229, 232

Learner needs, 43–116
  leadership and culture, 49–66
  new bottom line, 96–116
  race and gender plus, 67–83
  technology and learning communities, 83–95
Learner resistance, 83–88
  acknowledging the need for other types of learning, 87
  cause of, 84
  general resistance to all new technology, 84
  hybrid courses, 87
  increased student responsibility, 84–85
  just-in-time training and accommodation, 86–87
  learning the interface, 84
  personal relationship with students, 85–86
  personality and preferred learning style, 85
  reasonable accommodation, 86
  strategies for dealing with, 85
  virtual office experience, 85
Learning:
  social dimensions of, 161–163
    community of learning, 163
    contracting, 162
    peer questions observed, 163
    pre-work, 162–163
    relative progress, 163
    team work, 163
    at work coaching, 163
Learning community, 163
Learning Management Systems (LMS), 4, 22
Learning nugget, 158
Learning screen, e-learning, 9
Lee, Kathryn, 77
Lee, William W., 233
LeGault v. *Russo*, 234
Lehne, Ted, 175
Level III evaluation:
  purpose of, 219
  suggestions for, 220–222
  unpopularity of, 219–220
Lewis, Roosevelt, 74
Liemandt, Joe, 131–138
Lightspan learning programs, 183
Live e-learning, 185
Lockheed Martin, 71–72
Logue, Ann C., 76
Loknes, Regy, 157
Lolly-Harvey, Christine, 64
Lonesome online, 120, 161–167
Loose-structure cultures vs. tight-structure cultures, and training, 34–35
Lopez, Kimberly, 213

M
M-Learning (Mobile-Learning), 184
Mallet, Vince, 133–134
Management by objectives (MBO), 215
March, James, 16
Maricopa Center for Learning and Instruction, 197
Marquardt, Michael J., 25
Martin, Carolyn A., 66
Masie, Elliott, 9, 10, 89, 149, 161, 173, 191, 218, 230, 243–245
Maslow, Abraham, 83
MassWit, 80
Mayer, Rich, 231
McBaine, Neylan, 65
McCartney, Scott, 106
McCormick, Patricia, 83
McDonald, Pete, 110
McMorrow, John, 230
McNellis, Thomas, 207–208
Measurement paradox, 225–226, 227
Menager-Beeley, Rosemarie, 83
Mentoring, facilitated, 199–201
Mentoring yourself, 81–82
Merrill, David, 231
Merritt, Jennifer, 180
Merullo, Ralph, 178
Metz, Mike, 140–141, 145–147
Microsoft Certified Systems Engineer (MCSE), 5
Miles, Doc, 109
Mineta, Norman, 109–110
Mintzberg, Henry, 16
Module, 158
Mohrman, Chris, 73–74
Morgan Stanley Dean Witter, 98
Morse, Jodie, 182
Moshinski, Jim, 164
Multex.com, 94–95
Multimedia, use of, 122
Mura, Agnes, 217
Murray, Margo, 199

N
Nadler, Richard, 177
Napster and e-learning, 89–91
Napster's Universal Jukebox Model, 183
Nasser, Jacques, 60

Neal, Kenneth, 176
Network-based learning, 182
Networking Professionals Connection, 93
New kinds of learning, government action, 14–15
New York Institute of Finance (NYIF), 179
Nokia Corporation, 184
Non-profit organizations, 347–354
Northwest Airlines Corp, 73
Nunley, Roger H., 98

O

One-time flat fee, e-learning, 6–7
OneAnthem, 211–212
OneOnOne Computer Training, 183
Ong, Betty, 107, 111
Online attrition, 164–166
    after-course strategies, 164–165
        celebrating successful completion, 164
        reinforcement of learning, 165
        support, 164
        viewing e-learning as a process, 165
    metacognition, 165–166
        determining environmental favorability, 165–166
        examining strategies, 165
    motivation, 165–166
Online communities:
    essential tools for, 94
    facilitating, 92–95
    rules for successful communities, 93
Online course management systems, 154–156
    assessment rubrics, 156
    commenting on student documents, 155
    descriptive material, 154–155
    designing lessons for F2F, 156
    file exchange, 155
    peer review management, 155–156
Online facilitators, 198
Online library, 183
Online training, 175–179
    flexibility of, 177
    Onsite follow-up visit by trainer, 221
    OpenCourseWare (MIT), 183
    Opportunity Knocks program (First USA Bank), 62–64
    Organization, developing, 187–188
    Ornani, Fabrizio, 179
    Oseng, David, 73–74
    Owens, Diana L., 233
    Ozzie, Ray, 89

P

Paradox of group performance, 224–225, 227–228
Paradox of rewards, 226, 228
Paradox of roles, 224
Parallel paths, 10–13
Parfitt, Craig, 108
Participate.com, 94–95
Partner E-Learning Connection, Cisco, 145–146
Pasteur, Louis, 17
Pay as you go pricing, e-learning, 6–7
Payment based on time, e-learning, 7–8
Peach, Kathleen M., 73
Peer appraisal, 223–228,
    managing through paradoxes, 226–228
    measurement paradox, 225–226, 227
    paradox of group performance, 224–225, 227–228
    paradox of rewards, 226, 228
    paradox of roles, 224
    paradoxes in process, 223–224
    purpose of, 226–227
    scope of, 227–228
Peer questions observed, as social dimension of learning, 163
Peer to Peer (P2P) Networking, 89–91
    annotations, 90
    business model, 91
    content ownership issues, 91
    content structuring, 90
    culture issues, 91
    cumulative content, 91
    digital collaboration, 90
    media capture, 90–91
    quality of content, 91
    technology issues, 91
Peiperl, Maury A., 223
People-process-technology mix, e-learning, 9
PeopleLink, 94–95
Per server pricing, e-learning, 6–7
Performance assessment, 214–217
    behavioral-based, 215–216
    management by objectives (MBO), 215
    skill-based, 216–217
Performance Engineering Group, 97, 210
Performance evaluation standards, defining, 187
Performance improvement, quarterly evaluation of, 229
Performance Learning Systems (PLS), 175–177
Performance measurement, 233–239
    commercial use, training for, 237

content validity, 236
court rulings
   Bernard v. *Gulf Oil Corporation*, 235
   Evans v. *City of Evanston, Illinois*, 234
   LeGault v. *Russo*, 234
   Police Officers for Equal Rights v. *the City of Columbus, Ohio*, 234–235
ethical issues, 235–237
face validity, 236
individual needs, training for, 237
measurement variables, 237–238
organizational needs, training for, 237
predictive validity, 237
statistical measures, 237–238
test item validity, 236–237
validity measurement, types of, 236–237
Peterson, David B., 49–54
Phelps, Kyle, 111
Photographs, including, 188
Pink, Daniel H., 152
Police Officers for Equal Rights v. *the City of Columbus, Ohio*, 234–235
"Portraits of Grief" (New York Times), 44
Posttraining evaluation, 221
Power orientation, 166
Powered, Inc., 8
PowerPoint newsletter, 183
PPL Corporation, 99, 102
Practice, 122
  and e-learning, 9
  including opportunities, 187
Pre-work, as social dimension of learning, 162–163
Predictive validity, 237
Pretesting/posttesting, 232
Pretraining evaluation, 221
Price, defined, 5
Price per seat, e-learning, 6–7
Printing, 122
Privacy, and learning, 122
Productivity Point International (PPI), 102
Professional organizations, 249–258
Projects, 124–127
Purington, Cliff, 96–97, 209–210
Pyzdek, Thomas, 207

Q
QUALCOMM, 124–127
Quality of Life programs, 62
Quality standard in e-business, 207–208
Quantum ideas, 55

Quarterly evaluation of performance improvement, 229
Quicklearns, 97, 210

R
R. R. Donnelley & Sons Co., 74
Race and gender plus:
  affirmative action, training's role in, 75
  being your own mentor, 81–82
  girl gangs, 76–80
  Hispanics, diversity among, 68
  immigration, institutional effects of, 69–70
  racism in the workplace, 71–74
  U.S. Census, surprises in, 67–68
Racism in the workplace, 71–74
  in blue-collar industries, 72–73
  in offices, 73
  racial discrimination/harassment claims, settlement of, 72
  revenge, 74
  silence, 73–74
Randomized assessment of question pools, e-learning, 9
Raybourn, Cynthia, 213
Readability vs. irritability, 122–123
Recognition of each student, 188
Reinforcement/feedback, 122
Relative progress, as social dimension of learning, 163
Renfroe, Angela, 78
Repetition, opportunity for, 122
Results-oriented customer service training, 98–102
Richardi, Ralph, 109
Ritter, Greg, 9
Robison, Karyn-Siobhan, 14
Rockwell Collins, 96–97
Rockwell Collins business-driven learning strategy, 209–210
ROI factors in e-learning, 211–212
Rosen, Monte, 176, 178–179
Rosenberg, Marc J., 230
Rosenberg, Michael, 231
Rosier, Rich, 49–54
Roy, Bill, 108
Royal Dutch/Shell Group, 93–95
Rudd, John S., 14
Ryan, Liz, 79–80

S
Sammis, Stuart, 213
Samuelson, Robert J., 69–70

Sazen, Hanif, 9
Scalability, and e-learning, 9
Schelin, Elsa, 181
Schmitt, Eric, 67
Schneider, Mica, 180
Scholastic Aptitude Test (SAT), 205
Screen design, 123
Seegers, Harvey, 9, 11–13
"Seeing first", 17–18, 20–21
Seimen's knowledge management (KM) metrics, 213
Self pacing, 121
September 11 attacks, 2, 4, 44–47, 70, 98, 103, 106
Sessa, Valerie, 27
Shank, Patti, 127
Shank, Roger C., 2
Sharable Content Object Reference Model (SCORM), 205
Shell Corporation, blending training, 157–158
Sherbert, Ed, 214
Sims, Rod, 127–129
Simulations, 221
SiteScape, 93–95
Skill-based performance assessment, 216–217
Smith, Rita, 23
Snyder, Scott, 136
Social dimensions of learning:
　community of learning, 163
　contracting, 162
　peer questions observed, 163
　pre-work, 162–163
　relative progress, 163
　team work, 163
　at work coaching, 163
Soliday, Ed, 110
Sorrenti, M., 20
SourceForge, 95
Spence, Betty, 81
State of the Union, September 20, 2001, 112–116
Stopko, Alan, 49–54
Studdert, Andy, 108–109, 111
Student-to-student collaborations, 189
Sturm, Susan, 72
Sunoo, Brenda Paik, 98
Supportive managers, 23–24
Surry, Daniel, 128
Swain, Carol M., 73
Symonds, William C., 69

T

Tapley, Glen, 146
Tapscott, Don, 186
Teal, David, 159
Team Effectiveness Leadership Model, 28–29
Team work, as social dimension of learning, 163
Teams:
　computer-mediated teams vs. conventional teams, 28
　geographically dispersed teams (GDTs), 27–31
　　challenges faced by, 31
　　communication, 31
　　goals/objectives, 31
　　group effectiveness within, 28
　　rewards, 31
　group decision support systems, 28
　growth of, 30–31
　team composition, 29
　team design, 29–30
TechLearn 2001 Orlando Conference, 47
Techno-skeptic converts, 196–197
Technology and learning communities, 83–95
　DaimlerChrysler wellness program, 103–105
　learner resistance, 83–88
　Napster and e-learning, 89–91
　online communities, facilitating, 92–95
　results-oriented customer service training, 98–102
Technology tsunami, surviving, 195–199
Tenzing, 182
Test item validity, 236–237
Thinking change, 2–4, 14–21
　new kinds of learning, government action on, 14–15
　new ways of thinking at the top, 16–21
"Thinking first", 17, 20
360-degree feedback, 223–228
　managing through paradoxes, 226–228
　measurement paradox, 225–226
　paradox of group performance, 224–225
　paradox of rewards, 226
　paradox of roles, 224
　paradoxes in process, 223–224
Tichy, Noel M., 131
TigerDirect.com, 98
Topic, 158
Trading Partner Network (General Electric), 12
Trainer's Almanac, 247–393
　non-profit organizations, 347–354

professional organizations, 249–258
training conferences, 259–276
training for trainers, 309–345
training journals/magazines/newsletters, 367–380
training research and reference sources, 355–365
training Websites, 381–393
  e-learning Web resources, 382
  ratings of, 383–393
worldwide conference centers, 277–307
Trainers as facilitators of learning, 172, 191–202
TRAINING 2001 Industry Report, 4, 36–41
  delivery method, 38–41
  highlights, 37
Training across cultures, 32–35
  achievement vs. relationship, 34
  egalitarian cultures vs. hierarchical cultures, 32–33
  individualism vs. collectivism, 33–34
  loose-structure cultures vs. tight-structure cultures, 34–35
Training Audit, 23–24
  client relationship management, 24
  curriculum development, 23
  curriculum management, 24
  delivery, 24
  governing process, 23
  marketing and communications, 24
  measurement and evaluation, 24
  outsourcing/vendor management, 23
  report, 24
  students, 24
  training management system, 24
  training organization, 23
  training plan, 23
  training products/services, 23
Training budget breakdowns, 41
Training conferences, 259–276
Training evaluation, 203–245, 218–222
  action plan audit, 221
  current practice, 219
  e-learning evaluation, 204, 207–213
  follow-up assignment, 221
  internal referencing strategy, 221
  involving evaluators early, 220
  learner evaluation, 205, 214–229
  Level III evaluation
    purpose of, 219

  suggestions for, 220–222
  unpopularity of, 219–220
  onsite follow-up visit by trainer, 221
  pretraining/posttraining evaluation, 221
  simulations, 221
  tests/measures/certification, 230–245
  unobtrusive monitoring, 221–222
Training for trainers, 309–345
Training journals/magazines/newsletters, 367–380
Training management, 1–41
  digital structures, 22–24
  e-learning management, 5–13
  global connections, 25–35
  thinking change, 14–21
  TRAINING 2001 Industry Report, 36–41
Training program delivery, 169–202
  blended delivery, 173–180
  e-learning advances, 181–190
  trainers as facilitators of learning, 191–202
Training program design, 117–167
  e-learning design issues, 119, 139–153
  e-learning design nuts and bolts, 119–120, 154–160
  Instructional System Design (ISD), 118–119, 121–138
  lonesome online, 120, 161–167
Training research and reference sources, 355–365
Training Websites, 381–393
  e-learning Web resources, 382
  ratings of, 383–393
Traut, Terence R., 167
Trentin, Guglielmo, 182
Trilogy University, 131–138
  CarOrder.com, 136
  clarity on strategy, 137
  description of, 132
  Fast Cycle Time, 136
  first three months at, 132–135
  IveBeenGood.com, 136
  new-product pipeline, 135–136
  next generation of leaders, 136
  organizational transformation, 137
  "teachable point of view", 137
  Uberworks, 136
  virtuous teaching cycle, 137
Trust, building, 188
Tulgan, Bruce, 66

U

United Airlines, and September 11 attacks, 106–111
Universal Jukebox Model (Napster), 183
U.S. Census, 45
  color-blind society, moving toward, 67–68
  Hispanic, new broad meaning of, 67–68
  surprises in, 67–68
  work-life balance issues, 68

V

Van Buren, Mark, 9, 69, 178, 240
Van Unnik, Arjan, 93
Vigil, Raymond, 230
Virtual instructors, 195–198

W

Wal-Mart, ordering system, 11
Walden Institute, 198–199
Wallas, G., 17
Web-based learning, 182
Web-based training, 175–179
  flexibility of, 177
Webber, Alan, 46
WebCT site, 154–156
Weech, William A., 32
Weggen, Cornelia, 6
Weick, Karl, 18
Weinstein, Maddy, 230
Welch, Jack, 2, 9, 10–13, 207, 242
Welch, John F., 242
Wellington, Sheila, 81
Westley, Frances, 16
Widmayer, Sharon, 154
Wild Oats Markets, 99, 101–102
Wilson, Jennifer Neumann, 213
Wiltrakis, Jack N., 74
Wireless application protocol (WAP), 184
Woodwell, William Jr., 69
Work coaching, as social dimension of learning at, 163
Work-life balance issues, 68
Workplace changes, 2–4
Worldwide conference centers, 277–307

Y

Young, Doug, 198–199
Young, Kenneth, 103–104

Z

Zaniello, Ben, 136
Zatzkis, Ralph, 74
Zielinski, Dave, 195
Zimmerman, Eilene, 175